MY TIME

WITH

GOD

FOR STUDENTS

_____

BELONGS TO

_____

GIVEN BY

_____

DATE

_____

OCCASION

You [Lord] will teach me how to live a holy life. Being with you will fill me with joy;
at your right hand I will find pleasure forever.
—Psalm 16:11

MY TIME WITH GOD

Thomas Nelson
Since 1798

NCV™
NEW CENTURY VERSION®

NASHVILLE   DALLAS   MEXICO CITY   RIO DE JANEIRO   BEIJING

FOR STUDENTS

DEVOTIONS for the ENTIRE YEAR

MY TIME WITH GOD FOR STUDENTS

Copyright © 2006 by Thomas Nelson, Inc.

Published in Nashville, Tennessee, by Thomas Nelson. Thomas Nelson is a trademark of Thomas Nelson, Inc.

Editorial services provided by Amanda and Stephen Sorenson. Acknowledgments for devotional "Insights" begin on page 639. Design: Jay Smith-Juicebox Designs www.juiceboxdesigns.com

The preliminary research and development of the New Century Version was done by the World Bible Translation Center, Inc., Fort Worth, TX 76182.

Printed in the United States of America
2 3 4 5 6 7 8 9 — 12 11 10 09 08 07

CONTENTS

MY TIME WITH GOD IS TIME WELL SPENT!

Would you like to know God better . . . to explore exciting Bible truths each day and still meet your other demands and responsibilities . . . to be challenged (at a comfortable pace) to grow deeper in your faith?

My Time with God for Students has been designed to give you an ideal way to find out more about God and to engage yourself in exploring the treasures of his Word. You may begin your reading whenever you wish, and in a year's time you will have read the entire New Testament and related sections from the Old Testament. Plus you will have received insights from classical and contemporary writers.

There's a reading for Monday, Tuesday, Wednesday, Thursday, Friday, and one for Saturday/Sunday. (We know how busy weekends can be!)

Each two-page reading begins with the New Testament passage for the day and is followed by at least one Old Testament passage that reinforces the theme. This unique format allows you to see Scripture's truths unfold and to gain a new understanding of God's love and mercy throughout history.

If you wish, you may choose to read thematically. Maybe you're wrestling with a problem at school or at work, an issue of faith, or some kind of hurt or temptation. Or maybe you would like to study a particular biblical theme. Whatever your need or interest, the index that begins on page 627 will guide you to just the right reading.

Not only is *My Time with God for Students* a valuable aid in personal growth and inspirational study, it is helpful for small groups and Sunday school classes.

My Time with God for Students features the New Century Version, an accurate and easy-to-understand translation that is perfect for devotional reading. In fact, because of its smooth, familiar style, you may find it hard to stop at just one reading a day!

Most likely, you will recognize the names of many of the authors whose quotations we've included. Their insights—taken from more than one hundred seventy books—will challenge your thinking, broaden your understanding, and guide you to an even deeper relationship with God. And the credits at the end of the book show you where to go if you're interested in reading more from some of these great sources of wisdom and encouragement.

Questions, comments, and/or invitations to action that follow each reading will help you evaluate and apply what you've read. They are also excellent discussion starters for small group settings. We invite you now to spend time with God and discover what he has in store for you. It's the best investment you'll ever make!

For more resources about the Bible and to find a community of people who are interested in connecting their faith and life, visit www.myfaithandlife.com.

THE PUBLISHER

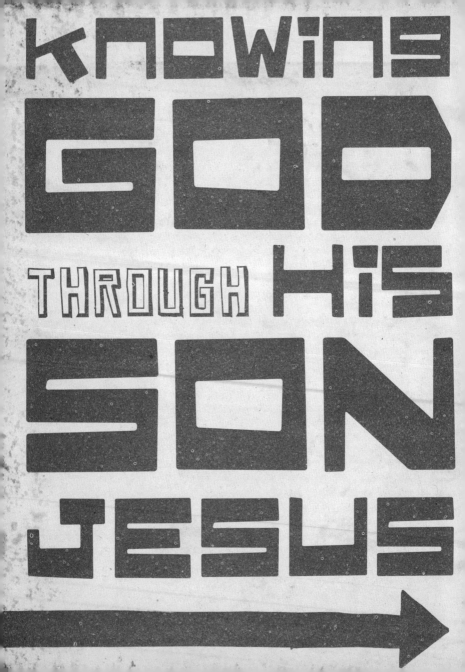

WHO IS JESUS?

The great theme of the Bible is the person of Jesus Christ and his work of salvation for humankind. Christianity is rooted in the person of Jesus, and the best reason for believing that Christianity is true is the life of Jesus. Throughout the Old Testament, the promises of his coming are foretold and graphically portrayed in numerous examples.

We can look at how God has made himself known in many ways: through the Jewish people, through the events of history, through the wonders of the universe itself, and through visions and personal encounters with him. But he has most supremely made himself known in and through Jesus Christ. Through the incarnation of Christ—coming as God in the flesh—God has intervened decisively and directly in the world he created.

Until recent times, the question "Who is Jesus?" was not much of an issue. Jesus has always been precisely who the Bible said he is. During his earthly ministry, Jesus was not only a man, but he was God himself who had come down from the glory of heaven to walk on this earth and show us what God is like. He lived a sinless life and performed the signs and miracles that the Gospels said he did.

Jesus taught what the New Testament said he taught, called together a group of followers, and was crucified, giving his life as a ransom for captive souls. He was resurrected three days later, continued to teach his followers, and then ascended into heaven back to God. Finally, he will come again a second time to usher in the complete reign of God over all of his creation.

Some people mistakenly believe that Jesus was merely a social reformer who came to change society and free those people who were bound by injustice, tyranny, and oppression. Others say he came to show us his acts of love so that we might know how we should live. Some even think that he was a misguided religious figure with no relevance for today.

But none of these theories alone are adequate to explain the Jesus Christ pictured clearly in the New Testament. In unmistakable language, it is pronounced that Jesus was God himself in human form. He is the one and only Son of God who came to earth to reveal the nature of God to people and save them from their fatal state as sinners.

Jesus took on himself the punishment for the sin of humankind when he died on the cross. God demonstrated beyond all doubt that Jesus is the divine Savior and

Lord of all by raising him from the dead, according to Scripture. "The Good News is about God's Son, Jesus Christ our Lord. As a man, he was born from the family of David. But through the Spirit of holiness he was declared to be God's Son with great power by rising from the dead" (Romans 1:3–4).

HOW DO I BECOME A FOLLOWER OF CHRIST?

You become a follower of Christ by embracing his teachings and pursuing a personal relationship with him. The cool thing about Christianity is that it is the only faith whose founder is alive! At its core, religion is humankind's attempt to reach God on its terms, but Christianity is all about a relationship with God through his Son, Jesus Christ.

All the founders of the religions of the world are dead and gone. But Jesus is alive and well, seated on his throne in heaven, where he prays for all people to see the light and follow him. Following Christ is a lot simpler than it has been made out to be. Think about what is involved with following a human leader, such as a pastor. You spend as much time with him as possible and study his teachings in order to put them into practice.

The same is true with following Jesus. You spend time with him in worship, offering prayer and praise to him. And you study his teaching by reading the Bible so you can learn how to act like he acted as a human. The term "Christian" actually means "Christlike," suggesting that believers walk the walk and don't simply talk the talk.

WHAT IS THE CHRISTIAN WALK ALL ABOUT?

As the term suggests, you can think of the Christian walk as a daily walk with Jesus. Perhaps the best example of what it means is the story of Adam and Eve in the Garden of Eden (Genesis 2 and 3). The Scriptures remind us that before they yielded to the devil and fell into sin, the first family used to walk and talk with God in the cool of the day. How cool is that? Well, that is a good picture of what it means to walk with Jesus.

Think of hanging out with the lover of your soul! Nothing is cooler than cultivating a close relationship with the one who died to save you from your sins. And Jesus is no reluctant redeemer. He longs for the type of intimate connection that he used to enjoy with humankind before sin entered the picture.

Your walk with Christ is uniquely your own, so don't allow others to pressure you into some manmade method for relating to your God. There are as many different ways of drawing closer to him as there are people. Abandon yourself to God, and he'll help you to gradually grow and become more like Jesus.

WHAT ABOUT THE RESURRECTION OF JESUS CHRIST?

The truth of Christianity lies in the resurrection of Jesus Christ from the grave. The question is not whether he was a good teacher or a prophet, but did he rise from the dead? The apostle Paul was perfectly clear about the importance of Christ's resurrection: "If Christ has not been raised, then your faith has nothing to it; you are still guilty of your sins" (1 Corinthians 15:17).

Jesus' own words leave no room for doubt concerning his understanding of himself and the work he came to do on this earth: "I am the way, and the truth, and the life. The only way to the Father is through me" (John 14:6). He also said, "I am the resurrection and the life. Those who believe in me will have life even if they die. And everyone who lives and believes in me will never die" (John 11:25–26).

The resurrection of Jesus is the pivotal event in human history that boldly demonstrates the existence of God and his provision for the salvation of people on earth. Even our time line is interpreted in light of Jesus, with B.C. representing the time before Christ and A.D. representing the time after his death and resurrection. What makes the Christian faith unique is that it is founded on this unprecedented historical event. No other faith can make such a claim.

With God's help, the first-century followers of Christ turned the world upside down, and the world has never been the same since. All of history bears testimony to the fact that the early Christians made the world a better place and that dignity, decency, and deliverance follow wherever Christianity spreads. Virtually every significant social movement in Western civilization—from the abolition of slavery to the creation of child labor laws—owes its origin to the influence of Jesus Christ and his followers.

HOW DO I INVITE JESUS INTO MY LIFE?

Inviting Jesus into your life is as simple as believing in his resurrection and asking him to become the Lord of your life. The text of Romans 10:9 describes the process plainly: "If you declare with your mouth, 'Jesus is Lord,' and if you believe in your heart that God raised Jesus from the dead, you will be saved." It doesn't get any plainer than that.

Interestingly, the term "lord" refers to a position of ownership, so when you invite Jesus into your life, it means much more than a casual relationship. No longer are you and your will seated on the throne of your heart. It is Jesus who is to get the last word on what you say and do.

The paradox about entering a personal relationship with Jesus Christ is that he doesn't "lord" it over you. If you want to sin, he will allow you to. But once you realize his goodness and faithfulness and experience for yourself how very much he loves you, the desire to commit sin loses its appeal.

HOW CAN I SHARE JESUS WITH OTHERS?

You can share Jesus with others in several ways. Matthew 5:16 suggests one way: "You should be a light for other people. Live so that they will see the good things you do and will praise your Father in heaven." You share Jesus as you allow the light from within you to shine out toward others by helping people in need.

Jesus himself gave us a list of good deeds we can do to show others his goodness, including feeding the hungry, giving water to the thirsty, visiting the lonely, clothing the naked, and caring for the sick and incarcerated. He even went so far as to say that when we do such deeds for others, it's as if we're doing them for him (see Matthew 25:31–40).

While speaking with others about Jesus is certainly one way to share the Good News, not backing up what you say with action can actually undermine your credibility with your audience. So be sure you are also modeling the message. A famous quote attributed to Saint Francis of Assisi drives home the point: "Preach the Gospel always, and if necessary, use words."

A NOTE ABOUT THE NEW CENTURY VERSION®

God never intended the Bible to be too difficult for his people. To make sure God's message was clear, the authors of the Bible recorded God's word in familiar everyday language. These books brought a message that the original readers could understand. These first readers knew that God spoke through these books. Down through the centuries, many people wanted a Bible so badly that they copied different Bible books by hand!

Today, now that the Bible is readily available, many Christians do not regularly read it. Many feel that the Bible is too hard to understand or irrelevant to life.

The *New Century Version* captures the clear and simple message that the very first readers understood. This version presents the Bible as God intended it: clear and dynamic.

A team of scholars from the World Bible Translation Center worked together with twenty-one other experienced Bible scholars from all over the world to translate the text directly from the best available Greek and Hebrew texts. You can trust that this Bible accurately presents God's Word as it came to us in the original languages.

Translators kept sentences short and simple. They avoided difficult words and worked to make the text easier to read. They used modern terms for places and measurements. And they put figures of speech and idiomatic expressions ("he was gathered to his people") in language that even children understand ("he died").

Following the tradition of other English versions, the *New Century Version* indicates the divine name, *Yahweh*, by putting LORD, and sometimes GOD, in capital letters. This distinguishes it from *Adonai*, another Hebrew word that is translated Lord.

We acknowledge the infallibility of God's Word and yet our own frailty. We pray that God will use this Bible to help you understand his rich truth for yourself. To God be the glory.

THE PUBLISHER

1

MATTHEW 1:1-25

The Family History of Jesus

This is the family history of Jesus Christ. He came from the family of David, and David came from the family of Abraham.

2 Abraham was the father of Isaac.

Isaac was the father of Jacob.

Jacob was the father of Judah and his brothers.

3 Judah was the father of Perez and Zerah.

(Their mother was Tamar.)

Perez was the father of Hezron.

Hezron was the father of Ram.

4 Ram was the father of Amminadab.

Amminadab was the father of Nahshon.

Nahshon was the father of Salmon.

5 Salmon was the father of Boaz.

(Boaz's mother was Rahab.)

Boaz was the father of Obed.

(Obed's mother was Ruth.)

Obed was the father of Jesse.

6 Jesse was the father of King David.

David was the father of Solomon.

(Solomon's mother had been Uriah's wife.)

7 Solomon was the father of Rehoboam.

Rehoboam was the father of Abijah.

Abijah was the father of Asa.

8 Asa was the father of Jehoshaphat.

Jehoshaphat was the father of Jehoram.

Jehoram was the ancestor of Uzziah.

9 Uzziah was the father of Jotham.

Jotham was the father of Ahaz.

Ahaz was the father of Hezekiah.

10 Hezekiah was the father of Manasseh.

Manasseh was the father of Amon.

Amon was the father of Josiah.

11 Josiah was the grandfather of Jehoiachin and his brothers.

(This was at the time that the people were taken to Babylon.)

12 After they were taken to Babylon:

Jehoiachin was the father of Shealtiel.

Shealtiel was the grandfather of Zerubbabel.

13 Zerubbabel was the father of Abiud.

Abiud was the father of Eliakim.

Eliakim was the father of Azor.

14 Azor was the father of Zadok.

Zadok was the father of Akim.

Akim was the father of Eliud.

15 Eliud was the father of Eleazar.

Eleazar was the father of Matthan.

Matthan was the father of Jacob.

16 Jacob was the father of Joseph.

Joseph was the husband of Mary,

and Mary was the mother of Jesus.

Jesus is called the Christ.

17 So there were fourteen generations from Abraham to David. And there were fourteen generations from David until the people were taken to Babylon. And there were fourteen generations from the time when the people were taken to Babylon until Christ was born.

The Birth of Jesus Christ

18 This is how the birth of Jesus Christ came about. His mother Mary was engaged to marry Joseph, but before they married, she learned she was pregnant by the power of the Holy Spirit. 19 Because Mary's husband, Joseph, was a good man, he did not want to disgrace her in public, so he planned to divorce her secretly.

20 While Joseph thought about these things, an angel of the Lord came to him in a dream. The angel said, "Joseph, descendant of David, don't be afraid to take Mary as your wife, because the baby in her is from the Holy Spirit. 21 She will give birth to a son, and you will name him Jesus, because he will save his people from their sins."

22 All this happened to bring about what the Lord had said through the prophet: 23 "The virgin will be pregnant. She will have a son, and they will name him Immanuel," which means "God is with us."

24 When Joseph woke up, he did what the Lord's angel had told him to do. Joseph took Mary as his wife, 25 but he did not have sexual relations with her until she gave birth to the son. And Joseph named him Jesus.

OLD TESTAMENT READING

Then Isaiah said, "Ahaz, descendant of David, listen carefully! Isn't it bad enough that you wear out the patience of people? Do you also have to wear out the patience of my God? 14 The Lord himself will give you a sign: The virgin will be pregnant. She will have a son, and she will name him Immanuel."

Isaiah 7:13–14

INSIGHTS

The doctrine of the virgin birth is crucial to our faith. The incarnation of the Son of God was accomplished by a creative act of the Holy Spirit in the body of Mary, a virgin. It was a special miracle performed by the third person of the Holy Trinity—the Holy Spirit—which enabled the second person of the Trinity—the eternal Son of God—to take upon Himself a genuine, although sinless, human nature. He was born of a virgin, as a man, without surrendering any aspect of His deity. . . .

. . . One with us, yet one with God. He had to become man because man was the one who had sinned. He had to be God because God was the only One who could do anything about the sin of man. Humanity had tried for centuries, and the situation only got worse! The only way God could bring about the salvation of the fallen human race was to assume the form of the race He was to redeem.

God has given us the means to know the truth. Jesus is the way to the Father, because He is our Redeemer. He is the truth because He is the fulfillment of all the prophecies concerning Him. He is the life because He overcame death. . . . Jesus has the fullness of God dwelling in Him bodily forever and ever. The Son of God became the Son of man so that the sons of men might become the sons of God.

TERRY FULLAM

PAUSE FOR REFLECTION

What does the virgin birth of Jesus signify for all people? In what ways have you and all nations been blessed through the children of Abraham?

MATTHEW 2:1-23

Wise Men Come to Visit Jesus

Jesus was born in the town of Bethlehem in Judea during the time when Herod was king. When Jesus was born, some wise men from the east came to Jerusalem. **2**They asked, "Where is the baby who was born to be the king of the Jews? We saw his star in the east and have come to worship him."

3When King Herod heard this, he was troubled, as were all the people in Jerusalem. **4**Herod called a meeting of all the leading priests and teachers of the law and asked them where the Christ would be born. **5**They answered, "In the town of Bethlehem in Judea. The prophet wrote about this in the Scriptures:

6'But you, Bethlehem, in the land of Judah,
    are not just an insignificant village in Judah.
A ruler will come from you
    who will be like a shepherd for my people
        Israel.'"   *Micah 5:2*

7Then Herod had a secret meeting with the wise men and learned from them the exact time they first saw the star. **8**He sent the wise men to Bethlehem, saying, "Look carefully for the child. When you find him, come tell me so I can worship him too."

9After the wise men heard the king, they left. The star that they had seen in the east went before them until it stopped above the place where the child was. **10**When the wise men saw the star, they were filled with joy. **11**They came to the house where the child was and saw him with his mother, Mary, and they bowed down and worshiped him. They opened their gifts and gave him treasures of gold, frankincense, and myrrh. **12**But God warned the wise men in a dream not to go back to Herod, so they returned to their own country by a different way.

Jesus' Parents Take Him to Egypt

13After they left, an angel of the Lord came to Joseph in a dream and said, "Get up! Take the child and his mother and escape to Egypt, because Herod is starting to look for the child so he can kill him. Stay in Egypt until I tell you to return."

14So Joseph got up and left for Egypt during the night with the child and his mother. **15**And Joseph stayed in Egypt until Herod died. This happened to bring about what the Lord had said through the prophet: "I called my son out of Egypt."

Herod Kills the Baby Boys

16When Herod saw that the wise men had tricked him, he was furious. So he gave an order to kill all the baby boys in Bethlehem and in the surrounding area who were two years old or younger. This was in keeping with the time he learned from the wise men. **17**So what God had said through the prophet Jeremiah came true:

18"A voice was heard in Ramah
    of painful crying and deep sadness:
Rachel crying for her children.
    She refused to be comforted,
    because her children are dead."
                            Jeremiah 31:15

Joseph and Mary Return

19After Herod died, an angel of the Lord spoke to Joseph in a dream while he was in Egypt. **20**The angel said, "Get up! Take the child and his mother and go to the land of Israel, because the people who were trying to kill the child are now dead."

21So Joseph took the child and his mother and went to Israel. **22**But he heard that Archelaus was now king in Judea since his father Herod had died. So Joseph was afraid to go there. After being warned in a dream, he went to the area of Galilee, **23**to a town called Nazareth, and lived there. And so what God had said through the prophets came true: "He will be called a Nazarene."

OLD TESTAMENT READING

But you, Bethlehem Ephrathah,
though you are too small to be among the
army groups from Judah,
from you will come one who will rule Israel
for me.
He comes from very old times,
from days long ago."

3The LORD will give up his people
until the one who is having a baby gives
birth;
then the rest of his relatives will return
to the people of Israel.
4At that time the ruler of Israel will stand
and take care of his people
with the LORD's strength
and with the power of the name of the
LORD his God.
The Israelites will live in safety,
because his greatness will reach all over
the earth.
5 He will bring peace.

Micah 5:2–5a

INSIGHTS

God has led. This is history's testimony. Looking back over lives, we can see how beautifully, wonderfully, lovingly God has led. "As for me, the LORD has led me," testified the servant of Abraham (Genesis 24:27).

God will lead. This is the testimony of doctrine. The Scriptures teach it by precept and example throughout Old and New Testaments. The word of God declares it to be so. Looking ahead—before the need, before the crunch—we can testify that God will lead.

God is leading! This is the testimony of faith, where the rubber meets the road. God has promised to lead, and I seek to be led—an unbeatable combination. God's promise, my submission.

God has led, for which I am grateful. I know God will lead, and for this I praise and thank Him.

God is leading! This is my confidence and joy . . . my rest.

RICHARD HALVERSON

PAUSE FOR REFLECTION

Note the instances in which God protected the child Jesus and how each of those also fulfilled prophecy. What does this reveal to you about God's sovereignty and faithfulness in protecting his own?

MATTHEW 3:1 — 4:11

The Work of John the Baptist

3 About that time John the Baptist began preaching in the desert area of Judea. ²John said, "Change your hearts and lives because the kingdom of heaven is near." ³John the Baptist is the one Isaiah the prophet was talking about when he said:

"This is a voice of one
  who calls out in the desert:
'Prepare the way for the Lord.
  Make the road straight for him.'"

Isaiah 40:3

⁴John's clothes were made from camel's hair, and he wore a leather belt around his waist. For food, he ate locusts and wild honey. ⁵Many people came from Jerusalem and Judea and all the area around the Jordan River to hear John. ⁶They confessed their sins, and he baptized them in the Jordan River.

⁷Many of the Pharisees and Sadducees came to the place where John was baptizing people. When John saw them, he said, "You are snakes! Who warned you to run away from God's coming punishment? ⁸Do the things that show you really have changed your hearts and lives. ⁹And don't think you can say to yourselves, 'Abraham is our father.' I tell you that God could make children for Abraham from these rocks. ¹⁰The ax is now ready to cut down the trees, and every tree that does not produce good fruit will be cut down and thrown into the fire.

¹¹"I baptize you with water to show that your hearts and lives have changed. But there is one coming after me who is greater than I am, whose sandals I am not good enough to carry. He will baptize you with the Holy Spirit and fire. ¹²He will come ready to clean the grain, separating the good grain from the chaff. He will put the good part of the grain into his barn, but he will burn the chaff with a fire that cannot be put out."

Jesus Is Baptized by John

¹³At that time Jesus came from Galilee to the Jordan River and wanted John to baptize him. ¹⁴But John tried to stop him, saying, "Why do you come to me to be baptized? I need to be baptized by you!"

¹⁵Jesus answered, "Let it be this way for now. We should do all things that are God's will." So John agreed to baptize Jesus.

¹⁶As soon as Jesus was baptized, he came up out of the water. Then heaven opened, and he saw God's Spirit coming down on him like a dove. ¹⁷And a voice from heaven said, "This is my Son, whom I love, and I am very pleased with him."

The Temptation of Jesus

4 Then the Spirit led Jesus into the desert to be tempted by the devil. ²Jesus fasted for forty days and nights. After this, he was very hungry. ³The devil came to Jesus to tempt him, saying, "If you are the Son of God, tell these rocks to become bread."

⁴Jesus answered, "It is written in the Scriptures, 'A person lives not on bread alone, but by everything God says.'"

⁵Then the devil led Jesus to the holy city of Jerusalem and put him on a high place of the

Temple. **6**The devil said, "If you are the Son of God, jump down, because it is written in the Scriptures:

'He has put his angels in charge of you.

They will catch you in their hands

so that you will not hit your foot on a rock.'"

Psalm 91:11–12

7Jesus answered him, "It also says in the Scriptures, 'Do not test the Lord your God.'"

8Then the devil led Jesus to the top of a very high mountain and showed him all the kingdoms of the world and all their splendor. **9**The devil said, "If you will bow down and worship me, I will give you all these things."

10Jesus said to the devil, "Go away from me, Satan! It is written in the Scriptures, 'You must worship the Lord your God and serve only him.'"

11So the devil left Jesus, and angels came and took care of him.

OLD TESTAMENT READING

Children, come and listen to me.

I will teach you to worship the LORD.

12You must do these things

to enjoy life and have many happy days.

13You must not say evil things,

and you must not tell lies.

14Stop doing evil and do good.

Look for peace and work for it.

Psalm 34:11–14

INSIGHTS

Jean, a small shopkeeper in Bordeaux, worked long hours with virtually nothing to show for his labors. Even his best efforts to beguile the Paris tax collector left him very little for his family. His life was depressing and without purpose, until the day when a missionary entered his shop to make a purchase.

Before leaving the shop, this foreigner shared his faith with Jean, and for the first time the shopkeeper realized that there was more to life than he had ever supposed. . . .

As he grew in faith, Jean became convinced that his lifestyle must be radically altered and that he could no longer lie about how much income he was making at his little shop. When the time came to submit his tax forms, he filled them out in full and paid the required amount of taxes. The local tax clerk was stunned, and word spread like wildfire among the shopkeepers. Jean's wife was outraged, and his neighbors were convinced that he had lost his mind. When they inquired about his foolish actions, he could only explain that God had made him a different man.

RUTH TUCKER

PAUSE FOR REFLECTION

What message from God did John bring to the people of his day? Was it different from the message of the Old Testament? Was it different from Jesus' message? What does it mean to have a changed heart and live a changed life today?

MATTHEW 4:12 — 5:12

Jesus Begins Work in Galilee

12When Jesus heard that John had been put in prison, he went back to Galilee. **13**He left Nazareth and went to live in Capernaum, a town near Lake Galilee, in the area near Zebulun and Naphtali. **14**Jesus did this to bring about what the prophet Isaiah had said:

15"Land of Zebulun and land of Naphtali
along the sea,
beyond the Jordan River.
This is Galilee where the non-Jewish
people live.
16 These people who live in darkness
will see a great light.
They live in a place covered with the shadows
of death,
but a light will shine on them."

Isaiah 9:1–2

Jesus Chooses Some Followers

17From that time Jesus began to preach, saying, "Change your hearts and lives, because the kingdom of heaven is near."

18As Jesus was walking by Lake Galilee, he saw two brothers, Simon (called Peter) and his brother Andrew. They were throwing a net into the lake because they were fishermen. **19**Jesus said, "Come follow me, and I will make you fish for people." **20**So Simon and Andrew immediately left their nets and followed him.

21As Jesus continued walking by Lake Galilee, he saw two other brothers, James and John, the sons of Zebedee. They were in a boat with their father Zebedee, mending their nets. Jesus told them to come with him. **22**Immediately they left the boat and their father, and they followed Jesus.

Jesus Teaches and Heals People

23Jesus went everywhere in Galilee, teaching in the synagogues, preaching the Good News about the kingdom of heaven, and healing all the people's diseases and sicknesses. **24**The news about Jesus spread all over Syria, and people brought all the sick to him. They were suffering from different kinds of diseases. Some were in great pain, some had demons, some were epileptics, and some were paralyzed. Jesus healed all of them. **25**Many people from Galilee, the Ten Towns, Jerusalem, Judea, and the land across the Jordan River followed him.

Jesus Teaches the People

5 When Jesus saw the crowds, he went up on a hill and sat down. His followers came to him, **2**and he began to teach them, saying:
3"They are blessed who realize their spiritual
poverty,
for the kingdom of heaven belongs to
them.
4 They are blessed who grieve,
for God will comfort them.
5 They are blessed who are humble,
for the whole earth will be theirs.
6 They are blessed who hunger and thirst after
justice,
for they will be satisfied.
7 They are blessed who show mercy to others,
for God will show mercy to them.

8 They are blessed whose thoughts are pure,
   for they will see God.
9 They are blessed who work for peace,
   for they will be called God's children.
10 They are blessed who are persecuted for
      doing good,
   for the kingdom of heaven belongs to
      them.

11 "People will insult you and hurt you. They will lie and say all kinds of evil things about you because you follow me. But when they do, you will be blessed. 12 Rejoice and be glad, because you have a great reward waiting for you in heaven. People did the same evil things to the prophets who lived before you."

OLD TESTAMENT READING

The LORD said to Abram, "Leave your country, your relatives, and your father's family, and go to the land I will show you.

2 I will make you a great nation,
   and I will bless you.
I will make you famous,
   and you will be a blessing to others."

4 So Abram left Haran as the LORD had told him, and Lot went with him. At this time Abram was 75 years old.

Genesis 12:1–2, 4

INSIGHTS

Today, in principle, the call of the Lord Jesus has not changed. He still says "Follow me", and adds, "whoever of you does not renounce all that he has cannot be my disciple". In practice, however, this does not mean for the majority of Christians a physical departure from their home or their job. It implies rather an inner surrender of both, and a refusal to allow either family or ambition to occupy the first place in our lives.

First, there must be a renunciation of sin. This, in a word, is repentance. It is the first part of Christian conversion. It can in no circumstances be bypassed. Repentance and faith belong together. We cannot follow Christ without forsaking sin. . . .

Second, there must be a renunciation of self. In order to follow Christ we must not only forsake isolated sins, but renounce the very principle of self-will which lies at the root of every act of sin. To follow Christ is to surrender to him the rights over our own lives. It is to abdicate the throne of our heart and do homage to him as our King. . . .

The full, inexorable demand of Jesus Christ is now laid bare. He does not call us to a sloppy half-heartedness, but to a vigorous, absolute commitment. He calls us to make him our Lord.

John Stott

ACTION POINT

What have you had to forsake in order to follow Jesus? Think about what occupies first place in your life now. Pray that you will make following Jesus most important.

MATTHEW 5:13-37

You Are Like Salt and Light

13"You are the salt of the earth. But if the salt loses its salty taste, it cannot be made salty again. It is good for nothing, except to be thrown out and walked on.

14"You are the light that gives light to the world. A city that is built on a hill cannot be hidden. **15**And people don't hide a light under a bowl. They put it on a lampstand so the light shines for all the people in the house. **16**In the same way, you should be a light for other people. Live so that they will see the good things you do and will praise your Father in heaven.

The Importance of the Law

17"Don't think that I have come to destroy the law of Moses or the teaching of the prophets. I have not come to destroy them but to bring about what they said. **18**I tell you the truth, nothing will disappear from the law until heaven and earth are gone. Not even the smallest letter or the smallest part of a letter will be lost until everything has happened. **19**Whoever refuses to obey any command and teaches other people not to obey that command will be the least important in the kingdom of heaven. But whoever obeys the commands and teaches other people to obey them will be great in the kingdom of heaven. **20**I tell you that if you are no more obedient than the teachers of the law and the Pharisees, you will never enter the kingdom of heaven.

Jesus Teaches About Anger

21"You have heard that it was said to our people long ago, 'You must not murder anyone. Anyone who murders another will be judged.' **22**But I tell you, if you are angry with a brother or sister, you will be judged. If you say bad things to a brother or sister, you will be judged by the council. And if you call someone a fool, you will be in danger of the fire of hell.

23"So when you offer your gift to God at the altar, and you remember that your brother or sister has something against you, **24**leave your gift there at the altar. Go and make peace with that person, and then come and offer your gift.

25"If your enemy is taking you to court, become friends quickly, before you go to court. Otherwise, your enemy might turn you over to the judge, and the judge might give you to a guard to put you in jail. **26**I tell you the truth, you will not leave there until you have paid everything you owe.

Jesus Teaches About Sexual Sin

27"You have heard that it was said, 'You must not be guilty of adultery.' **28**But I tell you that if anyone looks at a woman and wants to sin sexually with her, in his mind he has already done that sin with the woman. **29**If your right eye causes you to sin, take it out and throw it away. It is better to lose one part of your body than to have your whole body thrown into hell. **30**If your right hand causes you to sin, cut it off and throw it away. It is better to lose one part of your body than for your whole body to go into hell.

Jesus Teaches About Divorce

31"It was also said, 'Anyone who divorces his wife must give her a written divorce paper.' **32**But I tell you that anyone who divorces his wife forces her to be guilty of adultery. The only reason for a man to divorce his wife is if she has sexual relations with another man. And anyone who marries that divorced woman is guilty of adultery.

Make Promises Carefully

33"You have heard that it was said to our people long ago, 'Don't break your promises, but keep the promises you make to the Lord.' 34But I tell you, never swear an oath. Don't swear an oath using the name of heaven, because heaven is God's throne. 35Don't swear an oath using the name of the earth, because the earth belongs to God. Don't swear an oath using the name of Jerusalem, because that is the city of the great King. 36Don't even swear by your own head, because you cannot make one hair on your head become white or black. 37Say only yes if you mean yes, and no if you mean no. If you say more than yes or no, it is from the Evil One."

OLD TESTAMENT READING

People who love the LORD hate evil.
The LORD watches over those who follow him
and frees them from the power of the
wicked.
11Light shines on those who do right;
joy belongs to those who are honest.

Psalm 97:10–11

LORD, you give light to my lamp.
My God brightens the darkness around me.

Psalm 18:28

INSIGHTS

Nowhere in the Bible are we commanded to bring non-Christians into the church to get saved. In fact, there is not one instance in the Bible of anyone who ever got converted in a church or synagogue. For instance, in Luke 19, our Lord did not ask Zaccheus to meet Him at the synagogue on the Sabbath. Instead, he went to Zaccheus' home. The misconception is that the pagan is supposed to come and hear; the Biblical mandate for the believer is to go and tell.

If we are to be salt and light in our world, we need to go where the lost are. That might mean inviting them into your home for dinner, going next door to visit with them, playing miniature golf together, or doing something else with them. The Holy Spirit will start working in their lives as they watch our lives and try to figure out why we are different.

Robert Tamasy

APPLICATION

Think about what it means to be salt and light in the world today. What kind of lifestyle shines as a light to the world and shows people how to be saved? How do you need to change your life in order to be the salt and light God wants you to be?

MATTHEW 5:38 – 6:15

Don't Fight Back

38"You have heard that it was said, 'An eye for an eye, and a tooth for a tooth.' 39But I tell you, don't stand up against an evil person. If someone slaps you on the right cheek, turn to him the other cheek also. 40If someone wants to sue you in court and take your shirt, let him have your coat also. 41If someone forces you to go with him one mile, go with him two miles. 42If a person asks you for something, give it to him. Don't refuse to give to someone who wants to borrow from you.

Love All People

43"You have heard that it was said, 'Love your neighbor and hate your enemies.' 44But I say to you, love your enemies. Pray for those who hurt you. 45If you do this, you will be true children of your Father in heaven. He causes the sun to rise on good people and on evil people, and he sends rain to those who do right and to those who do wrong. 46If you love only the people who love you, you will get no reward. Even the tax collectors do that. 47And if you are nice only to your friends, you are no better than other people. Even those who don't know God are nice to their friends. 48So you must be perfect, just as your Father in heaven is perfect.

Jesus Teaches About Giving

"Be careful! When you do good things, don't do them in front of people to be seen by them. If you do that, you will have no reward from your Father in heaven.

2"When you give to the poor, don't be like the hypocrites. They blow trumpets in the synagogues and on the streets so that people will see them and honor them. I tell you the truth, those hypocrites already have their full reward. 3So when you give to the poor, don't let anyone know what you are doing. 4Your giving should be done in secret. Your Father can see what is done in secret, and he will reward you.

Jesus Teaches About Prayer

5"When you pray, don't be like the hypocrites. They love to stand in the synagogues and on the street corners and pray so people will see them. I tell you the truth, they already have their full reward. 6When you pray, you should go into your room and close the door and pray to your Father who cannot be seen. Your Father can see what is done in secret, and he will reward you.

7"And when you pray, don't be like those people who don't know God. They continue saying things that mean nothing, thinking that God will hear them because of their many words. 8Don't be like them, because your Father knows the things you need before you ask him. 9So when you pray, you should pray like this:

'Our Father in heaven,
    may your name always be kept holy.
10May your kingdom come
    and what you want be done,
        here on earth as it is in heaven.
11Give us the food we need for each day.
12Forgive us for our sins,
        just as we have forgiven those who sinned
            against us.

13And do not cause us to be tempted,
but save us from the Evil One.' [The kingdom,
the power, and the glory are yours
forever. Amen.]
14Yes, if you forgive others for their sins, your Father in heaven will also forgive you for your sins.
15But if you don't forgive others, your Father in heaven will not forgive your sins."

OLD TESTAMENT READING

Lord, tell me your ways.
Show me how to live.
5Guide me in your truth,
and teach me, my God, my Savior.
I trust you all day long.
6Lord, remember your mercy and love
that you have shown since long ago.
7Do not remember the sins
and wrong things I did when I was young.
But remember to love me always
because you are good, Lord.

Psalm 25:4–7

INSIGHTS

Scripture is realistic in its treatment of sin, whether in the believer or unbeliever. It recognizes that sin is a continuing problem, even for the believer. He is not forever done with sin when he is converted, because he never gets beyond the reach of temptation. True, he has experienced the joy of forgiveness. He revels in the assurance that his guilt has been removed, but he is nowhere promised exemption from the lure of temptation or the possibility of sinning. . . .

Then how is it possible for a God who hates sin and requires purity, to continue having dealings with a sin-prone believer, to say nothing of permitting a deepening intimacy? The answer is that in the multi-faceted death of His Son, provision is made for a cleaning so deep, so radical, so continuous that a believer can walk with God in unbroken communion and deepening fellowship.

J. OSWALD SANDERS

ACTION POINT

In your own words, describe how God wants his people to pray. Why do you think seeking God's forgiveness is an essential part of prayer? Approach God now in prayer. Make yourself pure before him and share with him all that is in your heart.

MATTHEW 6:16 – 7:6

Jesus Teaches About Worship

16"When you fast, don't put on a sad face like the hypocrites. They make their faces look sad to show people they are fasting. I tell you the truth, those hypocrites already have their full reward. **17**So when you fast, comb your hair and wash your face. **18**Then people will not know that you are fasting, but your Father, whom you cannot see, will see you. Your Father sees what is done in secret, and he will reward you.

God Is More Important than Money

19"Don't store treasures for yourselves here on earth where moths and rust will destroy them and thieves can break in and steal them. **20**But store your treasures in heaven where they cannot be destroyed by moths or rust and where thieves cannot break in and steal them. **21**Your heart will be where your treasure is.

22"The eye is a light for the body. If your eyes are good, your whole body will be full of light. **23**But if your eyes are evil, your whole body will be full of darkness. And if the only light you have is really darkness, then you have the worst darkness.

24"No one can serve two masters. The person will hate one master and love the other, or will follow one master and refuse to follow the other. You cannot serve both God and worldly riches.

Don't Worry

25"So I tell you, don't worry about the food or drink you need to live, or about the clothes you need for your body. Life is more than food, and the body is more than clothes. **26**Look at the birds in the air. They don't plant or harvest or store food in barns, but your heavenly Father feeds them. And you know that you are worth much more than the birds. **27**You cannot add any time to your life by worrying about it.

28"And why do you worry about clothes? Look at how the lilies in the field grow. They don't work or make clothes for themselves. **29**But I tell you that even Solomon with his riches was not dressed as beautifully as one of these flowers. **30**God clothes the grass in the field, which is alive today but tomorrow is thrown into the fire. So you can be even more sure that God will clothe you. Don't have so little faith! **31**Don't worry and say, 'What will we eat?' or 'What will we drink?' or 'What will we wear?' **32**The people who don't know God keep trying to get these things, and your Father in heaven knows you need them. **33**Seek first God's kingdom and what God wants. Then all your other needs will be met as well. **34**So don't worry about tomorrow, because tomorrow will have its own worries. Each day has enough trouble of its own.

Be Careful About Judging Others

7 "Don't judge others, or you will be judged. **2**You will be judged in the same way that you judge others, and the amount you give to others will be given to you.

3"Why do you notice the little piece of dust in your friend's eye, but you don't notice the big piece of wood in your own eye? **4**How can you say to your friend, 'Let me take that little piece of dust out of your eye'? Look at yourself! You still have that big piece of wood in your own eye. **5**You hypocrite!

First, take the wood out of your own eye. Then you will see clearly to take the dust out of your friend's eye.

⁶"Don't give holy things to dogs, and don't throw your pearls before pigs. Pigs will only trample on them, and dogs will turn to attack you."

OLD TESTAMENT READING

On the twenty-fourth day of that same month, the people of Israel gathered. They fasted, and they wore rough cloth and put dust on their heads to show their sadness. ²Those people whose ancestors were from Israel had separated themselves from all foreigners. They stood and confessed their sins and their ancestors' sins. ³For a fourth of the day they stood where they were and read from the Book of the Teachings of the LORD their God. For another fourth of the day they confessed their sins and worshiped the LORD their God.

Nehemiah 9:1–3

The LORD says, "Even now, come back to me
with all your heart.
Fast, cry, and be sad."

¹³Tearing your clothes is not enough to show
you are sad;
let your heart be broken.
Come back to the LORD your God,
because he is kind and shows mercy.
He doesn't become angry quickly,
and he has great love.

Joel 2:12–13c

INSIGHTS

Our problem is that we want to test God rather than trust him. We want to experiment with him rather than rely on him. We're like the boy who tests the doubtful ice instead of skating confidently where God is leading. What is our faith worth if we don't trust completely? It is perfectly natural to trust in our own understanding, to rely on our own natural strengths, gifts, or talents (and indeed some modern prophets tell us to do so!). But it is the walk of faith to trust his teaching and direction. Give him first place and let him have precedence. This is the secret of safe guidance and peaceful progression. Simple dependence upon him, committing our all to him, obeying him implicitly—this is how to acknowledge him "in all thy ways."

AL BRYANT

APPLICATION

Describe the kind of life that truly honors God. In what ways do you trust and seek God on a daily basis?

MATTHEW
7:7 – 8:4

Ask God for What You Need

7"Ask, and God will give to you. Search, and you will find. Knock, and the door will open for you. 8Yes, everyone who asks will receive. Everyone who searches will find. And everyone who knocks will have the door opened.

9"If your children ask for bread, which of you would give them a stone? 10Or if your children ask for a fish, would you give them a snake? 11Even though you are bad, you know how to give good gifts to your children. How much more your heavenly Father will give good things to those who ask him!

The Most Important Rule

12"Do to others what you want them to do to you. This is the meaning of the law of Moses and the teaching of the prophets.

The Way to Heaven Is Hard

13"Enter through the narrow gate. The gate is wide and the road is wide that leads to hell, and many people enter through that gate. 14But the gate is small and the road is narrow that leads to true life. Only a few people find that road.

People Know You by Your Actions

15"Be careful of false prophets. They come to you looking gentle like sheep, but they are really dangerous like wolves. 16You will know these people by what they do. Grapes don't come from thornbushes, and figs don't come from thorny weeds. 17In the same way, every good tree produces good fruit, but a bad tree produces bad fruit. 18A good tree cannot produce bad fruit, and a bad tree cannot produce good fruit. 19Every tree that does not produce good fruit is cut down and thrown into the fire. 20In the same way, you will know these false prophets by what they do.

21"Not all those who say 'You are our Lord' will enter the kingdom of heaven. The only people who will enter the kingdom of heaven are those who do what my Father in heaven wants. 22On the last day many people will say to me, 'Lord, Lord, we spoke for you, and through you we forced out demons and did many miracles.' 23Then I will tell them clearly, 'Get away from me, you who do evil. I never knew you.'

Two Kinds of People

24"Everyone who hears my words and obeys them is like a wise man who built his house on rock. 25It rained hard, the floods came, and the winds blew and hit that house. But it did not fall, because it was built on rock. 26Everyone who hears my words and does not obey them is like a foolish man who built his house on sand. 27It rained hard, the floods came, and the winds blew and hit that house, and it fell with a big crash."

28When Jesus finished saying these things, the people were amazed at his teaching, 29because he did not teach like their teachers of the law. He taught like a person who had authority.

Jesus Heals a Sick Man

8 When Jesus came down from the hill, great crowds followed him. 2Then a man with a skin disease came to Jesus. The

man bowed down before him and said, "Lord, you can heal me if you will."

³Jesus reached out his hand and touched the man and said, "I will. Be healed!" And immediately the man was healed from his disease. ⁴Then Jesus said to him, "Don't tell anyone about this. But go and show yourself to the priest and offer the gift Moses commanded for people who are made well. This will show the people what I have done."

OLD TESTAMENT READING

Happy are those who don't listen to the
        wicked,
    who don't go where sinners go,
    who don't do what evil people do.
²They love the LORD's teachings,
    and they think about those teachings day
        and night.
³They are strong, like a tree planted by a river.
    The tree produces fruit in season,
    and its leaves don't die.
Everything they do will succeed.

Psalm 1:1–3

When people's steps follow the LORD,
    God is pleased with their ways.
²⁴If they stumble, they will not fall,
    because the LORD holds their hand.

Psalm 37:23–24

INSIGHTS

It must be admitted that, in its first stages, the broad way is generally easy and rather delightful. The boat launched on the flowing stream sweeps merrily and pleasantly along, the gradient of the road slopes so as to make walking easy, the sun shines, and the path is filled with bright flowers. But to a life given up to self-indulgence, there is only one end—destruction.

There is a more excellent way, but it is too narrow to admit the trailing garments of passionate desire, too narrow for pride, self-indulgence, greed, and avarice—it is the Way of the Cross, but it leads to Life! We all want to see life—and the remarkable thing is that those who expect to get most out of it by self-indulgence miss everything; whilst those who seem to curtail their lives by following Christ, win everything. Few find and enter this path, is the lament of our Lord. Let us put our hand in His, that He may lead us into the path of life, "that shineth more and more unto the perfect day."

F. B. MEYER

APPLICATION

What good things does God promise to those who search for him and walk in his ways? What kind of person makes the decision to walk through the narrow gate and build on the Rock? What kind of person are you? On what path do you walk? What will be the reward of that path?

MATTHEW 8:5-27

Jesus Heals a Soldier's Servant

5When Jesus entered the city of Capernaum, an army officer came to him, begging for help. **6**The officer said, "Lord, my servant is at home in bed. He can't move his body and is in much pain."

7Jesus said to the officer, "I will go and heal him."

8The officer answered, "Lord, I am not worthy for you to come into my house. You only need to command it, and my servant will be healed. **9**I, too, am a man under the authority of others, and I have soldiers under my command. I tell one soldier, 'Go,' and he goes. I tell another soldier, 'Come,' and he comes. I say to my servant, 'Do this,' and my servant does it.

10When Jesus heard this, he was amazed. He said to those who were following him, "I tell you the truth, this is the greatest faith I have found, even in Israel. **11**Many people will come from the east and from the west and will sit and eat with Abraham, Isaac, and Jacob in the kingdom of heaven. **12**But those people who should be in the kingdom will be thrown outside into the darkness, where people will cry and grind their teeth with pain."

13Then Jesus said to the officer, "Go home. Your servant will be healed just as you believed he would." And his servant was healed that same hour.

Jesus Heals Many People

14When Jesus went to Peter's house, he saw that Peter's mother-in-law was sick in bed with a fever. **15**Jesus touched her hand, and the fever left her. Then she stood up and began to serve Jesus.

16That evening people brought to Jesus many who had demons. Jesus spoke and the demons left them, and he healed all the sick. **17**He did these things to bring about what Isaiah the prophet had said:

"He took our suffering on him
and carried our diseases."   *Isaiah 53:4*

People Want to Follow Jesus

18When Jesus saw the crowd around him, he told his followers to go to the other side of the lake. **19**Then a teacher of the law came to Jesus and said, "Teacher, I will follow you any place you go."

20Jesus said to him, "The foxes have holes to live in, and the birds have nests, but the Son of Man has no place to rest his head."

21Another man, one of Jesus' followers, said to him, "Lord, first let me go and bury my father."

22But Jesus told him, "Follow me, and let the people who are dead bury their own dead."

Jesus Calms a Storm

23Jesus got into a boat, and his followers went with him. **24**A great storm arose on the lake so that waves covered the boat, but Jesus was sleeping. **25**His followers went to him and woke him, saying, "Lord, save us! We will drown!"

26Jesus answered, "Why are you afraid? You don't have enough faith." Then Jesus got up and gave a command to the wind and the waves, and it became completely calm.

27The men were amazed and said, "What kind of man is this? Even the wind and the waves obey him!"

OLD TESTAMENT READING

My whole being, praise the LORD.
LORD my God, you are very great.
You are clothed with glory and majesty;
2 you wear light like a robe.
You stretch out the skies like a tent.
3 You build your room above the clouds.
You make the clouds your chariot,
and you ride on the wings of the wind.
4 You make the winds your messengers,
and flames of fire are your servants.

31 May the glory of the LORD be forever.
May the LORD enjoy what he has made.
32 He just looks at the earth, and it shakes.
He touches the mountains, and they
smoke.

33 I will sing to the LORD all my life;
I will sing praises to my God as long as I
live.

Psalm 104:1–4, 31–33

INSIGHTS

When Jesus was on earth He displayed remarkable powers. He raised Lazarus from the dead and performed many other miracles. His contemporaries noted an element of His power that we sometimes do not—the power of His speaking. The gospel writers reported that Jesus did not speak like the scribes and the Pharisees but as one "having authority" (see Matt. 7:29). . . .

Behind the authority of Jesus stood the omnipotent power of God, the link to Jesus' divine authority. The very word authority hints at a connection to the word authorship. God is the omnipotent author of His creation. He is the omnipotent redeemer of His creation. He exercises omnipotent authority over His creation.

R. C. SPROUL

PAUSE FOR REFLECTION

In what ways did Jesus' followers see his powerful authority demonstrated? In what did the psalmist recognize his authority? What reveals his authority to you? Is his authority as real to you as to the army officer?

MATTHEW
8:28 — 9:17

Jesus Heals Two Men with Demons

28When Jesus arrived at the other side of the lake in the area of the Gadarene people, two men who had demons in them met him. These men lived in the burial caves and were so dangerous that people could not use the road by those caves. **29**They shouted, "What do you want with us, Son of God? Did you come here to torture us before the right time?"

30Near that place there was a large herd of pigs feeding. **31**The demons begged Jesus, "If you make us leave these men, please send us into that herd of pigs."

32Jesus said to them, "Go!" So the demons left the men and went into the pigs. Then the whole herd rushed down the hill into the lake and were drowned. **33**The herdsmen ran away and went into town, where they told about all of this and what had happened to the men who had demons. **34**Then the whole town went out to see Jesus. When they saw him, they begged him to leave their area.

Jesus Heals a Paralyzed Man

9Jesus got into a boat and went back across the lake to his own town. **2**Some people brought to Jesus a man who was paralyzed and lying on a mat. When Jesus saw the faith of these people, he said to the paralyzed man, "Be encouraged, young man. Your sins are forgiven."

3Some of the teachers of the law said to themselves, "This man speaks as if he were God. That is blasphemy!"

4Knowing their thoughts, Jesus said, "Why are you thinking evil thoughts? **5**Which is easier: to say, 'Your sins are forgiven,' or to tell him, 'Stand up and walk'? **6**But I will prove to you that the Son of Man has authority on earth to forgive sins." Then Jesus said to the paralyzed man, "Stand up, take your mat, and go home." **7**And the man stood up and went home. **8**When the people saw this, they were amazed and praised God for giving power like this to human beings.

Jesus Chooses Matthew

9When Jesus was leaving, he saw a man named Matthew sitting in the tax collector's booth. Jesus said to him, "Follow me," and he stood up and followed Jesus.

10As Jesus was having dinner at Matthew's house, many tax collectors and "sinners" came and ate with Jesus and his followers. **11**When the Pharisees saw this, they asked Jesus' followers, "Why does your teacher eat with tax collectors and sinners?"

12When Jesus heard them, he said, "It is not the healthy people who need a doctor, but the sick. **13**Go and learn what this means: 'I want kindness more than I want animal sacrifices.' I did not come to invite good people but to invite sinners."

Jesus' Followers Are Criticized

14Then the followers of John came to Jesus and said, "Why do we and the Pharisees often fast for a certain time, but your followers don't?"

15Jesus answered, "The friends of the bridegroom are not sad while he is with them. But the time will come when the bridegroom will be taken from them, and then they will fast.

16"No one sews a patch of unshrunk cloth over a hole in an old coat. If he does, the patch will shrink and pull away from the coat, making the hole worse. **17**Also, people never pour new wine into old leather bags. Otherwise, the bags will break, the wine will spill, and the wine bags will be ruined. But people always pour new wine into new wine bags. Then both will continue to be good."

OLD TESTAMENT READING

The LORD shows mercy and is kind.
   He does not become angry quickly, and he
      has great love.
9He will not always accuse us,
   and he will not be angry forever.
10He has not punished us as our sins should be
      punished;
   he has not repaid us for the evil we have
      done.
11As high as the sky is above the earth,
   so great is his love for those who respect
      him.
12He has taken our sins away from us
   as far as the east is from west.
13The LORD has mercy on those who respect
      him,
   as a father has mercy on his children.

Psalm 103:8–13

INSIGHTS

Other faiths assume our ability to secure and retain God's favor by right action and give us detailed guidance as to how to do it; but Christianity has said that sin has so ruined us that we cannot do this. It is beyond our power to keep the law of God as we should; we are guilty and helpless, wholly unable to save ourselves, and so must be saved, if at all, by the action of another.

Other faiths direct us to follow the teaching of their founders—famous men long deceased; but Christianity, identifying its founder as God incarnate, who died for our sins and rose again to bestow forgiveness, proclaims him as alive and calls on us to trust him and his atoning work, making him the object of our worship and service. Redemption through the love of the Son of God, who became man, bore his Father's judgment on our sins, and rose from death to reign forever, is a theme without parallel in the world's religions.

Christianity proclaims that those who repent of sin and trust in Jesus Christ are created anew at the heart of their being by the Holy Spirit. They are united to Jesus Christ in his risen life, their inner nature is changed, so that their deepest impulse is not now to disobey God and serve self, but to deny self and obey God. There is nothing like this in any other religion.

J. I. PACKER

➤ APPLICATION

If Jesus is our example, what should our attitude toward sinners be?

MATTHEW
9:18 – 10:10

Jesus Gives Life to a Dead Girl and Heals a Sick Woman

18While Jesus was saying these things, a leader of the synagogue came to him. He bowed down before Jesus and said, "My daughter has just died. But if you come and lay your hand on her, she will live again." **19**So Jesus and his followers stood up and went with the leader.

20Then a woman who had been bleeding for twelve years came behind Jesus and touched the edge of his coat. **21**She was thinking, "If I can just touch his clothes, I will be healed."

22Jesus turned and saw the woman and said, "Be encouraged, dear woman. You are made well because you believed." And the woman was healed from that moment on.

23Jesus continued along with the leader and went into his house. There he saw the funeral musicians and many people crying. **24**Jesus said, "Go away. The girl is not dead, only asleep." But the people laughed at him. **25**After the crowd had been thrown out of the house, Jesus went into the girl's room and took hold of her hand, and she stood up. **26**The news about this spread all around the area.

Jesus Heals More People

27When Jesus was leaving there, two blind men followed him. They cried out, "Have mercy on us, Son of David!"

28After Jesus went inside, the blind men went with him. He asked the men, "Do you believe that I can make you see again?"

They answered, "Yes, Lord."

29Then Jesus touched their eyes and said, "Because you believe I can make you see again, it will happen." **30**Then the men were able to see. But Jesus warned them strongly, saying, "Don't tell anyone about this." **31**But the blind men left and spread the news about Jesus all around that area.

32When the two men were leaving, some people brought another man to Jesus. This man could not talk because he had a demon in him. **33**After Jesus forced the demon to leave the man, he was able to speak. The crowd was amazed and said, "We have never seen anything like this in Israel."

34But the Pharisees said, "The prince of demons is the one that gives him power to force demons out."

35Jesus traveled through all the towns and villages, teaching in their synagogues, preaching the Good News about the kingdom, and healing all kinds of diseases and sicknesses. **36**When he saw the crowds, he felt sorry for them because they were hurting and helpless, like sheep without a shepherd. **37**Jesus said to his followers, "There are many people to harvest but only a few workers to help harvest them. **38**Pray to the Lord, who owns the harvest, that he will send more workers to gather his harvest."

Jesus Sends Out His Apostles

10 Jesus called his twelve followers together and gave them authority to drive out evil spirits and to heal every kind of disease and sickness. **2**These are the names of the twelve apostles: Simon (also called

Peter) and his brother Andrew; James son of Zebedee, and his brother John; **3**Philip and Bartholomew; Thomas and Matthew, the tax collector; James son of Alphaeus, and Thaddaeus; **4**Simon the Zealot and Judas Iscariot, who turned against Jesus.

5Jesus sent out these twelve men with the following order: "Don't go to the non-Jewish people or to any town where the Samaritans live. **6**But go to the people of Israel, who are like lost sheep. **7**When you go, preach this: 'The kingdom of heaven is near.' **8**Heal the sick, raise the dead to life again, heal those who have skin diseases, and force demons out of people. I give you these powers freely, so help other people freely. **9**Don't carry any money with you—gold or silver or copper. **10**Don't carry a bag or extra clothes or sandals or a walking stick. Workers should be given what they need."

OLD TESTAMENT READING

I will feed my flock and lead them to rest, says the Lord GOD. **16**I will search for the lost, bring back those that strayed away, put bandages on those that were hurt, and make the weak strong. But I will destroy those sheep that are fat and strong. I will tend the sheep with fairness."

Ezekiel 34:15–16

INSIGHTS

The nature of God is to seek and to save sinners. From the opening pages of human history, it was God who sought the fallen couple in the garden. . . . The Almighty was portrayed as a Savior throughout the Old Testament (Psalm 106:21; Isaiah 43:11; Hosea 13:4), so it is appropriate that when Christ entered the world of men as God in human flesh, He was known first of all as a Savior.

Even His name was divinely chosen to be the name of a Savior. An angel told Joseph in a dream, "You shall call His name Jesus, for it is He who will save His people from their sins" (Matthew 1:21). The very heart of all redemptive teaching is that Jesus entered this world on a search-and-rescue mission for sinners. That truth is what characterizes the gospel as good news.

But it is good news only for those who perceive themselves as sinners. The unequivocal teaching of Jesus is that those who will not acknowledge and repent of their sin are beyond the reach of saving grace. All are sinners, but not all are willing to admit their depravity. If they do, He becomes their friend (cf. Matthew 11:19). Those who will not can know Him only as a Judge.

JOHN F. MACARTHUR, JR.

ACTION POINT

In what ways is God's compassion for the lost expressed in these passages of Scripture? How does God want to care for his people? Thank him for the ways he has shown his compassion to you.

MATTHEW 10:11-40

11"When you enter a city or town, find some worthy person there and stay in that home until you leave. **12**When you enter that home, say, 'Peace be with you.' **13**If the people there welcome you, let your peace stay there. But if they don't welcome you, take back the peace you wished for them. **14**And if a home or town refuses to welcome you or listen to you, leave that place and shake its dust off your feet. **15**I tell you the truth, on the Judgment Day it will be better for the towns of Sodom and Gomorrah than for the people of that town.

Jesus Warns His Apostles

16"Listen, I am sending you out like sheep among wolves. So be as clever as snakes and as innocent as doves. **17**Be careful of people, because they will arrest you and take you to court and whip you in their synagogues. **18**Because of me you will be taken to stand before governors and kings, and you will tell them and the non-Jewish people about me. **19**When you are arrested, don't worry about what to say or how to say it. At that time you will be given the things to say. **20**It will not really be you speaking but the Spirit of your Father speaking through you.

21"Brothers will give their own brothers to be killed, and fathers will give their own children to be killed. Children will fight against their own parents and have them put to death. **22**All people will hate you because you follow me, but those people who keep their faith until the end will be saved. **23**When you are treated badly in one city, run to another city. I tell you the truth, you will not finish

going through all the cities of Israel before the Son of Man comes.

24"A student is not better than his teacher, and a servant is not better than his master. **25**A student should be satisfied to become like his teacher; a servant should be satisfied to become like his master. If the head of the family is called Beelzebul, then the other members of the family will be called worse names!

Fear God, Not People

26"So don't be afraid of those people, because everything that is hidden will be shown. Everything that is secret will be made known. **27**I tell you these things in the dark, but I want you to tell them in the light. What you hear whispered in your ear you should shout from the housetops. **28**Don't be afraid of people, who can kill the body but cannot kill the soul. The only one you should fear is the one who can destroy the soul and the body in hell. **29**Two sparrows cost only a penny, but not even one of them can die without your Father's knowing it. **30**God even knows how many hairs are on your head. **31**So don't be afraid. You are worth much more than many sparrows.

Tell People About Your Faith

32"All those who stand before others and say they believe in me, I will say before my Father in heaven that they belong to me. **33**But all who stand before others and say they do not believe in me, I will say before my Father in heaven that they do not belong to me.

34"Don't think that I came to bring peace to the earth. I did not come to bring peace, but a sword. **35**I have come so that

'a son will be against his father,
a daughter will be against her mother,
a daughter-in-law will be against her mother-
in-law.
36 A person's enemies will be members of his
own family.'
Micah 7:6

37 "Those who love their father or mother more
than they love me are not worthy to be my followers. Those who love their son or daughter more
than they love me are not worthy to be my followers. **38** Whoever is not willing to carry the cross
and follow me is not worthy of me. **39** Those who
try to hold on to their lives will give up true life.
Those who give up their lives for me will hold on
to true life. **40** Whoever accepts you also accepts
me, and whoever accepts me also accepts the One
who sent me."

OLD TESTAMENT READING

tell the people about the message I received
from the LORD,
but this only brings me insults.
The people make fun of me all day long.
9 Sometimes I say to myself,
"I will forget about the LORD.
I will not speak anymore in his name."
But then his message becomes like a burning
fire inside me,
deep within my bones.
I get tired of trying to hold it inside of me,
and finally, I cannot hold it in.
Jeremiah 20:8c–9

INSIGHTS

In the Sermon on the Mount Jesus said that those who suffer unjust treatment will have a "great" reward in heaven (see Matt. 5:10). The elect who have been abused, abandoned, stolen from, taken advantage of—all will be rewarded for their pain. . . .

God knows when we suffer unjustly. . . . God has not abandoned you to the whims and wishes of those who are more powerful. He knows when His children are overlooked for advancement because of their religious views. Young lady, He knows when less talented women are advanced past you because you refuse to compromise morally. He sees the abandoned mother who never knows from month to month if her estranged husband is going to send a check. God is taking it all in. He has already appointed a prosecuting attorney, a jury, and a judge. And they are all the same person—the Lord Jesus. On that court date He will bring about justice for His elect.

Charles Stanley

PAUSE FOR REFLECTION

How intensely does the desire to speak about Jesus burn within you? What price are you willing to pay to follow Jesus? What gives you comfort as you seek to follow him? What is your reward?

MATTHEW
10:41—11:24

41Whoever meets a prophet and accepts him will receive the reward of a prophet. And whoever accepts a good person because that person is good will receive the reward of a good person. **42**Those who give one of these little ones a cup of cold water because they are my followers will truly get their reward."

Jesus and John the Baptist

11 After Jesus finished telling these things to his twelve followers, he left there and went to the towns in Galilee to teach and preach.

2John the Baptist was in prison, but he heard about what the Christ was doing. So John sent some of his followers to Jesus. **3**They asked him, "Are you the One who is to come, or should we wait for someone else?"

4Jesus answered them, "Go tell John what you hear and see: **5**The blind can see, the crippled can walk, and people with skin diseases are healed. The deaf can hear, the dead are raised to life, and the Good News is preached to the poor. **6**Those who do not stumble in their faith because of me are blessed."

7As John's followers were leaving, Jesus began talking to the people about John. Jesus said, "What did you go out into the desert to see? A reed blown by the wind? **8**What did you go out to see? A man dressed in fine clothes? No, those who wear fine clothes live in kings' palaces. **9**So why did you go out? To see a prophet? Yes, and I tell you, John is more than a prophet. **10**This was written about him:

'I will send my messenger ahead of you,
who will prepare the way for you.'

Malachi 3:1

11I tell you the truth, John the Baptist is greater than any other person ever born, but even the least important person in the kingdom of heaven is greater than John. **12**Since the time John the Baptist came until now, the kingdom of heaven has been going forward in strength, and people have been trying to take it by force. **13**All the prophets and the law of Moses told about what would happen until the time John came. **14**And if you will believe what they said, you will believe that John is Elijah, whom they said would come. **15**Let those with ears use them and listen!

16"What can I say about the people of this time? What are they like? They are like children sitting in the marketplace, who call out to each other,

17'We played music for you, but you did not dance;

we sang a sad song, but you did not cry.'
18John came and did not eat or drink like other people. So people say, 'He has a demon.' **19**The Son of Man came, eating and drinking, and people say, 'Look at him! He eats too much and drinks too much wine, and he is a friend of tax collectors and sinners.' But wisdom is proved to be right by what she does."

Jesus Warns Unbelievers

20Then Jesus criticized the cities where he did most of his miracles, because the people did not change their lives and stop sinning. **21**He said, "How terrible for you, Korazin! How terrible for you, Bethsaida! If the same miracles I did in you had happened in Tyre and Sidon, those people would have changed their lives a long time ago. They would have worn rough cloth and put ashes on themselves to show they had changed. **22**But I tell you, on the Judgment Day it will be better for Tyre and Sidon than for you. **23**And you, Capernaum, will you be lifted up to heaven? No, you will be thrown down to the depths. If the miracles I did in you had happened in Sodom, its people would have stopped sinning, and it would still be a city today. **24**But I tell you, on the Judgment Day it will be better for Sodom than for you."

OLD TESTAMENT READING

Y ou fools, how long will you be foolish?
24I called, but you refused to listen;
I held out my hand, but you paid no attention.
25You did not follow my advice
and did not listen when I corrected you.
26So I will laugh when you are in trouble.

28"Then you will call to me,
but I will not answer.
You will look for me,
but you will not find me.
29It is because you rejected knowledge
and did not choose to respect the LORD.
30You did not accept my advice,
and you rejected my correction.

31So you will get what you deserve;
you will get what you planned for others."

Proverbs 1:22a, 24–26a, 28–31

INSIGHTS

Generally speaking, God's kingdom is a synonym for God's rule. Those who choose to live in His kingdom (though still very much alive on Planet Earth) choose to live under His authority. . . .

. . . The kingdom is the invisible realm where God rules as supreme authority. That's helpful news. The bad news is that we, by nature, don't want Him to rule over us; we much prefer to please ourselves. . . .

. . . To put it bluntly, we don't want anybody other than ourselves ruling over us! Much like those people in a story Jesus once told, "We do not want this man to reign over us!" (Luke 19:14). Not until we experience a spiritual rebirth will we submit to God's rule.

CHARLES SWINDOLL

PAUSE FOR REFLECTION

What is the penalty for rejecting God's wisdom and knowledge? What does God promise to those who listen to him? What change occurs in those who accept God's kingdom? Has that change occurred in you?

MATTHEW 11:25 – 12:21

Jesus Offers Rest to People

25At that time Jesus said, "I praise you, Father, Lord of heaven and earth, because you have hidden these things from the people who are wise and smart. But you have shown them to those who are like little children. **26**Yes, Father, this is what you really wanted.

27"My Father has given me all things. No one knows the Son, except the Father. And no one knows the Father, except the Son and those whom the Son chooses to tell.

28"Come to me, all of you who are tired and have heavy loads, and I will give you rest. **29**Accept my teachings and learn from me, because I am gentle and humble in spirit, and you will find rest for your lives. **30**The burden that I ask you to accept is easy; the load I give you to carry is light."

Jesus Is Lord of the Sabbath

At that time Jesus was walking through some fields of grain on a Sabbath day. His followers were hungry, so they began to pick the grain and eat it. **2**When the Pharisees saw this, they said to Jesus, "Look! Your followers are doing what is unlawful to do on the Sabbath day."

3Jesus answered, "Have you not read what David did when he and the people with him were hungry? **4**He went into God's house, and he and those with him ate the holy bread, which was lawful only for priests to eat. **5**And have you not read

in the law of Moses that on every Sabbath day the priests in the Temple break this law about the Sabbath day? But the priests are not wrong for doing that. **6**I tell you that there is something here that is greater than the Temple. **7**The Scripture says, 'I want kindness more than I want animal sacrifices.' You don't really know what those words mean. If you understood them, you would not judge those who have done nothing wrong.

8"So the Son of Man is Lord of the Sabbath day."

Jesus Heals a Man's Hand

9Jesus left there and went into their synagogue, **10**where there was a man with a crippled hand. They were looking for a reason to accuse Jesus, so they asked him, "Is it right to heal on the Sabbath day?"

11Jesus answered, "If any of you has a sheep, and it falls into a ditch on the Sabbath day, you will help it out of the ditch. **12**Surely a human being is more important than a sheep. So it is lawful to do good things on the Sabbath day."

13Then Jesus said to the man with the crippled hand, "Hold out your hand." The man held out his hand, and it became well again, like the other hand. **14**But the Pharisees left and made plans to kill Jesus.

Jesus Is God's Chosen Servant

15Jesus knew what the Pharisees were doing, so he left that place. Many people followed him, and he healed all who were sick. **16**But Jesus warned the people not to tell who he was. **17**He did these things to bring about what Isaiah the prophet had said:
18"Here is my servant whom I have chosen.

I love him, and I am pleased with him.

I will put my Spirit upon him,
and he will tell of my justice to all people.

¹⁹ He will not argue or cry out;
no one will hear his voice in the streets.

²⁰ He will not break a crushed blade of grass
or put out even a weak flame
until he makes justice win the victory.

²¹ In him will the non-Jewish people find
hope."

Isaiah 42:1–4

OLD TESTAMENT READING

The sacrifice God wants is a broken spirit.
God, you will not reject a heart that is
broken and sorry for sin.

Psalm 51:17

INSIGHTS

"Lord," I said, "I want to be your
man, not my own.
So to you I give my money, my
car—even my home."
Then, smug and content. I relaxed
with a smile
And whispered to God, "I bet its
been a while,
Since anyone has given so much—
so freely?"
His answer surprised me. He
replied, "Not really."

"Not a day has gone by since the
beginning of time,
That someone hasn't offered
meager nickels and dimes,
Golden altars and crosses,
contributions and penance,
Stone monuments and steeples; but
why not repentance?

"Your lips know no prayers. Your
eyes, no compassion.
But you will go to church (when
church-going's in fashion).

"Just give me a tear—a heart ready
to mold.
And I'll give you a mission, a
message so bold
That a fire will be stirred where
there was only death,
And your heart will be flamed by my
life and my breath."

I stuck my hands in my pockets and
kicked at the dirt.
It's tough to be corrected (I guess
my feelings were hurt).
But it was worth the struggle to
realize the thought.
That the cross isn't for sale and
Christ's blood can't be bought.

MAX LUCADO

APPLICATION

What does God want from his people? Be specific! Think about what it means for
God to want those things from you. Pray that you will understand what he wants
and that your heart will be open to obey him.

MATTHEW 12:22-45

Jesus' Power Is from God

22Then some people brought to Jesus a man who was blind and could not talk, because he had a demon. Jesus healed the man so that he could talk and see. **23**All the people were amazed and said, "Perhaps this man is the Son of David!"

24When the Pharisees heard this, they said, "Jesus uses the power of Beelzebul, the ruler of demons, to force demons out of people."

25Jesus knew what the Pharisees were thinking, so he said to them, "Every kingdom that is divided against itself will be destroyed. And any city or family that is divided against itself will not continue. **26**And if Satan forces out himself, then Satan is divided against himself, and his kingdom will not continue. **27**You say that I use the power of Beelzebul to force out demons. If that is true, then what power do your people use to force out demons? So they will be your judges. **28**But if I use the power of God's Spirit to force out demons, then the kingdom of God has come to you.

29"If anyone wants to enter a strong person's house and steal his things, he must first tie up the strong person. Then he can steal the things from the house.

30"Whoever is not with me is against me. Whoever does not work with me is working against me. **31**So I tell you, people can be forgiven for every sin and everything they say against God. But whoever speaks against the Holy Spirit will not be forgiven. **32**Anyone who speaks against the Son of Man can be forgiven, but anyone who speaks against the Holy Spirit will not be forgiven, now or in the future.

People Know You by Your Words

33"If you want good fruit, you must make the tree good. If your tree is not good, it will have bad fruit. A tree is known by the kind of fruit it produces. **34**You snakes! You are evil people, so how can you say anything good? The mouth speaks the things that are in the heart. **35**Good people have good things in their hearts, and so they say good things. But evil people have evil in their hearts, so they say evil things. **36**And I tell you that on the Judgment Day people will be responsible for every careless thing they have said. **37**The words you have said will be used to judge you. Some of your words will prove you right, but some of your words will prove you guilty."

The People Ask for a Miracle

38Then some of the Pharisees and teachers of the law answered Jesus, saying, "Teacher, we want to see you work a miracle as a sign."

39Jesus answered, "Evil and sinful people are the ones who want to see a miracle for a sign. But no sign will be given to them, except the sign of the prophet Jonah. **40**Jonah was in the stomach of the big fish for three days and three nights. In the same way, the Son of Man will be in the grave three days and three nights. **41**On the Judgment Day the people from Nineveh will stand up with you people who live now, and they will show that you are guilty. When Jonah preached to them, they were sorry and changed their lives. And I tell you that someone greater than Jonah is here. **42**On the Judgment Day, the Queen of the South will stand up with you people who live today. She will show that you are guilty, because she came from far away to listen to Solomon's wise teaching. And I tell you that someone greater than Solomon is here.

People Today Are Full of Evil

43"When an evil spirit comes out of a person, it travels through dry places, looking for a place to rest, but it doesn't find it. 44So the spirit says, 'I will go back to the house I left.' When the spirit comes back, it finds the house still empty, swept clean, and made neat. 45Then the evil spirit goes out and brings seven other spirits even more evil than it is, and they go in and live there. So the person has even more trouble than before. It is the same way with the evil people who live today."

OLD TESTAMENT READING

The words of a good person are like pure
        silver,
    but an evil person's thoughts are worth
        very little.
21Good people's words will help many others,
    but fools will die because they don't have
        wisdom.

Proverbs 10:20–21

INSIGHTS

The tongue is the indicator of the person. What we talk about all the time is what we love. The words we use and the words we don't use define what we are thinking, feeling, and becoming. . . .

We Christians must learn to undergo rigorous self-examination; we must honestly discern what we are really saying if we are going to understand who we are. . . .

We must listen closely to the inner reminder of this Holy Spirit. In essence, what we are doing is sticking out our tongues for the Great Physician to examine. . . . If some symptoms indicate mouth disease, we must confess to him the words that were unpleasing to him and ask forgiveness. Then we should take a dose of medicine and read from those Scriptures that emphasize healthy mouth habits. We should place the medicinal verses dealing with word usage under our tongues nightly, and let them accomplish a cathartic cleaning as we sleep so that tomorrow we can begin the day with renewed strength to speak words of life.

KAREN BURTON MAINS

ACTION POINT

Are you intimidated by the thought of explaining every careless word you have said? Listen to your words today and write down what they reveal about your heart. Pray that your words will prove your heart to be innocent before God.

MATTHEW 12:46 — 13:17

Jesus' True Family

46While Jesus was talking to the people, his mother and brothers stood outside, trying to find a way to talk to him. **47**Someone told Jesus, "Your mother and brothers are standing outside, and they want to talk to you."

48He answered, "Who is my mother? Who are my brothers?" **49**Then he pointed to his followers and said, "Here are my mother and my brothers. **50**My true brother and sister and mother are those who do what my Father in heaven wants."

A Story About Planting Seed

13 That same day Jesus went out of the house and sat by the lake. **2**Large crowds gathered around him, so he got into a boat and sat down, while the people stood on the shore. **3**Then Jesus used stories to teach them many things. He said: "A farmer went out to plant his seed. **4**While he was planting, some seed fell by the road, and the birds came and ate it all up. **5**Some seed fell on rocky ground, where there wasn't much dirt. That seed grew very fast, because the ground was not deep. **6**But when the sun rose, the plants dried up, because they did not have deep roots. **7**Some other seed fell among thorny weeds, which grew and choked the good plants. **8**Some other seed fell on good ground where it grew and produced a crop. Some plants made a hundred times more, some made sixty times more, and some made thirty times more. **9**Let those with ears use them and listen."

Why Jesus Used Stories to Teach

10The followers came to Jesus and asked, "Why do you use stories to teach the people?"

11Jesus answered, "You have been chosen to know the secrets about the kingdom of heaven, but others cannot know these secrets. **12**Those who have understanding will be given more, and they will have all they need. But those who do not have understanding, even what they have will be taken away from them. **13**This is why I use stories to teach the people: They see, but they don't really see. They hear, but they don't really hear or understand. **14**So they show that the things Isaiah said about them are true:

'You will listen and listen, but you will not understand.
You will look and look, but you will not learn.
15For the minds of these people have become stubborn.
They do not hear with their ears,
and they have closed their eyes.
Otherwise they might really understand what they see with their eyes
and hear with their ears.
They might really understand in their minds and come back to me and be healed.'

Isaiah 6:9–10

16But you are blessed, because you see with your eyes and hear with your ears. **17**I tell you the truth, many prophets and good people wanted to see the things that you now see, but they did not see them. And they wanted to hear the things that you now hear, but they did not hear them."

OLD TESTAMENT READING

How I love your teachings!
I think about them all day long.
101 I have avoided every evil way
so I could obey your word.
103 Your promises are sweet to me,
sweeter than honey in my mouth!
104 Your orders give me understanding,
so I hate lying ways.

105 Your word is like a lamp for my feet
and a light for my path.

106 I will do what I have promised
and obey your fair laws.

Psalm 119:97, 101, 103–106

But they refused to pay attention; they were stubborn and did not want to listen anymore. **12** They made their hearts as hard as rock and would not listen to the teachings of the LORD All-Powerful. And they would not hear the words he sent by his Spirit through the earlier prophets. So the LORD All-Powerful became very angry."

Zechariah 7:11–12

INSIGHTS

Our Lord warns that the human heart can be so pounded and beaten down with the traffic of sin that it becomes completely insensitive to the gospel. This is the heart that knows no repentance, no sorrow over sin, no guilt, and no concern for the things of God. It allows itself to be trampled by an endless procession of evil thoughts, cherished sins, and ungodly activities. It is careless, callous, indifferent, never broken up or softened by conviction or sorrow for wrongdoing. This is the heart of the fool described in Proverbs. The fool hates knowledge, and resists instruction. The fool despises wisdom and says in his heart there is no God. He will not hear. His mind is closed. And he does not want to be bothered with a gospel invitation.

Many people have hearts like that. You can shower them with seed, but it just lies there. It does not penetrate. And it does not stay very long before Satan comes and takes it away completely. Each time you try to witness to such a person, you must start again at the beginning.

Dry, hard, soil on the edge of the field does not necessarily signify someone who is anti-religious. Some of the hardest individuals in the world remain on the fringes of true religion. But because sin has so hardened their hearts, they are utterly unproductive and unresponsive to God.

JOHN F. MACARTHUR, JR.

ACTION POINT

How are the teachings of Jesus received by those who follow him? Why is it that some people are unable to understand God's words? Pray for a soft heart that wants to understand all that God teaches.

MATTHEW 13:18-43

Jesus Explains the Seed Story

18"So listen to the meaning of that story about the farmer. **19**What is the seed that fell by the road? That seed is like the person who hears the message about the kingdom but does not understand it. The Evil One comes and takes away what was planted in that person's heart. **20**And what is the seed that fell on rocky ground? That seed is like the person who hears the teaching and quickly accepts it with joy. **21**But he does not let the teaching go deep into his life, so he keeps it only a short time. When trouble or persecution comes because of the teaching he accepted, he quickly gives up. **22**And what is the seed that fell among the thorny weeds? That seed is like the person who hears the teaching but lets worries about this life and the temptation of wealth stop that teaching from growing. So the teaching does not produce fruit in that person's life. **23**But what is the seed that fell on the good ground? That seed is like the person who hears the teaching and understands it. That person grows and produces fruit, sometimes a hundred times more, sometimes sixty times more, and sometimes thirty times more."

A Story About Wheat and Weeds

24Then Jesus told them another story: "The kingdom of heaven is like a man who planted good seed in his field. **25**That night, when everyone was asleep, his enemy came and planted weeds among the wheat and then left. **26**Later, the wheat sprouted and the heads of grain grew, but the weeds also grew. **27**Then the man's servants came to him and said, 'You planted good seed in your field. Where did the weeds come from?' **28**The man answered, 'An enemy planted weeds.' The servants asked, 'Do you want us to pull up the weeds?' **29**The man answered, 'No, because when you pull up the weeds, you might also pull up the wheat. **30**Let the weeds and the wheat grow together until the harvest time. At harvest time I will tell the workers, "First gather the weeds and tie them together to be burned. Then gather the wheat and bring it to my barn."'"

Stories of Mustard Seed and Yeast

31Then Jesus told another story: "The kingdom of heaven is like a mustard seed that a man planted in his field. **32**That seed is the smallest of all seeds, but when it grows, it is one of the largest garden plants. It becomes big enough for the wild birds to come and build nests in its branches."

33Then Jesus told another story: "The kingdom of heaven is like yeast that a woman took and hid in a large tub of flour until it made all the dough rise."

34Jesus used stories to tell all these things to the people; he always used stories to teach them. **35**This is as the prophet said:

"I will speak using stories;
I will tell things that have been secret since the world was made."   *Psalm 78:2*

Jesus Explains About the Weeds

36Then Jesus left the crowd and went into the house. His followers came to him and said, "Explain to us the meaning of the story about the weeds in the field."

37Jesus answered, "The man who planted the good seed in the field is the Son of Man. 38The field is the world, and the good seed are all of God's children who belong to the kingdom. The weeds are those people who belong to the Evil One. 39And the enemy who planted the bad seed is the devil. The harvest time is the end of the age, and the workers who gather are God's angels.

40"Just as the weeds are pulled up and burned in the fire, so it will be at the end of the age. 41The Son of Man will send out his angels, and they will gather out of his kingdom all who cause sin and all who do evil. 42The angels will throw them into the blazing furnace, where the people will cry and grind their teeth with pain. 43Then the good people will shine like the sun in the kingdom of their Father. Let those with ears use them and listen."

OLD TESTAMENT READING

Remember my words with your whole being. Write them down and tie them to your hands as a sign; tie them on your foreheads to remind you. 19Teach them well to your children, talking about them when you sit at home and walk along the road, when you lie down and when you get up. 20Write them on your doors and gates 21so that both you and your children will live a long time in the land the LORD promised your ancestors, as long as the skies are above the earth.

Deuteronomy 11:18–21

INSIGHTS

H. A. Ironside told of a godly man named Andrew Frazer who had come to southern California to recover from a serious illness. Though this Irishman was quite weak, he opened his worn Bible and began expounding the truths of God's Word in a way that Ironside had never heard before. So moved by Frazer's words was Ironside that his curiosity drove him to ask, "Where did you learn these things? Did you learn them in some college or seminary?" The sickly man said, "My dear young man, I learned these things on my knees on the mud floor of a little sod cottage in the north of Ireland. There with my open Bible before me I used to kneel for hours at a time and ask the Spirit of God to reveal Christ to my soul and to open the Word to my heart. He taught me more on my knees on that mud floor than I ever could have learned in all the seminaries or colleges in the world."

WOODROW KROLL

APPLICATION

What happens when a person understands and lives by God's teaching? What are you willing to do in order to remember God's Word with your whole heart?

MATTHEW
13:44 — 14:12

Stories of a Treasure and a Pearl

44"The kingdom of heaven is like a treasure hidden in a field. One day a man found the treasure, and then he hid it in the field again. He was so happy that he went and sold everything he owned to buy that field.

45"Also, the kingdom of heaven is like a man looking for fine pearls. **46**When he found a very valuable pearl, he went and sold everything he had and bought it.

A Story of a Fishing Net

47"Also, the kingdom of heaven is like a net that was put into the lake and caught many different kinds of fish. **48**When it was full, the fishermen pulled the net to the shore. They sat down and put all the good fish in baskets and threw away the bad fish. **49**It will be this way at the end of the age. The angels will come and separate the evil people from the good people. **50**The angels will throw the evil people into the blazing furnace, where people will cry and grind their teeth with pain."

51Jesus asked his followers, "Do you understand all these things?"

They answered, "Yes, we understand."

52Then Jesus said to them, "So every teacher of the law who has been taught about the kingdom of heaven is like the owner of a house. He brings out both new things and old things he has saved."

Jesus Goes to His Hometown

53When Jesus finished teaching with these stories, he left there. **54**He went to his hometown and taught the people in the synagogue, and they were amazed. They said, "Where did this man get this wisdom and this power to do miracles? **55**He is just the son of a carpenter. His mother is Mary, and his brothers are James, Joseph, Simon, and Judas. **56**And all his sisters are here with us. Where then does this man get all these things?" **57**So the people were upset with Jesus.

But Jesus said to them, "A prophet is honored everywhere except in his hometown and in his own home."

58So he did not do many miracles there because they had no faith.

How John the Baptist Was Killed

14 At that time Herod, the ruler of Galilee, heard the reports about Jesus. **2**So he said to his servants, "Jesus is John the Baptist, who has risen from the dead. That is why he can work these miracles."

3Sometime before this, Herod had arrested John, tied him up, and put him into prison. Herod did this because of Herodias, who had been the wife of Philip, Herod's brother. **4**John had been telling Herod, "It is not lawful for you to be married to Herodias." **5**Herod wanted to kill John, but he was afraid of the people, because they believed John was a prophet.

6On Herod's birthday, the daughter of Herodias danced for Herod and his guests, and she pleased him. **7**So he promised with an oath to give her anything she wanted. **8**Herodias told her daughter what to ask for, so she said to Herod, "Give me the head of John the Baptist here on a platter." **9**Although King Herod was very sad, he had made a promise, and his dinner guests had heard him. So Herod ordered that what she asked for be done. **10**He sent soldiers to the prison to cut off John's head. **11**And they brought it on a platter and gave it to the girl, and she took it to her mother. **12**John's followers came and got his body and buried it. Then they went and told Jesus.

OLD TESTAMENT READING

LORD, everything you have made will praise you;
  those who belong to you will bless you.
11They will tell about the glory of your kingdom
  and will speak about your power.
12Then everyone will know the mighty things you do
  and the glory and majesty of your kingdom.
13Your kingdom will go on and on,
  and you will rule forever.

Psalm 145:10–13a

INSIGHTS

During the Civil War, the army of the Union and the army of the Confederacy were locked in a vicious battle to the death just outside the city of Richmond. As night fell after the first day of the battle, cheers were heard from the Confederate lines. When General Grant asked what was going on behind the enemy's line, he was told that the wife of General George Pickett had given birth to a baby boy, and that his troops were celebrating. . . .

Upon receiving the news, General Grant ordered bonfires to be lit and a toast to be given. Cheers and hoorahs rang out all night long. For a few hours, the shooting stopped and warring soldiers were drawn together for a birthday party. The birth of Pickett's son only temporarily stopped a war. But it stands as evidence of what a good birthday party can do. . . .

The good news is that another Son was born, and there were some who stopped what they were doing and enjoyed a little bit of peace for just a little while. There was singing in the sky—at least some shepherds said there was. And some strange visitors came looking for a baby whom they nicknamed the Prince of Peace. Everyone has not gotten the message, so not everyone knows about the baby. But the baby started a movement and we know that someday everyone will come to His party and call Him the Lord of the feast.

There's a great day coming when the world will change. What started as a birthday party will end with a wedding feast. We will call it the "Kingdom of God." We must pray for it, and we must work for it.

TONY CAMPOLO

PAUSE FOR REFLECTION

What do you understand about God's kingdom from the three images Jesus presented to his followers? Is the coming of God's kingdom exciting enough for you to stop doing your own thing and celebrate?

MATTHEW 14:13 – 36

More than Five Thousand Fed

13When Jesus heard what had happened to John, he left in a boat and went to a lonely place by himself. But the crowds heard about it and followed him on foot from the towns. **14**When he arrived, he saw a great crowd waiting. He felt sorry for them and healed those who were sick.

15When it was evening, his followers came to him and said, "No one lives in this place, and it is already late. Send the people away so they can go to the towns and buy food for themselves."

16But Jesus answered, "They don't need to go away. You give them something to eat."

17They said to him, "But we have only five loaves of bread and two fish."

18Jesus said, "Bring the bread and the fish to me." **19**Then he told the people to sit down on the grass. He took the five loaves and the two fish and, looking to heaven, he thanked God for the food. Jesus divided the bread and gave it to his followers, who gave it to the people. **20**All the people ate and were satisfied. Then the followers filled twelve baskets with the leftover pieces of food. **21**There were about five thousand men there who ate, not counting women and children.

Jesus Walks on the Water

22Immediately Jesus told his followers to get into the boat and go ahead of him across the lake. He stayed there to send the people home. **23**After he had sent them away, he went by himself up into the hills to pray. It was late, and Jesus was there alone. **24**By this time, the boat was already far away from land. It was being hit by waves, because the wind was blowing against it.

25Between three and six o'clock in the morning, Jesus came to them, walking on the water. **26**When his followers saw him walking on the water, they were afraid. They said, "It's a ghost!" and cried out in fear.

27But Jesus quickly spoke to them, "Have courage! It is I. Do not be afraid."

28Peter said, "Lord, if it is really you, then command me to come to you on the water."

29Jesus said, "Come."

And Peter left the boat and walked on the water to Jesus. **30**But when Peter saw the wind and the waves, he became afraid and began to sink. He shouted, "Lord, save me!"

31Immediately Jesus reached out his hand and caught Peter. Jesus said, "Your faith is small. Why did you doubt?"

32After they got into the boat, the wind became calm. **33**Then those who were in the boat worshiped Jesus and said, "Truly you are the Son of God!"

34When they had crossed the lake, they came to shore at Gennesaret. **35**When the people there recognized Jesus, they told people all around there that Jesus had come, and they brought all their sick to him. **36**They begged Jesus to let them touch just the edge of his coat, and all who touched it were healed.

OLD TESTAMENT READING

You, LORD, give true peace
    to those who depend on you,
    because they trust you.
⁴So, trust the LORD always,
    because he is our Rock forever.

Isaiah 26:3–4

The LORD is kind and does what is right;
    our God is merciful.

⁶The LORD watches over the foolish;
    when I was helpless, he saved me.
⁷I said to myself, "Relax,
    because the LORD takes care of you."
⁸LORD, you saved me from death.
    You stopped my eyes from crying;
    you kept me from being defeated.
⁹So I will walk with the LORD
    in the land of the living.

Psalm 116:5–9

INSIGHTS

Today many fears fill our lives. We fear poverty, sickness, loneliness, death. We fear the dangers of the night and the pressures of the day.

David learned that the only way to be released from fears was to TRUST the Lord. "What time I am afraid, I will trust in thee." He changed the focus of his eyes from his situation to the Lord. Faith replaced fear. He PUT his trust in the Lord. This was an act of his will. "In God have I put my trust: I will not be afraid what man can do unto me" (Ps. 56:11).

Freedom from fear is the result of confidence and trust in God. We may be helpless against fear, but God is not. When trusting God, there is nothing to fear.

Faith is more than believing what God can do. It is trust in the Person of God Himself. "But without faith it is impossible to please him: for he that cometh to God must believe that He IS, and that He is a rewarder of them that diligently seek Him" (Heb. 11:6). . . .

One day a father discovered his little boy had climbed an old tree. The limbs were beginning to break under the boy's weight. The father held up his arms and called, "Jump! I'll catch you." The little son considered the offer for a moment. Then, as more limbs began to break, he said, "Shall I let go of everything, Daddy, and trust you?"

What a lesson for us. Our Heavenly Father wants us to let go of everything and trust Him.

MILLIE STAMM

PAUSE FOR REFLECTION

Think about the fears and needs in your life. In what ways have you "let go of everything" and put your trust in God to meet those needs? Pray or write your own psalm of trust to God. Praise him for his faithfulness to you.

MATTHEW 15:1-31

Obey God's Law

15 Then some Pharisees and teachers of the law came to Jesus from Jerusalem. They asked him, **2**"Why don't your followers obey the unwritten laws which have been handed down to us? They don't wash their hands before they eat."

3Jesus answered, "And why do you refuse to obey God's command so that you can follow your own teachings? **4**God said, 'Honor your father and your mother,' and 'Anyone who says cruel things to his father or mother must be put to death.' **5**But you say a person can tell his father or mother, 'I have something I could use to help you, but I have given it to God already.' **6**You teach that person not to honor his father or his mother. You rejected what God said for the sake of your own rules. **7**You are hypocrites! Isaiah was right when he said about you:

8'These people show honor to me with words,
  but their hearts are far from me.
9Their worship of me is worthless.
  The things they teach are nothing but
    human rules.'"   *Isaiah 29:13*

10After Jesus called the crowd to him, he said, "Listen and understand what I am saying. **11**It is not what people put into their mouths that makes them unclean. It is what comes out of their mouths that makes them unclean."

12Then his followers came to him and asked, "Do you know that the Pharisees are angry because of what you said?"

13Jesus answered, "Every plant that my Father in heaven has not planted himself will be pulled up by the roots. **14**Stay away from the Pharisees; they are blind leaders. And if a blind person leads a blind person, both will fall into a ditch."

15Peter said, "Explain the example to us."

16Jesus said, "Do you still not understand? **17**Surely you know that all the food that enters the mouth goes into the stomach and then goes out of the body. **18**But what people say with their mouths comes from the way they think; these are the things that make people unclean. **19**Out of the mind come evil thoughts, murder, adultery, sexual sins, stealing, lying, and speaking evil of others. **20**These things make people unclean; eating with unwashed hands does not make them unclean."

Jesus Helps a Non-Jewish Woman

21Jesus left that place and went to the area of Tyre and Sidon. **22**A Canaanite woman from that area came to Jesus and cried out, "Lord, Son of David, have mercy on me! My daughter has a demon, and she is suffering very much."

23But Jesus did not answer the woman. So his followers came to Jesus and begged him, "Tell the woman to go away. She is following us and shouting."

24Jesus answered, "God sent me only to the lost sheep, the people of Israel."

25Then the woman came to Jesus again and bowed before him and said, "Lord, help me!"

26Jesus answered, "It is not right to take the children's bread and give it to the dogs."

27The woman said, "Yes, Lord, but even the dogs eat the crumbs that fall from their masters' table."

28Then Jesus answered, "Woman, you have

great faith! I will do what you asked." And at that moment the woman's daughter was healed.

Jesus Heals Many People

29After leaving there, Jesus went along the shore of Lake Galilee. He went up on a hill and sat there.

30Great crowds came to Jesus, bringing with them the lame, the blind, the crippled, those who could not speak, and many others. They put them at Jesus' feet, and he healed them. 31The crowd was amazed when they saw that people who could not speak before were now able to speak. The crippled were made strong. The lame could walk, and the blind could see. And they praised the God of Israel for this.

OLD TESTAMENT READING

Those who hate you may try to fool you with
    their words,
    but in their minds they are planning
      evil.
25People's words may be kind, but don't believe
    them,
    because their minds are full of evil
      thoughts.
26Lies can hide hate,
    but the evil will be plain to everyone.

Proverbs 26:24–26

INSIGHTS

In the ancient Greek plays, the actors were called hypocrites. On the stage they professed to be something they weren't. Unfortunately, there are many people who go through life playacting. They profess to be something they are not. They are hypocrites. They fool no one with this false veneer, this facade, this hypocrisy, except themselves. What they really are is well-known to God and their acquaintances with the result that they are displeasing to both. . . .

. . . Through the years innumerable people have gone to a Christless grave to spend eternity in hell because of the hypocrisy of many who call themselves Christians.

It is said that Thomas K. Beecher could not stand deceit of any kind. When he discovered that the clock in his church ran habitually either too slow or too fast, he reportedly put a placard on the wall above it that read in large letters, "Don't blame my hands—the trouble lies deeper." Don't make the mistake of promising to be a better Christian. The trouble is not on the outside; it is in the inner recesses of a person's being. Only Christ can cure this malady. This He will do if a person in genuine repentance seeks His forgiveness and turns himself over to Him in simple childlike faith.

HAROLD FICKETT

APPLICATION

Why is hypocrisy so displeasing to God? Where does hypocrisy originate? What hypocrisy in your life needs to be healed?

MATTHEW
15:32 — 16:20

More than Four Thousand Fed

32Jesus called his followers to him and said, "I feel sorry for these people, because they have already been with me three days, and they have nothing to eat. I don't want to send them away hungry. They might faint while going home."

33His followers asked him, "How can we get enough bread to feed all these people? We are far away from any town."

34Jesus asked, "How many loaves of bread do you have?"

They answered, "Seven, and a few small fish."

35Jesus told the people to sit on the ground. **36**He took the seven loaves of bread and the fish and gave thanks to God. Then he divided the food and gave it to his followers, and they gave it to the people. **37**All the people ate and were satisfied. Then his followers filled seven baskets with the leftover pieces of food. **38**There were about four thousand men there who ate, besides women and children. **39**After sending the people home, Jesus got into the boat and went to the area of Magadan.

The Leaders Ask for a Miracle

The Pharisees and Sadducees came to Jesus, wanting to trick him. So they asked him to show them a miracle from God.

2Jesus answered, "At sunset you say we will have good weather, because the sky is red. **3**And in the morning you say that it will be a rainy day, because the sky is dark and red. You see these signs in the sky and know what they mean. In the same way, you see the things that I am doing now, but you don't know their meaning. **4**Evil and sinful people ask for a miracle as a sign, but they will not be given any sign, except the sign of Jonah." Then Jesus left them and went away.

Guard Against Wrong Teachings

5Jesus' followers went across the lake, but they had forgotten to bring bread. **6**Jesus said to them, "Be careful! Beware of the yeast of the Pharisees and the Sadducees."

7His followers discussed the meaning of this, saying, "He said this because we forgot to bring bread."

8Knowing what they were talking about, Jesus asked them, "Why are you talking about not having bread? Your faith is small. **9**Do you still not understand? Remember the five loaves of bread that fed the five thousand? And remember that you filled many baskets with the leftovers? **10**Or the seven loaves of bread that fed the four thousand and the many baskets you filled then also? **11**I was not talking to you about bread. Why don't you understand that? I am telling you to beware of the yeast of the Pharisees and the Sadducees." **12**Then the followers understood that Jesus was not telling them to beware of the yeast used in bread but to beware of the teaching of the Pharisees and the Sadducees.

Peter Says Jesus Is the Christ

13When Jesus came to the area of Caesarea Philippi, he asked his followers, "Who do people say the Son of Man is?"

14 They answered, "Some say you are John the Baptist. Others say you are Elijah, and still others say you are Jeremiah or one of the prophets."

15 Then Jesus asked them, "And who do you say I am?"

16 Simon Peter answered, "You are the Christ, the Son of the living God."

17 Jesus answered, "You are blessed, Simon son of Jonah, because no person taught you that. My Father in heaven showed you who I am. **18** So I tell you, you are Peter. On this rock I will build my church, and the power of death will not be able to defeat it. **19** I will give you the keys of the kingdom of heaven; the things you don't allow on earth will be the things that God does not allow, and the things you allow on earth will be the things that God allows." **20** Then Jesus warned his followers not to tell anyone he was the Christ.

OLD TESTAMENT READING

The LORD says, "All you who are thirsty, come and drink.
Those of you who do not have money, come, buy and eat!
Come buy wine and milk
without money and without cost.
2 Why spend your money on something that is not real food?
Why work for something that doesn't really satisfy you?
Listen closely to me, and you will eat what is good;
your soul will enjoy the rich food that satisfies."

Isaiah 55:1–2

INSIGHTS

Our Lord's mission of grace and truth was at its height. His help was sought with the utmost eagerness. Large numbers of sick were cast at his feet in hot haste. The crumb was given to the woman of Canaan, but whole loaves were distributed to the crowds of Jews, because it was befitting that they should have a full chance to appreciate and accept Christ. For a brief moment they glorified the God of Israel, but the spasm of gratitude was transient. "His own" rejected Jesus. They would have his miracles, but would not own his claims. Take care that you do not become content with getting his help; love him for himself.

Do not suppose that these miracles were confined to his earthly life. He is still the great storehouse of divine and healing energy. He is still moved with compassion, and longs to help each weary and sin-sick soul. His thought still is "lest they faint in the way." The wilderness can place no bar on "the saving strength of his right hand."

F. B. MEYER

APPLICATION

What does the "real food" that Jesus offers satisfy? How does a person receive that food? Why do you want to be close to Jesus? Do you want his miracles or his claims? Physical food or spiritual food?

MATTHEW
16:21 – 17:13

Jesus Says that He Must Die

21From that time on Jesus began telling his followers that he must go to Jerusalem, where the Jewish elders, the leading priests, and the teachers of the law would make him suffer many things. He told them he must be killed and then be raised from the dead on the third day.

22Peter took Jesus aside and told him not to talk like that. He said, "God save you from those things, Lord! Those things will never happen to you!"

23Then Jesus said to Peter, "Go away from me, Satan! You are not helping me! You don't care about the things of God, but only about the things people think are important."

24Then Jesus said to his followers, "If people want to follow me, they must give up the things they want. They must be willing even to give up their lives to follow me. **25**Those who want to save their lives will give up true life, and those who give up their lives for me will have true life. **26**It is worthless to have the whole world if they lose their souls. They could never pay enough to buy back their souls. **27**The Son of Man will come again with his Father's glory and with his angels. At that time, he will reward them for what they have done. **28**I tell you the truth, some people standing here will see the Son of Man coming with his kingdom before they die."

Jesus Talks with Moses and Elijah

17 Six days later, Jesus took Peter, James, and John, the brother of James, up on a high mountain by themselves. **2**While they watched, Jesus' appearance was changed; his face became bright like the sun, and his clothes became white as light. **3**Then Moses and Elijah appeared to them, talking with Jesus.

4Peter said to Jesus, "Lord, it is good that we are here. If you want, I will put up three tents here—one for you, one for Moses, and one for Elijah."

5While Peter was talking, a bright cloud covered them. A voice came from the cloud and said, "This is my Son, whom I love, and I am very pleased with him. Listen to him!"

6When his followers heard the voice, they were so frightened they fell to the ground. **7**But Jesus went to them and touched them and said, "Stand up. Don't be afraid." **8**When they looked up, they saw Jesus was now alone.

9As they were coming down the mountain, Jesus commanded them not to tell anyone about what they had seen until the Son of Man had risen from the dead.

10Then his followers asked him, "Why do the teachers of the law say that Elijah must come first?"

11Jesus answered, "They are right to say that Elijah is coming and that he will make everything the way it should be. **12**But I tell you that Elijah has already come, and they did not recognize him. They did to him whatever they wanted to do. It will be the same with the Son of Man; those same people will make the Son of Man suffer." **13**Then the followers understood that Jesus was talking about John the Baptist.

OLD TESTAMENT READING

We all have wandered away like sheep;
    each of us has gone his own way.
But the LORD has put on him the punishment
    for all the evil we have done.

[7] He was beaten down and punished,
    but he didn't say a word.
He was like a lamb being led to be killed.
    He was quiet, as a sheep is quiet while its
        wool is being cut;
    he never opened his mouth.
[8] Men took him away roughly and unfairly.
    He died without children to continue his
        family.
He was put to death;
    he was punished for the sins of my people.
[9] He was buried with wicked men,
    and he died with the rich.
He had done nothing wrong,
    and he had never lied.

[10] But it was the LORD who decided
    to crush him and make him suffer.
The LORD made his life a penalty offering,
    but he will still see his descendants and live a
        long life.
He will complete the things the LORD wants
    him to do.

Isaiah 53:6–10

INSIGHTS

The New Testament proclaims that at some unforeseeable time in the future God will ring down the final curtain on history, and there will come a Day on which all our days and all the judgments upon us and all our judgments upon each other will themselves be judged. The judge will be Christ. In other words, the one who judges us most finally will be the one who loves us most fully.

Romantic love is blind to everything except what is lovable and lovely, but Christ's love sees us with terrible clarity and sees us whole. Christ's love so wishes our joy that it is ruthless against everything in us that diminishes our joy. The worst sentence Love can pass is that we behold the suffering which Love has endured for our sake, and that is also our acquittal. The justice and mercy of the judge are ultimately one.

FREDERICK BUECHNER

ACTION POINT

What was most important to Jesus when he suffered and died for us? What did he promise would follow? Think about the statement, "the one who judges us most finally will be the one who loves us most fully." Pray now and thank God that our Judge is also our Savior!

MATTHEW 17:14 — 18:9

Jesus Heals a Sick Boy

14When Jesus and his followers came back to the crowd, a man came to Jesus and bowed before him. **15**The man said, "Lord, have mercy on my son. He has epilepsy and is suffering very much, because he often falls into the fire or into the water. **16**I brought him to your followers, but they could not cure him."

17Jesus answered, "You people have no faith, and your lives are all wrong. How long must I put up with you? How long must I continue to be patient with you? Bring the boy here." **18**Jesus commanded the demon inside the boy. Then the demon came out, and the boy was healed from that time on.

19The followers came to Jesus when he was alone and asked, "Why couldn't we force the demon out?"

20Jesus answered, "Because your faith is too small. I tell you the truth, if your faith is as big as a mustard seed, you can say to this mountain, 'Move from here to there,' and it will move. All things will be possible for you. [**21**That kind of spirit comes out only if you use prayer and fasting.]"

Jesus Talks About His Death

22While Jesus' followers were gathering in Galilee, he said to them, "The Son of Man will be handed over to people, **23**and they will kill him. But on the third day he will be raised from the dead." And the followers were filled with sadness.

Jesus Talks About Paying Taxes

24When Jesus and his followers came to Capernaum, the men who collected the Temple tax came to Peter. They asked, "Does your teacher pay the Temple tax?"

25Peter answered, "Yes, Jesus pays the tax."

Peter went into the house, but before he could speak, Jesus said to him, "What do you think? The kings of the earth collect different kinds of taxes. But who pays the taxes—the king's children or others?"

26Peter answered, "Other people pay the taxes."

Jesus said to Peter, "Then the children of the king don't have to pay taxes. **27**But we don't want to upset these tax collectors. So go to the lake and fish. After you catch the first fish, open its mouth and you will find a coin. Take that coin and give it to the tax collectors for you and me."

Who Is the Greatest?

18 At that time the followers came to Jesus and asked, "Who is greatest in the kingdom of heaven?"

2Jesus called a little child to him and stood the child before his followers. **3**Then he said, "I tell you the truth, you must change and become like little children. Otherwise, you will never enter the kingdom of heaven. **4**The greatest person in the kingdom of heaven is the one who makes himself humble like this child.

5"Whoever accepts a child in my name accepts me. **6**If one of these little children believes in me, and someone causes that child to sin, it would be better for that person to have a large stone tied around the neck and be drowned in the sea. **7**How terrible for the people of the world because of the things that cause them to sin. Such things will happen, but how terrible for the one who causes them to happen! **8**If your hand or your foot causes you to sin, cut it off and throw it away. It is better for you to lose part of your body and live forever than to have two hands and two feet and be thrown into the fire that burns forever. **9**If your eye causes you to sin, take it out and throw it away. It is better for you to have only one eye and live forever than to have two eyes and be thrown into the fire of hell."

OLD TESTAMENT READING

Pride will ruin people,
but those who are humble will be honored.

Proverbs 29:23

As Manasseh suffered, he begged the LORD his God for help and humbled himself before the God of his ancestors. **13**When Manasseh prayed, the LORD heard him and had pity on him. So the LORD let him return to Jerusalem and to his kingdom. Then Manasseh knew that the LORD is the true God.

2 Chronicles 33:12–13

INSIGHTS

I was once considering what the reason was our Lord loved humility in us so much. I suddenly remembered that He is essentially the supreme truth and that humility is just our walking in truth. For it is a very great truth that we have no good in us; we have only misery and nothingness. He who does not understand this walks in lies. But he who understands this the best is the most pleasing to the Supreme Truth. May God grant us this favor, sisters, never to be without the humbling knowledge of ourselves. . . .

His Majesty seeks and loves courageous souls. But they must be humble in all their ways and have no confidence in themselves. . . .

. . . I often used to think of those words of the Apostle Paul: "All things are possible with God" (Philippians 4:13). I saw clearly that I could do nothing of myself. This was of great help to me to see this. So also was the saying of Augustine: "Give me, Lord, what You command, and command what You desire." . . .

. . . But it is necessary that we should understand what this humility is like. For I believe Satan will try to do great harm. He hinders those who begin to pray from going forward by suggesting to them false notions of humility. He makes them think that it is pride to have spiritual ambitions, desires to imitate the saints, and longings to be like martyrs.

ST. TERESA OF AVILA

▶ ACTION POINT

How does God view pride? Why do you think he places such a high value on humility? Describe the attitudes and actions of true humility, and pray that God will cause you to want to be humble.

MATTHEW 18:10 - 35

A Lost Sheep

10"Be careful. Don't think these little children are worth nothing. I tell you that they have angels in heaven who are always with my Father in heaven. [**11**The Son of Man came to save lost people.]

12"If a man has a hundred sheep but one of the sheep gets lost, he will leave the other ninety-nine on the hill and go to look for the lost sheep. **13**I tell you the truth, if he finds it he is happier about that one sheep than about the ninety-nine that were never lost. **14**In the same way, your Father in heaven does not want any of these little children to be lost.

When a Person Sins Against You

15"If your fellow believer sins against you, go and tell him in private what he did wrong. If he listens to you, you have helped that person to be your brother or sister again. **16**But if he refuses to listen, go to him again and take one or two other people with you. 'Every case may be proved by two or three witnesses.' **17**If he refuses to listen to them, tell the church. If he refuses to listen to the church, then treat him like a person who does not believe in God or like a tax collector.

18"I tell you the truth, the things you don't allow on earth will be the things God does not allow. And the things you allow on earth will be the things that God allows.

19"Also, I tell you that if two of you on earth agree about something and pray for it, it will be done for you by my Father in heaven. **20**This is true because if two or three people come together in my name, I am there with them."

An Unforgiving Servant

21Then Peter came to Jesus and asked, "Lord, when my fellow believer sins against me, how many times must I forgive him? Should I forgive him as many as seven times?"

22Jesus answered, "I tell you, you must forgive him more than seven times. You must forgive him even if he wrongs you seventy times seven.

23"The kingdom of heaven is like a king who decided to collect the money his servants owed him. **24**When the king began to collect his money, a servant who owed him several million dollars was brought to him. **25**But the servant did not have enough money to pay his master, the king. So the master ordered that everything the servant owned should be sold, even the servant's wife and children. Then the money would be used to pay the king what the servant owed.

26"But the servant fell on his knees and begged, 'Be patient with me, and I will pay you everything I owe.' **27**The master felt sorry for his servant and told him he did not have to pay it back. Then he let the servant go free.

28"Later, that same servant found another servant who owed him a few dollars. The servant grabbed him around the neck and said, 'Pay me the money you owe me!'

29"The other servant fell on his knees and begged him, 'Be patient with me, and I will pay you everything I owe.'

30"But the first servant refused to be patient. He threw the other servant into prison until he could pay everything he owed. **31**When the other servants saw what had happened, they were very sorry. So they went and told their master all that had happened.

32"Then the master called his servant in and said, 'You evil servant! Because you begged me to forget what you owed, I told you that you did not have to pay anything. **33**You should have showed mercy to that other servant, just as I showed mercy to you.' **34**The master was very angry and put the servant in prison to be punished until he could pay everything he owed.

35"This king did what my heavenly Father will do to you if you do not forgive your brother or sister from your heart."

OLD TESTAMENT READING

ut suppose the wicked stop doing all the sins they have done and obey all my rules and do what is fair and right. Then they will surely live; they will not die. **22**Their sins will be forgotten. Because they have done what is right, they will live. **23**I do not really want the wicked to die, says the Lord GOD. I want them to stop their bad ways and live."

Ezekiel 18:21–23

INSIGHTS

Forgiving and being forgiven are all of one piece. They cannot be separated. In giving we receive. In accepting those who have injured us we open ourselves to God's acceptance.

It is not a matter of which comes first. There is no sequence of time or priority. The two are one. Anyone who loves God must also love his neighbor. Anyone who hates another does not and cannot love God. Love of God and our neighbor are interlocking and indivisible. We only learn to love as we learn to know God. And we truly learn to know God as we learn to love our brother and sister. It's all of a piece. The life that is open to the love of God is loving to others. The person who truly receives the forgiveness of God is truly forgiving of others. . . .

God's forgiveness gives us the freedom to love and live creatively. The rush of God's strength, which brings forgiveness, gives in turn the ability to forgive, and forgive, and forgive, not just seven times, as the apostle Peter once volunteered, but seventy times seven. . . .

The contrast between our debt to God and the debts others may owe us is immeasurable.

And when God has forgiven us the debt we owe Him, how can we be unforgiving to others who owe us so little in comparison?

DAVID AUGSBURGER

APPLICATION

As you think about the parable of the servants, what debt that God has forgiven you can serve as a model of how you ought to forgive others? In what ways does Ezekiel 18 affect how you think about God?

MATTHEW 19:1-26

Jesus Teaches About Divorce

19 After Jesus said all these things, he left Galilee and went into the area of Judea on the other side of the Jordan River. **2**Large crowds followed him, and he healed them there.

3Some Pharisees came to Jesus and tried to trick him. They asked, "Is it right for a man to divorce his wife for any reason he chooses?"

4Jesus answered, "Surely you have read in the Scriptures: When God made the world, 'he made them male and female.' **5**And God said, 'So a man will leave his father and mother and be united with his wife, and the two will become one body.' **6**So there are not two, but one. God has joined the two together, so no one should separate them."

7The Pharisees asked, "Why then did Moses give a command for a man to divorce his wife by giving her divorce papers?"

8Jesus answered, "Moses allowed you to divorce your wives because you refused to accept God's teaching, but divorce was not allowed in the beginning. **9**I tell you that anyone who divorces his wife and marries another woman is guilty of adultery. The only reason for a man to divorce his wife is if his wife has sexual relations with another man."

10The followers said to him, "If that is the only reason a man can divorce his wife, it is better not to marry."

11Jesus answered, "Not everyone can accept this teaching, but God has made some able to accept it. **12**There are different reasons why some men cannot marry. Some men were born without the ability to become fathers. Others were made that way later in life by other people. And some men have given up marriage because of the kingdom of heaven. But the person who can marry should accept this teaching about marriage."

Jesus Welcomes Children

13Then the people brought their little children to Jesus so he could put his hands on them and pray for them. His followers told them to stop, **14**but Jesus said, "Let the little children come to me. Don't stop them, because the kingdom of heaven belongs to people who are like these children." **15**After Jesus put his hands on the children, he left there.

A Rich Young Man's Question

16A man came to Jesus and asked, "Teacher, what good thing must I do to have life forever?"

17Jesus answered, "Why do you ask me about what is good? Only God is good. But if you want to have life forever, obey the commands."

18The man asked, "Which commands?"

Jesus answered, " 'You must not murder anyone; you must not be guilty of adultery; you must not steal; you must not tell lies about your neighbor; **19**honor your father and mother; and love your neighbor as you love yourself.' "

20The young man said, "I have obeyed all these things. What else do I need to do?"

21Jesus answered, "If you want to be perfect, then go and sell your possessions and give the money to the poor. If you do this, you will have treasure in heaven. Then come and follow me."

22But when the young man heard this, he left sorrowfully, because he was rich.

23Then Jesus said to his followers, "I tell you the truth, it will be hard for a rich person to enter the kingdom of heaven. **24**Yes, I tell you that it is easier for a camel to go through the eye of a needle than for a rich person to enter the kingdom of God."

25When Jesus' followers heard this, they were very surprised and asked, "Then who can be saved?"

26Jesus looked at them and said, "For people this is impossible, but for God all things are possible."

OLD TESTAMENT READING

This is another thing you do. You cover the LORD's altar with your tears. You cry and moan, because he does not accept your offerings and is not pleased with what you bring. **14**You ask, "Why?" It is because the LORD sees how you treated the wife you married when you were young. You broke your promise to her, even though she was your partner and you had an agreement with her. **15**God made husbands and wives to become one body and one spirit for his purpose—so they would have children who are true to God.

So be careful, and do not break your promise to the wife you married when you were young.

16The LORD God of Israel says, "I hate divorce. And I hate people who do cruel things as easily as they put on clothes," says the LORD All-Powerful.

So be careful. And do not break your trust.

Malachi 2:13–16

INSIGHTS

The marriage law must conform with the purpose for which marriage was instituted by God. It was instituted to create a new unity of two persons, and no provision was made for the dissolving of that unity. Jesus does not idealize marriage. He does not say that every marriage is made in heaven; he says that marriage itself is made in heaven—that is, instituted by God. To the question, "Is it lawful for a man to divorce his wife?" his answer, in effect, is "No; not for any cause." . . .

Is it wise to take Jesus's rulings on this or other practical issues and give them legislative force? Perhaps not. It is better probably, to let his words stand in the uncompromising rigour as the ideal at which his followers ought to aim. Legislation has to make provision for the hardness of men's hearts, but Jesus showed a more excellent way than the way of legislation and supplies the power to change the human heart and make his ideal a practical possibility.

F. F. BRUCE

PAUSE FOR REFLECTION

In what ways does knowing God's purpose for marriage affect your view of marriage and divorce?

MATTHEW 19:27 – 20:19

27Peter said to Jesus, "Look, we have left everything and followed you. So what will we have?"

28Jesus said to them, "I tell you the truth, when the age to come has arrived, the Son of Man will sit on his great throne. All of you who followed me will also sit on twelve thrones, judging the twelve tribes of Israel. **29**And all those who have left houses, brothers, sisters, father, mother, children, or farms to follow me will get much more than they left, and they will have life forever. **30**Many who are first now will be last in the future. And many who are last now will be first in the future.

A Story About Workers

20 "The kingdom of heaven is like a person who owned some land. One morning, he went out very early to hire some people to work in his vineyard. **2**The man agreed to pay the workers one coin for working that day. Then he sent them into the vineyard to work. **3**About nine o'clock the man went to the marketplace and saw some other people standing there, doing nothing. **4**So he said to them, 'If you go and work in my vineyard, I will pay you what your work is worth.' **5**So they went to work in the vineyard. The man went out again about twelve o'clock and three o'clock and did the same thing. **6**About five o'clock the man went to the marketplace again and saw others standing there. He asked them, 'Why did you stand here all day doing nothing?' **7**They answered, 'No one gave us a job.' The man said to them, 'Then you can go and work in my vineyard.'

8"At the end of the day, the owner of the vineyard said to the boss of all the workers, 'Call the workers and pay them. Start with the last people I hired and end with those I hired first.'

9"When the workers who were hired at five o'clock came to get their pay, each received one coin. **10**When the workers who were hired first came to get their pay, they thought they would be paid more than the others. But each one of them also received one coin. **11**When they got their coin, they complained to the man who owned the land. **12**They said, 'Those people were hired last and worked only one hour. But you paid them the same as you paid us who worked hard all day in the hot sun.' **13**But the man who owned the vineyard said to one of those workers, 'Friend, I am being fair to you. You agreed to work for one coin. **14**So take your pay and go. I want to give the man who was hired last the same pay that I gave you. **15**I can do what I want with my own money. Are you jealous because I am good to those people?'

16"So those who are last now will someday be first, and those who are first now will someday be last."

Jesus Talks About His Own Death

17While Jesus was going to Jerusalem, he took his twelve followers aside privately and said to them, **18**"Look, we are going to Jerusalem. The Son of Man will be turned over to the leading priests and the teachers of the law, and they will say that he must die. **19**They will give the Son of Man to the non-Jewish people to laugh at him and beat him with whips and crucify him. But on the third day, he will be raised to life again."

OLD TESTAMENT READING

There is no one holy like the LORD.
   There is no God but you;
      there is no Rock like our God.

6"The LORD sends death,
   and he brings to life.

He sends people to the grave,
   and he raises them to life again.
7The LORD makes some people poor,
   and others he makes rich.
He makes some people humble,
   and others he makes great.
8The LORD raises the poor up from the dust,
   and he lifts the needy from the ashes.
He lets the poor sit with princes
   and receive a throne of honor."

1 Samuel 2:2, 6–8b

INSIGHTS

The message of the parable is that the revolution of God brought by Jesus is a marvellously generous revolution, offering a full place and reward even to the late-comer or outsider. For the rich and the religious such egalitarian salvation did not always seem good news, since it meant giving up their present advantage and special position. . . . In the parable those who had worked all day complained of the master's unfair generosity. But for those in need of employment at the eleventh hour the master's generosity was good news indeed. . . .

. . . The revolution of God is a levelling revolution; not, however, a negatively levelling revolution bringing everyone down, but a positively levelling revolution in which God's amazing generosity welcomes even late-comers . . . and gives them the full day's wage. . . .

. . . To put it simply: entry into the kingdom of God is through God's generosity to sinners; being in the kingdom of God entails running the race to obtain the prize (1 Cor. 9:24). There is truth in the old saying that the entry fee to Christianity is completely free, but the annual subscription is everything we've got. No one will be in the coming kingdom of God on the basis of his or her own achievements, but only on the basis of God's generosity; but everyone will be called to account on the day of judgement and will be rewarded according to his or her response to the Lord's generosity.

DAVID WENHAM

ACTION POINT

Think about God's fairness and mercy. In what ways are you tempted to be jealous of his generosity shown to others? Pray for a greater understanding of his goodness, and extend his generosity to others.

MATTHEW
20:20 — 21:11

A Mother Asks Jesus a Favor

20Then the wife of Zebedee came to Jesus with her sons. She bowed before him and asked him to do something for her.

21Jesus asked, "What do you want?"

She said, "Promise that one of my sons will sit at your right side and the other will sit at your left side in your kingdom."

22But Jesus said, "You don't understand what you are asking. Can you drink the cup that I am about to drink?"

The sons answered, "Yes, we can."

23Jesus said to them, "You will drink from my cup. But I cannot choose who will sit at my right or my left; those places belong to those for whom my Father has prepared them."

24When the other ten followers heard this, they were angry with the two brothers.

25Jesus called all the followers together and said, "You know that the rulers of the non-Jewish people love to show their power over the people. And their important leaders love to use all their authority. **26**But it should not be that way among you. Whoever wants to become great among you must serve the rest of you like a servant. **27**Whoever wants to become first among you must serve the rest of you like a slave. **28**In the same way, the Son of Man did not come to be served. He came to serve others and to give his life as a ransom for many people."

Jesus Heals Two Blind Men

29When Jesus and his followers were leaving Jericho, a great many people followed him. **30**Two blind men sitting by the road heard that Jesus was going by, so they shouted, "Lord, Son of David, have mercy on us!"

31The people warned the blind men to be quiet, but they shouted even more, "Lord, Son of David, have mercy on us!"

32Jesus stopped and said to the blind men, "What do you want me to do for you?"

33They answered, "Lord, we want to see."

34Jesus felt sorry for the blind men and touched their eyes, and at once they could see. Then they followed Jesus.

Jesus Enters Jerusalem as a King

21 As Jesus and his followers were coming closer to Jerusalem, they stopped at Bethphage at the hill called the Mount of Olives. From there Jesus sent two of his followers **2**and said to them, "Go to the town you can see there. When you enter it, you will quickly find a donkey tied there with its colt. Untie them and bring them to me. **3**If anyone asks you why you are taking the donkeys, say that the Master needs them, and he will send them at once."

4This was to bring about what the prophet had said:

5"Tell the people of Jerusalem,
　'Your king is coming to you.
He is gentle and riding on a donkey,
　on the colt of a donkey.'"

Isaiah 62:11; Zechariah 9:9

6The followers went and did what Jesus told

them to do. **7**They brought the donkey and the colt to Jesus and laid their coats on them, and Jesus sat on them. **8**Many people spread their coats on the road. Others cut branches from the trees and spread them on the road. **9**The people were walking ahead of Jesus and behind him, shouting,

"Praise to the Son of David!

God bless the One who comes in the name of the Lord!   *Psalm 118:26*

Praise to God in heaven!"

10When Jesus entered Jerusalem, all the city was filled with excitement. The people asked, "Who is this man?"

11The crowd said, "This man is Jesus, the prophet from the town of Nazareth in Galilee."

OLD TESTAMENT READING

Come, let's sing for joy to the LORD.
    Let's shout praises to the Rock
        who saves us.
2Let's come to him with thanksgiving.
    Let's sing songs to him,
3because the LORD is the great God,
    the great King over all gods.

                                                  Psalm 95:1–3

This is the day that the LORD has made.
    Let us rejoice and be glad today!

                                                  Psalm 118:24

INSIGHTS

You can almost hear the roar of the crowds as Jesus proceeds slowly into Jerusalem, like a triumphant general returning from a great victory. . . .

From the dusty roads of this earth, where the lips of little children sang his praises, to the very throne of heaven where surely angel anthems rolled, this was Jesus' moment. . . .

Not only on this day of days, but down through the centuries, Jesus has reigned in triumph in the hearts of men and women who have accepted his glorious life and teaching. The Pharisees could hardly have realized how prophetic their words would be: "Look how the whole world has gone after him!"

And why wouldn't we follow Jesus? He leads us in triumph! Just when we think we have had all the trouble we can handle, Jesus reaches down and lifts us gently onto the colt he is riding into Jerusalem. Just when we think nobody cares, he opens our ears and we can hear the crowds shout, "Look who's riding with the King!" And just when we think there is no reward for being righteous, Jesus smiles and quietly reassures us, "My Father will honor the one who serves me."

F. LaGard Smith

ACTION POINT

List the ways Jesus has shown himself to be a king of triumph in your life. Spend some time in prayer, celebrating your praise to him. If you would like, write down your praises.

MATTHEW 21:12-32

Jesus Goes to the Temple

12Jesus went into the Temple and threw out all the people who were buying and selling there. He turned over the tables of those who were exchanging different kinds of money, and he upset the benches of those who were selling doves. **13**Jesus said to all the people there, "It is written in the Scriptures, 'My Temple will be called a house for prayer.' But you are changing it into a 'hideout for robbers.'"

14The blind and crippled people came to Jesus in the Temple, and he healed them. **15**The leading priests and the teachers of the law saw that Jesus was doing wonderful things and that the children were praising him in the Temple, saying, "Praise to the Son of David." All these things made the priests and the teachers of the law very angry.

16They asked Jesus, "Do you hear the things these children are saying?"

Jesus answered, "Yes. Haven't you read in the Scriptures, 'You have taught children and babies to sing praises'?"

17Then Jesus left and went out of the city to Bethany, where he spent the night.

The Power of Faith

18Early the next morning, as Jesus was going back to the city, he became hungry. **19**Seeing a fig tree beside the road, Jesus went to it, but there were no figs on the tree, only leaves. So Jesus said to the tree, "You will never again have fruit." The tree immediately dried up.

20When his followers saw this, they were amazed. They asked, "How did the fig tree dry up so quickly?"

21Jesus answered, "I tell you the truth, if you have faith and do not doubt, you will be able to do what I did to this tree and even more. You will be able to say to this mountain, 'Go, fall into the sea.' And if you have faith, it will happen. **22**If you believe, you will get anything you ask for in prayer."

Leaders Doubt Jesus' Authority

23Jesus went to the Temple, and while he was teaching there, the leading priests and the elders of the people came to him. They said, "What authority do you have to do these things? Who gave you this authority?"

24Jesus answered, "I also will ask you a question. If you answer me, then I will tell you what authority I have to do these things. **25**Tell me: When John baptized people, did that come from God or just from other people?"

They argued about Jesus' question, saying, "If we answer, 'John's baptism was from God,' Jesus will say, 'Then why didn't you believe him?' **26**But if we say, 'It was from people,' we are afraid of what the crowd will do because they all believe that John was a prophet."

27So they answered Jesus, "We don't know."

Jesus said to them, "Then I won't tell you what authority I have to do these things.

A Story About Two Sons

28"Tell me what you think about this: A man had two sons. He went to the first son and said, 'Son, go and work today in my vineyard.' **29**The son answered, 'I will not go.' But later the son changed his mind and went. **30**Then the father went to the other son and said, 'Son, go and work today in my vineyard.' The son answered, 'Yes, sir, I will go and work,' but he did not go. **31**Which of the two sons obeyed his father?"

The priests and leaders answered, "The first son."

Jesus said to them, "I tell you the truth, the tax collectors and the prostitutes will enter the kingdom of God before you do. **32**John came to show you the right way to live. You did not believe him, but the tax collectors and prostitutes believed him. Even after seeing this, you still refused to change your ways and believe him."

OLD TESTAMENT READING

LORD, I love the Temple where you live, where your glory is.

Psalm 26:8

If you do that, do you think you can come before me and stand in this place where I have chosen to be worshiped? Do you think you can say, "We are safe!" when you do all these hateful things? **11**This place where I have chosen to be worshiped is nothing more to you than a hideout for robbers. I have been watching you, says the LORD.

12" 'You people of Judah, go now to the town of Shiloh, where I first made a place to be worshiped. See what I did to it because of the evil things the people of Israel had done. **13**You people of Judah have done all these evil things too, says the LORD. I spoke to you again and again, but you did not listen to me. I called you, but you did not answer. **14**So I will destroy the place where I have chosen to be worshiped in Jerusalem.' "

Jeremiah 7:10–14a

INSIGHTS

In both the Old and New Testaments, God's purpose in revealing himself, in redeeming, and in bringing a people into existence was to create a worshiping community to be a sign of his redeeming work. For example, when God entered into a covenant with the people of Israel, they met him at Mt. Sinai in the first public meeting between God and his people. This meeting with God became the prototype for public worship in Israel. And it was through public worship that God's revelation, redemption, and covenant were remembered and passed down in history. . . .

. . . We go to worship in praise and thank God for what he has done, is doing, and will do.

Robert Webber

PAUSE FOR REFLECTION

In God's eyes, worship is no casual, Sunday-morning time filler! How does your worship experience stand as a continuing reminder of God's redeeming work in your life?

MATTHEW
21:33 — 22:14

A Story About God's Son

33"Listen to this story: There was a man who owned a vineyard. He put a wall around it and dug a hole for a winepress and built a tower. Then he leased the land to some farmers and left for a trip. **34**When it was time for the grapes to be picked, he sent his servants to the farmers to get his share of the grapes. **35**But the farmers grabbed the servants, beat one, killed another, and then killed a third servant with stones. **36**So the man sent some other servants to the farmers, even more than he sent the first time. But the farmers did the same thing to the servants that they had done before. **37**So the man decided to send his son to the farmers. He said, 'They will respect my son.' **38**But when the farmers saw the son, they said to each other, 'This son will inherit the vineyard. If we kill him, it will be ours!' **39**Then the farmers grabbed the son, threw him out of the vineyard, and killed him. **40**So what will the owner of the vineyard do to these farmers when he comes?"

41The priests and leaders said, "He will surely kill those evil men. Then he will lease the vineyard to some other farmers who will give him his share of the crop at harvest time."

42Jesus said to them, "Surely you have read this in the Scriptures:

'The stone that the builders rejected
    became the cornerstone.
The Lord did this,
    and it is wonderful to us.' *Psalm 118:22–23*

43"So I tell you that the kingdom of God will be taken away from you and given to people who do the things God wants in his kingdom. **44**The person who falls on this stone will be broken, and on whomever that stone falls, that person will be crushed."

45When the leading priests and the Pharisees heard these stories, they knew Jesus was talking about them. **46**They wanted to arrest him, but they were afraid of the people, because the people believed that Jesus was a prophet.

A Story About a Wedding Feast

22 Jesus again used stories to teach them. He said, **2**"The kingdom of heaven is like a king who prepared a wedding feast for his son. **3**The king invited some people to the feast. When the feast was ready, the king sent his servants to tell the people, but they refused to come.

4"Then the king sent other servants, saying, 'Tell those who have been invited that my feast is ready. I have killed my best bulls and calves for the dinner, and everything is ready. Come to the wedding feast.'

5"But the people refused to listen to the servants and left to do other things. One went to work in his field, and another went to his business. **6**Some of the other people grabbed the servants, beat them, and killed them. **7**The king was furious and sent his army to kill the murderers and burn their city.

8"After that, the king said to his servants, 'The wedding feast is ready. I invited those people, but they were not worthy to come. **9**So go to the street corners and invite everyone you find to come to my feast.' **10**So the servants went into the streets and gathered all the people they could find, both good and bad. And the wedding hall was filled with guests.

11"When the king came in to see the guests, he saw a man who was not dressed for a wedding. **12**The king said, 'Friend, how were you allowed to come in here? You are not dressed for a wedding.' But the man said nothing. **13**So the king told some servants, 'Tie this man's hands and feet. Throw him out into the darkness, where people will cry and grind their teeth with pain.'

14"Yes, many are invited, but only a few are chosen."

OLD TESTAMENT READING

Foreigners who have joined the LORD should not say,
  "The LORD will not accept me with his people."
The eunuch should not say,
  "Because I cannot have children, the LORD will not accept me."
4This is what the LORD says:
  "The eunuchs should obey the law about the Sabbath
    and do what I want
    and keep my agreement.
5If they do, I will make their names remembered
    within my Temple and its walls.
  It will be better for them than children.
I will give them a name that will last forever,
    that will never be forgotten.

Isaiah 56:3–5

INSIGHTS

Who can become a Christian? The answer in a nutshell is that anyone can. Anyone who wants to can "take the free gift of the water of life" (Revelation 22:17). Whosoever will may come. Everyone has an invitation to the marriage supper of the Lamb (Matthew 22:9). . . .

. . . It is certainly true that not all do make the decision to give their lives over to God. Some stubbornly insist on going their own way. "Whoever rejects the Son will not see life, for God's wrath remains on him" (John 3:36). Such people will not enjoy the salvation God has for the world. "Yet to all who received him, to those who believed in his name, he gave the right to become children of God" (John 1:12). . . .

Who can become a Christian? Anyone can, because God's grace closes nobody out. There are no limits to his grace except those that sinners impose upon themselves. Jesus Christ, our Advocate, has become "the atoning sacrifice for our sins, and not only for ours but also for the sins of the whole world" (1 John 2:2). Salvation is so broad as to encompass potentially the entire human race.

CLARK H. PINNOCK

APPLICATION

To whom is God's kingdom given? For what reasons do people refuse God's invitation? Are there ways by which you limit God's grace in your life?

MATTHEW 22:15-40

Is It Right to Pay Taxes or Not?

15Then the Pharisees left that place and made plans to trap Jesus in saying something wrong. **16**They sent some of their own followers and some people from the group called Herodians. They said, "Teacher, we know that you are an honest man and that you teach the truth about God's way. You are not afraid of what other people think about you, because you pay no attention to who they are. **17**So tell us what you think. Is it right to pay taxes to Caesar or not?"

18But knowing that these leaders were trying to trick him, Jesus said, "You hypocrites! Why are you trying to trap me? **19**Show me a coin used for paying the tax." So the men showed him a coin. **20**Then Jesus asked, "Whose image and name are on the coin?"

21The men answered, "Caesar's."

Then Jesus said to them, "Give to Caesar the things that are Caesar's, and give to God the things that are God's."

22When the men heard what Jesus said, they were amazed and left him and went away.

Some Sadducees Try to Trick Jesus

23That same day some Sadducees came to Jesus and asked him a question. (Sadducees believed that people would not rise from the dead.) **24**They said, "Teacher, Moses said if a married man dies without having children, his brother must marry the widow and have children for him.

25Once there were seven brothers among us. The first one married and died. Since he had no children, his brother married the widow. **26**Then the second brother also died. The same thing happened to the third brother and all the other brothers. **27**Finally, the woman died. **28**Since all seven men had married her, when people rise from the dead, whose wife will she be?"

29Jesus answered, "You don't understand, because you don't know what the Scriptures say, and you don't know about the power of God. **30**When people rise from the dead, they will not marry, nor will they be given to someone to marry. They will be like the angels in heaven. **31**Surely you have read what God said to you about rising from the dead. **32**God said, 'I am the God of Abraham, the God of Isaac, and the God of Jacob.' God is the God of the living, not the dead."

33When the people heard this, they were amazed at Jesus' teaching.

The Most Important Command

34When the Pharisees learned that the Sadducees could not argue with Jesus' answers to them, the Pharisees met together. **35**One Pharisee, who was an expert on the law of Moses, asked Jesus this question to test him: **36**"Teacher, which command in the law is the most important?"

37Jesus answered, " 'Love the Lord your God with all your heart, all your soul, and all your mind.' **38**This is the first and most important command. **39**And the second command is like the first: 'Love your neighbor as you love yourself.' **40**All the law and the writings of the prophets depend on these two commands."

OLD TESTAMENT READING

Listen, people of Israel! The LORD our God is the only LORD. ⁵Love the LORD your God with all your heart, all your soul, and all your strength. ⁶Always remember these commands I give you today. ⁷Teach them to your children, and talk about them when you sit at home and walk along the road, when you lie down and when you get up. ⁸Write them down and tie them to your hands as a sign. Tie them on your forehead to remind you, ⁹and write them on your doors and gates.

Deuteronomy 6:4–9

Then Joshua called a meeting of all the people from the tribes of Reuben, Gad, and East Manasseh. ²He said to them, "You have done everything Moses, the LORD's servant, told you to do. You have also obeyed all my commands. ⁵But be careful to obey the teachings and laws Moses, the LORD's servant, gave you: to love the LORD your God and obey his commands, to continue to follow him and serve him the very best you can."

Joshua 22:1–2, 5

I love those who love me,
and those who seek me find me.

Proverbs 8:17

INSIGHTS

I have tried giving myself to other gods—the gods of education and knowledge, success and money, accomplishment and work. I have given good works First Place in my affection. I have tried to get other people to be god for me; I have even let the church assume top priority in my time and energy. I have placed my neck in other worldly nooses and yokes, but only the yoke of Christ grants me freedom.

Surrendering my will to His yoke is a constant process. As I continue to allow the presence of God to permeate the various parts of my life, I am understanding more clearly that anything or anyone, other than God, to whom I turn for meaning, purpose, or strength will ultimately disappoint me or destroy me. God affirmed the first commandment for my benefit; He knew I would never be whole as long as I worshiped anything or anyone besides Himself. I have tried to fill my life with other people, pleasure, work, and acquisition, but these things only partially satisfy.

. . . I am learning that the God of Abraham, Joseph, and Isaac is indeed the Source of everything I need and that His intent is always for good.

JEANIE MILEY

APPLICATION

How do we demonstrate that we love God with all our heart, soul, and mind? How are you loving God today? How is he satisfying your soul?

MATTHEW
22:41 – 23:22

Jesus Questions the Pharisees

41While the Pharisees were together, Jesus asked them, **42**"What do you think about the Christ? Whose son is he?"

They answered, "The Christ is the Son of David."

43Then Jesus said to them, "Then why did David call him 'Lord'? David, speaking by the power of the Holy Spirit, said,

44'The Lord said to my Lord,

"Sit by me at my right side,

until I put your enemies under your

control." '   *Psalm 110:1*

45David calls the Christ 'Lord,' so how can the Christ be his son?"

46None of the Pharisees could answer Jesus' question, and after that day no one was brave enough to ask him any more questions.

Jesus Accuses Some Leaders

23 Then Jesus said to the crowds and to his followers, **2**"The teachers of the law and the Pharisees have the authority to tell you what the law of Moses says. **3**So you should obey and follow whatever they tell you, but their lives are not good examples for you to follow. They tell you to do things, but they themselves don't do them. **4**They make strict rules and try to force people to obey them, but they are unwilling to help those who struggle under the weight of their rules.

5"They do good things so that other people will see them. They enlarge the little boxes holding Scriptures that they wear, and they make their special prayer clothes very long. **6**Those Pharisees and teachers of the law love to have the most important seats at feasts and in the synagogues. **7**They love people to greet them with respect in the marketplaces, and they love to have people call them 'Teacher.'

8"But you must not be called 'Teacher,' because you have only one Teacher, and you are all brothers and sisters together. **9**And don't call any person on earth 'Father,' because you have one Father, who is in heaven. **10**And you should not be called 'Master,' because you have only one Master, the Christ. **11**Whoever is your servant is the greatest among you. **12**Whoever makes himself great will be made humble. Whoever makes himself humble will be made great.

13"How terrible for you, teachers of the law and Pharisees! You are hypocrites! You close the door for people to enter the kingdom of heaven. You yourselves don't enter, and you stop others who are trying to enter. [**14**How terrible for you, teachers of the law and Pharisees. You are hypocrites. You take away widows' houses, and you say long prayers so that people will notice you. So you will have a worse punishment.]

15"How terrible for you, teachers of the law and Pharisees! You are hypocrites! You travel across land and sea to find one person who will change to your ways. When you find that person, you make him more fit for hell than you are.

16"How terrible for you! You guide the people, but you are blind. You say, 'If people swear by the Temple when they make a promise, that means nothing. But if they swear by the gold that is in the

Temple, they must keep that promise.' **17**You are blind fools! Which is greater: the gold or the Temple that makes that gold holy? **18**And you say, 'If people swear by the altar when they make a promise, that means nothing. But if they swear by the gift on the altar, they must keep that promise.' **19**You are blind! Which is greater: the gift or the altar that makes the gift holy? **20**The person who swears by the altar is really using the altar and also everything on the altar. **21**And the person who swears by the Temple is really using the Temple and also everything in the Temple. **22**The person who swears by heaven is also using God's throne and the One who sits on that throne."

OLD TESTAMENT READING

A terrible and shocking thing
    has happened in the land of Judah:
31The prophets speak lies,
        and the priests take power into their own
            hands,
    and my people love it this way.
        But what will you do when the end
            comes?"

Jeremiah 5:30–31

INSIGHTS

From the Hallmark-card theology of a thousand churches to the nauseating nonsense of PTL, American evangelicalism is awash in a sloppy, sentimental, superficial theology that wouldn't empower a clockwork mouse, let alone a disciple of Christ in the tough, modern world. . . .

. . . Having visited almost all the countries in the English-speaking world, I would say that I know none where the churches are more full and the sermons more empty than in America. There are magnificent exceptions, of course. But by and large, I am never hungrier and rarely angrier than when I come out of an American evangelical church after what passes for the preaching of the Word of God.

The problem is not just the heresy, though doubtless there is some of that. Nor is it just the degree of entertainment, and there is lots of that. Nor is it even the appalling gaps in the theology, for there is far too much of that. The real problem is that in what is said there is almost no sense of announcement from God; and in what is shown, there is almost no sense of anointing by God.

Jeremiah attacked the false prophets of his day with the damning question, "Which of them has stood in the council of the LORD, seen him and heard his word?" (Jer. 23:18). Are we who profess a high view of authority much better in practice? Is such a standard too demanding?

OS GUINNESS

PAUSE FOR REFLECTION

Study these readings and list the things that God's teachers are supposed to do. Why will God punish false spiritual leaders? How well do you think today's religious leaders measure up?

MATTHEW
23:23 — 24:8

23"How terrible for you, teachers of the law and Pharisees! You are hypocrites! You give to God one-tenth of everything you earn—even your mint, dill, and cumin. But you don't obey the really important teachings of the law—justice, mercy, and being loyal. These are the things you should do, as well as those other things. **24**You guide the people, but you are blind! You are like a person who picks a fly out of a drink and then swallows a camel!

25"How terrible for you, teachers of the law and Pharisees! You are hypocrites! You wash the outside of your cups and dishes, but inside they are full of things you got by cheating others and by pleasing only yourselves. **26**Pharisees, you are blind! First make the inside of the cup clean, and then the outside of the cup can be truly clean.

27"How terrible for you, teachers of the law and Pharisees! You are hypocrites! You are like tombs that are painted white. Outside, those tombs look fine, but inside, they are full of the bones of dead people and all kinds of unclean things. **28**It is the same with you. People look at you and think you are good, but on the inside you are full of hypocrisy and evil.

29"How terrible for you, teachers of the law and Pharisees! You are hypocrites! You build tombs for the prophets, and you show honor to the graves of those who lived good lives. **30**You say, 'If we had lived during the time of our ancestors, we would not have helped them kill the prophets.' **31**But you give proof that you are descendants of those who murdered the prophets. **32**And you will complete the sin that your ancestors started.

33"You are snakes! A family of poisonous snakes! How are you going to escape God's judgment? **34**So I tell you this: I am sending to you prophets and wise men and teachers. Some of them you will kill and crucify. Some of them you will beat in your synagogues and chase from town to town. **35**So you will be guilty for the death of all the good people who have been killed on earth—from the murder of that good man Abel to the murder of Zechariah son of Berakiah, whom you murdered between the Temple and the altar. **36**I tell you the truth, all of these things will happen to you people who are living now.

Jesus Feels Sorry for Jerusalem

37"Jerusalem, Jerusalem! You kill the prophets and stone to death those who are sent to you. Many times I wanted to gather your people as a hen gathers her chicks under her wings, but you did not let me. **38**Now your house will be left completely empty. **39**I tell you, you will not see me again until that time when you will say, 'God bless the One who comes in the name of the Lord.'"

The Temple Will Be Destroyed

24 As Jesus left the Temple and was walking away, his followers came up to show him the Temple's buildings. **2**Jesus asked, "Do you see all these buildings? I tell you the truth, not one stone will be left on another. Every stone will be thrown down to the ground."

3Later, as Jesus was sitting on the Mount of

Olives, his followers came to be alone with him. They said, "Tell us, when will these things happen? And what will be the sign that it is time for you to come again and for this age to end?"

⁴Jesus answered, "Be careful that no one fools you. ⁵Many will come in my name, saying, 'I am the Christ,' and they will fool many people. ⁶You will hear about wars and stories of wars that are coming, but don't be afraid. These things must happen before the end comes. ⁷Nations will fight against other nations; kingdoms will fight against other kingdoms. There will be times when there is no food for people to eat, and there will be earthquakes in different places. ⁸These things are like the first pains when something new is about to be born."

OLD TESTAMENT READING

Crooked leaders cannot be your friends.
        They use the law to cause suffering.
²¹They join forces against people who do right
        and sentence to death the innocent.
²²But the LORD is my defender;
        my God is the rock of my protection.
²³God will pay them back for their sins
        and will destroy them for their evil.
        The LORD our God will destroy them.

Psalm 94:20–23

INSIGHTS

A young man came to D. L. Moody and said, "Mr. Moody, I want to be a Christian; but must I give up the world?" Moody characteristically replied, "Young man, if you live the out-and-out Christian life, the world will soon give you up." If we are popular with the crowd of worldlings, or if we are not penalised in some way for our attachment to Christ, we have good cause to inspect our discipleship. . . .

The world varies its ways of persecuting us. Sometimes it uses the sword, and sometimes the lip of scorn. Most of us can stand the sword far better than derision or sarcasm. . . .

Let us remember, also, that there is another side to this being penalised for Christian godliness. It is equally true that all who live ungodly, and persecute God's people, shall suffer punishment. Old Testament incidents, as Paul tells us, were recorded for our admonition, as warnings and examples to us. Under the old dispensation God frequently visited punishment upon persons immediately after their committing of wrongs, so that the connection between the sin and the punishment might be clearly seen. In this present age, the judgment of the ungodly may be deferred; but it is none the less certain, and will be awful when at last it falls.

J. SIDLOW BAXTER

PAUSE FOR REFLECTION

What are Jesus' accusations against the teachers and Pharisees? What are his warnings to them?

MATTHEW 24:9-35

9"Then people will arrest you, hand you over to be hurt, and kill you. They will hate you because you believe in me. **10**At that time, many will lose their faith, and they will turn against each other and hate each other. **11**Many false prophets will come and cause many people to believe lies. **12**There will be more and more evil in the world, so most people will stop showing their love for each other. **13**But those people who keep their faith until the end will be saved. **14**The Good News about God's kingdom will be preached in all the world, to every nation. Then the end will come.

15"Daniel the prophet spoke about 'a blasphemous object that brings destruction.' You will see this standing in the holy place." (You who read this should understand what it means.) **16**"At that time, the people in Judea should run away to the mountains. **17**If people are on the roofs of their houses, they must not go down to get anything out of their houses. **18**If people are in the fields, they must not go back to get their coats. **19**At that time, how terrible it will be for women who are pregnant or have nursing babies! **20**Pray that it will not be winter or a Sabbath day when these things happen and you have to run away, **21**because at that time there will be much trouble. There will be more trouble than there has ever been since the beginning of the world until now, and nothing as bad will ever happen again. **22**God has decided to make that terrible time short. Otherwise, no one would go on living. But God will

make that time short to help the people he has chosen. **23**At that time, someone might say to you, 'Look, there is the Christ!' Or another person might say, 'There he is!' But don't believe them. **24**False Christs and false prophets will come and perform great wonders and miracles. They will try to fool even the people God has chosen, if that is possible. **25**Now I have warned you about this before it happens.

26"If people tell you, 'The Christ is in the desert,' don't go there. If they say, 'The Christ is in the inner room,' don't believe it. **27**When the Son of Man comes, he will be seen by everyone, like lightning flashing from the east to the west. **28**Wherever the dead body is, there the vultures will gather.

29"Soon after the trouble of those days,

'the sun will grow dark,

and the moon will not give its light.

The stars will fall from the sky.

And the powers of the heavens will be

shaken.'   *Isaiah 13:10; 34:4*

30"At that time, the sign of the Son of Man will appear in the sky. Then all the peoples of the world will cry. They will see the Son of Man coming on clouds in the sky with great power and glory. **31**He will use a loud trumpet to send his angels all around the earth, and they will gather his chosen people from every part of the world.

32"Learn a lesson from the fig tree: When its branches become green and soft and new leaves appear, you know summer is near. **33**In the same way, when you see all these things happening, you will know that the time is near, ready to come. **34**I tell you the truth, all these things will happen while the people of this time are still living. ³⁵Earth and sky will be destroyed, but the words I have said will never be destroyed."

OLD TESTAMENT READING

Look, the LORD's day of judging is coming— a terrible day, a day of God's anger.

He will destroy the land
  and the sinners who live in it.
¹⁰The stars will not show their light;
  the skies will be dark.
The sun will grow dark as it rises,
  and the moon will not give its light.

Isaiah 13:9–10

INSIGHTS

To a unique degree this generation has witnessed the universal and dramatic fulfillment of prophecy. Many of the signs Jesus said would herald His return have developed before our eyes.

There is the evangelistic sign: "This gospel of the kingdom will be preached in the whole world as a testimony to all nations, and then the end will come" (Matthew 24:14).

This prophecy has been fulfilled in our generation to a degree that has never before been the case. There is now no major nation in which there is no Christian witness. . . .

There is the religious sign: "That day will not come until the rebellion occurs and the man of lawlessness is revealed" (2 Thessalonians 2:3).

Unfortunately, we can see this sign being fulfilled all around us. As Jesus foretold, the love of the many is growing cold (Matthew 24:12). . . .

Political signs abound. Could prevailing world conditions have been more accurately and comprehensively described than in our Lord's words in Luke 21:25–26? "There will be signs. . . . On the earth, nations will be in anguish and perplexity. . . . Men will faint from terror, apprehensive of what is coming on the world."

There is the Jewish sign: "Jerusalem will be trampled on by the Gentiles until the times of the Gentiles are fulfilled" (Luke 21:24). . . .

. . . For the first time in 2,500 years, Jerusalem is not dominated by Gentiles. . . .

Whatever view we hold regarding the details surrounding the second coming of Christ, history is moving rapidly—not to cataclysm merely, but to consummation.

J. OSWALD SANDERS

PAUSE FOR REFLECTION

Why did Jesus warn his followers about the end times? What event will be perfectly clear to all people? Despite the horror of these events, what glorious hope does Jesus promise to his people at the end?

MATTHEW
24:36 – 25:13

When Will Jesus Come Again?

36"No one knows when that day or time will be, not the angels in heaven, not even the Son. Only the Father knows. **37**When the Son of Man comes, it will be like what happened during Noah's time. **38**In those days before the flood, people were eating and drinking, marrying and giving their children to be married, until the day Noah entered the boat. **39**They knew nothing about what was happening until the flood came and destroyed them. It will be the same when the Son of Man comes. **40**Two men will be in the field. One will be taken, and the other will be left. **41**Two women will be grinding grain with a mill. One will be taken, and the other will be left.

42"So always be ready, because you don't know the day your Lord will come. **43**Remember this: If the owner of the house knew what time of night a thief was coming, the owner would watch and not let the thief break in. **44**So you also must be ready, because the Son of Man will come at a time you don't expect him.

45"Who is the wise and loyal servant that the master trusts to give the other servants their food at the right time? **46**When the master comes and finds the servant doing his work, the servant will be blessed. **47**I tell you the truth, the master will choose that servant to take care of everything he owns. **48**But suppose that evil servant thinks to himself, 'My master will not come back soon,' **49**and he begins to beat the other servants and eat and get drunk with others like him? **50**The master will come when that servant is not ready and is not expecting him. **51**Then the master will cut him in pieces and send him away to be with the hypocrites, where people will cry and grind their teeth with pain.

A Story About Ten Bridesmaids

25 "At that time the kingdom of heaven will be like ten bridesmaids who took their lamps and went to wait for the bridegroom. **2**Five of them were foolish and five were wise. **3**The five foolish bridesmaids took their lamps, but they did not take more oil for the lamps to burn. **4**The wise bridesmaids took their lamps and more oil in jars. **5**Because the bridegroom was late, they became sleepy and went to sleep.

6"At midnight someone cried out, 'The bridegroom is coming! Come and meet him!' **7**Then all the bridesmaids woke up and got their lamps ready. **8**But the foolish ones said to the wise, 'Give us some of your oil, because our lamps are going out.' **9**The wise bridesmaids answered, 'No, the oil we have might not be enough for all of us. Go to the people who sell oil and buy some for yourselves.'

10"So while the five foolish bridesmaids went to buy oil, the bridegroom came. The bridesmaids who were ready went in with the bridegroom to the wedding feast. Then the door was closed and locked.

11"Later the others came back and said, 'Sir, sir, open the door to let us in.' **12**But the bridegroom answered, 'I tell you the truth, I don't want to know you.'

13"So always be ready, because you don't know the day or the hour the Son of Man will come."

OLD TESTAMENT READING

The LORD All-Powerful says, "I will send my messenger, who will prepare the way for me. Suddenly, the Lord you are looking for will come to his Temple; the messenger of the agreement, whom you want, will come." **2**No one can live through that time; no one can survive when he comes. He will be like a purifying fire and like laundry soap. **5**The LORD All-Powerful says, "Then I will come to you and judge you. I will be quick to testify against those who take part in evil magic, adultery, and lying under oath, those who cheat workers of their pay and who cheat widows and orphans, those who are unfair to foreigners, and those who do not respect me."

16Then those who honored the LORD spoke with each other, and the LORD listened and heard them. The names of those who honored the LORD and respected him were written in his presence in a book to be remembered.

17The LORD All-Powerful says, "They belong to me; on that day they will be my very own. As a parent shows mercy to his child who serves him, I will show mercy to my people. **18**You will again see the difference between good and evil people, between those who serve God and those who don't."

Malachi 3:1–2, 5, 16–18

INSIGHTS

We look for the return of the Lord because He said many times that He would come—and because it is one of the most frequently mentioned subjects in the Bible. Christ is with us today through His Holy Spirit, and He will be with Christians and with the church down to the end of the age. When He ascended up into heaven, the disciples were told by two angels standing by that He would return again as they were now seeing Him go (see Acts 1:11).

The climactic event of history is yet in the future. It will be sudden and final—the culmination of the ages. It will take the unbelieving world by surprise, and people will try to hide from His holy presence. At the return of Christ the resurrection of believers will take place. They will be gathered together to be with the Lord forever. We can only speculate about the exact details of His return. The important thing is that He is coming again and that we yet have time to trust in Him as our Savior and Lord. The Bible says all people must face Him at that time—as either Savior or Judge: "When the Son of Man comes in his glory . . . he will sit on his throne in heavenly glory" (Matthew 25:31).

BILLY GRAHAM

APPLICATION

What do you want to be doing when Jesus comes again? Will you be with those who say it is useless to serve God, or will you stand with those who honor the Lord? Pray that you will remain faithful.

MATTHEW 25:14-40

A Story About Three Servants

14"The kingdom of heaven is like a man who was going to another place for a visit. Before he left, he called for his servants and told them to take care of his things while he was gone. **15**He gave one servant five bags of gold, another servant two bags of gold, and a third servant one bag of gold, to each one as much as he could handle. Then he left. **16**The servant who got five bags went quickly to invest the money and earned five more bags. **17**In the same way, the servant who had two bags invested them and earned two more. **18**But the servant who got one bag went out and dug a hole in the ground and hid the master's money.

19"After a long time the master came home and asked the servants what they did with his money. **20**The servant who was given five bags of gold brought five more bags to the master and said, 'Master, you trusted me to care for five bags of gold, so I used your five bags to earn five more.' **21**The master answered, 'You did well. You are a good and loyal servant. Because you were loyal with small things, I will let you care for much greater things. Come and share my joy with me.'

22"Then the servant who had been given two bags of gold came to the master and said, 'Master, you gave me two bags of gold to care for, so I used your two bags to earn two more.' **23**The master answered, 'You did well. You are a good and loyal servant. Because you were loyal with small things, I will let you care for much greater things. Come and share my joy with me.'

24"Then the servant who had been given one bag of gold came to the master and said, 'Master, I knew that you were a hard man. You harvest things you did not plant. You gather crops where you did not sow any seed. **25**So I was afraid and went and hid your money in the ground. Here is your bag of gold.' **26**The master answered, 'You are a wicked and lazy servant! You say you knew that I harvest things I did not plant and that I gather crops where I did not sow any seed. **27**So you should have put my gold in the bank. Then, when I came home, I would have received my gold back with interest.'

28"So the master told his other servants, 'Take the bag of gold from that servant and give it to the servant who has ten bags of gold. **29**Those who have much will get more, and they will have much more than they need. But those who do not have much will have everything taken away from them.' **30**Then the master said, 'Throw that useless servant outside, into the darkness where people will cry and grind their teeth with pain.'

The King Will Judge All People

31"The Son of Man will come again in his great glory, with all his angels. He will be King and sit on his great throne. **32**All the nations of the world will be gathered before him, and he will separate them into two groups as a shepherd separates the sheep from the goats. **33**The Son of Man will put the sheep on his right and the goats on his left.

34"Then the King will say to the people on his right, 'Come, my Father has given you his blessing. Receive the kingdom God has prepared for you since the world was made. **35**I was hungry, and you gave me food. I was thirsty, and you gave me something to drink. I was alone and away from home, and you invited me into your house. 36I was without clothes, and you gave me something to wear. I was sick, and you cared for me. I was in prison, and you visited me.'

37"Then the good people will answer, 'Lord, when did we see you hungry and give you food, or thirsty and give you something to drink? 38When did we see you alone and away from home and invite you into our house? When did we see you without clothes and give you something to wear? 39When did we see you sick or in prison and care for you?'

40"Then the King will answer, 'I tell you the truth, anything you did for even the least of my people here, you also did for me.'"

OLD TESTAMENT READING

Happy are those who think about the poor.
    When trouble comes, the LORD will save
        them.
2The LORD will protect them and spare their
        life
    and will bless them in the land.
    He will not let their enemies take them.
3The LORD will give them strength when they
        are sick,
    and he will make them well again.

Psalm 41:1–3

INSIGHTS

"One kind word can warm three winter months," says a Japanese proverb.

Kind words indeed warm the human spirit. Kindness is literally love in action, showing genuine friendship to others by regarding them as important in God's sight and worthy of dignity and respect. It involves treating others with courtesy, lending encouragement, and freely offering yourself or your resources to help a person in need, no strings attached. . . .

In the book of Proverbs, we read that kindness is a prime quality of a virtuous woman: "When she speaks, her words are wise, and kindness is the rule for everything she says" (Proverbs 31:26). Men, these virtues are for us, too!

Jim has discovered the pleasure of kindness. He makes a special effort to brighten someone's day with an unexpected kind word or gesture. . . . At work, he frequently expresses appreciation to others for the jobs they do. With his neighbors, he is quick to lend a helping hand or offer encouragement.

Imagine the impact Christians could have on the world if kindness were the rule in all we do!

BILL BRIGHT

APPLICATION

What in these readings shows that God considers mistreatment of the poor, homeless, sick, and downtrodden to be a personal insult? How does that inspire you to be merciful, kind, and generous?

MATTHEW
25:41 — 26:19

41"Then the King will say to those on his left, 'Go away from me. You will be punished. Go into the fire that burns forever that was prepared for the devil and his angels. **42**I was hungry, and you gave me nothing to eat. I was thirsty, and you gave me nothing to drink. **43**I was alone and away from home, and you did not invite me into your house. I was without clothes, and you gave me nothing to wear. I was sick and in prison, and you did not care for me.'

44"Then those people will answer, 'Lord, when did we see you hungry or thirsty or alone and away from home or without clothes or sick or in prison? When did we see these things and not help you?'

45"Then the King will answer, 'I tell you the truth, anything you refused to do for even the least of my people here, you refused to do for me.'

46"These people will go off to be punished forever, but the good people will go to live forever."

The Plan to Kill Jesus

26 After Jesus finished saying all these things, he told his followers, **2**"You know that the day after tomorrow is the day of the Passover Feast. On that day the Son of Man will be given to his enemies to be crucified."

3Then the leading priests and the elders had a meeting at the palace of the high priest, named Caiaphas. **4**At the meeting, they planned to set a trap to arrest Jesus and kill him. **5**But they said, "We must not do it during the feast, because the people might cause a riot."

Perfume for Jesus' Burial

6Jesus was in Bethany at the house of Simon, who had a skin disease. **7**While Jesus was there, a woman approached him with an alabaster jar filled with expensive perfume. She poured this perfume on Jesus' head while he was eating.

8His followers were upset when they saw the woman do this. They asked, "Why waste that perfume? **9**It could have been sold for a great deal of money and the money given to the poor."

10Knowing what had happened, Jesus said, "Why are you troubling this woman? She did an excellent thing for me. **11**You will always have the poor with you, but you will not always have me. **12**This woman poured perfume on my body to prepare me for burial. **13**I tell you the truth, wherever the Good News is preached in all the world, what this woman has done will be told, and people will remember her."

Judas Becomes an Enemy of Jesus

14Then one of the twelve apostles, Judas Iscariot, went to talk to the leading priests. **15**He said, "What will you pay me for giving Jesus to you?" And they gave him thirty silver coins. **16**After that, Judas watched for the best time to turn Jesus in.

Jesus Eats the Passover Meal

17On the first day of the Feast of Unleavened Bread, the followers came to Jesus. They said, "Where do you want us to prepare for you to eat the Passover meal?"

¹⁸Jesus answered, "Go into the city to a certain man and tell him, 'The Teacher says: "The chosen time is near. I will have the Passover with my followers at your house."'" ¹⁹The followers did what Jesus told them to do, and they prepared the Passover meal.

OLD TESTAMENT READING

Manoah said to the angel of the LORD, "We would like you to stay awhile so we can cook a young goat for you."

¹⁶The angel of the LORD answered, "Even if I stay awhile, I would not eat your food. But if you want to prepare something, offer a burnt offering to the LORD." (Manoah did not understand that the man was really the angel of the LORD.)

¹⁷Then Manoah asked the angel of the LORD, "What is your name? Then we will honor you when what you have said really happens."

¹⁸The angel of the LORD said, "Why do you ask my name? It is too amazing for you to understand." ¹⁹So Manoah sacrificed a young goat on a rock and offered some grain as a gift to the LORD. Then an amazing thing happened as Manoah and his wife watched. ²⁰The flames went up to the sky from the altar. As the fire burned, the angel of the LORD went up to heaven in the flame. When Manoah and his wife saw that, they bowed facedown on the ground. ²¹The angel of the LORD did not appear to them again. Then Manoah understood that the man was really the angel of the LORD. ²²Manoah said, "We have seen God, so we will surely die."

²³But his wife said to him, "If the LORD wanted to kill us, he would not have accepted our burnt offering or grain offering. He would not have shown us all these things or told us all this."

Judges 13:15–23

INSIGHTS

It was said of the soldiers of the first Napoleon that they were content to die in the ditch if only he rode over them to victory. With their last breath they cried, "Long live the Emperor!" It seemed as though they had lost all thought and care of their own interests, so long as glory was given to his name. So should it be of us. Higher than our own comfort, or success, or popularity, should be the one thought of the glory of our God. Let Christ be honored, loved, exalted, at whatever cost to us. . . .

. . . Live to please God, and He will breathe on you His peace. Seek His glory, and He will make your heart His home. Do His will, and thereby good shall come to you.

F. B. MEYER

ACTION POINT

Review the ways people honored God in these readings (including the Matthew 25 parable). Spend some time honoring God in prayer today. Then, list the ways you want to honor God. Start glorifying him today!

MATTHEW 26:20-46

20In the evening Jesus was sitting at the table with his twelve followers. **21**As they were eating, Jesus said, "I tell you the truth, one of you will turn against me."

22This made the followers very sad. Each one began to say to Jesus, "Surely, Lord, I am not the one who will turn against you, am I?"

23Jesus answered, "The man who has dipped his hand with me into the bowl is the one who will turn against me. **24**The Son of Man will die, just as the Scriptures say. But how terrible it will be for the person who hands the Son of Man over to be killed. It would be better for him if he had never been born."

25Then Judas, who would give Jesus to his enemies, said to Jesus, "Teacher, surely I am not the one, am I?"

Jesus answered, "Yes, it is you."

The Lord's Supper

26While they were eating, Jesus took some bread and thanked God for it and broke it. Then he gave it to his followers and said, "Take this bread and eat it; this is my body."

27Then Jesus took a cup and thanked God for it and gave it to the followers. He said, "Every one of you drink this. **28**This is my blood which is the new agreement that God makes with his people. This blood is poured out for many to forgive their sins. **29**I tell you this: I will not drink of this fruit of the vine again until that day when I drink it new with you in my Father's kingdom."

30After singing a hymn, they went out to the Mount of Olives.

Jesus' Followers Will Leave Him

31Jesus told his followers, "Tonight you will all stumble in your faith on account of me, because it is written in the Scriptures:

'I will kill the shepherd,
    and the sheep will scatter.'   *Zechariah 13:7*

32But after I rise from the dead, I will go ahead of you into Galilee."

33Peter said, "Everyone else may stumble in their faith because of you, but I will not."

34Jesus said, "I tell you the truth, tonight before the rooster crows you will say three times that you don't know me."

35But Peter said, "I will never say that I don't know you! I will even die with you!" And all the other followers said the same thing.

Jesus Prays Alone

36Then Jesus went with his followers to a place called Gethsemane. He said to them, "Sit here while I go over there and pray." **37**He took Peter and the two sons of Zebedee with him, and he began to be very sad and troubled. **38**He said to them, "My heart is full of sorrow, to the point of death. Stay here and watch with me."

39After walking a little farther away from them, Jesus fell to the ground and prayed, "My Father, if it is possible, do not give me this cup of suffering. But do what you want, not what I want." **40**Then Jesus went back to his followers and found them asleep. He said to Peter, "You men could not stay awake with me for one hour? **41**Stay awake and pray for strength against temptation.

The spirit wants to do what is right, but the body is weak."

42Then Jesus went away a second time and prayed, "My Father, if it is not possible for this painful thing to be taken from me, and if I must do it, I pray that what you want will be done."

43Then he went back to his followers, and again he found them asleep, because their eyes were heavy. **44**So Jesus left them and went away and prayed a third time, saying the same thing.

45Then Jesus went back to his followers and said, "Are you still sleeping and resting? The time has come for the Son of Man to be handed over to sinful people. **46**Get up, we must go. Look, here comes the man who has turned against me."

OLD TESTAMENT READING

This is what the Lord GOD says: I, myself, will search for my sheep and take care of them. **12**As a shepherd takes care of his scattered flock when it is found, I will take care of my sheep. I will save them from all the places where they were scattered on a cloudy and dark day. **16**I will search for the lost, bring back those that strayed away, put bandages on those that were hurt, and make the weak strong.'"

Ezekiel 34:11–12, 16a

INSIGHTS

Lambs are wont to lag behind, prone to wander, and apt to grow weary, but from all the danger of these infirmities the Shepherd protects them with His arm of power. He finds new-born souls, like young lambs, ready to perish—He nourishes them till life becomes vigorous; He finds weak minds ready to faint and die—He consoles them and renews their strength. All the little ones He gathers, for it is not the will of our heavenly Father that one of them should perish. What a quick eye He must have to see them all! What a tender heart to care for them all! What a far-reaching and po-tent arm, to gather them all! In His lifetime on earth He was a great gatherer of the weaker sort, and now that He dwells in heaven, His loving heart yearns towards the meek and contrite, the timid and feeble, the fearful and fainting here below. How gently did He gather me to Himself, to His truth, to His blood, to His love, to His church! With what effectual grace did He compel me to Himself? Since my first con-version, how frequently has He restored me from my wanderings, and once again folded me within the circle of His everlasting arm! The best of all is, that He does it all Himself personally, not delegating the task of love, but condescending Himself to rescue and preserve His most unworthy servant.

CHARLES SPURGEON

APPLICATION

How do these readings comfort you? Thank God that he promises to care for you.

TUESDAY

THE PAIN OF BEING BETRAYED BY FRIENDS

MATTHEW
26:47-68

Jesus Is Arrested

47While Jesus was still speaking, Judas, one of the twelve apostles, came up. With him were many people carrying swords and clubs who had been sent from the leading priests and the Jewish elders of the people. **48**Judas had planned to give them a signal, saying, "The man I kiss is Jesus. Arrest him." **49**At once Judas went to Jesus and said, "Greetings, Teacher!" and kissed him.

50Jesus answered, "Friend, do what you came to do."

Then the people came and grabbed Jesus and arrested him. **51**When that happened, one of Jesus' followers reached for his sword and pulled it out. He struck the servant of the high priest and cut off his ear.

52Jesus said to the man, "Put your sword back in its place. All who use swords will be killed with swords. **53**Surely you know I could ask my Father, and he would give me more than twelve armies of angels. **54**But it must happen this way to bring about what the Scriptures say."

55Then Jesus said to the crowd, "You came to get me with swords and clubs as if I were a criminal. Every day I sat in the Temple teaching, and you did not arrest me there. **56**But all these things have happened so that it will come about as the prophets wrote." Then all of Jesus' followers left him and ran away.

Jesus Before the Leaders

57Those people who arrested Jesus led him to the house of Caiaphas, the high priest, where the teachers of the law and the elders were gathered. **58**Peter followed far behind to the courtyard of the high priest's house, and he sat down with the guards to see what would happen to Jesus.

59The leading priests and the whole Jewish council tried to find something false against Jesus so they could kill him. **60**Many people came and told lies about him, but the council could find no real reason to kill him. Then two people came and said, **61**"This man said, 'I can destroy the Temple of God and build it again in three days.'"

62Then the high priest stood up and said to Jesus, "Aren't you going to answer? Don't you have something to say about their charges against you?" **63**But Jesus said nothing.

Again the high priest said to Jesus, "I command you by the power of the living God: Tell us if you are the Christ, the Son of God."

64Jesus answered, "Those are your words. But I tell you, in the future you will see the Son of Man sitting at the right hand of God, the Powerful One, and coming on clouds in the sky."

65When the high priest heard this, he tore his clothes and said, "This man has said things that are against God! We don't need any more witnesses; you all heard him say these things against God. **66**What do you think?"

The people answered, "He should die."

67Then the people there spat in Jesus' face and beat him with their fists. Others slapped him. **68**They said, "Prove to us that you are a prophet, you Christ! Tell us who hit you!"

OLD TESTAMENT READING

It was not an enemy insulting me.
   I could stand that.
It was not someone who hated me.
   I could hide from him.

13 But it is you, a person like me,
   my companion and good friend.
14 We had a good friendship
   and walked together to God's Temple.

20 The one who was my friend attacks his
      friends
   and breaks his promises.
21 His words are slippery like butter,
   but war is in his heart.
His words are smoother than oil,
   but they cut like knives.

Psalm 55:12–14, 20–21

INSIGHTS

Have you ever been betrayed by a friend? If so, you know the pain of separation which resembles the grief of death. When Judas agreed to betray Jesus, he might as well have hammered the spikes that would later be driven through Jesus' hands.

Have you ever wondered how it was possible for one of the apostles (who had witnessed Jesus' power, teaching, and love) to turn him over to his enemies for any amount of money? This, of course, was not Judas' first act of betrayal. As treasurer for the disciples, Judas had been dipping into the till all along. He was a dishonest and greedy man. Even so, the mind races: How in the world could he have betrayed Jesus? . . .

Perhaps we have a clue when we are told about others who refused to accept Jesus as the Christ: "Even after Jesus had done all these miraculous signs in their presence, they still would not believe in him." Judas was not the only one to betray Jesus. All those who refused to believe in him despite the overwhelming evidence of his deity might as well have picked up their own 30 silver coins when Judas did.

Even today there are those who, despite the evidence, continue to betray Jesus through disbelief. How is it possible? Why do they choose to ignore him? . . .

. . . We can choose Christ, or we can choose the world with its false allure. Yet it is not a choice that we make just once in a lifetime. Each day that Judas robbed Jesus was a day of betrayal. And for those who heard Jesus teach, and watched his miracles, yet refused to believe—for them, every day was a day of betrayal.

Do we believe in Jesus, yet live our lives as if we didn't? If so, we too betray Jesus. Will today be a day of faith or a day of betrayal?

F. LaGard Smith

PAUSE FOR REFLECTION

When Jesus answered Judas' betrayal with the words, "Friend, do the thing you came to do," Jesus showed that he knew exactly what was in Judas' heart. If Jesus said the same thing today about your plans, how would you be affected?

MATTHEW
26:69 — 27:20

Peter Says He Doesn't Know Jesus

69At that time, as Peter was sitting in the courtyard, a servant girl came to him and said, "You also were with Jesus of Galilee."

70But Peter said to all the people there that he was never with Jesus. He said, "I don't know what you are talking about."

71When he left the courtyard and was at the gate, another girl saw him. She said to the people there, "This man was with Jesus of Nazareth."

72Again, Peter said he was never with him, saying, "I swear I don't know this man Jesus!"

73A short time later, some people standing there went to Peter and said, "Surely you are one of those who followed Jesus. The way you talk shows it."

74Then Peter began to place a curse on himself and swear, "I don't know the man." At once, a rooster crowed. **75**And Peter remembered what Jesus had told him: "Before the rooster crows, you will say three times that you don't know me." Then Peter went outside and cried painfully.

Jesus Is Taken to Pilate

27 Early the next morning, all the leading priests and elders of the people decided that Jesus should die. **2**They tied him, led him away, and turned him over to Pilate, the governor.

Judas Kills Himself

3Judas, the one who had given Jesus to his enemies, saw that they had decided to kill Jesus. Then he was very sorry for what he had done. So he took the thirty silver coins back to the priests and the leaders, **4**saying, "I sinned; I handed over to you an innocent man."

The leaders answered, "What is that to us? That's your problem, not ours."

5So Judas threw the money into the Temple. Then he went off and hanged himself.

6The leading priests picked up the silver coins in the Temple and said, "Our law does not allow us to keep this money with the Temple money, because it has paid for a man's death." **7**So they decided to use the coins to buy Potter's Field as a place to bury strangers who died in Jerusalem. **8**That is why that field is still called the Field of Blood. **9**So what Jeremiah the prophet had said came true: "They took thirty silver coins. That is how little the Israelites thought he was worth. **10**They used those thirty silver coins to buy the potter's field, as the Lord commanded me."

Pilate Questions Jesus

11Jesus stood before Pilate the governor, and Pilate asked him, "Are you the king of the Jews?"

Jesus answered, "Those are your words."

12When the leading priests and the elders accused Jesus, he said nothing.

13So Pilate said to Jesus, "Don't you hear them accusing you of all these things?"

14But Jesus said nothing in answer to Pilate, and Pilate was very surprised at this.

Pilate Tries to Free Jesus

15Every year at the time of Passover the governor would free one prisoner whom the people chose. **16**At that time there was a man in prison,

named Barabbas, who was known to be very bad.
17When the people gathered at Pilate's house, Pilate said, "Whom do you want me to set free: Barabbas or Jesus who is called the Christ?" **18**Pilate knew that they turned Jesus in to him because they were jealous.

19While Pilate was sitting there on the judge's seat, his wife sent this message to him: "Don't do anything to that man, because he is innocent. Today I had a dream about him, and it troubled me very much."

20But the leading priests and elders convinced the crowd to ask for Barabbas to be freed and for Jesus to be killed.

OLD TESTAMENT READING

The king asked Daniel, who was also called Belteshazzar, "Are you able to tell me what I dreamed and what it means?"

27Daniel answered, "No wise man, magician, or fortune-teller can explain to the king the secret he has asked about. **28**But there is a God in heaven who explains secret things, and he has shown King Nebuchadnezzar what will happen at a later time."

Daniel 2:26–28a

INSIGHTS

On one occasion when I was in prayer, I had a vision in which I saw how all things are seen in God. I cannot explain what I saw, but what I saw remains to this day, deeply imprinted upon my soul. It was a great act of grace in God to give me that vision. It puts me to unspeakable confusion, shame, and horror whenever I recall that magnificent sight, and then think of my sin. I believe that had the Lord been pleased to send me that great revelation of Himself earlier in my life, it would have kept me back from much sin. . . .

Suppose the Godhead to be like a vast globe of light, a globe larger than the whole world, and that all our actions are seen in that all-embracing globe. . . I saw all my most filthy actions gathered up and reflected back upon me from that world of light. I tell you it was the most pitiful and dreadful thing to see. I did not know where to hide myself, for that shining light, in which there was no darkness at all, held the whole world within it, and all worlds. . . .

. . . Oh that those who commit deeds of darkness could be made to see this!
. . . Oh, the madness of committing sin in the immediate presence of a Majesty so great.

ST. TERESA OF AVILA

▶ PAUSE FOR REFLECTION

Why did Pilate ignore his wife's urgent warning? What important messages from God are you ignoring?

MATTHEW 27:21-44

²¹Pilate said, "I have Barabbas and Jesus. Which do you want me to set free for you?"

The people answered, "Barabbas."

²²Pilate asked, "So what should I do with Jesus, the one called the Christ?"

They all answered, "Crucify him!"

²³Pilate asked, "Why? What wrong has he done?"

But they shouted louder, "Crucify him!"

²⁴When Pilate saw that he could do nothing about this and that a riot was starting, he took some water and washed his hands in front of the crowd. Then he said, "I am not guilty of this man's death. You are the ones who are causing it!"

²⁵All the people answered, "We and our children will be responsible for his death."

²⁶Then he set Barabbas free. But Jesus was beaten with whips and handed over to the soldiers to be crucified.

²⁷The governor's soldiers took Jesus into the governor's palace, and they all gathered around him. ²⁸They took off his clothes and put a red robe on him. ²⁹Using thorny branches, they made a crown, put it on his head, and put a stick in his right hand. Then the soldiers bowed before Jesus and made fun of him, saying, "Hail, King of the Jews!" ³⁰They spat on Jesus. Then they took his stick and began to beat him on the head. ³¹After they finished, the soldiers took off the robe and put his own clothes on him again. Then they led him away to be crucified.

Jesus Is Crucified

³²As the soldiers were going out of the city with Jesus, they forced a man from Cyrene, named Simon, to carry the cross for Jesus. ³³They all came to the place called Golgotha, which means the Place of the Skull. ³⁴The soldiers gave Jesus wine mixed with gall to drink. He tasted the wine but refused to drink it. ³⁵When the soldiers had crucified him, they threw lots to decide who would get his clothes. ³⁶The soldiers sat there and continued watching him. ³⁷They put a sign above Jesus' head with a charge against him. It said: THIS IS JESUS, THE KING OF THE JEWS. ³⁸Two robbers were crucified beside Jesus, one on the right and the other on the left. ³⁹People walked by and insulted Jesus and shook their heads, ⁴⁰saying, "You said you could destroy the Temple and build it again in three days. So save yourself! Come down from that cross if you are really the Son of God!"

⁴¹The leading priests, the teachers of the law, and the Jewish elders were also making fun of Jesus. ⁴²They said, "He saved others, but he can't save himself! He says he is the king of Israel! If he is the king, let him come down now from the cross. Then we will believe in him. ⁴³He trusts in God, so let God save him now, if God really wants him. He himself said, 'I am the Son of God.'" ⁴⁴And in the same way, the robbers who were being crucified beside Jesus also insulted him.

OLD TESTAMENT READING

But I am like a worm instead of a man.
  People make fun of me and hate me.
7 Those who look at me laugh.
    They stick out their tongues and shake
      their heads.
8 They say, "Turn to the LORD for help.
    Maybe he will save you.
  If he likes you,
    maybe he will rescue you."

Psalm 22:6–8

Who would have believed what we heard?
  Who saw the LORD's power in this?
2 He grew up like a small plant before the LORD,
  like a root growing in a dry land.

He had no special beauty or form to make us
      notice him;
  there was nothing in his appearance to
    make us desire him.
3 He was hated and rejected by people.
  He had much pain and suffering.
People would not even look at him.
  He was hated, and we didn't even notice
    him.

5 But he was wounded for the wrong we did;
  he was crushed for the evil we did.
The punishment, which made us well, was
    given to him,
  and we are healed because of his
    wounds.

Isaiah 53:1–3, 5

INSIGHTS

While Francis Xavier was preaching one day in one of the cities of Japan, a man walked up to him as if he had something to say to him privately. As the missionary leaned closer to hear what he had to say, the man spat on his face.

Without a word or the least sign of annoyance, Xavier pulled out a handkerchief and wiped his face. Then he went on with his important message as if nothing had happened. The scorn of the audience was turned to admiration.

The most learned doctor of the city happened to be present.

"A law which teaches men such virtue, inspires them with such courage, and gives them such complete mastery over themselves," he said, "could not but be from God."

Supernatural power and enablement by God's Holy Spirit make that kind of behavior possible for every believer. Furthermore, that kind of behavior probably will do more to attract and influence an unbelieving world than words ever can.

With Christ as our example, love as our motive, and humility as our covering, let us depend on God's Holy Spirit for the wisdom and strength required to respond to mistreatment in a Christlike way. Then, and only then, are we in a position to reflect honor and glory to the Lord Jesus Christ.

BILL BRIGHT

ACTION POINT

Study the model of grace Christ provides. Pray for grace to bear whatever insults come your way.

MATTHEW 27:45 — 28:10

Jesus Dies

45At noon the whole country became dark, and the darkness lasted for three hours. **46**About three o'clock Jesus cried out in a loud voice, "Eli, Eli, lama sabachthani?" This means, "My God, my God, why have you abandoned me?"

47Some of the people standing there who heard this said, "He is calling Elijah."

48Quickly one of them ran and got a sponge and filled it with vinegar and tied it to a stick and gave it to Jesus to drink. **49**But the others said, "Don't bother him. We want to see if Elijah will come to save him."

50But Jesus cried out again in a loud voice and died.

51Then the curtain in the Temple was torn into two pieces, from the top to the bottom. Also, the earth shook and rocks broke apart. **52**The graves opened, and many of God's people who had died were raised from the dead. **53**They came out of the graves after Jesus was raised from the dead and went into the holy city, where they appeared to many people.

54When the army officer and the soldiers guarding Jesus saw this earthquake and everything else that happened, they were very frightened and said, "He really was the Son of God!"

55Many women who had followed Jesus from Galilee to help him were standing at a distance from the cross, watching. **56**Mary Magdalene, and Mary the mother of James and Joseph, and the mother of James and John were there.

Jesus Is Buried

57That evening a rich man named Joseph, a follower of Jesus from the town of Arimathea, came to Jerusalem. **58**Joseph went to Pilate and asked to have Jesus' body. So Pilate gave orders for the soldiers to give it to Joseph. **59**Then Joseph took the body and wrapped it in a clean linen cloth. **60**He put Jesus' body in a new tomb that he had cut out of a wall of rock, and he rolled a very large stone to block the entrance of the tomb. Then Joseph went away. **61**Mary Magdalene and the other woman named Mary were sitting near the tomb.

The Tomb of Jesus Is Guarded

62The next day, the day after Preparation Day, the leading priests and the Pharisees went to Pilate. **63**They said, "Sir, we remember that while that liar was still alive he said, 'After three days I will rise from the dead.' **64**So give the order for the tomb to be guarded closely till the third day. Otherwise, his followers might come and steal the body and tell people that he has risen from the dead. That lie would be even worse than the first one."

65Pilate said, "Take some soldiers and go guard the tomb the best way you know." **66**So they all went to the tomb and made it safe from thieves by sealing the stone in the entrance and putting soldiers there to guard it.

Jesus Rises from the Dead

 The day after the Sabbath day was the first day of the week. At dawn on the first day, Mary Magdalene and another woman named Mary went to look at the tomb.

2At that time there was a strong earthquake. An angel of the Lord came down from heaven, went to the tomb, and rolled the stone away from the entrance. Then he sat on the stone. **3**He was shining as bright as lightning, and his clothes were white as snow. **4**The soldiers guarding the tomb shook with fear because of the angel, and they became like dead men.

5The angel said to the women, "Don't be afraid. I know that you are looking for Jesus, who has been crucified. **6**He is not here. He has risen from the dead as he said he would. Come and see the place where his body was. **7**And go quickly and tell his followers, 'Jesus has risen from the dead. He is going into Galilee ahead of you, and you will see him there.'" Then the angel said, "Now I have told you."

8The women left the tomb quickly. They were afraid, but they were also very happy. They ran to tell Jesus' followers what had happened. **9**Suddenly, Jesus met them and said, "Greetings." The women came up to him, took hold of his feet, and worshiped him. **10**Then Jesus said to them, "Don't be afraid. Go and tell my followers to go on to Galilee, and they will see me there."

OLD TESTAMENT READING

I keep the LORD before me always.
>   Because he is close by my side,
>   I will not be hurt.
> **9**So I rejoice and am glad.
>   Even my body has hope,
> **10**because you will not leave me in the grave.
>   You will not let your holy one rot.

Psalm 16:8–10

INSIGHTS

The power of the resurrection is the power of personal regeneration. Resurrection spells regeneration. The two things must always be kept together: the new world and the new person. Resurrection is not just a passport to heaven, but a power to change us now. Paul says he wants to know Christ and the power of his resurrection. The two are the same. To know Christ today is to come under the influence of the same power that raised Him from the dead. What a cruel thing an example is without the power to live it. Christ is the best of all examples, but more than that, He can come within us and give us His own Spirit to fulfill the example. The result is we actually become like Him, we are able to do the things He did, and most of all, we are able to love as He loved.

LLOYD OGILVIE

PAUSE FOR REFLECTION

Why did the Pharisees fear the possibility of Jesus' resurrection? When he rose again, what did Jesus destroy forever? What difference did his resurrection make in the lives of his followers? How has his resurrection regenerated your life?

MATTHEW 28:11— MARK 1:20

The Soldiers Report to the Leaders

11While the women went to tell Jesus' followers, some of the soldiers who had been guarding the tomb went into the city to tell the leading priests everything that had happened. **12**Then the priests met with the elders and made a plan. They paid the soldiers a large amount of money **13**and said to them, "Tell the people that Jesus' followers came during the night and stole the body while you were asleep. **14**If the governor hears about this, we will satisfy him and save you from trouble." **15**So the soldiers kept the money and did as they were told. And that story is still spread among the people even today.

Jesus Talks to His Followers

16The eleven followers went to Galilee to the mountain where Jesus had told them to go. **17**On the mountain they saw Jesus and worshiped him, but some of them did not believe it was really Jesus. **18**Then Jesus came to them and said, "All power in heaven and on earth is given to me. **19**So go and make followers of all people in the world. Baptize them in the name of the Father and the Son and the Holy Spirit. **20**Teach them to obey everything that I have taught you, and I will be with you always, even until the end of this age."

John Prepares for Jesus

This is the beginning of the Good News about Jesus Christ, the Son of God, **2**as the prophet Isaiah wrote:

> "I will send my messenger ahead of you,
> who will prepare your way."   *Malachi 3:1*

3"This is a voice of one
  who calls out in the desert:
'Prepare the way for the Lord.
  Make the road straight for him.'"

Isaiah 40:3

4John was baptizing people in the desert and preaching a baptism of changed hearts and lives for the forgiveness of sins. **5**All the people from Judea and Jerusalem were going out to him. They confessed their sins and were baptized by him in the Jordan River. **6**John wore clothes made from camel's hair, had a leather belt around his waist, and ate locusts and wild honey. **7**This is what John preached to the people: "There is one coming after me who is greater than I; I am not good enough even to kneel down and untie his sandals. **8**I baptize you with water, but he will baptize you with the Holy Spirit."

Jesus Is Baptized

9At that time Jesus came from the town of Nazareth in Galilee and was baptized by John in the Jordan River. **10**Immediately, as Jesus was coming up out of the water, he saw heaven open. The Holy Spirit came down on him like a dove, **11**and a voice came from heaven: "You are my Son, whom I love, and I am very pleased with you."

12Then the Spirit sent Jesus into the desert. **13**He was in the desert forty days and was tempted by Satan. He was with the wild animals, and the angels came and took care of him.

Jesus Chooses Some Followers

14After John was put in prison, Jesus went into Galilee, preaching the Good News from God. **15**He said, "The right time has come. The kingdom of

God is near. Change your hearts and lives and believe the Good News!"

16When Jesus was walking by Lake Galilee, he saw Simon and his brother Andrew throwing a net into the lake because they were fishermen. **17**Jesus said to them, "Come follow me, and I will make you fish for people." **18**So Simon and Andrew immediately left their nets and followed him.

19Going a little farther, Jesus saw two more brothers, James and John, the sons of Zebedee. They were in a boat, mending their nets. **20**Jesus immediately called them, and they left their father in the boat with the hired workers and followed Jesus.

OLD TESTAMENT READING

Sing to the LORD, all the earth.
   Every day tell how he saves us.
24Tell the nations about his glory;
   tell all peoples the miracles he does.
25The LORD is great; he should be praised.
   He should be respected more than all the
      gods.

1 Chronicles 16:23–25

INSIGHTS

For the New Testament Christians, witness was not a sales pitch.

They simply shared, each in his own way, what they had received. Theirs was not a formally prepared, carefully worked-out presentation with a gimmick to manipulate conversation, and a "closer" for an on-the-spot-decision . . . but the spontaneous, irrepressible, effervescent enthusiasm of those who had met the most fascinating Person who ever lived.

The gospel is not theology. It's a Person. Theology doesn't save. Jesus Christ saves. The first-century disciples were totally involved with a Person. They were followers of Jesus. They were learners of Jesus. They were committed to Jesus. They were filled with Jesus.

They had encountered Jesus Christ and it simply could not be concealed. They witnessed not because they had to, but because they could not help it.

Their school of witnessing was the school of the Spirit where they learned continuously. Authentic Christian witness is born of the Spirit.

Madison Avenue, with all its sophisticated know-how, can't improve on the strategy. Nothing is more convincing than the simple, unembellished word of a satisfied customer.

RICHARD HALVERSON

ACTION POINT

Pray that God's salvation will be so real to you that you cannot help but tell others.

MARK 1:21-45

Jesus Forces Out an Evil Spirit

21Jesus and his followers went to Capernaum. On the Sabbath day he went to the synagogue and began to teach. 22The people were amazed at his teaching, because he taught like a person who had authority, not like their teachers of the law. 23Just then, a man was there in the synagogue who had an evil spirit in him. He shouted, 24"Jesus of Nazareth! What do you want with us? Did you come to destroy us? I know who you are—God's Holy One!"

25Jesus commanded the evil spirit, "Be quiet! Come out of the man!" 26The evil spirit shook the man violently, gave a loud cry, and then came out of him.

27The people were so amazed they asked each other, "What is happening here? This man is teaching something new, and with authority. He even gives commands to evil spirits, and they obey him." 28And the news about Jesus spread quickly everywhere in the area of Galilee.

Jesus Heals Many People

29As soon as Jesus and his followers left the synagogue, they went with James and John to the home of Simon and Andrew. 30Simon's mother-in-law was sick in bed with a fever, and the people told Jesus about her. 31So Jesus went to her bed, took her hand, and helped her up. The fever left her, and she began serving them.

32That evening, after the sun went down, the people brought to Jesus all who were sick and had demons in them. 33The whole town gathered at the door. 34Jesus healed many who had different kinds of sicknesses, and he forced many demons to leave people. But he would not allow the demons to speak, because they knew who he was.

35Early the next morning, while it was still dark, Jesus woke and left the house. He went to a lonely place, where he prayed. 36Simon and his friends went to look for Jesus. 37When they found him, they said, "Everyone is looking for you!"

38Jesus answered, "We should go to other towns around here so I can preach there too. That is the reason I came." 39So he went everywhere in Galilee, preaching in the synagogues and forcing out demons.

Jesus Heals a Sick Man

40A man with a skin disease came to Jesus. He fell to his knees and begged Jesus, "You can heal me if you will."

41Jesus felt sorry for the man, so he reached out his hand and touched him and said, "I will. Be healed!" 42Immediately the disease left the man, and he was healed.

43Jesus told the man to go away at once, but he warned him strongly, 44"Don't tell anyone about this. But go and show yourself to the priest. And offer the gift Moses commanded for people who are made well. This will show the people what I have done." 45The man left there, but he began to tell everyone that Jesus had healed him, and so he spread the news about Jesus. As a result, Jesus could not enter a town if people saw him. He stayed in places where nobody lived, but people came to him from everywhere.

OLD TESTAMENT READING

Come, let's go back to the Lord.
He has hurt us, but he will heal us.
He has wounded us, but he will bandage
our wounds.
2In two days he will put new life in us;
on the third day he will raise us up
so that we may live in his presence **3**and
know him.

Let's try to learn about the LORD;
he will come to us as surely as the dawn
comes.
He will come to us like rain,
like the spring rain that waters the ground."

Hosea 6:1–3

LORD, heal me, and I will truly be healed.
Save me, and I will truly be saved.
You are the one I praise.

Jeremiah 17:14

INSIGHTS

Bethlehem, Galilee, Gethsemane—He walked there. But today Christ walks the concrete sidewalks of Times Square, 47th Street, and Broadway. And as He walks, His feet are soiled—not with the sand of the seashore or the reddish dust of the Emmaus Road, but with the soot and filth of the city.

He walks the "Great White Way," and His face is lit by the gaudy neon signboards of materialism. He walks in the shadows of the dark alleyways, where faces are not lit at all. . . .

He is pushed and shoved through Grand Central Station, elbowed and ignored, yet in the crowd He feels a measure of virtue flow from His being and searches through the faces for an honest seeker passing by. . . .

Christ walks the city and . . . weaves the cloth that transforms rags into a lovely tapestry. . . . He acts the part that tells the story of how that Love invaded humankind, for only story tells the Story. Christ incarnate. Christ the living, walking parable, takes the stage to be the Story. . . .

. . . He is the broken, and He is the healer. He is the hungry, and He is the Bread of Life. He is the homeless, yet it is He who says "Come to Me all you who are overloaded, and I will be your resting place." He is the loser who makes losing the only way to win. He is the omnipotent who calls all who follow to choose powerlessness and teaches us by laying down all power in heaven and in earth. He is the sick, and He is the wholeness.

GLORIA GAITHER

ACTION POINT

Can there be any greater healing than that given by the Healer? Can you imagine any greater compassion than that shown in the love of his Son? Meditate on one of these readings and let it become your prayer of praise to God today.

MARK 2:1-22

Jesus Heals a Paralyzed Man

A few days later, when Jesus came back to Capernaum, the news spread that he was at home. **2**Many people gathered together so that there was no room in the house, not even outside the door. And Jesus was teaching them God's message. **3**Four people came, carrying a paralyzed man. **4**Since they could not get to Jesus because of the crowd, they dug a hole in the roof right above where he was speaking. When they got through, they lowered the mat with the paralyzed man on it. **5**When Jesus saw the faith of these people, he said to the paralyzed man, "Young man, your sins are forgiven."

6Some of the teachers of the law were sitting there, thinking to themselves, **7**"Why does this man say things like that? He is speaking as if he were God. Only God can forgive sins."

8Jesus knew immediately what these teachers of the law were thinking. So he said to them, "Why are you thinking these things? **9**Which is easier: to tell this paralyzed man, 'Your sins are forgiven,' or to tell him, 'Stand up. Take your mat and walk'? **10**But I will prove to you that the Son of Man has authority on earth to forgive sins." So Jesus said to the paralyzed man, **11**"I tell you, stand up, take your mat, and go home." **12**Immediately the paralyzed man stood up, took his mat, and walked out while everyone was watching him.

The people were amazed and praised God. They said, "We have never seen anything like this!"

13Jesus went to the lake again. The whole crowd followed him there, and he taught them. **14**While he was walking along, he saw a man named Levi son of Alphaeus, sitting in the tax collector's booth. Jesus said to him, "Follow me," and he stood up and followed Jesus.

15Later, as Jesus was having dinner at Levi's house, many tax collectors and "sinners" were eating there with Jesus and his followers. Many people like this followed Jesus. **16**When the teachers of the law who were Pharisees saw Jesus eating with the tax collectors and "sinners," they asked his followers, "Why does he eat with tax collectors and sinners?"

17Jesus heard this and said to them, "It is not the healthy people who need a doctor, but the sick. I did not come to invite good people but to invite sinners."

Jesus' Followers Are Criticized

18Now the followers of John and the Pharisees often fasted for a certain time. Some people came to Jesus and said, "Why do John's followers and the followers of the Pharisees often fast, but your followers don't?"

19Jesus answered, "The friends of the bridegroom do not fast while the bridegroom is still with them. As long as the bridegroom is with them, they cannot fast. **20**But the time will come when the bridegroom will be taken from them, and then they will fast.

21"No one sews a patch of unshrunk cloth over a hole in an old coat. Otherwise, the patch will shrink and pull away—the new patch will pull away from the old coat. Then the hole will be worse. **22**Also, no one ever pours new wine into old leather bags. Otherwise, the new wine will break the bags, and the wine will be ruined along with the bags. But new wine should be put into new leather bags."

OLD TESTAMENT READING

But it was the LORD who decided
 to crush him and make him suffer.
  The LORD made his life a penalty offering,
 but he will still see his descendants and live a
   long life.
  He will complete the things the LORD wants
   him to do.
11"After his soul suffers many things,
  he will see life and be satisfied.

My good servant will make many people right
  with God;
 he will carry away their sins.
12For this reason I will make him a great man
  among people,
 and he will share in all things with those
   who are strong.
He willingly gave his life
 and was treated like a criminal.
But he carried away the sins of many
  people
 and asked forgiveness for those who
  sinned."

Isaiah 53:10–12

INSIGHTS

Forgiveness is one of the first and most glorious blessings we receive from God. It is the transition from the old to the new life; the sign and pledge of God's love: with it we receive the right to all the spiritual gifts which are prepared for us in Christ. The believer can never forget, either here or in eternity, that he is a forgiven sinner. Nothing more inflames his love, awakens his joy, or strengthens his courage than the continually renewed experience of God's forgiving love. Every day, yes, every thought of God reminds him: I owe all to pardoning grace.

This forgiving love is one of the greatest manifestations of the divine nature. In it God finds His glory and blessedness and wants to share this with His redeemed people.

ANDREW MURRAY

APPLICATION

What is the most important characteristic of the good servant promised in Isaiah 53? Is it then surprising that Jesus forgave sins while he was on earth? Has your spirit been healed by Jesus' forgiveness of your sins?

MARK 2:23 – 3:27

Jesus Is Lord of the Sabbath

23One Sabbath day, as Jesus was walking through some fields of grain, his followers began to pick some grain to eat. **24**The Pharisees said to Jesus, "Why are your followers doing what is not lawful on the Sabbath day?"

25Jesus answered, "Have you never read what David did when he and those with him were hungry and needed food? **26**During the time of Abiathar the high priest, David went into God's house and ate the holy bread, which is lawful only for priests to eat. And David also gave some of the bread to those who were with him."

27Then Jesus said to the Pharisees, "The Sabbath day was made to help people; they were not made to be ruled by the Sabbath day. **28**So then, the Son of Man is Lord even of the Sabbath day."

Jesus Heals a Man's Hand

3Another time when Jesus went into a synagogue, a man with a crippled hand was there. **2**Some people watched Jesus closely to see if he would heal the man on the Sabbath day so they could accuse him.

3Jesus said to the man with the crippled hand, "Stand up here in the middle of everyone."

4Then Jesus asked the people, "Which is lawful on the Sabbath day: to do good or to do evil, to save a life or to kill?" But they said nothing to answer him.

5Jesus was angry as he looked at the people, and he felt very sad because they were stubborn. Then he said to the man, "Hold out your hand." The man held out his hand and it was healed. **6**Then the Pharisees left and began making plans with the Herodians about a way to kill Jesus.

Many People Follow Jesus

7Jesus left with his followers for the lake, and a large crowd from Galilee followed him. **8**Also many people came from Judea, from Jerusalem, from Idumea, from the lands across the Jordan River, and from the area of Tyre and Sidon. When they heard what Jesus was doing, many people came to him. **9**When Jesus saw the crowds, he told his followers to get a boat ready for him to keep people from crowding against him. **10**He had healed many people, so all the sick were pushing toward him to touch him. **11**When evil spirits saw Jesus, they fell down before him and shouted, "You are the Son of God!" **12**But Jesus strongly warned them not to tell who he was.

Jesus Chooses His Twelve Apostles

13Then Jesus went up on a mountain and called to him those he wanted, and they came to him. **14**Jesus chose twelve and called them apostles. He wanted them to be with him, and he wanted to send them out to preach **15**and to have the authority to force demons out of people. **16**These are the twelve men he chose: Simon (Jesus named him Peter), **17**James and John, the sons of Zebedee (Jesus named them Boanerges, which means "Sons of Thunder"), **18**Andrew, Philip, Bartholomew, Matthew, Thomas, James the son of Alphaeus, Thaddaeus, Simon the Zealot, **19**and Judas Iscariot, who later turned against Jesus.

Some People Say Jesus Has a Devil

20Then Jesus went home, but again a crowd gathered. There were so many people that Jesus and his followers could not eat. **21**When his family heard this, they went to get him because they thought he was out of his mind. **22**But the teachers of the law from Jerusalem were saying, "Beelzebul is living inside him! He uses power from the ruler of demons to force demons out of people."

23So Jesus called the people together and taught them with stories. He said, "Satan will not force himself out of people. **24**A kingdom that is divided cannot continue, **25**and a family that is divided cannot continue. **26**And if Satan is against himself and fights against his own people, he cannot continue; that is the end of Satan. **27**No one can enter a strong person's house and steal his things unless he first ties up the strong person. Then he can steal things from the house."

OLD TESTAMENT READING

This is what the LORD says:
"Give justice to all people,
    and do what is right,
because my salvation will come to you soon.
    Soon everyone will know that I do what is
        right.
2The person who obeys the law about
        the Sabbath
    will be blessed,
and the person who does no evil
    will be blessed."

Isaiah 56:1–2

INSIGHTS

Sabbath rest means worship with the Christian family. In proper worship we will have a chance to exercise all three aspects that lead to the rest of our private worlds: looking backward, upward, and ahead. Such worship is non-negotiable to the person committed to walking with God. . . .

. . . Sabbath means a deliberate acceptance of personal rest and tranquility within the individual life. Sabbath means a rest that brings peace into the private world. As Christ pressed stillness into a storm, order into a being of a demon-possessed maniac, health into a desperately sick woman, and life into a dead friend, so He seeks to press peace into [our] harried private world. . . . But there is a condition. We must accept this peace as a gift and take the time to receive it.

GORDON MACDONALD

APPLICATION

Think about Jesus' statement that the Sabbath was meant to help people. In what ways do you think keeping the Sabbath is good for us? How do you think Jesus feels about the way you keep the Sabbath?

MARK 3:28 — 4:20

28"I tell you the truth, all sins that people do and all the things people say against God can be forgiven. **29**But anyone who speaks against the Holy Spirit will never be forgiven; he is guilty of a sin that continues forever."

30Jesus said this because the teachers of the law said that he had an evil spirit inside him.

Jesus' True Family

31Then Jesus' mother and brothers arrived. Standing outside, they sent someone in to tell him to come out. **32**Many people were sitting around Jesus, and they said to him, "Your mother and brothers are waiting for you outside."

33Jesus asked, "Who are my mother and my brothers?" **34**Then he looked at those sitting around him and said, "Here are my mother and my brothers! **35**My true brother and sister and mother are those who do what God wants."

A Story About Planting Seed

Again Jesus began teaching by the lake. A great crowd gathered around him, so he sat down in a boat near the shore. All the people stayed on the shore close to the water. **2**Jesus taught them many things, using stories. He said, **3**"Listen! A farmer went out to plant his seed. **4**While he was planting, some seed fell by the road, and the birds came and ate it up. **5**Some seed fell on rocky ground where there wasn't much dirt. That seed grew very fast, because the ground was not deep. **6**But when the sun rose, the plants dried up because they did not have deep roots. **7**Some other seed fell among thorny weeds, which grew and choked the good plants. So those plants did not produce a crop. **8**Some other seed fell on good ground and began to grow. It got taller and produced a crop. Some plants made thirty times more, some made sixty times more, and some made a hundred times more."

9Then Jesus said, "Let those with ears use them and listen!"

Jesus Tells Why He Used Stories

10Later, when Jesus was alone, the twelve apostles and others around him asked him about the stories.

11Jesus said, "You can know the secret about the kingdom of God. But to other people I tell everything by using stories **12**so that:

'They will look and look, but they will not
learn.
They will listen and listen, but they will not
understand.
If they did learn and understand,
they would come back to me and be
forgiven.'" *Isaiah 6:9–10*

Jesus Explains the Seed Story

13Then Jesus said to his followers, "Don't you understand this story? If you don't, how will you understand any story? **14**The farmer is like a person who plants God's message in people. **15**Sometimes the teaching falls on the road. This is like the people who hear the teaching of God, but Satan quickly comes and takes away the teaching that was planted in them. **16**Others are like the seed planted on rocky ground. They hear the teaching and quickly accept it with joy. **17**But since they don't allow the teaching to go deep into their lives, they keep it only a short time. When trouble or persecution comes because of the teaching they accepted, they quickly give up. **18**Others are like the seed planted among the thorny weeds. They hear the teaching, **19**but the worries of this life, the temptation of wealth, and many other evil desires keep the teaching from growing and producing fruit in their lives. **20**Others are like the seed planted in the good ground. They hear the teaching and accept it. Then they grow and produce fruit—sometimes thirty times more, sometimes sixty times more, and sometimes a hundred times more."

OLD TESTAMENT READING

Then Moses went up on the mountain to God. The LORD called to him from the mountain and said, "Say this to the family of Jacob, and tell the people of Israel: **4**'Every one of you has seen what I did to the people of Egypt. You saw how I carried you out of Egypt, as if on eagle's wings. And I brought you here to me. **5**So now if you obey me and keep my agreement, you will be my own possession, chosen from all nations.'"

Exodus 19:3–5

INSIGHTS

The source of Christ's victory, the secret of His power, and of ours, lies in obedience. . . . In an obedient heart there is a way prepared for God. There are many Christians who always seek pleasure and satisfaction for themselves. These have not yet learned that only obedient children are happy children. That which in truth brings abiding happiness is nothing else than obedience toward God. For a healthy soul there is only one thing that counts—to be obedient. . . .

Why have so many of God's lambs so little assurance of salvation? Why are their souls not satisfied with the peace of God? God gives us the answer in Isaiah 48:18: "Oh, that thou hadst hearkened to my commandments! Then had thy peace been as a river, and thy righteousness as the waves of the sea." People say, "I lack faith. I have too little faith; therefore I have no assurance of salvation, no peace." But in most instances it is not faith which is lacking, for even with a trembling hand one can receive costly gifts. It is rather obedience which is lacking. There is something in their lives which they will not let go, and which hinders the Holy Spirit from giving them the assurance that they are God's children. . . . No one who is disobedient to God can have confidence in Him. Confidence is a result of obedience.

G. STEINBERGER

APPLICATION

What one thing does God require of those who would be his people? What do those who obey God receive from him? How's your obedience? Is it obvious that you belong to God?

MARK 4:21 — 5:10

Use What You Have

21Then Jesus said to them, "Do you hide a lamp under a bowl or under a bed? No! You put the lamp on a lampstand. **22**Everything that is hidden will be made clear and every secret thing will be made known. **23**Let those with ears use them and listen!

24"Think carefully about what you hear. The way you give to others is the way God will give to you, but God will give you even more. **25**Those who have understanding will be given more. But those who do not have understanding, even what they have will be taken away from them."

Jesus Uses a Story About Seed

26Then Jesus said, "The kingdom of God is like someone who plants seed in the ground. **27**Night and day, whether the person is asleep or awake, the seed still grows, but the person does not know how it grows. **28**By itself the earth produces grain. First the plant grows, then the head, and then all the grain in the head. **29**When the grain is ready, the farmer cuts it, because this is the harvest time."

A Story About Mustard Seed

30Then Jesus said, "How can I show you what the kingdom of God is like? What story can I use to explain it? **31**The kingdom of God is like a mustard seed, the smallest seed you plant in the ground. **32**But when planted, this seed grows and becomes the largest of all garden plants. It pro-duces large branches, and the wild birds can make nests in its shade."

33Jesus used many stories like these to teach the crowd God's message—as much as they could understand. **34**He always used stories to teach them. But when he and his followers were alone, Jesus explained everything to them.

Jesus Calms a Storm

35That evening, Jesus said to his followers, "Let's go across the lake." **36**Leaving the crowd behind, they took him in the boat just as he was. There were also other boats with them. **37**A very strong wind came up on the lake. The waves came over the sides and into the boat so that it was already full of water. **38**Jesus was at the back of the boat, sleeping with his head on a cushion. His followers woke him and said, "Teacher, don't you care that we are drowning!"

39Jesus stood up and commanded the wind and said to the waves, "Quiet! Be still!" Then the wind stopped, and it became completely calm.

40Jesus said to his followers, "Why are you afraid? Do you still have no faith?"

41The followers were very afraid and asked each other, "Who is this? Even the wind and the waves obey him!"

A Man with Demons Inside Him

Jesus and his followers went to the other side of the lake to the area of the Gerasene people. **2**When Jesus got out of the boat, instantly a man with an evil spirit came to him from the burial caves. **3**This man lived in the caves, and no one could tie him up, not even with a chain. **4**Many times people had used chains to tie the man's hands and feet, but he always broke them off. No one was strong enough to control him. **5**Day and night he would wander around the burial caves and on the hills, screaming and cutting himself with stones. **6**While Jesus was still far away, the man saw him, ran to him, and fell down before him.

7The man shouted in a loud voice, "What do you want with me, Jesus, Son of the Most High God? I command you in God's name not to torture me!" **8**He said this because Jesus was saying to him, "You evil spirit, come out of the man."

9Then Jesus asked him, "What is your name?"

He answered, "My name is Legion, because we are many spirits." **10**He begged Jesus again and again not to send them out of that area.

OLD TESTAMENT READING

The LORD's voice is heard over the sea.
The glorious God thunders;
the LORD thunders over the ocean.
4The LORD's voice is powerful;
the LORD's voice is majestic.
5The LORD's voice breaks the trees;
the LORD breaks the cedars of Lebanon.
7The LORD's voice makes the lightning flash.

10The LORD controls the flood.
The LORD will be King forever.

Psalm 29:3–5, 7, 10

INSIGHTS

There is a power that destroys. There is also a power that creates. The power that creates gives life and joy and peace. It is freedom and not bondage, life and not death, transformation and not coercion. The power that creates restores relationship and gives the gift of wholeness to all. The power that creates is spiritual power, the power that proceeds from God. . . .

In the crucifixion the power that creates reached its apex. At the cross Satan sought to use all the power at his disposal to destroy Christ, but God turned it into the ultimate act of creative power. The penalty for sin was paid; the justice of God was satisfied. Through the cross of Christ, you and I can receive forgiveness and know the restoring of our relationship to God. Christ died for our sins, and in that death we see the power that creates.

Our response to this supreme act of power is gratitude. It is "love divine, all loves excelling." We can never hope or want to duplicate this act of power. We simply thank God for what he has done.

RICHARD FOSTER

ACTION POINT

Think about the many kinds of awesome power God has at his disposal. How has he used his power to draw you to himself? Thank him for saving you by his power.

MARK 5:11-36

11A large herd of pigs was feeding on a hill near there. **12**The demons begged Jesus, "Send us into the pigs; let us go into them." **13**So Jesus allowed them to do this. The evil spirits left the man and went into the pigs. Then the herd of pigs—about two thousand of them—rushed down the hill into the lake and were drowned.

14The herdsmen ran away and went to the town and to the countryside, telling everyone about this. So people went out to see what had happened. **15**They came to Jesus and saw the man who used to have the many evil spirits, sitting, clothed, and in his right mind. And they were frightened. **16**The people who saw this told the others what had happened to the man who had the demons living in him, and they told about the pigs. **17**Then the people began to beg Jesus to leave their area.

18As Jesus was getting back into the boat, the man who was freed from the demons begged to go with him.

19But Jesus would not let him. He said, "Go home to your family and tell them how much the Lord has done for you and how he has had mercy on you." **20**So the man left and began to tell the people in the Ten Towns about what Jesus had done for him. And everyone was amazed.

Jesus Gives Life to a Dead Girl and Heals a Sick Woman

21When Jesus went in the boat back to the other side of the lake, a large crowd gathered around him there. **22**A leader of the synagogue, named Jairus, came there, saw Jesus, and fell at his feet. **23**He begged Jesus, saying again and again, "My daughter is dying. Please come and put your hands on her so she will be healed and will live." **24**So Jesus went with him.

A large crowd followed Jesus and pushed very close around him. **25**Among them was a woman who had been bleeding for twelve years. **26**She had suffered very much from many doctors and had spent all the money she had, but instead of improving, she was getting worse. **27**When the woman heard about Jesus, she came up behind him in the crowd and touched his coat. **28**She thought, "If I can just touch his clothes, I will be healed." **29**Instantly her bleeding stopped, and she felt in her body that she was healed from her disease.

30At once Jesus felt power go out from him. So he turned around in the crowd and asked, "Who touched my clothes?"

31His followers said, "Look at how many people are pushing against you! And you ask, 'Who touched me?'"

32But Jesus continued looking around to see who had touched him. **33**The woman, knowing that she was healed, came and fell at Jesus' feet. Shaking with fear, she told him the whole truth. **34**Jesus said to her, "Dear woman, you are made well because you believed. Go in peace; be healed of your disease."

35While Jesus was still speaking, some people came from the house of the synagogue leader. They said, "Your daughter is dead. There is no need to bother the teacher anymore."

36But Jesus paid no attention to what they said. He told the synagogue leader, "Don't be afraid; just believe."

OLD TESTAMENT READING

When Goliath looked at David and saw that he was only a boy, tanned and handsome, he looked down on David with disgust. 43He said, "Do you think I am a dog, that you come at me with a stick?" He used his gods' names to curse David. 44He said to David, "Come here. I'll feed your body to the birds of the air and the wild animals!"

45But David said to him, "You come to me using a sword and two spears. But I come to you in the name of the LORD All-Powerful, the God of the armies of Israel! You have spoken against him. 46Today the LORD will hand you over to me, and I'll kill you and cut off your head. Today I'll feed the bodies of the Philistine soldiers to the birds of the air and the wild animals. Then all the world will know there is a God in Israel! 47Everyone gathered here will know the LORD does not need swords or spears to save people. The battle belongs to him, and he will hand you over to us."

50So David defeated the Philistine with only a sling and a stone. He hit him and killed him. He did not even have a sword in his hand.

1 Samuel 17:42–47, 50

INSIGHTS

The doctrine of the Bible is that Christ saves His people from sin through faith; that Christ's Spirit is received by faith to dwell in the heart. It is faith that works by love. Love is wrought and sustained by faith. By faith, Christians "overcome the world, the flesh, and the devil." It is by faith that they "quench all the fiery darts of the wicked." It is by faith that they "put on the Lord Jesus Christ, and put off the old man, with his deeds." It is by faith that we "stand," by resolutions we fall. This is the victory that overcometh the world, even our faith.

It is by faith that the flesh is kept under and carnal desires subdued, and by faith that we receive the Spirit of Christ to work in us to will and to do, according to His good pleasure. He sheds abroad His own love in our hearts, and thereby enkindles ours. . . . Nothing but the life and energy of the Spirit of Christ can save us from sin, and trust is the universal condition for the working of His saving energy within us. . . .

. . . When we open the door by implicit trust, He enters in and takes up His abode with us and in us. By shedding abroad His love, He quickens our souls into sympathy with himself and in this way, and in this way alone, He purifies our hearts through faith.

CHARLES FINNEY

PAUSE FOR REFLECTION

What has the Lord done for you? How has he shown himself to you? How has he responded to your faith in him? In what way does his mercy amaze you? With whom does he want you to share your faith?

MARK 5:37 – 6:20

37Jesus let only Peter, James, and John the brother of James go with him. **38**When they came to the house of the synagogue leader, Jesus found many people there making lots of noise and crying loudly. **39**Jesus entered the house and said to them, "Why are you crying and making so much noise? The child is not dead, only asleep." **40**But they laughed at him. So, after throwing them out of the house, Jesus took the child's father and mother and his three followers into the room where the child was. **41**Taking hold of the girl's hand, he said to her, "Talitha, koum!" (This means, "Young girl, I tell you to stand up!") **42**At once the girl stood right up and began walking. (She was twelve years old.) Everyone was completely amazed. **43**Jesus gave them strict orders not to tell people about this. Then he told them to give the girl something to eat.

Jesus Goes to His Hometown

6 Jesus left there and went to his hometown, and his followers went with him. **2**On the Sabbath day he taught in the synagogue. Many people heard him and were amazed, saying, "Where did this man get these teachings? What is this wisdom that has been given to him? And where did he get the power to do miracles? **3**He is just the carpenter, the son of Mary and the brother of James, Joseph, Judas, and Simon. And his sisters are here with us." So the people were upset with Jesus.

4Jesus said to them, "A prophet is honored everywhere except in his hometown and with his own people and in his own home." **5**So Jesus was not able to work any miracles there except to heal a few sick people by putting his hands on them. **6**He was amazed at how many people had no faith.

Then Jesus went to other villages in that area and taught. **7**He called his twelve followers together and got ready to send them out two by two and gave them authority over evil spirits. **8**This is what Jesus commanded them: "Take nothing for your trip except a walking stick. Take no bread, no bag, and no money in your pockets. **9**Wear sandals, but take only the clothes you are wearing. **10**When you enter a house, stay there until you leave that town. **11**If the people in a certain place refuse to welcome you or listen to you, leave that place. Shake its dust off your feet as a warning to them."

12So the followers went out and preached that people should change their hearts and lives. **13**They forced many demons out and put olive oil on many sick people and healed them.

How John the Baptist Was Killed

14King Herod heard about Jesus, because he was now well known. Some people said, "He is John the Baptist, who has risen from the dead. That is why he can work these miracles."

15Others said, "He is Elijah."

Other people said, "Jesus is a prophet, like the prophets who lived long ago."

16When Herod heard this, he said, "I killed John by cutting off his head. Now he has risen from the dead!"

17Herod himself had ordered his soldiers to arrest John and put him in prison in order to please his wife, Herodias. She had been the wife of Philip,

Herod's brother, but then Herod had married her. **18**John had been telling Herod, "It is not lawful for you to be married to your brother's wife." **19**So Herodias hated John and wanted to kill him. But she couldn't, **20**because Herod was afraid of John and protected him. He knew John was a good and holy man. Also, though John's preaching always bothered him, he enjoyed listening to John.

OLD TESTAMENT READING

ut the LORD said to me, "Tell the people, 'You must not go up there and fight. I will not be with you, and your enemies will defeat you.'"

43So I told you, but you would not listen. You would not obey the LORD's command. You were proud, so you went on up into the mountains, **44**and the Amorites who lived in those mountains came out and fought you. They chased you like bees and defeated you from Edom to Hormah. **45**So you came back and cried before the LORD, but the LORD did not listen to you; he refused to pay attention to you.

Deuteronomy 1:42–45

INSIGHTS

God had told the people to enter and possess the land, but they preferred to spy it out just to see if God was really telling the truth! Well, He was—it was a rich land, a beautiful land, and a fruitful land. But there were giants! "We are not able to overcome!" This was the majority report.

The minority report came from Caleb and Joshua, and Moses agreed with them: "We are well able to overcome it!" This is the Old Testament version of Romans 8:31: "If God be for us, who can be against us?" The majority saw the obstacles, and they were bigger than their God. The minority saw God, and the obstacles disappeared!

Unbelief always cries and complains. It plays the same tune: "We are not able!" The nation had the promises of God to lean on and the presence of God to depend on, but they preferred to walk by sight. It cost them forty years in the wilderness, the world's longest funeral march!

Christians do not fight for victory; we fight from victory. Jesus said, "In the world ye shall have tribulation: but be of good cheer; I have overcome the world" (John 16:33). John said, "This is the victory that overcometh the world, even our faith" (1 John 5:4).

Either we are overcomers—or overcome.

warren wiersbe

APPLICATION

List the consequences of unbelief described in these Scripture readings. What are the rewards of faith? What about your life? Are you reaping consequences or rewards? Will you be an overcomer or be overcome?

MARK 6:21-44

21Then the perfect time came for Herodias to cause John's death. On Herod's birthday, he gave a dinner party for the most important government leaders, the commanders of his army, and the most important people in Galilee. 22When the daughter of Herodias came in and danced, she pleased Herod and the people eating with him.

So King Herod said to the girl, "Ask me for anything you want, and I will give it to you." 23He promised her, "Anything you ask for I will give to you—up to half of my kingdom."

24The girl went to her mother and asked, "What should I ask for?"

Her mother answered, "Ask for the head of John the Baptist."

25At once the girl went back to the king and said to him, "I want the head of John the Baptist right now on a platter."

26Although the king was very sad, he had made a promise, and his dinner guests had heard it. So he did not want to refuse what she asked. 27Immediately the king sent a soldier to bring John's head. The soldier went and cut off John's head in the prison 28and brought it back on a platter. He gave it to the girl, and the girl gave it to her mother. 29When John's followers heard this, they came and got John's body and put it in a tomb.

More than Five Thousand Fed

30The apostles gathered around Jesus and told him about all the things they had done and taught. 31Crowds of people were coming and going so that Jesus and his followers did not even have time to eat. He said to them, "Come away by yourselves, and we will go to a lonely place to get some rest."

32So they went in a boat by themselves to a lonely place. 33But many people saw them leave and recognized them. So from all the towns they ran to the place where Jesus was going, and they got there before him. 34When he arrived, he saw a great crowd waiting. He felt sorry for them, because they were like sheep without a shepherd. So he began to teach them many things.

35When it was late in the day, his followers came to him and said, "No one lives in this place, and it is already very late. 36Send the people away so they can go to the countryside and towns around here to buy themselves something to eat."

37But Jesus answered, "You give them something to eat."

They said to him, "We would all have to work a month to earn enough money to buy that much bread!"

38Jesus asked them, "How many loaves of bread do you have? Go and see."

When they found out, they said, "Five loaves and two fish."

39Then Jesus told his followers to have the people sit in groups on the green grass. 40So they sat in groups of fifty or a hundred. 41Jesus took the five loaves and two fish and, looking up to heaven, he thanked God for the food. He divided the bread and gave it to his followers for them to give to the people. Then he divided the two fish among them all. 42All the people ate and were satisfied. 43The followers filled twelve baskets with the leftover pieces of bread and fish. 44There were five thousand men who ate.

OLD TESTAMENT READING

I praise your greatness, my God the King;
   I will praise you forever and ever.
²I will praise you every day;
   I will praise you forever and ever.
³The LORD is great and worthy of our praise;
   no one can understand how great he is.

⁴Parents will tell their children what you have
         done.
   They will retell your mighty acts,
⁵wonderful majesty, and glory.
   And I will think about your miracles.
⁶They will tell about the amazing things you
         do,
   and I will tell how great you are.

Psalm 145:1–6

Let them give thanks to the LORD for his love
   and for the miracles he does for
         people.
⁹He satisfies the thirsty
   and fills up the hungry.

Psalm 107:8–9

INSIGHTS

It is better to trust in God than to accumulate riches. . . .

Trust in God gives clearness of vision. When we are thinking partly of doing God's work in the world, and partly of lining our own nest, we are in the condition of the man whose eyes do not look in the same direction. . . . We are endeavouring to serve two masters, and our judgment is therefore distorted. Who has not often experienced this? You have tried to ascertain God's will, or to form a right judgment about your life, but constantly your perception of duty has been obscured by the thought that, if you decided in a certain direction, you would interfere with your interests in another. Your eye has not been single, and you have walked in darkness. When, however, you feel so absorbed in God's interests that you are indifferent to your own, all becomes clear, and you leave Him to care for all results. . . .

Let us not think that God is niggardly and stinting in His gifts. He gives fish as well as bread when He feeds the crowds; colours as well as leaves when He clothes the flowers. You have been adopted into His Family, and may call Him "Abba, Father." Surely this act of grace shows a special love on His part. Would He have taken such care of the spiritual, and have none for the physical? The ungodly may worry about the maintenance; but a child of God may be sure that His needs will be supplied.

F. B. MEYER

APPLICATION

What is the difference between Jesus' perspective on feeding the crowd and his disciples' perspective? Do you face similar conflict between feeling a need to provide for yourself and trusting God to provide? Let these psalms be your prayer of trust and thanks for God's provision!

WEDNESDAY

GOD'S MERCY, EVEN TO THOSE WHO DON'T UNDERSTAND

> ## MARK 6:45 — 7:13

Jesus Walks on the Water

45Immediately Jesus told his followers to get into the boat and go ahead of him to Bethsaida across the lake. He stayed there to send the people home. **46**After sending them away, he went into the hills to pray.

47That night, the boat was in the middle of the lake, and Jesus was alone on the land. **48**He saw his followers struggling hard to row the boat, because the wind was blowing against them. Between three and six o'clock in the morning, Jesus came to them, walking on the water, and he wanted to walk past the boat. **49**But when they saw him walking on the water, they thought he was a ghost and cried out. **50**They all saw him and were afraid. But quickly Jesus spoke to them and said, "Have courage! It is I. Do not be afraid." **51**Then he got into the boat with them, and the wind became calm. The followers were greatly amazed. **52**They did not understand about the miracle of the five loaves, because their minds were closed.

53When they had crossed the lake, they came to shore at Gennesaret and tied the boat there. **54**When they got out of the boat, people immediately recognized Jesus. **55**They ran everywhere in that area and began to bring sick people on mats wherever they heard he was. **56**And everywhere he went—into towns, cities, or countryside—the people brought the sick to the marketplaces. They begged him to let them touch just the edge of his coat, and all who touched it were healed.

Obey God's Law

7When some Pharisees and some teachers of the law came from Jerusalem, they gathered around Jesus. **2**They saw that some of Jesus' followers ate food with hands that were not clean, that is, they hadn't washed them. **3**(The Pharisees and all the Jews never eat before washing their hands in the way required by their unwritten laws. **4**And when they buy something in the market, they never eat it until they wash themselves in a special way. They also follow many other unwritten laws, such as the washing of cups, pitchers, and pots.)

5The Pharisees and the teachers of the law said to Jesus, "Why don't your followers obey the unwritten laws which have been handed down to us? Why do your followers eat their food with hands that are not clean?"

6Jesus answered, "Isaiah was right when he spoke about you hypocrites. He wrote,

'These people show honor to me with words,
but their hearts are far from me.
7 Their worship of me is worthless.
The things they teach are nothing but
human rules.'   *Isaiah 29:13*

8You have stopped following the commands of God, and you follow only human teachings."

9Then Jesus said to them, "You cleverly ignore the commands of God so you can follow your own teachings. **10**Moses said, 'Honor your father and your mother,' and 'Anyone who says cruel things to his father or mother must be put to death.' **11**But you say a person can tell his father or mother, 'I have something I could use to help you, but it is Corban—a gift to God.' **12**You no longer let that person use that money for his father or his mother. **13**By your own rules, which you teach people, you are rejecting what God said. And you do many things like that."

OLD TESTAMENT READING

ut they kept on sinning;
they did not believe even with the miracles.
33So he ended their days without meaning
and their years in terror.
34Anytime he killed them, they would look to
him for help;
they would come back to God and follow
him.
35They would remember that God was their
Rock,
that God Most High had saved them.
36But their words were false,
and their tongues lied to him.
37Their hearts were not really loyal to God;
they did not keep his agreement.
38Still God was merciful.
He forgave their sins
and did not destroy them.
Many times he held back his anger
and did not stir up all his anger.
39He remembered that they were only
human,
like a wind that blows and does not come
back.

Psalm 78:32–39

ACTION POINT

Did Jesus condemn his followers for their lack of faith and understanding? What did he do for those who want his healing and miracles, but little else? How was Jesus merciful to the Pharisees and teachers of the law? In what way is God merciful, even to those who don't live by his teachings? Write your own psalm of praise to God for his unending mercy.

MARK 7:14-37

14After Jesus called the crowd to him again, he said, "Every person should listen to me and understand what I am saying. **15**There is nothing people put into their bodies that makes them unclean. People are made unclean by the things that come out of them. [**16**Let those with ears use them and listen.]"

17When Jesus left the people and went into the house, his followers asked him about this story. **18**Jesus said, "Do you still not understand? Surely you know that nothing that enters someone from the outside can make that person unclean. **19**It does not go into the mind, but into the stomach. Then it goes out of the body." (When Jesus said this, he meant that no longer was any food unclean for people to eat.)

20And Jesus said, "The things that come out of people are the things that make them unclean. **21**All these evil things begin inside people, in the mind: evil thoughts, sexual sins, stealing, murder, adultery, **22**greed, evil actions, lying, doing sinful things, jealousy, speaking evil of others, pride, and foolish living. **23**All these evil things come from inside and make people unclean."

Jesus Helps a Non-Jewish Woman

24Jesus left that place and went to the area around Tyre. When he went into a house, he did not want anyone to know he was there, but he could not stay hidden. **25**A woman whose daughter had an evil spirit in her heard that he was there. So she quickly came to Jesus and fell at his feet. **26**She was Greek, born in Phoenicia, in Syria. She begged Jesus to force the demon out of her daughter.

27Jesus told the woman, "It is not right to take the children's bread and give it to the dogs. First let the children eat all they want."

28But she answered, "Yes, Lord, but even the dogs under the table can eat the children's crumbs."

29Then Jesus said, "Because of your answer, you may go. The demon has left your daughter."

30The woman went home and found her daughter lying in bed; the demon was gone.

Jesus Heals a Deaf Man

31Then Jesus left the area around Tyre and went through Sidon to Lake Galilee, to the area of the Ten Towns. **32**While he was there, some people brought a man to him who was deaf and could not talk plainly. The people begged Jesus to put his hand on the man to heal him.

33Jesus led the man away from the crowd, by himself. He put his fingers in the man's ears and then spit and touched the man's tongue. **34**Looking up to heaven, he sighed and said to the man, "Ephphatha!" (This means, "Be opened.") **35**Instantly the man was able to hear and to use his tongue so that he spoke clearly.

36Jesus commanded the people not to tell anyone about what happened. But the more he commanded them, the more they told about it. **37**They were completely amazed and said, "Jesus does everything well. He makes the deaf hear! And those who can't talk he makes able to speak."

OLD TESTAMENT READING

Some people are wicked and no good.
They go around telling lies,
¹³winking with their eyes, tapping with their
feet,
and making signs with their fingers.
¹⁴They make evil plans in their hearts
and are always starting arguments.
¹⁵So trouble will strike them in an instant;
suddenly they will be so hurt no one can
help them.

¹⁶There are six things the LORD hates.
There are seven things he cannot stand:

¹⁷ a proud look,
a lying tongue,
hands that kill innocent people,
¹⁸ a mind that thinks up evil plans,
feet that are quick to do evil,
¹⁹ a witness who lies,
and someone who starts arguments among
families.

Proverbs 6:12–19

More than anything else, a person's mind is
evil
and cannot be healed.
Who can understand it?"

Jeremiah 17:9

INSIGHTS

A friend received a significant honor. I can't remember struggling with envy and jealousy before, but on that day, I was swept up into a whirlwind of envy. I drove back to my office in a complete state of shock. Where in creation did that come from? It leaked through the pinholes of my otherwise good character. A Christian's good character is the character of Jesus breathed into each of us by the Holy Spirit. Once we stop allowing the Spirit to fill us with power, the pinholes leak sin from our old nature.

Accepting our total depravity—our capacity to sin, that our character is filled with pinholes—is essential to living a victorious Christian life. If we presume that when we become Christian we are now good, we have missed the point. Jesus Christ shed His blood to forgive our sin, not to remove our sin. We have a continuing sinful nature which requires us to guard our heart and mind. We must post a twenty-four-hour guard at the gate to our mind.

PATRICK MORLEY

APPLICATION

What evil things does Jesus say come from within a person? Why is it necessary to have a clean heart? Does your life show any evidence of "heart" trouble? What commitment will you make to guard those areas of weakness?

MARK 8:1-26

More than Four Thousand People Fed

 Another time there was a great crowd with Jesus that had nothing to eat. So Jesus called his followers and said, 2"I feel sorry for these people, because they have already been with me for three days, and they have nothing to eat. 3If I send them home hungry, they will faint on the way. Some of them live a long way from here."

4Jesus' followers answered, "How can we get enough bread to feed all these people? We are far away from any town."

5Jesus asked, "How many loaves of bread do you have?"

They answered, "Seven."

6Jesus told the people to sit on the ground. Then he took the seven loaves, gave thanks to God, and divided the bread. He gave the pieces to his followers to give to the people, and they did so. 7The followers also had a few small fish. After Jesus gave thanks for the fish, he told his followers to give them to the people also. 8All the people ate and were satisfied. Then his followers filled seven baskets with the leftover pieces of food. 9There were about four thousand people who ate. After they had eaten, Jesus sent them home. 10Then right away he got into a boat with his followers and went to the area of Dalmanutha.

The Leaders Ask for a Miracle

11The Pharisees came to Jesus and began to ask him questions. Hoping to trap him, they asked Jesus for a miracle from God. 12Jesus sighed deeply and said, "Why do you people ask for a miracle as a sign? I tell you the truth, no sign will be given to you." 13Then Jesus left the Pharisees and went in the boat to the other side of the lake.

Guard Against Wrong Teachings

14His followers had only one loaf of bread with them in the boat; they had forgotten to bring more. 15Jesus warned them, "Be careful! Beware of the yeast of the Pharisees and the yeast of Herod."

16His followers discussed the meaning of this, saying, "He said this because we have no bread."

17Knowing what they were talking about, Jesus asked them, "Why are you talking about not having bread? Do you still not see or understand? Are your minds closed? 18You have eyes, but you don't really see. You have ears, but you don't really listen. Remember when 19I divided five loaves of bread for the five thousand? How many baskets did you fill with leftover pieces of food?"

They answered, "Twelve."

20"And when I divided seven loaves of bread for the four thousand, how many baskets did you fill with leftover pieces of food?"

They answered, "Seven."

21Then Jesus said to them, "Don't you understand yet?"

Jesus Heals a Blind Man

22Jesus and his followers came to Bethsaida. There some people brought a blind man to Jesus and begged him to touch the man. 23So Jesus took the blind man's hand and led him out of the village. Then he spit on the man's eyes and put his hands on the man and asked, "Can you see now?"

24The man looked up and said, "Yes, I see people, but they look like trees walking around."

25Again Jesus put his hands on the man's eyes. Then the man opened his eyes wide and they were healed, and he was able to see everything clearly. ²⁶Jesus told him to go home, saying, "Don't go into the town."

OLD TESTAMENT READING

They turned against God so often in the desert
    and grieved him there.

⁴¹Again and again they tested God
    and brought pain to the Holy One of Israel.
⁴²They did not remember his power
    or the time he saved them from the enemy.
⁴³They forgot the signs he did in Egypt
    and his wonders in the fields of Zoan.

Psalm 78:40–43

INSIGHTS

For three years, day in and day out, he [Judas] occupied himself with Jesus Christ. He saw the Lord's miracles, heard His words, even participated in His ministry. In all that time, no one ever questioned his faith. He had the same status as the other disciples. Except for the Savior Himself who knew the thoughts of Judas's heart, no one ever suspected that this man would betray Christ.

Yet, while the others were growing into apostles, Judas was quietly becoming a vile, calculating tool of Satan. Whatever his character seemed to be at the beginning, his faith was not real (John 13:10–11). He was unregenerate, and his heart gradually hardened so that he became the treacherous man who sold the Savior for a fistful of coins. . . .

It was not the will of God apart from Judas's own choice that he should betray Christ. At every opportunity, Jesus warned Judas and entreated him to repent and be saved, but at every point Judas turned away. Judas had heard the gospel according to Jesus, yet he refused to turn from his sin and selfishness. Jesus' words in John 13 represent His final, loving appeal to this man. In the end, however, the Savior's merciful entreaty would condemn Judas in the hardness of his heart.

JOHN F. MACARTHUR, JR.

PAUSE FOR REFLECTION

Who has witnessed more miracles of God than the Israelites or those who walked with Jesus while he was on earth? Do miracles lead people to salvation? What is more important than miracles in causing a person to turn toward God?

MARK 8:27 — 9:13

Peter Says Jesus Is the Christ

27Jesus and his followers went to the towns around Caesarea Philippi. While they were traveling, Jesus asked them, "Who do people say I am?" **28**They answered, "Some say you are John the Baptist. Others say you are Elijah, and others say you are one of the prophets." **29**Then Jesus asked, "But who do you say I am?"

Peter answered, "You are the Christ."

30Jesus warned his followers not to tell anyone who he was.

31Then Jesus began to teach them that the Son of Man must suffer many things and that he would be rejected by the Jewish elders, the leading priests, and the teachers of the law. He told them that the Son of Man must be killed and then rise from the dead after three days. **32**Jesus told them plainly what would happen. Then Peter took Jesus aside and began to tell him not to talk like that. **33**But Jesus turned and looked at his followers. Then he told Peter not to talk that way. He said, "Go away from me, Satan! You don't care about the things of God, but only about things people think are important."

34Then Jesus called the crowd to him, along with his followers. He said, "If people want to follow me, they must give up the things they want. They must be willing even to give up their lives to follow me. **35**Those who want to save their lives will give up true life. But those who give up their lives for me and for the Good News will have true life. **36**It is worthless to have the whole world if they lose their souls. **37**They could never pay enough to buy back their souls. **38**The people who live now are living in a sinful and evil time. If people are ashamed of me and my teaching, the Son of Man will be ashamed of them when he comes with his Father's glory and with the holy angels."

9Then Jesus said to the people, "I tell you the truth, some people standing here will see the kingdom of God come with power before they die."

Jesus Talks with Moses and Elijah

2Six days later, Jesus took Peter, James, and John up on a high mountain by themselves. While they watched, Jesus' appearance was changed. **3**His clothes became shining white, whiter than any person could make them. **4**Then Elijah and Moses appeared to them, talking with Jesus.

5Peter said to Jesus, "Teacher, it is good that we are here. Let us make three tents—one for you, one for Moses, and one for Elijah." **6**Peter did not know what to say, because he and the others were so frightened.

7Then a cloud came and covered them, and a voice came from the cloud, saying, "This is my Son, whom I love. Listen to him!"

8Suddenly Peter, James, and John looked around, but they saw only Jesus there alone with them.

9As they were coming down the mountain,

Jesus commanded them not to tell anyone about what they had seen until the Son of Man had risen from the dead.

¹⁰So the followers obeyed Jesus, but they discussed what he meant about rising from the dead.

¹¹Then they asked Jesus, "Why do the teachers of the law say that Elijah must come first?"

¹²Jesus answered, "They are right to say that Elijah must come first and make everything the way it should be. But why does the Scripture say that the Son of Man will suffer much and that people will treat him as if he were nothing? ¹³I tell you that Elijah has already come. And people did to him whatever they wanted to do, just as the Scriptures said it would happen."

OLD TESTAMENT READING

Anything I saw and wanted, I got for myself;
     I did not miss any pleasure I desired.
I was pleased with everything I did,
     and this pleasure was the reward for all my
          hard work.
¹¹But then I looked at what I had done,
     and I thought about all the hard work.
Suddenly I realized it was useless, like chasing
          the wind.
     There is nothing to gain from anything we
          do here on earth.

Ecclesiastes 2:10–11

INSIGHTS

"I will hear what God the Lord will speak" (Ps. 85:8). Blessed is the soul which hears the Lord speaking within, and from His mouth receives the word of consolation. Blessed are the ears that catch the pulses of the divine whisper (Matt. 13:16, 17), and give no heed to the whisperings of this world. Blessed indeed are those ears which listen not after the voice which is sounding without, but for the truth teaching inwardly. Blessed are the eyes that are shut to outward things, but intent on things inward. Blessed are they that enter far into things within, and endeavor to prepare themselves more and more, by daily exercises, for the receiving of heavenly secrets. Blessed are they who are glad to have time to spare for God, and who shake off all worldly hindrances.

Consider these things, O my soul, and shut up the door of your sensual desires, that you may hear what the Lord your God speaks in you (Ps. 85:8).

Thus says your Beloved, "I am thy salvation," your Peace, and your Life: keep yourself with Me, and you shall find peace. Let go all transitory things, and seek the things eternal. What are all transitory objects but seductive things? And what can all creatures avail, if you are forsaken by the Creator?

Renounce therefore all things, and labor to please your Creator, and to be faithful unto Him, that you may be able to attain unto true blessedness.

Thomas à Kempis

ACTION POINT

List and evaluate the things in your life that seem worth pursuing. If you want to follow Jesus, what priorities do you need to rearrange?

MARK 9:14-37

Jesus Heals a Sick Boy

14When Jesus, Peter, James, and John came back to the other followers, they saw a great crowd around them and the teachers of the law arguing with them. **15**But as soon as the crowd saw Jesus, the people were surprised and ran to welcome him.

16Jesus asked, "What are you arguing about?"

17A man answered, "Teacher, I brought my son to you. He has an evil spirit in him that stops him from talking. **18**When the spirit attacks him, it throws him on the ground. Then my son foams at the mouth, grinds his teeth, and becomes very stiff. I asked your followers to force the evil spirit out, but they couldn't."

19Jesus answered, "You people have no faith. How long must I stay with you? How long must I put up with you? Bring the boy to me."

20So the followers brought him to Jesus. As soon as the evil spirit saw Jesus, it made the boy lose control of himself, and he fell down and rolled on the ground, foaming at the mouth.

21Jesus asked the boy's father, "How long has this been happening?"

The father answered, "Since he was very young. **22**The spirit often throws him into a fire or into water to kill him. If you can do anything for him, please have pity on us and help us."

23Jesus said to the father, "You said, 'If you can!' All things are possible for the one who believes."

24Immediately the father cried out, "I do believe! Help me to believe more!"

25When Jesus saw that a crowd was quickly gathering, he ordered the evil spirit, saying, "You spirit that makes people unable to hear or speak, I command you to come out of this boy and never enter him again!"

26The evil spirit screamed and caused the boy to fall on the ground again. Then the spirit came out. The boy looked as if he were dead, and many people said, "He is dead!" **27**But Jesus took hold of the boy's hand and helped him to stand up.

28When Jesus went into the house, his followers began asking him privately, "Why couldn't we force that evil spirit out?"

29Jesus answered, "That kind of spirit can only be forced out by prayer."

Jesus Talks About His Death

30Then Jesus and his followers left that place and went through Galilee. He didn't want anyone to know where he was, **31**because he was teaching his followers. He said to them, "The Son of Man will be handed over to people, and they will kill him. After three days, he will rise from the dead." **32**But the followers did not understand what Jesus meant, and they were afraid to ask him.

Who Is the Greatest?

33Jesus and his followers went to Capernaum. When they went into a house there, he asked them, "What were you arguing about on the road?" **34**But the followers did not answer, because their argument on the road was about which one of them was the greatest.

35Jesus sat down and called the twelve apostles to him. He said, "Whoever wants to be the most important must be last of all and servant of all."

36Then Jesus took a small child and had him stand among them. Taking the child in his arms, he said, 37"Whoever accepts a child like this in my name accepts me. And whoever accepts me accepts the One who sent me."

OLD TESTAMENT READING

Moses used to take a tent and set it up a long way outside the camp; he called it the "Meeting Tent." Anyone who wanted to ask the LORD about something would go to the Meeting Tent outside the camp. 8Whenever Moses went out to the Tent, all the people would rise and stand at the entrances of their tents, watching him until he entered the Meeting Tent. 9When Moses went into the Tent, the pillar of cloud would always come down and stay at the entrance of the Tent while the LORD spoke with Moses. 10Whenever the people saw the pillar of cloud at the entrance of the Tent, they stood and worshiped, each person at the entrance of his own tent.

11The LORD spoke to Moses face to face as a man speaks with his friend. Then Moses would return to the camp, but Moses' young helper, Joshua son of Nun, did not leave the Tent.

Exodus 33:7–11

INSIGHTS

The Father in heaven is so interested in His child, and so longs to have his life in step with His will and His love, that He is willing to keep the child's guidance entirely in His own hand. He knows so well that we do not do what is really holy and heavenly, except when He works it in us, that He intends His very demands to become promises of what He will do, in watching over and leading us all day long. We may count on Him to teach us His way and show us His path not only in special trials and hard times, but in everyday life. . . .

. . . So simple and delightful can it become to a soul that has practiced waiting on God, to walk all day in the enjoyment of God's light and leading. What is needed to help us find such a life is one thing: the real knowledge and faith of God as the only source of wisdom and goodness, as always ready and longing to be to us all that we can possibly need. Yes, this is the one thing we need.

ANDREW MURRAY

ACTION POINT

What special teaching did Jesus want to give his followers when they were alone? As you read Old Testament passages, think about how much God wants to teach his people. Thank him for his great outpouring of love. Pray that your heart will listen for his wisdom.

MARK 9:38 – 10:16

Anyone Not Against Us Is for Us

38Then John said, "Teacher, we saw someone using your name to force demons out of a person. We told him to stop, because he does not belong to our group."

39But Jesus said, "Don't stop him, because anyone who uses my name to do powerful things will not easily say evil things about me. **40**Whoever is not against us is with us. **41**I tell you the truth, whoever gives you a drink of water because you belong to the Christ will truly get his reward.

42"If one of these little children believes in me, and someone causes that child to sin, it would be better for that person to have a large stone tied around his neck and be drowned in the sea. **43**If your hand causes you to sin, cut it off. It is better for you to lose part of your body and live forever than to have two hands and go to hell, where the fire never goes out. [**44**In hell the worm does not die; the fire is never put out.] **45**If your foot causes you to sin, cut it off. It is better for you to lose part of your body and to live forever than to have two feet and be thrown into hell. [**46**In hell the worm does not die; the fire is never put out.] **47**If your eye causes you to sin, take it out. It is better for you to enter the kingdom of God with only one eye than to have two eyes and be thrown into hell. **48**In hell the worm does not die; the fire is never put out. **49**Every person will be salted with fire.

50"Salt is good, but if the salt loses its salty taste, you cannot make it salty again. So, be full of salt, and have peace with each other."

Jesus Teaches About Divorce

10 Then Jesus left that place and went into the area of Judea and across the Jordan River. Again, crowds came to him, and he taught them as he usually did.

2Some Pharisees came to Jesus and tried to trick him. They asked, "Is it right for a man to divorce his wife?"

3Jesus answered, "What did Moses command you to do?"

4They said, "Moses allowed a man to write out divorce papers and send her away."

5Jesus said, "Moses wrote that command for you because you were stubborn. **6**But when God made the world, 'he made them male and female.' **7**'So a man will leave his father and mother and be united with his wife, **8**and the two will become one body.' So there are not two, but one. **9**God has joined the two together, so no one should separate them."

10Later, in the house, his followers asked Jesus again about the question of divorce. **11**He answered, "Anyone who divorces his wife and marries another woman is guilty of adultery against her. **12**And the woman who divorces her husband and marries another man is also guilty of adultery."

Jesus Accepts Children

13Some people brought their little children to Jesus so he could touch them, but his followers told them to stop. **14**When Jesus saw this, he was upset and said to them, "Let the little children come to me. Don't stop them, because the kingdom of God belongs to people who are like these children. **15**I tell you the truth, you must accept the kingdom of God as if you were a little child, or you will never enter it." **16**Then Jesus took the children in his arms, put his hands on them, and blessed them.

OLD TESTAMENT READING

Now Joseph was well built and handsome. [7]After some time the wife of Joseph's master began to desire Joseph, and one day she said to him, "Have sexual relations with me."

[8]But Joseph refused and said to her, "My master trusts me with everything in his house. He has put me in charge of everything he owns. [9]There is no one in his house greater than I. He has not kept anything from me except you, because you are his wife. How can I do such an evil thing? It is a sin against God."

[10]The woman talked to Joseph every day, but he refused to have sexual relations with her or even spend time with her.

[11]One day Joseph went into the house to do his work as usual and was the only man in the house at that time. [12]His master's wife grabbed his coat and said to him, "Come and have sexual relations with me." But Joseph left his coat in her hand and ran out of the house.

Genesis 39:6b–12

INSIGHTS

Repentance is a definite turn from every thought, word, deed and habit which is known to be wrong. It is not sufficient to feel pangs of remorse or to make some kind of apology to God. Fundamentally, repentance is a matter neither of emotion nor of speech. It is an inward change of mind and attitude towards sin which leads to a change of behaviour.

There can be no compromise here. There may be sins in our lives which we do not think we ever could renounce; but we must be willing to let them go as we cry to God for deliverance from them. If you are in doubt regarding what is right and what is wrong, what must go and what may be retained, do not be too greatly influenced by the customs and conventions of Christians you may know. Go by the clear teaching of the Bible and by the prompting of your conscience, and Christ will gradually lead you further along the path of righteousness. When he puts his finger on anything, give it up. It may be some association or recreation, some literature we read, or some attitude of pride, jealousy or resentment, or an unforgiving spirit.

Jesus told his followers to pluck out their eye and cut off their hand or foot if these caused them to sin. We are not to obey this with dead literalism, of course, and mutilate our bodies. It is a vivid figure of speech for dealing ruthlessly with the avenues along which temptation comes to us.

JOHN STOTT

APPLICATION

How serious a problem does Jesus consider sin to be? Is there anything casual about his attitude? What about your attitude toward sin? Do you vigorously run from it or politely coexist with it?

MARK 10:17-41

A Rich Young Man's Question

17 As Jesus started to leave, a man ran to him and fell on his knees before Jesus. The man asked, "Good teacher, what must I do to have life forever?"

18 Jesus answered, "Why do you call me good? Only God is good. **19** You know the commands: 'You must not murder anyone. You must not be guilty of adultery. You must not steal. You must not tell lies about your neighbor. You must not cheat. Honor your father and mother.'"

20 The man said, "Teacher, I have obeyed all these things since I was a boy."

21 Jesus, looking at the man, loved him and said, "There is one more thing you need to do. Go and sell everything you have, and give the money to the poor, and you will have treasure in heaven. Then come and follow me."

22 He was very sad to hear Jesus say this, and he left sorrowfully, because he was rich.

23 Then Jesus looked at his followers and said, "How hard it will be for the rich to enter the kingdom of God!"

24 The followers were amazed at what Jesus said. But he said again, "My children, it is very hard to enter the kingdom of God! **25** It is easier for a camel to go through the eye of a needle than for a rich person to enter the kingdom of God."

26 The followers were even more surprised and said to each other, "Then who can be saved?"

27 Jesus looked at them and said, "For people this is impossible, but for God all things are possible."

28 Peter said to Jesus, "Look, we have left everything and followed you."

29 Jesus said, "I tell you the truth, all those who have left houses, brothers, sisters, mother, father, children, or farms for me and for the Good News **30** will get more than they left. Here in this world they will have a hundred times more homes, brothers, sisters, mothers, children, and fields. And with those things, they will also suffer for their belief. But in this age they will have life forever. **31** Many who are first now will be last in the future. And many who are last now will be first in the future."

Jesus Talks About His Death

32 As Jesus and the people with him were on the road to Jerusalem, he was leading the way. His followers were amazed, but others in the crowd who followed were afraid. Again Jesus took the twelve apostles aside and began to tell them what was about to happen in Jerusalem. **33** He said, "Look, we are going to Jerusalem. The Son of Man will be turned over to the leading priests and the teachers of the law. They will say that he must die, and they will turn him over to the non-Jewish people, **34** who will laugh at him and spit on him. They will beat him with whips and crucify him. But on the third day, he will rise to life again."

Two Followers Ask Jesus a Favor

35 Then James and John, sons of Zebedee, came to Jesus and said, "Teacher, we want to ask you to do something for us."

36 Jesus asked, "What do you want me to do for you?"

37 They answered, "Let one of us sit at your

right side and one of us sit at your left side in your glory in your kingdom."

38Jesus said, "You don't understand what you are asking. Can you drink the cup that I must drink? And can you be baptized with the same kind of baptism that I must go through?"

39They answered, "Yes, we can."

Jesus said to them, "You will drink the same cup that I will drink, and you will be baptized with the same baptism that I must go through. 40But I cannot choose who will sit at my right or my left; those places belong to those for whom they have been prepared."

41When the other ten followers heard this, they began to be angry with James and John.

OLD TESTAMENT READING

Then people will say,
"There really are rewards for doing what is right.
There really is a God who judges the world."

Psalm 58:11

INSIGHTS

Be not wearied by the labors which you have undertaken for my sake, nor let tribulations cast you down. But let My promise strengthen and comfort you under every circumstance. I am well able to reward you, above all measure and degree. . . .

Do in earnest what you do; labor faithfully in My vineyard (Matt. 20:7); I will be your recompense. Write, read, chant, mourn, keep silence, pray, endure crosses manfully. Life everlasting is worth all these battles, and greater than these. Peace shall come in one day which is known unto the Lord, and there shall be "not day, nor night" (Zech. 14:7) (that is, of this present time), but unceasing light, infinite brightness, steadfast peace, and secure rest. Then you shall not say: "Who shall deliver me from the body of this death?" (Rom. 7:24); nor cry: "Woe is me, that I sojourn in Mesech" (Ps. 120:5). For death shall be cast down headlong, and there shall be salvation which can never fail, no more anxiety, blessed joy, companionship sweet and noble. . . .

Lift up your face therefore to Heaven. Behold, I and all My saints with Me, who in this world had great conflict, do now rejoice, now are comforted, now secure, now at rest, and shall remain with Me everlastingly in the kingdom of My Father!

THOMAS à KEMPIS

▶ APPLICATION

What areas of personal commitment to God's kingdom do you find difficult? What is hard for you to leave behind? Pray that you will truly believe—deep inside—that God will reward your faithfulness far above what you can even imagine.

MARK 10:42 — 11:14

⁴²Jesus called them together and said, "The other nations have rulers. You know that those rulers love to show their power over the people, and their important leaders love to use all their authority. ⁴³But it should not be that way among you. Whoever wants to become great among you must serve the rest of you like a servant. ⁴⁴Whoever wants to become the first among you must serve all of you like a slave. ⁴⁵In the same way, the Son of Man did not come to be served. He came to serve others and to give his life as a ransom for many people."

Jesus Heals a Blind Man

⁴⁶Then they came to the town of Jericho. As Jesus was leaving there with his followers and a great many people, a blind beggar named Bartimaeus son of Timaeus was sitting by the road. ⁴⁷When he heard that Jesus from Nazareth was walking by, he began to shout, "Jesus, Son of David, have mercy on me!"

⁴⁸Many people warned the blind man to be quiet, but he shouted even more, "Son of David, have mercy on me!"

⁴⁹Jesus stopped and said, "Tell the man to come here."

So they called the blind man, saying, "Cheer up! Get to your feet. Jesus is calling you." ⁵⁰The blind man jumped up, left his coat there, and went to Jesus.

⁵¹Jesus asked him, "What do you want me to do for you?"

The blind man answered, "Teacher, I want to see."

⁵²Jesus said, "Go, you are healed because you believed." At once the man could see, and he followed Jesus on the road.

Jesus Enters Jerusalem as a King

11 As Jesus and his followers were coming closer to Jerusalem, they came to the towns of Bethphage and Bethany near the Mount of Olives. From there Jesus sent two of his followers ²and said to them, "Go to the town you can see there. When you enter it, you will quickly find a colt tied, which no one has ever ridden. Untie it and bring it here to me. ³If anyone asks you why you are doing this, tell him its Master needs the colt, and he will send it at once."

⁴The followers went into the town, found a colt tied in the street near the door of a house, and untied it. ⁵Some people were standing there and asked, "What are you doing? Why are you untying that colt?" ⁶The followers answered the way Jesus told them to answer, and the people let them take the colt.

⁷They brought the colt to Jesus and put their coats on it, and Jesus sat on it. ⁸Many people spread their coats on the road. Others cut branches in the fields and spread them on the road. ⁹The people were walking ahead of Jesus and behind him, shouting,

"Praise God!
God bless the One who comes in the name of
   the Lord! *Psalm 118:26*
¹⁰God bless the kingdom of our father David!
   That kingdom is coming!
Praise to God in heaven!"

11Jesus entered Jerusalem and went into the Temple. After he had looked at everything, since it was already late, he went out to Bethany with the twelve apostles.

12The next day as Jesus was leaving Bethany, he became hungry. **13**Seeing a fig tree in leaf from far away, he went to see if it had any figs on it. But he found no figs, only leaves, because it was not the right season for figs. **14**So Jesus said to the tree, "May no one ever eat fruit from you again." And Jesus' followers heard him say this.

OLD TESTAMENT READING

After these things God tested Abraham's faith. God said to him, "Abraham!"

And he answered, "Here I am."

2Then God said, "Take your only son, Isaac, the son you love, and go to the land of Moriah. Kill him there and offer him as a whole burnt offering on one of the mountains I will tell you about."

10Then Abraham took his knife and was about to kill his son.

11But the angel of the LORD called to him from heaven and said, "Abraham! Abraham!"

Abraham answered, "Yes."

12The angel said, "Don't kill your son or hurt him in any way. Now I can see that you trust God and that you have not kept your son, your only son, from me."

Genesis 22:1–2, 10–12

INSIGHTS

We must squarely face the fact that the thought of service, except as a token or temporary activity, is distasteful. To accept a lower place is bad enough, but to choose a lower place—preposterous!

Words like obey, submit, serve, or worse, the expression "know your place," are met with defiance from a people who are obsessed with their "rights." Of course these rights are not wrong, and it is appropriate that there is legislation to protect rights. The problem is that legislation can only protect us from the bad; it cannot produce good in us. And it certainly cannot suggest to us that there might be some value in renouncing our rights for something or someone else. The Cross is the best evidence that there is much more to love than justice, much more to right than rights. A person who has won a public battle for human rights has done a good thing. But a person who has won a personal battle and given up human rights in the interest of human obligation has done a great thing. More often than not, the action will be labeled demeaning or ridiculous. So was the Cross.

THOMAS SCHMIDT

APPLICATION

Who is our greatest example of being a servant of God? How far was he willing to go in serving others? What did God call his servant Abraham to do? How is God calling you to serve him? Are you willing to be his servant?

MARK 11:15 – 12:12

Jesus Goes to the Temple

15When Jesus returned to Jerusalem, he went into the Temple and began to throw out those who were buying and selling there. He turned over the tables of those who were exchanging different kinds of money, and he upset the benches of those who were selling doves. **16**Jesus refused to allow anyone to carry goods through the Temple courts. **17**Then he taught the people, saying, "It is written in the Scriptures, 'My Temple will be called a house for prayer for people from all nations.' But you are changing God's house into a 'hideout for robbers.'"

18The leading priests and the teachers of the law heard all this and began trying to find a way to kill Jesus. They were afraid of him, because all the people were amazed at his teaching. **19**That evening, Jesus and his followers left the city.

The Power of Faith

20The next morning as Jesus was passing by with his followers, they saw the fig tree dry and dead, even to the roots. **21**Peter remembered the tree and said to Jesus, "Teacher, look! The fig tree you cursed is dry and dead!"

22Jesus answered, "Have faith in God. **23**I tell you the truth, you can say to this mountain, 'Go, fall into the sea.' And if you have no doubts in your mind and believe that what you say will happen, God will do it for you. **24**So I tell you to believe that you have received the things you ask for in prayer, and God will give them to you. **25**When you are praying, if you are angry with someone,

forgive him so that your Father in heaven will also forgive your sins. [**26**But if you don't forgive other people, then your Father in heaven will not forgive your sins.]"

Leaders Doubt Jesus' Authority

27Jesus and his followers went again to Jerusalem. As Jesus was walking in the Temple, the leading priests, the teachers of the law, and the elders came to him. **28**They said to him, "What authority do you have to do these things? Who gave you this authority?"

29Jesus answered, "I will ask you one question. If you answer me, I will tell you what authority I have to do these things. **30**Tell me: When John baptized people, was that authority from God or just from other people?"

31They argued about Jesus' question, saying, "If we answer, 'John's baptism was from God,' Jesus will say, 'Then why didn't you believe him?' **32**But if we say, 'It was from other people,' the crowd will be against us." (These leaders were afraid of the people, because all the people believed that John was a prophet.)

33So they answered Jesus, "We don't know."

Jesus said to them, "Then I won't tell you what authority I have to do these things."

A Story About God's Son

12 Jesus began to use stories to teach the people. He said, "A man planted a vineyard. He put a wall around it and dug a hole for a winepress and built a tower. Then he leased the land to some farmers and left for a trip. **2**When it was time for the grapes to be picked, he sent a servant to the farmers to get his share of the grapes. **3**But the farmers grabbed the servant and beat him and sent him away empty-handed. **4**Then the man sent another servant. They hit him on the head and showed no respect for him. **5**So the man sent another servant, whom they killed. The man sent many other servants; the farmers beat some of them and killed others.

6"The man had one person left to send, his son whom he loved. He sent him last of all, saying, 'They will respect my son.'

7"But the farmers said to each other, 'This son will inherit the vineyard. If we kill him, it will be ours.' **8**So they took the son, killed him, and threw him out of the vineyard.

9"So what will the owner of the vineyard do? He will come and kill those farmers and will give the vineyard to other farmers. **10**Surely you have read this Scripture:

'The stone that the builders rejected
    became the cornerstone.
11The Lord did this,
    and it is wonderful to us.'"

Psalm 118:22–23

12The Jewish leaders knew that the story was about them. So they wanted to find a way to arrest Jesus, but they were afraid of the people. So the leaders left him and went away.

OLD TESTAMENT READING

The LORD is close to everyone who prays to
    him,
  to all who truly pray to him.
19He gives those who respect him
    what they want.
  He listens when they cry, and he saves them.

Psalm 145:18–19

INSIGHTS

How do you pray a prayer so filled with faith that it can move a mountain? By shifting the focus from the size of your mountain to the sufficiency of the mountain mover, and by stepping forward in obedience. . . .

While the children of Israel are perched on the edge of the Promised Land, twelve spies go out to survey it. Ten come back saying, "You wouldn't believe the size of the cities, the armies, the giants. We'd better look somewhere else." Two come back saying, "The God who is faithful promised he would give us the land, so let's go in his strength." Ten looked at the size of the mountain and fell back; only two looked at the sufficiency of the mountain mover and wanted to move forward. . . .

I challenge you to shift the focus of your prayer. Don't spend a lot of time describing your mountain to the Lord. He knows what it is. Instead, focus your attention on the mountain mover—his glory, power and faithfulness. Then start walking in faith, following his leading, and watch that mountain step aside.

BILL HYBELS

ACTION POINT

How does God want us to ask him for what we need? In what remarkable ways has God answered your prayers? Make a list of them.

MARK 12:13–31

Is It Right to Pay Taxes or Not?

13Later, the Jewish leaders sent some Pharisees and Herodians to Jesus to trap him in saying something wrong. **14**They came to him and said, "Teacher, we know that you are an honest man. You are not afraid of what other people think about you, because you pay no attention to who they are. And you teach the truth about God's way. Tell us: Is it right to pay taxes to Caesar or not? **15**Should we pay them, or not?"

But knowing what these men were really trying to do, Jesus said to them, "Why are you trying to trap me? Bring me a coin to look at." **16**They gave Jesus a coin, and he asked, "Whose image and name are on the coin?"

They answered, "Caesar's."

17Then Jesus said to them, "Give to Caesar the things that are Caesar's, and give to God the things that are God's." The men were amazed at what Jesus said.

Some Sadducees Try to Trick Jesus

18Then some Sadducees came to Jesus and asked him a question. (Sadducees believed that people would not rise from the dead.) **19**They said, "Teacher, Moses wrote that if a man's brother dies, leaving a wife but no children, then that man must marry the widow and have children for his brother. **20**Once there were seven brothers. The first brother married and died, leaving no children. **21**So the second brother married the widow, but he also died and had no children. The same thing happened with the third brother. **22**All seven brothers married her and died, and none of the brothers had any children. Finally the woman died too. **23**Since all seven brothers had married her, when people rise from the dead, whose wife will she be?"

24Jesus answered, "Why don't you understand? Don't you know what the Scriptures say, and don't you know about the power of God? **25**When people rise from the dead, they will not marry, nor will they be given to someone to marry. They will be like the angels in heaven. **26**Surely you have read what God said about people rising from the dead. In the book in which Moses wrote about the burning bush, it says that God told Moses, 'I am the God of Abraham, the God of Isaac, and the God of Jacob.' **27**God is the God of the living, not the dead. You Sadducees are wrong!"

The Most Important Command

28One of the teachers of the law came and heard Jesus arguing with the Sadducees. Seeing that Jesus gave good answers to their questions, he asked Jesus, "Which of the commands is most important?"

29Jesus answered, "The most important command is this: 'Listen, people of Israel! The Lord our God is the only Lord. **30**Love the Lord your God with all your heart, all your soul, all your mind, and all your strength.' **31**The second command is this: 'Love your neighbor as you love yourself.' There are no commands more important than these."

OLD TESTAMENT READING

Those who lead good people to do wrong
will be ruined by their own evil,
but the innocent will be rewarded with
good things.

Proverbs 28:10

LORD, rescue me from evil people;
protect me from cruel people
²who make evil plans,
who always start fights.
³They make their tongues sharp as a
snake's;
their words are like snake poison. *Selah*

⁴LORD, guard me from the power of wicked
people;
protect me from cruel people
who plan to trip me up.
⁵The proud hid a trap for me.
They spread out a net beside the road;
they set traps for me. *Selah*

⁶I said to the LORD, "You are my God."
LORD, listen to my prayer for help.
⁷LORD God, my mighty savior,
you protect me in battle.
⁸LORD, do not give the wicked what they want.
Don't let their plans succeed,
or they will become proud. *Selah*

Psalm 140:1–8

INSIGHTS

The reproach we experience is the natural resentment in the hearts of men toward all that is godly and righteous. This is the cross we are to bear. This is why Christians are often persecuted. . . .

Let us not forget that there is happiness and blessing in persecution. As George MacDonald puts it, we become "hearty through hardship." . . .

Our Lord instructs the persecuted to be happy. "Rejoice," He said, "and be exceeding glad: for great is your reward in heaven: for so persecuted they the prophets which were before you" (Matthew 5:12).

The word joy has all but disappeared from our current Christian vocabulary. One of the reasons is that we have thought that joy and happiness were found in comfort, ease and luxury. James did not say, "Count it all joy when you fall into an easy chair," but he said, "Count it all joy when you fall into divers temptations" (James 1:2).

The persecuted are happy because they are being processed for heaven. Persecution is one of the natural consequences of living the Christian life. It is to the Christian what "growing pains" are to the growing child. No pain, no development. No suffering, no glory. No struggle, no victory. No persecution, no reward! Jesus predicted that if they persecuted Him, they would persecute you who follow Him, too.

BILLY GRAHAM

► APPLICATION

Have you ever felt that you've unwittingly walked into a trap designed to test your Christian commitment? If so, be glad you must be an effective witness! Pray for strength to face such encounters.

MARK 12:32 – 13:10

32The man answered, "That was a good answer, Teacher. You were right when you said God is the only Lord and there is no other God besides him. **33**One must love God with all his heart, all his mind, and all his strength. And one must love his neighbor as he loves himself. These commands are more important than all the animals and sacrifices we offer to God."

34When Jesus saw that the man answered him wisely, Jesus said to him "You are close to the kingdom of God." And after that, no one was brave enough to ask Jesus any more questions.

35As Jesus was teaching in the Temple, he asked, "Why do the teachers of the law say that the Christ is the son of David? **36**David himself, speaking by the Holy Spirit, said:

'The Lord said to my Lord,
"Sit by me at my right side,
until I put your enemies under your
control." '   *Psalm 110:1*

37David himself calls the Christ 'Lord,' so how can the Christ be his son?" The large crowd listened to Jesus with pleasure.

38Jesus continued teaching and said, "Beware of the teachers of the law. They like to walk around wearing fancy clothes, and they love for people to greet them with respect in the marketplaces. **39**They love to have the most important seats in the synagogues and at feasts. **40**But they cheat widows and steal their houses and then try to make themselves look good by saying long prayers. They will receive a greater punishment."

True Giving

41Jesus sat near the Temple money box and watched the people put in their money. Many rich people gave large sums of money. **42**Then a poor widow came and put in two small copper coins, which were only worth a few cents.

43Calling his followers to him, Jesus said, "I tell you the truth, this poor widow gave more than all those rich people. **44**They gave only what they did not need. This woman is very poor, but she gave all she had; she gave all she had to live on."

The Temple Will Be Destroyed

13 As Jesus was leaving the Temple, one of his followers said to him, "Look, Teacher! How beautiful the buildings are! How big the stones are!"

2Jesus said, "Do you see all these great buildings? Not one stone will be left on another. Every stone will be thrown down to the ground."

3Later, as Jesus was sitting on the Mount of Olives, opposite the Temple, he was alone with Peter, James, John, and Andrew. They asked Jesus, **4**"Tell us, when will these things happen? And what will be the sign that they are going to happen?"

5Jesus began to answer them, "Be careful that no one fools you. **6**Many people will come in my name, saying, 'I am the One,' and they will fool many people. **7**When you hear about wars and stories of wars that are coming, don't be afraid. These things must happen before the end comes. **8**Nations will fight against other nations, and kingdoms against other kingdoms. There will be earthquakes in different places, and there will be times when there is no food for people to eat. These things are like the first pains when something new is about to be born.

9"You must be careful. People will arrest you and take you to court and beat you in their synagogues. You will be forced to stand before kings and governors, to tell them about me. This will happen to you because you follow me. 10But before these things happen, the Good News must be told to all people."

OLD TESTAMENT READING

The people continued to bring gifts each morning because they wanted to. 4So all the skilled workers left the work they were doing on the Holy Tent, 5and they said to Moses, "The people are bringing more than we need to do the work the LORD commanded."

6Then Moses sent this command throughout the camp: "No man or woman should make anything else as a gift for the Holy Tent." So the people were kept from giving more, 7because what they had was already more than enough to do all the work.

Exodus 36:3b–7

INSIGHTS

Many beloved saints are depriving themselves of wondrous spiritual blessing by not giving as stewards what is entrusted to them. They act as if it were their own, as if all belonged to them, as if already they were in possession of the inheritance incorruptible and undefiled; forgetting that they have nothing whatever which is their own, that they are bought by the precious blood of Christ, and all they possess— their bodily strength, their time, their talents, their business, their professions, their eyes, their hands, their feet, all belong to the Lord Jesus Christ; because He has bought them with his precious blood. . . .

Just as we are constrained by the love of Christ, so God condescends to use us; and as we give, He is pleased to entrust to us more and more. . . .

My advice is this: if the reader has as yet but little knowledge and little grace, let him accordingly begin with a small percentage, yea, though it were ever so small a percentage, only let him be true to God, and put aside for Him habitually as He may be pleased to prosper him. In this way blessing for the soul will be reaped, will be abundantly reaped, and soon will the desire spring up in the heart to increase the proportion of returns to the Lord. This way will more and more lead the heart to such a state to be only a steward for the Lord, and to be willing to stand with all we have and are before the Lord as His stewards.

GEORGE MÜLLER

PAUSE FOR REFLECTION

What does God promise to those who give generously to him? To those who do not? Reread the Exodus passage. Can you imagine God's people today giving so much that they would have to be told to stop?

MARK 13:11-37

[11]"When you are arrested and judged, don't worry ahead of time about what you should say. Say whatever is given you to say at that time, because it will not really be you speaking; it will be the Holy Spirit.

[12]"Brothers will give their own brothers to be killed, and fathers will give their own children to be killed. Children will fight against their own parents and cause them to be put to death. [13]All people will hate you because you follow me, but those people who keep their faith until the end will be saved.

[14]"You will see 'a blasphemous object that brings destruction' standing where it should not be." (You who read this should understand what it means.) "At that time, the people in Judea should run away to the mountains. [15]If people are on the roofs of their houses, they must not go down or go inside to get anything out of their houses. [16]If people are in the fields, they must not go back to get their coats. [17]At that time, how terrible it will be for women who are pregnant or have nursing babies! [18]Pray that these things will not happen in winter, [19]because those days will be full of trouble. There will be more trouble than there has ever been since the beginning, when God made the world, until now, and nothing as bad will ever happen again. [20]God has decided to make that terrible time short. Otherwise, no one would go on living. But God will make that time short to help the people he has chosen. [21]At that time,

someone might say to you, 'Look, there is the Christ!' Or another person might say, 'There he is!' But don't believe them. [22]False Christs and false prophets will come and perform great wonders and miracles. They will try to fool even the people God has chosen, if that is possible. [23]So be careful. I have warned you about all this before it happens.

[24]"During the days after this trouble comes,

'the sun will grow dark,

and the moon will not give its light.
[25]The stars will fall from the sky.

And the powers of the heavens will be
shaken.'   *Isaiah 13:10; 34:4*

[26]"Then people will see the Son of Man coming in clouds with great power and glory. [27]Then he will send his angels all around the earth to gather his chosen people from every part of the earth and from every part of heaven.

[28]"Learn a lesson from the fig tree: When its branches become green and soft and new leaves appear, you know summer is near. [29]In the same way, when you see these things happening, you will know that the time is near, ready to come. [30]I tell you the truth, all these things will happen while the people of this time are still living. [31]Earth and sky will be destroyed, but the words I have said will never be destroyed.

[32]"No one knows when that day or time will be, not the angels in heaven, not even the Son. Only the Father knows. [33]Be careful! Always be ready, because you don't know when that time will be. [34]It is like a man who goes on a trip. He leaves his house and lets his servants take care of it, giving each one a special job to do. The man

tells the servant guarding the door always to be watchful. **35**So always be ready, because you don't know when the owner of the house will come back. It might be in the evening, or at midnight, or in the morning while it is still dark, or when the sun rises. **36**Always be ready. Otherwise he might come back suddenly and find you sleeping. **37**I tell you this, and I say this to everyone: 'Be ready!'"

OLD TESTAMENT READING

Those who are wise will help the others understand what is happening. But they will be killed with swords, or burned, or taken captive, or robbed of their homes and possessions. These things will continue for many days. **34**When the wise ones are suffering, they will get a little help, but many who join the wise ones will not help them in their time of need. **35**Some of the wise ones will be killed. But the hard times must come so they can be made stronger and purer and without faults until the time of the end comes. Then, at the right time, the end will come."

Daniel 11:33–35

INSIGHTS

My hope is built on nothing less
Than Jesus' blood and righteousness;
I dare not trust the sweetest frame,
But wholly lean on Jesus' name.
On Christ, the solid Rock, I stand:
All other ground is sinking sand.

When darkness veils His lovely face,
I rest on His unchanging grace;
In ev'ry high and stormy gale,
My anchor holds within the veil.
On Christ, the solid Rock, I stand:
All other ground is sinking sand.

His oath, His covenant, His blood,
Support me in the whelming flood;
When all around my soul gives way,
He then is all my hope and stay.
On Christ, the solid Rock I stand:
All other ground is sinking sand.

When He shall come with trumpet sound,
O may I then in Him be found:
Dressed in His righteousness alone,
Faultless to stand before the throne.
On Christ, the solid Rock, I stand:
All other ground is sinking sand.

EDWARD MOTE

PAUSE FOR REFLECTION

What are God's people to be and do during the end times? What is the purpose of their suffering during that time? On what can God's righteous ones depend during that time?

MARK 14:1-26

The Plan to Kill Jesus

14 It was now only two days before the Passover and the Feast of Unleavened Bread. The leading priests and teachers of the law were trying to find a trick to arrest Jesus and kill him. **2** But they said, "We must not do it during the feast, because the people might cause a riot."

A Woman with Perfume for Jesus

3 Jesus was in Bethany at the house of Simon, who had a skin disease. While Jesus was eating there, a woman approached him with an alabaster jar filled with very expensive perfume, made of pure nard. She opened the jar and poured the perfume on Jesus' head.

4 Some who were there became upset and said to each other, "Why waste that perfume? **5** It was worth a full year's work. It could have been sold and the money given to the poor." And they got very angry with the woman.

6 Jesus said, "Leave her alone. Why are you troubling her? She did an excellent thing for me. **7** You will always have the poor with you, and you can help them anytime you want. But you will not always have me. **8** This woman did the only thing she could do for me; she poured perfume on my body to prepare me for burial. **9** I tell you the truth, wherever the Good News is preached in all the world, what this woman has done will be told, and people will remember her."

Judas Becomes an Enemy of Jesus

10 One of the twelve apostles, Judas Iscariot, went to talk to the leading priests to offer to hand Jesus over to them. **11** These priests were pleased about this and promised to pay Judas money. So he watched for the best time to turn Jesus in.

Jesus Eats the Passover Meal

12 It was now the first day of the Feast of Unleavened Bread when the Passover lamb was sacrificed. Jesus' followers said to him, "Where do you want us to go and prepare for you to eat the Passover meal?"

13 Jesus sent two of his followers and said to them, "Go into the city and a man carrying a jar of water will meet you. Follow him. **14** When he goes into a house, tell the owner of the house, 'The Teacher says: "Where is my guest room in which I can eat the Passover meal with my followers?" ' **15** The owner will show you a large room upstairs that is furnished and ready. Prepare the food for us there."

16 So the followers left and went into the city. Everything happened as Jesus had said, so they prepared the Passover meal.

17 In the evening, Jesus went to that house with the twelve. **18** While they were all eating, Jesus said, "I tell you the truth, one of you will turn against me—one of you eating with me now."

19 The followers were very sad to hear this. Each one began to say to Jesus, "I am not the one, am I?"

20 Jesus answered, "It is one of the twelve—the one who dips his bread into the bowl with me.

²¹The Son of Man will die, just as the Scriptures say. But how terrible it will be for the person who hands the Son of Man over to be killed. It would be better for him if he had never been born."

The Lord's Supper

²²While they were eating, Jesus took some bread and thanked God for it and broke it. Then he gave it to his followers and said, "Take it; this is my body."

²³Then Jesus took a cup and thanked God for it and gave it to the followers, and they all drank from the cup.

²⁴Then Jesus said, "This is my blood which is the new agreement that God makes with his people. This blood is poured out for many. ²⁵I tell you the truth, I will not drink of this fruit of the vine again until that day when I drink it new in the kingdom of God."

²⁶After singing a hymn, they went out to the Mount of Olives.

OLD TESTAMENT READING

You are always to remember this day and celebrate it with a feast to the LORD. Your descendants are to honor the LORD with this feast from now on.

²⁵"Do this when you go to the land the LORD has promised to give you. ²⁶When your children ask you, 'Why are we doing these things?' ²⁷you will say, 'This is the Passover sacrifice to honor the LORD. When we were in Egypt, the LORD passed over the houses of Israel, and when he killed the Egyptians, he saved our homes.' " Then the people bowed down and worshiped the LORD.

Exodus 12:14, 25–27

INSIGHTS

Right down to the present, Jews re-enact the Passover event in celebration of their redemption from Egypt. . . .

In this service, words are connected with ritual, symbol, and gesture. It is a drama, a reenactment of the flight of Israel from the land of Pharaoh. It is not only a past event, but a present reality. For, although the Exodus happened in the past, its power and meaning reach down into history and change the lives of people now as did the original event. Reenactment of the action still has the power to change lives. . . .

The church has also retained the Old Testament principle that the event being celebrated becomes contemporaneous: Paul referred to the Table as a "participation" in Christ (1 Cor. 10:16). It is important to understand, though, that the death and resurrection of Jesus Christ is not an event which we memorialize. Its power, like that of the Exodus, reaches down through history and becomes a present reality to the people who celebrate it in faith.

Robert Webber

PAUSE FOR REFLECTION

Reread the full account of the Passover (Exodus 12:1–27) and try to feel the drama and significance of the Passover celebration. What feelings and awareness related to Jesus' celebration of the Lord's Supper (Mark 14:22–26) does this stir within you?

MARK 14:27-52

Jesus' Followers Will Leave Him

27Then Jesus told the followers, "You will all stumble in your faith, because it is written in the Scriptures:

'I will kill the shepherd,
    and the sheep will scatter.'   *Zechariah 13:7*
28But after I rise from the dead, I will go ahead of you into Galilee."

29Peter said, "Everyone else may stumble in their faith, but I will not."

30Jesus answered, "I tell you the truth, tonight before the rooster crows twice you will say three times you don't know me."

31But Peter insisted, "I will never say that I don't know you! I will even die with you!" And all the other followers said the same thing.

Jesus Prays Alone

32Jesus and his followers went to a place called Gethsemane. He said to them, "Sit here while I pray." **33**Jesus took Peter, James, and John with him, and he began to be very sad and troubled. **34**He said to them, "My heart is full of sorrow, to the point of death. Stay here and watch."

35After walking a little farther away from them, Jesus fell to the ground and prayed that, if possible, he would not have this time of suffering. **36**He prayed, "Abba, Father! You can do all things. Take away this cup of suffering. But do what you want, not what I want."

37Then Jesus went back to his followers and found them asleep. He said to Peter, "Simon, are you sleeping? Couldn't you stay awake with me for one hour? **38**Stay awake and pray for strength against temptation. The spirit wants to do what is right, but the body is weak."

39Again Jesus went away and prayed the same thing. **40**Then he went back to his followers, and again he found them asleep, because their eyes were very heavy. And they did not know what to say to him.

41After Jesus prayed a third time, he went back to his followers and said to them, "Are you still sleeping and resting? That's enough. The time has come for the Son of Man to be handed over to sinful people. **42**Get up, we must go. Look, here comes the man who has turned against me."

Jesus Is Arrested

43At once, while Jesus was still speaking, Judas, one of the twelve apostles, came up. With him were many people carrying swords and clubs who had been sent from the leading priests, the teachers of the law, and the Jewish elders.

44Judas had planned a signal for them, saying, "The man I kiss is Jesus. Arrest him and guard him while you lead him away." **45**So Judas went straight to Jesus and said, "Teacher!" and kissed him. **46**Then the people grabbed Jesus and arrested him. **47**One of his followers standing nearby pulled out his sword and struck the servant of the high priest and cut off his ear.

48Then Jesus said, "You came to get me with swords and clubs as if I were a criminal. **49**Every day I was with you teaching in the Temple, and you did not arrest me there. But all these things have happened to make the Scriptures come true." **50**Then all of Jesus' followers left him and ran away.

51A young man, wearing only a linen cloth, was following Jesus, and the people also grabbed him. 52But the cloth he was wearing came off, and he ran away naked.

OLD TESTAMENT READING

Solomon prayed this prayer to the LORD, kneeling in front of the altar with his arms raised toward heaven. When he finished praying, he got up. 55Then, in a loud voice, he stood and blessed all the people of Israel, saying: 56"Praise the LORD! He promised he would give rest to his people Israel, and he has given us rest. The LORD has kept all the good promises he gave through his servant Moses. 57May the LORD our God be with us as he was with our ancestors. May he never leave us, 58and may he turn us to himself so we will follow him. Let us obey all the laws and commands he gave our ancestors. 59May the LORD our God remember this prayer day and night and do what is right for his servant and his people Israel day by day."

1 Kings 8:54–59

Three times each day Daniel would kneel down to pray and thank God, just as he always had done.

Daniel 6:10b

INSIGHTS

The powerful reality grips me, Lord
That when I kneel in Your presence
To ask Your forgiveness
I am utterly stripped of facade.
You accept no big-name references
No high-caliber recommendations.
Extenuating circumstances
Crumble to dust
In Your court of appeal . . .
I am forgiven never
Because of inherited tendencies
Or emotional discomfort
Or nagging weakness . . .
I can never plead
Corrupt environment
Or life's strange twistings
Or my own unbelievable stupidity . . .
Ultimately I have one solitary defense.
Only one—
But always one:
Forgive me, God
For Jesus' sake.
Like a song unending
The words keep singing . . .
I am totally forgiven
I am continually cleansed
Just for Jesus' sake.

RUTH CALKIN

► PAUSE FOR REFLECTION

What physical posture did these men of God assume when they offered their heart-felt prayers to God? Do you think there is a difference between kneeling, sitting, or standing before God in prayer? How do you pray most earnestly to God?

MARK 14:53—15:5

Jesus Before the Leaders

53The people who arrested Jesus led him to the house of the high priest, where all the leading priests, the elders, and the teachers of the law were gathered. **54**Peter followed far behind and entered the courtyard of the high priest's house. There he sat with the guards, warming himself by the fire.

55The leading priests and the whole Jewish council tried to find something that Jesus had done wrong so they could kill him. But the council could find no proof of anything. **56**Many people came and told false things about him, but all said different things—none of them agreed.

57Then some people stood up and lied about Jesus, saying, **58**"We heard this man say, 'I will destroy this Temple that people made. And three days later, I will build another Temple not made by people.'" **59**But even the things these people said did not agree.

60Then the high priest stood before them and asked Jesus, "Aren't you going to answer? Don't you have something to say about their charges against you?" **61**But Jesus said nothing; he did not answer.

The high priest asked Jesus another question: "Are you the Christ, the Son of the blessed God?"

62Jesus answered, "I am. And in the future you will see the Son of Man sitting at the right hand of God, the Powerful One, and coming on clouds in the sky."

63When the high priest heard this, he tore his clothes and said, "We don't need any more witnesses! **64**You all heard him say these things against God. What do you think?"

They all said that Jesus was guilty and should die. **65**Some of the people there began to spit at Jesus. They blindfolded him and beat him with their fists and said, "Prove you are a prophet!" Then the guards led Jesus away and beat him.

Peter Says He Doesn't Know Jesus

66While Peter was in the courtyard, a servant girl of the high priest came there. **67**She saw Peter warming himself at the fire and looked closely at him.

Then she said, "You also were with Jesus, that man from Nazareth."

68But Peter said that he was never with Jesus. He said, "I don't know or understand what you are talking about." Then Peter left and went toward the entrance of the courtyard. And the rooster crowed.

69The servant girl saw Peter there, and again she said to the people who were standing nearby, "This man is one of those who followed Jesus." **70**Again Peter said that it was not true.

A short time later, some people were standing near Peter saying, "Surely you are one of those who followed Jesus, because you are from Galilee, too."

71Then Peter began to place a curse on himself and swear, "I don't know this man you're talking about!"

72At once, the rooster crowed the second time. Then Peter remembered what Jesus had told him: "Before the rooster crows twice, you will say three times that you don't know me." Then Peter lost control of himself and began to cry.

Pilate Questions Jesus

15 Very early in the morning, the leading priests, the elders, the teachers of the law, and all the Jewish council decided what to do with Jesus. They tied him, led him away, and turned him over to Pilate, the governor.

2Pilate asked Jesus, "Are you the king of the Jews?"

Jesus answered, "Those are your words."

3The leading priests accused Jesus of many things. **4**So Pilate asked Jesus another question, "You can see that they are accusing you of many things. Aren't you going to answer?"

5But Jesus still said nothing, so Pilate was very surprised.

OLD TESTAMENT READING

LORD, defend me because I have lived an innocent life.
I have trusted the LORD and never doubted.
2LORD, try me and test me;
look closely into my heart and mind.

Psalm 26:1–2

INSIGHTS

Here is a secret to the spiritual strength that willingly suffers wrong: accustom yourself in everything that happens to recognize the hand and will of God. Whether it be some great wrong that is done you, or some little offense that you meet in daily life, before you consider the person who did it, first be still and remember, God allows me to come into this trouble to see if I will glorify Him in it. This trial, be it great or small, is allowed by God and is His will concerning me. Let me first recognize and submit to God's will in it. Then with the peace of God which this gives, I will receive wisdom to know how to behave in it. With my eye turned from man to God, suffering wrong takes on this new dimension.

. . . Jesus saw beyond the temporal injustice and was satisfied to leave the vindication of His rights and honor in God's hands; He knew they were safe with Him. Peter writes, "He committed himself to him that judgeth righteously" (2:23). It was settled between the Father and the Son: the Son was not to care for His own honor, but only for the Father's. The Father would care for the Son's honor. Let the believer follow Christ's example in this; it will give him such rest and peace. Commit your right and your honor into God's keeping. Meet every offense that man commits against you with the firm trust that God will watch over and care for you.

ANDREW MURRAY

PAUSE FOR REFLECTION

How important is innocence in God's eyes? Think about the total trust Jesus had in his Father—trust that enabled him to stand innocent before God without having to prove his innocence to his accusers.

MARK 15:6-32

Pilate Tries to Free Jesus

6Every year at the time of the Passover the governor would free one prisoner whom the people chose. **7**At that time, there was a man named Barabbas in prison who was a rebel and had committed murder during a riot. **8**The crowd came to Pilate and began to ask him to free a prisoner as he always did.

9So Pilate asked them, "Do you want me to free the king of the Jews?" **10**Pilate knew that the leading priests had turned Jesus in to him because they were jealous. **11**But the leading priests had persuaded the people to ask Pilate to free Barabbas, not Jesus.

12Then Pilate asked the crowd again, "So what should I do with this man you call the king of the Jews?"

13They shouted, "Crucify him!"

14Pilate asked, "Why? What wrong has he done?"

But they shouted even louder, "Crucify him!"

15Pilate wanted to please the crowd, so he freed Barabbas for them. After having Jesus beaten with whips, he handed Jesus over to the soldiers to be crucified.

16The soldiers took Jesus into the governor's palace (called the Praetorium) and called all the other soldiers together. **17**They put a purple robe on Jesus and used thorny branches to make a crown for his head. **18**They began to call out to him, "Hail, King of the Jews!" **19**The soldiers beat Jesus on the head many times with a stick. They spit on him and made fun of him by bowing on their knees and worshiping him. **20**After they finished, the soldiers took off the purple robe and put his own clothes on him again. Then they led him out of the palace to be crucified.

Jesus Is Crucified

21A man named Simon from Cyrene, the father of Alexander and Rufus, was coming from the fields to the city. The soldiers forced Simon to carry the cross for Jesus. **22**They led Jesus to the place called Golgotha, which means the Place of the Skull. **23**The soldiers tried to give Jesus wine mixed with myrrh to drink, but he refused. **24**The soldiers crucified Jesus and divided his clothes among themselves, throwing lots to decide what each soldier would get.

25It was nine o'clock in the morning when they crucified Jesus. **26**There was a sign with this charge against Jesus written on it: THE KING OF THE JEWS. **27**They also put two robbers on crosses beside Jesus, one on the right, and the other on the left. [**28**And the Scripture came true that says, "They put him with criminals."] **29**People walked by and insulted Jesus and shook their heads, saying, "You said you could destroy the Temple and build it again in three days. **30**So save yourself! Come down from that cross!"

31The leading priests and the teachers of the law were also making fun of Jesus. They said to each other, "He saved other people, but he can't save himself. **32**If he is really the Christ, the king of Israel, let him come down now from the cross. When we see this, we will believe in him." The robbers who were being crucified beside Jesus also insulted him.

OLD TESTAMENT READING

Evil people have surrounded me;
like dogs they have trapped me.
They have bitten my arms and legs.

¹⁷I can count all my bones;
people look and stare at me.
¹⁸They divided my clothes among them,
and they threw lots for my clothing.

Psalm 22:16–18

INSIGHTS

Think of the love that God must have had when He gave His son to die for the world! I used to think a good deal more of Christ than I did of the Father. Somehow or other I had the idea that God was a stern judge; that Christ came between me and God, and appeased the anger of God. But after I became a father, and for years had an only son, as I looked at my boy I thought of the Father giving His Son to die, and it seemed to me as if it required more love for the Father to give His Son than for the Son to die. Oh, the love that God must have had for the world when He gave His Son to die for it! "God so loved the world, that He gave His only begotten Son, that whosoever believeth in Him should not perish, but have everlasting life" (John 3:16). I have never been able to preach from that text. I have often thought I would, but it is so high that I can never climb to its height, I have just quoted it and passed on. Who can fathom the depth of those words: "God so loved the world"? We can never scale the heights of His love, or fathom its depths. Paul prayed that he might know the height, the depth, the length, and the breadth of the love of God; but it was past his finding out. . . .

Nothing speaks to us of the love of God like the Cross of Christ. Come with me to Calvary, and look upon the Son of God as He hangs there. Can you hear that piercing cry from His dying lips: "Father, forgive them; for they know not what they do!" and say that He does not love you? "Greater love hath no man than this, that a man lay down his life for his friends" (John 15:13). But Jesus Christ laid down His life for His enemies.

Another thought is this: He loved us long before we ever thought of Him. The idea that He does not love us until we first love Him is not to be found in Scripture. In 1 John 4:10 it is written: "Herein is love, not that we love God, but that He loved us, and sent His Son to be the propitiation for our sins." He loved us before we ever thought of loving Him. You loved your children before they knew anything about your love. And so, long before we ever thought of God, we were in His thoughts.

D. L. MOODY

PAUSE FOR REFLECTION

How does your image of God's love change as you read about the way Jesus suffered injury, insult, and degradation in order to save you? Perhaps now would be a good time for a thoughtful prayer of thanks for God's love.

MARK 15:33 — 16:8

Jesus Dies

33At noon the whole country became dark, and the darkness lasted for three hours. **34**At three o'clock Jesus cried in a loud voice, "Eloi, Eloi, lama sabachthani." This means, "My God, my God, why have you abandoned me?"

35When some of the people standing there heard this, they said, "Listen! He is calling Elijah."

36Someone there ran and got a sponge, filled it with vinegar, tied it to a stick, and gave it to Jesus to drink. He said, "We want to see if Elijah will come to take him down from the cross."

37Then Jesus cried in a loud voice and died.

38The curtain in the Temple was torn into two pieces, from the top to the bottom. **39**When the army officer who was standing in front of the cross saw what happened when Jesus died, he said, "This man really was the Son of God!"

40Some women were standing at a distance from the cross, watching; among them were Mary Magdalene, Salome, and Mary the mother of James and Joseph. (James was her youngest son.) **41**These women had followed Jesus in Galilee and helped him. Many other women were also there who had come with Jesus to Jerusalem.

Jesus Is Buried

42This was Preparation Day. (That means the day before the Sabbath day.) That evening, **43**Joseph from Arimathea was brave enough to go to Pilate and ask for Jesus' body. Joseph, an important member of the Jewish council, was one of the people who was waiting for the kingdom of God to come. **44**Pilate was amazed that Jesus would have already died, so he called the army officer who had guarded Jesus and asked him if Jesus had already died. **45**The officer told Pilate that he was dead, so Pilate told Joseph he could have the body. **46**Joseph bought some linen cloth, took the body down from the cross, and wrapped it in the linen. He put the body in a tomb that was cut out of a wall of rock. Then he rolled a very large stone to block the entrance of the tomb. **47**And Mary Magdalene and Mary the mother of Joseph saw the place where Jesus was laid.

Jesus Rises from the Dead

16 The day after the Sabbath day, Mary Magdalene, Mary the mother of James, and Salome bought some sweet-smelling spices to put on Jesus' body. **2**Very early on that day, the first day of the week, soon after sunrise, the women were on their way to the tomb. **3**They said to each other, "Who will roll away for us the stone that covers the entrance of the tomb?"

4Then the women looked and saw that the stone had already been rolled away, even though it was very large. **5**The women entered the tomb and saw a young man wearing a white robe and sitting on the right side, and they were afraid.

6But the man said, "Don't be afraid. You are looking for Jesus from Nazareth, who has been crucified. He has risen from the dead; he is not here. Look, here is the place they laid him. **7**Now go and tell his followers and Peter, 'Jesus is going into Galilee ahead of you, and you will see him there as he told you before.'"

8The women were confused and shaking with fear, so they left the tomb and ran away. They did not tell anyone about what happened, because they were afraid.

OLD TESTAMENT READING

The burning desert will have pools of water,
and the dry ground will have springs.
Where wild dogs once lived,
grass and water plants will grow.
8A road will be there;
this highway will be called "The Road to Being Holy."
Evil people will not be allowed to walk on that road;
only good people will walk on it.
No fools will go on it.
9No lions will be there,
nor will dangerous animals be on that road.
They will not be found there.
That road will be for the people God saves;
10   the people the LORD has freed will return there.
They will enter Jerusalem with joy,
and their happiness will last forever.
Their gladness and joy will fill them completely,
and sorrow and sadness will go far away.

Isaiah 35:7–10

INSIGHTS

I will never forget the day that I looked into the tomb. It changed my whole ministry. It came to me that my Savior was really alive, that His work on the cross for sinners so satisfied divine justice and divine character and divine righteousness, that I would never see my sins again. God raised Him from the dead as a guarantee to me personally that death has no more authority over the man in Christ. It has been shorn of its power. . . . At the cross we see His love, but in resurrection we see His power.

We've been joined to a risen Savior. That is why the apostles gave witness with such great power in the book of Acts. Paul stood before Felix, before Festus, before Agrippa, before the Sanhedrin, before the philosophers of Athens, and before the corrupt Corinthians with only one message. He preached the risen Christ.

. . . The cross is a tragedy if there is no resurrection. Would to God that His people would continually rejoice that our Savior is alive forevermore.

JOHN G. MITCHELL

ACTION POINT

Meditate on the Isaiah 35 reading until you begin to understand the awesome reality of Christ's resurrection. Pray now and thank God that Jesus not only died, but that he lives today!

MARK 16:9 —
LUKE 1:13

Verses 9–20 are not included in some of the earliest surviving Greek copies of Mark.

Some Followers See Jesus

[9After Jesus rose from the dead early on the first day of the week, he showed himself first to Mary Magdalene. One time in the past, he had forced seven demons out of her. 10After Mary saw Jesus, she went and told his followers, who were very sad and were crying. 11But Mary told them that Jesus was alive. She said that she had seen him, but the followers did not believe her.

12Later, Jesus showed himself to two of his followers while they were walking in the country, but he did not look the same as before. 13These followers went back to the others and told them what had happened, but again, the followers did not believe them.

Jesus Talks to the Apostles

14Later Jesus showed himself to the eleven apostles while they were eating, and he criticized them because they had no faith. They were stubborn and refused to believe those who had seen him after he had risen from the dead.

15Jesus said to his followers, "Go everywhere in the world, and tell the Good News to everyone. 16Anyone who believes and is baptized will be saved, but anyone who does not believe will be punished. 17And those who believe will be able to do these things as proof: They will use my name to force out demons. They will speak in new languages. 18They will pick up snakes and drink poison without being hurt. They will touch the sick, and the sick will be healed."

19After the Lord Jesus said these things to his followers, he was carried up into heaven, and he sat at the right side of God. 20The followers went everywhere in the world and told the Good News to people, and the Lord helped them. The Lord proved that the Good News they told was true by giving them power to work miracles.]

Luke Writes About Jesus' Life

Many have tried to report on the things that happened among us. 2They have written the same things that we learned from others—the people who saw those things from the beginning and served God by telling people his message. 3Since I myself have studied everything carefully from the beginning, most excellent Theophilus, it seemed good for me to write it out for you. I arranged it in order, 4to help you know that what you have been taught is true.

Zechariah and Elizabeth

5During the time Herod ruled Judea, there was a priest named Zechariah who belonged to Abijah's group.n Zechariah's wife, Elizabeth, came from the family of Aaron. 6Zechariah and Elizabeth truly did what God said was good. They did everything the Lord commanded and were without fault in keeping his law. 7But they had no children, because Elizabeth could not have a baby, and both of them were very old.

8One day Zechariah was serving as a priest before God, because his group was on duty. 9According to the custom of the priests, he was chosen by lot to go into the Temple of the Lord and burn incense. **10**There were a great many people outside praying at the time the incense was offered. **11**Then an angel of the Lord appeared to Zechariah, standing on the right side of the incense table. **12**When he saw the angel, Zechariah was startled and frightened. **13**But the angel said to him, "Zechariah, don't be afraid. God has heard your prayer. Your wife, Elizabeth, will give birth to a son, and you will name him John."

OLD TESTAMENT READING

Joshua son of Nun and Caleb son of Jephunneh, who had explored the land, tore their clothes. **7**They said to all of the Israelites, "The land we explored is very good. **9**Don't turn against the LORD! Don't be afraid of the people in that land! We will chew them up. They have no protection, but the LORD is with us. So don't be afraid of them."

11The LORD said to Moses, "How long will these people ignore me? How long will they not believe me in spite of the miracles I have done among them?"

20The LORD answered, "I have forgiven them as you asked. **21**But, as surely as I live and as surely as my glory fills the whole earth, I make this promise: **22**All these people saw my glory and the miracles I did in Egypt and in the desert, but they disobeyed me and tested me ten times. **23**So not one of them will see the land I promised to their ancestors. No one who rejected me will see that land. **24**But my servant Caleb thinks differently and follows me completely. So I will bring him into the land he has already seen, and his children will own that land."

Numbers 14:6–7, 9, 11, 20–24

INSIGHTS

You may ask how people wind up in hell if God is a loving God. People wind up in hell by trampling the love of God instead of treasuring it. They ignore it, spurn it, yawn over it, close their hearts to it, keep saying "someday, someday, someday."

The Bible says there will be a someday. It's a day of reckoning. To those who have spurned His love, God will say in effect, "I loved you every day of your life. I loved you with a perfect love. I extended Myself to you. I made My wisdom available to you. I made My comfort and My strength and My Spirit available to you. I made My offer of salvation to you. But you trampled and spurned My love. You had it your way on earth, so now you can have it your way in eternity."

Are you facing that scenario? Will you continue to trample the love of God? That's the question of the ages, and it is one you yourself must answer.

BILL HYBELS

PAUSE FOR REFLECTION

What is the essential message of the Good News? After Jesus returned to heaven, how did he prove that the Good News was true? Is it really easier to believe God when we see his miracles? What is the fate of all those who—even though they have witnessed miracles—choose to reject God?

LUKE 1:14-45

14"He will bring you joy and gladness, and many people will be happy because of his birth. **15**John will be a great man for the Lord. He will never drink wine or beer, and even from birth, he will be filled with the Holy Spirit. **16**He will help many people of Israel return to the Lord their God. **17**He will go before the Lord in spirit and power like Elijah. He will make peace between parents and their children and will bring those who are not obeying God back to the right way of thinking, to make a people ready for the coming of the Lord."

18Zechariah said to the angel, "How can I know that what you say is true? I am an old man, and my wife is old, too."

19The angel answered him, "I am Gabriel. I stand before God, who sent me to talk to you and to tell you this good news. **20**Now, listen! You will not be able to speak until the day these things happen, because you did not believe what I told you. But they will really happen."

21Outside, the people were still waiting for Zechariah and were surprised that he was staying so long in the Temple. **22**When Zechariah came outside, he could not speak to them, and they knew he had seen a vision in the Temple. He could only make signs to them and remained unable to speak. **23**When his time of service at the Temple was finished, he went home.

24Later, Zechariah's wife, Elizabeth, became pregnant and did not go out of her house for five months. Elizabeth said, **25**"Look what the Lord has done for me! My people were ashamed of me, but now the Lord has taken away that shame."

An Angel Appears to Mary

26During Elizabeth's sixth month of pregnancy, God sent the angel Gabriel to Nazareth, a town in Galilee, **27**to a virgin. She was engaged to marry a man named Joseph from the family of David. Her name was Mary. **28**The angel came to her and said, "Greetings! The Lord has blessed you and is with you."

29But Mary was very startled by what the angel said and wondered what this greeting might mean.

30The angel said to her, "Don't be afraid, Mary; God has shown you his grace. **31**Listen! You will become pregnant and give birth to a son, and you will name him Jesus. **32**He will be great and will be called the Son of the Most High. The Lord God will give him the throne of King David, his ancestor. **33**He will rule over the people of Jacob forever, and his kingdom will never end."

34Mary said to the angel, "How will this happen since I am a virgin?"

35The angel said to Mary, "The Holy Spirit will come upon you, and the power of the Most High will cover you. For this reason the baby will be holy and will be called the Son of God. **36**Now Elizabeth, your relative, is also pregnant with a son though she is very old. Everyone thought she could not have a baby, but she has been pregnant for six months. **37**God can do anything!"

38Mary said, "I am the servant of the Lord. Let this happen to me as you say!" Then the angel went away.

Mary Visits Elizabeth

39Mary got up and went quickly to a town in the hills of Judea. **40**She came to Zechariah's house and greeted Elizabeth. **41**When Elizabeth heard Mary's greeting, the unborn baby inside her jumped, and Elizabeth was filled with the Holy Spirit. **42**She cried out in a loud voice, "God has blessed you more than any other woman, and he has blessed the baby to which you will give birth. **43**Why has this good thing happened to me, that the mother of my Lord comes to me? **44**When I heard your voice, the baby inside me jumped with joy. **45**You are blessed because you believed that what the Lord said to you would really happen."

OLD TESTAMENT READING

ut I will send you Elijah the prophet before that great and terrifying day of the LORD's judging. **6**Elijah will help parents love their children and children love their parents. Otherwise, I will come and put a curse on the land."

Malachi 4:5–6

INSIGHTS

Reports continually flow to my attention from many places around the world telling of visitors of the angelic order appearing, ministering, fellowshiping and disappearing. They warn of God's impending judgment; they spell out the tenderness of His love; they meet a desperate need; then they are gone. Of one thing we can be sure: angels never draw attention to themselves but ascribe glory to God and press His message upon the hearers as a delivering and sustaining word of the highest order.

Demonic activity and Satan worship are on the increase in all parts of the world. The devil is alive and more at work than at any other time. The Bible says that since he realizes his time is short, his activity will increase. Through his demonic influences he does succeed in turning many away from true faith; but we can still say that his evil activities are countered for the people of God by His ministering spirits, the holy ones of the angelic order. They are vigorous in delivering the heirs of salvation from the stratagems of evil men. They cannot fail.

Believers, look up—take courage. The angels are nearer than you think. For after all, God has given "his angels charge of you, to guard you in all your ways. On their hands they will bear you up, lest you dash your foot against a stone" (Psalm 91:11, 12, RSV).

BILLY GRAHAM

APPLICATION

When an angel delivers God's message to a person, what response does God expect? What are the consequences of believing or doubting God's message? Are you open to receiving his message for you?

LUKE 1:46-77

Mary Praises God

⁴⁶Then Mary said,

"My soul praises the Lord;

⁴⁷ my heart rejoices in God my Savior,

⁴⁸because he has shown his concern for his
humble servant girl.

From now on, all people will say that I am
blessed,

⁴⁹ because the Powerful One has done great
things for me.

His name is holy.

⁵⁰God will show his mercy forever and ever
to those who worship and serve him.

⁵¹He has done mighty deeds by his power.

He has scattered the people who are proud
and think great things about themselves.

⁵²He has brought down rulers from their
thrones
and raised up the humble.

⁵³He has filled the hungry with good things
and sent the rich away with nothing.

⁵⁴He has helped his servant, the people of
Israel,

remembering to show them mercy

⁵⁵as he promised to our ancestors,
to Abraham and to his children forever."

⁵⁶Mary stayed with Elizabeth for about three
months and then returned home.

The Birth of John

⁵⁷When it was time for Elizabeth to give birth,
she had a boy. ⁵⁸Her neighbors and relatives
heard how good the Lord was to her, and they rejoiced with her.

⁵⁹When the baby was eight days old, they
came to circumcise him. They wanted to name
him Zechariah because this was his father's name,
⁶⁰but his mother said, "No! He will be named
John."

⁶¹The people said to Elizabeth, "But no one in
your family has this name." ⁶²Then they made
signs to his father to find out what he would like
to name him.

⁶³Zechariah asked for a writing tablet and
wrote, "His name is John," and everyone was surprised. ⁶⁴Immediately Zechariah could talk
again, and he began praising God. ⁶⁵All their
neighbors became alarmed, and in all the mountains of Judea people continued talking about all
these things. ⁶⁶The people who heard about them
wondered, saying, "What will this child be?" because the Lord was with him.

Zechariah Praises God

⁶⁷Then Zechariah, John's father, was filled with
the Holy Spirit and prophesied:

⁶⁸"Let us praise the Lord, the God of Israel,
because he has come to help his people
and has given them freedom.

⁶⁹He has given us a powerful Savior
from the family of God's servant David.

⁷⁰He said that he would do this
through his holy prophets who lived long
ago:

⁷¹He promised he would save us from our
enemies
and from the power of all those who hate
us.

⁷²He said he would give mercy to our ancestors
and that he would remember his holy
promise.
⁷³God promised Abraham, our father,
⁷⁴   that he would save us from the power of
our enemies
so we could serve him without fear,
⁷⁵being holy and good before God as long as we
live.

⁷⁶"Now you, child, will be called a prophet of
the Most High God.
You will go before the Lord to prepare his
way.
⁷⁷You will make his people know that they will
be saved
by having their sins forgiven."

OLD TESTAMENT READING

ut I have hope
when I think of this:

²²The LORD's love never ends;
his mercies never stop.
²³They are new every morning;
LORD, your loyalty is great.
²⁴I say to myself, "The LORD is mine,
so I hope in him."

²⁵The LORD is good to those who hope in him,
to those who seek him.
²⁶It is good to wait quietly
for the LORD to save.

Lamentations 3:21–26

INSIGHTS

The Israelites were always worshiping the idols of the peoples around them in spite of the warning and the pleadings of the prophets. It wasn't until their captivity in Babylon that they were cured of these dangerous liaisons with "other gods." From the days of their captivity until now—two-and-a-half millennia—the Jews have never again been guilty of this sin. But in many places in Scripture, the Holy Spirit takes up the refrain to make sure the people of God would never slip back. . . .

God is still dealing mercifully with those who wander away in rebellion and pride, but return in humility and faith. We have our Golden Calves, our substitutes for the living God. We have things in our lives that seem more important because they promise more immediate gratification. We, too, grow discouraged in a wilderness—a treadmill of monotonous busyness without tangible or meaningful results. To banish our sense of emptiness and lostness in this secular world, we may have looked for satisfaction in lesser gods, although we would never call them Golden Calves. Even so, God is patiently waiting for us to forsake these idols. He may discipline us, but in His mercy, He will never forsake us.

WILLIAM STODDARD

▶ PAUSE FOR REFLECTION

Do you sense how greatly Mary, Elizabeth, and Zechariah felt God's mercy to them and to all of God's people? Thank God that no matter how greatly we sin he is merciful and forgiving to everyone who repents!

LUKE 1:78 – 2:26

78 "With the loving mercy of our God,
    a new day from heaven will dawn upon us.
79 It will shine on those who live in darkness,
    in the shadow of death.
  It will guide us into the path of peace."

80 And so the child grew up and became strong in spirit. John lived in the desert until the time when he came out to preach to Israel.

The Birth of Jesus

At that time, Augustus Caesar sent an order that all people in the countries under Roman rule must list their names in a register. 2 This was the first registration; it was taken while Quirinius was governor of Syria. 3 And all went to their own towns to be registered.

4 So Joseph left Nazareth, a town in Galilee, and went to the town of Bethlehem in Judea, known as the town of David. Joseph went there because he was from the family of David. 5 Joseph registered with Mary, to whom he was engaged and who was now pregnant. 6 While they were in Bethlehem, the time came for Mary to have the baby, 7 and she gave birth to her first son. Because there were no rooms left in the inn, she wrapped the baby with pieces of cloth and laid him in a feeding trough.

Shepherds Hear About Jesus

8 That night, some shepherds were in the fields nearby watching their sheep. 9 Then an angel of the Lord stood before them. The glory of the Lord was shining around them, and they became very frightened. 10 The angel said to them, "Do not be afraid. I am bringing you good news that will be a great joy to all the people. 11 Today your Savior was born in the town of David. He is Christ, the Lord. 12 This is how you will know him: You will find a baby wrapped in pieces of cloth and lying in a feeding box."

13 Then a very large group of angels from heaven joined the first angel, praising God and saying:

14 "Give glory to God in heaven,
        and on earth let there be peace among the
            people who please God."

15 When the angels left them and went back to heaven, the shepherds said to each other, "Let's go to Bethlehem. Let's see this thing that has happened which the Lord has told us about."

16 So the shepherds went quickly and found Mary and Joseph and the baby, who was lying in a feeding trough. 17 When they had seen him, they told what the angels had said about this child. 18 Everyone was amazed at what the shepherds said to them. 19 But Mary treasured these things and continued to think about them. 20 Then the shepherds went back to their sheep, praising God and thanking him for everything they had seen and heard. It had been just as the angel had told them.

21 When the baby was eight days old, he was circumcised and was named Jesus, the name given by the angel before the baby began to grow inside Mary.

Jesus Is Presented in the Temple

22 When the time came for Mary and Joseph to do what the law of Moses taught about being

made pure, they took Jesus to Jerusalem to present him to the Lord. **23**(It is written in the law of the Lord: "Every firstborn male shall be given to the Lord.") **24**Mary and Joseph also went to offer a sacrifice, as the law of the Lord says: "You must sacrifice two doves or two young pigeons."

Simeon Sees Jesus

25In Jerusalem lived a man named Simeon who was a good man and godly. He was waiting for the time when God would take away Israel's sorrow, and the Holy Spirit was in him. **26**Simeon had been told by the Holy Spirit that he would not die before he saw the Christ promised by the Lord.

OLD TESTAMENT READING

The LORD, the LORD gives me strength and makes me sing.
He has saved me."
3You will receive your salvation with joy as you would draw water from a well.
4At that time you will say,
"Praise the LORD and worship him.
Tell everyone what he has done and how great he is.
5Sing praise to the LORD, because he has done great things.

Isaiah 12:2b–5a

INSIGHTS

In His holiness and love God could not wink at sin. He could not compromise either His justice or His mercy. Therefore, out of grace He sent His Son. . . . By God's mercy, He came in Christ to pay the full price, and at the cross, exposed His heart. God abhors, condemns, and judges sin, and yet by the power of the cross, He forgives sinners—people like you and me! . . .

. . . We have all gone over the line in breaking the Ten Commandments and Jesus' commandment to love. We've brought hurt, pain and suffering to ourselves and others by what we've done or said or refused to be. We've broken His heart. And even before we asked Him, He forgave us. He reconciled us. He exonerated us. We stutter out our yearning to be free in response to His cross, melted by His love, and healed by His forgiveness.

The same voice that cried. "Father forgive them," from Calvary, says to us with the commanding power of His cross-shaped heart, "The ransom has been paid for all time. And now in this propitious moment in your time it is a pardon for you. You are forgiven. You are free!"

Oh, the wonder of it all, indeed!

LLOYD OGILVIE

ACTION POINT

Think about all the things Jesus' birth represented to his parents, the shepherds, and Simeon. What does Jesus' coming to earth signify to you? Meditate on the wonder of it all. Thank him for his salvation.

LUKE 2:27-52

27The Spirit led Simeon to the Temple. When Mary and Joseph brought the baby Jesus to the Temple to do what the law said they must do, **28**Simeon took the baby in his arms and thanked God:

29"Now, Lord, you can let me, your servant,
die in peace as you said.
30With my own eyes I have seen your salvation,
31 which you prepared before all people.
32It is a light for the non-Jewish people to see
and an honor for your people, the
Israelites."

33Jesus' father and mother were amazed at what Simeon had said about him. **34**Then Simeon blessed them and said to Mary, "God has chosen this child to cause the fall and rise of many in Israel. He will be a sign from God that many people will not accept **35**so that the thoughts of many will be made known. And the things that will happen will make your heart sad, too."

Anna Sees Jesus

36There was a prophetess, Anna, from the family of Phanuel in the tribe of Asher. Anna was very old. She had once been married for seven years. **37**Then her husband died, and she was a widow for eighty-four years. Anna never left the Temple but worshiped God, going without food and praying day and night. **38**Standing there at that time, she thanked God and spoke about Jesus to all who were waiting for God to free Jerusalem.

Joseph and Mary Return Home

39When Joseph and Mary had done everything the law of the Lord commanded, they went home to Nazareth, their own town in Galilee. **40**The little child grew and became strong. He was filled with wisdom, and God's goodness was upon him.

Jesus As a Boy

41Every year Jesus' parents went to Jerusalem for the Passover Feast. **42**When he was twelve years old, they went to the feast as they always did. **43**After the feast days were over, they started home. The boy Jesus stayed behind in Jerusalem, but his parents did not know it. **44**Thinking that Jesus was with them in the group, they traveled for a whole day. Then they began to look for him among their family and friends. **45**When they did not find him, they went back to Jerusalem to look for him there. **46**After three days they found Jesus sitting in the Temple with the teachers, listening to them and asking them questions. **47**All who heard him were amazed at his understanding and answers. **48**When Jesus' parents saw him, they were astonished. His mother said to him, "Son, why did you do this to us? Your father and I were very worried about you and have been looking for you."

49Jesus said to them, "Why were you looking for me? Didn't you know that I must be in my Father's house?" **50**But they did not understand the meaning of what he said.

51Jesus went with them to Nazareth and was obedient to them. But his mother kept in her mind all that had happened. **52**Jesus became wiser and grew physically. People liked him, and he pleased God.

OLD TESTAMENT READING

When Samuel was old enough to eat, Hannah took him to the house of the LORD at Shiloh, along with a three-year-old bull, one-half bushel of flour, and a leather bag filled with wine. 25After they had killed the bull for the sacrifice, Hannah brought Samuel to Eli. 26She said to Eli, "As surely as you live, sir, I am the same woman who stood near you praying to the LORD. 27I prayed for this child, and the LORD answered my prayer and gave him to me. 28Now I give him back to the LORD. He will belong to the LORD all his life." And he worshiped the LORD there.

1 Samuel 1:24–28

INSIGHTS

Many people have the idea that God only calls preachers and missionaries, and the rest of us can do whatever we want to. But God has a calling for all of His children. . . .

. . . The people that God calls, the people God uses and chooses, His all-stars, are common ordinary people. . . .

. . . I thank God for the wise, noble, and mighty who love the Lord. I thank God for any athlete, movie star, or millionaire who will give his or her life to Christ. But God's work is going to be done primarily not through the superstar preachers, evangelists, or celebrities; God's work is going to be done through His ordinary everyday run-of-the-mill people. . . .

. . . God called a timid man with a stutter—a speech impediment—by the name of Moses and made him the greatest leader in the Old Testament. God called David, a little shepherd boy, right out of the pasture and made him the greatest king who ever ruled over Israel. . . . God's ways are above our ways, His thoughts are above our thoughts, and His calling confounds the wise. . . .

When I think of the weak I recall the life of Jonathan Edwards. He was one of the greatest revival preachers America or the world has ever known. . . .

He was an asthmatic. Whenever he would preach he would cough and hack and wheeze during most of the message. He was a very thin, frail man. He had horrible eyesight. . . .

. . . Jonathan Edwards' sermons, despite his disabilities, caused people to come writhing in anguish down the aisles wanting to get right with God. . . .

. . . The people that God uses and chooses, God's all-stars, are not people of ability; they are people of availability who have learned the secret of giving their praise to God. If you use your life for the glory of God, God will use your life for His glory.

JAMES MERRITT

ACTION POINT

Jesus knew he was called to do the Father's work. So did Samuel. What about you? Do you long for his clear call?

LUKE 3:1-22

The Preaching of John

It was the fifteenth year of the rule of Tiberius Caesar. These men were under Caesar: Pontius Pilate, the ruler of Judea; Herod, the ruler of Galilee; Philip, Herod's brother, the ruler of Iturea and Traconitis; and Lysanias, the ruler of Abilene. **2**Annas and Caiaphas were the high priests. At this time, the word of God came to John son of Zechariah in the desert. **3**He went all over the area around the Jordan River preaching a baptism of changed hearts and lives for the forgiveness of sins. **4**As it is written in the book of Isaiah the prophet:

"This is a voice of one
who calls out in the desert:
'Prepare the way for the Lord.
Make the road straight for him.
5Every valley should be filled in,
and every mountain and hill should be
made flat.
Roads with turns should be made straight,
and rough roads should be made smooth.
6And all people will know about the salvation
of God!'"   *Isaiah 40:3–5*

7To the crowds of people who came to be baptized by John, he said, "You are all snakes! Who warned you to run away from God's coming punishment? **8**Do the things that show you really have changed your hearts and lives. Don't begin to say to yourselves, 'Abraham is our father.' I tell you that God could make children for Abraham from these rocks. **9**The ax is now ready to cut down the trees, and every tree that does not produce good fruit will be cut down and thrown into the fire."

10The people asked John, "Then what should we do?"

11John answered, "If you have two shirts, share with the person who does not have one. If you have food, share that also."

12Even tax collectors came to John to be baptized. They said to him, "Teacher, what should we do?"

13John said to them, "Don't take more taxes from people than you have been ordered to take."

14The soldiers asked John, "What about us? What should we do?"

John said to them, "Don't force people to give you money, and don't lie about them. Be satisfied with the pay you get."

15Since the people were hoping for the Christ to come, they wondered if John might be the one.

16John answered everyone, "I baptize you with water, but there is one coming who is greater than I am. I am not good enough to untie his sandals. He will baptize you with the Holy Spirit and fire. **17**He will come ready to clean the grain, separating the good grain from the chaff. He will put the good part of the grain into his barn, but he will burn the chaff with a fire that cannot be put out."

18And John continued to preach the Good News, saying many other things to encourage the people.

19But John spoke against Herod, the governor, because of his sin with Herodias, the wife of Herod's brother, and because of the many other evil things Herod did. **20**So Herod did something even worse: He put John in prison.

Jesus Is Baptized by John

21When all the people were being baptized by John, Jesus also was baptized. While Jesus was praying, heaven opened **22**and the Holy Spirit came down on him in the form of a dove. Then a voice came from heaven, saying, "You are my Son, whom I love, and I am very pleased with you."

OLD TESTAMENT READING

A voice says, "Cry out!"
    Then I said, "What shall I cry out?"

"Say all people are like the grass,
    and all their glory is like the flowers of the field.
8The grass dies and the flowers fall,
    but the word of our God will live forever."
Shout it out and don't be afraid.
    Say to the towns of Judah,
    "Here is your God."
10Look, the Lord GOD is coming with power
    to rule all the people.
Look, he will bring reward for his people;
    he will have their payment with him.

Isaiah 40:6, 8, 9c–10

INSIGHTS

Is it a waste to focus on the Lord's descent? Quite the contrary. It's biblical; it's the very thing Titus 2:13 says we ought to do.

When's the last time you—on your own—meditated on that fact? If you're like me it's been too long. People who are more practical than mystical, who are realistic rather than idealistic, tend to shove that stuff to times like funerals or near-death experiences. . . . Listen, this Bible of ours is full and running over with promises and encouragements directly related to the return of our Lord Christ. . . .

Critics have denied it. Cynics have laughed at it. Scholars have ignored it. Liberal theologians have explained it away (they call that "rethinking" it) and fanatics have perverted it. . . . But there it stands, solid as a stone, soon to be fulfilled, ready to offer us hope and encouragement amidst despair and unbelief.

"Okay, swell. But what do I do in the meantime?" I can hear a dozen or more pragmatists asking that question. First, it might be best for you to understand what you don't do. You don't sit around, listening for some bugle call. You don't keep staring up into the sky, looking for the rapture cloud. . . .

You do get your act together. You do live every day (as if it's your last) for His glory. You do work diligently . . . (as if He isn't coming for another ten years) for His Name's sake. You do shake salt out every chance you get . . . and do shine the light . . . and remain balanced, cheerful, winsome, and stable, anticipating His return day by day.

CHARLES SWINDOLL

APPLICATION

Do you feel the excitement of John's listeners? Do you await Christ's second coming with a yawn, or are you living each day as he wants you to?

LUKE 3:23-38

The Family History of Jesus

23 When Jesus began his ministry, he was about thirty years old. People thought that Jesus was Joseph's son.

Joseph was the son of Heli.

24 Heli was the son of Matthat.
Matthat was the son of Levi.
Levi was the son of Melki.
Melki was the son of Jannai.
Jannai was the son of Joseph.

25 Joseph was the son of Mattathias.
Mattathias was the son of Amos.
Amos was the son of Nahum.
Nahum was the son of Esli.
Esli was the son of Naggai.

26 Naggai was the son of Maath.
Maath was the son of Mattathias.
Mattathias was the son of Semein.
Semein was the son of Josech.
Josech was the son of Joda.

27 Joda was the son of Joanan.
Joanan was the son of Rhesa.
Rhesa was the son of Zerubbabel.
Zerubbabel was the grandson of Shealtiel.
Shealtiel was the son of Neri.

28 Neri was the son of Melki.
Melki was the son of Addi.
Addi was the son of Cosam.
Cosam was the son of Elmadam.
Elmadam was the son of Er.

29 Er was the son of Joshua.
Joshua was the son of Eliezer.
Eliezer was the son of Jorim.
Jorim was the son of Matthat.
Matthat was the son of Levi.

30 Levi was the son of Simeon.
Simeon was the son of Judah.
Judah was the son of Joseph.
Joseph was the son of Jonam.
Jonam was the son of Eliakim.

31 Eliakim was the son of Melea.
Melea was the son of Menna.
Menna was the son of Mattatha.
Mattatha was the son of Nathan.
Nathan was the son of David.

32 David was the son of Jesse.
Jesse was the son of Obed.
Obed was the son of Boaz.
Boaz was the son of Salmon.
Salmon was the son of Nahshon.

33 Nahshon was the son of Amminadab.
Amminadab was the son of Admin.
Admin was the son of Arni.
Arni was the son of Hezron.
Hezron was the son of Perez.
Perez was the son of Judah.

34 Judah was the son of Jacob.
Jacob was the son of Isaac.
Isaac was the son of Abraham.
Abraham was the son of Terah.
Terah was the son of Nahor.

35 Nahor was the son of Serug.
Serug was the son of Reu.
Reu was the son of Peleg.
Peleg was the son of Eber.
Eber was the son of Shelah.

36 Shelah was the son of Cainan.
Cainan was the son of Arphaxad.
Arphaxad was the son of Shem.
Shem was the son of Noah.
Noah was the son of Lamech.

37 Lamech was the son of Methuselah.
Methuselah was the son of Enoch.
Enoch was the son of Jared.

Jared was the son of Mahalalel.
Mahalalel was the son of Kenan.
³⁸Kenan was the son of Enosh.
Enosh was the son of Seth.
Seth was the son of Adam.
Adam was the son of God.

OLD TESTAMENT READING

A new branch will grow
    from a stump of a tree;
so a new king will come
    from the family of Jesse.
²The Spirit of the LORD will rest upon that king.
    The Spirit will give him wisdom and
        understanding, guidance and power.

The Spirit will teach him to know and
    respect the LORD.
³This king will be glad to obey the LORD.
    He will not judge by the way things look
        or decide by what he hears.
⁴But he will judge the poor honestly;
    he will be fair in his decisions for the poor
        people of the land.
At his command evil people will be punished,
    and by his words the wicked will be put to
        death.
⁵Goodness and fairness will give him
    strength,
    like a belt around his waist.

Isaiah 11:1–5

INSIGHTS

In coming to the kingdom-phase of Satan's antagonism, we believe that he was aware of Jacob's prophetic utterance in Genesis 49:10.

With the abandonment of Saul, the throne of Israel is transferred from Benjamin to Judah (1 Sam. 16). David, a man after God's own heart, is chosen and anointed king (1 Sam. 16:13; 2 Sam. 2:4; 5:2). And with such a change, there commences the desperate and determined attack of Satan upon "the seed royal," that is, the house of Judah, from which the Messiah must spring. . . .

Saul, the God-forsaken, Satan-possessed monarch (1 Sam. 16:14), tried his utmost to destroy the Lord's anointed one, and thus David is obliged to flee as a fugitive, hiding in caves and holes from his father-in-law. . . .

In the union of Jehoram and Athaliah, the daughter of Ahab, king of Israel, Satan continues his assault upon the house of Judah. . . .

At this critical moment, God's word appears to be at stake. Those of the royal seed are becoming fewer and fewer. In fact, the light was almost quenched, for Athaliah "arose and destroyed all the seed royal of the house of Judah" (2 Chron. 22:10). What followed?

Carefully he is hid and cared for while Athaliah reigns on in blissful ignorance until the day dawns when Joash is presented and crowned as king over Judah and Athaliah is slain (2 Kings 11:4–16; 2 Chron. 23:11, 15). Thus God, in a marvelous way, defeated the evil tactics of the devil, thereby fulfilling the promise of giving a light forever (2 Chron. 21:7).

HERBERT LOCKYER

PAUSE FOR REFLECTION

Although family history may not be very important to you, a king must be able to prove his royal heritage. What do these prophetic and genealogical verses tell you about the nature of Jesus' kingship?

LUKE 4:1-30

Jesus Is Tempted by the Devil

4 Jesus, filled with the Holy Spirit, returned from the Jordan River. The Spirit led Jesus into the desert ²where the devil tempted Jesus for forty days. Jesus ate nothing during that time, and when those days were ended, he was very hungry.

³The devil said to Jesus, "If you are the Son of God, tell this rock to become bread."

⁴Jesus answered, "It is written in the Scriptures: 'A person does not live on bread alone.'"

⁵Then the devil took Jesus and showed him all the kingdoms of the world in an instant. ⁶The devil said to Jesus, "I will give you all these kingdoms and all their power and glory. It has all been given to me, and I can give it to anyone I wish. ⁷If you worship me, then it will all be yours."

⁸Jesus answered, "It is written in the Scriptures: 'You must worship the Lord your God and serve only him.'"

⁹Then the devil led Jesus to Jerusalem and put him on a high place of the Temple. He said to Jesus, "If you are the Son of God, jump down. ¹⁰It is written in the Scriptures:

'He has put his angels in charge of you
   to watch over you.'   *Psalm 91:11*
¹¹It is also written:
'They will catch you in their hands
   so that you will not hit your foot on a
      rock.'"   *Psalm 91:12*

¹²Jesus answered, "But it also says in the Scriptures: 'Do not test the Lord your God.'"

¹³After the devil had tempted Jesus in every way, he left him to wait until a better time.

Jesus Teaches the People

¹⁴Jesus returned to Galilee in the power of the Holy Spirit, and stories about him spread all through the area. ¹⁵He began to teach in their synagogues, and everyone praised him.

¹⁶Jesus traveled to Nazareth, where he had grown up. On the Sabbath day he went to the synagogue, as he always did, and stood up to read. ¹⁷The book of Isaiah the prophet was given to him. He opened the book and found the place where this is written:

¹⁸"The Lord has put his Spirit in me,
   because he appointed me to tell the Good
      News to the poor.
He has sent me to tell the captives they are free
   and to tell the blind that they can see
      again.   *Isaiah 61:1*
God sent me to free those who have been
      treated unfairly   *Isaiah 58:6*
¹⁹ and to announce the time when the Lord
      will show his kindness."   *Isaiah 61:2*

²⁰Jesus closed the book, gave it back to the assistant, and sat down. Everyone in the synagogue was watching Jesus closely. ²¹He began to say to them, "While you heard these words just now, they were coming true!"

²²All the people spoke well of Jesus and were amazed at the words of grace he spoke. They asked, "Isn't this Joseph's son?"

²³Jesus said to them, "I know that you will tell me the old saying: 'Doctor, heal yourself.' You want to say, 'We heard about the things you did in Capernaum. Do those things here in your own town!'" ²⁴Then Jesus said, "I tell you the truth, a

prophet is not accepted in his hometown. **25**But I tell you the truth, there were many widows in Israel during the time of Elijah. It did not rain in Israel for three and one-half years, and there was no food anywhere in the whole country. **26**But Elijah was sent to none of those widows, only to a widow in Zarephath, a town in Sidon. **27**And there were many with skin diseases living in Israel during the time of the prophet Elisha. But none of them were healed, only Naaman, who was from the country of Syria."

28When all the people in the synagogue heard these things, they became very angry. **29**They got up, forced Jesus out of town, and took him to the edge of the cliff on which the town was built. They planned to throw him off the edge, **30**but Jesus walked through the crowd and went on his way.

OLD TESTAMENT READING

The Lord GOD has put his Spirit in me,
  because the LORD has appointed me to tell
    the good news to the poor.
  He has sent me to comfort those whose
    hearts are broken,
  to tell the captives they are free,
    and to tell the prisoners they are released.
2He has sent me to announce the time
    when the LORD will show his
    kindness
  and the time when our God will punish
    evil people.
  He has sent me to comfort all those
    who are sad
3   and to help the sorrowing people of
    Jerusalem.

Isaiah 61:1–3a

INSIGHTS

Jesus' words in the synagogue at Nazareth, spoken near the beginning of his public ministry, throb with hope for the poor. . . . Jesus informed his audience that this Scripture was now fulfilled in himself. The mission of the Incarnate One was to free the oppressed. . . .

Jesus' actual ministry corresponded precisely to the words of Luke 4. He spent most of his time not among the rich and powerful in Jerusalem, but among the poor in the cultural and economic backwater of Galilee. He healed the sick and blind. He fed the hungry. And he warned his followers in the strongest possible words that those who do not feed the hungry, clothe the naked, and visit the prisoners will experience eternal damnation (Matt. 25:31–46).

At the supreme moment of history when God took on human flesh, the God of Israel was still liberating the poor and oppressed and summoning his people to do the same.

RONALD SIDER

PAUSE FOR REFLECTION

Why do you think Jesus so clearly proclaimed who he was in the synagogue at Nazareth? Why do you think he identified himself with these particular portions of Isaiah?

LUKE 4:31–5:11

Jesus Forces Out an Evil Spirit

31Jesus went to Capernaum, a city in Galilee, and on the Sabbath day, he taught the people. **32**They were amazed at his teaching, because he spoke with authority. **33**In the synagogue a man who had within him an evil spirit shouted in a loud voice, **34**"Jesus of Nazareth! What do you want with us? Did you come to destroy us? I know who you are—God's Holy One!"

35Jesus commanded the evil spirit, "Be quiet! Come out of the man!" The evil spirit threw the man down to the ground before all the people and then left the man without hurting him.

36The people were amazed and said to each other, "What does this mean? With authority and power he commands evil spirits, and they come out." **37**And so the news about Jesus spread to every place in the whole area.

Jesus Heals Many People

38Jesus left the synagogue and went to the home of Simon. Simon's mother-in-law was sick with a high fever, and they asked Jesus to help her. **39**He came to her side and commanded the fever to leave. It left her, and immediately she got up and began serving them.

40When the sun went down, the people brought those who were sick to Jesus. Putting his hands on each sick person, he healed every one of them. **41**Demons came out of many people, shouting, "You are the Son of God." But Jesus commanded the demons and would not allow them to speak, because they knew Jesus was the Christ.

42At daybreak, Jesus went to a lonely place, but the people looked for him. When they found him, they tried to keep him from leaving. **43**But Jesus said to them, "I must preach about God's kingdom to other towns, too. This is why I was sent."

44Then he kept on preaching in the synagogues of Judea.

Jesus' First Followers

5 One day while Jesus was standing beside Lake Galilee, many people were pressing all around him to hear the word of God. **2**Jesus saw two boats at the shore of the lake. The fishermen had left them and were washing their nets. **3**Jesus got into one of the boats, the one that belonged to Simon, and asked him to push off a little from the land. Then Jesus sat down and continued to teach the people from the boat.

4When Jesus had finished speaking, he said to Simon, "Take the boat into deep water, and put your nets in the water to catch some fish."

5Simon answered, "Master, we worked hard all night trying to catch fish, and we caught nothing. But you say to put the nets in the water, so I will." **6**When the fishermen did as Jesus told them, they caught so many fish that the nets began to break. **7**They called to their partners in the other boat to come and help them. They came and filled both boats so full that they were almost sinking.

8When Simon Peter saw what had happened, he bowed down before Jesus and said, "Go away from me, Lord. I am a sinful man!" **9**He and the other fishermen were amazed at the many fish they caught, as were **10**James and John, the sons of Zebedee, Simon's partners.

Jesus said to Simon, "Don't be afraid. From now on you will fish for people." **11**When the men brought their boats to the shore, they left everything and followed Jesus.

OLD TESTAMENT READING

Elisha sent Naaman a messenger who said, "Go and wash in the Jordan River seven times. Then your skin will be healed, and you will be clean."

¹¹Naaman became angry and left.

¹³Naaman's servants came near and said to him, "My father, if the prophet had told you to do some great thing, wouldn't you have done it? Doesn't it make more sense just to do it? After all, he only told you, 'Wash, and you will be clean.'" ¹⁴So Naaman went down and dipped in the Jordan seven times, just as Elisha had said. Then his skin became new again, like the skin of a child. And he was clean.

2 Kings 5:10–11a, 13–14

INSIGHTS

"Trust and obey, for there's no other way
To be happy in Jesus, but to trust and obey."

All too often we glibly sing the words of this familiar Christian hymn without giving them much thought. These important words convey exactly what the Bible teaches. The secret of spiritual happiness and blessing is simply trusting and obeying the Lord. . . . The divine method for happiness and blessing is full trust in God and complete obedience to His Word. Lack of faith and partial obedience not only result in unhappiness and loss of blessing; they bring serious consequences in the life of the believer.

The Bible contains many passages that teach the trust-and-obey-for-happiness principle (see Psalm 119, for instance). In addition, many character studies from the Scriptures illustrate this same truth. Jacob is one such example. Jacob was a believer who had to learn over and over again throughout his life that halfway trust and obedience do not bring happiness and blessing. . . .

. . . God had stated in no uncertain terms His promises to Jacob, and yet Jacob had the audacity to hold back with an "if" type of faith and obedience. But let's not mock Jacob's faith and obedience before we examine our own. Can we say without reservation that we simply trust and obey, or must we confess that we selfishly bargain with God? . . .

. . . God does not expect us to question or change or compromise His commands; He expects us to simply trust Him and obey Him. That's the way to find spiritual blessing and happiness.

DAVID REID

PAUSE FOR REFLECTION

Did Naaman and Simon expect God to work the way he did? Do you think anything less than total obedience will accomplish God's work and blessing in your life?

LUKE 5:12-35

Jesus Heals a Sick Man

12When Jesus was in one of the towns, there was a man covered with a skin disease. When he saw Jesus, he bowed before him and begged him, "Lord, you can heal me if you will."

13Jesus reached out his hand and touched the man and said, "I will. Be healed!" Immediately the disease disappeared. **14**Then Jesus said, "Don't tell anyone about this, but go and show yourself to the priest and offer a gift for your healing, as Moses commanded. This will show the people what I have done."

15But the news about Jesus spread even more. Many people came to hear Jesus and to be healed of their sicknesses, **16**but Jesus often slipped away to be alone so he could pray.

Jesus Heals a Paralyzed Man

17One day as Jesus was teaching the people, the Pharisees and teachers of the law from every town in Galilee and Judea and from Jerusalem were there. The Lord was giving Jesus the power to heal people. **18**Just then, some men were carrying on a mat a man who was paralyzed. They tried to bring him in and put him down before Jesus. **19**But because there were so many people there, they could not find a way in. So they went up on the roof and lowered the man on his mat through the ceiling into the middle of the crowd right before Jesus. **20**Seeing their faith, Jesus said, "Friend, your sins are forgiven."

21The Jewish teachers of the law and the Pharisees thought to themselves, "Who is this man who is speaking as if he were God? Only God can forgive sins."

22But Jesus knew what they were thinking and said, "Why are you thinking these things? **23**Which is easier: to say, 'Your sins are forgiven,' or to say, 'Stand up and walk'? **24**But I will prove to you that the Son of Man has authority on earth to forgive sins." So Jesus said to the paralyzed man, "I tell you, stand up, take your mat, and go home."

25At once the man stood up before them, picked up his mat, and went home, praising God. **26**All the people were fully amazed and began to praise God. They were filled with much respect and said, "Today we have seen amazing things!"

Levi Follows Jesus

27After this, Jesus went out and saw a tax collector named Levi sitting in the tax collector's booth. Jesus said to him, "Follow me!" **28**So Levi got up, left everything, and followed him.

29Then Levi gave a big dinner for Jesus at his house. Many tax collectors and other people were eating there, too. **30**But the Pharisees and the men who taught the law for the Pharisees began to complain to Jesus' followers, "Why do you eat and drink with tax collectors and sinners?"

31Jesus answered them, "It is not the healthy people who need a doctor, but the sick. **32**I have not come to invite good people but sinners to change their hearts and lives."

Jesus Answers a Question

33They said to Jesus, "John's followers often fast for a certain time and pray, just as the Pharisees do. But your followers eat and drink all the time."

34Jesus said to them, "You cannot make the friends of the bridegroom fast while he is still with them. **35**But the time will come when the bridegroom will be taken away from them, and then they will fast."

OLD TESTAMENT READING

Lord, I call to you with all my heart.
Answer me, and I will keep your demands.
146I call to you.
Save me so I can obey your rules.

147I wake up early in the morning and cry out.
I hope in your word.
148I stay awake all night
so I can think about your promises.
149 Listen to me because of your love;
Lord, give me life by your laws.
150 Those who love evil are near,
but they are far from your teachings.
151 But, Lord, you are also near,
and all your commands are true.

Psalm 119:145–151

INSIGHTS

Jesus needed solitude simply because he was human—the only fully human person who has ever lived. He sought solitude. . . .

He went apart to cure his loneliness. He needed the silence of eternity as a thirsting man in the desert needs water. And he essentially needed the silence of eternity which was interpreted by love. For he who was love incarnate had his own needs to love and be loved. His deepest need, and likewise ours, could be met only by God. Ultimately no human being, no matter how close or dear, can fully satisfy our need for love. Those who imagine they can end up devouring one another.

Jesus longed for time apart to bask and sunbathe in his Father's love, to soak in it and repose in it. No matter how drained he felt, it seems that this deep, silent communion refreshed him more than a good night's sleep. . . .

. . . Human love and friendship indeed enrich our lives and partly meet this need—but not entirely, for at the core of our being [is] . . . a lovelonging for God which will only be met by converting our loneliness into deep solitude, by fleeing the sweets and cordials that may give temporary satisfaction, and finding the real thing in him.

MARGARET MAGDALEN

PAUSE FOR REFLECTION

It seems as if the psalmist thrived on his time with God, doesn't it? What is in your heart and on your lips when you slip away from life's demands to bask in the nearness of God's love? Isn't it about time you again slipped away to be refreshed by solitude with God?

LUKE 5:36 — 6:23

36 Jesus told them this story: "No one takes cloth off a new coat to cover a hole in an old coat. Otherwise, he ruins the new coat, and the cloth from the new coat will not be the same as the old cloth. **37** Also, no one ever pours new wine into old leather bags. Otherwise, the new wine will break the bags, the wine will spill out, and the leather bags will be ruined. **38** New wine must be put into new leather bags. **39** No one after drinking old wine wants new wine, because he says, 'The old wine is better.'"

Jesus Is Lord over the Sabbath

One Sabbath day Jesus was walking through some fields of grain. His followers picked the heads of grain, rubbed them in their hands, and ate them. **2** Some Pharisees said, "Why do you do what is not lawful on the Sabbath day?"

3 Jesus answered, "Have you not read what David did when he and those with him were hungry? **4** He went into God's house and took and ate the holy bread, which is lawful only for priests to eat. And he gave some to the people who were with him." **5** Then Jesus said to the Pharisees, "The Son of Man is Lord of the Sabbath day."

Jesus Heals a Man's Hand

6 On another Sabbath day Jesus went into the synagogue and was teaching, and a man with a crippled right hand was there. **7** The teachers of the law and the Pharisees were watching closely to see if Jesus would heal on the Sabbath day so they could accuse him. **8** But he knew what they were thinking, and he said to the man with the crippled hand, "Stand up here in the middle of everyone." The man got up and stood there. **9** Then Jesus said to them, "I ask you, which is lawful on the Sabbath day: to do good or to do evil, to save a life or to destroy it?" **10** Jesus looked around at all of them and said to the man, "Hold out your hand." The man held out his hand, and it was healed.

11 But the Pharisees and the teachers of the law were very angry and discussed with each other what they could do to Jesus.

Jesus Chooses His Apostles

12 At that time Jesus went off to a mountain to pray, and he spent the night praying to God. **13** The next morning, Jesus called his followers to him and chose twelve of them, whom he named apostles: **14** Simon (Jesus named him Peter), his brother Andrew, James, John, Philip, Bartholomew, **15** Matthew, Thomas, James son of Alphaeus, Simon (called the Zealot), **16** Judas son of James, and Judas Iscariot, who later turned Jesus over to his enemies.

Jesus Teaches and Heals

17 Jesus and the apostles came down from the mountain, and he stood on level ground. A large group of his followers was there, as well as many people from all around Judea, Jerusalem, and the seacoast cities of Tyre and Sidon. **18** They all came to hear Jesus teach and to be healed of their sicknesses, and he healed those who were troubled by evil spirits. **19** All the people were trying to touch Jesus, because power was coming from him and healing them all.

20Jesus looked at his followers and said,
"You people who are poor are blessed,
    because the kingdom of God belongs to
        you.
21You people who are now hungry are blessed,
    because you will be satisfied.
You people who are now crying are blessed,
    because you will laugh with joy.
22"People will hate you, shut you out, insult
you, and say you are evil because you follow the
Son of Man. But when they do, you will be blessed.
23Be full of joy at that time, because you have a
great reward in heaven. Their ancestors did the
same things to the prophets.

OLD TESTAMENT READING

In a little while the wicked will be no more.
    You may look for them, but they will be gone.
11People who are not proud will inherit the land
    and will enjoy complete peace.

12The wicked make evil plans against good
        people.
    They grind their teeth at them in anger.
13But the Lord laughs at the wicked,
    because he sees that their day is coming.

Psalm 37:10–13

INSIGHTS

The representations of the Bible with regard to the final doom of the wicked are exceedingly striking. Spiritual truths are revealed by natural objects: e.g., the gates and walls of the New Jerusalem, to present the splendours and glories of the heavenly state. A spiritual telescope is put into our hands; we are permitted to point it towards the glorious city "whose builder and Maker is God"; we may survey its inner sanctuary, where the worshipping hosts praise God without ceasing. We see their flowing robes of white—the palms of victory in their hands—the beaming joy of their faces—the manifestations of ineffable bliss in their souls. . . .

Then we have the other side. The veil is lifted, and you come to the very verge of hell to see what is there. Whereas on the one hand all was glorious, on the other all is fearful, and full of horrors.

There is a bottomless pit. A deathless soul is cast therein; it sinks and sinks and sinks, going down that awful pit which knows no bottom, weeping and wailing as it descends, and you hear its groans as they echo and re-echo from the sides of that dread cavern of woe!

CHARLES FINNEY

PAUSE FOR REFLECTION

Study the contrasting images of reward and suffering on earth and in heaven for both the wicked and God's people. What do these images reveal to you about God's love and compassion? Thank God that he sees all and cares for those who love him.

LUKE 6:24-45

24"But how terrible it will be for you who are
    rich,
    because you have had your easy life.
25 How terrible it will be for you who are full
    now,
    because you will be hungry.
How terrible it will be for you who are
    laughing now,
    because you will be sad and cry.

26"How terrible when everyone says only good
things about you, because their ancestors said the
same things about the false prophets.

Love Your Enemies

27"But I say to you who are listening, love your
enemies. Do good to those who hate you, 28bless
those who curse you, pray for those who are cruel
to you. 29If anyone slaps you on one cheek, offer
him the other cheek, too. If someone takes your
coat, do not stop him from taking your shirt.
30Give to everyone who asks you, and when
someone takes something that is yours, don't ask
for it back. 31Do to others what you would want
them to do to you. 32If you love only the people
who love you, what praise should you get? Even
sinners love the people who love them. 33If you do
good only to those who do good to you, what
praise should you get? Even sinners do that! 34If
you lend things to people, always hoping to get
something back, what praise should you get? Even
sinners lend to other sinners so that they can get
back the same amount! 35But love your enemies,
do good to them, and lend to them without hoping to get anything back. Then you will have a
great reward, and you will be children of the Most
High God, because he is kind even to people who
are ungrateful and full of sin. 36Show mercy, just
as your Father shows mercy.

Look at Yourselves

37"Don't judge others, and you will not be
judged. Don't accuse others of being guilty, and
you will not be accused of being guilty. Forgive,
and you will be forgiven. 38Give, and you will receive. You will be given much. Pressed down,
shaken together, and running over, it will spill into
your lap. The way you give to others is the way
God will give to you."

39Jesus told them this story: "Can a blind person lead another blind person? No! Both of them
will fall into a ditch. 40A student is not better than
the teacher, but the student who has been fully
trained will be like the teacher.

41"Why do you notice the little piece of dust in
your friend's eye, but you don't notice the big piece
of wood in your own eye? 42How can you say to
your friend, 'Friend, let me take that little piece of
dust out of your eye' when you cannot see that big
piece of wood in your own eye! You hypocrite! First,
take the wood out of your own eye. Then you will
see clearly to take the dust out of your friend's eye.

Two Kinds of Fruit

43"A good tree does not produce bad fruit, nor
does a bad tree produce good fruit. 44Each tree is
known by its own fruit. People don't gather figs
from thornbushes, and they don't get grapes from
bushes. 45Good people bring good things out of
the good they stored in their hearts. But evil people bring evil things out of the evil they stored in

their hearts. People speak the things that are in their hearts."

OLD TESTAMENT READING

But this made Jonah very unhappy, and he became angry. [2]He prayed to the LORD, "When I was still in my own country this is what I said would happen, and that is why I quickly ran away to Tarshish. I knew that you are a God who is kind and shows mercy. You don't become angry quickly, and you have great love. I knew you would choose not to cause harm."

Jonah 4:1–2

INSIGHTS

Mercy is concern for people in need. It is ministry to the miserable. Offering help for those who hurt . . .

Those special servants of God who extend mercy to the miserable often do so with much encouragement because they identify with the sorrowing—they "get inside their skin." Rather than watching from a distance or keeping the needy safely at arm's length, they get in touch, involved, and offer assistance that alleviates some of the pain.

A large group of the collegians in our church in Fullerton, California, pile into our bus one weekend a month and travel together—not to a mountain resort or the beach for fun-n-games, but to a garbage dump in Tijuana, Mexico, where hundreds of poverty-stricken Mexican families live. Our young adults, under the encouraging leadership of Kenneth Kemp (one of our pastoral staff team members), bring apples and other foodstuff plus money they have collected to share with those in that miserable existence. . . .

What are they doing? They are showing mercy . . . a ministry to others that is born out of the womb of identification. . . .

And what do they get in return? What does Christ promise? ". . . they shall receive mercy." Those who remain detached, distant, and disinterested in others will receive like treatment. But God promises that those who reach out and demonstrate mercy will, in turn, receive it. . . .

That is exactly what Jesus, our Savior, did for us when He came to earth. By becoming human. He got right inside our skin, literally. That made it possible for Him to see life through our eyes, feel the sting of our pain, and identify with the anguish of human need. He understands.

CHARLES SWINDOLL

ACTION POINT

Who is our model for mercy? Are any of his instructions in mercy difficult for you to practice? Pray that God will continue to reveal his mercy to you and enable you to be merciful—to those who suffer as well as to those who hate you.

LUKE 6:46 – 7:23

Two Kinds of People

46"Why do you call me, 'Lord, Lord,' but do not do what I say? **47**I will show you what everyone is like who comes to me and hears my words and obeys. **48**That person is like a man building a house who dug deep and laid the foundation on rock. When the floods came, the water tried to wash the house away, but it could not shake it, because the house was built well. **49**But the one who hears my words and does not obey is like a man who built his house on the ground without a foundation. When the floods came, the house quickly fell and was completely destroyed."

Jesus Heals a Soldier's Servant

7 When Jesus finished saying all these things to the people, he went to Capernaum. **2**There was an army officer who had a servant who was very important to him. The servant was so sick he was nearly dead. **3**When the officer heard about Jesus, he sent some Jewish elders to him to ask Jesus to come and heal his servant. **4**The men went to Jesus and begged him, saying, "This officer is worthy of your help. **5**He loves our people, and he built us a synagogue."

6So Jesus went with the men. He was getting near the officer's house when the officer sent friends to say, "Lord, don't trouble yourself, because I am not worthy to have you come into my house. **7**That is why I did not come to you myself. But you only need to command it, and my servant will be healed. **8**I, too, am a man under the authority of others, and I have soldiers under my command. I tell one soldier, 'Go,' and he goes. I tell another soldier, 'Come,' and he comes. I say to my servant, 'Do this,' and my servant does it."

9When Jesus heard this, he was amazed. Turning to the crowd that was following him, he said, "I tell you, this is the greatest faith I have found anywhere, even in Israel."

10Those who had been sent to Jesus went back to the house where they found the servant in good health.

Jesus Brings a Man Back to Life

11Soon afterwards Jesus went to a town called Nain, and his followers and a large crowd traveled with him. **12**When he came near the town gate, he saw a funeral. A mother, who was a widow, had lost her only son. A large crowd from the town was with the mother while her son was being carried out. **13**When the Lord saw her, he felt very sorry for her and said, "Don't cry." **14**He went up and touched the coffin, and the people who were carrying it stopped. Jesus said, "Young man, I tell you, get up!" **15**And the son sat up and began to talk. Then Jesus gave him back to his mother.

16All the people were amazed and began praising God, saying, "A great prophet has come to us! God has come to help his people."

17This news about Jesus spread through all Judea and into all the places around there.

John Asks a Question

18John's followers told him about all these things. He called for two of his followers **19**and sent them to the Lord to ask, "Are you the One who is to come, or should we wait for someone else?"

20When the men came to Jesus, they said, "John the Baptist sent us to you with this question: 'Are you the One who is to come, or should we wait for someone else?'"

21At that time, Jesus healed many people of their sicknesses, diseases, and evil spirits, and he gave sight to many blind people. 22Then Jesus answered John's followers, "Go tell John what you saw and heard here. The blind can see, the crippled can walk, and people with skin diseases are healed. The deaf can hear, the dead are raised to life, and the Good News is preached to the poor. 23Those who do not stumble in their faith because of me are blessed!"

OLD TESTAMENT READING

The LORD lives!
  May my Rock be praised.
  Praise the God who saves me!

Psalm 18:46

INSIGHTS

Suppose it were possible for a man never to have seen any season but summer. Then suppose that this man was called upon to advise in the erection of a building. You can imagine his procedure; everything is to be light, because he never heard a high wind. Waterpipes may be exposed, for he never felt the severity of frost. The most flimsy roof will be sufficient, for he knows nothing of the great rains of winter and spring.

Tell such a man that the winds will become stormy, that the rivers will be chilled into ice, that his windows will be blinded with snow, and that floods will beat upon his roof. If he is a wise man, he will say, "I must not build for one season, but for all seasons. I must not build for fine days, but for days that will be tempestuous. I must, as far as possible, prepare for the most inclement and trying weather." That is simple common sense.

Why be less sensible in building a character than in building a house? We build our bricks for severity as well as for sunshine, so why build our character with less care? If in summer we think about the frost, why not in prosperity have some thought for adversity? If in July we prepare for December, why not in the flattering hour of exultation think of the judgment that is at once infallible and irresistible?

As he would be infinitely foolish who would build his house without thinking of the natural forces that will try its strength, so is he cursed with insanity who builds his character without thinking of the fire with which God will try every man's work.

JOSEPH PARKER

ACTION POINT

On what are you building your life? Will your house stand firm against any storm? Write your own psalm that reminds you both of God's steadfast protection and your need to follow his ways.

LUKE 7:24-50

24When John's followers left, Jesus began talking to the people about John: "What did you go out into the desert to see? A reed blown by the wind? **25**What did you go out to see? A man dressed in fine clothes? No, people who have fine clothes and much wealth live in kings' palaces. **26**But what did you go out to see? A prophet? Yes, and I tell you, John is more than a prophet. **27**This was written about him:

'I will send my messenger ahead of you,
who will prepare the way for you.'

Malachi 3:1

28I tell you, John is greater than any other person ever born, but even the least important person in the kingdom of God is greater than John."

29(When the people, including the tax collectors, heard this, they all agreed that God's teaching was good, because they had been baptized by John. **30**But the Pharisees and experts on the law refused to accept God's plan for themselves; they did not let John baptize them.)

31Then Jesus said, "What shall I say about the people of this time? What are they like? **32**They are like children sitting in the marketplace, calling to one another and saying,

'We played music for you, but you did not dance;

we sang a sad song, but you did not cry.'

33John the Baptist came and did not eat bread or drink wine, and you say, 'He has a demon in him.' **34**The Son of Man came eating and drinking, and you say, 'Look at him! He eats too much and drinks too much wine, and he is a friend of tax collectors and sinners!' **35**But wisdom is proved to be right by what it does."

A Woman Washes Jesus' Feet

36One of the Pharisees asked Jesus to eat with him, so Jesus went into the Pharisee's house and sat at the table. **37**A sinful woman in the town learned that Jesus was eating at the Pharisee's house. So she brought an alabaster jar of perfume **38**and stood behind Jesus at his feet, crying. She began to wash his feet with her tears, and she dried them with her hair, kissing them many times and rubbing them with the perfume. **39**When the Pharisee who asked Jesus to come to his house saw this, he thought to himself, "If Jesus were a prophet, he would know that the woman touching him is a sinner!"

40Jesus said to the Pharisee, "Simon, I have something to say to you."

Simon said, "Teacher, tell me."

41Jesus said, "Two people owed money to the same banker. One owed five hundred coins and the other owed fifty. **42**They had no money to pay what they owed, but the banker told both of them they did not have to pay him. Which person will love the banker more?"

43Simon, the Pharisee, answered, "I think it would be the one who owed him the most money."

Jesus said to Simon, "You are right." **44**Then Jesus turned toward the woman and said to Simon, "Do you see this woman? When I came into your house, you gave me no water for my feet, but she washed my feet with her tears and dried them with her hair. **45**You gave me no kiss of greeting, but she has been kissing my feet since I came in. **46**You did not put oil on my head, but she poured perfume on my feet. **47**I tell you that her many sins are forgiven, so she showed great love. But the person who is forgiven only a little will love only a little."

48Then Jesus said to her, "Your sins are forgiven."

49The people sitting at the table began to say among themselves, "Who is this who even forgives sins?"

50Jesus said to the woman, "Because you believed, you are saved from your sins. Go in peace."

OLD TESTAMENT READING

You say, 'My teachings are right,
and I am clean in God's sight.'
5I wish God would speak
and open his lips against you
6and tell you the secrets of wisdom,
because wisdom has two sides.
Know this: God has even forgotten some of
your sin.

Job 11:4–6

INSIGHTS

Before I can become wise, I must first realize that I am foolish. Before I can receive power, I must first confess that I am powerless. I must lament my sins before I can rejoice in a Savior. Mourning, in God's sequence, always comes before exultation. Blessed are those who mourn their unworthiness, their helplessness, and their inadequacy.

Isaiah, the mighty prophet of God, knew by experience that one must bow the knee in mourning before one can lift the voice in jubilation. When his sin appeared ugly and venomous in the bright light of God's holiness, he said: "Woe is me! for I am undone; because I am a man of unclean lips: for mine eyes have seen the King, the LORD of hosts" (Isaiah 6:5).

We cannot be satisfied with our goodness after beholding the holiness of God. But our mourning over our unworthiness and sinfulness should be of short duration, for God has said: "I, even I, am he that blotteth out thy transgressions for mine own sake, and will not remember thy sins" (Isaiah 43:25).

Isaiah had to experience the mourning inadequacy before he could realize the joy of forgiveness. . . .

In God's economy, a person must go down into the valley of grief before he or she can scale the heights of spiritual glory. One must become tired and weary of living without Christ before he or she can seek and find His fellowship. One must come to the end of "self" before one can really begin to live.

BILLY GRAHAM

ACTION POINT

Are you, like the Pharisees, ever tempted to brush your sins off as being of little consequence? Pray that you will truly mourn the burden of your sin and love God deeply because of his great forgiveness.

LUKE 8:1-21

The Group with Jesus

 After this, while Jesus was traveling through some cities and small towns, he preached and told the Good News about God's kingdom. The twelve apostles were with him, **2**and also some women who had been healed of sicknesses and evil spirits: Mary, called Magdalene, from whom seven demons had gone out; **3**Joanna, the wife of Cuza (the manager of Herod's house); Susanna; and many others. These women used their own money to help Jesus and his apostles.

A Story About Planting Seed

4When a great crowd was gathered, and people were coming to Jesus from every town, he told them this story:

5"A farmer went out to plant his seed. While he was planting, some seed fell by the road. People walked on the seed, and the birds ate it up. **6**Some seed fell on rock, and when it began to grow, it died because it had no water. **7**Some seed fell among thorny weeds, but the weeds grew up with it and choked the good plants. **8**And some seed fell on good ground and grew and made a hundred times more."

As Jesus finished the story, he called out, "Let those with ears use them and listen!"

9Jesus' followers asked him what this story meant.

10Jesus said, "You have been chosen to know the secrets about the kingdom of God. But I use stories to speak to other people so that:

'They will look, but they may not see.

They will listen, but they may not understand.'   *Isaiah 6:9*

11"This is what the story means: The seed is God's message. **12**The seed that fell beside the road is like the people who hear God's teaching, but the devil comes and takes it away from them so they cannot believe it and be saved. **13**The seed that fell on rock is like those who hear God's teaching and accept it gladly, but they don't allow the teaching to go deep into their lives. They believe for a while, but when trouble comes, they give up. **14**The seed that fell among the thorny weeds is like those who hear God's teaching, but they let the worries, riches, and pleasures of this life keep them from growing and producing good fruit. **15**And the seed that fell on the good ground is like those who hear God's teaching with good, honest hearts and obey it and patiently produce good fruit.

Use What You Have

16"No one after lighting a lamp covers it with a bowl or hides it under a bed. Instead, the person puts it on a lampstand so those who come in will see the light. **17**Everything that is hidden will become clear, and every secret thing will be made known. **18**So be careful how you listen. Those who have understanding will be given more. But those who do not have understanding, even what they think they have will be taken away from them."

Jesus' True Family

19Jesus' mother and brothers came to see him, but there was such a crowd they could not get to him. **20**Someone said to Jesus, "Your mother and your brothers are standing outside, wanting to see you."

21Jesus answered them, "My mother and my

brothers are those who listen to God's teaching and obey it!"

OLD TESTAMENT READING

My people, listen to my teaching;
listen to what I say.
²I will speak using stories;
I will tell secret things from long ago.

³We have heard them and known them
by what our ancestors have told us.
⁴We will not keep them from our children;
we will tell those who come later
about the praises of the LORD.
We will tell about his power
and the miracles he has done.

Psalm 78:1–4

INSIGHTS

Not all of Christ's parables are explained. In fact, most are not. But this one is....

The first type of soil represents the hard heart.... What is it that makes the human heart hard? Sin hardens the heart, and the heart that is hardened sins even more.

... That type of person is described in the first chapter of Romans. He or she begins by suppressing the truth about God that may be known from nature (vv. 18–20), plunges inevitably into spiritual ignorance and moral degradation (vv. 21–31), and eventually comes not only to practice the sins of the heathen but to approve them as well (v. 32). Here we see both halves of the circle; sin leads to a rejection of God and God's truth, and the rejection of God's truth leads to even greater sin. What is it that leads such a person to reject the truth of God in the first place? According to Paul, it is a determined opposition to the nature of God Himself which the apostle describes as human "godlessness and wickedness" (Rom. 1:18).

So rather than repent of sin and turn for mercy to a God who is altogether sovereign, holy, knowing, and unchangeable, men and women suppress what knowledge they have and refuse to seek out that additional knowledge that could be the salvation of their souls....

... When Jesus came preaching the kingdom of God, He came preaching God's right to rule over the minds and hearts of all people. But that is precisely what the people involved did not want....

So it is also today. That is probably the greatest reason for the rejection of the gospel of God's grace in Jesus Christ.

JAMES BOICE

APPLICATION

Why do you think Jesus twice warns his hearers to listen to his teaching carefully? What message do you think Jesus wants you to hear? What difference do his words make in your heart and life?

LUKE 8:22-48

Jesus Calms a Storm

22One day Jesus and his followers got into a boat, and he said to them, "Let's go across the lake." And so they started across. **23**While they were sailing, Jesus fell asleep. A very strong wind blew up on the lake, causing the boat to fill with water, and they were in danger.

24The followers went to Jesus and woke him, saying, "Master! Master! We will drown!"

Jesus got up and gave a command to the wind and the waves. They stopped, and it became calm. **25**Jesus said to his followers, "Where is your faith?"

The followers were afraid and amazed and said to each other, "Who is this that commands even the wind and the water, and they obey him?"

A Man with Demons Inside Him

26Jesus and his followers sailed across the lake from Galilee to the area of the Gerasene people. **27**When Jesus got out on the land, a man from the town who had demons inside him came to Jesus. For a long time he had worn no clothes and had lived in the burial caves, not in a house. **28**When he saw Jesus, he cried out and fell down before him. He said with a loud voice, "What do you want with me, Jesus, Son of the Most High God? I beg you, don't torture me!" **29**He said this because Jesus was commanding the evil spirit to come out of the man. Many times it had taken hold of him. Though he had been kept under guard and chained hand and foot, he had broken his chains and had been forced by the demon out into a lonely place.

30Jesus asked him, "What is your name?"

He answered, "Legion," because many demons were in him. **31**The demons begged Jesus not to send them into eternal darkness. **32**A large herd of pigs was feeding on a hill, and the demons begged Jesus to allow them to go into the pigs. So Jesus allowed them to do this. **33**When the demons came out of the man, they went into the pigs, and the herd ran down the hill into the lake and was drowned.

34When the herdsmen saw what had happened, they ran away and told about this in the town and the countryside. **35**And people went to see what had happened. When they came to Jesus, they found the man sitting at Jesus' feet, clothed and in his right mind, because the demons were gone. But the people were frightened. **36**The people who saw this happen told the others how Jesus had made the man well. **37**All the people of the Gerasene country asked Jesus to leave, because they were all very afraid. So Jesus got into the boat and went back to Galilee.

38The man whom Jesus had healed begged to go with him, but Jesus sent him away, saying, **39**"Go back home and tell people how much God has done for you." So the man went all over town telling how much Jesus had done for him.

Jesus Gives Life to a Dead Girl and Heals a Sick Woman

40When Jesus got back to Galilee, a crowd welcomed him, because everyone was waiting for him. **41**A man named Jairus, a leader of the synagogue, came to Jesus and fell at his feet, begging him to come to his house. **42**Jairus' only daughter, about twelve years old, was dying.

While Jesus was on his way to Jairus' house, the people were crowding all around him. **43**A woman was in the crowd who had been bleeding for twelve years, but no one was able to heal her. **44**She came up behind Jesus and touched the edge of his coat, and instantly her bleeding stopped. **45**Then Jesus said, "Who touched me?"

When all the people said they had not touched him, Peter said, "Master, the people are all around you and are pushing against you."

46But Jesus said, "Someone did touch me, because I felt power go out from me." **47**When the woman saw she could not hide, she came forward, shaking, and fell down before Jesus. While all the people listened, she told why she had touched him and how she had been instantly healed. **48**Jesus said to her, "Dear woman, you are made well because you believed. Go in peace."

OLD TESTAMENT READING

The LORD defends those who suffer;
   he defends them in times of trouble.

Psalm 9:9

INSIGHTS

The image Jesus left with the world, the cross, . . . is proof that God cares about our suffering and pain. He died of it. . . .

. . . Jesus, who had said He could call down angels at any moment and rescue Himself from the horror, chose not to—because of us. For God so loved us, that He sent His only Son to die for us.

And thus the cross, an eternal stumbling block to some, became the cornerstone of our faith. . . .

By taking it on Himself, Jesus in a sense dignified pain. Of all the kinds of lives He could have lived, He chose a suffering one. . . . Even though Jesus died, His death became the great victory of history, pulling man and God together. God made a supreme good out of that awful day.

Jesus' followers are not insulated from the tragedies of this world, just as He was not. God has never promised that tornados will skip our houses on the way to our pagan neighbors'. Microbes do not flee from Christian bodies. Rather, Peter could say to suffering Christians, "This suffering is all part of the work God has given you. Christ, who suffered for you, is your example. Follow in his steps" (1 Peter 2:21 LB).

PHILIP YANCEY

PAUSE FOR REFLECTION

These verses show Jesus surrounded by suffering. How did he respond? How much does he care about your suffering? Thank him that he not only relieves our suffering, but took our greatest suffering upon himself on the cross.

LUKE 8:49 – 9:17

49 While Jesus was still speaking, someone came from the house of the synagogue leader and said to him, "Your daughter is dead. Don't bother the teacher anymore."

50 When Jesus heard this, he said to Jairus, "Don't be afraid. Just believe, and your daughter will be well."

51 When Jesus went to the house, he let only Peter, John, James, and the girl's father and mother go inside with him. **52** All the people were crying and feeling sad because the girl was dead, but Jesus said, "Stop crying. She is not dead, only asleep."

53 The people laughed at Jesus because they knew the girl was dead. **54** But Jesus took hold of her hand and called to her, "My child, stand up!" **55** Her spirit came back into her, and she stood up at once. Then Jesus ordered that she be given something to eat. **56** The girl's parents were amazed, but Jesus told them not to tell anyone what had happened.

Jesus Sends Out the Apostles

 Jesus called the twelve apostles together and gave them power and authority over all demons and the ability to heal sicknesses. **2** He sent the apostles out to tell about God's kingdom and to heal the sick. **3** He said to them, "Take nothing for your trip, neither a walking stick, bag, bread, money, or extra clothes. **4** When you enter a house, stay there until it is time to leave. **5** If people do not welcome you, shake the dust off of your feet as you leave the town, as a warning to them."

6 So the apostles went out and traveled through all the towns, preaching the Good News and healing people everywhere.

Herod Is Confused About Jesus

7 Herod, the governor, heard about all the things that were happening and was confused, because some people said, "John the Baptist has risen from the dead." **8** Others said, "Elijah has come to us." And still others said, "One of the prophets who lived long ago has risen from the dead." **9** Herod said, "I cut off John's head, so who is this man I hear such things about?" And Herod kept trying to see Jesus.

More than Five Thousand Fed

10 When the apostles returned, they told Jesus everything they had done. Then Jesus took them with him to a town called Bethsaida where they could be alone together. **11** But the people learned where Jesus went and followed him. He welcomed them and talked with them about God's kingdom and healed those who needed to be healed.

12 Late in the afternoon, the twelve apostles came to Jesus and said, "Send the people away. They need to go to the towns and countryside around here and find places to sleep and something to eat, because no one lives in this place."

13 But Jesus said to them, "You give them something to eat."

They said, "We have only five loaves of bread and two fish, unless we go buy food for all these people." **14** (There were about five thousand men there.)

Jesus said to his followers, "Tell the people to sit in groups of about fifty people."

15 So the followers did this, and all the people sat down. **16** Then Jesus took the five loaves of bread and two fish, and looking up to heaven, he thanked God for the food. Then he divided the food and gave it to the followers to give to the people. [17] They all ate and were satisfied, and what was left over was gathered up, filling twelve baskets.

OLD TESTAMENT READING

[B]ut ask the animals, and they will teach you,

or ask the birds of the air, and they will tell you.
[8] Speak to the earth, and it will teach you,
or let the fish of the sea tell you.
[9] Every one of these knows
that the hand of the LORD has done this.
[10] The life of every creature
and the breath of all people are in God's hand."

Job 12:7–10

INSIGHTS

No two days were ever exactly the same on my bit of beach. Part of its great appeal lay in the ever-changing appearance of its shoreline.

The subtle play of sunlight and shadow on the cliff faces altered their contours. Some mornings the rugged rocks seemed softened by the muted shades of the rising sun. They glowed warm, golden, wrapped in sunshine and serenity.

Other days the same rock buttresses stood gray and forbidding in the fog and mist that swirled in off the sea. The shoreline looked almost black, dark with dampness, soaked with sea spray.

Always, always, always the ocean is at work on the land. Summer and winter, spring and autumn the changing tides rise and ebb, shaping the character of the coast. Their force is utterly relentless—their power immeasurable—their titanic thrust untamed.

Great mysteries surround the majestic, awesome action of the tides. With incredible precision they move billions of tons of water from surface to surface upon the sea. They are the reflection of gigantic energy within the cosmos that knows no rest, that never slumbers, that never sleeps.

In the same overshadowing way, our Father watches over His children, quietly overseeing the events of their lives that they might accomplish His purposes for Him.

W. PHILLIP KELLER

ACTION POINT

What do these readings show that God controls? Is there anything more for him to control? What experience in your life or image from nature reminds you that God is in control? Think of it often, and praise God for his great sovereignty!

LUKE 9:18-43a

Jesus Is the Christ

18One time when Jesus was praying alone, his followers were with him, and he asked them, "Who do the people say I am?"

19They answered, "Some say you are John the Baptist. Others say you are Elijah. And others say you are one of the prophets from long ago who has come back to life."

20Then Jesus asked, "But who do you say I am?" Peter answered, "You are the Christ from God."

21Jesus warned them not to tell anyone, saying, **22**"The Son of Man must suffer many things. He will be rejected by the Jewish elders, the leading priests, and the teachers of the law. He will be killed and after three days will be raised from the dead."

23Jesus said to all of them, "If people want to follow me, they must give up the things they want. They must be willing to give up their lives daily to follow me. **24**Those who want to save their lives will give up true life. But those who give up their lives for me will have true life. **25**It is worthless to have the whole world if they themselves are destroyed or lost. **26**If people are ashamed of me and my teaching, then the Son of Man will be ashamed of them when he comes in his glory and with the glory of the Father and the holy angels. **27**I tell you the truth, some people standing here will see the kingdom of God before they die."

Jesus Talks with Moses and Elijah

28About eight days after Jesus said these things, he took Peter, John, and James and went up on a mountain to pray. **29**While Jesus was praying, the appearance of his face changed, and his clothes became shining white. **30**Then two men, Moses and Elijah, were talking with Jesus. **31**They appeared in heavenly glory, talking about his departure which he would soon bring about in Jerusalem. **32**Peter and the others were very sleepy, but when they awoke fully, they saw the glory of Jesus and the two men standing with him. **33**When Moses and Elijah were about to leave, Peter said to Jesus, "Master, it is good that we are here. Let us make three tents—one for you, one for Moses, and one for Elijah." (Peter did not know what he was talking about.)

34While he was saying these things, a cloud came and covered them, and they became afraid as the cloud covered them. **35**A voice came from the cloud, saying, "This is my Son, whom I have chosen. Listen to him!"

36When the voice finished speaking, only Jesus was there. Peter, John, and James said nothing and told no one at that time what they had seen.

Jesus Heals a Sick Boy

37The next day, when they came down from the mountain, a large crowd met Jesus. **38**A man in the crowd shouted to him, "Teacher, please come and look at my son, because he is my only child. **39**An evil spirit seizes my son, and suddenly he screams. It causes him to lose control of himself and foam at the mouth. The evil spirit keeps on hurting him and almost never leaves him. **40**I begged your followers to force the evil spirit out, but they could not do it."

41Jesus answered, "You people have no faith, and your lives are all wrong. How long must I stay with you and put up with you? Bring your son here."

42While the boy was coming, the demon threw him on the ground and made him lose control of himself. But Jesus gave a strong command to the evil spirit and healed the boy and gave him back to his father. **43**All the people were amazed at the great power of God.

OLD TESTAMENT READING

Y ou were patient with them for many years
and warned them by your Spirit through
the prophets,

but they did not pay attention.
So you handed them over to other
countries.
31But because your mercy is great, you did not
kill them all or leave them.
You are a kind and merciful God."

Nehemiah 9:30–31

INSIGHTS

In Judaism it was the custom for the pupil to select the rabbi of his choice and attach himself to him for instruction. Thus Paul sat "at the feet of Gamaliel" (Acts 22:3, KJV). But here it was Jesus and not the disciples who took the initiative. "When day came, He called His disciples to Him; and chose twelve of them" (Luke 6:13). . . . He called them personally and bound them to Him with bonds of affection that stood the test of time. Thus He chose to invest His life and channel it into that little group of men. . . .

. . . They were not theologians or political leaders—just ordinary men who became extraordinary under the molding hand of the Master Potter. That makes His selection of them the more wonderful. . . .

Their imperfections were painfully apparent, but those did not debar them from His fellowship and friendship. If God required perfection before He admitted us into the circle of His fellowship, who would qualify? Quirks of temperament did not disqualify them, or Peter with his volatile nature would not have been counted in. Nor would James and John with their selfish ambition and callous racism. Thomas's disbelief would have placed him outside the circle. But Jesus welcomed them all into the circle of His love and intimacy.

J. OSWALD SANDERS

PAUSE FOR REFLECTION

Chronicle your own spiritual journey in a way similar to Nehemiah's account of God's dealings with the children of Israel (9:19–31). In what ways has God stood beside you as a patient, wise, and ever-merciful teacher? Thank him for claiming you as his own.

LUKE 9:43b – 10:7

Jesus Talks About His Death

While everyone was wondering about all that Jesus did, he said to his followers, **44**"Don't forget what I tell you now: The Son of Man will be handed over to people." **45**But the followers did not understand what this meant; the meaning was hidden from them so they could not understand. But they were afraid to ask Jesus about it.

Who Is the Greatest?

46Jesus' followers began to have an argument about which one of them was the greatest. **47**Jesus knew what they were thinking, so he took a little child and stood the child beside him. **48**Then Jesus said, "Whoever accepts this little child in my name accepts me. And whoever accepts me accepts the One who sent me, because whoever is least among you all is really the greatest."

Anyone Not Against Us Is for Us

49John answered, "Master, we saw someone using your name to force demons out of people. We told him to stop, because he does not belong to our group."

50But Jesus said to him, "Don't stop him, because whoever is not against you is for you."

A Town Rejects Jesus

51When the time was coming near for Jesus to depart, he was determined to go to Jerusalem. **52**He sent some messengers ahead of him, who went into a town in Samaria to make everything ready for him. **53**But the people there would not welcome him, because he was set on going to Jerusalem.

54When James and John, followers of Jesus, saw this, they said, "Lord, do you want us to call fire down from heaven and destroy those people?"

55But Jesus turned and scolded them. [And Jesus said, "You don't know what kind of spirit you belong to. **56**The Son of Man did not come to destroy the souls of people but to save them."] Then they went to another town.

Following Jesus

57As they were going along the road, someone said to Jesus, "I will follow you any place you go."

58Jesus said to them, "The foxes have holes to live in, and the birds have nests, but the Son of Man has no place to rest his head."

59Jesus said to another man, "Follow me!"

But he said, "Lord, first let me go and bury my father."

60But Jesus said to him, "Let the people who are dead bury their own dead. You must go and tell about the kingdom of God."

61Another man said, "I will follow you, Lord, but first let me go and say good-bye to my family."

62Jesus said, "Anyone who begins to plow a field but keeps looking back is of no use in the kingdom of God."

Jesus Sends Out the Seventy-Two

10 After this, the Lord chose seventy-two others and sent them out in pairs ahead of him into every town and place where he planned to go. **2**He said to them, "There are a great many people to harvest, but there are only a few workers. So pray to God, who owns the harvest, that he will send more workers to help gather his harvest. **3**Go now, but listen! I am sending you out like sheep among wolves.

⁴Don't carry a purse, a bag, or sandals, and don't waste time talking with people on the road. ⁵Before you go into a house, say, 'Peace be with this house.' ⁶If peace-loving people live there, your blessing of peace will stay with them, but if not, then your blessing will come back to you. ⁷Stay in the same house, eating and drinking what the people there give you. A worker should be given his pay. Don't move from house to house."

INSIGHTS

When you begin to pray, your life can take on all kinds of perils and problems that you never had before. Think about it. As far as we know, Abraham was living a comfortable, trouble-free life until he began to pray. It was through prayer that he heard God's message to leave home, move out, hit the road for an unknown destination, and start a journey of indeterminate length. His life became exceedingly difficult and dangerous. . . .

Prayer was the launching pad for Moses as well. He was quietly tending sheep in the Midian hills, leading a settled life with his wife and sons and his father-in-law. Things changed when he started to pray. It started dramatically enough at a burning bush, where he heard God speak to him and entrust him with an impossible task— that of leading the Israelites out of Egypt. From one perspective, that was the last really comfortable day of Moses' life. . . .

Peter, James, John, and Andrew were comfortable, middle-class businessmen, settled and respected in their community, until their dialog with Jesus began. As they responded to his invitation to, "Follow me," all of that ended. They embarked on three years of intense ministry and then carried out the commission to "go and make disciples of all nations" (Matt. 28:19) in the face of unimaginable adversity and persecution. . . .

That is the peril of prayer. . . . As we begin to talk to God and hear him speak to us, life may never be the same.

BRUCE LARSON

OLD TESTAMENT READING

At that time Hanani the seer came to Asa king of Judah and said to him, "You depended on the king of Aram to help you and not on the LORD your God. So the king of Aram's army escaped from you. ⁸The Cushites and Libyans had a large and powerful army and many chariots and horsemen. But you depended on the LORD to help you, so he handed them over to you. ⁹The LORD searches all the earth for people who have given themselves completely to him. He wants to make them strong."

2 Chronicles 16:7–9b

APPLICATION

When Jesus walked on earth, he literally called his disciples to follow him. How does he call people when he isn't living on earth? Is God calling you, through your prayers, to break out into new territory, to follow him more faithfully?

LUKE 10:8-29

8"If you go into a town and the people welcome you, eat what they give you. 9Heal the sick who live there, and tell them, 'The kingdom of God is near you.' 10But if you go into a town, and the people don't welcome you, then go into the streets and say, 11'Even the dirt from your town that sticks to our feet we wipe off against you. But remember that the kingdom of God is near.' 12I tell you, on the Judgment Day it will be better for the people of Sodom than for the people of that town.

Jesus Warns Unbelievers

13"How terrible for you, Korazin! How terrible for you, Bethsaida! If the miracles I did in you had happened in Tyre and Sidon, those people would have changed their lives long ago. They would have worn rough cloth and put ashes on themselves to show they had changed. 14But on the Judgment Day it will be better for Tyre and Sidon than for you. 15And you, Capernaum, will you be lifted up to heaven? No! You will be thrown down to the depths!

16"Whoever listens to you listens to me, and whoever refuses to accept you refuses to accept me. And whoever refuses to accept me refuses to accept the One who sent me."

Satan Falls

17When the seventy-two came back, they were very happy and said, "Lord, even the demons obeyed us when we used your name!"

18Jesus said, "I saw Satan fall like lightning from heaven. 19Listen, I have given you power to walk on snakes and scorpions, power that is greater than the enemy has. So nothing will hurt you. 20But you should not be happy because the spirits obey you but because your names are written in heaven."

Jesus Prays to the Father

21Then Jesus rejoiced in the Holy Spirit and said, "I praise you, Father, Lord of heaven and earth, because you have hidden these things from the people who are wise and smart. But you have shown them to those who are like little children. Yes, Father, this is what you really wanted.

22"My Father has given me all things. No one knows who the Son is, except the Father. And no one knows who the Father is, except the Son and those whom the Son chooses to tell."

23Then Jesus turned to his followers and said privately, "You are blessed to see what you now see. 24I tell you, many prophets and kings wanted to see what you now see, but they did not, and they wanted to hear what you now hear, but they did not."

The Good Samaritan

25Then an expert on the law stood up to test Jesus, saying, "Teacher, what must I do to get life forever?"

26Jesus said, "What is written in the law? What do you read there?"

27The man answered, "Love the Lord your God with all your heart, all your soul, all your strength, and all your mind." Also, "Love your neighbor as you love yourself."

28Jesus said to him, "Your answer is right. Do this and you will live."

29But the man, wanting to show the importance of his question, said to Jesus, "And who is my neighbor?"

OLD TESTAMENT READING

God gave Solomon great wisdom so he could understand many things. His wisdom was as hard to measure as the grains of sand on the seashore. 30His wisdom was greater than any wisdom of the East, or any wisdom in Egypt. 31He was wiser than anyone on earth. He was even wiser than Ethan the Ezrahite, as well as Heman, Calcol, and Darda—the three sons of Mahol. King Solomon became famous in all the surrounding countries. 32During his life he spoke three thousand wise sayings and also wrote one thousand five songs. 33He taught about many kinds of plants—everything from the great cedar trees of Lebanon to the weeds that grow out of the walls. He also taught about animals, birds, crawling things, and fish. 34People from all nations came to listen to King Solomon's wisdom. The kings of all nations sent them to him, because they had heard of Solomon's wisdom.

1 Kings 4:29–34

INSIGHTS

Too many Christians do not believe Christ's promise that He would endue the Church with spiritual power; they doubt that His promise is to every believer. Consequently, they have no faith to lay hold of Christ's power. If His promise does not belong to all, how can they know to whom it does belong? Of course, with this limited understanding they cannot lay hold of the promise by faith.

Another lack in Christians is persistence in waiting upon God for that which He has promised to us in the Scriptures. People give up before they have prevailed, and hence, the enduement of spiritual power is not received.

Of great concern also is the extent to which the Church has practically lost sight of the necessity of the enduement of spiritual power. Much is said about our dependence upon the Holy Spirit by almost everybody, but how little is this dependence realized. Christians and even ministers go to work without any spiritual power. I mourn to be obliged to say that the ranks of the ministry seem to be filling up with those who do not possess spiritual power. May the Lord have mercy upon us! Will this last remark be thought uncharitable? If so, let the current state of the Church and her success in evangelism be heard on this subject. Surely, something is wrong.

CHARLES FINNEY

APPLICATION

What is the source of the believer's wisdom and power? What is the believer's true reason for happiness? Take a look at your life. In what do you find happiness? Is spiritual power evident in your life? Pray that God's spirit will be alive in you.

LUKE 10:30 – 11:13

30Jesus answered, "As a man was going down from Jerusalem to Jericho, some robbers attacked him. They tore off his clothes, beat him, and left him lying there, almost dead. **31**It happened that a priest was going down that road. When he saw the man, he walked by on the other side. **32**Next, a Levite came there, and after he went over and looked at the man, he walked by on the other side of the road. **33**Then a Samaritan traveling down the road came to where the hurt man was. When he saw the man, he felt very sorry for him. **34**The Samaritan went to him, poured olive oil and wine on his wounds, and bandaged them. Then he put the hurt man on his own donkey and took him to an inn where he cared for him. **35**The next day, the Samaritan brought out two coins, gave them to the innkeeper, and said, 'Take care of this man. If you spend more money on him, I will pay it back to you when I come again.'"

36Then Jesus said, "Which one of these three men do you think was a neighbor to the man who was attacked by the robbers?"

37The expert on the law answered, "The one who showed him mercy."

Jesus said to him, "Then go and do what he did."

Mary and Martha

38While Jesus and his followers were traveling, Jesus went into a town. A woman named Martha let Jesus stay at her house. **39**Martha had a sister named Mary, who was sitting at Jesus' feet and lis-tening to him teach. **40**But Martha was busy with all the work to be done. She went in and said, "Lord, don't you care that my sister has left me alone to do all the work? Tell her to help me."

41But the Lord answered her, "Martha, Martha, you are worried and upset about many things. **42**Only one thing is important. Mary has chosen the better thing, and it will never be taken away from her."

Jesus Teaches About Prayer

11 One time Jesus was praying in a certain place. When he finished, one of his fol-lowers said to him, "Lord, teach us to pray as John taught his followers."

2Jesus said to them, "When you pray, say:
'Father, may your name always be kept holy.
May your kingdom come.
3Give us the food we need for each day.
4Forgive us for our sins,
  because we forgive everyone who has done
    wrong to us.
And do not cause us to be tempted.'"

Continue to Ask

5Then Jesus said to them, "Suppose one of you went to your friend's house at midnight and said to him, 'Friend, loan me three loaves of bread. **6**A friend of mine has come into town to visit me, but I have nothing for him to eat.' **7**Your friend inside the house answers, 'Don't bother me! The door is already locked, and my children and I are in bed. I cannot get up and give you anything.' **8**I tell you, if friendship is not enough to make him get up to give you the bread, your boldness will make him get up and give you whatever you need. **9**So I tell you, ask, and God will give to you. Search, and you will find. Knock, and the door will open for you. **10**Yes, everyone who asks will receive. The one who searches will find. And everyone who knocks will have the door opened. **11**If your children ask for a fish, which of you would give them a snake instead? **12**Or, if your children ask for an egg, would you give them a scorpion? **13**Even though you are bad, you know how to give good things to your children. How much more your heavenly Father will give the Holy Spirit to those who ask him!"

OLD TESTAMENT READING

Whenever you are able,
   do good to people who need help.
28If you have what your neighbor asks for,
   don't say, "Come back later.
   I will give it to you tomorrow."

Proverbs 3:27–28

INSIGHTS

Kindness is a sincere desire for the happiness of others; goodness is the activity calculated to advance that happiness. . . .

. . . The New Testament has much to say about the kindness of God. The first mention is in Luke 6: Jesus says that God "is kind to the ungrateful and wicked." Next we find that God's kindness leads sinners toward repentance (Romans 2:4). In Ephesians 2:7, in the context of our utter lostness and sin, Paul speaks of the incomparable riches of God's grace, expressed in his kindness to us in Christ Jesus. . . .

What lesson can we draw from these accounts of the kindness of God? He is kind to all men—the ungrateful, the wicked, the utterly lost and hopeless, the rebellious—without distinction. . . .

Our natural inclination is to show kindness only to those for whom we have some natural affinity—family, friends, likable neighbors. But God shows kindness to those who are most despicable—the ungrateful and wicked. Have you ever tried to be kind to someone who was ungrateful? Unless God's grace was working in your heart in a significant way, your reaction to his ingratitude may well have been, "I'll never do anything for him again!" But God doesn't turn his back on the ungrateful. . . .

We need to develop a kind disposition, to be sensitive to others and truly desire their happiness. But sensitivity alone is not enough: the grace of goodness impels us to take action to meet those needs.

JERRY BRIDGES

ACTION POINT

Think about contemporary parallels to the story of the good Samaritan that show what it means for you to do good to anyone who needs help even when it is inconvenient or unpleasant. Diligently pray that you will seek ways to express God's kindness.

LUKE 11:14-36

Jesus' Power Is from God

14One time Jesus was sending out a demon who could not talk. When the demon came out, the man who had been unable to speak, then spoke. The people were amazed. **15**But some of them said, "Jesus uses the power of Beelzebul, the ruler of demons, to force demons out of people."

16Other people, wanting to test Jesus, asked him to give them a sign from heaven. **17**But knowing their thoughts, he said to them, "Every kingdom that is divided against itself will be destroyed. And a family that is divided against itself will not continue. **18**So if Satan is divided against himself, his kingdom will not continue. You say that I use the power of Beelzebul to force out demons. **19**But if I use the power of Beelzebul to force out demons, what power do your people use to force demons out? So they will be your judges. **20**But if I use the power of God to force out demons, then the kingdom of God has come to you.

21"When a strong person with many weapons guards his own house, his possessions are safe. **22**But when someone stronger comes and defeats him, the stronger one will take away the weapons the first man trusted and will give away the possessions.

23"Anyone who is not with me is against me, and anyone who does not work with me is working against me.

The Empty Person

24"When an evil spirit comes out of a person, it travels through dry places, looking for a place to rest. But when it finds no place, it says, 'I will go back to the house I left.' **25**And when it comes back, it finds that house swept clean and made neat. **26**Then the evil spirit goes out and brings seven other spirits more evil than it is, and they go in and live there. So the person has even more trouble than before."

People Who Are Truly Blessed

27As Jesus was saying these things, a woman in the crowd called out to Jesus, "Blessed is the mother who gave birth to you and nursed you."

28But Jesus said, "No, blessed are those who hear the teaching of God and obey it."

The People Want a Miracle

29As the crowd grew larger, Jesus said, "The people who live today are evil. They want to see a miracle for a sign, but no sign will be given them, except the sign of Jonah. **30**As Jonah was a sign for those people who lived in Nineveh, the Son of Man will be a sign for the people of this time. **31**On the Judgment Day the Queen of the South will stand up with the people who live now. She will show they are guilty, because she came from far away to listen to Solomon's wise teaching. And I tell you that someone greater than Solomon is here. **32**On the Judgment Day the people of Nineveh will stand up with the people who live now, and they will show that you are guilty. When Jonah preached to them, they were sorry and changed their lives. And I tell you that someone greater than Jonah is here.

Be a Light for the World

33"No one lights a lamp and puts it in a secret place or under a bowl, but on a lampstand so the people who come in can see. **34**Your eye is a light for the body. When your eyes are good, your whole body will be full of light. But when your eyes are evil, your whole body will be full of darkness. **35**So be careful not to let the light in you become darkness. **36**If your whole body is full of light, and none of it is dark, then you will shine bright, as when a lamp shines on you."

OLD TESTAMENT READING

Keep your eyes focused on what is right,
    and look straight ahead to what is good.
26Be careful what you do,
    and always do what is right.
27Don't turn off the road of goodness;
    keep away from evil paths.

Proverbs 4:25–27

INSIGHTS

The nature of the Christian life is Christ's life taking hold upon all the inner life of a man, changing, dominating, pulsating. It is seen therefore, and I do not think we can be too careful in emphasizing this, that Christian life is neither human imitation of Christ, nor correct intellectual positions concerning Christ. Neither is it a cult, or a system of thought. I may attempt to imitate Christ sincerely through long years, and yet never be a Christian. I may hold absolutely correct intellectual views concerning Christ as a person, and His power, and yet never be a Christian. It is possible for me to admire Him, and attempt with all the power of my life to imitate Him, and yet never realize Him. It is quite possible for a person to believe most sincerely in His Deity, and in the fact of His atoning work, and moreover, in the necessity for regeneration, and yet never be submitted to His Lordship, never to have personal share in the work of His atonement, never to be born again.

Nothing short of the coming into life of the individual of Christ Himself constitutes a Christian. If Jesus Christ is external to your life there will be times when the world will not see Him and hear Him, and will not know you belong to Him. But if Christ be in you, living, reigning there absolutely, and you are obeying Him, there never will be a moment when the truth will not be evident. You cannot hide Christ if once He comes within. If the light is there, it simply must shine.

G. CAMPBELL MORGAN

APPLICATION

What happens when a person focuses his or her eyes on the good things of God? Is your body filled with the light of Christ? What practical reminder will help you keep your eyes focused on God?

LUKE 11:37–12:7

Jesus Accuses the Pharisees

37After Jesus had finished speaking, a Pharisee asked Jesus to eat with him. So Jesus went in and sat at the table. **38**But the Pharisee was surprised when he saw that Jesus did not wash his hands before the meal. **39**The Lord said to him, "You Pharisees clean the outside of the cup and the dish, but inside you are full of greed and evil. **40**You foolish people! The same one who made what is outside also made what is inside. **41**So give what is in your dishes to the poor, and then you will be fully clean. **42**How terrible for you Pharisees! You give God one-tenth of even your mint, your rue, and every other plant in your garden. But you fail to be fair to others and to love God. These are the things you should do while continuing to do those other things. **43**How terrible for you Pharisees, because you love to have the most important seats in the synagogues, and you love to be greeted with respect in the marketplaces. **44**How terrible for you, because you are like hidden graves, which people walk on without knowing."

Jesus Talks to Experts on the Law

45One of the experts on the law said to Jesus, "Teacher, when you say these things, you are insulting us, too."

46Jesus answered, "How terrible for you, you experts on the law! You make strict rules that are very hard for people to obey, but you yourselves don't even try to follow those rules. **47**How terrible for you, because you build tombs for the prophets whom your ancestors killed! **48**And now you show that you approve of what your ancestors did. They killed the prophets, and you build tombs for them! **49**This is why in his wisdom God said, 'I will send prophets and apostles to them. They will kill some, and they will treat others cruelly.' **50**So you who live now will be punished for the deaths of all the prophets who were killed since the beginning of the world— **51**from the killing of Abel to the killing of Zechariah, who died between the altar and the Temple. Yes, I tell you that you who are alive now will be punished for them all.

52"How terrible for you, you experts on the law. You have taken away the key to learning about God. You yourselves would not learn, and you stopped others from learning, too."

53When Jesus left, the teachers of the law and the Pharisees began to give him trouble, asking him questions about many things, **54**trying to catch him saying something wrong.

Don't Be Like the Pharisees

12 So many thousands of people had gathered that they were stepping on each other. Jesus spoke first to his followers, saying, "Beware of the yeast of the Pharisees, because they are hypocrites. **2**Everything that is hidden will be shown, and everything that is secret will be made known. **3**What you have said in the dark will be heard in the light, and what you have whispered in an inner room will be shouted from the housetops.

4"I tell you, my friends, don't be afraid of people who can kill the body but after that can do nothing more to hurt you. **5**I will show you the one to fear. Fear the one who has the power to kill you and also to throw you into hell. Yes, this is the one you should fear.

[6]"Five sparrows are sold for only two pennies, and God does not forget any of them. [7]But God even knows how many hairs you have on your head. Don't be afraid. You are worth much more than many sparrows."

OLD TESTAMENT READING

The LORD says, "I am the one who comforts you.

So why should you be afraid of people, who die?
Why should you fear people who die like the grass?
[13]Have you forgotten the LORD who made you,
who stretched out the skies
and made the earth?

Isaiah 51:12–13a

INSIGHTS

Many of us have lost the fear of the Lord. We have forgotten our deep awe for the character of God, His holiness, His eternality, His sovereignty over all the affairs of men. We let Him get smaller. We let our impression of ourselves get bigger. We see ourselves as larger in intellect and capabilities, as more technologically advanced and more scientific. As we prosper, we don't need God as we once did.

What is the fear of the Lord? And how can we get it into our lives? The fear of the Lord is to love what God loves and to hate what God hates. The fear of the Lord is both positive and negative. . . .

The positive is to love what God loves—wisdom. God loves wisdom. The fear of the Lord is to love wisdom. "My son, if you accept my words and store up my commands within you, turning your ear to wisdom and applying your heart to understanding . . . then you will understand the fear of the Lord and find the knowledge of God. For the Lord gives wisdom" (Proverbs 2:1–2, 5–6). . . .

The negative is to hate what God hates—evil. God hates evil. "To fear the Lord is to hate evil" (Proverbs 8:13). "Through the fear of the Lord a man avoids evil" (Proverbs 16:6). "To shun evil is understanding" (Job 28:28). The person who would understand the fear of the Lord will hate what God hates. God hates evil, so he will hate evil. . . .

The person gripped by godly fear cannot tolerate evil because God does not tolerate evil. He hates evil with the intensity that God hates evil, or at least he tries to. He is a reformer, not a recluse. His hatred of evil sanctions him no occasion to tolerate.

PATRICK MORLEY

PAUSE FOR REFLECTION

What kind of fear of God did Jesus tell the Pharisees and teachers of the law they should have? In your own words, describe the two kinds of fear that those who trust the Lord should have.

LUKE 12:8-34

Don't Be Ashamed of Jesus

8"I tell you, all those who stand before others and say they believe in me, I, the Son of Man, will say before the angels of God that they belong to me. **9**But all who stand before others and say they do not believe in me, I will say before the angels of God that they do not belong to me.

10"Anyone who speaks against the Son of Man can be forgiven, but anyone who speaks against the Holy Spirit will not be forgiven.

11"When you are brought into the synagogues before the leaders and other powerful people, don't worry about how to defend yourself or what to say. **12**At that time the Holy Spirit will teach you what you must say."

Jesus Warns Against Selfishness

13Someone in the crowd said to Jesus, "Teacher, tell my brother to divide with me the property our father left us."

14But Jesus said to him, "Who said I should judge or decide between you?" **15**Then Jesus said to them, "Be careful and guard against all kinds of greed. Life is not measured by how much one owns."

16Then Jesus told this story: "There was a rich man who had some land, which grew a good crop. **17**He thought to himself, 'What will I do? I have no place to keep all my crops.' **18**Then he said, 'This is what I will do: I will tear down my barns and build bigger ones, and there I will store all my grain and other goods. **19**Then I can say to myself,

"I have enough good things stored to last for many years. Rest, eat, drink, and enjoy life!"'

20"But God said to him, 'Foolish man! Tonight your life will be taken from you. So who will get those things you have prepared for yourself?'

21"This is how it will be for those who store up things for themselves and are not rich toward God."

Don't Worry

22Jesus said to his followers, "So I tell you, don't worry about the food you need to live, or about the clothes you need for your body. **23**Life is more than food, and the body is more than clothes. **24**Look at the birds. They don't plant or harvest, they don't have storerooms or barns, but God feeds them. And you are worth much more than birds. **25**You cannot add any time to your life by worrying about it. **26**If you cannot do even the little things, then why worry about the big things? **27**Consider how the lilies grow; they don't work or make clothes for themselves. But I tell you that even Solomon with his riches was not dressed as beautifully as one of these flowers. **28**God clothes the grass in the field, which is alive today but tomorrow is thrown into the fire. So how much more will God clothe you? Don't have so little faith! **29**Don't always think about what you will eat or what you will drink, and don't keep worrying. **30**All the people in the world are trying to get these things, and your Father knows you need them. **31**But seek God's kingdom, and all your other needs will be met as well.

Don't Trust in Money

32"Don't fear, little flock, because your Father wants to give you the kingdom. **33**Sell your possessions and give to the poor. Get for yourselves purses that will not wear out, the treasure in heaven that never runs out, where thieves can't steal and moths can't destroy. **34** Your heart will be where your treasure is."

OLD TESTAMENT READING

Whoever loves money
will never have enough money;

Whoever loves wealth
will not be satisfied with it.
This is also useless.
11 The more wealth people have,
the more friends they have to help
spend it.
So what do people really gain?
They gain nothing except to look at their
riches.

Ecclesiastes 5:10–11

INSIGHTS

Constantly the Bible deals decisively with the inner spirit of slavery that an idolatrous attachment to wealth brings. "If riches increase, set not your heart on them," counsels the psalmist (Ps. 62:10). . . .

. . . Jesus . . . saw the grip that wealth can have on a person. He knew that "where your treasure is, there will your heart be also," which is precisely why he commanded his followers: "Do not lay up for yourselves treasures on earth" (Matt. 6:21, 19). He is not saying that the heart should or should not be where the treasure is. He is stating the plain fact that wherever you find the treasure, you will find the heart.

He exhorted the rich young ruler not just to have an inner attitude of detachment from his possessions, but literally to get rid of his possessions if he wanted the kingdom of God (Matt. 19:16–22). . . . He counseled people who came seeking God, "Sell your possessions, and give alms; provide yourselves with purses that do not grow old, with a treasure in the heavens that does not fail . . ." (Luke 12:33). He told the parable of the rich farmer whose life centered in hoarding—we would call him prudent; Jesus called him a fool (Luke 12:16–21). He states that if we really want the kingdom of God we must, like a merchant in search of fine pearls, be willing to sell everything we have to get it (Matt. 13:45, 46). He calls all who would follow him to a joyful life of carefree unconcern for possessions: "Give to every one who begs from you; and of him who takes away your goods do not ask them again" (Luke 6:30).

RICHARD FOSTER

PAUSE FOR REFLECTION

What things does God say are important in life? What causes people to be greedy? What necessities are we to trust God to provide? Why is it important for those who follow Christ to guard against greed?

LUKE 12:35-56

Always Be Ready

35"Be dressed, ready for service, and have your lamps shining. **36**Be like servants who are waiting for their master to come home from a wedding party. When he comes and knocks, the servants immediately open the door for him. **37**They will be blessed when their master comes home, because he sees that they were watching for him. I tell you the truth, the master will dress himself to serve and tell the servants to sit at the table, and he will serve them. **38**Those servants will be blessed when he comes in and finds them still waiting, even if it is midnight or later.

39"Remember this: If the owner of the house knew what time a thief was coming, he would not allow the thief to enter his house. **40**So you also must be ready, because the Son of Man will come at a time when you don't expect him!"

Who Is the Trusted Servant?

41Peter said, "Lord, did you tell this story to us or to all people?"

42The Lord said, "Who is the wise and trusted servant that the master trusts to give the other servants their food at the right time? **43**When the master comes and finds the servant doing his work, the servant will be blessed. **44**I tell you the truth, the master will choose that servant to take care of everything he owns. **45**But suppose the servant thinks to himself, 'My master will not come back soon,' and he begins to beat the other servants, men and women, and to eat and drink

and get drunk. **46**The master will come when that servant is not ready and is not expecting him. Then the master will cut him in pieces and send him away to be with the others who don't obey.

47"The servant who knows what his master wants but is not ready, or who does not do what the master wants, will be beaten with many blows! **48**But the servant who does not know what his master wants and does things that should be punished will be beaten with few blows. From everyone who has been given much, much will be demanded. And from the one trusted with much, much more will be expected.

Jesus Causes Division

49"I came to set fire to the world, and I wish it were already burning! **50**I have a baptism to suffer through, and I feel very troubled until it is over. **51**Do you think I came to give peace to the earth? No, I tell you, I came to divide it. **52**From now on, a family with five people will be divided, three against two, and two against three. **53**They will be divided: father against son and son against father, mother against daughter and daughter against mother, mother-in-law against daughter-in-law and daughter-in-law against mother-in-law."

Understanding the Times

54Then Jesus said to the people, "When you see clouds coming up in the west, you say, 'It's going to rain,' and it happens. **55**When you feel the wind begin to blow from the south, you say, 'It will be a hot day,' and it happens. **56**Hypocrites! You know how to understand the appearance of the earth and sky. Why don't you understand what is happening now?"

OLD TESTAMENT READING

The earth belongs to the LORD, and everything
   in it—
   the world and all its people.
²He built it on the waters
   and set it on the rivers.

³Who may go up on the mountain of the LORD?
   Who may stand in his holy Temple?
⁴Only those with clean hands and pure hearts,
who have not worshiped idols,
who have not made promises in the name
   of a false god.
⁵They will receive a blessing from the LORD;
   the God who saves them will declare them
   right.
⁶They try to follow God;
   they look to the God of Jacob for help.

Selah

Psalm 24:1–6

INSIGHTS

The last message the risen Christ gave his people was the promise of his soon return. Couple this with Paul's admonition to the Thessalonian Christians and you get a
good rule for life: Live both expectantly and patiently, and you will be fulfilling the
Lord's will until he returns.

What are some of the blessings awaiting the believer when Jesus Christ comes
back? First of all, the faithful ones can confidently expect to be rewarded for their
faithfulness. . . .

There is also a clear-cut promise of reward to the obedient Christian. . . .

But in addition to waiting expectantly, we are also admonished to wait patiently,
to "occupy 'til he comes." And while we are waiting, we are to be yielded to the
"love of God" operative in our lives. If the love of God flows through us, we will find
ourselves sharing that love with those around us, for God is love, and that love is bigger than its container, the Christian, so it must overflow. Those around us long for
love, for our world is full of hate, Satan's legacy since the Garden of Eden episode.
Let us as Christians share God's love as we await the return of his Son from heaven.

AL BRYANT

PAUSE FOR REFLECTION

What warnings does Jesus give to servants who are not ready for his return? What
does he promise to those who are ready? What must your life be like in order to
obey Jesus' words, "Be dressed, ready for service, and have your lamps shining"?

LUKE
12:57 — 13:21

Settle Your Problems

57"Why can't you decide for yourselves what is right? **58**If your enemy is taking you to court, try hard to settle it on the way. If you don't, your enemy might take you to the judge, and the judge might turn you over to the officer, and the officer might throw you into jail. **59**I tell you, you will not get out of there until you have paid everything you owe."

Change Your Hearts

13 At that time some people were there who told Jesus that Pilate had killed some people from Galilee while they were worshiping. He mixed their blood with the blood of the animals they were sacrificing to God. **2**Jesus answered, "Do you think this happened to them because they were more sinful than all others from Galilee? **3**No, I tell you. But unless you change your hearts and lives, you will be destroyed as they were! **4**What about those eighteen people who died when the tower of Siloam fell on them? Do you think they were more sinful than all the others who live in Jerusalem? **5**No, I tell you. But unless you change your hearts and lives, you will all be destroyed too!"

The Useless Tree

6Jesus told this story: "A man had a fig tree planted in his vineyard. He came looking for some fruit on the tree, but he found none. **7**So the man said to his gardener, 'I have been looking for fruit on this tree for three years, but I never find any.

Cut it down. Why should it waste the ground?' **8**But the servant answered, 'Master, let the tree have one more year to produce fruit. Let me dig up the dirt around it and put on some fertilizer. **9**If the tree produces fruit next year, good. But if not, you can cut it down.'"

Jesus Heals on the Sabbath

10Jesus was teaching in one of the synagogues on the Sabbath day. **11**A woman was there who, for eighteen years, had an evil spirit in her that made her crippled. Her back was always bent; she could not stand up straight. **12**When Jesus saw her, he called her over and said, "Woman, you are free from your sickness." **13**Jesus put his hands on her, and immediately she was able to stand up straight and began praising God.

14The synagogue leader was angry because Jesus healed on the Sabbath day. He said to the people, "There are six days when one has to work. So come to be healed on one of those days, and not on the Sabbath day."

15The Lord answered, "You hypocrites! Doesn't each of you untie your work animals and lead them to drink water every day—even on the Sabbath day? **16**This woman that I healed, a daughter of Abraham, has been held by Satan for eighteen years. Surely it is not wrong for her to be freed from her sickness on a Sabbath day!" **17**When Jesus said this, all of those who were criticizing him were ashamed, but the entire crowd rejoiced at all the wonderful things Jesus was doing.

Stories of Mustard Seed and Yeast

18Then Jesus said, "What is God's kingdom like? What can I compare it with? **19**It is like a mustard seed that a man plants in his garden. The seed grows and becomes a tree, and the wild birds build nests in its branches."

20Jesus said again, "What can I compare God's kingdom with? **21**It is like yeast that a woman took and hid in a large tub of flour until it made all the dough rise."

OLD TESTAMENT READING

The vineyard belonging to the LORD All-Powerful
is the nation of Israel;
the garden that he loves

is the people of Judah.
He looked for justice, but there was only killing.
He hoped for right living, but there were only cries of pain.

15So the common people and the great people
will be brought down;
those who are proud will be humbled.
16The LORD All-Powerful will receive glory by judging fairly;
the holy God will show himself holy by doing what is right.

Isaiah 5:7, 15–16

INSIGHTS

We all know what fruit is. The produce of the branch, by which men are refreshed and nourished. The fruit is not for the branch, but for those who come to carry it away. As soon as the fruit is ripe, the branch gives it off, to commence afresh its work of beneficence, and anew prepare its fruit for another season. A fruit-bearing tree lives not for itself but wholly for those to whom its fruit brings refreshment and life. And so the branch exists only and entirely for the sake of the fruit. To make glad the heart of the husbandman is its object, its safety, and its glory.

Beautiful image of the believer, abiding in Christ! He not only grows in strength, the union with the vine becoming ever surer and firmer, he also bears fruit, yea, much fruit. He has the power to offer that to others of which they can eat and live. Amid all who surround him he becomes like a tree of life, of which they can taste and be refreshed. He is in his circle a centre of life and of blessing, and that simply because he abides in Christ, and receives from Him the Spirit and the life of which he can impart to others. Learn thus, if you would bless others, to abide in Christ, and that if you do abide, you shall surely bless.

ANDREW MURRAY

APPLICATION

What result did Christ's healing work have on the people? Does he expect anything less from those who follow him? What does he do to nurture his people so they will bear good fruit? What does he promise if they don't? Are you bearing the fruit Christ has prepared you to bear?

LUKE
13:22 — 14:14

The Narrow Door

22Jesus was teaching in every town and village as he traveled toward Jerusalem. **23**Someone said to Jesus, "Lord, will only a few people be saved?"

Jesus said, **24**"Try hard to enter through the narrow door, because many people will try to enter there, but they will not be able. **25**When the owner of the house gets up and closes the door, you can stand outside and knock on the door and say, 'Sir, open the door for us.' But he will answer, 'I don't know you or where you come from.' **26**Then you will say, 'We ate and drank with you, and you taught in the streets of our town.' **27**But he will say to you, 'I don't know you or where you come from. Go away from me, all you who do evil!' **28**You will cry and grind your teeth with pain when you see Abraham, Isaac, Jacob, and all the prophets in God's kingdom, but you yourselves thrown outside. **29**People will come from the east, west, north, and south and will sit down at the table in the kingdom of God. **30**There are those who are last now who will be first in the future. And there are those who are first now who will be last in the future."

Jesus Will Die in Jerusalem

31At that time some Pharisees came to Jesus and said, "Go away from here! Herod wants to kill you!"

32Jesus said to them, "Go tell that fox Herod, 'Today and tomorrow I am forcing demons out and healing people. Then, on the third day, I will reach my goal.' **33**Yet I must be on my way today and tomorrow and the next day. Surely it cannot be right for a prophet to be killed anywhere except in Jerusalem.

34"Jerusalem, Jerusalem! You kill the prophets and stone to death those who are sent to you. Many times I wanted to gather your people as a hen gathers her chicks under her wings, but you would not let me. **35**Now your house is left completely empty. I tell you, you will not see me until that time when you will say, 'God bless the One who comes in the name of the Lord.'"

Healing on the Sabbath

14 On a Sabbath day, when Jesus went to eat at the home of a leading Pharisee, the people were watching Jesus very closely. **2**And in front of him was a man with dropsy. **3**Jesus said to the Pharisees and experts on the law, "Is it right or wrong to heal on the Sabbath day?" **4**But they would not answer his question. So Jesus took the man, healed him, and sent him away. **5**Jesus said to the Pharisees and teachers of the law, "If your child or ox falls into a well on the Sabbath day, will you not pull him out quickly?" **6**And they could not answer him.

Don't Make Yourself Important

7When Jesus noticed that some of the guests were choosing the best places to sit, he told this story: **8**"When someone invites you to a wedding feast, don't take the most important seat, because someone more important than you may have been invited. **9**The host, who invited both of you, will come to you and say, 'Give this person your seat.' Then you will be embarrassed and will have to move to the last place. **10**So when you are invited, go sit in a seat that is not important. When the host comes to you, he may say, 'Friend, move up here to a more important place.' Then all the other guests will respect you. **11**All who make themselves great will be made humble, but those who make themselves humble will be made great."

You Will Be Rewarded

12Then Jesus said to the man who had invited him, "When you give a lunch or a dinner, don't invite only your friends, your family, your other relatives, and your rich neighbors. At another time they will invite you to eat with them, and you will be repaid. **13**Instead, when you give a feast, invite the poor, the crippled, the lame, and the blind.

14Then you will be blessed, because they have nothing and cannot pay you back. But you will be repaid when the good people rise from the dead."

OLD TESTAMENT READING

Proud people will be ruined,
but the humble will be honored.

Proverbs 18:12

The LORD laughs at those who laugh at him,
but he gives grace to those who are not
proud.

Proverbs 3:34

INSIGHTS

God does not denigrate pride in its positive sense. The Bible has a hundred ways to illustrate the quiet feeling of competence that lies behind one's ability to do what he knows he has to do and can do. The apostle Paul's ministry was grounded on the assurance that Christ would help him finish what he had started. If that is what is meant by pride, we should certainly cultivate it and thank God for it. . . .

Pride in the dictionary sense of conceited and overbearing behavior . . . brings out the worst in antisocial relationships. Such pride is not the answer to the human problem; it is the human problem. . . . All of the major transgressions to inflict woe upon the human race—fear, greed, avarice, cruelty, lust, unbelief—can be traced to runaway pride. . . .

As to whether or not our pride is sin, the answer ultimately rests with each of us. The Christian knows the condition of his own heart. He measures it by the Word of God. Is he at peace? Is his conscience clear? Is he filled with the Spirit? . . . Then his personal life should reflect the modest, open, worshipful, loving stance of a humble creature of God who has been in the presence of his Creator.

SHERWOOD WIRT

PAUSE FOR REFLECTION

Why do you think Jesus spoke out against the seemingly mild form of pride he saw at the Pharisee's dinner? Why does God so detest pride? Why is humility necessary in the lives of those who belong to God? How does God honor humility?

LUKE 14:15 – 15:10

A Story About a Big Banquet

15One of those at the table with Jesus heard these things and said to him, "Blessed are the people who will share in the meal in God's kingdom."

16Jesus said to him, "A man gave a big banquet and invited many people. **17**When it was time to eat, the man sent his servant to tell the guests, 'Come. Everything is ready.'

18"But all the guests made excuses. The first one said, 'I have just bought a field, and I must go look at it. Please excuse me.' **19**Another said, 'I have just bought five pairs of oxen; I must go and try them. Please excuse me.' **20**A third person said, 'I just got married; I can't come.' **21**So the servant returned and told his master what had happened. Then the master became angry and said, 'Go at once into the streets and alleys of the town, and bring in the poor, the crippled, the blind, and the lame.' **22**Later the servant said to him, 'Master, I did what you commanded, but we still have room.' **23**The master said to the servant, 'Go out to the roads and country lanes, and urge the people there to come so my house will be full. **24**I tell you, none of those whom I invited first will eat with me.'"

The Cost of Being Jesus' Follower

25Large crowds were traveling with Jesus, and he turned and said to them, **26**"If anyone comes to me but loves his father, mother, wife, children, brothers, or sisters—or even life—more than me, he cannot be my follower. **27**Whoever is not willing to carry his cross and follow me cannot be my follower. **28**If you want to build a tower, you first sit down and decide how much it will cost, to see if you have enough money to finish the job. **29**If you don't, you might lay the foundation, but you would not be able to finish. Then all who would see it would make fun of you, **30**saying, 'This person began to build but was not able to finish.'

31"If a king is going to fight another king, first he will sit down and plan. He will decide if he and his ten thousand soldiers can defeat the other king who has twenty thousand soldiers. **32**If he can't, then while the other king is still far away, he will send some people to speak to him and ask for peace. **33**In the same way, you must give up everything you have to be my follower.

Don't Lose Your Influence

34"Salt is good, but if it loses its salty taste, you cannot make it salty again. **35**It is no good for the soil or for manure; it is thrown away.

"Let those with ears use them and listen."

A Lost Sheep, a Lost Coin

15The tax collectors and sinners all came to listen to Jesus. **2**But the Pharisees and the teachers of the law began to complain: "Look, this man welcomes sinners and even eats with them."

3Then Jesus told them this story: **4**"Suppose one of you has a hundred sheep but loses one of them. Then he will leave the other ninety-nine sheep in the open field and go out and look for the lost sheep until he finds it. **5**And when he finds it, he happily puts it on his shoulders **6**and goes home. He calls to his friends and neighbors and says, 'Be happy with me because I found my lost sheep.' **7**In the same way, I tell you there is more joy in heaven over one sinner who changes his heart and life, than over ninety-nine good people who don't need to change.

8"Suppose a woman has ten silver coins, but loses one. She will light a lamp, sweep the house, and look carefully for the coin until she finds it. **9**And when she finds it, she will call her friends and neighbors and say, 'Be happy with me because I have found the coin that I lost.' **10**In the same way, there is joy in the presence of the angels of God when one sinner changes his heart and life."

OLD TESTAMENT READING

Shadrach, Meshach, and Abednego answered the king, saying, "Nebuchadnezzar, we do not need to defend ourselves to you. **17**If you throw us into the blazing furnace, the God we serve is able to save us from the furnace. He will save us from your power, O king. **18**But even if God does not save us, we want you, O king, to know this: We will not serve your gods or worship the gold statue you have set up."

Daniel 3:16–18

INSIGHTS

When Christ said time after time that one must "deny himself and take up his cross and follow me" He was indicating that it is not easy to be His true follower. The apostle Paul warned, "Everyone who wants to live a godly life in Christ Jesus will be persecuted" (2 Timothy 3:12). He offers no cheap grace, no easy life. As someone has said, "Salvation is free but not cheap. . . ."

The Christian faith brings its own "blood, sweat and tears" to those who would follow Jesus Christ. Christ calls us to discipleship. When we come to Him, He takes away one set of burdens—the burden of sin, the burden of guilt, the burden of separation from God, the burden of hopelessness. But He also calls upon us to "Take my yoke upon you and learn from me" (Matthew 11:29). It is not a yoke that is too heavy for us to bear, for Christ bears it with us: "For my yoke is easy and my burden is light" (Matthew 11:30). Nevertheless, Christ calls us to follow Him, regardless of the cost, and He has never promised that our path will always be smooth. . . .

But in the midst of the suffering, trials and temptations, He will provide His peace, joy and fellowship. . . . In the midst of every situation of life He can give an inner calm and strength that you could never imagine apart from Him.

BILLY GRAHAM

APPLICATION

What price were Shadrach, Meshach, and Abednego willing to pay to serve God? What might it cost you to serve Christ, given your family or social setting? Are you willing to pay that price?

LUKE 15:11 — 16:8

The Son Who Left Home

11Then Jesus said, "A man had two sons. **12**The younger son said to his father, 'Give me my share of the property.' So the father divided the property between his two sons. **13**Then the younger son gathered up all that was his and traveled far away to another country. There he wasted his money in foolish living. **14**After he had spent everything, a time came when there was no food anywhere in the country, and the son was poor and hungry. **15**So he got a job with one of the citizens there who sent the son into the fields to feed pigs. **16**The son was so hungry that he wanted to eat the pods the pigs were eating, but no one gave him anything. **17**When he realized what he was doing, he thought, 'All of my father's servants have plenty of food. But I am here, almost dying with hunger. **18**I will leave and return to my father and say to him, "Father, I have sinned against God and against you. **19**I am no longer worthy to be called your son, but let me be like one of your servants."' **20**So the son left and went to his father.

"While the son was still a long way off, his father saw him and felt sorry for his son. So the father ran to him and hugged and kissed him. **21**The son said, 'Father, I have sinned against God and against you. I am no longer worthy to be called your son.' **22**But the father said to his servants, 'Hurry! Bring the best clothes and put them on him. Also, put a ring on his finger and sandals on his feet. **23**And get our fat calf and kill it so we can have a feast and celebrate. **24**My son was dead, but now he is alive again! He was lost, but now he is found!' So they began to celebrate.

25"The older son was in the field, and as he came closer to the house, he heard the sound of music and dancing. **26**So he called to one of the servants and asked what all this meant. **27**The servant said, 'Your brother has come back, and your father killed the fat calf, because your brother came home safely.' **28**The older son was angry and would not go in to the feast. So his father went out and begged him to come in. **29**But the older son said to his father, 'I have served you like a slave for many years and have always obeyed your commands. But you never gave me even a young goat to have at a feast with my friends. **30**But your other son, who wasted all your money on prostitutes, comes home, and you kill the fat calf for him!' **31**The father said to him, 'Son, you are always with me, and all that I have is yours. **32**We had to celebrate and be happy because your brother was dead, but now he is alive. He was lost, but now he is found.'"

True Wealth

16 Jesus also said to his followers, "Once there was a rich man who had a manager to take care of his business. This manager was accused of cheating him. **2**So he called the manager in and said to him, 'What is this I hear about you? Give me a report of what you have done with my money, because you can't be my manager any longer.' **3**The manager thought to himself, 'What will I do since my master is taking my job away from me? I am not strong enough to dig ditches, and I am ashamed to beg. **4**I know what I'll do so that when I lose my job people will welcome me into their homes.'

5"So the manager called in everyone who owed the master any money. He asked the first one,

'How much do you owe?' 6He answered, 'Eight hundred gallons of olive oil.' The manager said to him, 'Take your bill, sit down quickly, and write four hundred gallons.' 7Then the manager asked another one, 'How much do you owe?' He answered, 'One thousand bushels of wheat.' Then the manager said to him, 'Take your bill and write eight hundred bushels.' 8So, the master praised the dishonest manager for being clever. Yes, worldly people are more clever with their own kind than spiritual people are."

OLD TESTAMENT READING

For example, they may return what somebody gave them as a promise to repay a loan, or pay back what they stole. If they live by the rules that give life and do not sin, then they will surely live, and they will not die."

Ezekiel 33:15

INSIGHTS

Repentance is a rather dramatic word. It refers to the act of traveling in one direction and then suddenly changing to go the opposite way. Both John the Baptizer and Jesus used repentance as the centerpoint of their teaching because they were talking to a generation of people whose personal worlds were terribly broken. Yet the people would not face up to the changes necessary to make their worlds come back together again. Stubborn people do not repent very easily, and those people were stubborn.

Repentance is activated, first, in the act of confession: the candid acknowledgment before God, and perhaps to others, that one has sinned and is in need of forgiveness. Both by example and by teaching, the Scriptures place a high priority on confessing, for in so doing, one actually reveals the secrets of the heart. And until the heart is voluntarily opened up, the process of rebuilding a broken world cannot begin. . . .

. . . Restoration looks to the damage done in a broken-world experience and asks how it can be repaired. Broken relationships must be examined and, if possible, glued back together again. Forgiveness must be requested and granted, and that requires people to come together and offer mercy and grace to one another. These are not simple or easy things to give . . .

But restoration is one of the unique acts of the Christian community. In the final analysis, it cannot be demanded or even earned by the broken-world person; it must be freely given as God once freely gave grace to whoever wished to receive it.

Gordon MacDonald

PAUSE FOR REFLECTION

What does God want every person to do? What does he promise to those who confess and reject their sins? Is repentance a one-time or ongoing action? How freely do you extend mercy to restore repentant sinners?

LUKE 16:9 — 17:4

9"I tell you, make friends for yourselves using worldly riches so that when those riches are gone, you will be welcomed in those homes that continue forever. **10**Whoever can be trusted with a little can also be trusted with a lot, and whoever is dishonest with a little is dishonest with a lot. **11**If you cannot be trusted with worldly riches, then who will trust you with true riches? **12**And if you cannot be trusted with things that belong to someone else, who will give you things of your own?

13"No servant can serve two masters. The servant will hate one master and love the other, or will follow one master and refuse to follow the other. You cannot serve both God and worldly riches."

God's Law Cannot Be Changed

14The Pharisees, who loved money, were listening to all these things and made fun of Jesus. **15**He said to them, "You make yourselves look good in front of people, but God knows what is really in your hearts. What is important to people is hateful in God's sight.

16"The law of Moses and the writings of the prophets were preached until John came. Since then the Good News about the kingdom of God is being told, and everyone tries to enter it by force. **17**It would be easier for heaven and earth to pass away than for the smallest part of a letter in the law to be changed.

Divorce and Remarriage

18"If a man divorces his wife and marries another woman, he is guilty of adultery, and the man who marries a divorced woman is also guilty of adultery."

The Rich Man and Lazarus

19Jesus said, "There was a rich man who always dressed in the finest clothes and lived in luxury every day. **20**And a very poor man named Lazarus, whose body was covered with sores, was laid at the rich man's gate. **21**He wanted to eat only the small pieces of food that fell from the rich man's table. And the dogs would come and lick his sores. **22**Later, Lazarus died, and the angels carried him to the arms of Abraham. The rich man died, too, and was buried. **23**In the place of the dead, he was in much pain. The rich man saw Abraham far away with Lazarus at his side. **24**He called, 'Father Abraham, have mercy on me! Send Lazarus to dip his finger in water and cool my tongue, because I am suffering in this fire!' **25**But Abraham said, 'Child, remember when you were alive you had the good things in life, but bad things happened to Lazarus. Now he is comforted here, and you are suffering. **26**Besides, there is a big pit between you and us, so no one can cross over to you, and no one can leave there and come here.' **27**The rich man said, 'Father, then please send Lazarus to my father's house. **28**I have five brothers, and Lazarus could warn them so that they will not come to this place of pain.' **29**But Abraham said, 'They have the law of Moses and the writings of the prophets; let them learn from them.' **30**The rich man said, 'No, father Abraham! If someone goes to them from the dead, they would believe and change their hearts and lives.'

³¹But Abraham said to him, 'If they will not listen to Moses and the prophets, they will not listen to someone who comes back from the dead.'"

Sin and Forgiveness

17 Jesus said to his followers, "Things that cause people to sin will happen, but how terrible for the person who causes them to happen! ²It would be better for you to be thrown into the sea with a large stone around your neck than to cause one of these little ones to sin. ³So be careful!

"If another follower sins, warn him, and if he is sorry and stops sinning, forgive him. ⁴If he sins against you seven times in one day and says that he is sorry each time, forgive him."

OLD TESTAMENT READING

God, examine me and know my heart;
    test me and know my anxious thoughts.
²⁴See if there is any bad thing in me.
    Lead me on the road to everlasting life.

Psalm 139:23–24

INSIGHTS

Making good judgments in this world is sometimes a hit-and-miss proposition. Often we fail. In baseball, a hitter is constantly trying to guess what the pitcher will throw next. In football, a defensive coach tries to predict where the offense will run next. Basketball coaches continually try to outmaneuver each other. Sometimes they are right, and sometimes they are wrong. We fail because we seldom have all the facts. We have no idea what the other person is thinking. We're looking for a fast ball, and the pitcher throws a curve ball, or we're looking for a pass and they run! . . . We don't know all the facts, we don't know the future, and sometimes we don't even react properly when we do know! But with God, life is not a guessing game. His judgments are sure, because He knows all the facts. God knows everything about us. He knows our thoughts before we think them (Psalm 139:1–6). No one can escape His sight (Psalm 139:7–12). He even judges the thoughts and intentions of our hearts (Hebrews 4:12–13). God's judgment is always perfect, because He knows all the facts. Those who think they are getting away with something may escape our notice, but they will never escape the notice of God. The eyes of the Lord are in every place, watching the evil and the good (Proverbs 15:3). Take comfort, righteous ones, for goodness will be vindicated and evil will be punished!

ELLIOT JOHNSON / AL SCHIERBAUM

ACTION POINT

What feelings do you have when you realize that God knows what is in your heart and that he knows it even better than you do? Pray that God's knowledge of you will lead you closer to him. Take comfort that he not only knows you, but loves you! Praise him for his amazing knowledge!

LUKE 17:5-37

How Big Is Your Faith?

5The apostles said to the Lord, "Give us more faith!"

6The Lord said, "If your faith were the size of a mustard seed, you could say to this mulberry tree, 'Dig yourself up and plant yourself in the sea,' and it would obey you.

Be Good Servants

7"Suppose one of you has a servant who has been plowing the ground or caring for the sheep. When the servant comes in from working in the field, would you say, 'Come in and sit down to eat'? **8**No, you would say to him, 'Prepare something for me to eat. Then get yourself ready and serve me. After I finish eating and drinking, you can eat.' **9**The servant does not get any special thanks for doing what his master commanded. **10**It is the same with you. When you have done everything you are told to do, you should say, 'We are unworthy servants; we have only done the work we should do.'"

Be Thankful

11While Jesus was on his way to Jerusalem, he was going through the area between Samaria and Galilee. **12**As he came into a small town, ten men who had a skin disease met him there. They did not come close to Jesus **13**but called to him, "Jesus! Master! Have mercy on us!"

14When Jesus saw the men, he said, "Go and show yourselves to the priests."

As the ten men were going, they were healed.

15When one of them saw that he was healed, he went back to Jesus, praising God in a loud voice. **16**Then he bowed down at Jesus' feet and thanked him. (And this man was a Samaritan.) **17**Jesus said, "Weren't ten men healed? Where are the other nine? **18**Is this Samaritan the only one who came back to thank God?" **19**Then Jesus said to him, "Stand up and go on your way. You were healed because you believed."

God's Kingdom Is Within You

20Some of the Pharisees asked Jesus, "When will the kingdom of God come?"

Jesus answered, "God's kingdom is coming, but not in a way that you will be able to see with your eyes. **21**People will not say, 'Look, here it is!' or, 'There it is!' because God's kingdom is within you."

22Then Jesus said to his followers, "The time will come when you will want very much to see one of the days of the Son of Man. But you will not see it. **23**People will say to you, 'Look, there he is!' or, 'Look, here he is!' Stay where you are; don't go away and search.

When Jesus Comes Again

24"When the Son of Man comes again, he will shine like lightning, which flashes across the sky and lights it up from one side to the other. **25**But first he must suffer many things and be rejected by the people of this time. **26**When the Son of Man comes again, it will be as it was when Noah lived. **27**People were eating, drinking, marrying, and giving their children to be married until the day Noah entered the boat. Then the flood came and killed them all. **28**It will be the same as during the time of Lot. People were eating, drinking, buying, selling, planting, and building. **29**But the day Lot left Sodom, fire and sulfur rained down from the sky and killed them all. **30**This is how it will be when the Son of Man comes again.

31"On that day, a person who is on the roof and whose belongings are in the house should not go inside to get them. A person who is in the field should not go back home. **32**Remember Lot's wife. **33**Those who try to keep their lives will lose them. But those who give up their lives will save them. **34**I tell you, on that night two people will be sleeping in one bed; one will be taken and the other will be left. **35**There will be two women grinding grain together; one will be taken, and the other will be left. [**36**Two people will be in the field. One will be taken, and the other will be left.]"

37The followers asked Jesus, "Where will this be, Lord?"

Jesus answered, "Where there is a dead body, there the vultures will gather."

OLD TESTAMENT READING

The two men said to Lot, "Do you have any other relatives in this city? Do you have any sons-in-law, sons, daughters, or any other relatives? If you do, tell them to leave now, **13**because we are about to destroy this city. The LORD has heard of all the evil that is here, so he has sent us to destroy it."

Genesis 19:12–13

INSIGHTS

In John's vision . . . you will get a feeling for the absolute horror of this final judgment for those who do not believe. Picture it. Carefully the Lamb opens the sixth seal (Revelation 6:12–17). Suddenly, chaos grips the universe. An earthquake shakes the entire world, no Richter scale could measure its fury. There is a complete eclipse of the sun. . . .

The world is trembling with terror. The great cities collapse. John sees kings, princes, generals; the rich, the mighty, slave and free—every human being left on the earth running to escape the horror of God's final judgment. They flee to mountain caves. They cower behind rocks and boulders. But there is no escape. Desperately they cry out, "Hide us from the face of him who sits on the throne and from the wrath of the Lamb! For the great day of their wrath has come, and who can stand?" (Revelation 6:16, 17).

There will be a day of reckoning when God closes His books on time and judges every creature, living and dead.

BILLY GRAHAM

APPLICATION

When God decides it's time for judgment, is there any room for doubt about what he is doing? Will there be any doubt about his coming judgment? How does Jesus' warning about his coming judgment affect your everyday life?

LUKE 18:1-25

God Will Answer His People

18 Then Jesus used this story to teach his followers that they should always pray and never lose hope. **2**"In a certain town there was a judge who did not respect God or care about people. **3**In that same town there was a widow who kept coming to this judge, saying, 'Give me my rights against my enemy.' **4**For a while the judge refused to help her. But afterwards, he thought to himself, 'Even though I don't respect God or care about people, **5**I will see that she gets her rights. Otherwise she will continue to bother me until I am worn out.'"

6The Lord said, "Listen to what the unfair judge said. **7**God will always give what is right to his people who cry to him night and day, and he will not be slow to answer them. **8**I tell you, God will help his people quickly. But when the Son of Man comes again, will he find those on earth who believe in him?"

Being Right with God

9Jesus told this story to some people who thought they were very good and looked down on everyone else: **10**"A Pharisee and a tax collector both went to the Temple to pray. **11**The Pharisee stood alone and prayed, 'God, I thank you that I am not like other people who steal, cheat, or take part in adultery, or even like this tax collector. **12**I fast twice a week, and I give one-tenth of everything I get!'

13"The tax collector, standing at a distance, would not even look up to heaven. But he beat on his chest because he was so sad. He said, 'God, have mercy on me, a sinner.' **14**I tell you, when this man went home, he was right with God, but the Pharisee was not. All who make themselves great will be made humble, but all who make themselves humble will be made great."

Who Will Enter God's Kingdom?

15Some people brought even their babies to Jesus so he could touch them. When the followers saw this, they told them to stop. **16**But Jesus called for the children, saying, "Let the little children come to me. Don't stop them, because the kingdom of God belongs to people who are like these children. **17**I tell you the truth, you must accept the kingdom of God as if you were a child, or you will never enter it."

A Rich Man's Question

18A certain leader asked Jesus, "Good Teacher, what must I do to have life forever?"

19Jesus said to him, "Why do you call me good? Only God is good. **20**You know the commands: 'You must not be guilty of adultery. You must not murder anyone. You must not steal. You must not tell lies about your neighbor. Honor your father and mother.'"

21But the leader said, "I have obeyed all these commands since I was a boy."

22When Jesus heard this, he said to him, "There is still one more thing you need to do. Sell everything you have and give it to the poor, and you will have treasure in heaven. Then come and follow me." **23**But when the man heard this, he became very sad, because he was very rich.

24Jesus looked at him and said, "It is very hard for rich people to enter the kingdom of God. **25**It is easier for a camel to go through the eye of a needle than for a rich person to enter the kingdom of God."

OLD TESTAMENT READING

This is what the LORD says:
"The wise must not brag about their
    wisdom.
The strong must not brag about their
    strength.
The rich must not brag about their money.
24But if people want to brag, let them brag
    that they understand and know me.

Jeremiah 9:23–24a

INSIGHTS

To receive what we have as a gift from God is the first inner attitude of simplicity. We work but we know that it is not our work that gives us what we have. We live by grace even when it comes to "daily bread." We are dependent upon God for the simplest elements of life: water, sun. What we have is not the result of our labor, but of the gracious care of God. When we are tempted to think that what we own is the result of our personal efforts, it takes only a little drought or a small accident to show us once again how utterly dependent we are for everything.

To know that it is God's business, and not ours, to care for what we have is the second inner attitude of simplicity. God is able to protect what we possess. We can trust him. . . . Obviously, these matters are not restricted to possessions but include such things as our reputation and our employment. Simplicity means the freedom to trust God for these (and all) things.

To have our goods available to others marks the third inner attitude of simplicity. If our goods are not available to the community when it is clearly right and good, then they are stolen goods. . . . We cling to our possessions rather than sharing them because we are anxious about tomorrow. But if we truly believe that God is who Jesus says he is, then we do not need to be afraid. When we come to see God as the almighty Creator and our loving Father, we can share because we know that he will care for us. . . .

When we are seeking first the kingdom of God, these three attitudes will characterize our lives. Taken together they define what Jesus means by "do not be anxious." They comprise the inner reality of Christian simplicity.

RICHARD FOSTER

APPLICATION

Can we truly achieve anything for ourselves? What is the next step for you to take in trusting God?

LUKE 18:26 — 19:10

Who Can Be Saved?

26When the people heard this, they asked, "Then who can be saved?"

27Jesus answered, "The things impossible for people are possible for God."

28Peter said, "Look, we have left everything and followed you."

29Jesus said, "I tell you the truth, all those who have left houses, wives, brothers, parents, or children for the kingdom of God **30**will get much more in this life. And in the age that is coming, they will have life forever."

Jesus Will Rise from the Dead

31Then Jesus took the twelve apostles aside and said to them, "We are going to Jerusalem. Everything the prophets wrote about the Son of Man will happen. **32**He will be turned over to those who are evil. They will laugh at him, insult him, spit on him, **33**beat him with whips, and kill him. But on the third day, he will rise to life again." **34**The apostles did not understand this; the meaning was hidden from them, and they did not realize what was said.

Jesus Heals a Blind Man

35As Jesus came near the city of Jericho, a blind man was sitting beside the road, begging. **36**When he heard the people coming down the road, he asked, "What is happening?"

37They told him, "Jesus, from Nazareth, is going by."

38The blind man cried out, "Jesus, Son of David, have mercy on me!"

39The people leading the group warned the blind man to be quiet. But the blind man shouted even more, "Son of David, have mercy on me!"

40Jesus stopped and ordered the blind man to be brought to him. When he came near, Jesus asked him, **41**"What do you want me to do for you?"

He said, "Lord, I want to see."

42Jesus said to him, "Then see. You are healed because you believed."

43At once the man was able to see, and he followed Jesus, thanking God. All the people who saw this praised God.

Zacchaeus Meets Jesus

19 Jesus was going through the city of Jericho. **2**A man was there named Zacchaeus, who was a very important tax collector, and he was wealthy. **3**He wanted to see who Jesus was, but he was not able because he was too short to see above the crowd. **4**He ran ahead to a place where Jesus would come, and he climbed a sycamore tree so he could see him. **5**When Jesus came to that place, he looked up and said to him, "Zacchaeus, hurry and come down! I must stay at your house today."

6Zacchaeus came down quickly and welcomed him gladly. **7**All the people saw this and began to complain, "Jesus is staying with a sinner!"

8But Zacchaeus stood and said to the Lord, "I will give half of my possessions to the poor. And if I have cheated anyone, I will pay back four times more."

9Jesus said to him, "Salvation has come to this

house today, because this man also belongs to the family of Abraham. **10**The Son of Man came to find lost people and save them."

OLD TESTAMENT READING

After Jonah had entered the city and walked for one day, he preached to the people, saying, "After forty days, Nineveh will be destroyed!"

5The people of Nineveh believed God. They announced that they would fast for a while, and they put on rough cloth to show their sadness. All the people in the city did this, from the most important to the least important.

10When God saw what the people did, that they stopped doing evil, he changed his mind and did not do what he had warned. He did not punish them.

Jonah 3:4–5, 10

When the Passover celebration was finished, all the Israelites in Jerusalem went out to the towns of Judah. There they smashed the stone pillars used to worship gods. They cut down the Asherah idols and destroyed the altars and places for worshiping gods in all of Judah, Benjamin, Ephraim, and Manasseh. After they had destroyed all of them, the Israelites returned to their own towns and homes.

2 Chronicles 31:1

INSIGHTS

True repentance occurs when we begin to see sin from God's point of view— when we see the way our sin has broken his heart. Perhaps the idea that God's heart can be broken by our sin is new to you. In Genesis 6:5–6 we are told, "Then the LORD saw that the wickedness of man was great on the earth, and that every intent of the thoughts of his heart was only evil continually. And the LORD was sorry that he had made man on the earth, and he was grieved in his heart" (NASB). God was so disappointed with what he saw that there was a grief or sorrow in his heart.

Jesus also was brokenhearted as he wept over Jerusalem. "O Jerusalem, Jerusalem, you who kill the prophets and stone those sent to you, how often I have longed to gather your children together, as a hen gathers her chicks under her wings, but you were not willing!" (Lk. 13:34). God's heart aches over our sin. It alienates us from him and from our fellow believers.

If we want to have victory over sin and turn our lives wholeheartedly over to God, then we must see our sin from God's perspective. No sermon on hell can ever change a person's heart like seeing the grief sin has brought to the heart of the One who created us. We must ask God to show us what our sin does to him. As we do this and begin to understand his great love for us, despite how much we have hurt and grieved his heart, turning away from that sin is the natural thing to do. This is the test of our sincerity and of the level of our desperation to be right with God.

FLOYD MCCLUNG

ACTION POINT

Do you think the people mentioned in these passages recognized that their sin grieved God? What in your life grieves God?

LUKE 19:11-40

A Story About Three Servants

11As the people were listening to this, Jesus told them a story because he was near Jerusalem and they thought God's kingdom would appear immediately. **12**He said: "A very important man went to a country far away to be made a king and then to return home. **13**So he called ten of his servants and gave a coin to each servant. He said, 'Do business with this money until I get back.' **14**But the people in the kingdom hated the man. So they sent a group to follow him and say, 'We don't want this man to be our king.'

15"But the man became king. When he returned home, he said, 'Call those servants who have my money so I can know how much they earned with it.'

16"The first servant came and said, 'Sir, I earned ten coins with the one you gave me.' **17**The king said to the servant, 'Excellent! You are a good servant. Since I can trust you with small things, I will let you rule over ten of my cities.'

18"The second servant said, 'Sir, I earned five coins with your one.' **19**The king said to this servant, 'You can rule over five cities.'

20"Then another servant came in and said to the king, 'Sir, here is your coin which I wrapped in a piece of cloth and hid. **21**I was afraid of you, because you are a hard man. You even take money that you didn't earn and gather food that you didn't plant.' **22**Then the king said to the servant, 'I will condemn you by your own words, you evil servant. You knew that I am a hard man, taking money that I didn't earn and gathering food that I didn't plant. **23**Why then didn't you put my money in the bank? Then when I came back, my money would have earned some interest.'

24"The king said to the men who were standing by, 'Take the coin away from this servant and give it to the servant who earned ten coins.' **25**They said, 'But sir, that servant already has ten coins.' **26**The king said, 'Those who have will be given more, but those who do not have anything will have everything taken away from them. **27**Now where are my enemies who didn't want me to be king? Bring them here and kill them before me.'"

Jesus Enters Jerusalem as a King

28After Jesus said this, he went on toward Jerusalem. **29**As Jesus came near Bethphage and Bethany, towns near the hill called the Mount of Olives, he sent out two of his followers. **30**He said, "Go to the town you can see there. When you enter it, you will find a colt tied there, which no one has ever ridden. Untie it and bring it here to me. **31**If anyone asks you why you are untying it, say that the Master needs it."

32The two followers went into town and found the colt just as Jesus had told them. **33**As they were untying it, its owners came out and asked the followers, "Why are you untying our colt?"

34The followers answered, "The Master needs it." **35**So they brought it to Jesus, threw their coats on the colt's back, and put Jesus on it. **36**As Jesus rode toward Jerusalem, others spread their coats on the road before him.

37As he was coming close to Jerusalem, on the way down the Mount of Olives, the whole crowd of followers began joyfully shouting praise to God for all the miracles they had seen. **38**They said,

"God bless the king who comes in the name of
the Lord!   *Psalm 118:26*
There is peace in heaven and glory to God!".

39Some of the Pharisees in the crowd said to Jesus, "Teacher, tell your followers not to say these things."

40But Jesus answered, "I tell you, if my followers didn't say these things, then the stones would cry out."

OLD TESTAMENT READING

People will be rewarded for what they say,
and they will also be rewarded for what
they do.

Proverbs 12:14

Tell those who do what is right that things will
go well for them,
because they will receive a reward for what
they do.
11But how terrible it will be for the wicked!
They will be punished for all the wrong
they have done.

Isaiah 3:10–11

INSIGHTS

How does free forgiveness and justification by faith square with judgment according to works? The answer seems to be as follows. First, the gift of justification certainly shields believers from being condemned and banished from God's presence as sinners. This appears from the vision of judgment in Revelation 20:11–15, where alongside "the books" recording each man's work "the book of life" is opened, and those whose names are written there are not "cast into the lake of fire" as the rest of men are. But, second, the gift of justification does not at all shield believers from being assessed as Christians, and from forfeiting good which others will enjoy if it turns out that as Christians they have been slack, mischievous and destructive. This appears from Paul's warning to the Corinthians to be careful what life-style they build on Christ, the one foundation. "If any man builds upon this foundation . . . If any man's work abide . . . he shall receive a reward. If any man's work shall be burned, he shall suffer loss: but he himself shall be saved; yet so as by fire" (1 Corinthians 3:12–15). "Reward" and "loss" signify an enriched or impoverished relationship with God, though in what ways it is beyond our present power to know.

J. I. Packer

APPLICATION

For what does God punish or reward people? What do you think God expects his servants to do while they wait for his return? What kind of servant do you want to be for your Lord? How can you be a better one?

LUKE 19:41—20:19

Jesus Cries for Jerusalem

41As Jesus came near Jerusalem, he saw the city and cried for it, **42**saying, "I wish you knew today what would bring you peace. But now it is hidden from you. **43**The time is coming when your enemies will build a wall around you and will hold you in on all sides. **44**They will destroy you and all your people, and not one stone will be left on another. All this will happen because you did not recognize the time when God came to save you."

Jesus Goes to the Temple

45Jesus went into the Temple and began to throw out the people who were selling things there. **46**He said, "It is written in the Scriptures, 'My Temple will be a house for prayer.' But you have changed it into a 'hideout for robbers'!"

47Jesus taught in the Temple every day. The leading priests, the experts on the law, and some of the leaders of the people wanted to kill Jesus. **48**But they did not know how they could do it, because all the people were listening closely to him.

Jewish Leaders Question Jesus

 One day Jesus was in the Temple, teaching the people and telling them the Good News. The leading priests, teachers of the law, and elders came up to talk with him, **2**saying, "Tell us what authority you have to do these things? Who gave you this authority?"

3Jesus answered, "I will also ask you a question. Tell me: **4**When John baptized people, was that authority from God or just from other people?"

5They argued about this, saying, "If we answer, 'John's baptism was from God,' Jesus will say, 'Then why did you not believe him?' **6**But if we say, 'It was from other people,' all the people will stone us to death, because they believe John was a prophet." **7**So they answered that they didn't know where it came from.

8Jesus said to them, "Then I won't tell you what authority I have to do these things."

A Story About God's Son

9Then Jesus told the people this story: "A man planted a vineyard and leased it to some farmers. Then he went away for a long time. **10**When it was time for the grapes to be picked, he sent a servant to the farmers to get some of the grapes. But they beat the servant and sent him away empty-handed. **11**Then he sent another servant. They beat this servant also, and showed no respect for him, and sent him away empty-handed. **12**So the man sent a third servant. The farmers wounded him and threw him out. **13**The owner of the vineyard said, 'What will I do now? I will send my son whom I love. Maybe they will respect him.' **14**But when the farmers saw the son, they said to each other, 'This son will inherit the vineyard. If we kill him, it will be ours.' **15**So the farmers threw the son out of the vineyard and killed him.

"What will the owner of this vineyard do to them? **16**He will come and kill those farmers and will give the vineyard to other farmers."

When the people heard this story, they said, "Let this never happen!"

17But Jesus looked at them and said, "Then what does this verse mean:

'The stone that the builders rejected became the cornerstone'? *Psalm 118:22*

18Everyone who falls on that stone will be broken, and the person on whom it falls, that person will be crushed!"

19The teachers of the law and the leading priests wanted to arrest Jesus at once, because they knew the story was about them. But they were afraid of what the people would do.

OLD TESTAMENT READING

Jerusalem, your rulers are like those of Sodom,
and your people are like those of Gomorrah.
Hear the word of the LORD;
listen to the teaching of our God!
Even if you say many prayers,
I will not listen to you,
because your hands are full of blood.
16Wash yourselves and make yourselves clean.
Stop doing the evil things I see you do.
Stop doing wrong.

Isaiah 1:10, 15b–16

INSIGHTS

Jesus did not come to change Israel's politics, He came to change men's hearts. When He rode into Jerusalem, Jesus presented Himself as a humble king, not a violent conqueror. Led by the spiritually blind rulers, the nation rejected Him and said, "We have no king but Caesar!"

What were the consequences of this rebellion? In a few years, Jerusalem was reduced to shambles by the Roman armies and the temple was destroyed. The Jewish nation was dispersed across the face of the earth to wander "many days, without a king, and without a prince" (Hosea 3:4).

But there is a much wider application. When the Lord returns, He will have to punish those who will not bow before Him and submit to His will. . . .

Sad to say, most of the people in our world want nothing to do with Jesus Christ. "There is none that understandeth, there is none that seeketh after God" (Rom. 3:11). But God is seeking after men! "For the Son of man is come to seek and to save that which was lost." . . .

When the Lord returns, it will mean reward for the faithful, loss of reward for the unfaithful, and terrible judgment for the unbelieving, rebellious people who rejected Him . . . (2 Thes. 1:8–9).

WARREN WIERSBE

APPLICATION

Jerusalem is identified in Scripture as God's holy city. For what reasons did Jesus weep over it? In a broader sense, what does this scene reveal about how Jesus views sin? Does Jesus weep or rejoice over the condition of your heart?

LUKE 20:20-47

Is It Right to Pay Taxes or Not?

20So they watched Jesus and sent some spies who acted as if they were sincere. They wanted to trap Jesus in saying something wrong so they could hand him over to the authority and power of the governor. **21**So the spies asked Jesus, "Teacher, we know that what you say and teach is true. You pay no attention to who people are, and you always teach the truth about God's way. **22**Tell us, is it right for us to pay taxes to Caesar or not?"

23But Jesus, knowing they were trying to trick him, said, **24**"Show me a coin. Whose image and name are on it?"

They said, "Caesar's."

25Jesus said to them, "Then give to Caesar the things that are Caesar's, and give to God the things that are God's."

26So they were not able to trap Jesus in anything he said in the presence of the people. And being amazed at his answer, they became silent.

Some Sadducees Try to Trick Jesus

27Some Sadducees, who believed people would not rise from the dead, came to Jesus. **28**They asked, "Teacher, Moses wrote that if a man's brother dies and leaves a wife but no children, then that man must marry the widow and have children for his brother. **29**Once there were seven brothers. The first brother married and died, but had no children. **30**Then the second brother married the widow, and he died. **31**And the third brother married the widow, and he died. The same thing happened with all seven brothers; they died and had no children. **32**Finally, the woman died also. **33**Since all seven brothers had married her, whose wife will she be when people rise from the dead?"

34Jesus said to them, "On earth, people marry and are given to someone to marry. **35**But those who will be worthy to be raised from the dead and live again will not marry, nor will they be given to someone to marry. **36**In that life they are like angels and cannot die. They are children of God, because they have been raised from the dead. **37**Even Moses clearly showed that the dead are raised to life. When he wrote about the burning bush, he said that the Lord is 'the God of Abraham, the God of Isaac, and the God of Jacob.' **38**God is the God of the living, not the dead, because all people are alive to him."

39Some of the teachers of the law said, "Teacher, your answer was good." **40**No one was brave enough to ask him another question.

Is the Christ the Son of David?

41Then Jesus said, "Why do people say that the Christ is the Son of David? **42**In the book of Psalms, David himself says:

'The Lord said to my Lord,

"Sit by me at my right side,

43   until I put your enemies under your
                control."'   *Psalm 110:1*

44David calls the Christ 'Lord,' so how can the Christ be his son?"

Jesus Accuses Some Leaders

45While all the people were listening, Jesus said to his followers, **46**"Beware of the teachers of the law. They like to walk around wearing fancy clothes, and they love for people to greet them with respect in the marketplaces. They love to have the most important seats in the synagogues and at feasts. **47** But they cheat widows and steal their houses and then try to make themselves look good by saying long prayers. They will receive a greater punishment."

OLD TESTAMENT READING

How terrible it will be for people who plan wickedness,
  who lie on their beds and make evil plans.
When the morning light comes, they do what they planned,
  because they have the power to do so.
2 They want fields, so they take them;
  they want houses, so they take them away.
They cheat people to get their houses;
  they rob them even of their property.
3 That is why the LORD says:
"Look, I am planning trouble against such people,
  and you won't be able to save yourselves.
You will no longer walk proudly,
  because it will be a terrible time."

Micah 2:1–3

INSIGHTS

Not long ago a discerning man said that his minister preaches against sin, but he does not tell what sin is. He preaches against sin in general, but never against any particular sin. He denounces it in the aggregate, but never meddles with it in detail as it exists among his people. . . .

Do you see the importance of praying continually for a quick and tender and powerful conscience? Do you see the importance of great watchfulness lest we should abuse and seduce our conscience by indulgence in sin? Do you see the great importance of faithful dealings with the consciences all around you, so as to keep your own and their consciences fully awake and as quick and sensitive as the apple of the eye? . . .

It is impossible for me to understand how some could really be in love with the law of God, earnestly and honestly engaged in supporting it in all the length and breadth of its claims, and yet indulge in so many forms of violating it with so little compunction or misgiving. Is there not, my beloved brethren, some delusion in this?

CHARLES FINNEY

ACTION POINT

What are the leaders of God's people responsible to do? What does God promise to spiritual leaders who plan wickedness? Pray that God will open your eyes and protect you from the blinding influence of false spiritual leaders.

LUKE 21:1-28

True Giving

21 As Jesus looked up, he saw some rich people putting their gifts into the Temple money box. **2**Then he saw a poor widow putting two small copper coins into the box. **3**He said, "I tell you the truth, this poor widow gave more than all those rich people. **4**They gave only what they did not need. This woman is very poor, but she gave all she had to live on."

The Temple Will Be Destroyed

5Some people were talking about the Temple and how it was decorated with beautiful stones and gifts offered to God.

But Jesus said, **6**"As for these things you are looking at, the time will come when not one stone will be left on another. Every stone will be thrown down."

7They asked Jesus, "Teacher, when will these things happen? What will be the sign that they are about to take place?"

8Jesus said, "Be careful so you are not fooled. Many people will come in my name, saying, 'I am the One' and, 'The time has come!' But don't follow them. **9**When you hear about wars and riots, don't be afraid, because these things must happen first, but the end will come later."

10Then he said to them, "Nations will fight against other nations, and kingdoms against other kingdoms. **11**In various places there will be great earthquakes, sicknesses, and a lack of food. Fearful events and great signs will come from heaven.

12"But before all these things happen, people will arrest you and treat you cruelly. They will judge you in their synagogues and put you in jail and force you to stand before kings and governors, because you follow me. **13**But this will give you an opportunity to tell about me. **14**Make up your minds not to worry ahead of time about what you will say. **15**I will give you the wisdom to say things that none of your enemies will be able to stand against or prove wrong. **16**Even your parents, brothers, relatives, and friends will turn against you, and they will kill some of you. **17**All people will hate you because you follow me. **18**But none of these things can really harm you. **19**By continuing to have faith you will save your lives.

Jerusalem Will Be Destroyed

20"When you see armies all around Jerusalem, you will know it will soon be destroyed. **21**At that time, the people in Judea should run away to the mountains. The people in Jerusalem must get out, and those who are near the city should not go in. **22**These are the days of punishment to bring about all that is written in the Scriptures. **23**How terrible it will be for women who are pregnant or have nursing babies! Great trouble will come upon this land, and God will be angry with these people. **24**They will be killed by the sword and taken as prisoners to all nations. Jerusalem will be crushed by non-Jewish people until their time is over.

Don't Fear

25"There will be signs in the sun, moon, and stars. On earth, nations will be afraid and confused because of the roar and fury of the sea. [26]People will be so afraid they will faint, wondering what is happening to the world, because the powers of the heavens will be shaken. [27]Then people will see the Son of Man coming in a cloud with power and great glory. [28]When these things begin to happen, look up and hold your heads high, because the time when God will free you is near!"

OLD TESTAMENT READING

ut Moses said to the LORD, "Please, Lord, I have never been a skilled speaker. Even now, after talking to you, I cannot speak well. I speak slowly and can't find the best words."

[11]Then the LORD said to him, "Who made a person's mouth? And who makes someone deaf or not able to speak? Or who gives a person sight or blindness? It is I, the LORD."

[14]The LORD became angry with Moses and said, "Your brother Aaron, from the family of Levi, is a skilled speaker. He is already coming to meet you, and he will be happy when he sees you. [15]You will speak to Aaron and tell him what to say. I will help both of you to speak and will teach you what to do."

Exodus 4:10–11, 14–15

INSIGHTS

"What in the world will I say?"
At some time in life we're all confronted with this challenge. . . .

In today's passage Jesus is talking about our concern over what to say when we are faced with giving testimony about Him in a setting which is hostile to the Christian faith. He assures us that the Holy Spirit will give us the thoughts, the words, and the courage which we so often lack. . . . There may be times when you are concerned about sharing your faith in Christ with someone or when you are challenged in your faith by other people. Rely upon the fact that God is the source of your thoughts and words at those times. Dr. Lloyd Ogilvie says:

Our only task is to open our minds in calm expectation of wisdom beyond our own capacity. We were never meant to be adequate on our own. It is when we think we are adequate that we get into trouble. A Christian is not one who works for the Lord but one in whom and through whom the Lord works. We are not to speak for God but to yield our tongues to express the thoughts the Lord has implanted.

What can we draw from these words? Listen to the Lord before you speak and, after you have heard Him, speak with confidence and concern.

H. NORMAN WRIGHT

ACTION POINT

What did God promise to do for both Moses and Aaron? Have you ever been (or are you) worried about what to say? Pray for a willing spirit that God can use; then trust him to give his message through you!

LUKE
21:29 — 22:20

Jesus' Words Will Live Forever

29Then Jesus told this story: "Look at the fig tree and all the other trees. **30**When their leaves appear, you know that summer is near. **31**In the same way, when you see these things happening, you will know that God's kingdom is near.

32"I tell you the truth, all these things will happen while the people of this time are still living. **33**Earth and sky will be destroyed, but the words I have spoken will never be destroyed.

Be Ready All the Time

34"Be careful not to spend your time feasting, drinking, or worrying about worldly things. If you do, that day might come on you suddenly, **35**like a trap on all people on earth. **36**So be ready all the time. Pray that you will be strong enough to escape all these things that will happen and that you will be able to stand before the Son of Man."

37During the day, Jesus taught the people in the Temple, and at night he went out of the city and stayed on the Mount of Olives. **38**Every morning all the people got up early to go to the Temple to listen to him.

Judas Becomes an Enemy of Jesus

It was almost time for the Feast of Unleavened Bread, called the Passover Feast. **2**The leading priests and teachers of the law were trying to find a way to kill Jesus, because they were afraid of the people.

3Satan entered Judas Iscariot, one of Jesus' twelve apostles. **4**Judas went to the leading priests and some of the soldiers who guarded the Temple and talked to them about a way to hand Jesus over to them. **5**They were pleased and agreed to give Judas money. **6**He agreed and watched for the best time to hand Jesus over to them when he was away from the crowd.

Jesus Eats the Passover Meal

7The Day of Unleavened Bread came when the Passover lambs had to be sacrificed. **8**Jesus said to Peter and John, "Go and prepare the Passover meal for us to eat."

9They asked, "Where do you want us to prepare it?" **10**Jesus said to them, "After you go into the city, a man carrying a jar of water will meet you. Follow him into the house that he enters, **11**and tell the owner of the house, 'The Teacher says: "Where is the guest room in which I may eat the Passover meal with my followers?" ' **12**Then he will show you a large, furnished room upstairs. Prepare the Passover meal there."

13So Peter and John left and found everything as Jesus had said. And they prepared the Passover meal.

The Lord's Supper

14When the time came, Jesus and the apostles were sitting at the table. **15**He said to them, "I wanted very much to eat this Passover meal with you before I suffer. **16**I will not eat another

Passover meal until it is given its true meaning in the kingdom of God."

17 Then Jesus took a cup, gave thanks, and said, "Take this cup and share it among yourselves. **18** I will not drink again from the fruit of the vine until God's kingdom comes."

19 Then Jesus took some bread, gave thanks, broke it, and gave it to the apostles, saying, "This is my body, which I am giving for you. Do this to remember me." **20** In the same way, after supper, Jesus took the cup and said, "This cup is the new agreement that God makes with his people. This new agreement begins with my blood which is poured out for you."

OLD TESTAMENT READING

LORD, you are my share in life;
   I have promised to obey your words.
58 I prayed to you with all my heart.
   Have mercy on me as you have promised.
59 I thought about my life,
   and I decided to follow your rules.
60 I hurried and did not wait
   to obey your commands.

Psalm 119:57–60

INSIGHTS

The coming of God's Son is the real hope of the believers. . . . The early Christians constantly looked forward to it. The Church in its first love waited for its Lord. How often too Jesus Himself and His apostles admonished us to wait for His coming and to hasten to meet Him! The return of the Lord is not a theme with which certain specialists occupy themselves, but it is the great theme of Scripture and it must also become ours. We are all deeply aware of the fact that our congregations need a spiritual renewal. "How can this take place?" I asked a missionary. "When the hope of the Lord's return becomes living in our congregations," he answered. . . .

Think of a congregation of three hundred in which there were thirty who really were waiting for the Lord. What holiness and what light these could give to a congregation! John says, "Everyone that hath this hope set on him purifieth himself even as he is pure." He that does not have this hope, does not cleanse himself. Those who are really waiting need not be exhorted to cleanse themselves; they do it without outward prompting. They do not need to be urged to press forward, to deny themselves, to humble themselves; they just naturally strive to be like the Lamb. . . . As long as we do not have this Hope, we are really without hope; and the state of such persons is known to us all. . . .

Hitherto many of us have been like the brother who once said: "For many years I have known that I was converted, but I did not know for what purpose. I have long known that I was sealed with the Holy Spirit, but not to what end. But I understood it when 1 Thess. 1:9–10 and Eph. 4:30 became clear to me: we are converted to serve the true and living God, and to wait for His Son from Heaven."

G. Steinberger

ACTION POINT

What must we do to be ready for Jesus return? Will you pray daily to be ready?

LUKE 22:21-53

Who Will Turn Against Jesus?

21"But one of you will turn against me, and his hand is with mine on the table. **22**What God has planned for the Son of Man will happen, but how terrible it will be for that one who turns against the Son of Man."

23Then the apostles asked each other which one of them would do that.

Be Like a Servant

24The apostles also began to argue about which one of them was the most important. **25**But Jesus said to them, "The kings of the non-Jewish people rule over them, and those who have authority over others like to be called 'friends of the people.' **26**But you must not be like that. Instead, the greatest among you should be like the youngest, and the leader should be like the servant. **27**Who is more important: the one sitting at the table or the one serving? You think the one at the table is more important, but I am like a servant among you.

28"You have stayed with me through my struggles. **29**Just as my Father has given me a kingdom, I also give you a kingdom **30**so you may eat and drink at my table in my kingdom. And you will sit on thrones, judging the twelve tribes of Israel.

Don't Lose Your Faith!

31"Simon, Simon, Satan has asked to test all of you as a farmer sifts his wheat. **32**I have prayed that you will not lose your faith! Help your brothers be stronger when you come back to me."

33But Peter said to Jesus, "Lord, I am ready to go with you to prison and even to die with you!"

34But Jesus said, "Peter, before the rooster crows this day, you will say three times that you don't know me."

Be Ready for Trouble

35Then Jesus said to the apostles, "When I sent you out without a purse, a bag, or sandals, did you need anything?"

They said, "No."

36He said to them, "But now if you have a purse or a bag, carry that with you. If you don't have a sword, sell your coat and buy one. **37**The Scripture says, 'He was treated like a criminal,' and I tell you this scripture must have its full meaning. It was written about me, and it is happening now."

38His followers said, "Look, Lord, here are two swords."

He said to them, "That is enough."

Jesus Prays Alone

39Jesus left the city and went to the Mount of Olives, as he often did, and his followers went with him. **40**When he reached the place, he said to them, "Pray for strength against temptation."

41Then Jesus went about a stone's throw away from them. He kneeled down and prayed, **42**"Father, if you are willing, take away this cup of suffering. But do what you want, not what I want." **43**Then an angel from heaven appeared to him to strengthen him. **44**Being full of pain, Jesus prayed even harder. His sweat was like drops of blood falling to the ground. **45**When he finished praying, he went to his followers and found them asleep because of their sadness. **46**Jesus said to them, "Why are you sleeping? Get up and pray for strength against temptation."

Jesus Is Arrested

47While Jesus was speaking, a crowd came up, and Judas, one of the twelve apostles, was leading them. He came close to Jesus so he could kiss him.

48But Jesus said to him, "Judas, are you using the kiss to give the Son of Man to his enemies?"

49When those who were standing around him saw what was happening, they said, "Lord, should we strike them with our swords?" **50**And one of them struck the servant of the high priest and cut off his right ear.

51Jesus said, "Stop! No more of this." Then he touched the servant's ear and healed him.

52Those who came to arrest Jesus were the leading priests, the soldiers who guarded the Temple, and the elders. Jesus said to them, "You came out here with swords and clubs as though I were a criminal. **53**I was with you every day in the Temple, and you didn't arrest me there. But this is your time—the time when darkness rules."

OLD TESTAMENT READING

Lord, save me from my enemies;
    I hide in you.
10Teach me to do what you want,
    because you are my God.
Let your good Spirit
    lead me on level ground.

Psalm 143:9–10

INSIGHTS

I seek at the beginning to get my heart in such a state that it has no will of its own in regard to a given matter. Nine tenths of the trouble with people generally is just here. Nine tenths of the difficulties are overcome when our hearts are ready to do the Lord's will, whatever it may be. When one is truly in this state, it is usually but a little way to the knowledge of what His will is.

Having done this, I do not leave the result to feeling or simple impression. If so, I make myself liable to great delusions.

I seek the will of the Spirit of God through, or in connection with, the Word of God. The Spirit and the Word must be combined. If I look to the Spirit alone without the Word, I lay myself open to great delusions also. If the Holy Spirit guides us at all, He will do it according to the Scriptures and never contrary to them.

Next I take into account providential circumstances. These often plainly indicate God's will in connection with His Word and Spirit.

I ask God in prayer to reveal His will to me aright.

Thus through prayer to God, the study of the Word, and reflection, I come to a deliberate judgment according to the best of my ability and knowledge; and if my mind is thus at peace, and continues so after two or three more petitions, I proceed accordingly.

GEORGE MÜLLER

PAUSE FOR REFLECTION

What did Jesus do to know God's will? What do you do to discover God's will?

LUKE
22:54 — 23:12

Peter Says He Doesn't Know Jesus

54They arrested Jesus, and led him away, and brought him into the house of the high priest. Peter followed far behind them. **55**After the soldiers started a fire in the middle of the courtyard and sat together, Peter sat with them. **56**A servant girl saw Peter sitting there in the firelight, and looking closely at him, she said, "This man was also with him."

57But Peter said this was not true; he said, "Woman, I don't know him."

58A short time later, another person saw Peter and said, "You are also one of them."

But Peter said, "Man, I am not!"

59About an hour later, another man insisted, "Certainly this man was with him, because he is from Galilee, too."

60But Peter said, "Man, I don't know what you are talking about!"

At once, while Peter was still speaking, a rooster crowed. **61**Then the Lord turned and looked straight at Peter. And Peter remembered what the Lord had said: "Before the rooster crows this day, you will say three times that you don't know me." **62**Then Peter went outside and cried painfully.

The People Make Fun of Jesus

63The men who were guarding Jesus began making fun of him and beating him.

64They blindfolded him and said, "Prove that you are a prophet, and tell us who hit you." **65**They said many cruel things to Jesus.

Jesus Before the Leaders

66When day came, the council of the elders of the people, both the leading priests and the teachers of the law, came together and led Jesus to their highest court. **67**They said, "If you are the Christ, tell us."

Jesus said to them, "If I tell you, you will not believe me. **68**And if I ask you, you will not answer. **69**But from now on, the Son of Man will sit at the right hand of the powerful God."

70They all said, "Then are you the Son of God?"

Jesus said to them, "You say that I am."

71They said, "Why do we need witnesses now? We ourselves heard him say this."

Pilate Questions Jesus

23 Then the whole group stood up and led Jesus to Pilate. **2**They began to accuse Jesus, saying, "We caught this man telling things that mislead our people. He says that we should not pay taxes to Caesar, and he calls himself the Christ, a king."

3Pilate asked Jesus, "Are you the king of the Jews?"

Jesus answered, "Those are your words."

4Pilate said to the leading priests and the people, "I find nothing against this man."

5They were insisting, saying, "But Jesus makes trouble with the people, teaching all around Judea. He began in Galilee, and now he is here."

Pilate Sends Jesus to Herod

6Pilate heard this and asked if Jesus was from Galilee. **7**Since Jesus was under Herod's authority, Pilate sent Jesus to Herod, who was in Jerusalem at that time. **8**When Herod saw Jesus, he was very glad, because he had heard about Jesus and had wanted to meet him for a long time. He was hoping to see Jesus work a miracle. **9**Herod asked Jesus many questions, but Jesus said nothing. **10**The leading priests and teachers of the law were standing there, strongly accusing Jesus. **11**After Herod and his soldiers had made fun of Jesus, they dressed him in a kingly robe and sent him back to Pilate. **12**In the past, Pilate and Herod had always been enemies, but on that day they became friends.

OLD TESTAMENT READING

ut Isaac said, "Your brother came and tricked me. He has taken your blessing."

36Esau said, "Jacob is the right name for him. He has tricked me these two times. He took away my share of everything you own, and now he has taken away my blessing." Then Esau asked, "Haven't you saved a blessing for me?"

37Isaac answered, "I gave Jacob the power to be master over you, and all his brothers will be his servants. And I kept him strong with grain and new wine. There is nothing left to give you, my son."

41After that Esau hated Jacob because of the blessing from Isaac. He thought to himself, "My father will soon die, and I will be sad for him. Then I will kill Jacob."

Genesis 27:35–37, 41

INSIGHTS

For the Old Testament Jew, truth was a sacred matter. Truth involved a proper understanding of reality, but it also involved much more than that. For the Jew truth also had a personal dimension, an emotional dimension, and an ethical dimension.

Truth is personal—it is a special part of any close human relationship. Trust is a by-product of truth, and personal relationships are built upon trust. I trust people who demonstrate that they are truthful. I do not trust people who show themselves to be habitual liars.

Broken truth hurts. Satan, "the father of lies," loves to attack and distort truth. The Scripture says that Satan was a liar from the beginning. It is painful for anybody to invest his heart in a lie. A broken truth often means a broken heart. This is the problem with lies. We do invest our hearts in the promises people make and the stories they tell us. When the promises are not kept and the stories prove to be false, we are hurt. We are disillusioned. We sometimes grow bitter. Trust is a fragile commodity and is as precious as it is delicate. Deep levels of trust take years to develop. Yet, such trust can be smashed to pieces in seconds.

R. C. SPROUL

PAUSE FOR REFLECTION

How did deceit in Isaac's family change the family relationships? When Peter lied about knowing Jesus, how did he feel? How did his relationship with Jesus change? Thank Jesus that his trust never fails!

LUKE 23:13-43

Jesus Must Die

13Pilate called the people together with the leading priests and the rulers. **14**He said to them, "You brought this man to me, saying he makes trouble among the people. But I have questioned him before you all, and I have not found him guilty of what you say. **15**Also, Herod found nothing wrong with him; he sent him back to us. Look, he has done nothing for which he should die. **16**So, after I punish him, I will let him go free." [**17**Every year at the Passover Feast, Pilate had to release one prisoner to the people.]

18But the people shouted together, "Take this man away! Let Barabbas go free!" **19**(Barabbas was a man who was in prison for his part in a riot in the city and for murder.)

20Pilate wanted to let Jesus go free and told this to the crowd. **21**But they shouted again, "Crucify him! Crucify him!"

22A third time Pilate said to them, "Why? What wrong has he done? I can find no reason to kill him. So I will have him punished and set him free."

23But they continued to shout, demanding that Jesus be crucified. Their yelling became so loud that **24**Pilate decided to give them what they wanted. **25**He set free the man who was in jail for rioting and murder, and he handed Jesus over to them to do with him as they wished.

Jesus Is Crucified

26As they led Jesus away, Simon, a man from Cyrene, was coming in from the fields. They forced him to carry Jesus' cross and to walk behind him.

27A large crowd of people was following Jesus, including some women who were sad and crying for him. **28**But Jesus turned and said to them, "Women of Jerusalem, don't cry for me. Cry for yourselves and for your children. **29**The time is coming when people will say, 'Blessed are the women who cannot have children and who have no babies to nurse.' **30**Then people will say to the mountains, 'Fall on us!' And they will say to the hills, 'Cover us!' **31**If they act like this now when life is good, what will happen when bad times come?"

32There were also two criminals led out with Jesus to be put to death. **33**When they came to a place called the Skull, the soldiers crucified Jesus and the criminals—one on his right and the other on his left. **34**Jesus said, "Father, forgive them, because they don't know what they are doing."

The soldiers threw lots to decide who would get his clothes. **35**The people stood there watching. And the leaders made fun of Jesus, saying, "He saved others. Let him save himself if he is God's Chosen One, the Christ."

36The soldiers also made fun of him, coming to Jesus and offering him some vinegar. **37**They said, "If you are the king of the Jews, save yourself!" **38**At the top of the cross these words were written: THIS IS THE KING OF THE JEWS.

39One of the criminals on a cross began to shout insults at Jesus: "Aren't you the Christ? Then save yourself and us."

40But the other criminal stopped him and said, "You should fear God! You are getting the same punishment he is. **41**We are punished justly, getting what we deserve for what we did. But this man has done nothing wrong." **42**Then he said, "Jesus, remember me when you come into your kingdom."

43Jesus said to him, "I tell you the truth, today you will be with me in paradise."

OLD TESTAMENT READING

This is what the Lord GOD, the Holy One of Israel, says:

"If you come back to me and trust me, you
　　will be saved.
　If you will be calm and trust me, you will
　　be strong."
　But you don't want to do that.
18The LORD wants to show his mercy to you.
　He wants to rise and comfort you.
The LORD is a fair God,
　and everyone who waits for his help will be
　　happy.

Isaiah 30:15, 18

INSIGHTS

The prisoners in the Montinlupa Prison who gathered for a large assembly were astonished to see a woman in her seventies make her way up the steps of the platform to address them. What would an old woman have to say to them? . . .

. . . She told how she and her family had hidden Jews from the Nazis during World War II and how German police, because of a tip from two of her fellow citizens, had pounded on their door one frigid February day in 1944 with warrants for their arrest. The speaker was Corrie ten Boom. . . .

After the war was over, the two Dutchmen who had betrayed her family were taken into custody and put on trial. . . . "My sister Nollie," Corrie told her audience, "heard of the trial of these two men who told the Gestapo about us, and she wrote a letter to both of them. . . . She told them that we had forgiven them and that we could do this because of Jesus, who is in our hearts."

Both men responded. One wrote: "I have received Jesus as my Savior. When you can give such ability to forgive to people like Corrie ten Boom and her sister, then there is hope for me. I brought my sins to Him." The other letter gave an opposite viewpoint: "I know what I have done to your family, that I have caused the death of several of you who have saved Jews, and above that I have helped to kill many hundreds of Jewish people. The only thing I regret is that I have not been able to kill more of your kind." Corrie went on to challenge the prisoners that every one of them—even as those criminals who had been on the cross—could accept or reject Christ and his forgiveness.

RUTH TUCKER

APPLICATION

How much evil will God forgive? What does he require to receive forgiveness? Are you willing to turn away from a life of sin and trust God for your salvation?

LUKE 23:44 — 24:12

Jesus Dies

44It was about noon, and the whole land became dark until three o'clock in the afternoon, **45**because the sun did not shine. The curtain in the Temple was torn in two. **46**Jesus cried out in a loud voice, "Father, I give you my life." After Jesus said this, he died.

47When the army officer there saw what happened, he praised God, saying, "Surely this was a good man!"

48When all the people who had gathered there to watch saw what happened, they returned home, beating their chests because they were so sad. **49**But those who were close friends of Jesus, including the women who had followed him from Galilee, stood at a distance and watched.

Joseph Takes Jesus' Body

50There was a good and religious man named Joseph who was a member of the council. **51**But he had not agreed to the other leaders' plans and actions against Jesus. He was from the town of Arimathea and was waiting for the kingdom of God to come. **52**Joseph went to Pilate to ask for the body of Jesus. **53**He took the body down from the cross, wrapped it in cloth, and put it in a tomb that was cut out of a wall of rock. This tomb had never been used before. **54**This was late on Preparation Day, and when the sun went down, the Sabbath day would begin.

55The women who had come from Galilee with Jesus followed Joseph and saw the tomb and how Jesus' body was laid. **56**Then the women left to prepare spices and perfumes.

On the Sabbath day they rested, as the law of Moses commanded.

Jesus Rises from the Dead

24 Very early on the first day of the week, at dawn, the women came to the tomb, bringing the spices they had prepared. **2**They found the stone rolled away from the entrance of the tomb, **3**but when they went in, they did not find the body of the Lord Jesus. **4**While they were wondering about this, two men in shining clothes suddenly stood beside them. **5**The women were very afraid and bowed their heads to the ground. The men said to them, "Why are you looking for a living person in this place for the dead? **6**He is not here; he has risen from the dead. Do you remember what he told you in Galilee? **7**He said the Son of Man must be handed over to sinful people, be crucified, and rise from the dead on the third day." **8**Then the women remembered what Jesus had said.

9The women left the tomb and told all these things to the eleven apostles and the other followers. **10**It was Mary Magdalene, Joanna, Mary the mother of James, and some other women who told the apostles everything that had happened at the tomb. **11**But they did not believe the women, because it sounded like nonsense. **12**But Peter got up and ran to the tomb. Bending down and looking in, he saw only the cloth that Jesus' body had been wrapped in. Peter went away to his home, wondering about what had happened.

OLD TESTAMENT READING

Here is my servant, the one I support.
He is the one I chose, and I am pleased
  with him.
I have put my Spirit upon him,
  and he will bring justice to all nations.
²He will not cry out or yell
  or speak loudly in the streets.
³He will not break a crushed blade of grass
  or put out even a weak flame.
He will truly bring justice;
⁴ he will not lose hope or give up
  until he brings justice to the world.

And people far away will trust his
  teachings."

⁶The LORD says, "I, the LORD, called you to do
  right,
  and I will hold your hand
 and protect you.
  You will be the sign of my agreement with
    the people,
  a light to shine for all people.
⁷You will help the blind to see.
  You will free those who are in prison,
  and you will lead those who live in
    darkness out of their prison.

Isaiah 42:1–4, 6–7

INSIGHTS

Never underestimate the power of a seed.

God didn't. When his kingdom was ravaged and his people had forgotten his name, he planted his seed. When the soil of the human heart had grown crusty, he planted his seed. When religion had become a ritual and the temple a trading post, he planted his seed.

Want to see a miracle? Watch him as he places the seed of his own self in the fertile womb of a Jewish girl.

Up it grew, "like a tender green shoot, sprouting from a root in dry and sterile ground." The seed spent a lifetime pushing back the stones that tried to keep it underground. The seed made a ministry out of shoving away the rocks that cluttered his father's soil.

The stones of legalism that burdened backs.

The stones of oppression that broke bones.

The stones of prejudice that fenced out the needy.

But it was the final stone that proved to be the supreme test of the seed. The stone of death—rolled by humans and sealed by Satan in front of the tomb. For a moment it appeared the seed would be stuck in the earth. For a moment, it looked like this rock was too big to be budged.

But then, somewhere in the heart of the earth, the seed of God stirred, shoved, and sprouted. The ground trembled, and the rock of the tomb tumbled. And the flower of Easter blossomed.

Never underestimate the power of a seed.

MAX LUCADO

▶ PAUSE FOR REFLECTION

What warnings did Jesus' followers have that he would die and rise again? When you ponder Christ's awesome salvation, do you, like Peter, take time alone to take it all in?

LUKE 24:13 - 53

Jesus on the Road to Emmaus

13That same day two of Jesus' followers were going to a town named Emmaus, about seven miles from Jerusalem. **14**They were talking about everything that had happened. **15**While they were talking and discussing, Jesus himself came near and began walking with them, **16**but they were kept from recognizing him. **17**Then he said, "What are these things you are talking about while you walk?"

The two followers stopped, looking very sad. **18**The one named Cleopas answered, "Are you the only visitor in Jerusalem who does not know what just happened there?"

19Jesus said to them, "What are you talking about?"

They said, "About Jesus of Nazareth. He was a prophet who said and did many powerful things before God and all the people. **20**Our leaders and the leading priests handed him over to be sentenced to death, and they crucified him. **21**But we were hoping that he would free Israel. Besides this, it is now the third day since this happened. **22**And today some women among us amazed us. Early this morning they went to the tomb, **23**but they did not find his body there. They came and told us that they had seen a vision of angels who said that Jesus was alive! **24**So some of our group went to the tomb, too. They found it just as the women said, but they did not see Jesus."

25Then Jesus said to them, "You are foolish and slow to believe everything the prophets said. **26**They said that the Christ must suffer these things before he enters his glory." **27**Then starting with what Moses and all the prophets had said about him, Jesus began to explain everything that had been written about himself in the Scriptures.

28They came near the town of Emmaus, and Jesus acted as if he were going farther. **29**But they begged him, "Stay with us, because it is late; it is almost night." So he went in to stay with them.

30When Jesus was at the table with them, he took some bread, gave thanks, divided it, and gave it to them. **31**And then, they were allowed to recognize Jesus. But when they saw who he was, he disappeared. **32**They said to each other, "It felt like a fire burning in us when Jesus talked to us on the road and explained the Scriptures to us."

33So the two followers got up at once and went back to Jerusalem. There they found the eleven apostles and others gathered. **34**They were saying, "The Lord really has risen from the dead! He showed himself to Simon."

35Then the two followers told what had happened on the road and how they recognized Jesus when he divided the bread.

Jesus Appears to His Followers

36While the two followers were telling this, Jesus himself stood right in the middle of them and said, "Peace be with you."

37They were fearful and terrified and thought they were seeing a ghost. **38**But Jesus said, "Why are you troubled? Why do you doubt what you see? **39**Look at my hands and my feet. It is I myself! Touch me and see, because a ghost does not have a living body as you see I have."

40After Jesus said this, he showed them his hands and feet. **41**While they still could not believe it because they were amazed and happy, Jesus said to them, "Do you have any food here?" **42**They gave him a piece of broiled fish. **43**While the followers watched, Jesus took the fish and ate it.

44He said to them, "Remember when I was with you before? I said that everything written about me must happen—everything in the law of Moses, the books of the prophets, and the Psalms."

45Then Jesus opened their minds so they could understand the Scriptures. **46**He said to them, "It is written that the Christ would suffer and rise from the dead on the third day **47**and that a change of hearts and lives and forgiveness of sins would be preached in his name to all nations, starting at Jerusalem. **48**You are witnesses of these things. **49**I will send you what my Father has promised, but you must stay in Jerusalem until you have received that power from heaven."

Jesus Goes Back to Heaven

50Jesus led his followers as far as Bethany, and he raised his hands and blessed them.

51While he was blessing them, he was separated from them and carried into heaven. **52**They worshiped him and returned to Jerusalem very happy. **53**They stayed in the Temple all the time, praising God.

OLD TESTAMENT READING

Jerusalem, you have good news to tell.
    Go up on a high mountain.
Jerusalem, you have good news to tell.
    Shout out loud the good news.
Shout it out and don't be afraid.
    Say to the towns of Judah,
    "Here is your God."
10Look, the Lord GOD is coming with power
    to rule all the people.

Isaiah 40:9–10a

INSIGHTS

Everyone has the great responsibility to win as many people as possible to Christ. This is the great privilege and the great duty of all disciples of Christ. . . .

I fear I must say that the great mass of people professing to be believers seem never to have been impressed with this truth. The work of saving souls is something they feel they can leave to ministers.

Many believers suppose it belongs only to those who are called to preach the gospel as a life work. They fail to realize that all are called to preach the gospel, that the whole life of every believer is to be a proclamation of the glad tidings.

CHARLES FINNEY

ACTION POINT

Write, in your own words, the essential message of salvation that Jesus wants his followers to proclaim. To whom does he want you to deliver that message? Will you?

JOHN 1:1-28

Christ Comes to the World

In the beginning there was the Word. The Word was with God, and the Word was God. **2**He was with God in the beginning. **3**All things were made by him, and nothing was made without him. **4**In him there was life, and that life was the light of all people. **5**The Light shines in the darkness, and the darkness has not overpowered it.

6There was a man named John who was sent by God. **7**He came to tell people the truth about the Light so that through him all people could hear about the Light and believe. **8**John was not the Light, but he came to tell people the truth about the Light. **9**The true Light that gives light to all was coming into the world!

10The Word was in the world, and the world was made by him, but the world did not know him. **11**He came to the world that was his own, but his own people did not accept him. **12**But to all who did accept him and believe in him he gave the right to become children of God. **13**They did not become his children in any human way—by any human parents or human desire. They were born of God.

14The Word became a human and lived among us. We saw his glory—the glory that belongs to the only Son of the Father—and he was full of grace and truth. **15**John tells the truth about him and cries out, saying, "This is the One I told you about: 'The One who comes after me is greater than I am, because he was living before me.'"

16Because he was full of grace and truth, from him we all received one gift after another. **17**The law was given through Moses, but grace and truth came through Jesus Christ. **18**No one has ever seen God. But God the only Son is very close to the Father, and he has shown us what God is like.

John Tells People About Jesus

19Here is the truth John told when the leaders in Jerusalem sent priests and Levites to ask him, "Who are you?"

20John spoke freely and did not refuse to answer. He said, "I am not the Christ."

21So they asked him, "Then who are you? Are you Elijah?"

He answered, "No, I am not."

"Are you the Prophet?" they asked.

He answered, "No."

22Then they said, "Who are you? Give us an answer to tell those who sent us. What do you say about yourself?"

23John told them in the words of the prophet Isaiah:

"I am the voice of one
    calling out in the desert:
'Make the road straight for the Lord.'"

Isaiah 40:3

24Some Pharisees who had been sent asked John: **25**"If you are not the Christ or Elijah or the Prophet, why do you baptize people?"

26John answered, "I baptize with water, but there is one here with you that you don't know about. **27**He is the One who comes after me. I am not good enough to untie the strings of his sandals."

28This all happened at Bethany on the other side of the Jordan River, where John was baptizing people.

OLD TESTAMENT READING

Before those people lived in darkness,
but now they have seen a great light.
They lived in a dark land,
but a light has shined on them.
⁶A child has been born to us;

God has given a son to us.
He will be responsible for leading the
people.
His name will be Wonderful Counselor,
Powerful God,
Father Who Lives Forever, Prince of Peace.

Isaiah 9:2, 6

INSIGHTS

Thanks to the great mercy and marvel of the Incarnation, the cosmic scene is resolved into a human drama. God reaches down to relate himself to man, and man reaches up to relate himself to God. Time looks into eternity and eternity into time, making now always and always now. Everything is transformed by this sublime drama of the Incarnation, God's special parable for fallen man in a fallen world. The way opens before us that was charted in the birth, ministry, death, and resurrection of Jesus Christ, a way that successive generations of believers have striven to follow. They have derived therefrom the moral, spiritual, and intellectual creativity out of which has come everything truly great in our art, our literature, our music. . . .

. . . Whatever may happen, however seemingly inimical to it may be the world's going and those who preside over the world's affairs, the truth of the Incarnation remains intact and inviolate. . . .

. . . Christ shows what life really is, and what our true destiny is. We escape from the cave. We emerge from the darkness and instead of shadows we have all around us the glory of God's creation. Instead of darkness we have light; instead of despair, hope; instead of time and the clocks ticking inexorably on, eternity, which never began and never ends and yet is sublimely now. . . . By identifying ourselves with Christ, by absorbing ourselves in his teaching, by living out the drama of his life with him, including especially the passion, that powerhouse of love and creativity—by living with, by, and in him, we can be reborn to become new men and women in a new world.

MALCOLM MUGGERIDGE

PAUSE FOR REFLECTION

In what ways would you say Christ's coming to earth enlightened the world? What did Christ's coming reveal? What difference does being reborn of God—becoming one of his children—make in your life?

JOHN 1:29 - 51

²⁹The next day John saw Jesus coming toward him. John said, "Look, the Lamb of God, who takes away the sin of the world! ³⁰This is the One I was talking about when I said, 'A man will come after me, but he is greater than I am, because he was living before me.' ³¹Even I did not know who he was, although I came baptizing with water so that the people of Israel would know who he is."

³²⁻³³Then John said, "I saw the Spirit come down from heaven in the form of a dove and rest on him. Until then I did not know who the Christ was. But the God who sent me to baptize with water told me, 'You will see the Spirit come down and rest on a man; he is the One who will baptize with the Holy Spirit.' ³⁴I have seen this happen, and I tell you the truth: This man is the Son of God."

The First Followers of Jesus

³⁵The next day John was there again with two of his followers. ³⁶When he saw Jesus walking by, he said, "Look, the Lamb of God!"

³⁷The two followers heard John say this, so they followed Jesus. ³⁸When Jesus turned and saw them following him, he asked, "What are you looking for?"

They said, "Rabbi, where are you staying?" ("Rabbi" means "Teacher.")

³⁹He answered, "Come and see." So the two men went with Jesus and saw where he was staying and stayed there with him that day. It was about four o'clock in the afternoon.

⁴⁰One of the two men who followed Jesus after they heard John speak about him was Andrew, Simon Peter's brother. ⁴¹The first thing Andrew did was to find his brother Simon and say to him, "We have found the Messiah." ("Messiah" means "Christ.")

⁴²Then Andrew took Simon to Jesus. Jesus looked at him and said, "You are Simon son of John. You will be called Cephas." ("Cephas" means "Peter.")

⁴³The next day Jesus decided to go to Galilee. He found Philip and said to him, "Follow me."

⁴⁴Philip was from the town of Bethsaida, where Andrew and Peter lived. ⁴⁵Philip found Nathanael and told him, "We have found the man that Moses wrote about in the law, and the prophets also wrote about him. He is Jesus, the son of Joseph, from Nazareth."

⁴⁶But Nathanael said to Philip, "Can anything good come from Nazareth?"

Philip answered, "Come and see."

⁴⁷As Jesus saw Nathanael coming toward him, he said, "Here is truly an Israelite. There is nothing false in him."

⁴⁸Nathanael asked, "How do you know me?"

Jesus answered, "I saw you when you were under the fig tree, before Philip told you about me."

⁴⁹Then Nathanael said to Jesus, "Teacher, you are the Son of God; you are the King of Israel."

⁵⁰Jesus said to Nathanael, "Do you believe simply because I told you I saw you under the fig tree? You will see greater things than that." ⁵¹And Jesus said to them, "I tell you the truth, you will all see heaven open and 'angels of God going up and coming down' on the Son of Man."

OLD TESTAMENT READING

We all have wandered away like sheep;
   each of us has gone his own way.
But the LORD has put on him the punishment
   for all the evil we have done.

7He was beaten down and punished,
   but he didn't say a word.
He was like a lamb being led to be killed.

He was quiet, as a sheep is quiet while its
   wool is being cut;
he never opened his mouth.
8Men took him away roughly and unfairly.
   He died without children to continue his
      family.
He was put to death;
   he was punished for the sins of my
      people.

Isaiah 53:6–8

INSIGHTS

It was never meant
to burst from the body
so fiercely, to pour
unchannelled from
the five wounds
and the unbandaged brow,
drowning the dark wood,
staining the stones
and the gravel below,
clotting in the air
dark with God's absence.

It was created for
a closed system—
the unbroken
rhythms of human blood
binding the body
of God, circulating

hot, brilliant,
saline, without
interruption
between heart, lungs
and all cells.

But because he
was once emptied
I am each day refilled;
my spirit-arteries
pulse with the vital red
of love; poured out,
it is his life
that now pumps through
my own heart's core.
He bled, and died, and I
have been transfused.

LUCI SHAW

▶ PAUSE FOR REFLECTION

What an awesome thing to be saved by the Lamb of God! How well do you know the Lamb of God? As certainly as John, Andrew, and Philip did? Or are you a bit skeptical, as Nathanael was? Reread the Isaiah passage and pray for a renewed knowledge of the Lamb of God—in your mind and in your heart.

JOHN 2:1-25

The Wedding at Cana

Two days later there was a wedding in the town of Cana in Galilee. Jesus' mother was there, **2**and Jesus and his followers were also invited to the wedding. **3**When all the wine was gone, Jesus' mother said to him, "They have no more wine."

4Jesus answered, "Dear woman, why come to me? My time has not yet come."

5His mother said to the servants, "Do whatever he tells you to do."

6In that place there were six stone water jars that the Jews used in their washing ceremony. Each jar held about twenty or thirty gallons.

7Jesus said to the servants, "Fill the jars with water." So they filled the jars to the top.

8Then he said to them, "Now take some out and give it to the master of the feast."

So they took the water to the master. **9**When he tasted it, the water had become wine. He did not know where the wine came from, but the servants who had brought the water knew. The master of the wedding called the bridegroom **10**and said to him, "People always serve the best wine first. Later, after the guests have been drinking awhile, they serve the cheaper wine. But you have saved the best wine till now."

11So in Cana of Galilee Jesus did his first miracle. There he showed his glory, and his followers believed in him.

Jesus in the Temple

12After this, Jesus went to the town of Capernaum with his mother, brothers, and followers. They stayed there for just a few days. **13**When it was almost time for the Jewish Passover Feast, Jesus went to Jerusalem. **14**In the Temple he found people selling cattle, sheep, and doves. He saw others sitting at tables, exchanging different kinds of money. **15**Jesus made a whip out of cords and forced all of them, both the sheep and cattle, to leave the Temple. He turned over the tables and scattered the money of those who were exchanging it. **16**Then he said to those who were selling pigeons, "Take these things out of here! Don't make my Father's house a place for buying and selling!"

17When this happened, the followers remembered what was written in the Scriptures: "My strong love for your Temple completely controls me."

18Some of his people said to Jesus, "Show us a miracle to prove you have the right to do these things."

19Jesus answered them, "Destroy this temple, and I will build it again in three days."

20They answered, "It took forty-six years to build this Temple! Do you really believe you can build it again in three days?"

21(But the temple Jesus meant was his own body. **22**After Jesus was raised from the dead, his followers remembered that Jesus had said this. Then they believed the Scripture and the words Jesus had said.)

23When Jesus was in Jerusalem for the Passover Feast, many people believed in him because they saw the miracles he did. **24**But Jesus did not believe in them because he knew them all. **25**He did not need anyone to tell him about people, because he knew what was in people's minds.

OLD TESTAMENT READING

I will look for trustworthy people
so I can live with them in the land.
Only those who live innocent lives
will be my servants.

[7] No one who is dishonest will live in my house;
no liars will stay around me.
[8] Every morning I will destroy the wicked in
the land.
I will rid the LORD's city of people who do
evil.

Psalm 101:6–8

INSIGHTS

In Cana Jesus manifested His power as the Creator. Now He came to manifest His authority as the Messiah, the Son of God. Not only did He drive the sheep and oxen out of the temple, but He whipped the merchants out of the place. These Jews knew that He was right. The law and their consciences were witnesses against them. Christ was filled with righteous indignation in His zeal for His Father's house.

Christ cleansed the temple by crying, "Make not my Father's house an house of merchandise." Mark that He calls the temple "My Father's house." Christ was claiming a unique relationship with the Living God. . . .

When Christ drove the merchandisers out of the temple, they experienced something of the terror of the Lord. In the future men will cry to the mountains and rocks to hide them "from the face of him that sitteth on the throne, and from the wrath of the Lamb: For the great day of his wrath is come; and who shall be able to stand?" (Revelation 6:16–17).

Sometimes we forget that He is a righteous God and that every one of us must one day stand in His presence and give an account to Him. "It is a fearful thing to fall into the hands of the living God" (Hebrews 10:31). . . .

. . . Christ cleansed the temple when men sinned and made it unclean. Similarly, the Lord has a right to cleanse us when we sin. It is much better for us to willingly confess our sins so that He may forgive and cleanse us. And He is willing and ready to do just that. How wonderful it is to know that the blood of Jesus Christ, God's Son, cleanseth us from all sin (1 John 1:7).

JOHN G. MITCHELL

ACTION POINT

What was revealed by the Jews' demand that Jesus prove he had the right to cleanse God's temple? In what ways do you demand that Jesus prove his right to purge the sin from your heart (which is also his temple)? Ask for his forgiveness.

JOHN 3:1-30

Nicodemus Comes to Jesus

3 There was a man named Nicodemus who was one of the Pharisees and an important Jewish leader. **2**One night Nicodemus came to Jesus and said, "Teacher, we know you are a teacher sent from God, because no one can do the miracles you do unless God is with him."

3Jesus answered, "I tell you the truth, unless you are born again, you cannot be in God's kingdom."

4Nicodemus said, "But if a person is already old, how can he be born again? He cannot enter his mother's womb again. So how can a person be born a second time?"

5But Jesus answered, "I tell you the truth, unless you are born from water and the Spirit, you cannot enter God's kingdom. **6**Human life comes from human parents, but spiritual life comes from the Spirit. **7**Don't be surprised when I tell you, 'You must all be born again.' **8**The wind blows where it wants to and you hear the sound of it, but you don't know where the wind comes from or where it is going. It is the same with every person who is born from the Spirit."

9Nicodemus asked, "How can this happen?"

10Jesus said, "You are an important teacher in Israel, and you don't understand these things? **11**I tell you the truth, we talk about what we know, and we tell about what we have seen, but you don't accept what we tell you. **12**I have told you about things here on earth, and you do not believe me. So you will not believe me if I tell you about things

of heaven. **13**The only one who has ever gone up to heaven is the One who came down from heaven—the Son of Man.

14"Just as Moses lifted up the snake in the desert, the Son of Man must also be lifted up. **15**So that everyone who believes can have eternal life in him.

16"God loved the world so much that he gave his one and only Son so that whoever believes in him may not be lost, but have eternal life. **17**God did not send his Son into the world to judge the world guilty, but to save the world through him. **18**People who believe in God's Son are not judged guilty. Those who do not believe have already been judged guilty, because they have not believed in God's one and only Son. **19**They are judged by this fact: The Light has come into the world, but they did not want light. They wanted darkness, because they were doing evil things. **20**All who do evil hate the light and will not come to the light, because it will show all the evil things they do. **21**But those who follow the true way come to the light, and it shows that the things they do were done through God."

Jesus and John the Baptist

22After this, Jesus and his followers went into the area of Judea, where he stayed with his followers and baptized people. **23**John was also baptizing in Aenon, near Salim, because there was plenty of water there. People were going there to be baptized. **24**(This was before John was put into prison.)

25Some of John's followers had an argument with a Jew about religious washing. **26**So they came to John and said, "Teacher, remember the man who was with you on the other side of the

Jordan River, the one you spoke about so much? He is baptizing, and everyone is going to him."

27John answered, "A man can get only what God gives him. **28**You yourselves heard me say, 'I am not the Christ, but I am the one sent to prepare the way for him.' **29**The bride belongs only to the bridegroom. But the friend who helps the bridegroom stands by and listens to him. He is thrilled that he gets to hear the bridegroom's voice. In the same way, I am really happy. **30**He must become greater, and I must become less important."

OLD TESTAMENT READING

The LORD looked and could not find any justice,
> and he was displeased.

16He could not find anyone to help the people,
> and he was surprised that there was no one
> to help.

So he used his own power to save the people;
> his own goodness gave him strength.

17He covered himself with goodness like armor.
> He put the helmet of salvation on his head.

He put on his clothes for punishing
> and wrapped himself in the coat of his
> strong love.

Isaiah 59:15b–17

INSIGHTS

God loves us, not only as a host of human beings who are living on the earth at this time, but as individuals whom He knows by name. He has a personal interest in each one. He has a perfect plan for every detail in the life of each individual. He is not willing that any should perish, but wants all mankind to be saved and come to the knowledge of the truth (1 Timothy 2:4).

The greatest and most profound expression of God's love for us is in the death of Christ on the cross. Men rejected the Lord Jesus Christ as God's Son, falsely accused Him, condemned Him to death, beat Him, crowned Him with thorns, spit on Him, made sport of Him, crucified Him with thieves, and ridiculed Him. While they were doing this, He forgave them and paid the penalty of their sin by dying for them.

This speaks most powerfully of the extent of God's unchanging, everlasting love. There is no greater expression of love than for a man to lay down his life for his friends.

LUCILLE SOLLENBERGER

ACTION POINT

What motivated God to use his own power, to send his own son, to save us? Why do some reject God's salvation? Reread Isaiah 59:15b–17 and as you do, ask God for his forgiveness of your wrongs and praise him for offering himself to save you.

JOHN 3:31—4:26

The One Who Comes from Heaven

31"The One who comes from above is greater than all. The one who is from the earth belongs to the earth and talks about things on the earth. But the One who comes from heaven is greater than all. **32**He tells what he has seen and heard, but no one accepts what he says. **33**Whoever accepts what he says has proven that God is true. **34**The One whom God sent speaks the words of God, because God gives him the Spirit fully. **35**The Father loves the Son and has given him power over everything. **36**Those who believe in the Son have eternal life, but those who do not obey the Son will never have life. God's anger stays on them."

Jesus and a Samaritan Woman

4 The Pharisees heard that Jesus was making and baptizing more followers than John, **2**although Jesus himself did not baptize people, but his followers did. **3**Jesus knew that the Pharisees had heard about him, so he left Judea and went back to Galilee. **4**But on the way he had to go through the country of Samaria.

5In Samaria Jesus came to the town called Sychar, which is near the field Jacob gave to his son Joseph. **6**Jacob's well was there. Jesus was tired from his long trip, so he sat down beside the well. It was about twelve o'clock noon. **7**When a Samaritan woman came to the well to get some water, Jesus said to her, "Please give me a drink." **8**(This happened while Jesus' followers were in town buying some food.)

9The woman said, "I am surprised that you ask me for a drink, since you are a Jewish man and I am a Samaritan woman." (Jewish people are not friends with Samaritans.)

10Jesus said, "If you only knew the free gift of God and who it is that is asking you for water, you would have asked him, and he would have given you living water."

11The woman said, "Sir, where will you get this living water? The well is very deep, and you have nothing to get water with. **12**Are you greater than Jacob, our father, who gave us this well and drank from it himself along with his sons and flocks?"

13Jesus answered, "Everyone who drinks this water will be thirsty again, **14**but whoever drinks the water I give will never be thirsty. The water I give will become a spring of water gushing up inside that person, giving eternal life."

15The woman said to him, "Sir, give me this water so I will never be thirsty again and will not have to come back here to get more water."

16Jesus told her, "Go get your husband and come back here."

17The woman answered, "I have no husband." Jesus said to her, "You are right to say you have no husband. **18**Really you have had five husbands, and the man you live with now is not your husband. You told the truth."

19The woman said, "Sir, I can see that you are a prophet. **20**Our ancestors worshiped on this mountain, but you say that Jerusalem is the place where people must worship."

21Jesus said, "Believe me, woman. The time is coming when neither in Jerusalem nor on this mountain will you actually worship the Father.

22You Samaritans worship something you don't understand. We understand what we worship, because salvation comes from the Jews. 23The time is coming when the true worshipers will worship the Father in spirit and truth, and that time is here already. You see, the Father too is actively seeking such people to worship him. 24God is spirit, and those who worship him must worship in spirit and truth."

25The woman said, "I know that the Messiah is coming." (Messiah is the One called Christ.) "When the Messiah comes, he will explain everything to us."

26Then Jesus said, "I am he—I, the one talking to you."

OLD TESTAMENT READING

Skies, be shocked at the things that have happened
    and shake with great fear!" says the LORD.
13"My people have done two evils:
    They have turned away from me,
        the spring of living water.
    And they have dug their own wells,
        which are broken wells that cannot hold water.
18It did not help to go to Egypt
    and drink from the Shihor River.
    It did not help to go to Assyria
        and drink from the Euphrates River.
19Your evil will bring punishment to you,
    and the wrong you have done will teach you a lesson.
    Think about it and understand
    that it is a terrible evil to turn away from the
        LORD your God.
    It is wrong not to fear me,"
    says the Lord GOD All-Powerful.

Jeremiah 2:12–13, 18–19

INSIGHTS

The flow of life surging and pulsing through me to refresh this weary old world must be from God Himself. It must be the continuous outpouring of His Presence by His Spirit which touches and transforms all around me. Any person naive enough, arrogant enough, stupid enough to believe that it is his or her own charm, charisma, or capabilities that change and enliven others, lives in utter self-delusion.

One of the terrible tragedies of human behavior is for people to turn to other human beings in an effort to find sustenance for their spirits. They are always deluded, ever disappointed. Our spirits can only find life in the Living Spirit of the Living Lord. Our eternal quest for life-giving water can only be quenched by the eternal life of God Himself coming to us through the hidden springs of His own person who indwells those who are open channels for His life.

W. PHILLIP KELLER

PAUSE FOR REFLECTION

What do those who drink of Jesus' living water receive? How does one receive living water? What is the source of your sustenance?

JOHN 4:27-54

27Just then his followers came back from town and were surprised to see him talking with a woman. But none of them asked, "What do you want?" or "Why are you talking with her?"

28Then the woman left her water jar and went back to town. She said to the people, **29**"Come and see a man who told me everything I ever did. Do you think he might be the Christ?" **30**So the people left the town and went to see Jesus.

31Meanwhile, his followers were begging him, "Teacher, eat something."

32But Jesus answered, "I have food to eat that you know nothing about."

33So the followers asked themselves, "Did somebody already bring him food?"

34Jesus said, "My food is to do what the One who sent me wants me to do and to finish his work. **35**You have a saying, 'Four more months till harvest.' But I tell you, open your eyes and look at the fields ready for harvest now. **36**Already, the one who harvests is being paid and is gathering crops for eternal life. So the one who plants and the one who harvests celebrate at the same time. **37**Here the saying is true, 'One person plants, and another harvests.' **38**I sent you to harvest a crop that you did not work on. Others did the work, and you get to finish up their work."

39Many of the Samaritans in that town believed in Jesus because of what the woman said: "He told me everything I ever did." **40**When the Samaritans came to Jesus, they begged him to stay with them, so he stayed there two more days. **41**And many more believed because of the things he said.

42They said to the woman, "First we believed in Jesus because of what you said, but now we believe because we heard him ourselves. We know that this man really is the Savior of the world."

Jesus Heals an Officer's Son

43Two days later, Jesus left and went to Galilee. **44**(Jesus had said before that a prophet is not respected in his own country.) **45**When Jesus arrived in Galilee, the people there welcomed him. They had seen all the things he did at the Passover Feast in Jerusalem, because they had been there, too.

46Jesus went again to visit Cana in Galilee where he had changed the water into wine. One of the king's important officers lived in the city of Capernaum, and his son was sick. **47**When he heard that Jesus had come from Judea to Galilee, he went to Jesus and begged him to come to Capernaum and heal his son, because his son was almost dead. **48**Jesus said to him, "You people must see signs and miracles before you will believe in me."

49The officer said, "Sir, come before my child dies."

50Jesus answered, "Go. Your son will live."

The man believed what Jesus told him and went home. **51**On the way the man's servants came and met him and told him, "Your son is alive."

52The man asked, "What time did my son begin to get well?"

They answered, "Yesterday at one o'clock the fever left him."

53The father knew that one o'clock was the exact time that Jesus had said, "Your son will live." So the man and all the people who lived in his house believed in Jesus.

54That was the second miracle Jesus did after coming from Judea to Galilee.

OLD TESTAMENT READING

Jehoshaphat's army went out into the Desert of Tekoa early in the morning. As they were starting out, Jehoshaphat stood and said, "Listen to me, people of Judah and Jerusalem. Have faith in the LORD your God, and you will stand strong. Have faith in his prophets, and you will succeed."

21Jehoshaphat listened to the people's advice. Then he chose men to be singers to the LORD, to praise him because he is holy and wonderful. As they marched in front of the army, they said,

"Thank the LORD,
    because his love continues forever."

22As they began to sing and praise God, the LORD set ambushes for the people of Ammon, Moab, and Edom who had come to attack Judah. And they were defeated.

2 Chronicles 20:20–22

INSIGHTS

As Joshua 3 opens, the Israelites are camped on the bank of the Jordan River. . . . They are in sight of the Promised Land, Canaan, but they have an enormous problem: a river is right in their path, and there's no convenient way around it.

To make matters worse, it is flood season, and any usual fording places are impassable. The waters are deep and turbulent and menacing.

God could easily make the river subside right before their eyes. He could throw a wide bridge across it. But he doesn't. Instead, he gives Joshua some strange orders that he passes on. . . .

. . . Joshua commands the priests to pick up the ark and go stand in the river. . . .

In spite of the problems, the priests had faith enough to obey, and this is what happened: "As soon as the priests who carried the ark reached the Jordan and their feet touched the water's edge, the water from upstream stopped flowing. . . . The priests who carried the ark of the covenant of the LORD stood firm on dry ground in the middle of the Jordan, while all Israel passed by until the whole nation had completed the crossing on dry ground" (Josh 3:15–17).

God didn't give the priests absolute proof or even overwhelming evidence that the waters would part. He did nothing until they put their feet in the water, taking the first step of commitment and obedience. Only then did he stop the flow of the river. In the same way, mountain-moving faith will be given to us as we step out and follow the Lord's direction.

BILL HYBELS

PAUSE FOR REFLECTION

Whoever heard of an army singing its way into battle? A flooding river that stopped instantly? An adulterous woman bringing others to Christ? For what do you believe God?

JOHN 5:1-29

Jesus Heals a Man at a Pool

5 Later Jesus went to Jerusalem for a special feast. **2**In Jerusalem there is a pool with five covered porches, which is called Bethesda in the Hebrew language. This pool is near the Sheep Gate. **3**Many sick people were lying on the porches beside the pool. Some were blind, some were crippled, and some were paralyzed [, and they waited for the water to move. **4**Sometimes an angel of the Lord came down to the pool and stirred up the water. After the angel did this, the first person to go into the pool was healed from any sickness he had]. **5**A man was lying there who had been sick for thirty-eight years. **6**When Jesus saw the man and knew that he had been sick for such a long time, Jesus asked him, "Do you want to be well?"

7The sick man answered, "Sir, there is no one to help me get into the pool when the water starts moving. While I am coming to the water, someone else always gets in before me."

8Then Jesus said, "Stand up. Pick up your mat and walk." **9**And immediately the man was well; he picked up his mat and began to walk.

The day this happened was a Sabbath day. **10**So the Jews said to the man who had been healed, "Today is the Sabbath. It is against our law for you to carry your mat on the Sabbath day."

11But he answered, "The man who made me well told me, 'Pick up your mat and walk.'"

12Then they asked him, "Who is the man who told you to pick up your mat and walk?"

13But the man who had been healed did not know who it was, because there were many people in that place, and Jesus had left.

14Later, Jesus found the man at the Temple and said to him, "See, you are well now. Stop sinning so that something worse does not happen to you."

15Then the man left and told his people that Jesus was the one who had made him well.

16Because Jesus was doing this on the Sabbath day, some evil people began to persecute him. **17**But Jesus said to them, "My Father never stops working, and so I keep working, too."

18This made them try still harder to kill him. They said, "First Jesus was breaking the law about the Sabbath day. Now he says that God is his own Father, making himself equal with God!"

Jesus Has God's Authority

19But Jesus said, "I tell you the truth, the Son can do nothing alone. The Son does only what he sees the Father doing, because the Son does whatever the Father does. **20**The Father loves the Son and shows the Son all the things he himself does. But the Father will show the Son even greater things than this so that you can all be amazed. **21**Just as the Father raises the dead and gives them life, so also the Son gives life to those he wants to. **22**In fact, the Father judges no one, but he has given the Son power to do all the judging **23**so that all people will honor the Son as much as they honor the Father. Anyone who does not honor the Son does not honor the Father who sent him.

24"I tell you the truth, whoever hears what I say and believes in the One who sent me has eternal life. That person will not be judged guilty but has already left death and entered life. **25**I tell you the truth, the time is coming and is already here when the dead will hear the voice of the Son of God, and those who hear will have life. **26**Life comes from the Father himself, and he has allowed the Son to have life in himself as well. **27**And the Father has given the Son the approval to judge, because he is the Son of Man. **28**Don't be surprised at this: A time is coming when all who are dead and in their graves will hear his voice. **29**Then they will come out of their graves. Those who did good will rise and have life forever, but those who did evil will rise to be judged guilty."

OLD TESTAMENT READING

Evil will kill the wicked;
   those who hate good people will be judged
      guilty.
22But the LORD saves his servants' lives;
   no one who trusts him will be judged
      guilty.

Psalm 34:21–22

The LORD is my light and the one who saves
      me.
   So why should I fear anyone?
The LORD protects my life.
   So why should I be afraid?

Psalm 27:1

INSIGHTS

The New Testament teaching is not that everyone has eternal life, but that those who come to God through Jesus Christ are given eternal life as a gift. Many passages contain this teaching; it is not found in only one or two texts. The new birth, being "born of the Spirit," is to have the life of God given to us. Not all are born of the Spirit. The Scripture rejects the idea that everybody has a spark of deity within. In fact, the Bible says that man, in his natural condition, is "dead to God" and that re-birth, an action of the Holy Spirit, is required to plant the life of God.

That "the gift of God is eternal life" doesn't mean that our lives just go on and on and on. It means that we share in the divine nature of God, which is itself eternal. It is His life, then, that is lived in our bodies. That's what's meant by eternal life. We don't begin eternal life when we die; we begin it while we still live. Eternity begins with belief in Christ. . . .

. . . Eternal life comes to those who believe in the Son of Man, who has been lifted up on the cross—that act of obedience to the Father, His death, that brought salvation to all who believe in Him. It belongs to those who will share in the resurrection victory of Jesus Christ over death.

TERRY FULLER

APPLICATION

In the Old Testament, God is clearly recognized as the source and giver of life. What claims does Jesus make regarding his ability to give eternal life? Have you accepted Jesus' daring offer of eternal life?

JOHN 5:30 – 6:15

Jesus Is God's Son

30"I can do nothing alone. I judge only the way I am told, so my judgment is fair. I don't try to please myself, but I try to please the One who sent me.

31"If only I tell people about myself, what I say is not true. **32**But there is another who tells about me, and I know that the things he says about me are true.

33"You have sent people to John, and he has told you the truth. **34**It is not that I need what humans say; I tell you this so you can be saved. **35**John was like a burning and shining lamp, and you were happy to enjoy his light for a while.

36"But I have a proof about myself that is greater than that of John. The things I do, which are the things my Father gave me to do, prove that the Father sent me. **37**And the Father himself who sent me has given proof about me. You have never heard his voice or seen what he looks like. **38**His teaching does not live in you, because you don't believe in the One the Father sent. **39**You carefully study the Scriptures because you think they give you eternal life. They do in fact tell about me, **40**but you refuse to come to me to have that life.

41"I don't need praise from people. **42**But I know you—I know that you don't have God's love in you. **43**I have come from my Father and speak for him, but you don't accept me. But when another person comes, speaking only for himself, you will accept him. **44**You try to get praise from each other, but you do not try to get the praise that

comes from the only God. So how can you believe? **45**Don't think that I will stand before the Father and say you are wrong. The one who says you are wrong is Moses, the one you hoped would save you. **46**If you really believed Moses, you would believe me, because Moses wrote about me. **47**But if you don't believe what Moses wrote, how can you believe what I say?"

More than Five Thousand Fed

6 After this, Jesus went across Lake Galilee (or, Lake Tiberias). **2**Many people followed him because they saw the miracles he did to heal the sick. **3**Jesus went up on a hill and sat down there with his followers. **4**It was almost the time for the Jewish Passover Feast.

5When Jesus looked up and saw a large crowd coming toward him, he said to Philip, "Where can we buy enough bread for all these people to eat?" **6**(Jesus asked Philip this question to test him, because Jesus already knew what he planned to do.)

7Philip answered, "Someone would have to work almost a year to buy enough bread for each person to have only a little piece."

8Another one of his followers, Andrew, Simon Peter's brother, said, **9**"Here is a boy with five loaves of barley bread and two little fish, but that is not enough for so many people."

10Jesus said, "Tell the people to sit down." There was plenty of grass there, and about five thousand men sat down there. **11**Then Jesus took the loaves of bread, thanked God for them, and gave them to the people who were sitting there. He did the same with the fish, giving as much as the people wanted.

12When they had all had enough to eat, Jesus

said to his followers, "Gather the leftover pieces of fish and bread so that nothing is wasted." **13**So they gathered up the pieces and filled twelve baskets with the pieces left from the five barley loaves.

14When the people saw this miracle that Jesus did, they said, "He must truly be the Prophet who is coming into the world."

15Jesus knew that the people planned to come and take him by force and make him their king, so he left and went into the hills alone.

OLD TESTAMENT READING

Judah is like a young lion.
    You have returned from killing, my son.
Like a lion, he stretches out and lies down to rest,
    and no one is brave enough to wake him.
10Kings will come from Judah's family;
    someone from Judah will always be on the throne.
Judah will rule until Shiloh comes,
    and the nations will obey him.

Genesis 49:9–10

INSIGHTS

What God did makes sense. It makes sense that Jesus would be our sacrifice because a sacrifice was needed to justify man's presence before God. It makes sense that God would use the Old Law to tutor Israel on their need for grace. It makes sense that Jesus would be our High Priest. What God did makes sense. It can be taught, charted, and put in books on systematic theology.

However, why God did it is absolutely absurd. When one leaves the method and examines the motive, the carefully stacked blocks of logic begin to tumble. That type of love isn't logical; it can't be neatly outlined in a sermon or explained in a term paper. . . .

Even after generations of people had spit in his face, he still loved them. After a nation of chosen ones had stripped him naked and ripped his incarnated flesh, he still died for them. And even today, after billions have chosen to prostitute themselves before pimps of power, fame, and wealth, he still waits for them.

It is inexplicable. It doesn't have a drop of logic nor a thread of rationality. . . .

Bloodstained royalty. A God with tears. A creator with a heart. God became earth's mockery to save his children.

How absurd to think that such nobility would go to such poverty to share such a treasure with such thankless souls.

But he did.

In fact, the only thing more absurd than the gift is our stubborn unwillingness to receive it.

MAX LUCADO

APPLICATION

What evidence from his life and from the Scriptures proves that Jesus was who he said he was? Why didn't most Jews believe Jesus? Do you believe and trust him?

➤ # JOHN 6:16-40

Jesus Walks on the Water

16That evening Jesus' followers went down to Lake Galilee. **17**It was dark now, and Jesus had not yet come to them. The followers got into a boat and started across the lake to Capernaum. **18**By now a strong wind was blowing, and the waves on the lake were getting bigger. **19**When they had rowed the boat about three or four miles, they saw Jesus walking on the water, coming toward the boat. The followers were afraid, **20**but Jesus said to them, "It is I. Do not be afraid." **21**Then they were glad to take him into the boat. At once the boat came to land at the place where they wanted to go.

The People Seek Jesus

22The next day the people who had stayed on the other side of the lake knew that Jesus had not gone in the boat with his followers but that they had left without him. And they knew that only one boat had been there. **23**But then some boats came from Tiberias and landed near the place where the people had eaten the bread after the Lord had given thanks. **24**When the people saw that Jesus and his followers were not there now, they got into boats and went to Capernaum to find Jesus.

Jesus, the Bread of Life

25When the people found Jesus on the other side of the lake, they asked him, "Teacher, when did you come here?"

26Jesus answered, "I tell you the truth, you aren't looking for me because you saw me do miracles. You are looking for me because you ate the bread and were satisfied. **27**Don't work for the food that spoils. Work for the food that stays good always and gives eternal life. The Son of Man will give you this food, because on him God the Father has put his power."

28The people asked Jesus, "What are the things God wants us to do?"

29Jesus answered, "The work God wants you to do is this: Believe the One he sent."

30So the people asked, "What miracle will you do? If we see a miracle, we will believe you. What will you do? **31**Our ancestors ate the manna in the desert. This is written in the Scriptures: 'He gave them bread from heaven to eat.'"

32Jesus said, "I tell you the truth, it was not Moses who gave you bread from heaven; it is my Father who is giving you the true bread from heaven. **33**God's bread is the One who comes down from heaven and gives life to the world."

34The people said, "Sir, give us this bread always."

35Then Jesus said, "I am the bread that gives life. Whoever comes to me will never be hungry, and whoever believes in me will never be thirsty. **36**But as I told you before, you have seen me and still don't believe. **37**The Father gives me the people who are mine. Every one of them will come to me, and I will always accept them. **38**I came down from heaven to do what God wants me to do, not what I want to do. **39**Here is what the One who sent me wants me to do: I must not lose even one whom God gave me, but I must raise them all on the last day. **40**Those who see the Son and believe in him have eternal life, and I will raise them on the last day. This is what my Father wants."

OLD TESTAMENT READING

Give thanks to the LORD and pray to him.
Tell the nations what he has done.
[9]Sing to him; sing praises to him.
Tell about all his miracles.

[10]Be glad that you are his;
let those who seek the LORD be happy.
[11]Depend on the LORD and his strength;
always go to him for help.
[12]Remember the miracles he has done,
his wonders, and his decisions.

1 Chronicles 16:8–12

INSIGHTS

"Mom, I need new shoes," Nicky announced as he burst through the door after school. "Miss Bell says it's dangerous to run in gym with my toe sticking out."

I looked down at my son's blue tennies. Hadn't I just bought them last month? But the protruding toe, a slit along the side, and tattered laces told me he'd had them longer. "You're right, Nicky. It's time for some new tennies, but you'll have to wait until our next paycheck. . . ."

"But, Mother," Nicky protested, "I can't wear these shoes for gym anymore. Miss Bell said!"

I launched into an elaborate discourse on budgeting principles. "So you see, Nicky," I concluded, "that's how Mommy and Daddy spend money. Tennis shoes are not in the budget this time; next time they will be."

"Then I'll pray about my shoes," Nicky announced. "I'll tell God I need the money by tomorrow." . . .

. . . When he left for school the next morning, new tennis shoes were still uppermost on his mind. "Can we buy my shoes tonight? You'll get the money today, because I prayed about it."

"We'll see, Nicky," I replied as I kissed him goodbye. There wasn't time to explain just then.

But the need to explain didn't come; Nicky's answer came instead. "This is long overdue . . . sorry for the oversight," said the note I received in the mail that afternoon. The enclosed check, payment for an article I'd written long ago and forgotten, was more than enough to pay for Nicky's new shoes.

After school, Nicky's blue eyes danced. "See, Mom I told you it would come. Now can we buy my shoes?"

Today Nicky wears new blue-and-gold tennis shoes poignant reminders of a child's simple trust and of my need to continually relearn what faith is all about.

RUTH SENTER

ACTION POINT

What is your psalm of praise to the God of miracles? What wonders has he done for you? Praise him with joy! Believe him and seek after the food that gives eternal life.

JOHN 6:41-71

⁴¹Some people began to complain about Jesus because he said, "I am the bread that comes down from heaven." ⁴²They said, "This is Jesus, the son of Joseph. We know his father and mother. How can he say, 'I came down from heaven'?"

⁴³But Jesus answered, "Stop complaining to each other. ⁴⁴The Father is the One who sent me. No one can come to me unless the Father draws him to me, and I will raise that person up on the last day. ⁴⁵It is written in the prophets, 'They will all be taught by God.' Everyone who listens to the Father and learns from him comes to me. ⁴⁶No one has seen the Father except the One who is from God; only he has seen the Father. ⁴⁷I tell you the truth, whoever believes has eternal life. ⁴⁸I am the bread that gives life. ⁴⁹Your ancestors ate the manna in the desert, but still they died. ⁵⁰Here is the bread that comes down from heaven. Anyone who eats this bread will never die. ⁵¹I am the living bread that came down from heaven. Anyone who eats this bread will live forever. This bread is my flesh, which I will give up so that the world may have life."

⁵²Then the evil people began to argue among themselves, saying, "How can this man give us his flesh to eat?"

⁵³Jesus said, "I tell you the truth, you must eat the flesh of the Son of Man and drink his blood. Otherwise, you won't have real life in you. ⁵⁴Those who eat my flesh and drink my blood have eternal life, and I will raise them up on the last day. ⁵⁵My flesh is true food, and my blood is true drink.

⁵⁶Those who eat my flesh and drink my blood live in me, and I live in them. ⁵⁷The living Father sent me, and I live because of the Father. So whoever eats me will live because of me. ⁵⁸I am not like the bread your ancestors ate. They ate that bread and still died. I am the bread that came down from heaven, and whoever eats this bread will live forever." ⁵⁹Jesus said all these things while he was teaching in the synagogue in Capernaum.

The Words of Eternal Life

⁶⁰When the followers of Jesus heard this, many of them said, "This teaching is hard. Who can accept it?"

⁶¹Knowing that his followers were complaining about this, Jesus said, "Does this teaching bother you? ⁶²Then will it also bother you to see the Son of Man going back to the place where he came from? ⁶³It is the Spirit that gives life. The flesh doesn't give life. The words I told you are spirit, and they give life. ⁶⁴But some of you don't believe." (Jesus knew from the beginning who did not believe and who would turn against him.) ⁶⁵Jesus said, "That is the reason I said, 'If the Father does not bring a person to me, that one cannot come.'"

⁶⁶After Jesus said this, many of his followers left him and stopped following him.

⁶⁷Jesus asked the twelve followers, "Do you want to leave, too?"

⁶⁸Simon Peter answered him, "Lord, who would we go to? You have the words that give eternal life. ⁶⁹We believe and know that you are the Holy One from God."

⁷⁰Then Jesus answered, "I chose all twelve of you, but one of you is a devil."

⁷¹Jesus was talking about Judas, the son of Simon Iscariot. Judas was one of the twelve, but later he was going to turn against Jesus.

OLD TESTAMENT READING

That night all the people in the camp began crying loudly. ²All the Israelites complained against Moses and Aaron, and all the people said to them, "We wish we had died in Egypt or in this desert. ³Why is the LORD bringing us to this land to be killed with swords? Our wives and children will be taken away. We would be better off going back to Egypt." ⁴They said to each other, "Let's choose a leader and go back to Egypt."

Numbers 14:1–4

INSIGHTS

As God's children, through having accepted Christ's work for us, accusations are definitely always off limits. As we stand before the Creator of the universe, the all-wise, perfectly holy, mighty God, who made us in His image, who upholds the universe, who understands all things, who has shown His compassion in providing a way for us to come to Him through the Messiah, the Lamb . . . how dare we shake our fist in His face? How dare we question God and say, "Why did you do this to me?" . . .

. . . We can be angry at a person when we are caught in the awful results of cause-and-effect history following the Fall, or following attacks of Satan, or following human choices of one kind or another—but that person is never God. We may not understand our tragic situation. We may not feel we can face life after a terrible shock. We may not feel that we know how to cope in the midst of a war, or avalanche, or earthquake, or famine. But it is always off limits to blame God. We are not to run away from God, shaking our fist at Him and screaming. We are to run to Him when we are shaking with grief or trembling with fear.

He is our refuge and strength; a very present help in trouble. Our help is to come from Him as we run into the shelter of His arms, away from the noise of the battle, or the storm. He has promised us comfort, and we need to climb on His lap as a weeping, hurt child, not to kick at Him.

EDITH SCHAEFFER

PAUSE FOR REFLECTION

What difficulties or lack of understanding in life have tempted you to turn away from God? Did you reject or run toward God? What gives you confidence that Jesus is the "Holy One from God," the one on whom you can believe, the one you can run to for shelter?

JOHN 7:1-31

Jesus' Brothers Don't Believe

7 After this, Jesus traveled around Galilee. He did not want to travel in Judea, because some evil people there wanted to kill him. **2**It was time for the Feast of Shelters. **3**So Jesus' brothers said to him, "You should leave here and go to Judea so your followers there can see the miracles you do. **4**Anyone who wants to be well known does not hide what he does. If you are doing these things, show yourself to the world." **5**(Even Jesus' brothers did not believe in him.)

6Jesus said to his brothers, "The right time for me has not yet come, but any time is right for you. **7**The world cannot hate you, but it hates me, because I tell it the evil things it does. **8**So you go to the feast. I will not go yet to this feast, because the right time for me has not yet come." **9**After saying this, Jesus stayed in Galilee.

10But after Jesus' brothers had gone to the feast, Jesus went also. But he did not let people see him. **11**At the feast some people were looking for him and saying, "Where is that man?"

12Within the large crowd there, many people were whispering to each other about Jesus. Some said, "He is a good man."

Others said, "No, he fools the people." **13**But no one was brave enough to talk about Jesus openly, because they were afraid of the elders.

Jesus Teaches at the Feast

14When the feast was about half over, Jesus went to the Temple and began to teach. **15**The people were amazed and said, "This man has never studied in school. How did he learn so much?"

16Jesus answered, "The things I teach are not my own, but they come from him who sent me. **17**If people choose to do what God wants, they will know that my teaching comes from God and not from me. **18**Those who teach their own ideas are trying to get honor for themselves. But those who try to bring honor to the one who sent them speak the truth, and there is nothing false in them. **19**Moses gave you the law, but none of you obeys that law. Why are you trying to kill me?"

20The people answered, "A demon has come into you. We are not trying to kill you."

21Jesus said to them, "I did one miracle, and you are all amazed. **22**Moses gave you the law about circumcision. (But really Moses did not give you circumcision; it came from our ancestors.) And yet you circumcise a baby boy on a Sabbath day. **23**If a baby boy can be circumcised on a Sabbath day to obey the law of Moses, why are you angry at me for healing a person's whole body on the Sabbath day? **24**Stop judging by the way things look, but judge by what is really right."

Is Jesus the Christ?

25Then some of the people who lived in Jerusalem said, "This is the man they are trying to kill. **26**But he is teaching where everyone can see and hear him, and no one is trying to stop him. Maybe the leaders have decided he really is the Christ. **27**But we know where this man is from. Yet when the real Christ comes, no one will know where he comes from."

28Jesus, teaching in the Temple, cried out, "Yes, you know me, and you know where I am from. But I have not come by my own authority. I was sent by the One who is true, whom you don't know. 29But I know him, because I am from him, and he sent me."

30When Jesus said this, they tried to seize him. But no one was able to touch him, because it was not yet the right time. 31But many of the people believed in Jesus. They said, "When the Christ comes, will he do more miracles than this man has done?"

INSIGHTS

A few years ago one of the leading golfers on the professional tour was invited to play in a foursome with Gerald Ford, then president of the United States, Jack Nicklaus, and Billy Graham. . . .

OLD TESTAMENT READING

But Jehoshaphat asked, "Isn't there a prophet of the LORD here? Let's ask him what we should do."

8Then King Ahab said to Jehoshaphat, "There is one other prophet. We could ask the LORD through him, but I hate him. He never prophesies anything good about me, but something bad. He is Micaiah son of Imlah."

Jehoshaphat said, "King Ahab, you shouldn't say that!"

1 Kings 22:7–8

After the round of golf was finished, one of the other pros came up to the golfer and asked, "Hey, what was it like playing with the president and with Billy Graham?"

The pro unleashed a torrent of cursing, and in a disgusted manner said, "I don't need Billy Graham stuffing religion down my throat." With that he turned on his heel and stormed off, heading for the practice tee. . . .

Astonishing. Billy Graham had said not a word about God, Jesus, or religion, yet the pro had stormed away after the game accusing Billy of trying to ram religion down his throat. How can we explain this? It's really not difficult. Billy Graham didn't have to say a word; he didn't have to give a single sideward glance to make the pro feel uncomfortable. Billy Graham is so identified with religion, so associated with the things of God, that his very presence is enough to smother the wicked man who flees when no man pursues. . . .

. . . The greater the holiness the greater the human hostility toward it. It seems insane. No man was ever more loving than Jesus Christ. Yet even His love provoked men to anger. His love was a perfect love, a transcendent and holy love, but His very love brought trauma to people. This kind of love is so majestic we can't stand it.

R. C. SPROUL

PAUSE FOR REFLECTION

For what reasons did the leaders of the Jews hate Jesus? Is your life holy enough to incur the wrath of the unrighteous?

JOHN 7:32 — 8:11

The Leaders Try to Arrest Jesus

32The Pharisees heard the crowd whispering these things about Jesus. So the leading priests and the Pharisees sent some Temple guards to arrest him. **33**Jesus said, "I will be with you a little while longer. Then I will go back to the One who sent me. **34**You will look for me, but you will not find me. And you cannot come where I am."

35Some people said to each other, "Where will this man go so we cannot find him? Will he go to the Greek cities where our people live and teach the Greek people there? **36**What did he mean when he said, 'You will look for me, but you will not find me,' and 'You cannot come where I am'?"

Jesus Talks About the Spirit

37On the last and most important day of the feast Jesus stood up and said in a loud voice, "Let anyone who is thirsty come to me and drink. **38**If anyone believes in me, rivers of living water will flow out from that person's heart, as the Scripture says." **39**Jesus was talking about the Holy Spirit. The Spirit had not yet been given, because Jesus had not yet been raised to glory. But later, those who believed in Jesus would receive the Spirit.

The People Argue About Jesus

40When the people heard Jesus' words, some of them said, "This man really is the Prophet."

41Others said, "He is the Christ."

Still others said, "The Christ will not come from Galilee. **42**The Scripture says that the Christ will come from David's family and from Bethlehem, the town where David lived." **43**So the people did not agree with each other about Jesus. **44**Some of them wanted to arrest him, but no one was able to touch him.

Some Leaders Won't Believe

45The Temple guards went back to the leading priests and the Pharisees, who asked, "Why didn't you bring Jesus?"

46The guards answered, "The words he says are greater than the words of any other person who has ever spoken!"

47The Pharisees answered, "So Jesus has fooled you also! **48**Have any of the leaders or the Pharisees believed in him? No! **49**But these people, who know nothing about the law, are under God's curse."

50Nicodemus, who had gone to see Jesus before, was in that group. He said, **51**"Our law does not judge a person without hearing him and knowing what he has done."

52They answered, "Are you from Galilee, too? Study the Scriptures, and you will learn that no prophet comes from Galilee."

———

Some of the earliest surviving Greek copies do not contain 7:53—8:11.

[**53**And everyone left and went home.

The Woman Caught in Adultery

8 Jesus went to the Mount of Olives. **2**But early in the morning he went back to the Temple, and all the people came to him, and he sat and taught them. **3**The teachers of the law and the Pharisees brought a woman who had been caught in adultery. They forced her to stand before the people. **4**They said to Jesus, "Teacher, this woman was caught having sexual relations with a man who is not her husband. **5**The law of Moses commands that we stone to death every woman who does this. What do you say we should do?" **6**They were asking this to trick Jesus so that they could have some charge against him.

But Jesus bent over and started writing on the ground with his finger. **7**When they continued to ask Jesus their question, he raised up and said, "Anyone here who has never sinned can throw the first stone at her." **8**Then Jesus bent over again and wrote on the ground.

9Those who heard Jesus began to leave one by one, first the older men and then the others. Jesus was left there alone with the woman standing before him. **10**Jesus raised up again and asked her, "Woman, where are they? Has no one judged you guilty?"

11She answered, "No one, sir."

Then Jesus said, "I also don't judge you guilty. You may go now, but don't sin anymore."]

OLD TESTAMENT READING

No one can say, "I am innocent;
I have never done anything wrong."
Proverbs 20:9

INSIGHTS

The same sin that Adam introduced has polluted the entire human race. No one is immune to the sin disease. And no human accomplishment can erase the internal stain that separates us from God. Because Adam sinned, all have sinned. This leads to one conclusion: We all need help. We need forgiveness. We need a Savior.

So . . . how do we get out of this mess? Read the next two verses slowly and carefully.

So then as through one transgression there resulted condemnation to all men, even so through one act of righteousness there resulted justification of life to all men. For as through the one man's disobedience the many were made sinners, even so through the obedience of the One the many will be made righteous. (Rom. 5:18–19)

Wonderful! Marvelous reassurance!

"You're telling me, Chuck, that by simply believing in Jesus Christ I can have eternal life with God, my sins forgiven, a destiny secure in heaven, all of this and much more without my working for that?" Yes, that is precisely what Scripture teaches. I remind you, it is called grace. Its what the Protestant Reformation was all about. Salvation is offered by divine grace, not by human works.

CHARLES SWINDOLL

PAUSE FOR REFLECTION

List the ways Scripture readings show that every person has sinned. What did Jesus say to the woman caught in adultery? Is it different than what he says to you? How have you responded?

JOHN 8:12 - 41

Jesus Is the Light of the World

12Later, Jesus talked to the people again, saying, "I am the light of the world. The person who follows me will never live in darkness but will have the light that gives life."

13The Pharisees said to Jesus, "When you talk about yourself, you are the only one to say these things are true. We cannot accept what you say."

14Jesus answered, "Yes, I am saying these things about myself, but they are true. I know where I came from and where I am going. But you don't know where I came from or where I am going. **15**You judge by human standards. I am not judging anyone. **16**But when I do judge, I judge truthfully, because I am not alone. The Father who sent me is with me. **17**Your own law says that when two witnesses say the same thing, you must accept what they say. **18**I am one of the witnesses who speaks about myself, and the Father who sent me is the other witness."

19They asked, "Where is your father?"

Jesus answered, "You don't know me or my Father. If you knew me, you would know my Father, too." **20**Jesus said these things while he was teaching in the Temple, near where the money is kept. But no one arrested him, because the right time for him had not yet come.

The People Misunderstand Jesus

21Again, Jesus said to the people, "I will leave you, and you will look for me, but you will die in your sins. You cannot come where I am going."

22So the Jews asked, "Will he kill himself? Is that why he said, 'You cannot come where I am going'?"

23Jesus said, "You people are from here below, but I am from above. You belong to this world, but I don't belong to this world. **24**So I told you that you would die in your sins. Yes, you will die in your sins if you don't believe that I am he."

25They asked, "Then who are you?"

Jesus answered, "I am what I have told you from the beginning. **26**I have many things to say and decide about you. But I tell people only the things I have heard from the One who sent me, and he speaks the truth."

27The people did not understand that he was talking to them about the Father. **28**So Jesus said to them, "When you lift up the Son of Man, you will know that I am he. You will know that these things I do are not by my own authority but that I say only what the Father has taught me. **29**The One who sent me is with me. I always do what is pleasing to him, so he has not left me alone." **30**While Jesus was saying these things, many people believed in him.

Freedom from Sin

31So Jesus said to the Jews who believed in him, "If you continue to obey my teaching, you are truly my followers. **32**Then you will know the truth, and the truth will make you free."

33They answered, "We are Abraham's children, and we have never been anyone's slaves. So why do you say we will be free?"

34Jesus answered, "I tell you the truth, everyone who lives in sin is a slave to sin. **35**A slave does not stay with a family forever, but a son belongs to the family forever. **36**So if the Son makes you free, you will be truly free. **37**I know you are Abraham's children, but you want to kill me because you don't accept my teaching. **38**I am telling you what my Father has shown me, but you do what your father has told you."

39They answered, "Our father is Abraham."

Jesus said, "If you were really Abraham's children, you would do the things Abraham did. **40**I am a man who has told you the truth which I heard from God, but you are trying to kill me. Abraham did nothing like that. **41**So you are doing the things your own father did."

But they said, "We are not like children who never knew who their father was. God is our Father; he is the only Father we have."

OLD TESTAMENT READING

So, kings, be wise;
   rulers, learn this lesson.
11Obey the LORD with great fear.
   Be happy, but tremble.
12Show that you are loyal to his son,
   or you will be destroyed by his anger,
because he can quickly become angry.
   But happy are those who trust him for
      protection.

Psalm 2:10–12

INSIGHTS

Think first of the origin of that life of Christ in the Father. They were one—one in life and one in love. In this His abiding in the Father had its root. Though dwelling here on earth, He knew that He was one with the Father; that the Father's life was in Him, and His love on Him. . . .

. . . The Son is not afraid of losing aught by giving up all to the Father, for He knows that the Father loves Him, and can have no interest apart from that of the beloved Son. He knows that as complete as is the dependence on His part is the communication on the part of the Father of all He possesses. Hence when He had said, "The Son can do nothing of Himself, except he see the Father do it," He adds at once, "Whatsoever things the Father doeth, them also doeth the Son likewise: for the Father loveth the Son, and showeth Him all things that Himself doeth." . . .

. . . Christ was the revelation of the Father on earth. He could not be this if there were not the most perfect unity, the most complete communication of all the Father had to the Son. He could be it because the Father loved Him, and He abode in that love.

ANDREW MURRAY

PAUSE FOR REFLECTION

How many different ways in this passage did Jesus tell the people he was the Son of God? How does God say the people of earth are to treat his son? What convinced you that Jesus is God's son?

JOHN 8:42 — 9:12

42Jesus said to them, "If God were really your Father, you would love me, because I came from God and now I am here. I did not come by my own authority; God sent me. **43**You don't understand what I say, because you cannot accept my teaching. **44**You belong to your father the devil, and you want to do what he wants. He was a murderer from the beginning and was against the truth, because there is no truth in him. When he tells a lie, he shows what he is really like, because he is a liar and the father of lies. **45**But because I speak the truth, you don't believe me. **46**Can any of you prove that I am guilty of sin? If I am telling the truth, why don't you believe me? **47**The person who belongs to God accepts what God says. But you don't accept what God says, because you don't belong to God."

Jesus Is Greater than Abraham

48They answered, "We say you are a Samaritan and have a demon in you. Are we not right?"

49Jesus answered, "I have no demon in me. I give honor to my Father, but you dishonor me. **50**I am not trying to get honor for myself. There is One who wants this honor for me, and he is the judge. **51**I tell you the truth, whoever obeys my teaching will never die."

52They said to Jesus, "Now we know that you have a demon in you! Even Abraham and the prophets died. But you say, 'Whoever obeys my teaching will never die.' **53**Do you think you are greater than our father Abraham, who died? And the prophets died, too. Who do you think you are?"

54Jesus answered, "If I give honor to myself, that honor is worth nothing. The One who gives me honor is my Father, and you say he is your God. **55**You don't really know him, but I know him. If I said I did not know him, I would be a liar like you. But I do know him, and I obey what he says. **56**Your father Abraham was very happy that he would see my day. He saw that day and was glad."

57They said to him, "You have never seen Abraham! You are not even fifty years old."

58Jesus answered, "I tell you the truth, before Abraham was even born, I am!" **59**When Jesus said this, the people picked up stones to throw at him. But Jesus hid himself, and then he left the Temple.

Jesus Heals a Man Born Blind

9 As Jesus was walking along, he saw a man who had been born blind. **2**His followers asked him, "Teacher, whose sin caused this man to be born blind—his own sin or his parents' sin?"

3Jesus answered, "It is not this man's sin or his parents' sin that made him blind. This man was born blind so that God's power could be shown in him. **4**While it is daytime, we must continue doing the work of the One who sent me. Night is coming, when no one can work. **5**While I am in the world, I am the light of the world."

6After Jesus said this, he spit on the ground and made some mud with it and put the mud on the man's eyes. **7**Then he told the man, "Go and wash in the Pool of Siloam." (Siloam means Sent.) So the man went, washed, and came back seeing.

8The neighbors and some people who had earlier seen this man begging said, "Isn't this the same man who used to sit and beg?"

9Some said, "He is the one," but others said, "No, he only looks like him."

The man himself said, "I am the man."

10They asked, "How did you get your sight?"

11He answered, "The man named Jesus made some mud and put it on my eyes. Then he told me to go to Siloam and wash. So I went and washed, and then I could see."

12They asked him, "Where is this man?"

"I don't know," he answered.

OLD TESTAMENT READING

The LORD said to Moses, **11**"Phinehas son of Eleazar, the son of Aaron, the priest, has saved the Israelites from my anger. He hates sin as much as I do. Since he tried to save my honor among them, I will not kill them. **12**So tell Phinehas that I am making my peace agreement with him."

Numbers 25:10–12

INSIGHTS

Jesus glorified God by giving himself for the work of His redeeming love. God's glory is His holiness, and God's holiness is His redeeming love—love that triumphs over sin by conquering the sin and rescuing the sinner. Jesus not only told of the Father being the righteous One, whose condemnation must rest on sin, and the loving One, who saves everyone who turns from his sin, but He gave himself to be a sacrifice to that righteousness, a servant to that love, even unto death. It was not only in acts of obedience or words of confession that He glorified God, but in giving himself to magnify the holiness of God, to vindicate at once His law and His love by His atonement. He gave himself, His whole life and being, to show how the Father loved, how the Father must condemn the sin, and yet would save the sinner. He counted nothing too great a sacrifice. He lived and died only that the glory of the Father, the glory of His holiness, of His redeeming love, might break through the dark veil of sin and flesh, and shine into the hearts of the children. . . .

If we want to know the way, let us again study Jesus. He obeyed the Father. Let simple obedience mark our whole life. Let humble, childlike waiting for direction, a Christlike dependence on the Father's showing us His way, be our daily attitude. Let everything be done to the Lord, according to His will, for His glory, in direct relationship to himself. Let God's glory shine out in the holiness of our life.

ANDREW MURRAY

ACTION POINT

What brings honor to God? How did Jesus honor God? How do you think God wants you to honor him? Are you willing to honor him with a holy life?

JOHN 9:13 - 41

Pharisees Question the Healing

13Then the people took to the Pharisees the man who had been blind. **14**The day Jesus had made mud and healed his eyes was a Sabbath day. **15**So now the Pharisees asked the man, "How did you get your sight?"

He answered, "He put mud on my eyes, I washed, and now I see."

16So some of the Pharisees were saying, "This man does not keep the Sabbath day, so he is not from God."

But others said, "A man who is a sinner can't do miracles like these." So they could not agree with each other.

17They asked the man again, "What do you say about him since it was your eyes he opened?"

The man answered, "He is a prophet."

18These leaders did not believe that he had been blind and could now see again. So they sent for the man's parents **19**and asked them, "Is this your son who you say was born blind? Then how does he now see?"

20His parents answered, "We know that this is our son and that he was born blind. **21**But we don't know how he can now see. We don't know who opened his eyes. Ask him. He is old enough to speak for himself." **22**His parents said this because they were afraid of the elders, who had already decided that anyone who said Jesus was the Christ would be avoided. **23**That is why his parents said, "He is old enough. Ask him."

24So for the second time, they called the man who had been blind. They said, "You should give God the glory by telling the truth. We know that this man is a sinner."

25He answered, "I don't know if he is a sinner. One thing I do know: I was blind, and now I see."

26They asked, "What did he do to you? How did he make you see again?"

27He answered, "I already told you, and you didn't listen. Why do you want to hear it again? Do you want to become his followers, too?"

28Then they insulted him and said, "You are his follower, but we are followers of Moses. **29**We know that God spoke to Moses, but we don't even know where this man comes from."

30The man answered, "This is a very strange thing. You don't know where he comes from, and yet he opened my eyes. **31**We all know that God does not listen to sinners, but he listens to anyone who worships and obeys him. **32**Nobody has ever heard of anyone giving sight to a man born blind. **33**If this man were not from God, he could do nothing."

34They answered, "You were born full of sin! Are you trying to teach us?" And they threw him out.

Spiritual Blindness

35When Jesus heard that they had thrown him out, Jesus found him and said, "Do you believe in the Son of Man?"

36He asked, "Who is the Son of Man, sir, so that I can believe in him?"

37Jesus said to him, "You have seen him. The Son of Man is the one talking with you."

38He said, "Lord, I believe!" Then the man worshiped Jesus.

39Jesus said, "I came into this world so that the world could be judged. I came so that the blind would see and so that those who see will become blind."

40Some of the Pharisees who were nearby heard Jesus say this and asked, "Are you saying we are blind, too?"

41Jesus said, "If you were blind, you would not be guilty of sin. But since you keep saying you see, your guilt remains."

OLD TESTAMENT READING

Do good to me, your servant, so I can live, so I can obey your word.
18Open my eyes to see
the miracles in your teachings.
19I am a stranger on earth.
Do not hide your commands from me.
20I wear myself out with desire
for your laws all the time.
21You scold proud people;
those who ignore your commands are
cursed.
22Don't let me be insulted and hated
because I keep your rules.
23Even if princes speak against me,
I, your servant, will think about your
demands.
24Your rules give me pleasure;
they give me good advice.

Psalm 119:17–24

APPLICATION

What words of faith and wisdom did the blind man speak to the Jewish leaders? Why do you think Jesus looked for him after he was thrown out of the temple? Pray that you will see how much Jesus wants you to believe and trust him.

JOHN 10:1-33

The Shepherd and His Sheep

10 Jesus said, "I tell you the truth, the person who does not enter the sheepfold by the door, but climbs in some other way, is a thief and a robber. **2**The one who enters by the door is the shepherd of the sheep. **3**The one who guards the door opens it for him. And the sheep listen to the voice of the shepherd. He calls his own sheep by name and leads them out. **4**When he brings all his sheep out, he goes ahead of them, and they follow him because they know his voice. **5**But they will never follow a stranger. They will run away from him because they don't know his voice." **6**Jesus told the people this story, but they did not understand what it meant.

Jesus Is the Good Shepherd

7So Jesus said again, "I tell you the truth, I am the door for the sheep. **8**All the people who came before me were thieves and robbers. The sheep did not listen to them. **9**I am the door, and the person who enters through me will be saved and will be able to come in and go out and find pasture. **10**A thief comes to steal and kill and destroy, but I came to give life—life in all its fullness.

11"I am the good shepherd. The good shepherd gives his life for the sheep. **12**The worker who is paid to keep the sheep is different from the shepherd who owns them. When the worker sees a wolf coming, he runs away and leaves the sheep alone. Then the wolf attacks the sheep and scatters them. **13**The man runs away because he is only a paid worker and does not really care about the sheep.

14"I am the good shepherd. I know my sheep, and my sheep know me, **15**just as the Father knows me, and I know the Father. I give my life for the sheep. **16**I have other sheep that are not in this flock, and I must bring them also. They will listen to my voice, and there will be one flock and one shepherd. **17**The Father loves me because I give my life so that I can take it back again. **18**No one takes it away from me; I give my own life freely. I have the right to give my life, and I have the right to take it back. This is what my Father commanded me to do."

19Again the leaders did not agree with each other because of these words of Jesus. **20**Many of them said, "A demon has come into him and made him crazy. Why listen to him?"

21But others said, "A man who is crazy with a demon does not say things like this. Can a demon open the eyes of the blind?"

Jesus Is Rejected

22The time came for the Feast of Dedication at Jerusalem. It was winter, **23**and Jesus was walking in the Temple in Solomon's Porch. **24**Some people gathered around him and said, "How long will you make us wonder about you? If you are the Christ, tell us plainly."

25Jesus answered, "I told you already, but you did not believe. The miracles I do in my Father's name show who I am. **26**But you don't believe, because you are not my sheep. **27**My sheep listen to my voice; I know them, and they follow me. **28**I give them eternal life, and they will never die, and no one can steal them out of my hand. **29**My Father gave my sheep to me. He is greater than all, and no person can steal my sheep out of my Father's hand. **30**The Father and I are one."

31Again some of the people picked up stones to kill Jesus. **32**But he said to them, "I have done many good works from the Father. Which of these good works are you killing me for?"

33They answered, "We are not killing you because of any good work you did, but because you speak against God. You are only a human, but you say you are the same as God!"

OLD TESTAMENT READING

He takes care of his people like a shepherd.
He gathers them like lambs in his arms
and carries them close to him.
He gently leads the mothers of the lambs.

Isaiah 40:11

INSIGHTS

Do you need guidance as to your path? Look unto Jesus; it is always possible to discern His form, though partially veiled in mist; and when it is lost, be sure to stand still until He comes back to find and re-establish the blessed connection. . . . Do not get anxious or flurried. Put the government of your life upon His shoulder, and leave Him to execute His plan.

Sometimes He guides us to the rest of the green pastures, and the quiet of the still waters. In other words, we are left through happy months and years to fulfil the ordinary commonplaces of life, content to fill a little space, and receiving great increments of spiritual force for future service. At other times, we are guided from the lowland pastures up into the hills. The way is sunny, above us the precipitous cliffs, beneath the dark turbid stream; but this is well; we would not always be lying in the pastures or walking softly by the waters. It is good to climb the heights with their far view and bracing air.

In the late afternoon the Shepherd may lead his flock back into the valleys, through the dark woods, where the branches meet overhead and the wild beast lurks in ambush, but we know that in one hand He has the rod or club, with which to belabour anything that may attack; and in the other the crook to drag us out of the hole. He would not lead us into the dark valley which He had not explored, and whose perils He was not prepared to overcome. Darkness, sorrow, or death do not prove that we have missed His guidance, or have taken the wrong path, but rather that He accounts us able to bear the trial by faith in Himself.

F. B. MEYER

PAUSE FOR REFLECTION

What does Jesus promise to give his sheep who follow him? Study the qualities of the good shepherd that Jesus describes and think about the ways Jesus has been your shepherd. Praise him for his goodness!

JOHN 10:34 — 11:27

34Jesus answered, "It is written in your law that God said, 'I said, you are gods.' **35**This Scripture called those people gods who received God's message, and Scripture is always true. **36**So why do you say that I speak against God because I said, 'I am God's Son'? I am the one God chose and sent into the world. **37**If I don't do what my Father does, then don't believe me. **38**But if I do what my Father does, even though you don't believe in me, believe what I do. Then you will know and understand that the Father is in me and I am in the Father."

39They tried to take Jesus again, but he escaped from them.

40Then he went back across the Jordan River to the place where John had first baptized. Jesus stayed there, **41**and many people came to him and said, "John never did a miracle, but everything John said about this man is true." **42**And in that place many believed in Jesus.

The Death of Lazarus

11 A man named Lazarus was sick. He lived in the town of Bethany, where Mary and her sister Martha lived. **2**Mary was the woman who later put perfume on the Lord and wiped his feet with her hair. Mary's brother was Lazarus, the man who was now sick. **3**So Mary and Martha sent someone to tell Jesus, "Lord, the one you love is sick."

4When Jesus heard this, he said, "This sickness will not end in death. It is for the glory of God, to bring glory to the Son of God." **5**Jesus loved Martha and her sister and Lazarus. **6**But when he heard that Lazarus was sick, he stayed where he was for two more days. **7**Then Jesus said to his followers, "Let's go back to Judea."

8The followers said, "But Teacher, some people there tried to stone you to death only a short time ago. Now you want to go back there?"

9Jesus answered, "Are there not twelve hours in the day? If anyone walks in the daylight, he will not stumble, because he can see by this world's light. **10**But if anyone walks at night, he stumbles because there is no light to help him see."

11After Jesus said this, he added, "Our friend Lazarus has fallen asleep, but I am going there to wake him."

12The followers said, "But Lord, if he is only asleep, he will be all right."

13Jesus meant that Lazarus was dead, but his followers thought he meant Lazarus was really sleeping. **14**So then Jesus said plainly, "Lazarus is dead. **15**And I am glad for your sakes I was not there so that you may believe. But let's go to him now."

16Then Thomas (the one called Didymus) said to the other followers, "Let us also go so that we can die with him."

Jesus in Bethany

17When Jesus arrived, he learned that Lazarus had already been dead and in the tomb for four days. **18**Bethany was about two miles from Jerusalem. **19**Many of the Jews had come there to comfort Martha and Mary about their brother.

20When Martha heard that Jesus was coming, she went out to meet him, but Mary stayed home.

21Martha said to Jesus, "Lord, if you had been here, my brother would not have died. 22But I know that even now God will give you anything you ask."

23Jesus said, "Your brother will rise and live again."

24Martha answered, "I know that he will rise and live again in the resurrection on the last day."

25Jesus said to her, "I am the resurrection and the life. Those who believe in me will have life even if they die. 26And everyone who lives and believes in me will never die. Martha, do you believe this?"

27Martha answered, "Yes, Lord. I believe that you are the Christ, the Son of God, the One coming to the world."

OLD TESTAMENT READING

I waited patiently for the LORD.
  He turned to me and heard my cry.
2He lifted me out of the pit of destruction,
  out of the sticky mud.
He stood me on a rock
  and made my feet steady.
3He put a new song in my mouth,
  a song of praise to our God.
Many people will see this and worship him.
  Then they will trust the LORD.

Psalm 40:1–3

INSIGHTS

A pair of scientists and botanists were exploring in the Alps for some special kinds of flowers. One day they spied through their field glass a flower of rare beauty. But it was in a ravine with perpendicular cliffs on both sides. Someone must be lowered over the cliff to get it.

A native boy was watching. They said to him, "We will give you five pounds if you will let us lower you into the valley to get the flower." The boy looked into the valley and said, "Just a moment. I'll be back." He soon returned with a man. "I'll go over the cliff," he said, "and get the flower for you if this man holds the rope. He's my dad." Have we learned to trust the Lord as this little boy did his father?

Sometimes we find ourselves putting our confidence in man and what we think he can do for us. But man can let us down. Man can disappoint us. Not so the Lord. Needs may be pressing in but we can look up, trusting an all-wise, all-loving God to do all for our good and His glory.

We can trust the rope of our circumstances to Him. Man may become weary and let the rope drop; or he may be distracted or become impatient. But God never wearies of holding the rope. We can confidently leave it in His strong hand.

MILLIE STAMM

PAUSE FOR REFLECTION

How long had Lazarus been dead before Jesus reached out and saved him? Doesn't that stretch your ability to trust in his protection? Can you, like the psalmist, confidently praise God for his protection?

JOHN 11:28-57

Jesus Cries

28After Martha said this, she went back and talked to her sister Mary alone. Martha said, "The Teacher is here and he is asking for you." **29**When Mary heard this, she got up quickly and went to Jesus. **30**Jesus had not yet come into the town but was still at the place where Martha had met him. **31**The Jews were with Mary in the house, comforting her. When they saw her stand and leave quickly, they followed her, thinking she was going to the tomb to cry there.

32But Mary went to the place where Jesus was. When she saw him, she fell at his feet and said, "Lord, if you had been here, my brother would not have died."

33When Jesus saw Mary crying and the Jews who came with her also crying, he was upset and was deeply troubled. **34**He asked, "Where did you bury him?"

"Come and see, Lord," they said.

35Jesus cried.

36So the Jews said, "See how much he loved him."

37But some of them said, "If Jesus opened the eyes of the blind man, why couldn't he keep Lazarus from dying?"

Jesus Raises Lazarus

38Again feeling very upset, Jesus came to the tomb. It was a cave with a large stone covering the entrance. **39**Jesus said, "Move the stone away."

Martha, the sister of the dead man, said, "But, Lord, it has been four days since he died. There will be a bad smell."

40Then Jesus said to her, "Didn't I tell you that if you believed you would see the glory of God?"

41So they moved the stone away from the entrance. Then Jesus looked up and said, "Father, I thank you that you heard me. **42**I know that you always hear me, but I said these things because of the people here around me. I want them to believe that you sent me." **43**After Jesus said this, he cried out in a loud voice, "Lazarus, come out!" **44**The dead man came out, his hands and feet wrapped with pieces of cloth, and a cloth around his face.

Jesus said to them, "Take the cloth off of him and let him go."

The Plan to Kill Jesus

45Many of the people, who had come to visit Mary and saw what Jesus did, believed in him. **46**But some of them went to the Pharisees and told them what Jesus had done. **47**Then the leading priests and Pharisees called a meeting of the council. They asked, "What should we do? This man is doing many miracles. **48**If we let him continue doing these things, everyone will believe in him. Then the Romans will come and take away our Temple and our nation."

49One of the men there was Caiaphas, the high priest that year. He said, "You people know nothing! **50**You don't realize that it is better for one man to die for the people than for the whole nation to be destroyed."

51Caiaphas did not think of this himself. As high priest that year, he was really prophesying that Jesus would die for their nation **52**and for God's scattered children to bring them all together and make them one.

53That day they started planning to kill Jesus. **54**So Jesus no longer traveled openly among the people. He left there and went to a place near the desert, to a town called Ephraim and stayed there with his followers.

55It was almost time for the Passover Feast. Many from the country went up to Jerusalem before the Passover to do the special things to make themselves pure. **56**The people looked for Jesus and stood in the Temple asking each other, "Is he coming to the Feast? What do you think?" **57**But the leading priests and the Pharisees had given orders that if anyone knew where Jesus was, he must tell them. Then they could arrest him.

OLD TESTAMENT READING

Then Elijah lay on top of the boy three times. He prayed to the LORD, "LORD my God, let this boy live again!"

22The LORD answered Elijah's prayer; the boy began breathing again and was alive.

24"Now I know you really are a man from God," the woman said to Elijah. "I know that the LORD truly speaks through you!"

1 Kings 17:21–22, 24

INSIGHTS

Faith is man's response to God's initiative. . . .

To realize that faith is your response to something God does or says, will take pressure off you and enable you to adopt a more constructive attitude to it. Do not look inside yourself and ask, "How much faith do I have?" Look to God and ask, "What is he saying to me? What would he have me do?" When Jesus praised the great faith of different men and women in the Gospels, he was not praising a mystical inner state. He was usually commenting on a concrete action by which someone responded to him. . . .

Once you understand this you will also begin to see why the amount of faith you have is a less crucial issue than you might have thought. The saying of Jesus about the grain of mustard seed begins to make sense. . . .

How much faith did Martha need to get Lazarus back from the dead? Precious little (Jn. 11:38–40). If we are to go by mystical inner states, every evidence points to Martha having no faith at all. No, what she needed (and what she had) was enough faith to give orders for the tombstone to be moved, in spite of the doubts she felt. And Lazarus was raised from the dead. . . .

Faith then is your decision to respond to God's Word. The decision may either manifest itself in some outward action or else in what we might call an "interior action"—like the committing of your eternal destiny into the hands of Christ. In time the decision grows into an attitude, an attitude of always being ready to respond positively to God's Word.

JOHN WHITE

PAUSE FOR REFLECTION

When Jesus came to them, did Mary and Martha believe he had come to raise Lazarus from the dead? What faith did they have in Jesus? Is your faith in Jesus enough for him to accomplish his purposes?

JOHN 12:1-26

Jesus with Friends in Bethany

12 Six days before the Passover Feast, Jesus went to Bethany, where Lazarus lived. (Lazarus is the man Jesus raised from the dead.) **2** There they had a dinner for Jesus. Martha served the food, and Lazarus was one of the people eating with Jesus. **3** Mary brought in a pint of very expensive perfume made from pure nard. She poured the perfume on Jesus' feet, and then she wiped his feet with her hair. And the sweet smell from the perfume filled the whole house.

4 Judas Iscariot, one of Jesus' followers who would later turn against him, was there. Judas said, **5** "This perfume was worth an entire year's wages. Why wasn't it sold and the money given to the poor?" **6** But Judas did not really care about the poor; he said this because he was a thief. He was the one who kept the money box, and he often stole from it.

7 Jesus answered, "Leave her alone. It was right for her to save this perfume for today, the day for me to be prepared for burial. **8** You will always have the poor with you, but you will not always have me."

The Plot Against Lazarus

9 A large crowd of people heard that Jesus was in Bethany. So they went there to see not only Jesus but Lazarus, whom Jesus raised from the dead. **10** So the leading priests made plans to kill Lazarus, too. **11** Because of Lazarus many of the Jews were leaving them and believing in Jesus.

Jesus Enters Jerusalem

12 The next day a great crowd who had come to Jerusalem for the Passover Feast heard that Jesus was coming there. **13** So they took branches of palm trees and went out to meet Jesus, shouting,

"Praise God!

God bless the One who comes in the name of the Lord!

God bless the King of Israel!" *Psalm 118:25–26*

14 Jesus found a colt and sat on it. This was as the Scripture says,

15 "Don't be afraid, people of Jerusalem!

Your king is coming,

sitting on the colt of a donkey."

Zechariah 9:9

16 The followers of Jesus did not understand this at first. But after Jesus was raised to glory, they remembered that this had been written about him and that they had done these things to him.

People Tell About Jesus

17 There had been many people with Jesus when he raised Lazarus from the dead and told him to come out of the tomb. Now they were telling others about what Jesus did. **18** Many people went out to meet Jesus, because they had heard about this miracle. **19** So the Pharisees said to each other, "You can see that nothing is going right for us. Look! The whole world is following him."

Jesus Talks About His Death

20 There were some Greek people, too, who came to Jerusalem to worship at the Passover

Feast. **21**They went to Philip, who was from Bethsaida in Galilee, and said, "Sir, we would like to see Jesus." **22**Philip told Andrew, and then Andrew and Philip told Jesus.

23Jesus said to them, "The time has come for the Son of Man to receive his glory. **24**I tell you the truth, a grain of wheat must fall to the ground and die to make many seeds. But if it never dies, it remains only a single seed. **25**Those who love their lives will lose them, but those who hate their lives in this world will keep true life forever. **26**Whoever serves me must follow me. Then my servant will be with me everywhere I am. My Father will honor anyone who serves me."

OLD TESTAMENT READING

Lord, rise up and punish the wicked.
Don't forget those who need help.
13Why do wicked people hate God?
They say to themselves, "God won't punish us."
14Lord, surely you see these cruel and evil things;
look at them and do something.
People in trouble look to you for help.
You are the one who helps the orphans.
15Break the power of wicked people.
Punish them for the evil they have done.

Psalm 10:12–15

PAUSE FOR REFLECTION
Why did the religious leaders of the day hate Jesus and Lazarus? From whom does persecution come in your life? What portion of Scripture encourages and comforts you during such times?

JOHN 12:27 – 13:5

27"Now I am very troubled. Should I say, 'Father, save me from this time'? No, I came to this time so I could suffer. 28Father, bring glory to your name!"

Then a voice came from heaven, "I have brought glory to it, and I will do it again."

29The crowd standing there, who heard the voice, said it was thunder.

But others said, "An angel has spoken to him."

30Jesus said, "That voice was for your sake, not mine. 31Now is the time for the world to be judged; now the ruler of this world will be thrown down. 32If I am lifted up from the earth, I will draw all people toward me." 33Jesus said this to show how he would die.

34The crowd said, "We have heard from the law that the Christ will live forever. So why do you say, 'The Son of Man must be lifted up'? Who is this 'Son of Man'?"

35Then Jesus said, "The light will be with you for a little longer, so walk while you have the light. Then the darkness will not catch you. If you walk in the darkness, you will not know where you are going. 36Believe in the light while you still have it so that you will become children of light." When Jesus had said this, he left and hid himself from them.

Some People Won't Believe in Jesus

37Though Jesus had done many miracles in front of the people, they still did not believe in him. 38This was to bring about what Isaiah the prophet had said:

"Lord, who believed what we told them?
Who saw the Lord's power in this?"

Isaiah 53:1

39This is why the people could not believe: Isaiah also had said,

40"He has blinded their eyes,
and he has closed their minds.
Otherwise they would see with their eyes
and understand in their minds
and come back to me and be healed."

Isaiah 6:10

41Isaiah said this because he saw Jesus' glory and spoke about him.

42But many believed in Jesus, even many of the leaders. But because of the Pharisees, they did not say they believed in him for fear they would be put out of the synagogue. 43They loved praise from people more than praise from God.

44Then Jesus cried out, "Whoever believes in me is really believing in the One who sent me. 45Whoever sees me sees the One who sent me. 46I have come as light into the world so that whoever believes in me would not stay in darkness.

47"Anyone who hears my words and does not obey them, I do not judge, because I did not come to judge the world, but to save the world. 48There is a judge for those who refuse to believe in me and do not accept my words. The word I have taught will be their judge on the last day. 49The things I taught were not from myself. The Father who sent me told me what to say and what to teach. 50And I know that eternal life comes from what the Father commands. So whatever I say is what the Father told me to say."

Jesus Washes His Followers' Feet

13 It was almost time for the Passover Feast. Jesus knew that it was time for him to leave this world and go back to the Father. He had always loved those who were his own in the world, and he loved them all the way to the end.

²Jesus and his followers were at the evening meal. The devil had already persuaded Judas Iscariot, the son of Simon, to turn against Jesus. ³Jesus knew that the Father had given him power over everything and that he had come from God and was going back to God. ⁴So during the meal Jesus stood up and took off his outer clothing. Taking a towel, he wrapped it around his waist. ⁵Then he poured water into a bowl and began to wash the followers' feet, drying them with the towel that was wrapped around him.

OLD TESTAMENT READING

Moses heard every family crying as they stood in the entrances of their tents. Then the LORD became very angry, and Moses got upset. ¹¹He asked the LORD, "Why have you brought me, your servant, this trouble? What have I done wrong that you made me responsible for all these people? ¹³ᵇThey keep crying to me, 'We want meat!' ¹⁴I can't take care of all these people alone. It is too much for me. ¹⁵If you are going to continue doing this to me, then kill me now. If you care about me, put me to death, and then I won't have any more troubles."

¹⁶The LORD said to Moses, . . .

¹⁸"Tell the people this: 'Make yourselves holy for tomorrow, and you will eat meat. You cried to the LORD, "We want meat! We were better off in Egypt!" So now the LORD will give you meat to eat.'"

²¹Moses said, "LORD, here are six hundred thousand people standing around me, and you say, 'I will give them enough meat to eat for a month!' ²²If we killed all the flocks and herds, that would not be enough. If we caught all the fish in the sea, that would not be enough."

²³But the LORD said to Moses, "Do you think I'm weak? Now you will see if I can do what I say."

Numbers 11:10–11, 13b–16a, 18, 21–23

INSIGHTS

The late Dr. Heugh, of Glasgow, a short time before he breathed his last, said, "There is nothing I feel more than the criminality of not trusting Christ without doubt—without doubt. Oh, to think what Christ is, what he did, and whom he did it for, and then not to believe him, not to trust him! There is no wickedness like the wickedness of unbelief!"

CHARLES SPURGEON

PAUSE FOR REFLECTION

Does it surprise you that Moses, even after all the miracles he had seen (and been a part of), still struggled with unbelief? Why is it important for us to believe Jesus? In what ways do you find it difficult to trust and believe Jesus? What "miracles" have you seen that ought to strengthen your belief?

JOHN 13:6-35

⁶Jesus came to Simon Peter, who said to him, "Lord, are you going to wash my feet?"

⁷Jesus answered, "You don't understand now what I am doing, but you will understand later."

⁸Peter said, "No, you will never wash my feet."

Jesus answered, "If I don't wash your feet, you are not one of my people."

⁹Simon Peter answered, "Lord, then wash not only my feet, but wash my hands and my head, too!"

¹⁰Jesus said, "After a person has had a bath, his whole body is clean. He needs only to wash his feet. And you men are clean, but not all of you." ¹¹Jesus knew who would turn against him, and that is why he said, "Not all of you are clean."

¹²When he had finished washing their feet, he put on his clothes and sat down again. He asked, "Do you understand what I have just done for you? ¹³You call me 'Teacher' and 'Lord,' and you are right, because that is what I am. ¹⁴If I, your Lord and Teacher, have washed your feet, you also should wash each other's feet. ¹⁵I did this as an example so that you should do as I have done for you. ¹⁶I tell you the truth, a servant is not greater than his master. A messenger is not greater than the one who sent him. ¹⁷If you know these things, you will be blessed if you do them.

¹⁸"I am not talking about all of you. I know those I have chosen. But this is to bring about what the Scripture said: 'The man who ate at my table has turned against me.' ¹⁹I am telling you this now before it happens so that when it happens, you will believe that I am he. ²⁰I tell you the truth, whoever accepts anyone I send also accepts me. And whoever accepts me also accepts the One who sent me."

Jesus Talks About His Death

²¹After Jesus said this, he was very troubled. He said openly, "I tell you the truth, one of you will turn against me."

²²The followers all looked at each other, because they did not know whom Jesus was talking about. ²³One of the followers sitting next to Jesus was the follower Jesus loved. ²⁴Simon Peter motioned to him to ask Jesus whom he was talking about.

²⁵That follower leaned closer to Jesus and asked, "Lord, who is it?"

²⁶Jesus answered, "I will dip this bread into the dish. The man I give it to is the man who will turn against me." So Jesus took a piece of bread, dipped it, and gave it to Judas Iscariot, the son of Simon. ²⁷As soon as Judas took the bread, Satan entered him. Jesus said to him, "The thing that you will do—do it quickly." ²⁸No one at the table understood why Jesus said this to Judas. ²⁹Since he was the one who kept the money box, some of the followers thought Jesus was telling him to buy what was needed for the feast or to give something to the poor.

³⁰Judas took the bread Jesus gave him and immediately went out. It was night.

³¹When Judas was gone, Jesus said, "Now the Son of Man receives his glory, and God receives glory through him. ³²If God receives glory through him, then God will give glory to the Son

through himself. And God will give him glory quickly."

³³Jesus said, "My children, I will be with you only a little longer. You will look for me, and what I told the Jews, I tell you now: Where I am going you cannot come.

³⁴"I give you a new command: Love each other. You must love each other as I have loved you. ³⁵All people will know that you are my followers if you love each other."

INSIGHTS

With the resurrection of the Lord Jesus and the day of Pentecost came a breath of heavenly love. Those who received Jesus, the incarnation of love, into their lives and who chose to obey His command began to love one another. The pagan world looked on in amazement and said of the believers, "How they love one another!"

Within a few years following this command to love one another, the gospel had spread like a prairie fire throughout the known world. The miracle of God's love, His supernatural agape, had captivated multitudes throughout the decadent, wicked Roman Empire.

Tragically, today one seldom hears "How they love one another!" about Christians. Instead there is far too much suspicion, jealousy, criticism and conflict between Christians, churches and denominations. The unbelieving world often laughs at our publicized conflicts.

But those individuals who do demonstrate this supernatural love are usually warmly received by non-believers as well as believers. The churches that obey our Lord's command to "love one another" usually are filled to overflowing and are making a great impact for good and for the glory of God. They represent a highly desirable alternative to secular society.

How does one love supernaturally? By faith. God's Word commands us to love (John 13:34, 35). God's Word promises that He will enable us to do what He commands us to do (1 John 5:14, 15).

BILL BRIGHT

OLD TESTAMENT READING

You must not have any other gods except me. ⁵You must not worship or serve any idol, because I, the LORD your God, am a jealous God.

⁷"You must not use the name of the LORD your God thoughtlessly.

⁸"Remember to keep the Sabbath holy.

¹²"Honor your father and your mother.

¹³"You must not murder anyone.

¹⁴"You must not be guilty of adultery.

¹⁵"You must not steal.

¹⁶"You must not tell lies about your neighbor.

¹⁷"You must not want to take your neighbor's house."

Exodus 20:3, 5a, 7a, 8, 12a, 13–17a

APPLICATION

As Jesus prepared to leave his disciples, what one command did he give them? How can you more fully follow this command?

JOHN 13:36 — 14:26

Peter Will Say He Doesn't Know Jesus

36Simon Peter asked Jesus, "Lord, where are you going?"

Jesus answered, "Where I am going you cannot follow now, but you will follow later."

37Peter asked, "Lord, why can't I follow you now? I am ready to die for you!"

38Jesus answered, "Are you ready to die for me? I tell you the truth, before the rooster crows, you will say three times that you don't know me."

Jesus Comforts His Followers

14 Jesus said, "Don't let your hearts be troubled. Trust in God, and trust in me. **2**There are many rooms in my Father's house; I would not tell you this if it were not true. I am going there to prepare a place for you. **3**After I go and prepare a place for you, I will come back and take you to be with me so that you may be where I am. **4**You know the way to the place where I am going."

5Thomas said to Jesus, "Lord, we don't know where you are going. So how can we know the way?"

6Jesus answered, "I am the way, and the truth, and the life. The only way to the Father is through me. **7**If you really knew me, you would know my Father, too. But now you do know him, and you have seen him."

8Philip said to him, "Lord, show us the Father. That is all we need."

9Jesus answered, "I have been with you a long time now. Do you still not know me, Philip? Whoever has seen me has seen the Father. So why do you say, 'Show us the Father'? **10**Don't you believe that I am in the Father and the Father is in me? The words I say to you don't come from me, but the Father lives in me and does his own work. **11**Believe me when I say that I am in the Father and the Father is in me. Or believe because of the miracles I have done. **12**I tell you the truth, whoever believes in me will do the same things that I do. Those who believe will do even greater things than these, because I am going to the Father. **13**And if you ask for anything in my name, I will do it for you so that the Father's glory will be shown through the Son. **14**If you ask me for anything in my name, I will do it.

The Promise of the Holy Spirit

15"If you love me, you will obey my commands. **16**I will ask the Father, and he will give you another Helper to be with you forever— **17**the Spirit of truth. The world cannot accept him, because it does not see him or know him. But you know him, because he lives with you and he will be in you.

18"I will not leave you all alone like orphans; I will come back to you. **19**In a little while the world will not see me anymore, but you will see me. Because I live, you will live, too. **20**On that day you will know that I am in my Father, and that you are in me and I am in you. **21**Those who know my commands and obey them are the ones who love me, and my Father will love those who love me. I will love them and will show myself to them."

22Then Judas (not Judas Iscariot) said, "But, Lord, why do you plan to show yourself to us and not to the rest of the world?"

23Jesus answered, "If people love me, they will obey my teaching. My Father will love them, and we will come to them and make our home with them. 24Those who do not love me do not obey my teaching. This teaching that you hear is not really mine; it is from my Father, who sent me.

25"I have told you all these things while I am with you. 26But the Helper will teach you everything and will cause you to remember all that I told you. This Helper is the Holy Spirit whom the Father will send in my name."

OLD TESTAMENT READING

If you carefully obey the commands I am giving you today and love the LORD your God and serve him with your whole being, 14then he will send rain on your land at the right time, in the fall and spring, and you will be able to gather your grain, new wine, and oil.

Deuteronomy 11:13–14

INSIGHTS

The Master has revealed Himself to you, and is calling for your complete surrender, and you shrink and hesitate. A measure of surrender you are willing to make, and think indeed it is fit and proper that you should. But an utter abandonment, without any reserves, seems to you too much to be asked for. You are afraid of it. It involves too much, you think, and is too great a risk. . . .

. . . Your Lord says, "He that hath my commandments, and keepeth them, he it is that loveth me; and he that loveth me shall be loved of my Father, and I will love him, and will manifest myself to him. . . ."

He loves you with more than the love of friendship. . . . He has given you all, and He asks for all in return. The slightest reserve will grieve Him to the heart. He spared not Himself and how can you spare yourself? . . .

Oh, be generous in your self-surrender! Meet His measureless devotion for you with a measureless devotion to Him. . . . Whatever there is of you, let Him have it all. Give up forever everything that is separate from Him. . . .

. . . The obligations of love will be to you its sweetest privileges; and the right you have acquired to lavish the uttermost wealth of abandonment of all that you have upon your Lord will seem to lift you into a region of unspeakable glory. The perfect happiness of perfect obedience will dawn upon your soul, and you will begin to know something of what Jesus meant when He said, "I delight to do thy will, O my God."

HANNAH WHITALL SMITH

PAUSE FOR REFLECTION

Why do you obey God? Out of obligation? Because it is the "right" thing to do? God wants us to obey him simply because we love him! Pray for such a love-filled heart that obedience will be a delight!

JOHN 14:27 — 15:27

27"I leave you peace; my peace I give you. I do not give it to you as the world does. So don't let your hearts be troubled or afraid. 28You heard me say to you, 'I am going, but I am coming back to you.' If you loved me, you should be happy that I am going back to the Father, because he is greater than I am. 29I have told you this now, before it happens, so that when it happens, you will believe. 30I will not talk with you much longer, because the ruler of this world is coming. He has no power over me, 31but the world must know that I love the Father, so I do exactly what the Father told me to do.

"Come now, let us go.

Jesus Is Like a Vine

15 "I am the true vine; my Father is the gardener. 2He cuts off every branch of mine that does not produce fruit. And he trims and cleans every branch that produces fruit so that it will produce even more fruit. 3You are already clean because of the words I have spoken to you. 4Remain in me, and I will remain in you. A branch cannot produce fruit alone but must remain in the vine. In the same way, you cannot produce fruit alone but must remain in me.

5"I am the vine, and you are the branches. If any remain in me and I remain in them, they produce much fruit. But without me they can do nothing. 6If any do not remain in me, they are like a branch that is thrown away and then dies. Peo-ple pick up dead branches, throw them into the fire, and burn them. 7If you remain in me and follow my teachings, you can ask anything you want, and it will be given to you. 8You should produce much fruit and show that you are my followers, which brings glory to my Father. 9I loved you as the Father loved me. Now remain in my love. 10I have obeyed my Father's commands, and I remain in his love. In the same way, if you obey my commands, you will remain in my love. 11I have told you these things so that you can have the same joy I have and so that your joy will be the fullest possible joy.

12"This is my command: Love each other as I have loved you. 13The greatest love a person can show is to die for his friends. 14You are my friends if you do what I command you. 15I no longer call you servants, because a servant does not know what his master is doing. But I call you friends, because I have made known to you everything I heard from my Father. 16You did not choose me; I chose you. And I gave you this work: to go and produce fruit, fruit that will last. Then the Father will give you anything you ask for in my name. 17This is my command: Love each other.

Jesus Warns His Followers

18"If the world hates you, remember that it hated me first. 19If you belonged to the world, it would love you as it loves its own. But I have chosen you out of the world, so you don't belong to it. That is why the world hates you. 20Remember what I told you: A servant is not greater than his master. If people did wrong to me, they will do wrong to you, too. And if they obeyed my teaching, they will obey yours, too. 21They will do all

This is page 279. The top shows "JOHN" in stylized text.

this to you on account of me, because they do not know the One who sent me. **22**If I had not come and spoken to them, they would not be guilty of sin, but now they have no excuse for their sin. **23**Whoever hates me also hates my Father. **24**I did works among them that no one else has ever done. If I had not done these works, they would not be guilty of sin. But now they have seen what I have done, and yet they have hated both me and my Father. **25**But this happened so that what is written in their law would be true: 'They hated me for no reason.'

26"I will send you the Helper from the Father; he is the Spirit of truth who comes from the Father. When he comes, he will tell about me, **27**and you also must tell people about me, because you have been with me from the beginning."

OLD TESTAMENT READING

Create in me a pure heart, God,
and make my spirit right again.
11Do not send me away from you
or take your Holy Spirit away from me.
12Give me back the joy of your salvation.
Keep me strong by giving me a willing
spirit.
13Then I will teach your ways to those who do
wrong,
and sinners will turn back to you.

Psalm 51:10–13

INSIGHTS

If anyone asks the question, "How can I be a happy Christian?" our Lord's answer is very simple: . . . "You cannot have My joy without My life. Abide in Me, and let Me abide in you, and My joy will be in you." . . .

. . . There is no joy like love. There is no joy but love. Christ had just spoken of the Father's love and His own abiding in it, and of His having loved us with that same love. His joy is nothing but the joy of love, of being loved and of loving. It was the joy of receiving His Father's love and abiding in it, and then the joy of passing on that love and pouring it out on sinners. It is this joy He wants us to share: the joy of being loved of the Father and of Him; the joy of in our turn loving and living for those around us. . . .

. . . How sad that we should so need to be reminded that as God alone is the fountain of all joy, "God our exceeding joy," the only way to be perfectly happy is to have as much of God, as much of His will and fellowship, as possible! Religion is meant to be in everyday life a thing of unspeakable joy. And why do so many complain that it is not so? Because they do not believe that there is no joy like the joy of abiding in Christ and in His love, and being branches through whom He can pour out His love on a dying world.

ANDREW MURRAY

PAUSE FOR REFLECTION

In what ways do you think the peace that Jesus promises (John 14:27) differs from the world's peace? What does Jesus say about the relationship between love, joy, and obedience to God?

JOHN 16:1-28

16 "I have told you these things to keep you from giving up. ²People will put you out of their synagogues. Yes, the time is coming when those who kill you will think they are offering service to God. ³They will do this because they have not known the Father and they have not known me. ⁴I have told you these things now so that when the time comes you will remember that I warned you.

The Work of the Holy Spirit

"I did not tell you these things at the beginning, because I was with you then. ⁵Now I am going back to the One who sent me. But none of you asks me, 'Where are you going?' ⁶Your hearts are filled with sadness because I have told you these things. ⁷But I tell you the truth, it is better for you that I go away. When I go away, I will send the Helper to you. If I do not go away, the Helper will not come. ⁸When the Helper comes, he will prove to the people of the world the truth about sin, about being right with God, and about judgment. ⁹He will prove to them that sin is not believing in me. ¹⁰He will prove to them that being right with God comes from my going to the Father and not being seen anymore. ¹¹And the Helper will prove to them that judgment happened when the ruler of this world was judged.

¹²"I have many more things to say to you, but they are too much for you now. ¹³But when the Spirit of truth comes, he will lead you into all truth. He will not speak his own words, but he will speak only what he hears, and he will tell you what is to come. ¹⁴The Spirit of truth will bring glory to me, because he will take what I have to say and tell it to you. ¹⁵All that the Father has is mine. That is why I said that the Spirit will take what I have to say and tell it to you.

Sadness Will Become Happiness

¹⁶"After a little while you will not see me, and then after a little while you will see me again."

¹⁷Some of the followers said to each other, "What does Jesus mean when he says, 'After a little while you will not see me, and then after a little while you will see me again'? And what does he mean when he says, 'Because I am going to the Father'?" ¹⁸They also asked, "What does he mean by 'a little while'? We don't understand what he is saying."

¹⁹Jesus saw that the followers wanted to ask him about this, so he said to them, "Are you asking each other what I meant when I said, 'After a little while you will not see me, and then after a little while you will see me again'? ²⁰I tell you the truth, you will cry and be sad, but the world will be happy. You will be sad, but your sadness will become joy. ²¹When a woman gives birth to a baby, she has pain, because her time has come. But when her baby is born, she forgets the pain, because she is so happy that a child has been born into the world. ²²It is the same with you. Now you are sad, but I will see you again and you will be happy, and no one will take away your joy. ²³In that day you will not ask me for anything. I tell you the truth, my Father will give you anything you ask for in my name. ²⁴Until now you have not asked for any-

thing in my name. Ask and you will receive, so that your joy will be the fullest possible joy.

Victory over the World

25"I have told you these things indirectly in stories. But the time will come when I will not use stories like that to tell you things; I will speak to you in plain words about the Father. 26In that day you will ask the Father for things in my name. I mean, I will not need to ask the Father for you. 27The Father himself loves you. He loves you because you loved me and believed that I came from God. 28I came from the Father into the world. Now I am leaving the world and going back to the Father."

OLD TESTAMENT READING

Trust the LORD and do good.
Live in the land and feed on truth.
4Enjoy serving the LORD,
and he will give you what you want.
5Depend on the LORD;
trust him, and he will take care of you.
6Then your goodness will shine like the sun,
and your fairness like the noonday sun.

Psalm 37:3–6

INSIGHTS

How often have you answered the question, "How are you today?" with "Fine, thanks!" when you were not fine at all? What if you said, "Not well, actually. I'm having a hard day"? How would that person respond? What if he or she said, "What's concerning you? I'm here for you"? What would you say next, after experiencing such sincerity?

Can you imagine us communicating this honestly with one another on a regular basis? This is what Jesus invites us to do with him every day. He meets us where we are, asking us not to hide.

What troubles you today, underneath your smile and your ready response of "Fine, thanks"? Family issues? Strained relationships? Money? Your workload? Your decisions?

Whatever your burden, face the situation squarely and invite God to be Lord over it. Do not believe the lie that you are trapped by your circumstances or your past. Do not try to be someone else when you talk with God. Ask him to help you trust the Holy Spirit as your Comforter. Unashamedly declare your dependence on God. You will find joy in your sadness and strength in your weakness as Jesus' power lives in you (2 Cor. 12:9–10).

The Helper has come, just as Jesus promised. He walks us purposefully through the reality of life, filling us with more and more of himself. He is waiting to respond to our cry for help.

Now, how are you really doing? Take it to the Comforter.

BETSY ZENZ

PAUSE FOR REFLECTION

Who did Jesus promise to send to his followers? What would he do for them? Why does God love Jesus' followers? What does God do for those he loves? How is he comforting and caring for you today?

JOHN 16:29 — 17:20

29Then the followers of Jesus said, "You are speaking clearly to us now and are not using stories that are hard to understand. 30We can see now that you know all things. You can answer a person's question even before it is asked. This makes us believe you came from God."

31Jesus answered, "So now you believe? 32Listen to me; a time is coming when you will be scattered, each to your own home. That time is now here. You will leave me alone, but I am never really alone, because the Father is with me.

33"I told you these things so that you can have peace in me. In this world you will have trouble, but be brave! I have defeated the world."

Jesus Prays for His Followers

 After Jesus said these things, he looked toward heaven and prayed, "Father, the time has come. Give glory to your Son so that the Son can give glory to you. 2You gave the Son power over all people so that the Son could give eternal life to all those you gave him. 3And this is eternal life: that people know you, the only true God, and that they know Jesus Christ, the One you sent. 4Having finished the work you gave me to do, I brought you glory on earth. 5And now, Father, give me glory with you; give me the glory I had with you before the world was made.

6"I showed what you are like to those you gave me from the world. They belonged to you, and you gave them to me, and they have obeyed your teaching. 7Now they know that everything you gave me comes from you. 8I gave them the teachings you gave me, and they accepted them. They knew that I truly came from you, and they believed that you sent me. 9I am praying for them. I am not praying for people in the world but for those you gave me, because they are yours. 10All I have is yours, and all you have is mine. And my glory is shown through them. 11I am coming to you; I will not stay in the world any longer. But they are still in the world. Holy Father, keep them safe by the power of your name, the name you gave me, so that they will be one, just as you and I are one. 12While I was with them, I kept them safe by the power of your name, the name you gave me. I protected them, and only one of them, the one worthy of destruction, was lost so that the Scripture would come true.

13"I am coming to you now. But I pray these things while I am still in the world so that these followers can have all of my joy in them. 14I have given them your teaching. And the world has hated them, because they don't belong to the world, just as I don't belong to the world. 15I am not asking you to take them out of the world but to keep them safe from the Evil One. 16They don't belong to the world, just as I don't belong to the world. 17Make them ready for your service through your truth; your teaching is truth. 18I have sent them into the world, just as you sent me into the world. 19For their sake, I am making myself ready to serve so that they can be ready for their service of the truth.

20"I pray for these followers, but I am also praying for all those who will believe in me because of their teaching."

OLD TESTAMENT READING

Those who go to God Most High for safety
will be protected by the Almighty.
[2] I will say to the LORD, "You are my place of
safety and protection.
You are my God and I trust you."

[3] God will save you from hidden traps
and from deadly diseases.
[4] He will cover you with his feathers,
and under his wings you can hide.
His truth will be your shield and protection.

[5] You will not fear any danger by night
or an arrow during the day.
[6] You will not be afraid of diseases that come in
the dark
or sickness that strikes at noon.
[7] At your side one thousand people may
die,
or even ten thousand right beside you,
but you will not be hurt.
[8] You will only watch
and see the wicked punished.

Psalm 91:1–8

INSIGHTS

Someone has said that Psalm 91 is an expanded commentary on the great cry of the apostle Paul: "If God is for us, who can be against us?" (Rom. 8:31). What is the message of the Psalm? . . .

. . . God promises us shelter, covering, and comprehensive protection based on His very nature. Those who claim the promise and dwell in the shelter of the Most High will rest in the shadow of the Almighty. God offers us security, says the psalmist, by providing secret shelter. . . .

. . . Almighty God is saying, in effect, "When you dwell in My most secret place, I promise to be your divine host with the sacred responsibility of covering and caring for you." When we deposit our trust in Him, then He guarantees He will give us His sheltering protection against all that harms us—until our duty is done and our race is finished in His service.

We will still go through trials. That is part of life. But . . . if we are "dwelling" in communion with God, if we are accepting the shelter only He can give, then we will be safe until our work for the Lord is over, until our time on this earth is done. . . .

Our security does not rest in our weak, feeble, timid, fragile, finite humanity—not for a moment. Our security is in clinging to a God who takes care of those who take the conscious step of faith to believe.

JOEL GREGORY

PAUSE FOR REFLECTION

Why did Jesus pray for protection for all of his followers? What kind of protection did Jesus want for his followers? What assurances does Psalm 91 give to you? As you read Jesus' prayer, do you feel his personal love and care for you? Thank him.

JOHN 17:21—18:18

21Father, I pray that they can be one. As you are in me and I am in you, I pray that they can also be one in us. Then the world will believe that you sent me. 22I have given these people the glory that you gave me so that they can be one, just as you and I are one. 23I will be in them and you will be in me so that they will be completely one. Then the world will know that you sent me and that you loved them just as much as you loved me.

24"Father, I want these people that you gave me to be with me where I am. I want them to see my glory, which you gave me because you loved me before the world was made. 25Father, you are the One who is good. The world does not know you, but I know you, and these people know you sent me. 26I showed them what you are like, and I will show them again. Then they will have the same love that you have for me, and I will live in them."

Jesus Is Arrested

When Jesus finished praying, he went with his followers across the Kidron Valley. On the other side there was a garden, and Jesus and his followers went into it.

2Judas knew where this place was, because Jesus met there often with his followers. Judas was the one who turned against Jesus. 3So Judas came there with a group of soldiers and some guards from the leading priests and the Pharisees. They were carrying torches, lanterns, and weapons.

4Knowing everything that would happen to him, Jesus went out and asked, "Who is it you are looking for?"

5They answered, "Jesus from Nazareth."

"I am he," Jesus said. (Judas, the one who turned against Jesus, was standing there with them.) 6When Jesus said, "I am he," they moved back and fell to the ground.

7Jesus asked them again, "Who is it you are looking for?"

They said, "Jesus of Nazareth."

8"I told you that I am he," Jesus said. "So if you are looking for me, let the others go." 9This happened so that the words Jesus said before would come true: "I have not lost any of the ones you gave me."

10Simon Peter, who had a sword, pulled it out and struck the servant of the high priest, cutting off his right ear. (The servant's name was Malchus.) 11Jesus said to Peter, "Put your sword back. Shouldn't I drink the cup the Father gave me?"

Jesus Is Brought Before Annas

12Then the soldiers with their commander and the guards arrested Jesus. They tied him 13and led him first to Annas, the father-in-law of Caiaphas, the high priest that year. 14Caiaphas was the one who told the Jews that it would be better if one man died for all the people.

Peter Says He Doesn't Know Jesus

15Simon Peter and another one of Jesus' followers went along after Jesus. This follower knew the high priest, so he went with Jesus into the high priest's courtyard. 16But Peter waited outside near the door. The follower who knew the high priest came back outside, spoke to the girl at the door, and brought Peter inside. **17**The girl at the door said to Peter, "Aren't you also one of that man's followers?"

Peter answered, "No, I am not!"

18It was cold, so the servants and guards had built a fire and were standing around it, warming themselves. Peter also was standing with them, warming himself.

OLD TESTAMENT READING

It is good and pleasant
> when God's people live together in peace!
2It is like perfumed oil poured on the priest's head
> and running down his beard.
It ran down Aaron's beard
> and on to the collar of his robes.
3It is like the dew of Mount Hermon
> falling on the hills of Jerusalem.
There the LORD gives his blessing
> of life forever.

Psalm 133:1–3

INSIGHTS

Our God is a God of unity. It is against His nature to work in the midst of division. That is why in His high priestly prayer (John 17) Jesus repeatedly prayed that "they may be one, just as We are one." Jesus knew that Satan would try to destroy the church through disunity. Thus, He earnestly prayed that the church would be a unified body through which God could accomplish His work.

God's insistence on unity is why so much of the New Testament gives instruction for maintaining the unity of the church. For example, 1 Corinthians 14:40 instructs the church to do all things properly and in order. Ephesians 4:3 exhorts believers to be "diligent to preserve the unity of the Spirit in the bond of peace." . . .

Satan recognizes the power of God's people. He knows that we are the only ones in the world who can keep him from messing up God's plan. So he is desperate to stop us. That is why the church is always under attack from Satan. He wants to get choir folks fighting each other. He wants to get church leaders fighting each other. He wants to get members fighting each other. He wants husbands and wives to be fighting each other. If he succeeds, God's people become ineffective.

As God's people, we must overcome disunity before we can fight any other battles. When we see disunity, we should not join Satan's side and keep it going. We should stop, recognize the source, and act under God's authority to restore our unity so He can continue His work through us.

ANTHONY EVANS

ACTION POINT

Why does Jesus want his followers to be one? In what ways does disunity limit God's work through your life? Prayerfully read Psalm 133 and begin working for the unity that is such a precious blessing to God.

JOHN 18:19 — 19:3

The High Priest Questions Jesus

19The high priest asked Jesus questions about his followers and his teaching. **20**Jesus answered, "I have spoken openly to everyone. I have always taught in synagogues and in the Temple, where all the Jews come together. I never said anything in secret. **21**So why do you question me? Ask the people who heard my teaching. They know what I said."

22When Jesus said this, one of the guards standing there hit him. The guard said, "Is that the way you answer the high priest?"

23Jesus answered him, "If I said something wrong, then show what it was. But if what I said is true, why do you hit me?"

24Then Annas sent Jesus, who was still tied, to Caiaphas the high priest.

Peter Says Again He Doesn't Know Jesus

25As Simon Peter was standing and warming himself, they said to him, "Aren't you one of that man's followers?"

Peter said it was not true; he said, "No, I am not."

26One of the servants of the high priest was there. This servant was a relative of the man whose ear Peter had cut off. The servant said, "Didn't I see you with him in the garden?"

27Again Peter said it wasn't true. At once a rooster crowed.

Jesus Is Brought Before Pilate

28Early in the morning they led Jesus from Caiaphas's house to the Roman governor's palace. They would not go inside the palace, because they did not want to make themselves unclean; they wanted to eat the Passover meal. **29**So Pilate went outside to them and asked, "What charges do you bring against this man?"

30They answered, "If he were not a criminal, we wouldn't have brought him to you."

31Pilate said to them, "Take him yourselves and judge him by your own law."

"But we are not allowed to put anyone to death," the Jews answered. **32**(This happened so that what Jesus said about how he would die would come true.)

33Then Pilate went back inside the palace and called Jesus to him and asked, "Are you the king of the Jews?"

34Jesus said, "Is that your own question, or did others tell you about me?"

35Pilate answered, "I am not one of you. It was your own people and their leading priests who handed you over to me. What have you done wrong?"

36Jesus answered, "My kingdom does not belong to this world. If it belonged to this world, my servants would have fought to keep me from being given over to the Jewish leaders. But my kingdom is from another place."

37Pilate said, "So you are a king!"

Jesus answered, "You are the one saying I am a king. This is why I was born and came into the world: to tell people the truth. And everyone who belongs to the truth listens to me."

38Pilate said, "What is truth?" After he said this, he went out to the crowd again and said to them, "I find nothing against this man. **39**But it is your custom that I free one prisoner to you at Passover time. Do you want me to free the 'king of the Jews'?"

40They shouted back, "No, not him! Let Barabbas go free!" (Barabbas was a robber.)

19 Then Pilate ordered that Jesus be taken away and whipped. **2**The soldiers made a crown from some thorny branches and put it on Jesus' head and put a purple robe around him. **3**Then they came to him many times and said, "Hail, King of the Jews!" and hit him in the face.

OLD TESTAMENT READING

All you nations, praise the LORD.
  All you people, praise him
2because the LORD loves us very much,
  and his truth is everlasting.

Praise the LORD!

Psalm 117:1–2

LORD, you do what is right,
  and your laws are fair.
138 The rules you commanded are right
  and completely trustworthy.
139I am so upset I am worn out,
  because my enemies have forgotten your
    words.
140 Your promises are proven,
  so I, your servant, love them.
141I am unimportant and hated,
  but I have not forgotten your orders.
142 Your goodness continues forever,
  and your teachings are true.

Psalm 119:137–142

INSIGHTS

What is truth? I have often wondered how Pilate asked this question. What was his tone of voice? What kind of expression did he have on his face? Was the question raised in jest? Was it cynical? Was Pilate pensive for a moment? We don't really know. If Pilate was momentarily concerned for truth, his mood soon gave way to a spirit of expediency. If he cared about knowing the truth, he certainly didn't care much about doing the truth. . . .

To declare that Jesus was without fault and then minutes later to turn Him over to a barbarous mob was to slaughter the truth. Pilate judged the Truth. He sentenced the Truth. He scourged the Truth. He mocked the Truth. He crucified the Truth.

The irony is that at the very moment he asked his question "What is truth?" he was staring at the pure incarnation of Truth. The One who is the Truth had just said to him, "Everyone who is of the truth hears My voice."

Pilate missed that voice. The words bounced off his ears. He was not "of the truth."

R. C. SPROUL

APPLICATION

How ironic that Pilate was so close to the God of truth, yet failed to understand truth. What claims to truth does God make? Does he make his truth available to people? How? Pray that you will draw close to God and trust his truth.

→ ## JOHN 19:4-27

4Again Pilate came out and said to them, "Look, I am bringing Jesus out to you. I want you to know that I find nothing against him." **5**So Jesus came out, wearing the crown of thorns and the purple robe. Pilate said to them, "Here is the man!"

6When the leading priests and the guards saw Jesus, they shouted, "Crucify him! Crucify him!"

But Pilate answered, "Crucify him yourselves, because I find nothing against him."

7The leaders answered, "We have a law that says he should die, because he said he is the Son of God."

8When Pilate heard this, he was even more afraid. **9**He went back inside the palace and asked Jesus, "Where do you come from?" But Jesus did not answer him. **10**Pilate said, "You refuse to speak to me? Don't you know I have power to set you free and power to have you crucified?"

11Jesus answered, "The only power you have over me is the power given to you by God. The man who turned me in to you is guilty of a greater sin."

12After this, Pilate tried to let Jesus go. But some in the crowd cried out, "Anyone who makes himself king is against Caesar. If you let this man go, you are no friend of Caesar."

13When Pilate heard what they were saying, he brought Jesus out and sat down on the judge's seat at the place called The Stone Pavement. (In the Hebrew language the name is Gabbatha.) **14**It was about noon on Preparation Day of Passover week. Pilate said to the crowd, "Here is your king!"

15They shouted, "Take him away! Take him away! Crucify him!"

Pilate asked them, "Do you want me to crucify your king?"

The leading priests answered, "The only king we have is Caesar."

16So Pilate handed Jesus over to them to be crucified.

Jesus Is Crucified

The soldiers took charge of Jesus. **17**Carrying his own cross, Jesus went out to a place called The Place of the Skull, which in the Hebrew language is called Golgotha. **18**There they crucified Jesus. They also crucified two other men, one on each side, with Jesus in the middle. **19**Pilate wrote a sign and put it on the cross. It read: JESUS OF NAZARETH, THE KING OF THE JEWS. **20**The sign was written in Hebrew, in Latin, and in Greek. Many of the people read the sign, because the place where Jesus was crucified was near the city. **21**The leading priests said to Pilate, "Don't write, 'The King of the Jews.' But write, 'This man said, "I am the King of the Jews." ' "

22Pilate answered, "What I have written, I have written."

23After the soldiers crucified Jesus, they took his clothes and divided them into four parts, with each soldier getting one part. They also took his long shirt, which was all one piece of cloth, woven from top to bottom. **24**So the soldiers said to each other, "We should not tear this into parts. Let's throw lots to see who will get it."

This happened so that this Scripture would come true:

"They divided my clothes among them,
and they threw lots for my clothing."

Psalm 22:18

So the soldiers did this.

25 Standing near his cross were Jesus' mother, his mother's sister, Mary the wife of Clopas, and Mary Magdalene. 26 When Jesus saw his mother and the follower he loved standing nearby, he said to his mother, "Dear woman, here is your son." 27 Then he said to the follower, "Here is your mother." From that time on, the follower took her to live in his home.

OLD TESTAMENT READING

Tell them to give this message to their masters: 'The LORD All-Powerful, the God of Israel, says: "Tell your masters: 5 I made the earth, its people, and all its animals with my great power and strength. I can give the earth to anyone I want. 6 Now I have given all these lands to Nebuchadnezzar king of Babylon, my servant. I will make even the wild animals obey him. 7 All nations will serve Nebuchadnezzar and his son and grandson. Then the time will come for Babylon to be defeated, and many nations and great kings will make Babylon their servant."'"

Jeremiah 27:4–7

INSIGHTS

Our sovereign Lord . . . exerts control over His entire universe from beginning to end! His sovereignty means that He either causes or He allows all things to happen that do happen. He is absolutely independent, subject to no one, and influenced by no one. Despite the suffering, violence, and filth of this world, God remains in control—whether or not we acknowledge him. Before time began, God was in control. He has ruled over all creation ever since He created heaven and earth. . . .

The Israelites must have wondered whether God was in control, as they spent four hundred years of bondage in Egypt. Driven day after day by cruel taskmasters, they surely asked, "If there is a God, where is He?" . . . They probably reasoned that either there is no God, or that God did not have the power to stop the madness. But what happened? The sovereign God who controls every circumstance led Israel out of Egypt with mighty demonstrations of His power! Israel never forgot His deliverance. The entire world was shaken! Nations trembled at the prospect of confronting God's people.

ELLIOT JOHNSON /
AL SCHIERBAUM

PAUSE FOR REFLECTION

Who holds the only real power there is? Why does God give power to certain people for a time? What happens to those who think their power is their own? Submit your heart to his power today!

JOHN 19:28 – 20:9

Jesus Dies

28After this, Jesus knew that everything had been done. So that the Scripture would come true, he said, "I am thirsty." **29**There was a jar full of vinegar there, so the soldiers soaked a sponge in it, put the sponge on a branch of a hyssop plant, and lifted it to Jesus' mouth. **30**When Jesus tasted the vinegar, he said, "It is finished." Then he bowed his head and died.

31This day was Preparation Day, and the next day was a special Sabbath day. Since the religious leaders did not want the bodies to stay on the cross on the Sabbath day, they asked Pilate to order that the legs of the men be broken and the bodies be taken away. **32**So the soldiers came and broke the legs of the first man on the cross beside Jesus. Then they broke the legs of the man on the other cross beside Jesus. **33**But when the soldiers came to Jesus and saw that he was already dead, they did not break his legs. **34**But one of the soldiers stuck his spear into Jesus' side, and at once blood and water came out. **35**(The one who saw this happen is the one who told us this, and whatever he says is true. And he knows that he tells the truth, and he tells it so that you might believe.) **36**These things happened to make the Scripture come true: "Not one of his bones will be broken." **37**And another Scripture says, "They will look at the one they stabbed."

Jesus Is Buried

38Later, Joseph from Arimathea asked Pilate if he could take the body of Jesus. (Joseph was a secret follower of Jesus, because he was afraid of some of the leaders.) Pilate gave his permission, so Joseph came and took Jesus' body away. **39**Nicodemus, who earlier had come to Jesus at night, went with Joseph. He brought about seventy-five pounds of myrrh and aloes. **40**These two men took Jesus' body and wrapped it with the spices in pieces of linen cloth, which is how they bury the dead. **41**In the place where Jesus was crucified, there was a garden. In the garden was a new tomb that had never been used before. **42**The men laid Jesus in that tomb because it was nearby, and they were preparing to start their Sabbath day.

Jesus' Tomb Is Empty

Early on the first day of the week, Mary Magdalene went to the tomb while it was still dark. When she saw that the large stone had been moved away from the tomb, **2**she ran to Simon Peter and the follower whom Jesus loved. Mary said, "They have taken the Lord out of the tomb, and we don't know where they have put him."

3So Peter and the other follower started for the tomb. **4**They were both running, but the other follower ran faster than Peter and reached the tomb first. **5**He bent down and looked in and saw the strips of linen cloth lying there, but he did not go in. **6**Then following him, Simon Peter arrived and went into the tomb and saw the strips of linen lying there. **7**He also saw the cloth that had been around Jesus' head, which was folded up and laid in a different place from the strips of linen. **8**Then the other follower, who had reached the tomb first, also went in. He saw and believed. **9**(They did not yet understand from the Scriptures that Jesus must rise from the dead.)

OLD TESTAMENT READING

Clap your hands, all you people.
Shout to God with joy.
²The LORD Most High is wonderful.
He is the great King over all the earth!
³He defeated nations for us
and put them under our control.
⁴He chose the land we would inherit.
We are the children of Jacob, whom he
loved.   *Selah*

⁵God has risen with a shout of joy;
the LORD has risen as the trumpets sounded.
⁶Sing praises to God. Sing praises.
Sing praises to our King. Sing praises.
⁷God is King of all the earth,
so sing a song of praise to him.
⁸God is King over the nations.
God sits on his holy throne.
⁹The leaders of the nations meet
with the people of the God of Abraham,
because the leaders of the earth belong to
God.
He is supreme.

Psalm 47:1–9

I know that my Defender lives,
and in the end he will stand upon the
earth.
²⁶Even after my skin has been destroyed,
in my flesh I will see God.
²⁷I will see him myself;
I will see him with my very own eyes.
How my heart wants that to happen!"

Job 19:25–27

INSIGHTS

Christ is risen:
The world below lies desolate.
Christ is risen:
The spirits of evil are fallen.
Christ is risen:
The angels of God are rejoicing.
Christ is risen:
The tombs of the dead are empty.
Christ is risen indeed from the dead,
The first of the sleepers.
Glory and power are his forever and
ever.
Amen.

HIPPOLYTUS OF ROME

ACTION POINT

When Mary revealed the stunning news that Jesus was no longer in the tomb, the disciples took off running to see it for themselves! Does the realization that Jesus is truly alive set your heart racing? Ask God to renew your excitement and joy in Jesus' resurrection.

JOHN 20:10 — 21:3

Jesus Appears to Mary Magdalene

10Then the followers went back home. **11**But Mary stood outside the tomb, crying. As she was crying, she bent down and looked inside the tomb. **12**She saw two angels dressed in white, sitting where Jesus' body had been, one at the head and one at the feet.

13They asked her, "Woman, why are you crying?"

She answered, "They have taken away my Lord, and I don't know where they have put him." **14**When Mary said this, she turned around and saw Jesus standing there, but she did not know it was Jesus.

15Jesus asked her, "Woman, why are you crying? Whom are you looking for?"

Thinking he was the gardener, she said to him, "Did you take him away, sir? Tell me where you put him, and I will get him."

16Jesus said to her, "Mary."

Mary turned toward Jesus and said in the Hebrew language, "Rabboni." (This means "Teacher.")

17Jesus said to her, "Don't hold on to me, because I have not yet gone up to the Father. But go to my brothers and tell them, 'I am going back to my Father and your Father, to my God and your God.'"

18Mary Magdalene went and said to the followers, "I saw the Lord!" And she told them what Jesus had said to her.

Jesus Appears to His Followers

19When it was evening on the first day of the week, Jesus' followers were together. The doors were locked, because they were afraid of the elders. Then Jesus came and stood right in the middle of them and said, "Peace be with you." **20**After he said this, he showed them his hands and his side. His followers were thrilled when they saw the Lord.

21Then Jesus said again, "Peace be with you. As the Father sent me, I now send you." **22**After he said this, he breathed on them and said, "Receive the Holy Spirit. **23**If you forgive anyone his sins, they are forgiven. If you don't forgive them, they are not forgiven."

Jesus Appears to Thomas

24Thomas (called Didymus), who was one of the twelve, was not with them when Jesus came. **25**The other followers kept telling Thomas, "We saw the Lord."

But Thomas said, "I will not believe it until I see the nail marks in his hands and put my finger where the nails were and put my hand into his side."

26A week later the followers were in the house again, and Thomas was with them. The doors were locked, but Jesus came in and stood right in the middle of them. He said, "Peace be with you." **27**Then he said to Thomas, "Put your finger here, and look at my hands. Put your hand here in my side. Stop being an unbeliever and believe."

28Thomas said to him, "My Lord and my God!"

29Then Jesus told him, "You believe because you see me. Those who believe without seeing me will be truly blessed."

Why John Wrote This Book

30Jesus did many other miracles in the presence of his followers that are not written in this book. **31**But these are written so that you may believe that Jesus is the Christ, the Son of God. Then, by believing, you may have life through his name.

Jesus Appears to Seven Followers

21 Later, Jesus showed himself to his followers again—this time at Lake Galilee. This is how he showed himself: **2**Some of the followers were together: Simon Peter, Thomas (called Didymus), Nathanael from Cana in Galilee, the two sons of Zebedee, and two other followers. **3**Simon Peter said, "I am going out to fish."

The others said, "We will go with you." So they went out and got into the boat. They fished that night but caught nothing.

OLD TESTAMENT READING

Then Gideon said to God, "You said you would help me save Israel. **37**I will put some wool on the threshing floor. If there is dew only on the wool but all of the ground is dry, then I will know that you will use me to save Israel, as you said." **38**And that is just what happened. When Gideon got up early the next morning and squeezed the wool, he got a full bowl of water from it.

39Then Gideon said to God, "Don't be angry with me if I ask just one more thing. Please let me make one more test. Let only the wool be dry while the ground around it gets wet with dew." **40**That night God did that very thing. Just the wool was dry, but the ground around it was wet with dew.

Judges 6:36–40

INSIGHTS

Give your whole being to God without holding back and without doubting. He will prove himself to you, and work in you that which is pleasing in His sight through Jesus Christ. Keep His ways as you know them in the Word. Keep His ways, as nature teaches them, in always doing what appears right. Keep His ways as providence points them out. Keep His ways as the Holy Spirit suggests. Do not think of waiting on God while you say you are not willing to walk in His path. However weak you feel, only be willing, and he who has worked to will, will work to do by His power. . . .

. . . So come with every temptation you feel in yourself, every memory of unwillingness, unwatchfulness, unfaithfulness, and all that causes your unceasing self-condemnation. Put your powerlessness in God's almighty power, and find in waiting on God your deliverance.

ANDREW MURRAY

ACTION POINT

How does God treat those who doubt? What did he do for Gideon, for Mary, for Thomas? What was their response? Do you struggle with unbelief? Ask God to prove himself to you; his answer will overwhelm you!

JOHN 21:4-25

⁴Early the next morning Jesus stood on the shore, but the followers did not know it was Jesus. ⁵Then he said to them, "Friends, did you catch any fish?"

They answered, "No."

⁶He said, "Throw your net on the right side of the boat, and you will find some." So they did, and they caught so many fish they could not pull the net back into the boat.

⁷The follower whom Jesus loved said to Peter, "It is the Lord!" When Peter heard him say this, he wrapped his coat around himself. (Peter had taken his clothes off.) Then he jumped into the water. ⁸The other followers went to shore in the boat, dragging the net full of fish. They were not very far from shore, only about a hundred yards. ⁹When the followers stepped out of the boat and onto the shore, they saw a fire of hot coals. There were fish on the fire, and there was bread.

¹⁰Then Jesus said, "Bring some of the fish you just caught."

¹¹Simon Peter went into the boat and pulled the net to the shore. It was full of big fish, one hundred fifty-three in all, but even though there were so many, the net did not tear. ¹²Jesus said to them, "Come and eat." None of the followers dared ask him, "Who are you?" because they knew it was the Lord. ¹³Jesus came and took the bread and gave it to them, along with the fish.

¹⁴This was now the third time Jesus showed himself to his followers after he was raised from the dead.

Jesus Talks to Peter

¹⁵When they finished eating, Jesus said to Simon Peter, "Simon son of John, do you love me more than these?"

He answered, "Yes, Lord, you know that I love you."

Jesus said, "Feed my lambs."

¹⁶Again Jesus said, "Simon son of John, do you love me?"

He answered, "Yes, Lord, you know that I love you."

Jesus said, "Take care of my sheep."

¹⁷A third time he said, "Simon son of John, do you love me?"

Peter was hurt because Jesus asked him the third time, "Do you love me?" Peter said, "Lord, you know everything; you know that I love you!"

He said to him, "Feed my sheep. ¹⁸I tell you the truth, when you were younger, you tied your own belt and went where you wanted. But when you are old, you will put out your hands and someone else will tie you and take you where you don't want to go." ¹⁹(Jesus said this to show how Peter would die to give glory to God.) Then Jesus said to Peter, "Follow me!"

²⁰Peter turned and saw that the follower Jesus loved was walking behind them. (This was the follower who had leaned against Jesus at the supper and had said, "Lord, who will turn against you?") ²¹When Peter saw him behind them, he asked Jesus, "Lord, what about him?"

²²Jesus answered, "If I want him to live until I come back, that is not your business. You follow me."

²³So a story spread among the followers that

this one would not die. But Jesus did not say he would not die. He only said, "If I want him to live until I come back, that is not your business."

24That follower is the one who is telling these things and who has now written them down. We know that what he says is true.

25There are many other things Jesus did. If every one of them were written down, I suppose the whole world would not be big enough for all the books that would be written.

OLD TESTAMENT READING

Moses said to the LORD, **16**"The LORD is the God of the spirits of all people. May he choose a leader for these people, **17**who will go in and out before them. He must lead them out like sheep and bring them in; the LORD's people must not be like sheep without a shepherd."

Numbers 27:15–17

Then they will know that I, the LORD their God, am with them. The nation of Israel will know that they are my people, says the Lord GOD. **31**You, my human sheep, are the sheep I care for, and I am your God, says the Lord GOD.'"

Ezekiel 34:30–31

INSIGHTS

The shepherd is at the very center of the life of the sheep. He provides for their every need, satisfying them completely.

Sheep will not lie down if they have cause to be fearful. They are easily frightened. However, as soon as the shepherd appears and moves in the midst of the restless flock, they become quiet.

. . . Our Good Shepherd appears, saying, "Fear THOU not; for I am with thee" (Isa. 41:10). His presence in the midst of our need removes fear and gives rest.

Sheep will not lie down if they are hungry. The shepherd searches for the best pasture land available for his sheep. Our Good Shepherd knows we need to be well nourished for inner satisfaction. He provides nourishment for us from the green pastures of His Word. Nourished by it, we can lie down in quiet contentment.

Occasionally He has to MAKE us lie down. It may take illness, loneliness, heartache, or sorrow to accomplish this.

Not only does the shepherd lead his sheep in the green meadows of nourishment and rest, but beside the still waters. We are refreshed at the waters of quietness. . . .

Our Good Shepherd loves to see His sheep contented and relaxed, refreshed and satisfied with Him.

MILLIE STAMM

PAUSE FOR REFLECTION

Why is it important that God's people be led by a shepherd? How will a good shepherd lead the Lord's sheep? What relationship do you see between loving Jesus and caring for his sheep?

ACTS 1:1-26

Luke Writes Another Book

To Theophilus.

The first book I wrote was about everything Jesus began to do and teach ²until the day he was taken up into heaven. Before this, with the help of the Holy Spirit, Jesus told the apostles he had chosen what they should do. ³After his death, he showed himself to them and proved in many ways that he was alive. The apostles saw Jesus during the forty days after he was raised from the dead, and he spoke to them about the kingdom of God. ⁴Once when he was eating with them, he told them not to leave Jerusalem. He said, "Wait here to receive the promise from the Father which I told you about. ⁵John baptized people with water, but in a few days you will be baptized with the Holy Spirit."

Jesus Is Taken Up into Heaven

⁶When the apostles were all together, they asked Jesus, "Lord, are you now going to give the kingdom back to Israel?"

⁷Jesus said to them, "The Father is the only One who has the authority to decide dates and times. These things are not for you to know. ⁸But when the Holy Spirit comes to you, you will receive power. You will be my witnesses—in Jerusalem, in all of Judea, in Samaria, and in every part of the world."

⁹After he said this, as they were watching, he was lifted up, and a cloud hid him from their sight. ¹⁰As he was going, they were looking into the sky. Suddenly, two men wearing white clothes stood beside them. ¹¹They said, "Men of Galilee, why are you standing here looking into the sky? Jesus, whom you saw taken up from you into heaven, will come back in the same way you saw him go."

A New Apostle Is Chosen

¹²Then they went back to Jerusalem from the Mount of Olives. (This mountain is about half a mile from Jerusalem.) ¹³When they entered the city, they went to the upstairs room where they were staying. Peter, John, James, Andrew, Philip, Thomas, Bartholomew, Matthew, James son of Alphaeus, Simon (known as the Zealot), and Judas son of James were there. ¹⁴They all continued praying together with some women, including Mary the mother of Jesus, and Jesus' brothers.

¹⁵During this time there was a meeting of the believers (about one hundred twenty of them). Peter stood up and said, ¹⁶⁻¹⁷"Brothers and sisters, in the Scriptures the Holy Spirit said through David something that must happen involving Judas. He was one of our own group and served together with us. He led those who arrested Jesus." ¹⁸(Judas bought a field with the money he got for his evil act. But he fell to his death, his body burst open, and all his intestines poured out. ¹⁹Everyone in Jerusalem learned about this so they named this place Akeldama. In their language Akeldama means "Field of Blood.") ²⁰"In the Book of Psalms," Peter said, "this is written:

'May his place be empty;
    leave no one to live in it.'   *Psalm 69:25*

And it is also written:

'Let another man replace him as leader.'
                                          Psalm 109:8

21-22"So now a man must become a witness with us of Jesus' being raised from the dead. He must be one of the men who were part of our group during all the time the Lord Jesus was among us— from the time John was baptizing people until the day Jesus was taken up from us to heaven."

23They put the names of two men before the group. One was Joseph Barsabbas, who was also called Justus. The other was Matthias. **24-25**The apostles prayed, "Lord, you know the thoughts of everyone. Show us which one of these two you have chosen to do this work. Show us who should be an apostle in place of Judas, who turned away and went where he belongs." **26**Then they used lots to choose between them, and the lots showed that Matthias was the one. So he became an apostle with the other eleven.

OLD TESTAMENT READING

Let the fields and everything in them rejoice. Then all the trees of the forest will sing for joy

13 before the LORD, because he is coming.
He is coming to judge the world;
he will judge the world with fairness
and the peoples with truth.

Psalm 96:12–13

INSIGHTS

All true Christians believe that Jesus Christ is coming again. They may differ in their views of when certain promised events will occur, but they all agree that He is returning as He promised. Furthermore, all Christians agree that this faith in future glory ought to motivate the church. . . .

Because we do not know the day or the hour of our Lord's return, we must constantly be ready. The believer who starts to neglect the "blessed hope" (Titus 2:13) will gradually develop a cold heart, a worldly attitude, and an unfaithful life (Luke 12:35–48). . . .

Not only should this expectant attitude make a difference in our conduct, but it should also make a difference in our witness. . . .

Since this is the day of salvation, we must be diligent to do all we can to win the lost. . . . We must understand what the Bible teaches about God's program for this present age, and we must be motivated by a love for the lost (2 Cor. 5:14) and a desire to be pleasing to Him when He returns.

WARREN WIERSBE

ACTION POINT

What were Jesus' last words to his apostles? After he went up into heaven, what did God's messengers promise them? Praise God that his people still take his message into every part of the world!

ACTS 2:1-28

The Coming of the Holy Spirit

When the day of Pentecost came, they were all together in one place. **2**Suddenly a noise like a strong, blowing wind came from heaven and filled the whole house where they were sitting. **3**They saw something like flames of fire that were separated and stood over each person there. **4**They were all filled with the Holy Spirit, and they began to speak different languages by the power the Holy Spirit was giving them.

5There were some religious Jews staying in Jerusalem who were from every country in the world. **6**When they heard this noise, a crowd came together. They were all surprised, because each one heard them speaking in his own language. **7**They were completely amazed at this. They said, "Look! Aren't all these people that we hear speaking from Galilee? **8**Then how is it possible that we each hear them in our own languages? We are from different places: **9**Parthia, Media, Elam, Mesopotamia, Judea, Cappadocia, Pontus, Asia, **10**Phrygia, Pamphylia, Egypt, the areas of Libya near Cyrene, Rome **11**(both Jews and those who had become Jews), Crete, and Arabia. But we hear them telling in our own languages about the great things God has done!" **12**They were all amazed and confused, asking each other, "What does this mean?"

13But others were making fun of them, saying, "They have had too much wine."

Peter Speaks to the People

14But Peter stood up with the eleven apostles, and in a loud voice he spoke to the crowd: "My fellow Jews, and all of you who are in Jerusalem, listen to me. Pay attention to what I have to say. **15**These people are not drunk, as you think; it is only nine o'clock in the morning! **16**But Joel the prophet wrote about what is happening here today:

17'God says: In the last days
> I will pour out my Spirit on all kinds of
> people.
> Your sons and daughters will prophesy.
> Your young men will see visions,
> and your old men will dream dreams.

18At that time I will pour out my Spirit
> also on my male slaves and female slaves,
> and they will prophesy.

19I will show miracles
> in the sky and on the earth:
> blood, fire, and thick smoke.

20The sun will become dark,
> the moon red as blood,
> before the overwhelming and glorious day
> of the Lord will come.

21Then anyone who calls on the Lord will be
> saved.'   *Joel 2:28–32*

22"People of Israel, listen to these words: Jesus from Nazareth was a very special man. God clearly showed this to you by the miracles, wonders, and signs he did through Jesus. You all know this, because it happened right here among you. **23**Jesus was given to you, and with the help of those who don't know the law, you put him to death by nailing him to a cross. But this was God's plan which he had made long ago; he knew all this would happen. **24**God raised Jesus from the dead and set him free from the pain of death, because death could not hold him. **25**For David said this about him:

'I keep the Lord before me always.
Because he is close by my side,
I will not be hurt.
26So I am glad, and I rejoice.
Even my body has hope,
27because you will not leave me in the grave.
You will not let your Holy One rot.
28You will teach me how to live a holy life.
Being with you will fill me with joy.' "

Psalm 16:8–11

OLD TESTAMENT READING

The LORD says, "People of Jacob, you are my servants. Listen to me!
People of Israel, I chose you."
2This is what the LORD says, who made you,
who formed you in your mother's body,
who will help you:
"People of Jacob, my servants, don't be afraid.
Israel, I chose you.
3I will pour out water for the thirsty land
and make streams flow on dry land.
I will pour out my Spirit into your children
and my blessing on your descendants."

Isaiah 44:1–3

INSIGHTS

One day while I was sailing, the wind went down and the sea became calm and flat. There was nothing to do but sit in irons and wait for the wind. "Irons" is a sailing term for a windless time of drifting. While waiting for the wind, I drifted past another sailboat that was floating aimlessly. The people on board the craft waved and made a flat of the hand gesture of complaint about the lack of wind. One man stood by the sails and blew on them.

I thought about that for a long time afterward. How like many Christians and far too many churches. Human breath blowing on the sails—no wonder we make so little progress!

The Spirit of God in Hebrew is ruach, meaning "breath" and "wind." At Pentecost the power of the Holy Spirit was like a mighty wind. The Spirit filled the disciples and got them moving again. What we need is a mighty wind—a fresh, bracing wind of a new Pentecost. . . .

. . . So stop blowing your own breath into the sails of your life or your church. Ask for a fresh wind to fill the sails. Without the Holy Spirit, we'll drift in irons and be lost at sea. . . .

LLOYD OGILVIE

ACTION POINT

What did God's Spirit enable the believers to do? For what purpose? Has your life been renewed by God's Spirit? Pray that God's Spirit will fill you, direct you, and enable you to complete God's work in your life!

ACTS 2:29 – 3:10

29"Brothers and sisters, I can tell you truly that David, our ancestor, died and was buried. His grave is still here with us today. **30**He was a prophet and knew God had promised him that he would make a person from David's family a king just as he was. **31**Knowing this before it happened, David talked about the Christ rising from the dead. He said:

'He was not left in the grave.

His body did not rot.'

32So Jesus is the One whom God raised from the dead. And we are all witnesses to this. **33**Jesus was lifted up to heaven and is now at God's right side. The Father has given the Holy Spirit to Jesus as he promised. So Jesus has poured out that Spirit, and this is what you now see and hear. **34**David was not the one who was lifted up to heaven, but he said:

'The Lord said to my Lord,

"Sit by me at my right side,

35 until I put your enemies under your control."' *Psalm 110:1*

36"So, all the people of Israel should know this truly: God has made Jesus—the man you nailed to the cross—both Lord and Christ."

37When the people heard this, they felt guilty and asked Peter and the other apostles, "What shall we do?"

38Peter said to them, "Change your hearts and lives and be baptized, each one of you, in the name of Jesus Christ for the forgiveness of your sins. And you will receive the gift of the Holy Spirit. **39**This promise is for you, for your children, and for all who are far away. It is for everyone the Lord our God calls to himself."

40Peter warned them with many other words. He begged them, "Save yourselves from the evil of today's people!" **41**Then those people who accepted what Peter said were baptized. About three thousand people were added to the number of believers that day. **42**They spent their time learning the apostles' teaching, sharing, breaking bread, and praying together.

The Believers Share

43The apostles were doing many miracles and signs, and everyone felt great respect for God. **44**All the believers were together and shared everything. **45**They would sell their land and the things they owned and then divide the money and give it to anyone who needed it. **46**The believers met together in the Temple every day. They ate together in their homes, happy to share their food with joyful hearts. **47**They praised God and were liked by all the people. Every day the Lord added those who were being saved to the group of believers.

Peter Heals a Crippled Man

3 One day Peter and John went to the Temple at three o'clock, the time set each day for the afternoon prayer service. **2**There, at the Temple gate called Beautiful Gate, was a man who had been crippled all his life. Every day he was carried to this gate to beg for money from the people going into the Temple. **3**The man saw Peter and John going into the Temple and asked them for money. **4**Peter and John looked straight at him and said, "Look at us!" **5**The man looked at them, thinking they were going to give him some money. **6**But Peter said, "I don't have any silver or gold, but I do have something else I can give you. By the power of Jesus Christ from Nazareth, stand up and walk!" **7**Then Peter took the man's right hand and lifted him up. Immediately the man's feet and ankles became strong. **8**He jumped up, stood on his feet, and began to walk. He went into the Temple with them, walking and jumping and praising God. **9-10**All the people recognized him as the crippled man who always sat by the Beautiful Gate begging for money. Now they saw this same man walking and praising God, and they were amazed. They wondered how this could happen.

OLD TESTAMENT READING

Come, let's go back to the LORD.
  He has hurt us, but he will heal us.
  He has wounded us, but he will bandage
    our wounds.
2In two days he will put new life in us;
  on the third day he will raise us up
  so that we may live in his presence **3**and
    know him.
  Let's try to learn about the LORD;
  he will come to us as surely as the dawn
    comes."

Hosea 6:1–3b

INSIGHTS

Are you running on empty because of sin in your life that you think is well hidden? God sees and knows all about it. He wants you to face it, name it, confess it, turn from it, and, where you can, put things right. Self-flagellation will not make any lasting difference. Listen to David: "You do not delight in sacrifice, or I would bring it; you do not take pleasure in burnt offerings. The sacrifices of God are a broken spirit; a broken and contrite heart, O God, you will not despise" (Ps. 51:16–17).

God looks for brokenness of spirit—for a contrite, humble heart that, quickened by the Holy Spirit, teaches us to regard our sin as He does. We learn to pray, in the words of the old hymn:

Throw light into the darkened cells,
Where passion reigns within;
Quicken my conscience till it feels
The loathsomeness of sin.

And when we have seen our sin for what it is and rejected it, God will help us to have the right spirit in our hearts. Then we will be able to add:

Thus prostrate I shall learn of Thee,
What now I feebly prove,
That God alone in Christ can be
Unutterable love.

JILL BRISCOE

ACTION POINT

How did Peter's audience respond when they learned the truth about Christ? What did he tell them to do? Do your sins make you sick at heart? Then there is hope for you! Peter's message applies to you as well. Do what he says!

ACTS 3:11 – 4:12

Peter Speaks to the People

[11]While the man was holding on to Peter and John, all the people were amazed and ran to them at Solomon's Porch. [12]When Peter saw this, he said to them, "People of Israel, why are you surprised? You are looking at us as if it were our own power or goodness that made this man walk. [13]The God of Abraham, Isaac, and Jacob, the God of our ancestors, gave glory to Jesus, his servant. But you handed him over to be killed. Pilate decided to let him go free, but you told Pilate you did not want Jesus. [14]You did not want the One who is holy and good but asked Pilate to give you a murderer instead. [15]And so you killed the One who gives life, but God raised him from the dead. We are witnesses to this. [16]It was faith in Jesus that made this crippled man well. You can see this man, and you know him. He was made completely well because of trust in Jesus, and you all saw it happen!

[17]"Brothers and sisters, I know you did those things to Jesus because neither you nor your leaders understood what you were doing. [18]God said through the prophets that his Christ would suffer and die. And now God has made these things come true in this way. [19]So you must change your hearts and lives! Come back to God, and he will forgive your sins. Then the Lord will send the time of rest. [20]And he will send Jesus, the One he chose to be the Christ. [21]But Jesus must stay in heaven until the time comes when all things will be made right again. God told about this time long ago when he spoke through his holy prophets. [22]Moses said, 'The Lord your God will give you a prophet like me, who is one of your own people. You must listen to everything he tells you. [23]Anyone who does not listen to that prophet will die, cut off from God's people.' [24]Samuel, and all the other prophets who spoke for God after Samuel, told about this time now. [25]You are descendants of the prophets. You have received the agreement God made with your ancestors. He said to your father Abraham, 'Through your descendants all the nations on the earth will be blessed.' [26]God has raised up his servant Jesus and sent him to you first to bless you by turning each of you away from doing evil."

Peter and John at the Council

4 While Peter and John were speaking to the people, priests, the captain of the soldiers that guarded the Temple, and Sadducees came up to them. [2]They were upset because the two apostles were teaching the people and were preaching that people will rise from the dead through the power of Jesus. [3]The older leaders grabbed Peter and John and put them in jail. Since it was already night, they kept them in jail until the next day. [4]But many of those who had heard Peter and John preach believed the things they said. There were now about five thousand in the group of believers.

[5]The next day the rulers, the elders, and the teachers of the law met in Jerusalem. [6]Annas the high priest, Caiaphas, John, and Alexander were there, as well as everyone from the high priest's family. [7]They made Peter and John stand before

them and then asked them, "By what power or authority did you do this?"

8Then Peter, filled with the Holy Spirit, said to them, "Rulers of the people and you elders, **9**are you questioning us about a good thing that was done to a crippled man? Are you asking us who made him well? **10**We want all of you and all the people to know that this man was made well by the power of Jesus Christ from Nazareth. You crucified him, but God raised him from the dead. This man was crippled, but he is now well and able to stand here before you because of the power of Jesus. **11**Jesus is

'the stone that you builders rejected,
which has become the cornerstone.'
Psalm 118:22

12Jesus is the only One who can save people. No one else in the world is able to save us."

OLD TESTAMENT READING

Because of these things, this is what the Lord GOD says:

"I will put a stone in the ground in Jerusalem,
a tested stone.
Everything will be built on this important and
precious rock.
Anyone who trusts in it will never be
disappointed.
17I will use justice as a measuring line
and goodness as the standard.
The lies you hide behind will be destroyed as
if by hail.
They will be washed away as if in a flood."
Isaiah 28:16–17

INSIGHTS

"I am the way and the truth and the life. No one comes to the Father except through me" (John 14:6). . . .

. . . Jesus did not merely show the way to God; He said, "I am the way." He did not claim merely to know the truth; He said, "I am the truth." He did not merely point to the abundant life; He said, "I am the life." Therefore, within Christianity if there is no Christ, there is no way to God, no truth about God, and no vitality.

How could Jesus make such claims? If He was only a man, His claims are preposterous. But if He is who He said He is, and if He did what He said He would do, His claims make sense. Jesus claimed to be God and to have come to earth to die for our own sin. We deserve to die for our own sin, but Jesus died in our place. He who was sinless accepted the guilt of our sin and died for us. No one else could do it, but He could and did. Thus, He literally became the door by which sinful men and women can approach the Father.

JAMES BOICE

APPLICATION

Who is the rock on whom God's salvation is built? What is the way of salvation? Why does no other way of salvation exist?

ACTS 4:13-37

13The leaders saw that Peter and John were not afraid to speak, and they understood that these men had no special training or education. So they were amazed. Then they realized that Peter and John had been with Jesus. **14**Because they saw the healed man standing there beside the two apostles, they could say nothing against them. **15**After the leaders ordered them to leave the meeting, they began to talk to each other. **16**They said, "What shall we do with these men? Everyone in Jerusalem knows they have done a great miracle, and we cannot say it is not true. **17**But to keep it from spreading among the people, we must warn them not to talk to people anymore using that name."

18So they called Peter and John in again and told them not to speak or to teach at all in the name of Jesus. **19**But Peter and John answered them, "You decide what God would want. Should we obey you or God? **20**We cannot keep quiet. We must speak about what we have seen and heard." **21**The leaders warned the apostles again and let them go free. They could not find a way to punish them, because all the people were praising God for what had been done. **22**The man who received the miracle of healing was more than forty years old.

The Believers Pray

23After Peter and John left the meeting of leaders, they went to their own group and told them everything the leading priests and the elders had said to them. **24**When the believers heard this, they prayed to God together, "Lord, you are the One who made the sky, the earth, the sea, and everything in them. **25**By the Holy Spirit, through our father David your servant, you said:

'Why are the nations so angry?
    Why are the people making useless plans?
26 The kings of the earth prepare to fight,
    and their leaders make plans together
against the Lord
    and his Christ.'   *Psalm 2:1–2*

27 These things really happened when Herod, Pontius Pilate, and some Jews and non-Jews all came together against Jesus here in Jerusalem. Jesus is your holy servant, the One you made to be the Christ. **28** These people made your plan happen because of your power and your will. **29**And now, Lord, listen to their threats. Lord, help us, your servants, to speak your word without fear. **30**Show us your power to heal. Give proofs and make miracles happen by the power of Jesus, your holy servant."

31After they had prayed, the place where they were meeting was shaken. They were all filled with the Holy Spirit, and they spoke God's word without fear.

The Believers Share

32The group of believers were united in their hearts and spirit. All those in the group acted as though their private property belonged to everyone in the group. In fact, they shared everything. **33**With great power the apostles were telling people that the Lord Jesus was truly raised from the dead. And God blessed all the believers very much. **34**There were no needy people among them. From time to time those who owned fields or houses sold them, brought the money, 35and gave it to the apostles. Then the money was given to anyone who needed it.

36One of the believers was named Joseph, a Levite born in Cyprus. The apostles called him Barnabas (which means "one who encourages"). 37Joseph owned a field, sold it, brought the money, and gave it to the apostles.

OLD TESTAMENT READING

ecause you are precious to me,
  because I give you honor and love you,
I will give other people in your place;
  I will give other nations to save your life.
5Don't be afraid, because I am with you.
  I will bring your children from the east
  and gather you from the west.
6I will tell the north: Give my people to me.
  I will tell the south: Don't keep my people
    in prison.
Bring my sons from far away
  and my daughters from faraway places.
7Bring to me all the people who are mine,
  whom I made for my glory,
  whom I formed and made."

Isaiah 43:4–7

INSIGHTS

If we are Christians, we have all been delivered to be deliverers! The Word of God commands us to tell people they are in bondage to sin and that God would love to set them free from that taskmaster. . . .

Sometimes this is disappointing work. The people we go to may not want us to deliver them. Moses knew that particular scenario (Exod. 2:13–14). Or it can even be dangerous work. We may not be in danger of losing our life . . . but we may be in danger of losing our popularity, our friends, or in some extreme cases, even our job. Yes, a delivering work can be a disappointing work and even a dangerous work. But it is above all, a directed work, and that's what helps. To have a sense of God's direction when we are disappointed or in danger is a huge boost to our morale. The inner thrill that God has invited us to cooperate with Him takes the worry out of the work. People work is His work, and He will show us what to do, and even how to do it.

JILL BRISCOE

PAUSE FOR REFLECTION

Notice how, in these readings, the recitation of one's spiritual heritage served as encouragement to be God's fearless witness. How does your spiritual heritage encourage you to bravely proclaim God's truth?

ACTS 5:1-26

Ananias and Sapphira Die

5 But a man named Ananias and his wife Sapphira sold some land. **2**He kept back part of the money for himself; his wife knew about this and agreed to it. But he brought the rest of the money and gave it to the apostles. **3**Peter said, "Ananias, why did you let Satan rule your thoughts to lie to the Holy Spirit and to keep for yourself part of the money you received for the land? **4**Before you sold the land, it belonged to you. And even after you sold it, you could have used the money any way you wanted. Why did you think of doing this? You lied to God, not to us!" **5-6**When Ananias heard this, he fell down and died. Some young men came in, wrapped up his body, carried it out, and buried it. And everyone who heard about this was filled with fear.

7About three hours later his wife came in, but she did not know what had happened. **8**Peter said to her, "Tell me, was the money you got for your field this much?"

Sapphira answered, "Yes, that was the price."

9Peter said to her, "Why did you and your husband agree to test the Spirit of the Lord? Look! The men who buried your husband are at the door, and they will carry you out." **10**At that moment Sapphira fell down by his feet and died. When the young men came in and saw that she was dead, they carried her out and buried her beside her husband. **11**The whole church and all the others who heard about these things were filled with fear.

The Apostles Heal Many

12The apostles did many signs and miracles among the people. And they would all meet together on Solomon's Porch. **13**None of the others dared to join them, but all the people respected them. **14**More and more men and women believed in the Lord and were added to the group of believers. **15**The people placed their sick on beds and mats in the streets, hoping that when Peter passed by at least his shadow might fall on them. **16**Crowds came from all the towns around Jerusalem, bringing their sick and those who were bothered by evil spirits, and all of them were healed.

Leaders Try to Stop the Apostles

17The high priest and all his friends (a group called the Sadducees) became very jealous. **18**They took the apostles and put them in jail. **19**But during the night, an angel of the Lord opened the doors of the jail and led the apostles outside. The angel said, **20**"Go stand in the Temple and tell the people everything about this new life." **21**When the apostles heard this, they obeyed and went into the Temple early in the morning and continued teaching.

When the high priest and his friends arrived, they called a meeting of the leaders and all the important elders. They sent some men to the jail to bring the apostles to them. **22**But, upon arriving, the officers could not find the apostles. So they went back and reported to the leaders. **23**They said, "The jail was closed and locked, and the guards were standing at the doors. But when we opened the doors, the jail was empty!" **24**Hearing this, the captain of the Temple guards and the leading priests were confused and wondered what was happening.

25Then someone came and told them, "Listen! The men you put in jail are standing in the Temple teaching the people." **26**Then the captain and his men went out and brought the apostles back. But the soldiers did not use force, because they were afraid the people would stone them to death.

OLD TESTAMENT READING

Achan answered, "It is true! I have sinned against the LORD, the God of Israel. This is what I did: **21**Among the things I saw was a beautiful coat from Babylonia and about five pounds of silver and more than one and one-fourth pounds of gold. I wanted these things very much for myself, so I took them. You will find them buried in the ground under my tent, with the silver underneath."

24Then Joshua and all the people led Achan son of Zerah to the Valley of Trouble. They also took the silver, the coat, the gold, Achan's sons, daughters, cattle, donkeys, sheep, tent, and everything he owned. **25**Joshua said, "I don't know why you caused so much trouble for us, but now the LORD will bring trouble to you." Then all the people threw stones at Achan and his family until they died. Then the people burned them.

Joshua 7:20–21, 24–25

INSIGHTS

"When I have made it, I'll have time for . . ." How was that again?

"I want to make a lot of money for God. I must make money now so I can give money later." What was that again?

A farmer was explaining to a minister, "Well, if I'd get enough, I'd give half to the Lord."

"If you had two thousand acres of oil wells," asked the preacher, "would you give revenues from one thousand acres to the Lord?"

"Why, sure," the farmer gloated. "Anyone could live off a thousand acres of oil."

"If you had two hogs, would you give one to the Lord?" queried the minister.

At that, the farmer complained, "That's not fair. You know I have two pigs!"

We don't suddenly, someday, have an abundance of time and money to give. We begin with the little pieces. We are in training now, learning bit by bit to manage money, power, time, relationships and temptation. Then maybe someday we will find ourselves competent to manage life on a grander scale.

LYNN ANDERSON

PAUSE FOR REFLECTION

What was Ananias and Sapphira's sin against God? Achan's sin? Are you waiting to acquire enough to satisfy yourself before you give to God? What do you have now that you give to him?

ACTS 5:27 – 6:7

²⁷The soldiers brought the apostles to the meeting and made them stand before the leaders. The high priest questioned them, ²⁸saying, "We gave you strict orders not to continue teaching in that name. But look, you have filled Jerusalem with your teaching and are trying to make us responsible for this man's death."

²⁹Peter and the other apostles answered, "We must obey God, not human authority! ³⁰You killed Jesus by hanging him on a cross. But God, the God of our ancestors, raised Jesus up from the dead! ³¹Jesus is the One whom God raised to be on his right side, as Leader and Savior. Through him, all people could change their hearts and lives and have their sins forgiven. ³²We saw all these things happen. The Holy Spirit, whom God has given to all who obey him, also proves these things are true."

³³When the leaders heard this, they became angry and wanted to kill them. ³⁴But a Pharisee named Gamaliel stood up in the meeting. He was a teacher of the law, and all the people respected him. He ordered the apostles to leave the meeting for a little while. ³⁵Then he said, "People of Israel, be careful what you are planning to do to these men. ³⁶Remember when Theudas appeared? He said he was a great man, and about four hundred men joined him. But he was killed, and all his followers were scattered; they were able to do nothing. ³⁷Later, a man named Judas came from Galilee at the time of the registration. He also led a group of followers and was killed, and all his followers were scattered. ³⁸And so now I tell you:

Stay away from these men, and leave them alone. If their plan comes from human authority, it will fail. ³⁹But if it is from God, you will not be able to stop them. You might even be fighting against God himself!"

The leaders agreed with what Gamaliel said. ⁴⁰They called the apostles in, beat them, and told them not to speak in the name of Jesus again. Then they let them go free. ⁴¹The apostles left the meeting full of joy because they were given the honor of suffering disgrace for Jesus. ⁴²Every day in the Temple and in people's homes they continued teaching the people and telling the Good News—that Jesus is the Christ.

Seven Leaders Are Chosen

The number of followers was growing. But during this same time, the Greek-speaking followers had an argument with the other followers. The Greek-speaking widows were not getting their share of the food that was given out every day. ²The twelve apostles called the whole group of followers together and said, "It is not right for us to stop our work of teaching God's word in order to serve tables. ³So, brothers and sisters, choose seven of your own men who are good, full of the Spirit and full of wisdom. We will put them in charge of this work. ⁴Then we can continue to pray and to teach the word of God."

⁵The whole group liked the idea, so they chose these seven men: Stephen (a man with great faith and full of the Holy Spirit), Philip, Procorus, Nicanor, Timon, Parmenas, and Nicolas (a man from Antioch who had become a follower of the Jewish religion). ⁶Then they put these men before the apostles, who prayed and laid their hands on them.

7The word of God was continuing to spread. The group of followers in Jerusalem increased, and a great number of the Jewish priests believed and obeyed.

INSIGHTS

The Lord's thoughts are all working toward "an expected end." . . . God is working with a motive. All things are working together for one object: the good of those who love God. We see only the beginning; God sees the end from the beginning. He knows every letter of the Book of Providence; He sees not only what He is doing, but what will come of what He is doing.

As to our present pain and grief God sees not these things exclusively, but He sees the future joy and usefulness which will come of them. He regards not only the tearing up of the soil with the plow, but the clothing of that soil with the golden harvest. He sees the after consequences of affliction, and He accounts those painful incidents to be blessed which lead up to so much of happiness. Let us comfort ourselves with this. . . .

You have never seen the Great Artist's masterpiece; you have seen the rough marble, you have marked the chippings that fall on the ground; you have felt the edge of His chisel, you know the weight of His hammer, and you are full of the memory of these things; but oh, could you see that glorious image as it will be when He has put the finishing stroke to it, you would then understand the chisel, and the hammer, and the Worker better than you now do!

CHARLES SPURGEON

OLD TESTAMENT READING

Remember this, and do not forget it!
   Think about these things, you who turn
      against God.
9Remember what happened long ago.
   Remember that I am God, and there is no
      other God.
   I am God, and there is no one like
      me.
10From the beginning I told you what would
      happen in the end.
   A long time ago I told you things that have
      not yet happened.
When I plan something, it happens.
   What I want to do, I will do.
11I am calling a man from the east to carry out
      my plan;
   he will come like a hawk from a country
      far away.
I will make what I have said come true;
   I will do what I have planned."

Isaiah 46:8–11

APPLICATION

Did Gamaliel speak to the Jews with true wisdom? What do you learn about God's sovereign will in these readings? Pray to remember that God is working toward "an expected end" and to understand that what happens in your life is part of his work.

ACTS 6:8 – 7:16

Stephen Is Accused

8Stephen was richly blessed by God who gave him the power to do great miracles and signs among the people. **9**But some people were against him. They belonged to the synagogue of Free Men (as it was called), which included people from Cyrene, Alexandria, Cilicia, and Asia. They all came and argued with Stephen.

10But the Spirit was helping him to speak with wisdom, and his words were so strong that they could not argue with him. **11**So they secretly urged some men to say, "We heard Stephen speak against Moses and against God."

12This upset the people, the elders, and the teachers of the law. They came and grabbed Stephen and brought him to a meeting of the leaders. **13**They brought in some people to tell lies about Stephen, saying, "This man is always speaking against this holy place and the law of Moses. **14**We heard him say that Jesus from Nazareth will destroy this place and that Jesus will change the customs Moses gave us." **15**All the people in the meeting were watching Stephen closely and saw that his face looked like the face of an angel.

Stephen's Speech

7 The high priest said to Stephen, "Are these things true?"

2Stephen answered, "Brothers and fathers, listen to me. Our glorious God appeared to Abraham, our ancestor, in Mesopotamia before he lived in Haran. **3**God said to Abraham, 'Leave your country and your relatives, and go to the land I will show you.' **4**So Abraham left the country of Chaldea and went to live in Haran. After Abraham's father died, God sent him to this place where you now live. **5**God did not give Abraham any of this land, not even a foot of it. But God promised that he would give this land to him and his descendants, even before Abraham had a child. **6**This is what God said to him: 'Your descendants will be strangers in a land they don't own. The people there will make them slaves and will mistreat them for four hundred years. **7**But I will punish the nation where they are slaves. Then your descendants will leave that land and will worship me in this place.' **8**God made an agreement with Abraham, the sign of which was circumcision. And so when Abraham had his son Isaac, Abraham circumcised him when he was eight days old. Isaac also circumcised his son Jacob, and Jacob did the same for his sons, the twelve ancestors of our people.

9"Jacob's sons became jealous of Joseph and sold him to be a slave in Egypt. But God was with him **10**and saved him from all his troubles. The king of Egypt liked Joseph and respected him because of the wisdom God gave him. The king made him governor of Egypt and put him in charge of all the people in his palace.

11"Then all the land of Egypt and Canaan became so dry that nothing would grow, and the people suffered very much. Jacob's sons, our ancestors, could not find anything to eat. **12**But when Jacob heard there was grain in Egypt, he sent his sons there. This was their first trip to Egypt. **13**When they went there a second time, Joseph told his brothers who he was, and the king learned about Joseph's family. **14**Then Joseph sent messengers to invite Jacob, his father, to come to Egypt along with all his relatives (seventy-five persons altogether). **15**So Jacob went down to Egypt, where he and his sons died. **16**Later their bodies were moved to Shechem and put in a grave there. (It was the same grave Abraham had bought for a sum of money from the sons of Hamor in Shechem.)"

OLD TESTAMENT READING

Give thanks to the LORD and pray to him.
Tell the nations what he has done.
2Sing to him; sing praises to him.
Tell about all his miracles.
3Be glad that you are his;
let those who seek the LORD be happy.
4Depend on the LORD and his strength;
always go to him for help.

Psalm 105:1–4

INSIGHTS

What appears to be foolish in the eyes of society is often that which is most effective in the work of the kingdom. The ignorant, the uneducated, the despised of the world are sometimes God's choicest servants. So it was with Sophie "the scrubwoman" Lichtenfels, "whose sermons rose not from an exalted podium or pulpit but from callused hands and knees and with the rhythm of a lowly washtub and scrub brush." . . .

. . . Her testimony was simple.

"God called me to scrub and preach. I was born a preacher, but since I was poor I had to work. My work is good and I can be trusted, so they want me. But if they have me, they must hear me preach. No preach, no work. I scrub as unto the Lord and I preach to all in the house. When I am out of work I tell my father. He is the best employment office. You don't have to pay or wait. . . .

"Sometimes we pray so foolish. For 12 years I prayed the Lord make me a foreign missionary. One day I prayed like that and my Father said, 'Stop Sophie. Where were you born?' 'In Germany,' I replied. 'And where are you now?' 'In America.' 'Well, aren't you already a foreign missionary?' Then He said to me, 'Who lives on the floor above you?' 'A family of Swedes.' 'And above them?' 'Some Swiss.' . . .

" 'Yes, and in back are Italians, and a block away Chinese. You have never spoken to them about My Son. Do you think I'll send you a thousand miles away when you've got foreigners, even heathen all around you?' "

RUTH TUCKER

PAUSE FOR REFLECTION

Stephen was a powerful witness for God among Jews from many nations. What message did both Stephen and the psalmist have to share? What message has God given you to share to the "nations" around you?

ACTS 7:17-42a

17"The promise God made to Abraham was soon to come true, and the number of people in Egypt grew large. 18Then a new king, who did not know who Joseph was, began to rule Egypt. 19This king tricked our people and was cruel to our ancestors, forcing them to leave their babies outside to die. 20At this time Moses was born, and he was very beautiful. For three months Moses was cared for in his father's house. 21When they put Moses outside, the king's daughter adopted him and raised him as if he were her own son. 22The Egyptians taught Moses everything they knew, and he was a powerful man in what he said and did.

23"When Moses was about forty years old, he thought it would be good to visit his own people, the people of Israel. 24Moses saw an Egyptian mistreating one of his people, so he defended the Israelite and punished the Egyptian by killing him. 25Moses thought his own people would understand that God was using him to save them, but they did not. 26The next day when Moses saw two men of Israel fighting, he tried to make peace between them. He said, 'Men, you are brothers. Why are you hurting each other?' 27The man who was hurting the other pushed Moses away and said, 'Who made you our ruler and judge? 28Are you going to kill me as you killed the Egyptian yesterday?' 29When Moses heard him say this, he left Egypt and went to live in the land of Midian where he was a stranger. While Moses lived in Midian, he had two sons.

30"Forty years later an angel appeared to Moses in the flames of a burning bush as he was in the desert near Mount Sinai. 31When Moses saw this, he was amazed and went near to look closer. Moses heard the Lord's voice say, 32'I am the God of your ancestors, the God of Abraham, Isaac, and Jacob.' Moses began to shake with fear and was afraid to look. 33The Lord said to him, 'Take off your sandals, because you are standing on holy ground. 34I have seen the troubles my people have suffered in Egypt. I have heard their cries and have come down to save them. And now, Moses, I am sending you back to Egypt.'

35"This Moses was the same man the two men of Israel rejected, saying, 'Who made you a ruler and judge?' Moses is the same man God sent to be a ruler and savior, with the help of the angel that Moses saw in the burning bush. 36So Moses led the people out of Egypt. He worked miracles and signs in Egypt, at the Red Sea, and then in the desert for forty years. 37This is the same Moses that said to the people of Israel, 'God will give you a prophet like me, who is one of your own people.' 38This is the Moses who was with the gathering of the Israelites in the desert. He was with the angel that spoke to him at Mount Sinai, and he was with our ancestors. He received commands from God that give life, and he gave those commands to us.

39"But our ancestors did not want to obey Moses. They rejected him and wanted to go back to Egypt. 40They said to Aaron, 'Make us gods who will lead us. Moses led us out of Egypt, but we don't know what has happened to him.' 41So the people made an idol that looked like a calf. Then they brought sacrifices to it and were proud of what they had made with their own hands. **⁴²**But God turned against them and did not try to stop them from worshiping the sun, moon, and stars."

OLD TESTAMENT READING

The LORD sent darkness and made the land dark,
but the Egyptians turned against what he said.

²⁹So he changed their water into blood
and made their fish die.

³⁰Then their country was filled with frogs,
even in the bedrooms of their rulers.

³¹The LORD spoke and flies came,
and gnats were everywhere in the country.

³²He made hail fall like rain
and sent lightning through their land.

³³He struck down their grapevines and fig trees,
and he destroyed every tree in the country.

³⁴He spoke and grasshoppers came;
the locusts were too many to count.

³⁵They ate all the plants in the land
and everything the earth produced.

³⁶The LORD also killed all the firstborn sons in the land,
the oldest son of each family.

³⁷Then he brought his people out,
and they carried with them silver and gold.
Not one of his people stumbled.

Psalm 105:28–37

INSIGHTS

Great is Thy faithfulness, O God my Father,
There is no shadow of turning with Thee;
Thou changest not, Thy compassions they fail not;
As Thou hast been Thou forever wilt be.

Summer and winter, and springtime and harvest,
Sun, moon and stars in their courses above
Join with all nature in manifold witness
To Thy great faithfulness, mercy and love.

Pardon for sin and a peace that endureth,
Thy own dear presence to cheer and to guide;
Strength for today and bright hope for tomorrow,
Blessings all mine, with ten thousand beside!

Great is Thy faithfulness! Great is Thy faithfulness!
Morning by morning new mercies I see;
All I have needed Thy hand hath provided.
Great is Thy faithfulness, Lord, unto me!

THOMAS O. CHISHOLM

ACTION POINT

From what trials did God, in his faithfulness, deliver the people of Israel? List as many as you can. When you doubt his faithfulness in your life, reread your list and believe that God is and always will be faithful!

ACTS 7:42b — 8:1

"This is what is written in the book of the prophets: God says,

'People of Israel, you did not bring me
sacrifices and offerings
while you traveled in the desert for forty
years.
43You have carried with you
the tent to worship Molech
and the idols of the star god Rephan that
you made to worship.
So I will send you away beyond Babylon.'

Amos 5:25–27

44"The Holy Tent where God spoke to our ancestors was with them in the desert. God told Moses how to make this Tent, and he made it like the plan God showed him. **45**Later, Joshua led our ancestors to capture the lands of the other nations. Our people went in, and God forced the other people out. When our people went into this new land, they took with them this same Tent they had received from their ancestors. They kept it until the time of David, **46**who pleased God and asked God to let him build a house for him, the God of Jacob. **47**But Solomon was the one who built the Temple.

48"But the Most High does not live in houses that people build with their hands. As the prophet says:

49'Heaven is my throne,
and the earth is my footstool.
So do you think you can build a house for me?
says the Lord.
Do I need a place to rest?

50Remember, my hand made all these things!'"

Isaiah 66:1–2

51Stephen continued speaking: "You stubborn people! You have not given your hearts to God, nor will you listen to him! You are always against what the Holy Spirit is trying to tell you, just as your ancestors were. **52**Your ancestors tried to hurt every prophet who ever lived. Those prophets said long ago that the One who is good would come, but your ancestors killed them. And now you have turned against and killed the One who is good. **53**You received the law of Moses, which God gave you through his angels, but you haven't obeyed it."

Stephen Is Killed

54When the leaders heard this, they became furious. They were so mad they were grinding their teeth at Stephen. **55**But Stephen was full of the Holy Spirit. He looked up to heaven and saw the glory of God and Jesus standing at God's right side. **56**He said, "Look! I see heaven open and the Son of Man standing at God's right side."

57Then they shouted loudly and covered their ears and all ran at Stephen. **58**They took him out of the city and began to throw stones at him to kill him. And those who told lies against Stephen left their coats with a young man named Saul. **59**While they were throwing stones, Stephen prayed, "Lord Jesus, receive my spirit." **60**He fell on his knees and cried in a loud voice, "Lord, do not hold this sin against them." After Stephen said this, he died.

 Saul agreed that the killing of Stephen was good.

Troubles for the Believers

On that day the church of Jerusalem began to be persecuted, and all the believers, except the apostles, were scattered throughout Judea and Samaria.

OLD TESTAMENT READING

The king and these leaders stopped worshiping in the Temple of the LORD, the God of their ancestors. Instead, they began to worship the Asherah idols and other idols. Because they did wrong, God was angry with the people of Judah and Jerusalem. **19**Even though the LORD sent prophets to the people to turn them back to him and even though the prophets warned them, they refused to listen.

20Then the Spirit of God entered Zechariah son of Jehoiada the priest. Zechariah stood before the people and said, "This is what God says: 'Why do you disobey the LORD's commands? You will not be successful. Because you have left the LORD, he has also left you.'"

21But the king and his officers made plans against Zechariah. At the king's command they threw stones at him in the courtyard of the Temple of the LORD until he died.

2 Chronicles 24:18–21

INSIGHTS

In his remarkable and eloquent sermon, Stephen revealed his accurate grasp of Jewish history and its relevance to the new faith he had embraced. He turned the tables on his attackers and charged them with being the guilty ones. He refuted their charges in a closely reasoned, eloquent speech that reviewed their history from the time of Abraham onward. From it he demonstrated that the presence of the eternal God cannot be localized and confined to an earthly temple, be it ever so magnificent.

He cited God's presence with Joseph even when he was in Egypt. He reminded them that as a nation they had persistently rejected and resisted the messengers of God. They had envied and mistreated Joseph, whom God had sent as their preserver. They had rebelled against Moses and rejected his message. They had stoned the prophets and abused the functions of the Temple. They boasted of the angelic mediation of the Law, yet they failed to keep it. . . .

When Stephen delivered his final, blistering denunciation, he did it with his eyes open. He knew what the inevitable reaction of those bigoted men would be when he told them that they were stiff-necked, uncircumcised in heart, and murderers and betrayers of the Righteous One (Acts 7:51–52).

J. OSWALD SANDERS

PAUSE FOR REFLECTION

Was Stephen's martyrdom a unique event in Jewish history? Why did the religious leaders kill him? Why did they kill those who had preceded him? Is your heart in any way hardened to God's message today?

ACTS 8:2-25

2And some religious people buried Stephen and cried loudly for him. **3**Saul was also trying to destroy the church, going from house to house, dragging out men and women and putting them in jail. **4**And wherever they were scattered, they told people the Good News.

Philip Preaches in Samaria

5Philip went to the city of Samaria and preached about the Christ. **6**When the people there heard Philip and saw the miracles he was doing, they all listened carefully to what he said. **7**Many of these people had evil spirits in them, but Philip made the evil spirits leave. The spirits made a loud noise when they came out. Philip also healed many weak and crippled people there. **8**So the people in that city were very happy.

9But there was a man named Simon in that city. Before Philip came there, Simon had practiced magic and amazed all the people of Samaria. He bragged and called himself a great man. **10**All the people—the least important and the most important—paid attention to Simon, saying, "This man has the power of God, called 'the Great Power'!" **11**Simon had amazed them with his magic so long that the people became his followers. **12**But when Philip told them the Good News about the kingdom of God and the power of Jesus Christ, men and women believed Philip and were baptized. **13**Simon himself believed, and after he was baptized, he stayed very close to Philip. When he saw the miracles and the powerful things Philip did, Simon was amazed.

14When the apostles who were still in Jerusalem heard that the people of Samaria had accepted the word of God, they sent Peter and John to them. **15**When Peter and John arrived, they prayed that the Samaritan believers might receive the Holy Spirit. **16**These people had been baptized in the name of the Lord Jesus, but the Holy Spirit had not yet come upon any of them. **17**Then, when the two apostles began laying their hands on the people, they received the Holy Spirit.

18Simon saw that the Spirit was given to people when the apostles laid their hands on them. So he offered the apostles money, **19**saying, "Give me also this power so that anyone on whom I lay my hands will receive the Holy Spirit."

20Peter said to him, "You and your money should both be destroyed, because you thought you could buy God's gift with money. **21**You cannot share with us in this work since your heart is not right before God. **22**Change your heart! Turn away from this evil thing you have done, and pray to the Lord. Maybe he will forgive you for thinking this. **23**I see that you are full of bitter jealousy and ruled by sin."

24Simon answered, "Both of you pray for me to the Lord so the things you have said will not happen to me."

25After Peter and John told the people what they had seen Jesus do and after they had spoken the message of the Lord, they went back to Jerusalem. On the way, they went through many Samaritan towns and preached the Good News to the people.

OLD TESTAMENT READING

Korah, Dathan, Abiram, and On turned against Moses. **2**These men gathered two hundred fifty other Israelite men, well-known leaders chosen by the community, and challenged Moses. **3**They came as a group to speak to Moses and Aaron and said, "You have gone too far. All the people are holy, every one of them, and the LORD is among them. So why do you put yourselves above all the people of the LORD?"

8Moses also said to Korah, "Listen, you Levites. **9**The God of Israel has separated you from the rest of the Israelites. He brought you near to himself to do the work in the LORD's Holy Tent and to stand before all the Israelites and serve them. Isn't that enough?

28Then Moses said, "Now you will know that the LORD has sent me to do all these things; it was not my idea. **29**If these men die a normal death— the way men usually die—then the LORD did not really send me. **30**But if the LORD does something new, you will know they have insulted the LORD. The ground will open and swallow them. They will be buried alive and will go to the place of the dead, and everything that belongs to them will go with them."

Numbers 16:1a, 2–3, 8–9, 28–30

INSIGHTS

Delight yourself in the spiritual
  victories of others:
  Delight in all triumphs in Christ Jesus.
Rejoice when another's success is
  greater than yours:
  Be glad when another receives what
  you need.
Remain at peace when another
  receives the attention you think you
  deserve.
You must not strive:
You must war against
  all jealousy and contention.

Say today:
  I will not be jealous.
  I will not contend.
  I will not strive.
  I will rejoice at another's victories.
  I will delight in the success of others.
  I will not think others less worthy or
    less important than I.
  I will not see my work as more
    important than someone else's.
  I will pray for those who are my
    competitors.
  I will rejoice in my relationship with
    the Lord.

And so it will be.

Marie Chapian

ACTION POINT

Before reading Numbers 16, did you know that God considers jealousy of his chosen servants to be an insult to him, not an insult to his servants? God takes the bitter sin of jealousy quite seriously, doesn't he? For what sins of jealousy do you need to ask God's forgiveness?

ACTS 8:26 — 9:9

Philip Teaches an Ethiopian

26An angel of the Lord said to Philip, "Get ready and go south to the road that leads down to Gaza from Jerusalem—the desert road." **27**So Philip got ready and went. On the road he saw a man from Ethiopia, a eunuch. He was an important officer in the service of Candace, the queen of the Ethiopians; he was responsible for taking care of all her money. He had gone to Jerusalem to worship. **28**Now, as he was on his way home, he was sitting in his chariot reading from the Book of Isaiah, the prophet. **29**The Spirit said to Philip, "Go to that chariot and stay near it."

30So when Philip ran toward the chariot, he heard the man reading from Isaiah the prophet. Philip asked, "Do you understand what you are reading?"

31He answered, "How can I understand unless someone explains it to me?" Then he invited Philip to climb in and sit with him. **32**The portion of Scripture he was reading was this:

"He was like a sheep being led to be killed.

He was quiet, as a lamb is quiet while its
wool is being cut;

he never opened his mouth.

33 He was shamed and was treated unfairly.

He died without children to continue his
family.

His life on earth has ended." *Isaiah 53:7–8*

34The officer said to Philip, "Please tell me, who is the prophet talking about—himself or someone else?" **35**Philip began to speak, and starting with this same Scripture, he told the man the Good News about Jesus.

36While they were traveling down the road, they came to some water. The officer said, "Look, here is water. What is stopping me from being baptized?" [**37**Philip answered, "If you believe with all your heart, you can." The officer said, "I believe that Jesus Christ is the Son of God."] **38**Then the officer commanded the chariot to stop. Both Philip and the officer went down into the water, and Philip baptized him. **39**When they came up out of the water, the Spirit of the Lord took Philip away; the officer never saw him again. And the officer continued on his way home, full of joy. **40**But Philip appeared in a city called Azotus and preached the Good News in all the towns on the way from Azotus to Caesarea.

Saul Is Converted

 In Jerusalem Saul was still threatening the followers of the Lord by saying he would kill them. So he went to the high priest **2**and asked him to write letters to the synagogues in the city of Damascus. Then if Saul found any followers of Christ's Way, men or women, he would arrest them and bring them back to Jerusalem.

3So Saul headed toward Damascus. As he came near the city, a bright light from heaven suddenly flashed around him. **4**Saul fell to the ground and heard a voice saying to him, "Saul, Saul! Why are you persecuting me?"

5Saul said, "Who are you, Lord?"

The voice answered, "I am Jesus, whom you are persecuting. **6**Get up now and go into the city. Someone there will tell you what you must do."

[7] The people traveling with Saul stood there but said nothing. They heard the voice, but they saw no one. [8] Saul got up from the ground and opened his eyes, but he could not see. So those with Saul took his hand and led him into Damascus. [9] For three days Saul could not see and did not eat or drink.

OLD TESTAMENT READING

These Levites explained the Teachings to the people as they stood there: Jeshua, Bani, Sherebiah, Jamin, Akkub, Shabbethai, Hodiah, Maaseiah, Kelita, Azariah, Jozabad, Hanan, and Pelaiah. [8] They read from the Book of the Teachings of God and explained what it meant so the people understood what was being read.

[9] Then Nehemiah the governor, Ezra the priest and teacher, and the Levites who were teaching said to all the people, "This is a holy day to the LORD your God. Don't be sad or cry." All the people had been crying as they listened to the words of the Teachings.

[10] Nehemiah said, "Go and enjoy good food and sweet drinks. Send some to people who have none, because today is a holy day to the Lord. Don't be sad, because the joy of the LORD will make you strong."

[11] The Levites helped calm the people, saying, "Be quiet, because this is a holy day. Don't be sad."

[12] Then all the people went away to eat and drink, to send some of their food to others, and to celebrate with great joy. They finally understood what they had been taught.

Nehemiah 8:7–12

INSIGHTS

The Word of God is a constant and continuing source of joy for the Christian. I don't think I've ever met a joyless Christian who was regularly employed in searching the Scriptures. The result of such searching is to see beyond the words the One who inspired them. Of all the habits the Christian can cultivate, this is one of the most blessed and profitable. Some books are exhausting and exhaustible. The Bible is the only Book that rewards the student with increasing insight as he allows the Word of God to flow through and cleanse him. Indeed, it is the only Book that can cleanse and purify the life of its reader. Other books can inform, but only the Scripture can transform, infill, and inspire.

AL BRYANT

ACTION POINT

Why were the Israelites saddened when they first heard the Lord's teachings? What enabled them to be joyous? What brought great joy to the Ethiopian officer? Who has helped you understand God's Word? Thank God for that person and pray that you will experience the joy of living by God's Word.

ACTS 9:10-35

[10]There was a follower of Jesus in Damascus named Ananias. The Lord spoke to Ananias in a vision, "Ananias!"

Ananias answered, "Here I am, Lord."

[11]The Lord said to him, "Get up and go to Straight Street. Find the house of Judas, and ask for a man named Saul from the city of Tarsus. He is there now, praying. [12]Saul has seen a vision in which a man named Ananias comes to him and lays his hands on him. Then he is able to see again."

[13]But Ananias answered, "Lord, many people have told me about this man and the terrible things he did to your holy people in Jerusalem. [14]Now he has come here to Damascus, and the leading priests have given him the power to arrest everyone who worships you."

[15]But the Lord said to Ananias, "Go! I have chosen Saul for an important work. He must tell about me to those who are not Jews, to kings, and to the people of Israel. [16]I will show him how much he must suffer for my name."

[17]So Ananias went to the house of Judas. He laid his hands on Saul and said, "Brother Saul, the Lord Jesus sent me. He is the one you saw on the road on your way here. He sent me so that you can see again and be filled with the Holy Spirit." [18]Immediately, something that looked like fish scales fell from Saul's eyes, and he was able to see again! Then Saul got up and was baptized. [19]After he ate some food, his strength returned.

Saul Preaches in Damascus

Saul stayed with the followers of Jesus in Damascus for a few days. [20]Soon he began to preach about Jesus in the synagogues, saying, "Jesus is the Son of God."

[21]All the people who heard him were amazed. They said, "This is the man who was in Jerusalem trying to destroy those who trust in this name! He came here to arrest the followers of Jesus and take them back to the leading priests."

[22]But Saul grew more powerful. His proofs that Jesus is the Christ were so strong that his own people in Damascus could not argue with him.

[23]After many days, they made plans to kill Saul. [24]They were watching the city gates day and night, but Saul learned about their plan. [25]One night some followers of Saul helped him leave the city by lowering him in a basket through an opening in the city wall.

Saul Preaches in Jerusalem

[26]When Saul went to Jerusalem, he tried to join the group of followers, but they were all afraid of him. They did not believe he was really a follower. [27]But Barnabas accepted Saul and took him to the apostles. Barnabas explained to them that Saul had seen the Lord on the road and the Lord had spoken to Saul. Then he told them how boldly Saul had preached in the name of Jesus in Damascus.

[28]And so Saul stayed with the followers, going everywhere in Jerusalem, preaching boldly in the name of the Lord. [29]He would often talk and argue with the Jewish people who spoke Greek, but they were trying to kill him. [30]When the fol-

lowers learned about this, they took Saul to Caesarea and from there sent him to Tarsus.

31The church everywhere in Judea, Galilee, and Samaria had a time of peace and became stronger. Respecting the Lord by the way they lived, and being encouraged by the Holy Spirit, the group of believers continued to grow.

Peter Heals Aeneas

32As Peter was traveling through all the area, he visited God's people who lived in Lydda. **33**There he met a man named Aeneas, who was paralyzed and had not been able to leave his bed for the past eight years. **34**Peter said to him, "Aeneas, Jesus Christ heals you. Stand up and make your bed." Aeneas stood up immediately. **35**All the

people living in Lydda and on the Plain of Sharon saw him and turned to the Lord.

OLD TESTAMENT READING

The LORD said to Samuel, "Go, appoint him, because he is the one."

13So Samuel took the container of olive oil and poured it on Jesse's youngest son to appoint him in front of his brothers. From that day on, the LORD's Spirit worked in David. Samuel then went back to Ramah.

1 Samuel 16:12c–13

INSIGHTS

Blessed and happy are they who have a sweet faith in Jesus, intertwined with deep affection for Him, for this is a restful confidence. These lovers of Jesus are charmed with His character and delighted with His mission; they are carried away by the loving-kindness that He has manifested, and therefore they cannot help trusting Him because they so much admire, revere, and love Him. . . .

. . . We love Him and He loves us, and therefore we put ourselves into His hands, accept whatever He prescribes, and do whatever He bids. We feel that nothing can be wrongly ordered while He is the Director of our affairs, for He loves us too well to let us perish or suffer a single needless pang.

Faith is the root of obedience, and this may be clearly seen in the affairs of life. When a captain trusts a pilot to steer his vessel into port, he manages the vessel according to his direction. When a traveler trusts a guide to conduct him over a difficult pass, he follows the track which his guide points out. When a patient believes in a physician, he carefully follows his prescriptions and directions. Faith which refuses to obey the commands of the Saviour is a mere pretence and will never save the soul.

CHARLES SPURGEON

APPLICATION

What kind of faith is needed to earnestly say the words, "Here I am, Lord"? Is your faith sufficient to do anything your Savior may ask? What objections to complete obedience must you overcome?

ACTS 9:36 — 10:23a

Peter Heals Tabitha

36In the city of Joppa there was a follower named Tabitha (whose Greek name was Dorcas). She was always doing good deeds and kind acts. **37**While Peter was in Lydda, Tabitha became sick and died. Her body was washed and put in a room upstairs. **38**Since Lydda is near Joppa and the followers in Joppa heard that Peter was in Lydda, they sent two messengers to Peter. They begged him, "Hurry, please come to us!" **39**So Peter got ready and went with them. When he arrived, they took him to the upstairs room where all the widows stood around Peter, crying. They showed him the shirts and coats Tabitha had made when she was still alive. **40**Peter sent everyone out of the room and kneeled and prayed. Then he turned to the body and said, "Tabitha, stand up." She opened her eyes, and when she saw Peter, she sat up. **41**He gave her his hand and helped her up. Then he called the saints and the widows into the room and showed them that Tabitha was alive. **42**People everywhere in Joppa learned about this, and many believed in the Lord. **43**Peter stayed in Joppa for many days with a man named Simon who was a tanner.

Peter Teaches Cornelius

10 At Caesarea there was a man named Cornelius, an officer in the Italian group of the Roman army. **2**Cornelius was a religious man. He and all the other people who lived in his house worshiped the true God. He gave much of his money to the poor and prayed to God often. **3**One afternoon about three o'clock, Cornelius clearly saw a vision. An angel of God came to him and said, "Cornelius!"

4Cornelius stared at the angel. He became afraid and said, "What do you want, Lord?"

The angel said, "God has heard your prayers. He has seen that you give to the poor, and he remembers you. **5**Send some men now to Joppa to bring back a man named Simon who is also called Peter. **6**He is staying with a man, also named Simon, who is a tanner and has a house beside the sea." **7**When the angel who spoke to Cornelius left, Cornelius called two of his servants and a soldier, a religious man who worked for him. **8**Cornelius explained everything to them and sent them to Joppa.

9About noon the next day as they came near Joppa, Peter was going up to the roof to pray. **10**He was hungry and wanted to eat, but while the food was being prepared, he had a vision. **11**He saw heaven opened and something coming down that looked like a big sheet being lowered to earth by its four corners. **12**In it were all kinds of animals, reptiles, and birds. **13**Then a voice said to Peter, "Get up, Peter; kill and eat."

14But Peter said, "No, Lord! I have never eaten food that is unholy or unclean."

15But the voice said to him again, "God has made these things clean, so don't call them 'unholy'!" **16**This happened three times, and at once the sheet was taken back to heaven.

17While Peter was wondering what this vision meant, the men Cornelius sent had found Simon's house and were standing at the gate. **18**They asked, "Is Simon Peter staying here?"

19 While Peter was still thinking about the vision, the Spirit said to him, "Listen, three men are looking for you. **20** Get up and go downstairs. Go with them without doubting, because I have sent them to you."

21 So Peter went down to the men and said, "I am the one you are looking for. Why did you come here?"

22 They said, "A holy angel spoke to Cornelius, an army officer and a good man; he worships God. All the people respect him. The angel told Cornelius to ask you to come to his house so that he can hear what you have to say." **23** So Peter asked the men to come in and spend the night.

OLD TESTAMENT READING

Solomon finished building the Temple of the LORD and his royal palace and everything he wanted to build. **2** Then the LORD appeared to him again just as he had done before, in Gibeon. **3** The LORD said to him: "I have heard your prayer and what you have asked me to do. You built this Temple, and I have made it a holy place. I will be worshiped there forever and will watch over it and protect it always."

1 Kings 9:1–3

INSIGHTS

The Lord God of the universe, the Creator and Sustainer of all things, . . . not only commands us to pray, but also invites us to make our requests known. Jesus says that we have not because we ask not. James tells us that the effectual, fervent prayer of a righteous man accomplishes much. Time and again the Bible says that prayer is an effective tool. It is useful; it works. . . .

Prayer, like everything else in the Christian life, is for God's glory and for our benefit, in that order. Everything that God does, everything that God allows and ordains, is in the supreme sense for His glory. It is also true that while God seeks His own glory supremely, man benefits when God is glorified. We pray to glorify God, but also to receive the benefits of prayer from His hand. . . .

One of the great themes of the Reformation was the idea that all of our life is to be lived under the authority of God, to the glory of God, in the presence of God. . . . Prayer is discourse with the personal God Himself. There, in the act and dynamic of praying, I bring my whole life under His gaze. Yes, He knows what is in my mind, but I still have the privilege of articulating to Him what is there. He says, "Come. Speak to Me. Make your requests known to Me." And so, we come in order to know Him and to be known by Him.

R. C. SPROUL

ACTION POINT

Do you feel that your prayers are really in touch with God—powerful enough to raise the dead? No? Then take these Scriptures to heart. Pray as if God is the ultimate reality in your life. Then listen. His response will come!

ACTS 10:23b - 48

The next day Peter got ready and went with them, and some of the followers from Joppa joined him. **24**On the following day they came to Caesarea. Cornelius was waiting for them and had called together his relatives and close friends. **25**When Peter entered, Cornelius met him, fell at his feet, and worshiped him. **26**But Peter helped him up, saying, "Stand up. I too am only a human." **27**As he talked with Cornelius, Peter went inside where he saw many people gathered. **28**He said, "You people understand that it is against our law for Jewish people to associate with or visit anyone who is not Jewish. But God has shown me that I should not call any person 'unholy' or 'unclean.' **29**That is why I did not argue when I was asked to come here. Now, please tell me why you sent for me."

30Cornelius said, "Four days ago, I was praying in my house at this same time—three o'clock in the afternoon. Suddenly, there was a man standing before me wearing shining clothes. **31**He said, 'Cornelius, God has heard your prayer and has seen that you give to the poor and remembers you. **32**So send some men to Joppa and ask Simon Peter to come. Peter is staying in the house of a man, also named Simon, who is a tanner and has a house beside the sea.' **33**So I sent for you immediately, and it was very good of you to come. Now we are all here before God to hear everything the Lord has commanded you to tell us."

34Peter began to speak: "I really understand now that to God every person is the same. **35**In every country God accepts anyone who worships him and does what is right. **36**You know the message that God has sent to the people of Israel is the Good News that peace has come through Jesus Christ. Jesus is the Lord of all people! **37**You know what has happened all over Judea, beginning in Galilee after John preached to the people about baptism. **38**You know about Jesus from Nazareth, that God gave him the Holy Spirit and power. You know how Jesus went everywhere doing good and healing those who were ruled by the devil, because God was with him. **39**We saw what Jesus did in Judea and in Jerusalem, but the Jews in Jerusalem killed him by hanging him on a cross. **40**Yet, on the third day, God raised Jesus to life and caused him to be seen, **41**not by all the people, but only by the witnesses God had already chosen. And we are those witnesses who ate and drank with him after he was raised from the dead. **42**He told us to preach to the people and to tell them that he is the one whom God chose to be the judge of the living and the dead. **43**All the prophets say it is true that all who believe in Jesus will be forgiven of their sins through Jesus' name."

44While Peter was still saying this, the Holy Spirit came down on all those who were listening. **45**The Jewish believers who came with Peter were amazed that the gift of the Holy Spirit had been given even to the nations. **46**These believers heard them speaking in different languages and praising God. Then Peter said, **47**"Can anyone keep these people from being baptized with water? They have received the Holy Spirit just as we did!" **48**So Peter ordered that they be baptized in the name of Jesus Christ. Then they asked Peter to stay with them for a few days.

OLD TESTAMENT READING

The LORD says,
"Come, let us talk about these things.
Though your sins are like scarlet,
they can be as white as snow.
Though your sins are deep red,
they can be white like wool.

19If you become willing and obey me,
you will eat good crops from the land.
20But if you refuse to obey and if you turn
against me,
you will be destroyed by your enemies'
swords."
The LORD himself said these things.

Isaiah 1:18–20

INSIGHTS

At the heart of God is the desire to give and to forgive. Because of this, he set into motion the entire redemptive process that culminated in the cross and was confirmed in the resurrection. The usual notion of what Jesus did on the cross runs something like this: people were so bad and so mean and God was so angry with them that he could not forgive them unless somebody big enough took the rap for the whole lot of them.

Nothing could be further from the truth. Love, not anger, brought Jesus to the cross. Golgotha came as a result of God's great desire to forgive, not his reluctance. Jesus knew that by his vicarious suffering he could actually absorb all the evil of humanity and so heal it, forgive it, redeem it. . . .

Having accomplished this greatest of all his works, Jesus then took refreshment. "It is finished," he announced. That is, this great work of redemption was completed. He could feel the last dregs of the misery of humankind flow through him and into the care of the Father. The last twinges of evil, hostility, anger, and fear drained out of him, and he was able to turn again into the light of God's presence. . . .

This redemptive process is a great mystery hidden in the heart of God. But I know that it is true. I know this not only because the Bible says it is true, but because I have seen its effects in the lives of many people, including myself. It is the ground upon which we can know that confession and forgiveness are realities that transform us. Without the cross the Discipline of confession would be only psychologically therapeutic. But it is so much more. It involves an objective change in our relationship with God and a subjective change in us. It is a means of healing and transforming the inner spirit.

RICHARD FOSTER

PAUSE FOR REFLECTION

Peter was one of Jesus' closest disciples, yet we see here that he discovers a new, wonderful, and unexpected truth about God's forgiveness. What is it? Thank God for his awesome gift of salvation to you!

ACTS 11:1-30

Peter Returns to Jerusalem

11 The apostles and the believers in Judea heard that some who were not Jewish had accepted God's teaching too. **2**But when Peter came to Jerusalem, some people argued with him. **3**They said, "You went into the homes of people who are not circumcised and ate with them!"

4So Peter explained the whole story to them. **5**He said, "I was in the city of Joppa, and while I was praying, I had a vision. I saw something that looked like a big sheet being lowered from heaven by its four corners. It came very close to me. **6**I looked inside it and saw animals, wild beasts, reptiles, and birds. **7**I heard a voice say to me, 'Get up, Peter. Kill and eat.' **8**But I said, 'No, Lord! I have never eaten anything that is unholy or unclean.' **9**But the voice from heaven spoke again, 'God has made these things clean, so don't call them unholy.' **10**This happened three times. Then the whole thing was taken back to heaven. **11**Right then three men who were sent to me from Caesarea came to the house where I was staying. **12**The Spirit told me to go with them without doubting. These six believers here also went with me, and we entered the house of Cornelius. **13**He told us about the angel he saw standing in his house. The angel said to him, 'Send some men to Joppa and invite Simon Peter to come. **14**By the words he will say to you, you and all your family will be saved.' **15**When I began my speech, the Holy Spirit came on them just as he came on us at the beginning. **16**Then I remembered the words of the Lord. He said, 'John baptized with water, but you will be baptized with the Holy Spirit.' **17**Since God gave them the same gift he gave us who believed in the Lord Jesus Christ, how could I stop the work of God?"

18When the believers heard this, they stopped arguing. They praised God and said, "So God is allowing even other nations to turn to him and live."

The Good News Comes to Antioch

19Many of the believers were scattered when they were persecuted after Stephen was killed. Some of them went as far as Phoenicia, Cyprus, and Antioch telling the message to others, but only to Jews. **20**Some of these believers were people from Cyprus and Cyrene. When they came to Antioch, they spoke also to Greeks, telling them the Good News about the Lord Jesus. **21**The Lord was helping the believers, and a large group of people believed and turned to the Lord.

22The church in Jerusalem heard about all of this, so they sent Barnabas to Antioch. **23-24**Barnabas was a good man, full of the Holy Spirit and full of faith. When he reached Antioch and saw how God had blessed the people, he was glad. He encouraged all the believers in Antioch always to obey the Lord with all their hearts, and many people became followers of the Lord.

25Then Barnabas went to the city of Tarsus to look for Saul, **26**and when he found Saul, he brought him to Antioch. For a whole year Saul and Barnabas met with the church and taught many people there. In Antioch the followers were called Christians for the first time.

27About that time some prophets came from

Jerusalem to Antioch. **28**One of them, named Agabus, stood up and spoke with the help of the Holy Spirit. He said, "A very hard time is coming to the whole world. There will be no food to eat." (This happened when Claudius ruled.) **29**The followers all decided to help the believers who lived in Judea, as much as each one could. **30**They gathered the money and gave it to Barnabas and Saul, who brought it to the elders in Judea.

OLD TESTAMENT READING

enerous people will be blessed,
because they share their food with the poor.

Proverbs 22:9

INSIGHTS

Someone has said, "We have no permission from Jesus to be selective in our compassion." It is our natural tendency, however, to choose whom we will reach out to. Perhaps this was the problem of the priest and the Levite in the parable of the good Samaritan. In any event, we know it is often our problem. Jesus mingled with all men, the rich and the poor, the socially acceptable and the backward and undesirable. This willingness to enter into others' lives is costly. . . .

Our God wants to dislodge us from our comfortable, smug existence, to move us to mingle with our needy brothers, to stir us to touch those we might otherwise shun. Another poet, whose name is lost in history, expresses the challenge well: "Love has a hem to her garment that trails in the very dust; it can reach the stains of the streets and lanes, and because it can, it must." This is clearly the brand of compassion Jesus exemplified, and it is the kind of loving outreach he calls us to in our modern world. Answering his call is often a struggle for us. We may pay lip service to such compassion, but the performance is often costly, and we're inclined to back away. . . .

True compassion is an expression of the life of our Lord Jesus Christ. It is always ready to give, and always willing to sacrifice.

WILLIAM FLETCHER

ACTION POINT

When has God shaken up your view of how you are to live for him or to care for others? Does your view of Christian compassion need some adjustment? Pray for a heart that will gladly give and sacrifice for Jesus' sake.

ACTS 12:1-25

Herod Agrippa Hurts the Church

12 During that same time King Herod began to mistreat some who belonged to the church. **2**He ordered James, the brother of John, to be killed by the sword. **3**Herod saw that some of the people liked this, so he decided to arrest Peter, too. (This happened during the time of the Feast of Unleavened Bread.)

4After Herod arrested Peter, he put him in jail and handed him over to be guarded by sixteen soldiers. Herod planned to bring Peter before the people for trial after the Passover Feast. **5**So Peter was kept in jail, but the church prayed earnestly to God for him.

Peter Leaves the Jail

6The night before Herod was to bring him to trial, Peter was sleeping between two soldiers, bound with two chains. Other soldiers were guarding the door of the jail. **7**Suddenly, an angel of the Lord stood there, and a light shined in the cell. The angel struck Peter on the side and woke him up. "Hurry! Get up!" the angel said. And the chains fell off Peter's hands. **8**Then the angel told him, "Get dressed and put on your sandals." And Peter did. Then the angel said, "Put on your coat and follow me." **9**So Peter followed him out, but he did not know if what the angel was doing was real; he thought he might be seeing a vision. **10**They went past the first and second guards and came to the iron gate that separated them from the city.

The gate opened by itself for them, and they went through it. When they had walked down one street, the angel suddenly left him.

11Then Peter realized what had happened. He thought, "Now I know that the Lord really sent his angel to me. He rescued me from Herod and from all the things the people thought would happen."

12When he considered this, he went to the home of Mary, the mother of John Mark. Many people were gathered there, praying. **13**Peter knocked on the outside door, and a servant girl named Rhoda came to answer it. **14**When she recognized Peter's voice, she was so happy she forgot to open the door. Instead, she ran inside and told the group, "Peter is at the door!"

15They said to her, "You are crazy!" But she kept on saying it was true, so they said, "It must be Peter's angel."

16Peter continued to knock, and when they opened the door, they saw him and were amazed. **17**Peter made a sign with his hand to tell them to be quiet. He explained how the Lord led him out of the jail, and he said, "Tell James and the other believers what happened." Then he left to go to another place.

18The next day the soldiers were very upset and wondered what had happened to Peter. **19**Herod looked everywhere for him but could not find him. So he questioned the guards and ordered that they be killed.

The Death of Herod Agrippa

Later Herod moved from Judea and went to the city of Caesarea, where he stayed. **20**Herod was very angry with the people of Tyre and Sidon, but the people of those cities all came in a group to him. After convincing Blastus, the king's personal servant, to be on their side, they asked Herod for peace, because their country got its food from his country.

21On a chosen day Herod put on his royal robes, sat on his throne, and made a speech to the people. **22**They shouted, "This is the voice of a god, not a human!" **23**Because Herod did not give the glory to God, an angel of the Lord immediately caused him to become sick, and he was eaten by worms and died.

INSIGHTS

Interestingly, the Book of Daniel opens with a story of the Babylonian invasion of Judah. In the invasion the Babylonians were totally successful and a number of the children of Israel were deported into captivity, including Daniel and his three friends. . . . These young men understood that they were not in Babylon by chance. God had put them there. . . .

God knew what kind of persecution His children were facing and what He would have to do to deliver them out of it. . . . The fiery furnace, the intensity of the heat, and the anger of Nebuchadnezzar were all human efforts to thwart the will of God. But He overcame them all! At the moment of His children's greatest need, He sent His Son to deliver them from the fire. In so doing, God gives us a beautiful picture of His working in our lives. He does not always choose to keep us from the fire, but often brings about our deliverance while we are in the fire itself.

If God could deliver these young men from a fiery furnace, it should seem evident He can deliver us from whatever trouble we find ourselves in. . . .

. . . He may use these difficulties to teach us great lessons and to bring us to a point of repentance, but ultimately, He can also use these difficulties to produce a wonderful result that only He could bring to pass.

RICHARD LEE

24God's message continued to spread and reach people.

25After Barnabas and Saul finished their task in Jerusalem, they returned to Antioch, taking John Mark with them.

OLD TESTAMENT READING

But the Israelites crossed the sea on dry land, with a wall of water on their right and on their left. **30**So that day the LORD saved the Israelites from the Egyptians, and the Israelites saw the Egyptians lying dead on the seashore. **31**When the Israelites saw the great power the LORD had used against the Egyptians, they feared the LORD, and they trusted him and his servant Moses.

Exodus 14:29–31

PAUSE FOR REFLECTION

How did God's miraculous deliverance in each of these instances build up the faith of those involved? What result does his intervention bring about in your life?

ACTS 13:1-25

Barnabas and Saul Are Chosen

13 In the church at Antioch there were these prophets and teachers: Barnabas, Simeon (also called Niger), Lucius (from the city of Cyrene), Manaen (who had grown up with Herod, the ruler), and Saul. **2**They were all worshiping the Lord and fasting for a certain time. During this time the Holy Spirit said to them, "Set apart for me Barnabas and Saul to do a special work for which I have chosen them."

3So after they fasted and prayed, they laid their hands on Barnabas and Saul and sent them out.

Barnabas and Saul in Cyprus

4Barnabas and Saul, sent out by the Holy Spirit, went to the city of Seleucia. From there they sailed to the island of Cyprus. **5**When they came to Salamis, they preached the Good News of God in the synagogues. John Mark was with them to help.

6They went across the whole island to Paphos where they met a magician named Bar-Jesus. He was a false prophet **7**who always stayed close to Sergius Paulus, the governor and a smart man. He asked Barnabas and Saul to come to him, because he wanted to hear the message of God. **8**But Elymas, the magician, was against them. (Elymas is the name for Bar-Jesus in the Greek language.) He tried to stop the governor from believing in Jesus. **9**But Saul, who was also called Paul, was filled with the Holy Spirit. He looked straight at Elymas **10**and said, "You son of the devil! You are an enemy of everything that is right! You are full of evil tricks and lies, always trying to change the Lord's truths into lies. **11**Now the Lord will touch you, and you will be blind. For a time you will not be able to see anything—not even the light from the sun."

Then everything became dark for Elymas, and he walked around, trying to find someone to lead him by the hand. **12**When the governor saw this, he believed because he was amazed at the teaching about the Lord.

Paul and Barnabas Leave Cyprus

13Paul and those with him sailed from Paphos and came to Perga, in Pamphylia. There John Mark left them to return to Jerusalem. **14**They continued their trip from Perga and went to Antioch, a city in Pisidia. On the Sabbath day they went into the synagogue and sat down. **15**After the law of Moses and the writings of the prophets were read, the leaders of the synagogue sent a message to Paul and Barnabas: "Brothers, if you have any message that will encourage the people, please speak."

16Paul stood up, raised his hand, and said, "You Israelites and you who worship God, please listen! **17**The God of the Israelites chose our ancestors. He made the people great during the time they lived in Egypt, and he brought them out of that country with great power. **18**And he was patient with them for forty years in the desert. **19**God destroyed seven nations in the land of Canaan and gave the land to his people. **20**All this happened in about four hundred fifty years.

"After this, God gave them judges until the time of Samuel the prophet. **21**Then the people asked for a king, so God gave them Saul son of Kish. Saul was from the tribe of Benjamin and was king for forty years. **22**After God took him away, God made David their king. God said about him: 'I have found in David son of Jesse the kind of man I want. He will do all I want him to do.' **23**So God has brought Jesus, one of David's descendants, to Israel to be its Savior, as he promised. **24**Before Jesus came, John preached to all the people of Israel about a baptism of changed hearts and lives. **25**When he was finishing his work, he said, 'Who do you think I am? I am not the Christ. He is coming later, and I am not worthy to untie his sandals.'"

OLD TESTAMENT READING

ur ancestors in Egypt
did not learn from your miracles.
They did not remember all your kindnesses,
so they turned against you at the Red Sea.
8But the LORD saved them for his own sake,
to show his great power.

Psalm 106:7–8

oses and Aaron gathered all the elders of the Israelites, **30**and Aaron told them everything that the LORD had told Moses. Then Moses did the miracles for all the people to see, **31**and the Israelites believed. When they heard that the LORD was concerned about them and had seen their troubles, they bowed down and worshiped him.

Exodus 4:29–31

INSIGHTS

God, who made the visible heaven and earth, does not disdain to work visible miracles in heaven or earth, that He may thereby awaken the soul which is immersed in things visible to worship Himself, the Invisible. . . .

He restored to the blind those eyes which death was sure some time to close; He raised Lazarus from the dead, who was to die again. And whatever He did for the health of bodies, He did it not to the end that they should exist for evermore; whereas at the last He will give eternal health even to the body itself. But because those things which were not seen were not believed, by means of those temporal things which were seen He built up faith in those things which were not seen. Let no one therefore say that our Lord Jesus Christ doeth not those things now, and on this account prefer the former to the present ages of the Church. . . . The Lord did those things to invite us to the faith.

ST. AUGUSTINE

PAUSE FOR REFLECTION

In each of these passages, what did the miracles reveal about God? What was the result? In what way has God revealed himself to you? How have you responded?

ACTS 13:26-52

26"Brothers, sons of the family of Abraham, and others who worship God, listen! The news about this salvation has been sent to us. 27Those who live in Jerusalem and their leaders did not realize that Jesus was the Savior. They did not understand the words that the prophets wrote, which are read every Sabbath day. But they made them come true when they said Jesus was guilty. 28They could not find any real reason for Jesus to be put to death, but they asked Pilate to have him killed. 29When they had done to him all that the Scriptures had said, they took him down from the cross and laid him in a tomb. 30But God raised him up from the dead! 31After this, for many days, those who had gone with Jesus from Galilee to Jerusalem saw him. They are now his witnesses to the people. 32We tell you the Good News about the promise God made to our ancestors. 33God has made this promise come true for us, his children, by raising Jesus from the dead. We read about this also in Psalm 2:

'You are my Son.

Today I have become your Father.'

Psalm 2:7

34God raised Jesus from the dead, and he will never go back to the grave and become dust. So God said:

'I will give you the holy and sure blessings
     that I promised to David.'   *Isaiah 55:3*

35But in another place God says:

'You will not let your Holy One rot.'

Psalm 16:10

36David did God's will during his lifetime. Then he died and was buried beside his ancestors, and his body did rot in the grave. 37But the One God raised from the dead did not rot in the grave. 38-39Brothers, understand what we are telling you: You can have forgiveness of your sins through Jesus. The law of Moses could not free you from your sins. But through Jesus everyone who believes is free from all sins. 40Be careful! Don't let what the prophets said happen to you:

41'Listen, you people who doubt!

You can wonder, and then die.

I will do something in your lifetime
     that you won't believe even when you are
          told about it!'"   *Habakkuk 1:5*

42While Paul and Barnabas were leaving the synagogue, the people asked them to tell them more about these things on the next Sabbath. 43When the meeting was over, many people with those who had changed to worship God followed Paul and Barnabas from that place. Paul and Barnabas were persuading them to continue trusting in God's grace.

44On the next Sabbath day, almost everyone in the city came to hear the word of the Lord. 45Seeing the crowd, the Jewish people became very jealous and said insulting things and argued against what Paul said. 46But Paul and Barnabas spoke very boldly, saying, "We must speak the message of God to you first. But you refuse to listen. You are judging yourselves not worthy of having eternal life! So we will now go to the people of other nations. 47This is what the Lord told us to do, saying:

'I have made you a light for the nations;
you will show people all over the world the
way to be saved.'"   *Isaiah 49:6*

48When those who were not Jewish heard Paul say this, they were happy and gave honor to the message of the Lord. And the people who were chosen to have life forever believed the message.

49So the message of the Lord was spreading through the whole country. **50**But the Jewish people stirred up some of the important religious women and the leaders of the city. They started trouble against Paul and Barnabas and forced them out of their area. **51**So Paul and Barnabas shook the dust off their feet and went to Iconium. **52**But the followers were filled with joy and the Holy Spirit.

OLD TESTAMENT READING

Your words came to me, and I listened
carefully to them.
Your words made me very happy,
because I am called by your name,
LORD God All-Powerful.

Jeremiah 15:16

INSIGHTS

I'm convinced that enjoyment is the ultimate stage of knowledge. When we set out to learn the basic truths of an intellectual discipline, we are confounded by all we don't know. Little by little, we become more secure in ideas and theories. Then one day, we suddenly realize that we have captured the subject and know how to use our knowledge. . . .

. . . Enjoyment of our faith grows in the same way. In the beginning, God seems distant and aloof. Biblical and theological terms are like a foreign language. Our prayers are strained and shallow. . . . And then, with the touch of the Father's hand, we discover how much He loves us and wants us to know Him personally. Secondary theories about Him are replaced by an intimate relationship with Him. None of our awe and adoration is lost as we begin to enjoy Him. . . .

Enjoying God is really a vital expression of glorifying Him. The glory of God is the manifestation and revelation of all that He is as Creator, Sustainer, Redeemer, and Lord of all. We glorify Him when we worship Him for His lovingkindness, goodness, and mercifulness. Our worship becomes intimate when we joyfully experience God's nature and attributes. From that joy springs our desire to glorify Him by serving Him. Our faithful obedience becomes an enjoyable response.

LLOYD OGILVIE

▶ PAUSE FOR REFLECTION

How did the people respond when Paul and Barnabas spoke God's Word in Antioch? In what ways does the Lord make you happy? How has your happiness grown as you have come to know him better?

FRIDAY

SEEK GOD'S GUIDANCE WHEN MAKING DECISIONS

ACTS 14:1-28

Paul and Barnabas in Iconium

14 In Iconium, Paul and Barnabas went as usual to the synagogue. They spoke so well that a great many Jews and Greeks believed. **2**But some people who did not believe excited the others and turned them against the believers. **3**Paul and Barnabas stayed in Iconium a long time and spoke bravely for the Lord. He showed that their message about his grace was true by giving them the power to work miracles and signs. **4**But the city was divided. Some of the people agreed with the Jews, and others believed the apostles.

5Some who were not Jews, some Jews, and some of their rulers wanted to mistreat Paul and Barnabas and to stone them to death. **6**When Paul and Barnabas learned about this, they ran away to Lystra and Derbe, cities in Lycaonia, and to the areas around those cities. **7**They announced the Good News there, too.

Paul in Lystra and Derbe

8In Lystra there sat a man who had been born crippled; he had never walked. **9**As this man was listening to Paul speak, Paul looked straight at him and saw that he believed God could heal him. **10**So he cried out, "Stand up on your feet!" The man jumped up and began walking around. **11**When the crowds saw what Paul did, they shouted in the Lycaonian language, "The gods have become like humans and have come down to us!" **12**Then the people began to call Barnabas

"Zeus" and Paul "Hermes," because he was the main speaker. **13**The priest in the temple of Zeus, which was near the city, brought some bulls and flowers to the city gates. He and the people wanted to offer a sacrifice to Paul and Barnabas. **14**But when the apostles, Barnabas and Paul, heard about it, they tore their clothes. They ran in among the people, shouting, **15**"Friends, why are you doing these things? We are only human beings like you. We are bringing you the Good News and are telling you to turn away from these worthless things and turn to the living God. He is the One who made the sky, the earth, the sea, and everything in them. **16**In the past, God let all the nations do what they wanted. **17**Yet he proved he is real by showing kindness, by giving you rain from heaven and crops at the right times, by giving you food and filling your hearts with joy." **18**Even with these words, they were barely able to keep the crowd from offering sacrifices to them.

19Then some evil people came from Antioch and Iconium and persuaded the people to turn against Paul. So they threw stones at him and dragged him out of town, thinking they had killed him. **20**But the followers gathered around him, and he got up and went back into the town. The next day he and Barnabas left and went to the city of Derbe.

The Return to Antioch in Syria

21Paul and Barnabas told the Good News in Derbe, and many became followers. Paul and Barnabas returned to Lystra, Iconium, and Antioch, **22**making the followers of Jesus stronger and helping them stay in the faith. They said, "We must suffer many things to enter God's kingdom."

23They chose elders for each church, by praying and fasting for a certain time. These elders had trusted the Lord, so Paul and Barnabas put them in the Lord's care.

24Then they went through Pisidia and came to Pamphylia. **25**When they had preached the message in Perga, they went down to Attalia. **26**And from there they sailed away to Antioch where the believers had put them into God's care and had sent them out to do this work. Now they had finished.

27When they arrived in Antioch, Paul and Barnabas gathered the church together. They told the church all about what God had done with them and how God had made it possible for those who were not Jewish to believe. **28**And they stayed there a long time with the followers.

OLD TESTAMENT READING

Trust the LORD with all your heart,
 and don't depend on your own
  understanding.
6Remember the LORD in all you do,
 and he will give you success.

7Don't depend on your own wisdom.
 Respect the LORD and refuse to do
  wrong.

Proverbs 3:5–7

APPLICATION
Why do you think Paul and Barnabas especially sought God's guidance in choosing elders for the churches? For what decisions do you seek God's guidance? Should you be seeking his wisdom more?

ACTS 15:1-21

The Meeting at Jerusalem

15 Then some people came to Antioch from Judea and began teaching the non-Jewish believers: "You cannot be saved if you are not circumcised as Moses taught us." **2**Paul and Barnabas were against this teaching and argued with them about it. So the church decided to send Paul, Barnabas, and some others to Jerusalem where they could talk more about this with the apostles and elders.

3The church helped them leave on the trip, and they went through the countries of Phoenicia and Samaria, telling all about how the other nations had turned to God. This made all the believers very happy. **4**When they arrived in Jerusalem, they were welcomed by the apostles, the elders, and the church. Paul, Barnabas, and the others told about everything God had done with them. **5**But some of the believers who belonged to the Pharisee group came forward and said, "The non-Jewish believers must be circumcised. They must be told to obey the law of Moses."

6The apostles and the elders gathered to consider this problem. **7**After a long debate, Peter stood up and said to them, "Brothers, you know that in the early days God chose me from among you to preach the Good News to the nations. They heard the Good News from me, and they believed. **8**God, who knows the thoughts of everyone, accepted them. He showed this to us by giving them the Holy Spirit, just as he did to us. **9**To God, those people are not different from us. When they believed, he made their hearts pure. **10**So now why are you testing God by putting a heavy load around the necks of the non-Jewish believers? It is a load that neither we nor our ancestors were able to carry. **11**But we believe that we and they too will be saved by the grace of the Lord Jesus."

12Then the whole group became quiet. They listened to Paul and Barnabas tell about all the miracles and signs that God did through them among the people. **13**After they finished speaking, James said, "Brothers, listen to me. **14**Simon has told us how God showed his love for those people. For the first time he is accepting from among them a people to be his own. **15**The words of the prophets agree with this too:

16'After these things I will return.

The kingdom of David is like a fallen tent.
But I will rebuild its ruins,
  and I will set it up.

17 Then those people who are left alive may ask
    the Lord for help,
  and the other nations that belong to me,
says the Lord,
  who will make it happen.

18And these things have been known for a long
    time.' *Amos 9:11–12*

19"So I think we should not bother the other people who are turning to God. **20**Instead, we should write a letter to them telling them these things: Stay away from food that has been offered to idols (which makes it unclean), any kind of sexual sin, eating animals that have been strangled, and blood. **21**They should do these things, because for a long time in every city the law of Moses has been taught. And it is still read in the synagogue every Sabbath day."

OLD TESTAMENT READING

God, have mercy on us and bless us
and show us your kindness   *Selah*
²so the world will learn your ways,
and all nations will learn that you can save.

³God, the people should praise you;
all people should praise you.
⁴The nations should be glad and sing

because you judge people fairly.
You guide all the nations on earth.   *Selah*
⁵God, the people should praise you;
all people should praise you.

Psalm 67:1–5

All people everywhere,
follow me and be saved.
I am God. There is no other God."

Isaiah 45:22

INSIGHTS

The Law came and in bold letters etched by the finger of God it read, "This is ho-liness! Honor My Name by keeping My Law!" But the fact is, nobody could keep it, which explains the statement in Romans 5:20 that says "sin increased." The Law arouses sin but never arrests it. So how can the tailspin stop? What hope is there? The answer is found in the same verse: ". . . but where sin increased, grace abounded all the more." . . .

Let me amplify the scriptural statement even more. Where sin overflowed, grace flooded in. Where sin measurably increased, grace immeasurably increased. Where sin was finite, grace was infinite. Where sin was colossal, grace was supercolossal. Where sin abounds, grace superabounds. The sin identified by the Law in no way stopped the flow of the grace of God. Jesus' death on the cross was the sufficient payment for sin, putting grace into action that was not simply adequate but abun-dant. . . .

. . . God, in grace, offers you the free gift of forgiveness. All you can do is take it. Once you take it, you will be given the power to give up, to put on, to take off, to quit, to start—whatever. But don't confuse the issue of salvation. It is yours strictly on the basis of God's free gift. In spite of all the stuff you may hear to the contrary, the emphasis is not on what we do for God; instead, it is on what God has done for us.

CHARLES SWINDOLL

PAUSE FOR REFLECTION

To whom was the law of Moses given? Why? What evidence in the Old and New Testaments reveals that God offers salvation through Jesus Christ to all people—Jew and non-Jew?

ACTS 15:22 – 16:10

Letter to Non-Jewish Believers

22The apostles, the elders, and the whole church decided to send some of their men with Paul and Barnabas to Antioch. They chose Judas Barsabbas and Silas, who were respected by the believers. **23**They sent the following letter with them:

From the apostles and elders, your brothers.

To all the non-Jewish believers in Antioch, Syria, and Cilicia:

Greetings!

24 We have heard that some of our group have come to you and said things that trouble and upset you. But we did not tell them to do this. **25** We have all agreed to choose some messengers and send them to you with our dear friends Barnabas and Paul— **26**people who have given their lives to serve our Lord Jesus Christ. **27**So we are sending Judas and Silas, who will tell you the same things. **28** It has pleased the Holy Spirit that you should not have a heavy load to carry, and we agree. You need to do only these things: **29**Stay away from any food that has been offered to idols, eating any animals that have been strangled, and blood, and any kind of sexual sin. If you stay away from these things, you will do well.

Good-bye.

30So they left Jerusalem and went to Antioch where they gathered the church and gave them the letter. **31**When they read it, they were very happy because of the encouraging message. **32**Judas and Silas, who were also prophets, said many things to encourage the believers and make them stronger. **33**After some time Judas and Silas were sent off in peace by the believers, and they went back to those who had sent them [, **34**but Silas decided to remain there].

35But Paul and Barnabas stayed in Antioch and, along with many others, preached the Good News and taught the people the message of the Lord.

Paul and Barnabas Separate

36After some time, Paul said to Barnabas, "We should go back to all those towns where we preached the message of the Lord. Let's visit the believers and see how they are doing."

37Barnabas wanted to take John Mark with them, **38**but he had left them at Pamphylia; he did not continue with them in the work. So Paul did not think it was a good idea to take him. **39**Paul and Barnabas had such a serious argument about this that they separated and went different ways. Barnabas took Mark and sailed to Cyprus, **40**but Paul chose Silas and left. The believers in Antioch put Paul into the Lord's care, **41**and he went through Syria and Cilicia, giving strength to the churches.

Timothy Goes with Paul

16Paul came to Derbe and Lystra, where a follower named Timothy lived. Timothy's mother was Jewish and a believer, but his father was a Greek.

2The believers in Lystra and Iconium respected

Timothy and said good things about him. **3**Paul wanted Timothy to travel with him, but all the people living in that area knew that Timothy's father was Greek. So Paul circumcised Timothy to please his mother's people. **4**Paul and those with him traveled from town to town and gave the decisions made by the apostles and elders in Jerusalem for the people to obey. **5**So the churches became stronger in the faith and grew larger every day.

Paul Is Called Out of Asia

6Paul and those with him went through the areas of Phrygia and Galatia since the Holy Spirit did not let them preach the Good News in Asia. **7**When they came near the country of Mysia, they tried to go into Bithynia, but the Spirit of Jesus did not let them. **8**So they passed by Mysia and went to Troas. **9**That night Paul saw in a vision a man from Macedonia. The man stood and begged, "Come over to Macedonia and help us." **10**After Paul had seen the vision, we immediately prepared to leave for Macedonia, understanding that God had called us to tell the Good News to those people.

OLD TESTAMENT READING

The right word spoken at the right time
is as beautiful as gold apples in a silver
bowl.

Proverbs 25:11

INSIGHTS

I was rushing around trying to get dinner ready for my husband and houseguests. . . .

. . . Just as I began last-minute preparations, the doorbell rang. I ran to answer it. A friend had stopped by to drop off a folder of information for my husband.

"How are you, Doris?"

I began to tell her that I was a little tired and frazzled around the edges, when I noticed she wasn't listening. Before I could finish my response, she said, "That's good. It's nice to see you." And with that she left.

I walked slowly back to my kitchen, feeling lonely and deflated. My friend had let me down when I could have used just a word of encouragement, maybe even a quick prayer.

Mechanically, I began to set the table. Why didn't she hear me? Doesn't she care how I am? I just needed a little of her time.

And then I heard the words: Doris, you've done this to people, too. Let this be a lesson to you. Listen to those I send across your path. Give them at least five minutes, even if you are in a hurry. Stop and pray with them.

DORIS GREIG

APPLICATION

Our Proverbs reading summarizes the beauty of encouragement well, doesn't it? What has been your most encouraging experience? What kind of encouragement is offered in each of these examples? How do they help you know how to encourage others?

ACTS 16:11-34

Lydia Becomes a Christian

11We left Troas and sailed straight to the island of Samothrace. The next day we sailed to Neapolis. **12**Then we went by land to Philippi, a Roman colony and the leading city in that part of Macedonia. We stayed there for several days.

13On the Sabbath day we went outside the city gate to the river where we thought we would find a special place for prayer. Some women had gathered there, so we sat down and talked with them. **14**One of the listeners was a woman named Lydia from the city of Thyatira whose job was selling purple cloth. She worshiped God, and he opened her mind to pay attention to what Paul was saying. **15**She and all the people in her house were baptized. Then she invited us to her home, saying, "If you think I am truly a believer in the Lord, then come stay in my house." And she persuaded us to stay with her.

Paul and Silas in Jail

16Once, while we were going to the place for prayer, a servant girl met us. She had a special spirit in her, and she earned a lot of money for her owners by telling fortunes. **17**This girl followed Paul and us, shouting, "These men are servants of the Most High God. They are telling you how you can be saved."

18She kept this up for many days. This bothered Paul, so he turned and said to the spirit, "By the power of Jesus Christ, I command you to come out of her!" Immediately, the spirit came out.

19When the owners of the servant girl saw this, they knew that now they could not use her to make money. So they grabbed Paul and Silas and dragged them before the city rulers in the marketplace. **20**They brought Paul and Silas to the Roman rulers and said, "These men are Jews and are making trouble in our city. **21**They are teaching things that are not right for us as Romans to do."

22The crowd joined the attack against them. The Roman officers tore the clothes of Paul and Silas and had them beaten with rods. **23**Then Paul and Silas were thrown into jail, and the jailer was ordered to guard them carefully. **24**When he heard this order, he put them far inside the jail and pinned their feet down between large blocks of wood.

25About midnight Paul and Silas were praying and singing songs to God as the other prisoners listened. **26**Suddenly, there was a strong earthquake that shook the foundation of the jail. Then all the doors of the jail broke open, and all the prisoners were freed from their chains. **27**The jailer woke up and saw that the jail doors were open. Thinking that the prisoners had already escaped, he got his sword and was about to kill himself. **28**But Paul shouted, "Don't hurt yourself! We are all here."

29The jailer told someone to bring a light. Then he ran inside and, shaking with fear, fell down before Paul and Silas. **30**He brought them outside and said, "Men, what must I do to be saved?"

31They said to him, "Believe in the Lord Jesus and you will be saved—you and all the people in your house." **32**So Paul and Silas told the message of the Lord to the jailer and all the people in his house. **33**At that hour of the night the jailer took Paul and Silas and washed their wounds. Then he and all his people were baptized immediately. **34**After this the jailer took Paul and Silas home and gave them food. He and his family were very happy because they now believed in God.

OLD TESTAMENT READING

ne day Elisha went to Shunem, where an important woman lived. She begged Elisha to stay and eat. So every time Elisha passed by, he stopped there to eat. **9**The woman said to her husband, "I know that this is a holy man of God who passes by our house all the time. **10**Let's make a small room on the roof and put a bed in the room for him. We can put a table, a chair, and a lampstand there. Then when he comes by, he can stay there."

2 Kings 4:8–10

INSIGHTS

Emily is a young woman who desires to practice hospitality, though she did not grow up in a home that was especially welcoming to others. She actively pursues making her home inviting, and God is blessing her endeavors. Every week, many people are welcomed into Emily's home as she creates a genuine atmosphere of love for them.

Whether hospitality is a familiar or foreign concept, you have the opportunity to bless others by sharing your life with them. When you follow the Lord, he will open your mind to the needs of others. You can then be confident that you have something to offer to the people God puts in your path.

Provide a warm meal for a neighbor. Invite a friend over for tea. Lend a compassionate ear to that individual who needs it the most this week. Be ready at all times to welcome others into the place you call home. No matter what your living situation may be, ask God where there might be room in your life to give.

How many times has God blessed you through others? Just as God meets your needs through the people in your life, he also reaches others through your obedience.

Hospitality is extending to others what God has given to you. Like Emily, offer God your desire to serve him with the home you have been given. Cooperate with God. Watch expectantly for his activity. Be a dynamic part of what he is doing in your community . . . and be blessed.

BETSY ZENZ

ACTION POINT

What do you find particularly interesting about these examples of hospitality? What do you think it means to express Christian hospitality to people today? Pray about how God wants your family to use your home to serve him.

ACTS 16:35 – 17:15

35The next morning, the Roman officers sent the police to tell the jailer, "Let these men go free."

36The jailer said to Paul, "The officers have sent an order to let you go free. You can leave now. Go in peace."

37But Paul said to the police, "They beat us in public without a trial, even though we are Roman citizens. And they threw us in jail. Now they want to make us go away quietly. No! Let them come themselves and bring us out."

38The police told the Roman officers what Paul said. When the officers heard that Paul and Silas were Roman citizens, they were afraid. **39**So they came and told Paul and Silas they were sorry and took them out of jail and asked them to leave the city. **40**So when they came out of the jail, they went to Lydia's house where they saw some of the believers and encouraged them. Then they left.

Paul and Silas in Thessalonica

17 Paul and Silas traveled through Amphipolis and Apollonia and came to Thessalonica where there was a synagogue. **2**Paul went into the synagogue as he always did, and on each Sabbath day for three weeks, he talked with his fellow Jews about the Scriptures. **3**He explained and proved that the Christ must die and then rise from the dead. He said, "This Jesus I am telling you about is the Christ." **4**Some of them were convinced and joined Paul and Silas, along with many of the Greeks who worshiped God and many of the important women.

5But some others became jealous. So they got some evil men from the marketplace, formed a mob, and started a riot. They ran to Jason's house, looking for Paul and Silas, wanting to bring them out to the people. **6**But when they did not find them, they dragged Jason and some other believers to the leaders of the city. The people were yelling, "These people have made trouble everywhere in the world, and now they have come here too! **7**Jason is keeping them in his house. All of them do things against the laws of Caesar, saying there is another king, called Jesus."

8When the people and the leaders of the city heard these things, they became very upset. **9**They made Jason and the others put up a sum of money. Then they let the believers go free.

Paul and Silas Go to Berea

10That same night the believers sent Paul and Silas to Berea where they went to the synagogue. **11**These people were more willing to listen than the people in Thessalonica. The Bereans were eager to hear what Paul and Silas said and studied the Scriptures every day to find out if these things were true. **12**So, many of them believed, as well as many important Greek women and men. **13**But the people in Thessalonica learned that Paul was preaching the word of God in Berea, too. So they came there, upsetting the people and making trouble. **14**The believers quickly sent Paul away to the coast, but Silas and Timothy stayed in Berea. **15**The people leading Paul went with him to Athens. Then they carried a message from Paul back to Silas and Timothy for them to come to him as soon as they could.

OLD TESTAMENT READING

Rain and snow fall from the sky
and don't return without watering the
ground.
They cause the plants to sprout and grow,
making seeds for the farmer
and bread for the people.
11The same thing is true of the words I speak.
They will not return to me empty.
They make the things happen that I want to
happen,
and they succeed in doing what I send
them to do."

Isaiah 55:10–11

Your word is like a lamp for my feet
and a light for my path.
106I will do what I have promised
and obey your fair laws.
107I have suffered for a long time.
LORD, give me life by your word.
108LORD, accept my willing praise
and teach me your laws.

Psalm 119:105–108

INSIGHTS

I never pretend to make but one book my study. I read them occasionally, but have little time or inclination to read other books much while I have so much to learn of my Bible. I find it like a deep mine, the more I work it, the richer it grows. We must read that more than any or all other books. We must pause and pray over it, verse after verse, and compare part with part, dwell on it, digest it, and get it into our minds, till we feel that the Spirit of God has filled us with the spirit of holiness.

Will you do it? Will you lay your hearts open to God, and not give him rest, till he has filled you with divine knowledge? Will you search the scriptures? I have often been asked by young converts, and young men preparing for the ministry, what they should read. Read the Bible. I would give the same answer five hundred times. Over and above all other things, study the Bible.

CHARLES FINNEY

ACTION POINT

What was unusual about the Jews in Berea? Is it, then, surprising that many of them believed? What does God say about his word in Isaiah? How much do you treasure and seek after God's Word? Will you begin today to search after it more diligently?

ACTS 17:16 – 18:4

Paul Preaches in Athens

16While Paul was waiting for Silas and Timothy in Athens, he was troubled because he saw that the city was full of idols. 17In the synagogue, he talked with the Jews and the Greeks who worshiped God. He also talked every day with people in the marketplace.

18Some of the Epicurean and Stoic philosophers argued with him, saying, "This man doesn't know what he is talking about. What is he trying to say?" Others said, "He seems to be telling us about some other gods," because Paul was telling them about Jesus and his rising from the dead. 19They got Paul and took him to a meeting of the Areopagus, where they said, "Please explain to us this new idea you have been teaching. 20The things you are saying are new to us, and we want to know what this teaching means." 21(All the people of Athens and those from other countries who lived there always used their time to talk about the newest ideas.)

22Then Paul stood before the meeting of the Areopagus and said, "People of Athens, I can see you are very religious in all things. 23As I was going through your city, I saw the objects you worship. I found an altar that had these words written on it: TO A GOD WHO IS NOT KNOWN. You worship a god that you don't know, and this is the God I am telling you about! 24The God who made the whole world and everything in it is the Lord of the land and the sky. He does not live in temples built by human hands. 25This God is the One who gives life, breath, and everything else to people. He does not need any help from them; he has everything he needs. 26God began by making one person, and from him came all the different people who live everywhere in the world. God decided exactly when and where they must live. 27God wanted them to look for him and perhaps search all around for him and find him, though he is not far from any of us: 28'By his power we live and move and exist.' Some of your own poets have said: 'For we are his children.' 29Since we are God's children, you must not think that God is like something that people imagine or make from gold, silver, or rock. 30In the past, people did not understand God, and he ignored this. But now, God tells all people in the world to change their hearts and lives. 31God has set a day that he will judge all the world with fairness, by the man he chose long ago. And God has proved this to everyone by raising that man from the dead!"

32When the people heard about Jesus being raised from the dead, some of them laughed. But others said, "We will hear more about this from you later." 33So Paul went away from them. 34But some of the people believed Paul and joined him. Among those who believed was Dionysius, a member of the Areopagus, a woman named Damaris, and some others.

Paul in Corinth

18 Later Paul left Athens and went to Corinth. 2Here he met a Jew named Aquila who had been born in the

country of Pontus. But Aquila and his wife, Priscilla, had recently moved to Corinth from Italy, because Claudius commanded that all Jews must leave Rome. Paul went to visit Aquila and Priscilla. **3**Because they were tentmakers, just as he was, he stayed with them and worked with them. **4**Every Sabbath day he talked with the Jews and Greeks in the synagogue, trying to persuade them to believe in Jesus.

OLD TESTAMENT READING

This is the story of the creation of the sky and the earth. When the LORD God first made the earth and the sky, **5**there were still no plants on the earth. Nothing was growing in the fields because the LORD God had not yet made it rain on the land. And there was no person to care for the ground, **6**but a mist would rise up from the earth and water all the ground.

7Then the LORD God took dust from the ground and formed a man from it. He breathed the breath of life into the man's nose, and the man became a living person.

Genesis 2:4–7

INSIGHTS

I WILL WORSHIP

God, you are with me
    and you can help me;
You were with me when I was taken,
    and you are with me now.
You strengthen me.

The God I serve is everywhere—
    in heaven and earth and the sea,
but he is above them all,
    for all live in him:
All were created by him,
    and by him only do they remain.

I will worship only the true God;
    you will I carry in my heart;
No one on earth shall be able to
    separate me from you.

QUIRINUS OF SISCIA

MY COMFORT

Jesus Christ is my comfort.
It is you who created us all.
There is only you, one God,
    Father, Son, and Holy Spirit,
    to whom homage and praise are due.

JANUARIUS OF CORDOVA

▶ PAUSE FOR REFLECTION

In order to help them understand the Good News, what did Paul tell the philosophers and important people of Athens about the true God? What knowledge of God helps you to understand, trust, and worship him?

ACTS 18:5-28

5Silas and Timothy came from Macedonia and joined Paul in Corinth. After this, Paul spent all his time telling people the Good News, showing them that Jesus is the Christ. **6**But they would not accept Paul's teaching and said some evil things. So he shook off the dust from his clothes and said to them, "If you are not saved, it will be your own fault! I have done all I can do! After this, I will go to other nations." **7**Paul left the synagogue and moved into the home of Titius Justus, next to the synagogue. This man worshiped God. **8**Crispus was the leader of that synagogue, and he and all the people living in his house believed in the Lord. Many others in Corinth also listened to Paul and believed and were baptized.

9During the night, the Lord told Paul in a vision: "Don't be afraid. Continue talking to people and don't be quiet. **10**I am with you, and no one will hurt you because many of my people are in this city." **11**Paul stayed there for a year and a half, teaching God's word to the people.

Paul Is Brought Before Gallio

12When Gallio was the governor of the country of Southern Greece, some people came together against Paul and took him to the court. **13**They said, "This man is teaching people to worship God in a way that is against our law."

14Paul was about to say something, but Gallio spoke, saying, "I would listen to you if you were complaining about a crime or some wrong. **15**But the things you are saying are only questions about words and names—arguments about your own law. So you must solve this problem yourselves. I don't want to be a judge of these things." **16**And Gallio made them leave the court.

17Then they all grabbed Sosthenes, the leader of the synagogue, and beat him there before the court. But this did not bother Gallio.

Paul Returns to Antioch

18Paul stayed with the believers for many more days. Then he left and sailed for Syria, with Priscilla and Aquila. At Cenchrea Paul cut off his hair, because he had made a promise to God. **19**Then they went to Ephesus, where Paul left Priscilla and Aquila. While Paul was there, he went into the synagogue and talked with the people. **20**When they asked him to stay with them longer, he refused. **21**But as he left, he said, "I will come back to you again if God wants me to." And so he sailed away from Ephesus.

22When Paul landed at Caesarea, he went and gave greetings to the church in Jerusalem. After that, Paul went to Antioch. **23**He stayed there for a while and then left and went through the regions of Galatia and Phrygia. He traveled from town to town in these regions, giving strength to all the followers.

Apollos in Ephesus and Corinth

24A Jew named Apollos came to Ephesus. He was born in the city of Alexandria and was a good speaker who knew the Scriptures well. **25**He had been taught about the way of the Lord and was always very excited when he spoke and taught the truth about Jesus. But the only baptism Apollos knew about was the baptism that John taught. **26**Apollos began to speak very boldly in the synagogue, and when Priscilla and Aquila heard him, they took him to their home and helped him better understand the way of God. **27**Now Apollos wanted to go to the country of Southern Greece. So the believers helped him and wrote a letter to the followers there, asking them to accept him. These followers had believed in Jesus because of God's grace, and when Apollos arrived, he helped them very much. **28**He argued very strongly with the Jews before all the people, clearly proving with the Scriptures that Jesus is the Christ.

OLD TESTAMENT READING

I am with you and will protect you everywhere you go and will bring you back to this land. I will not leave you until I have done what I have promised you."

Genesis 28:15

The LORD guards you.
    The LORD is the shade that protects you
        from the sun.
6The sun cannot hurt you during the day,
    and the moon cannot hurt you at night.
7The LORD will protect you from all dangers;
    he will guard your life.
8The LORD will guard you as you come and go,
    both now and forever.

Psalm 121:5–8

INSIGHTS

How tenderly God soothes our fears! How sweetly He says, . . . "Fear thou not; for I am with thee: be not dismayed; for I am thy God: . . . I will uphold thee with the right hand of my righteousness" (Isaiah 41:10). And yet again, still with tender thoughtfulness, "I the Lord thy God will hold thy right hand, saying unto thee, Fear not; I will help thee" (Isaiah 41:13). He does not say it only once, but He keeps holding our right hand and repeating such promises.

The blessed Lord condensed it all into one single message of eternal comfort spoken to the disciples on the Sea of Galilee, It is I; be not afraid. He is the antidote to fear; He is the remedy for trouble; He is the substance and the sum of deliverance. We should, therefore, rise above fear. Let us keep our eyes fastened upon Him; let us abide continually in Him; let us be content with Him.

Let us cling closely to Him.

A. B. SIMPSON

ACTION POINT

What encouragement from the Lord have you received in times of fear? Which reading assures you that God is with you? Pray that you will always cling to God and feel the blessing of his presence!

ACTS 19:1-22

Paul in Ephesus

19 While Apollos was in Corinth, Paul was visiting some places on the way to Ephesus. There he found some followers **2**and asked them, "Did you receive the Holy Spirit when you believed?"

They said, "We have never even heard of a Holy Spirit."

3So he asked, "What kind of baptism did you have?"

They said, "It was the baptism that John taught."

4Paul said, "John's baptism was a baptism of changed hearts and lives. He told people to believe in the one who would come after him, and that one is Jesus."

5When they heard this, they were baptized in the name of the Lord Jesus. **6**Then Paul laid his hands on them, and the Holy Spirit came upon them. They began speaking different languages and prophesying. **7**There were about twelve people in this group.

8Paul went into the synagogue and spoke out boldly for three months. He talked with the people and persuaded them to accept the things he said about the kingdom of God. **9**But some of them became stubborn. They refused to believe and said evil things about the Way of Jesus before all the people. So Paul left them, and taking the followers with him, he went to the school of a man named Tyrannus. There Paul talked with people every day **10**for two years. Because of his work, every Jew and Greek in Asia heard the word of the Lord.

The Sons of Sceva

11God used Paul to do some very special miracles. **12**Some people took handkerchiefs and clothes that Paul had used and put them on the sick. When they did this, the sick were healed and evil spirits left them.

13But some people also were traveling around and making evil spirits go out of people. They tried to use the name of the Lord Jesus to force the evil spirits out. They would say, "By the same Jesus that Paul talks about, I order you to come out!" **14**Seven sons of Sceva, a leading priest, were doing this.

15But one time an evil spirit said to them, "I know Jesus, and I know about Paul, but who are you?"

16Then the man who had the evil spirit jumped on them. Because he was so much stronger than all of them, they ran away from the house naked and hurt. **17**All the people in Ephesus—Jews and Greeks—learned about this and were filled with fear and gave great honor to the Lord Jesus. **18**Many of the believers began to confess openly and tell all the evil things they had done. **19**Some of them who had used magic brought their magic books and burned them before everyone. Those books were worth about fifty thousand silver coins.

20So in a powerful way the word of the Lord kept spreading and growing.

21After these things, Paul decided to go to Jerusalem, planning to go through the countries of Macedonia and Southern Greece and then on to Jerusalem. He said, "After I have been to Jerusalem, I must also visit Rome." **22**Paul sent

Timothy and Erastus, two of his helpers, ahead to Macedonia, but he himself stayed in Asia for a while.

INSIGHTS

When I was a boy, each Saturday my father would make a list of chores for me to do before I could go and play. When he came home in the evening, he would take the list and—walking with me beside him—check how each job had been done. Sometimes he would point out a hidden, unswept corner that I had missed or find a small, untrimmed area of the yard that I had overlooked. When he did so, I would take a brush or clippers right then and finish the job properly. And you can be sure that, the next week, I would remember to carefully check those places I'd missed.

In checking on my work, my father was not being unkind or critical of what I'd done. He was helping me learn to do a job right the first time. And when I did, he would always encourage me and say, "That's good work, son."

That's how we should be with the Lord. We need to learn to be quick to take care of everything we see on the Father's "list" in his Word and then be open and ready for him to point out the things we have overlooked or neglected. We must offer daily confession, both for known sins that blot a day's activities and for sins we overlooked.

When we do these things, we know that through the blood of Christ we have instant and complete forgiveness: "If we confess our sins to him, he can be depended on to forgive us and to cleanse us from every wrong" (1 John 1:9).

"Hidden corners" do slip by unnoticed, and there are many believers caught up in sinful habits that at first they don't even recognize as sin. We might find, as we open to the Lord, that he begins to confront and adjust a pattern of our relationships, an aspect of our daily activities or entertainment, or some continued practice from childhood. We need to bring all aspects of our lives, regardless of what the world says is right or acceptable, under the searching eyes of the Lord.

JACK HAYFORD

OLD TESTAMENT READING

Then Jehoiada made an agreement between the LORD and the king and the people that they would be the LORD's special people. He also made an agreement between the king and the people. 18All the people of the land went to the temple of Baal and tore it down, smashing the altars and idols. They also killed Mattan, the priest of Baal, in front of the altars.

Then Jehoiada the priest placed guards at the Temple of the LORD.

2 Kings 11:17–18

▶ APPLICATION

What happens when God's people turn away from sin and truly seek to obey him? What sins in your life need to be put away?

ACTS 19:23 — 20:6

Trouble in Ephesus

23And during that time, there was some serious trouble in Ephesus about the Way of Jesus. **24**A man named Demetrius, who worked with silver, made little silver models that looked like the temple of the goddess Artemis. Those who did this work made much money. **25**Demetrius had a meeting with them and some others who did the same kind of work. He told them, "Men, you know that we make a lot of money from our business. **26**But look at what this man Paul is doing. He has convinced and turned away many people in Ephesus and in almost all of Asia! He says the gods made by human hands are not real. **27**There is a danger that our business will lose its good name, but there is also another danger: People will begin to think that the temple of the great goddess Artemis is not important. Her greatness will be destroyed, and Artemis is the goddess that everyone in Asia and the whole world worships."

28When the others heard this, they became very angry and shouted, "Artemis, the goddess of Ephesus, is great!" **29**The whole city became confused. The people grabbed Gaius and Aristarchus, who were from Macedonia and were traveling with Paul, and ran to the theater. **30**Paul wanted to go in and talk to the crowd, but the followers did not let him. **31**Also, some leaders of Asia who were friends of Paul sent him a message, begging him not to go into the theater. **32**Some people were shouting one thing, and some were shouting another. The meeting was completely confused; most of them did not know why they had come together. **33**They put a man named Alexander in front of the people, and some of them told him what to do. Alexander waved his hand so he could explain things to the people. **34**But when they saw that Alexander was a Jew, they all shouted the same thing for two hours: "Great is Artemis of Ephesus!"

35Then the city clerk made the crowd be quiet. He said, "People of Ephesus, everyone knows that Ephesus is the city that keeps the temple of the great goddess Artemis and her holy stone that fell from heaven. **36**Since no one can say this is not true, you should be quiet. Stop and think before you do anything. **37**You brought these men here, but they have not said anything evil against our goddess or stolen anything from her temple. **38**If Demetrius and those who work with him have a charge against anyone they should go to the courts and judges where they can argue with each other. **39**If there is something else you want to talk about, it can be decided at the regular town meeting of the people. **40**I say this because some people might see this trouble today and say that we are rioting. We could not explain this, because there is no real reason for this meeting." **41**After the city clerk said these things, he told the people to go home.

Paul in Macedonia and Greece

 When the trouble stopped, Paul sent for the followers to come to him. After he encouraged them and then told them good-bye, he left and went to the country of Macedonia. **2**He said many things to strengthen the followers in the different places on his way through Macedonia. Then he went to Greece, **3**where he stayed for three months. He was ready to sail for Syria, but some evil people were planning something against him. So Paul decided to go back through Macedonia to Syria. **4**The men who went with him were Sopater son of Pyrrhus, from the city of Berea; Aristarchus and Secundus, from the city of Thessalonica; Gaius, from Derbe; Timothy; and Tychicus and Trophimus, two men from Asia. **5**These men went on ahead and waited for us at Troas. **6**We sailed from Philippi after the Feast of Unleavened Bread. Five days later we met them in Troas, where we stayed for seven days.

OLD TESTAMENT READING

What if the Lord had not been on our side
  when we were attacked?
3When they were angry with us,
  they would have swallowed us alive.

6Praise the Lord,
  who did not let them chew us up.
7We escaped like a bird
  from the hunter's trap.
  The trap broke,
  and we escaped.
8Our help comes from the Lord,
  who made heaven and earth.

Psalm 124:2–3, 6–8

INSIGHTS

A mighty fortress is our God,
A bulwark never failing;
Our helper He amid the flood
Of mortal ills prevailing.
For still our ancient foe
Doth seek to work us woe—
His craft and pow'r are great,
And, armed with cruel hate,
On earth is not his equal.

Did we in our own strength confide,
Our striving would be losing,
Were not the right man on our side,
The man of God's own choosing.
Dost ask who that may be?
Christ Jesus, it is He—
Lord Sabaoth His name,
From age to age the same,
And He must win the battle.

And tho this world, with devils filled,
Should threaten to undo us,
We will not fear, for God hath willed
His truth to triumph thru us.
The prince of darkness grim,
We tremble not for him—
His rage we can endure,
For lo, his doom is sure:
One little word shall fell him.

MARTIN LUTHER

▶ PAUSE FOR REFLECTION

What motivated Demetrius to start the trouble in Ephesus? For what other reasons do people cause trouble for God's people? What comfort and strength do you find in Psalm 124 and Luther's famous hymn?

ACTS 20:7-38

Paul's Last Visit to Troas

7On the first day of the week, we all met together to break bread, and Paul spoke to the group. Because he was planning to leave the next day, he kept on talking until midnight. 8We were all together in a room upstairs, and there were many lamps in the room. 9A young man named Eutychus was sitting in the window. As Paul continued talking, Eutychus was falling into a deep sleep. Finally, he went sound asleep and fell to the ground from the third floor. When they picked him up, he was dead. 10Paul went down to Eutychus, knelt down, and put his arms around him. He said, "Don't worry. He is alive now." 11Then Paul went upstairs again, broke bread, and ate. He spoke to them a long time, until it was early morning, and then he left. 12They took the young man home alive and were greatly comforted.

The Trip from Troas to Miletus

13We went on ahead of Paul and sailed for the city of Assos, where he wanted to join us on the ship. Paul planned it this way because he wanted to go to Assos by land. 14When he met us there, we took him aboard and went to Mitylene. 15We sailed from Mitylene and the next day came to a place near Kios. The following day we sailed to Samos, and the next day we reached Miletus. 16Paul had already decided not to stop at Ephesus, because he did not want to stay too long in Asia. He was hurrying to be in Jerusalem on the day of Pentecost, if that were possible.

The Elders from Ephesus

17Now from Miletus Paul sent to Ephesus and called for the elders of the church. 18When they came to him, he said, "You know about my life from the first day I came to Asia. You know the way I lived all the time I was with you. 19The evil people made plans against me, which troubled me very much. But you know I always served the Lord unselfishly, and I often cried. 20You know I preached to you and did not hold back anything that would help you. You know that I taught you in public and in your homes. 21I warned both Jews and Greeks to change their lives and turn to God and believe in our Lord Jesus. 22But now I must obey the Holy Spirit and go to Jerusalem. I don't know what will happen to me there. 23I know only that in every city the Holy Spirit tells me that troubles and even jail wait for me. 24I don't care about my own life. The most important thing is that I complete my mission, the work that the Lord Jesus gave me—to tell people the Good News about God's grace.

25"And now, I know that none of you among whom I was preaching the kingdom of God will ever see me again. 26So today I tell you that if any of you should be lost, I am not responsible, 27because I have told you everything God wants you to know. 28Be careful for yourselves and for all the people the Holy Spirit has given to you to oversee. You must be like shepherds to the church of God, which he bought with the death of his own son. 29I know that after I leave, some people will come like wild wolves and try to destroy the flock. 30Also, some from your own group will rise up and twist the truth and will lead away followers after them. **31**So be careful! Always remember that for three years, day and night, I never stopped warning each of you, and I often cried over you.

32"Now I am putting you in the care of God and the message about his grace. It is able to give you strength, and it will give you the blessings God has for all his holy people. **33**When I was with you, I never wanted anyone's money or fine clothes. **34**You know I always worked to take care of my own needs and the needs of those who were with me. **35**I showed you in all things that you should work as I did and help the weak. I taught you to remember the words Jesus said: 'It is more blessed to give than to receive.'"

36When Paul had said this, he knelt down with all of them and prayed. **37-38**And they all cried because Paul had said they would never see him again. They put their arms around him and kissed him. Then they went with him to the ship.

OLD TESTAMENT READING

Then Elijah said, "Capture the prophets of Baal! Don't let any of them run away!" The people captured all the prophets. Then Elijah led them down to the Kishon Valley, where he killed them.

1 Kings 18:40

INSIGHTS

David Brainerd, early missionary to the Indians of the United States, was so consumed with a passion for the glory of Christ in the salvation of souls that he claimed: "I cared not how or where I lived, or what hardships I endured, so that I could but gain souls for Christ."

Paul was a passionately ambitious man, even before his conversion. . . .

. . . Whereas his old ambition had been to efface the name of Jesus and exterminate His church, now he had a passion to exalt the name of Jesus and establish and edify His church. His new ambition found its center in the glory of Christ and the advancement of His kingdom. . . .

Our Lord was gripped by a master ambition that integrated the whole of His life. It can be summarized in a single sentence: "I have come to do your will, O God" (Hebrews 10:7). When at life's end He offered His wonderful high-priestly prayer, He was able to report the complete achievement of this ambition: "I have brought you glory on earth by completing the work you gave me to do" (John 17:4).

J. OSWALD SANDERS

▶ PAUSE FOR REFLECTION

What was Paul's most important goal in life? What personal hardship did that commitment cost him? What sustains a person who makes such a commitment?

ACTS 21:1-25

Paul Goes to Jerusalem

21 After we all said good-bye to them, we sailed straight to the island of Cos. The next day we reached Rhodes, and from there we went to Patara. **2**There we found a ship going to Phoenicia, so we went aboard and sailed away. **3**We sailed near the island of Cyprus, seeing it to the north, but we sailed on to Syria. We stopped at Tyre because the ship needed to unload its cargo there. **4**We found some followers in Tyre and stayed with them for seven days. Through the Holy Spirit they warned Paul not to go to Jerusalem. **5**When we finished our visit, we left and continued our trip. All the followers, even the women and children, came outside the city with us. After we all knelt on the beach and prayed, **6**we said good-bye and got on the ship, and the followers went back home.

7We continued our trip from Tyre and arrived at Ptolemais, where we greeted the believers and stayed with them for a day. **8**The next day we left Ptolemais and went to the city of Caesarea. There we went into the home of Philip the preacher, one of the seven helpers, and stayed with him. **9**He had four unmarried daughters who had the gift of prophesying. **10**After we had been there for some time, a prophet named Agabus arrived from Judea. **11**He came to us and borrowed Paul's belt and used it to tie his own hands and feet. He said, "The Holy Spirit says, 'This is how evil people in Jerusalem will tie up the man who wears this belt. Then they will give him to the older leaders.'"

12When we all heard this, we and the people there begged Paul not to go to Jerusalem. **13**But he said, "Why are you crying and making me so sad? I am not only ready to be tied up in Jerusalem, I am ready to die for the Lord Jesus!"

14We could not persuade him to stay away from Jerusalem. So we stopped begging him and said, "We pray that what the Lord wants will be done."

15After this, we got ready and started on our way to Jerusalem. **16**Some of the followers from Caesarea went with us and took us to the home of Mnason, where we would stay. He was from Cyprus and was one of the first followers.

Paul Visits James

17In Jerusalem the believers were glad to see us. **18**The next day Paul went with us to visit James, and all the elders were there. **19**Paul greeted them and told them everything God had done among the other nations through him. **20**When they heard this, they praised God. Then they said to Paul, "Brother, you can see that many thousands of our people have become believers. And they think it is very important to obey the law of Moses. **21**They have heard about your teaching, that you tell our people who live among the nations to leave the law of Moses. They have heard that you tell them not to circumcise their children and not to obey customs. **22**What should we do? They will learn that you have come. **23**So we will tell you what to do: Four of our men have made a promise to God. **24**Take these men with you and share in their cleansing ceremony. Pay their expenses so they can shave their heads. Then it will prove to everyone that what they have heard about you is not true and that you follow the law of Moses in your own life. **25**We have already sent a letter to the non-Jewish believers. The letter said: 'Do not eat food that has been offered to idols, or blood, or animals that have been strangled. Do not take part in sexual sin.'"

OLD TESTAMENT READING

Then the LORD said to Moses, "Go down from this mountain, because your people, the people you brought out of the land of Egypt, have ruined themselves."

26So Moses stood at the entrance to the camp and said, "Let anyone who wants to follow the LORD come to me." And all the people from the family of Levi gathered around Moses.

27Then Moses said to them, "The LORD, the God of Israel, says this: 'Every man must put on his sword and go through the camp from one end to the other. Each man must kill his brother, his friend, and his neighbor.' " **29**Then Moses said, "Today you have been given for service to the LORD. You were willing to kill your own sons and brothers, and God has blessed you for this."

Exodus 32:7, 26–27, 29

INSIGHTS

Sometimes King Saul was among the prophets, easily turned into a prophet, and then afterwards among the witches; sometimes in one place and then another, and insincere in everything. How many such we have in every Christian assembly; men who are very easily molded. They have affectionate dispositions, very likely a tender conscience; but then the conscience is so remarkably tender, that when touched it seems to give, and you are afraid to probe deeper; it heals as soon as it is wounded. You may press then whichever way you wish, they are so elastic you can always win your purpose, but then they are not fixed in character and soon return to be what they were before.

Pray God to send a few men with "grit" in them; men, who when they know a thing to be right, will not turn away, or turn aside, or stop; men who will persevere all the more because there are difficulties to meet or foes to encounter; who stand all the more true to their Master because they are opposed; who, the more they are thrust into the fire, the hotter they become; who, just like the bow, the further the string is drawn the more powerfully it sends forth its arrows, and so the more they are trodden upon, the more mighty will they become in the cause of truth against error.

CHARLES SPURGEON

PAUSE FOR REFLECTION

Are you so convinced of the reality of God in your life that you would risk your life to serve him?

ACTS 21:26 — 22:5

26The next day Paul took the four men and shared in the cleansing ceremony with them. Then he went to the Temple and announced the time when the days of the cleansing ceremony would be finished. On the last day an offering would be given for each of the men.

27When the seven days were almost over, some of his people from Asia saw Paul at the Temple. They caused all the people to be upset and grabbed Paul. **28**They shouted, "People of Israel, help us! This is the man who goes everywhere teaching against the law of Moses, against our people, and against this Temple. Now he has brought some Greeks into the Temple and has made this holy place unclean!" **29**(They said this because they had seen Trophimus, a man from Ephesus, with Paul in Jerusalem. They thought that Paul had brought him into the Temple.)

30All the people in Jerusalem became upset. Together they ran, took Paul, and dragged him out of the Temple. The Temple doors were closed immediately. **31**While they were trying to kill Paul, the commander of the Roman army in Jerusalem learned that there was trouble in the whole city. **32**Immediately he took some officers and soldiers and ran to the place where the crowd was gathered. When the people saw them, they stopped beating Paul. **33**The commander went to Paul and arrested him. He told his soldiers to tie Paul with two chains. Then he asked who he was and what he had done wrong. **34**Some in the crowd were yelling one thing, and some were yelling another. Because of all this confusion and shouting, the commander could not learn what had happened. So he ordered the soldiers to take Paul to the army building. **35**When Paul came to the steps, the soldiers had to carry him because the people were ready to hurt him. **36**The whole mob was following them, shouting, "Kill him!"

37As the soldiers were about to take Paul into the army building, he spoke to the commander, "May I say something to you?"

The commander said, "Do you speak Greek? **38**I thought you were the Egyptian who started some trouble against the government not long ago and led four thousand killers out to the desert."

39Paul said, "No, I am a Jew from Tarsus in the country of Cilicia. I am a citizen of that important city. Please, let me speak to the people."

40The commander gave permission, so Paul stood on the steps and waved his hand to quiet the people. When there was silence, he spoke to them in the Hebrew language.

Paul Speaks to the People

 Paul said, "Brothers and fathers, listen to my defense to you." **2**When they heard him speaking the Hebrew language, they became very quiet. Paul said, **3**"I am a Jew, born in Tarsus in the country of Cilicia, but I grew up in this city. I was a student of Gamaliel, who carefully taught me everything about the law of our ancestors. I was very serious about serving God, just as are all of you here today. **4**I persecuted the people who followed the Way of Jesus, and some of them were even killed. I arrested men and women and put them in jail.

⁵The high priest and the whole council of elders can tell you this is true. They gave me letters to the brothers in Damascus. So I was going there to arrest these people and bring them back to Jerusalem to be punished."

OLD TESTAMENT READING

He said, "Human, I am sending you to the people of Israel. That nation has turned against me and broken away from me. They and their ancestors have sinned against me until this very day. ⁴I am sending you to people who are stubborn and who do not obey. You will say to them, 'This is what the Lord GOD says.' ⁵They may listen, or they may not, since they are a people who have turned against me. But they will know that a prophet has been among them."

Ezekiel 2:3–5

INSIGHTS

Johan is young, tall, blond, and Dutch. I got to know him through my cousin, who attended the same Bible school in England. Gifted and handsome, Johan could have carved out a comfortable youth ministry in his native Netherlands—or most anywhere in the world, for that matter.

Comfort, however, isn't one of Johan's major goals. He chose to take the gospel of Christ to the bedouins and nomads near Israel's desolate Sinai desert. A forgotten people in one of the most desolate corners of the world.

Johan works by an oasis near the sea, attracting travelers and bedouins by offering hot meals, clothing, and first aid. . . .

From the bedouins, Johan learned it is considered worse than murder if you know of a water source and yet neglect to tell your fellow man.

Few of us will ever line in a wilderness like the one where young Johan has pitched his tent. Not many among us will ever proclaim salvation to desert nomads. But all around us, no matter where we reside or work, there are thirsty men and women. The neighbor down the street, the man at the service station, the boy who carries our groceries, the secretary who types and files, or even the distant aunt who occasionally comes by for visits.

If these people don't know Christ, they're going to die of thirst. . . .

Do you know the Source of living water? If you do, please don't withhold a drink from somebody who is thirsty.

It's not just a matter of hospitality. It's a matter of life and death.

JONI EARECKSON TADA

APPLICATION
What difficulties did Paul and Ezekiel face in proclaiming God's message? Why did they speak God's Word, even at great personal risk? To whom is God leading you to share Christ? Will you take the risk?

ACTS 22:6-29

6"About noon when I came near Damascus, a bright light from heaven suddenly flashed all around me. 7I fell to the ground and heard a voice saying, 'Saul, Saul, why are you persecuting me?' 8I asked, 'Who are you, Lord?' The voice said, 'I am Jesus from Nazareth whom you are persecuting.' 9Those who were with me did not understand the voice, but they saw the light. 10I said, 'What shall I do, Lord?' The Lord answered, 'Get up and go to Damascus. There you will be told about all the things I have planned for you to do.' 11I could not see, because the bright light had made me blind. So my companions led me into Damascus.

12"There a man named Ananias came to me. He was a religious man; he obeyed the law of Moses, and all the Jews who lived there respected him. 13He stood by me and said, 'Brother Saul, see again!' Immediately I was able to see him. 14He said, 'The God of our ancestors chose you long ago to know his plan, to see the Righteous One, and to hear words from him. 15You will be his witness to all people, telling them about what you have seen and heard. 16Now, why wait any longer? Get up, be baptized, and wash your sins away, trusting in him to save you.'

17"Later, when I returned to Jerusalem, I was praying in the Temple, and I saw a vision. 18I saw the Lord saying to me, 'Hurry! Leave Jerusalem now! The people here will not accept the truth about me.' 19But I said, 'Lord, they know that in every synagogue I put the believers in jail and beat them. 20They also know I was there when Stephen, your witness, was killed. I stood there agreeing and holding the coats of those who were killing him!' 21But the Lord said to me, 'Leave now. I will send you far away to the other nations.'"

22The crowd listened to Paul until he said this. Then they began shouting, "Get rid of him! He doesn't deserve to live!" 23They shouted, threw off their coats, and threw dust into the air.

24Then the commander ordered the soldiers to take Paul into the army building and beat him. He wanted to make Paul tell why the people were shouting against him like this. 25But as the soldiers were tying him up, preparing to beat him, Paul said to an officer nearby, "Do you have the right to beat a Roman citizen who has not been proven guilty?"

26When the officer heard this, he went to the commander and reported it. The officer said, "Do you know what you are doing? This man is a Roman citizen."

27The commander came to Paul and said, "Tell me, are you really a Roman citizen?"

He answered, "Yes."

28The commander said, "I paid a lot of money to become a Roman citizen."

But Paul said, "I was born a citizen."

29The men who were preparing to question Paul moved away from him immediately. The commander was frightened because he had already tied Paul, and Paul was a Roman citizen.

OLD TESTAMENT READING

All the earth should worship the LORD;
the whole world should fear him.
⁹He spoke, and it happened.
He commanded, and it appeared.
¹⁰The LORD upsets the plans of nations;
he ruins all their plans.

¹¹But the LORD's plans will stand forever;
his ideas will last from now on.
¹²Happy is the nation whose God is the LORD,
the people he chose for his very own.

Psalm 33:8–12

People may make plans in their minds,
but the LORD decides what they will do.

Proverbs 16:9

INSIGHTS

God is at work in all the kaleidoscoping family transitions: not only in the high points but in the endings, beginnings, detours, dead ends, and in-between times. His powerful tools are not just the promotions and graduations but the failures and firings and losses and sicknesses and shocks and periods of boredom. In them all He's silently, busily, unceasingly encouraging, punishing, shaping. . . .

. . . And during all His working—all God's silent activity in the disappointments, surprises, delights, irritations—transformations are taking place. . . .

Do you feel as if nothing is happening . . . ?

I guess so does a lobster, encased in that ridiculous armor. As he grows it even gets crowded inside. But he sheds it fourteen times during his first year of life. Each shedding takes ten days, and each time in the period between shells—when he's naked, exposed, vulnerable—he grows about seven percent.

You feel stifled, unfulfilled? You don't know when you'll break out into change?

Wait for God.

Wait on God.

Wait with God.

Life is not fixed. Let it happen; don't rush it. "It is God who works in you to will and to act according to his good purpose. Do everything without complaining or arguing" (Phil. 2:13, 14). Keep your eyes fixed on Him, live in obedience as you see it, and then just be there.

ANNE ORTLUND

APPLICATION

Imagine yourself as Paul. How would you have taken the news that God had very different plans than what you had chosen? Pray that you will trust God's plans and obey them as they are revealed to you.

ACTS 22:30 — 23:22

Paul Speaks to Leaders

30The next day the commander decided to learn why the Jews were accusing Paul. So he ordered the leading priests and the council to meet. The commander took Paul's chains off. Then he brought Paul out and stood him before their meeting.

 Paul looked at the council and said, "Brothers, I have lived my life without guilt feelings before God up to this day." **2**Ananias, the high priest, heard this and told the men who were standing near Paul to hit him on the mouth. **3**Paul said to Ananias, "God will hit you, too! You are like a wall that has been painted white. You sit there and judge me, using the law of Moses, but you are telling them to hit me, and that is against the law."

4The men standing near Paul said to him, "You cannot insult God's high priest like that!"

5Paul said, "Brothers, I did not know this man was the high priest. It is written in the Scriptures, 'You must not curse a leader of your people.'"

6Some of the men in the meeting were Sadducees, and others were Pharisees. Knowing this, Paul shouted to them, "My brothers, I am a Pharisee, and my father was a Pharisee. I am on trial here because I believe that people will rise from the dead."

7When Paul said this, there was an argument between the Pharisees and the Sadducees, and the group was divided. **8**(The Sadducees do not believe in angels or spirits or that people will rise from the dead. But the Pharisees believe in them all.) **9**So there was a great uproar. Some of the teachers of the law, who were Pharisees, stood up and argued, "We find nothing wrong with this man. Maybe an angel or a spirit did speak to him."

10The argument was beginning to turn into such a fight that the commander was afraid some evil people would tear Paul to pieces. So he told the soldiers to go down and take Paul away and put him in the army building.

11The next night the Lord came and stood by Paul. He said, "Be brave! You have told people in Jerusalem about me. You must do the same in Rome."

12In the morning some evil people made a plan to kill Paul, and they took an oath not to eat or drink anything until they had killed him. **13**There were more than forty men who made this plan. **14**They went to the leading priests and the elders and said, "We have taken an oath not to eat or drink until we have killed Paul. **15**So this is what we want you to do: Send a message to the commander to bring Paul out to you as though you want to ask him more questions. We will be waiting to kill him while he is on the way here."

16But Paul's nephew heard about this plan and went to the army building and told Paul. **17**Then Paul called one of the officers and said, "Take this young man to the commander. He has a message for him."

18So the officer brought Paul's nephew to the commander and said, "The prisoner, Paul, asked me to bring this young man to you. He wants to tell you something."

19The commander took the young man's hand

and led him to a place where they could be alone. He asked, "What do you want to tell me?"

20The young man said, "The Jews have decided to ask you to bring Paul down to their council meeting tomorrow. They want you to think they are going to ask him more questions. **21**But don't believe them! More than forty men are hiding and waiting to kill Paul. They have all taken an oath not to eat or drink until they have killed him. Now they are waiting for you to agree."

22The commander sent the young man away, ordering him, "Don't tell anyone that you have told me about their plan."

OLD TESTAMENT READING

God, we thank you;
>   we thank you because you are near.
>   We tell about the miracles you do.

2You say, "I set the time for trial,
>   and I will judge fairly.
3The earth with all its people may shake,
>   but I am the one who holds it steady." *Selah*
>   *Psalm 75:1–3*

INSIGHTS

"Now on whom dost thou trust?" (2 Kings 18:20). Such was the challenge which the blatant Assyrian field-marshal, Rab-shakeh, flung at the beleaguered king Hezekiah, more than two-and-a-half millenniums ago. Little did he guess that before many more sunrises 185,000 of his proud army would be corpses, cut down by an invisible scythe of the Almighty! Hezekiah did not reply to Rab-shakeh, but despite the hopeless-looking circumstances his heart was fixed, trusting in Jehovah (18:5). This was his secret of victory.

Even so today, the first mark of the true Christian is reliance on Jehovah-Jesus. We rely on Him exclusively as the vicarious Sinbearer through whom we have the salvation of our souls.

But we are to rely on Him continually as our victorious Champion through whom we have victory in our daily life. . . . So long as we rely on Him we have victory. Temper, fear, lust, pride, envy, grudging, moodiness, impatience, despondency, worry; over all such we gain victory as we really rely on Jesus.

Again, we are to rely on Him as our vigilant Provider, who "supplies all our need" (Phil. 4:19; Ps. 34:22). He does not always employ ravens to feed His Elijahs, but by one means or another He sustains them if they really rely on Him.

J. SIDLOW BAXTER

ACTION POINT

In what ways has the Lord stood next to you and encouraged you to be brave for his sake? For what in your life do you need confidence that he is standing with you? Pray for his protection. Trust him. He will supply the victory!

ACTS 23:23 — 24:16

Paul Is Sent to Caesarea

23Then the commander called two officers and said, "I need some men to go to Caesarea. Get two hundred soldiers, seventy horsemen, and two hundred men with spears ready to leave at nine o'clock tonight. **24**Get some horses for Paul to ride so he can be taken to Governor Felix safely." **25**And he wrote a letter that said:

> **26**From Claudius Lysias.
> To the Most Excellent Governor Felix: Greetings.

27Some of the Jews had taken this man and planned to kill him. But I learned that he is a Roman citizen, so I went with my soldiers and saved him. **28**I wanted to know why they were accusing him, so I brought him before their council meeting. **29**I learned that these people said Paul did some things that were wrong by their own laws, but no charge was worthy of jail or death. **30**When I was told that some of them were planning to kill Paul, I sent him to you at once. I also told them to tell you what they have against him.

31So the soldiers did what they were told and took Paul and brought him to the city of Antipatris that night. **32**The next day the horsemen went with Paul to Caesarea, but the other soldiers went back to the army building in Jerusalem. **33**When the horsemen came to Caesarea and gave the letter to the governor, they turned Paul over to him. **34**The governor read the letter and asked Paul, "What area are you from?" When he learned that Paul was from Cilicia, **35**he said, "I will hear your case when those who are against you come here, too." Then the governor gave orders for Paul to be kept under guard in Herod's palace.

Paul Is Accused

24 Five days later Ananias, the high priest, went to the city of Caesarea with some of the elders and a lawyer named Tertullus. They had come to make charges against Paul before the governor. **2**Paul was called into the meeting, and Tertullus began to accuse him, saying, "Most Excellent Felix! Our people enjoy much peace because of you, and many wrong things in our country are being made right through your wise help. **3**We accept these things always and in every place, and we are thankful for them. **4**But not wanting to take any more of your time, I beg you to be kind and listen to our few words. **5**We have found this man to be a troublemaker, stirring up his people everywhere in the world. He is a leader of the Nazarene group. **6**Also, he was trying to make the Temple unclean, but we stopped him. [And we wanted to judge him by our own law. **7**But the officer Lysias came and used much force to take him from us. **8**And Lysias commanded those who wanted to accuse Paul to come to you.] By asking him questions yourself, you can decide if all these things are true." **9**The others agreed and said that all of this was true.

10When the governor made a sign for Paul to speak, Paul said, "Governor Felix, I know you have been a judge over this nation for a long time. So I am happy to defend myself before you. **11**You can learn for yourself that I went to worship in Jerusalem only twelve days ago. **12**Those who are accusing me did not find me arguing with anyone in the Temple or stirring up the people in the synagogues or in the city. ¹³They cannot prove the things they are saying against me now. ¹⁴But I will tell you this: I worship the God of our ancestors as a follower of the Way of Jesus. The others say that the Way of Jesus is not the right way. But I believe everything that is taught in the law of Moses and that is written in the books of the Prophets. ¹⁵I have the same hope in God that they have—the hope that all people, good and bad, will surely be raised from the dead. ¹⁶This is why I always try to do what I believe is right before God and people."

OLD TESTAMENT READING

Your father was satisfied to have food and drink.
He did what was right and fair,
so everything went well for him.
¹⁶He helped those who were poor and needy,
so everything went well for him.
That is what it means to know God,"
says the LORD.

Jeremiah 22:15b–16

INSIGHTS

Faithfully pleasing God is an activity, not just a nice set of beliefs. It must be a way of life.

. . . Twenty years ago, people were asking the question: Does God exist? Today that question has changed to: What difference does He make? The answer for too many people is: Not much. Even for many people who have an enormous amount of Bible knowledge, God makes little difference in how they actually live their lives.

. . . If Christ . . . makes absolutely no difference in the way I live and work, then pray tell, what difference does He make?! What's the point of playing a religious game that is all talk and no action?

I take the matter of obedience as an action quite seriously. I challenge you to do the same. Whenever you're exposed to Scripture, ask yourself: How can I apply this to my life? What practical thing can I do to embed this truth in my attitude, character, and behavior? Where does it need to make a difference? That's a commitment to life-change.

DOUG SHERMAN
WILLIAM HENDRICKS

ACTION POINT

Why did Paul try to do what was right before God and men? What does God say it means to know him (Jeremiah 22:16)? Pray that you will give yourself fully to obeying God's commands!

ACTS 24:17 – 25:12

17"After being away from Jerusalem for several years, I went back to bring money to my people and to offer sacrifices. **18**I was doing this when they found me in the Temple. I had finished the cleansing ceremony and had not made any trouble; no people were gathering around me. **19**But there were some people from Asia who should be here, standing before you. If I have really done anything wrong, they are the ones who should accuse me. **20**Or ask these people here if they found any wrong in me when I stood before the council in Jerusalem. **21**But I did shout one thing when I stood before them: 'You are judging me today because I believe that people will rise from the dead!'"

22Felix already understood much about the Way of Jesus. He stopped the trial and said, "When commander Lysias comes here, I will decide your case." **23**Felix told the officer to keep Paul guarded but to give him some freedom and to let his friends bring what he needed.

Paul Speaks to Felix and His Wife

24After some days Felix came with his wife, Drusilla, who was Jewish, and asked for Paul to be brought to him. He listened to Paul talk about believing in Christ Jesus. **25**But Felix became afraid when Paul spoke about living right, self-control, and the time when God will judge the world. He said, "Go away now. When I have more time, I will call for you." **26**At the same time Felix hoped that Paul would give him some money, so he often sent for Paul and talked with him.

27But after two years, Felix was replaced by Porcius Festus as governor. But Felix had left Paul in prison to please the Jews.

Paul Asks to See Caesar

25 Three days after Festus became governor, he went from Caesarea to Jerusalem. **2**There the leading priests and the important leaders made charges against Paul before Festus. **3**They asked Festus to do them a favor. They wanted him to send Paul back to Jerusalem, because they had a plan to kill him on the way. **4**But Festus answered that Paul would be kept in Caesarea and that he himself was returning there soon. **5**He said, "Some of your leaders should go with me. They can accuse the man there in Caesarea, if he has really done something wrong."

6Festus stayed in Jerusalem another eight or ten days and then went back to Caesarea. The next day he told the soldiers to bring Paul before him. Festus was seated on the judge's seat **7**when Paul came into the room. The people who had come from Jerusalem stood around him, making serious charges against him, which they could not prove. **8**This is what Paul said to defend himself: "I have done nothing wrong against the law, against the Temple, or against Caesar."

9But Festus wanted to please the people. So he asked Paul, "Do you want to go to Jerusalem for me to judge you there on these charges?"

10Paul said, "I am standing at Caesar's judgment seat now, where I should be judged. I have done nothing wrong to them; you know this is true. **11**If I have done something wrong and the law says I must die, I do not ask to be saved from death. But if these charges are not true, then no one can give me to them. I want Caesar to hear my case!"

¹²Festus talked about this with his advisers. Then he said, "You have asked to see Caesar, so you will go to Caesar!"

INSIGHTS

If our fathers emphasized God's "awful purity" at the expense of His love, we have emphasized His love at the expense of His "awful purity." We delight in these days to say, "Gentle, gentle, gentle, is the God and Father." We have almost forgotten that cherubim and seraphim, with veiled faces, continually cry, "Holy, holy, holy is the Lord of Hosts."

In our absorption in the thought of God as Father, we have almost lost sight of the fact that He is the Holy Sovereign, ruling the world in righteousness. The result has been that to a large extent we have lost the sense of religious awe, of reverence, and of godly fear. . . .

We have only to realize that God is the Holy Sovereign, and the awe is bound to come back. . . .

To believe that an Almighty God is on the throne, working out His own holy and perfect and acceptable righteousness—is there not enough in that to fill the hearts of sinful men with "godly fear"? Is there not enough in that to make us "tremble"?

The Puritan's religion was a serious religion. He was afraid of God—afraid of Him in a worthy sense. He conceived of God as with him and about him always, and he was afraid of sinning against His holiness.

And is there not enough in the mere realization of the fact that a Holy God sits upon the throne, a God who is actively and unceasingly asserting His holiness—is there not enough in that one fact to make us, who are so prone to sin, serious and fearful?

JOHN JONES

OLD TESTAMENT READING

Then, it was as if their eyes were opened. They realized they were naked, so they sewed fig leaves together and made something to cover themselves.

⁸Then they heard the LORD God walking in the garden during the cool part of the day, and the man and his wife hid from the LORD God among the trees in the garden. ⁹But the LORD God called to the man and said, "Where are you?"

¹⁰The man answered, "I heard you walking in the garden, and I was afraid because I was naked, so I hid."

Genesis 3:7–10

ACTION POINT
How do you respond to God's insistence on purity and his declarations of coming judgment? Pray that God will convince you of his holiness and your need for him!

ACTS 25:13 — 26:8

Paul Before King Agrippa

13A few days later King Agrippa and Bernice came to Caesarea to visit Festus. **14**They stayed there for some time, and Festus told the king about Paul's case. Festus said, "There is a man that Felix left in prison. **15**When I went to Jerusalem, the leading priests and the elders there made charges against him, asking me to sentence him to death. **16**But I answered, 'When a man is accused of a crime, Romans do not hand him over until he has been allowed to face his accusers and defend himself against their charges.' **17**So when these people came here to Caesarea for the trial, I did not waste time. The next day I sat on the judge's seat and commanded that the man be brought in. **18**They stood up and accused him, but not of any serious crime as I thought they would. **19**The things they said were about their own religion and about a man named Jesus who died. But Paul said that he is still alive. **20**Not knowing how to find out about these questions, I asked Paul, 'Do you want to go to Jerusalem and be judged there?' **21**But he asked to be kept in Caesarea. He wants a decision from the emperor. So I ordered that he be held until I could send him to Caesar."

22Agrippa said to Festus, "I would also like to hear this man myself."

Festus said, "Tomorrow you will hear him."

23The next day Agrippa and Bernice appeared with great show, acting like very important people. They went into the judgment room with the army leaders and the important men of Caesarea.

Then Festus ordered the soldiers to bring Paul in. **24**Festus said, "King Agrippa and all who are gathered here with us, you see this man. All the people, here and in Jerusalem, have complained to me about him, shouting that he should not live any longer. **25**When I judged him, I found no reason to order his death. But since he asked to be judged by Caesar, I decided to send him. **26**But I have nothing definite to write the emperor about him. So I have brought him before all of you— especially you, King Agrippa. I hope you can question him and give me something to write. **27**I think it is foolish to send a prisoner to Caesar without telling what charges are against him."

Paul Defends Himself

Agrippa said to Paul, "You may now speak to defend yourself."

Then Paul raised his hand and began to speak. **2**He said, "King Agrippa, I am very blessed to stand before you and will answer all the charges the evil people make against me. **3**You know so much about all the customs and the things they argue about, so please listen to me patiently.

4"All my people know about my whole life, how I lived from the beginning in my own country and later in Jerusalem. **5**They have known me for a long time. If they want to, they can tell you that I was a good Pharisee. And the Pharisees obey the laws of my tradition more carefully than any other group. **6**Now I am on trial because I hope for the promise that God made to our ancestors. **7**This is the promise that the twelve tribes of our people hope to receive as they serve God day and night. My king, they have accused me because I hope for this same promise! **8**Why do any of you people think it is impossible for God to raise people from the dead?"

OLD TESTAMENT READING

The LORD spared me because I did what was right.
> Because I have not done evil, he has rewarded me.

22I have followed the ways of the LORD;
> I have not done evil by turning from my God.

23I remember all his laws
> and have not broken his rules.

24I am innocent before him;
> I have kept myself from doing evil.

25The LORD rewarded me because I did what was right,
> because I did what the LORD said was right."

2 Samuel 22:21–25

Then the LORD said to Satan, "Have you noticed my servant Job? No one else on earth is like him. He is an honest and innocent man, honoring God and staying away from evil. You caused me to ruin him for no good reason, but he continues to be without blame."

Job 2:3

INSIGHTS

We must show nonbelievers what it looks like to be at peace with ourselves, and to truly love other people. The best means of creating an interest in Christ and the Christian way of life is to so thoroughly live and enjoy it that others will want to know how they, too, can have it.

. . . Most Americans believe that you cannot tell a born-again Christian from nonbelievers because there is no difference in the way they live. The only distinction, people say, is that Christians are more religious, more fanatical or more closed-minded. There is no widespread sense that the religious experience of Christians has changed the fabric of our thinking or the nature of our life-styles (other than requiring regular participation in church activities).

To convince a hardened and cynical world that we are not just different, but better off for those differences, we must allow them to see how our struggles in life have been altered for the better as a result of our relationship with Christ.

GEORGE BARNA

APPLICATION

How might Paul's testimony to King Agrippa have been different if he hadn't been so careful to live in a way that honored God? Is living in a way that pleases God most important to you? Pray that your life will make a positive difference in the world around you!

ACTS 26:9-32

9"I, too, thought I ought to do many things against Jesus from Nazareth. 10And that is what I did in Jerusalem. The leading priests gave me the power to put many of God's people in jail, and when they were being killed, I agreed it was a good thing. 11In every synagogue, I often punished them and tried to make them speak against Jesus. I was so angry against them I even went to other cities to find them and punish them.

12"One time the leading priests gave me permission and the power to go to Damascus. 13On the way there, at noon, I saw a light from heaven. It was brighter than the sun and flashed all around me and those who were traveling with me. 14We all fell to the ground. Then I heard a voice speaking to me in the Hebrew language, saying, 'Saul, Saul, why are you persecuting me? You are only hurting yourself by fighting me.' 15I said, 'Who are you, Lord?' The Lord said, 'I am Jesus, the one you are persecuting. 16Stand up! I have chosen you to be my servant and my witness— you will tell people the things that you have seen and the things that I will show you. This is why I have come to you today. 17I will keep you safe from your own people and also from the others. I am sending you to them 18to open their eyes so that they may turn away from darkness to the light, away from the power of Satan and to God. Then their sins can be forgiven, and they can have a place with those people who have been made holy by believing in me.'

19"King Agrippa, after I had this vision from heaven, I obeyed it. 20I began telling people that they should change their hearts and lives and turn to God and do things to show they really had changed. I told this first to those in Damascus, then in Jerusalem, and in every part of Judea, and also to the other people. 21This is why the Jews took me and were trying to kill me in the Temple. 22But God has helped me, and so I stand here today, telling all people, small and great, what I have seen. But I am saying only what Moses and the prophets said would happen— 23that the Christ would die, and as the first to rise from the dead, he would bring light to all people."

Paul Tries to Persuade Agrippa

24While Paul was saying these things to defend himself, Festus said loudly, "Paul, you are out of your mind! Too much study has driven you crazy!"

25Paul said, "Most excellent Festus, I am not crazy. My words are true and sensible. 26King Agrippa knows about these things, and I can speak freely to him. I know he has heard about all of these things, because they did not happen off in a corner. 27King Agrippa, do you believe what the prophets wrote? I know you believe."

28King Agrippa said to Paul, "Do you think you can persuade me to become a Christian in such a short time?"

29Paul said, "Whether it is a short or a long time, I pray to God that not only you but every person listening to me today would be saved and be like me—except for these chains I have."

30Then King Agrippa, Governor Festus, Ber-

nice, and all the people sitting with them stood up
³¹and left the room. Talking to each other, they said, "There is no reason why this man should die or be put in jail." ³²And Agrippa said to Festus, "We could let this man go free, but he has asked Caesar to hear his case."

OLD TESTAMENT READING

Are there any gods like you, Lord?
  There are no gods like you.
  You are wonderfully holy,
  amazingly powerful,
  a worker of miracles.
¹²You reached out with your right hand,
  and the earth swallowed our enemies.
¹³You keep your loving promise
  and lead the people you have saved.
  With your strength you will guide them
  to your holy place.

¹⁴"The other nations will hear this and tremble
  with fear."

Exodus 15:11–14a

Obey these laws carefully, in order to show the other nations that you have wisdom and understanding. When they hear about these laws, they will say, "This great nation of Israel is wise and understanding."

Deuteronomy 4:6

INSIGHTS

The best instrument for evangelism is the ordinary church member bearing witness to a vital faith. It always has been; it always will be. . . .

There is a high probability that if you are a Christian, it is because a member of the church invited you and then some of the people of the church loved you into making a decision for Christ. Generally, people are led into a personal relationship with Christ because there have been church members who cared enough to talk to them and love them into the Kingdom. . . .

. . . Our lifestyle as Christians should be a testimony to the validity of our message, but if we had to be spiritually perfect in order to witness for Christ, no one would qualify. . . . According to Paul, we must share the gospel while we are still in the process of changing into truly Christianized people. He wanted us to know that if we wait until we are the kind of people we ought to be before witnessing, we will never get the evangelistic job done. As imperfect people who are heirs to the grace of God, we are called to invite people to join us as we strive together to become more and more like Christ.

TONY CAMPOLO

APPLICATION

Have you ever felt unworthy to be God's witness? Despite your feelings, how is God making his name known through you? Pray to be a diligent and faithful witness!

ACTS 27:1-26

Paul Sails for Rome

27 It was decided that we would sail for Italy. An officer named Julius, who served in the emperor's army, guarded Paul and some other prisoners. **2**We got on a ship that was from the city of Adramyttium and was about to sail to different ports in Asia. Aristarchus, a man from the city of Thessalonica in Macedonia, went with us. **3**The next day we came to Sidon. Julius was very good to Paul and gave him freedom to go visit his friends, who took care of his needs. **4**We left Sidon and sailed close to the island of Cyprus, because the wind was blowing against us. **5**We went across the sea by Cilicia and Pamphylia and landed at the city of Myra, in Lycia. **6**There the officer found a ship from Alexandria that was going to Italy, so he put us on it.

7We sailed slowly for many days. We had a hard time reaching Cnidus because the wind was blowing against us, and we could not go any farther. So we sailed by the south side of the island of Crete near Salmone. **8**Sailing past it was hard. Then we came to a place called Fair Havens, near the city of Lasea.

9We had lost much time, and it was now dangerous to sail, because it was already after the Day of Cleansing. So Paul warned them, **10**"Men, I can see there will be a lot of trouble on this trip. The ship, the cargo, and even our lives may be lost." **11**But the captain and the owner of the ship did not agree with Paul, and the officer believed what the captain and owner of the ship said. **12**Since that harbor was not a good place for the ship to stay for the winter, most of the men decided that the ship should leave. They hoped we could go to Phoenix and stay there for the winter. Phoenix, a city on the island of Crete, had a harbor which faced southwest and northwest.

The Storm

13When a good wind began to blow from the south, the men on the ship thought, "This is the wind we wanted, and now we have it." So they pulled up the anchor, and we sailed very close to the island of Crete. **14**But then a very strong wind named the "northeaster" came from the island. **15**The ship was caught in it and could not sail against it. So we stopped trying and let the wind carry us. **16**When we went below a small island named Cauda, we were barely able to bring in the lifeboat. **17**After the men took the lifeboat in, they tied ropes around the ship to hold it together. The men were afraid that the ship would hit the sandbanks of Syrtis, so they lowered the sail and let the wind carry the ship. **18**The next day the storm was blowing us so hard that the men threw out some of the cargo. **19**A day later with their own hands they threw out the ship's equipment. **20**When we could not see the sun or the stars for many days, and the storm was very bad, we lost all hope of being saved.

21After the men had gone without food for a long time, Paul stood up before them and said, "Men, you should have listened to me. You should not have sailed from Crete. Then you would not have all this trouble and loss. **22**But now I tell you to cheer up because none of you will die. Only the ship will be lost. **23**Last night an angel came to me from the God I belong to and worship. **24**The angel said, 'Paul, do not be afraid. You must stand before Caesar. And God has promised you that he will save the lives of everyone sailing with you.' **25**So men, have courage. I trust in God that everything will happen as his angel told me. **26**But we will crash on an island."

INSIGHTS

The story of Jericho's conquest is a fine example of the completed promises of God. . . .

. . . On the seventh circuit of the seventh day the people shouted and the walls of Jericho fell down flat. The army of Israel entered the city unhindered and utterly destroyed all that was in the city, with one notable exception—the household of Rahab. Because they obeyed the Lord explicitly, the people saw two great promises of the Lord performed on the same day. The city of Jericho, the strongest outpost of the Canaanite defenses, had been utterly destroyed as God had promised. Likewise Rahab and her household had been spared destruction, as God had promised.

But there is one final promise of God that can be seen in the conquest of Jericho. . . . To show that God means business when He makes a promise, Joshua imprecated a solemn curse on anyone who would rebuild the now-destroyed Jericho. This curse was literally fulfilled in the fate of Heil, the Bethelite, who rebuilt Jericho in the reign of Ahab (about 925 B.C.). Heil's firstborn son, Abiram, died as he was laying the foundation for the rebuilding of Jericho. Also his youngest son, Segub, died while he was setting up the gates of the city (1 Kings 16:34). What God promises, God performs.

Whether the promise is for salvation, as in the case of Rahab, or for destruction, as in the case of Heil, the promises of God must never be taken lightly. Whatever God promises, God performs. You can count on it.

WOODROW KROLL

OLD TESTAMENT READING

Joshua, be strong and brave! You must lead these people so they can take the land that I promised their fathers I would give them. **7**Be strong and brave. Be sure to obey all the teachings my servant Moses gave you. If you follow them exactly, you will be successful in everything you do. **8**Always remember what is written in the Book of the Teachings. Study it day and night to be sure to obey everything that is written there. If you do this, you will be wise and successful in everything."

Joshua 1:6–8

PAUSE FOR REFLECTION

How did Paul and Joshua respond to God's promises? How well do you face great challenges with only the hope offered by a yet-to-be-fulfilled promise?

ACTS 27:27 — 28:11a

²⁷On the fourteenth night we were still being carried around in the Adriatic Sea. About midnight the sailors thought we were close to land, ²⁸so they lowered a rope with a weight on the end of it into the water. They found that the water was one hundred twenty feet deep. They went a little farther and lowered the rope again. It was ninety feet deep. ²⁹The sailors were afraid that we would hit the rocks, so they threw four anchors into the water and prayed for daylight to come. ³⁰Some of the sailors wanted to leave the ship, and they lowered the lifeboat, pretending they were throwing more anchors from the front of the ship. ³¹But Paul told the officer and the other soldiers, "If these men do not stay in the ship, your lives cannot be saved." ³²So the soldiers cut the ropes and let the lifeboat fall into the water.

³³Just before dawn Paul began persuading all the people to eat something. He said, "For the past fourteen days you have been waiting and watching and not eating. ³⁴Now I beg you to eat something. You need it to stay alive. None of you will lose even one hair off your heads." ³⁵After he said this, Paul took some bread and thanked God for it before all of them. He broke off a piece and began eating. ³⁶They all felt better and started eating, too. ³⁷There were two hundred seventy-six people on the ship. ³⁸When they had eaten all they wanted, they began making the ship lighter by throwing the grain into the sea.

The Ship Is Destroyed

³⁹When daylight came, the sailors saw land. They did not know what land it was, but they saw a bay with a beach and wanted to sail the ship to the beach if they could. ⁴⁰So they cut the ropes to the anchors and left the anchors in the sea. At the same time, they untied the ropes that were holding the rudders. Then they raised the front sail into the wind and sailed toward the beach. ⁴¹But the ship hit a sandbank. The front of the ship stuck there and could not move, but the back of the ship began to break up from the big waves.

⁴²The soldiers decided to kill the prisoners so none of them could swim away and escape. ⁴³But Julius, the officer, wanted to let Paul live and did not allow the soldiers to kill the prisoners. Instead he ordered everyone who could swim to jump into the water first and swim to land. ⁴⁴The rest were to follow using wooden boards or pieces of the ship, And this is how all the people made it safely to land.

Paul on the Island of Malta

 When we were safe on land, we learned that the island was called Malta. ²The people who lived there were very good to us. Because it was raining and very cold, they made a fire and welcomed all of us. ³Paul gathered a pile of sticks and was putting them on the fire when a poisonous snake came out because of the heat and bit him on the hand. ⁴The people living on the island saw the snake hanging from Paul's hand and said to each other, "This man must be a murderer! He did not die in the sea, but Justice does not want him to live." ⁵But Paul shook the snake off into the fire and was not hurt. **6**The people thought that Paul would swell up or fall down dead. They waited and watched him for a long time, but nothing bad happened to him. So they changed their minds and said, "He is a god!"

7There were some fields around there owned by Publius, an important man on the island. He welcomed us into his home and was very good to us for three days. **8**Publius' father was sick with a fever and dysentery. Paul went to him, prayed, and put his hands on the man and healed him. **9**After this, all the other sick people on the island came to Paul, and he healed them, too. **10-11**The people on the island gave us many honors. When we were ready to leave, three months later, they gave us the things we needed.

OLD TESTAMENT READING

So they picked up Jonah and threw him into the sea, and the sea became calm. **16**Then they began to fear the LORD very much; they offered a sacrifice to the LORD and made promises to him.

Jonah 1:15–16

INSIGHTS

Job did not understand the trials that came to him, but he passed the test because he could say, "'Though He slay me, I will hope in Him . . .'" (Job 13:15). Mary and Martha did not understand why Jesus waited until after Lazarus died before He came to them (John 11:21). The disciples did not understand why Jesus took them through Samaria, or why He waited at the well rather than go with them to buy food (John 4:8). Peter did not understand why Jesus let the soldiers arrest Him (John 18:10–11). Today, we understand the reason for these things because we can see the end result.

Job was tested because Satan said Job loved and served God only because of the protection and blessing God gave him. Job stood the test and Satan was defeated (Job 42:10–17).

After Jesus had raised Lazarus from the dead, Mary and Martha understood how the sickness and death of their brother had brought glory to God (John 11:43–45).

By the time they left Samaria, the disciples realized why they had to go through Samaria. A whole city, which otherwise would have been closed to them, heard the gospel and believed in Christ, all because Jesus talked to a woman while he waited at the well (John 4:39–41).

When difficulties come, we can know they have a purpose. We need not be confused. If we are in right relationship with God, we may not understand at the time, but we can know He will make all that happens to us work out for our good and His glory.

LUCILLE SOLLENBERGER

ACTION POINT

Notice how God used each of these adventures at sea to bring glory to himself. Pray for faithful confidence in God's perfect plan, even when you face the most difficult and confusing situations.

ACTS 28:11b - 31

Paul Goes to Rome

We got on a ship from Alexandria that had stayed on the island during the winter. On the front of the ship was the sign of the twin gods. **12**We stopped at Syracuse for three days. **13**From there we sailed to Rhegium. The next day a wind began to blow from the south, and a day later we came to Puteoli. **14**We found some believers there who asked us to stay with them for a week. Finally, we came to Rome. **15**The believers in Rome heard that we were there and came out as far as the Market of Appius and the Three Inns to meet us. When Paul saw them, he was encouraged and thanked God.

Paul in Rome

16When we arrived at Rome, Paul was allowed to live alone, with the soldier who guarded him.

17Three days later Paul sent for the leaders there. When they came together, he said, "Brothers, I have done nothing against our people or the customs of our ancestors. But I was arrested in Jerusalem and given to the Romans. **18**After they asked me many questions, they could find no reason why I should be killed. They wanted to let me go free, **19**but the evil people there argued against that. So I had to ask to come to Rome to have my trial before Caesar. But I have no charge to bring against my own people. **20**That is why I wanted to see you and talk with you. I am bound with this chain because I believe in the hope of Israel."

21They answered Paul, "We have received no letters from Judea about you. None of our Jewish brothers who have come from there brought news or told us anything bad about you. **22**But we want to hear your ideas, because we know that people everywhere are speaking against this religious group."

23Paul and the people chose a day for a meeting and on that day many more of the Jews met with Paul at the place he was staying. He spoke to them all day long. Using the law of Moses and the prophets' writings, he explained the kingdom of God, and he tried to persuade them to believe these things about Jesus. **24**Some believed what Paul said, but others did not. **25**So they argued and began leaving after Paul said one more thing to them: "The Holy Spirit spoke the truth to your ancestors through Isaiah the prophet, saying,

26'Go to this people and say:

You will listen and listen, but you will not
understand.
You will look and look, but you will not
learn,
27because these people have become stubborn.
They don't hear with their ears,
and they have closed their eyes.
Otherwise, they might really understand
what they see with their eyes
and hear with their ears.
They might really understand in their minds
and come back to me and be healed.'

Isaiah 6:9–10

28"I want you to know that God has also sent his salvation to all nations, and they will listen!" [**29**After Paul said this, the Jews left. They were arguing very much with each other.]

30Paul stayed two full years in his own rented house and welcomed all people who came to visit him. 31He boldly preached about the kingdom of God and taught about the Lord Jesus Christ, and no one stopped him.

INSIGHTS

Recently I finally got around to inviting a couple from our home church over for Sunday lunch. Sandy and Mike are young college graduates with promising careers and an adorable new baby. They are busy people and had not yet gotten involved in our church. I was ashamed to discover that although they'd been members of our church for nearly three years, ours was the first personal invitation they had received from anyone in our congregation. . . .

. . . In addition to providing examples of hospitality, Scripture gives us specific instructions to practice this kind of loving care for others. In his letters to Timothy and Titus, Paul listed it as a necessary qualification of an elder of the church. He combined encouragement and hospitality as important Christian traits in Titus 1:8–9. . . .

Paul's instructions in Romans 12:9–13 emphasize that this ministry of love in action belongs not just to elders, but should be a trademark of all believers. . . .

The emphasis in our practice of hospitality should be on how we give of ourselves to minister to others—not on how we perform to entertain others. The Bible commands us to carry out this ministry; it does not set up requirements for housing or meals. . . . The issue is not spending money, but spending our time—not giving things, but giving ourselves. . . .

. . . Focus on people, not preparations. In the Lord's hands, a few loaves and fishes go a long way.

RACHAEL CRABB

OLD TESTAMENT READING

Then Rebekah ran and told her mother's family about all these things. 29She had a brother named Laban. 30So he ran out to the well, and there was the man standing by the camels at the spring. 31Laban said, "Sir, you are welcome to come in; you don't have to stand outside. I have prepared the house for you and also a place for your camels."

32So Abraham's servant went into the house.

Genesis 24:28–29a, 30b–32a

PAUSE FOR REFLECTION

Do you think Paul, a prisoner, offered his guests luxurious accommodations? What do you think are the biblical standards for hospitality?

ROMANS 1:1-27

1 From Paul, a servant of Christ Jesus. God called me to be an apostle and chose me to tell the Good News.

²God promised this Good News long ago through his prophets, as it is written in the Holy Scriptures. ³⁻⁴The Good News is about God's Son, Jesus Christ our Lord. As a man, he was born from the family of David. But through the Spirit of holiness he was declared to be God's Son with great power by rising from the dead. ⁵Through Christ, God gave me the special work of an apostle, which was to lead people of all nations to believe and obey. I do this work for him. ⁶And you who are in Rome are also called to belong to Jesus Christ.

⁷To all of you in Rome whom God loves and has called to be his holy people:

Grace and peace to you from God our Father and the Lord Jesus Christ.

A Prayer of Thanks

⁸First I want to say that I thank my God through Jesus Christ for all of you, because people everywhere in the world are talking about your faith. ⁹God, whom I serve with my whole heart by telling the Good News about his Son, knows that I always mention you ¹⁰every time I pray. I pray that I will be allowed to come to you, and this will happen if God wants it. ¹¹I want very much to see you, to give you some spiritual gift to make you strong. ¹²I mean that I want us to help each other with the faith we have. Your faith will help me, and my faith will help you. ¹³Brothers and sisters, I want you to

know that I planned many times to come to you, but this has not been possible. I wanted to come so that I could help you grow spiritually as I have helped the other non-Jewish people.

¹⁴I have a duty to all people—Greeks and those who are not Greeks, the wise and the foolish. ¹⁵That is why I want so much to preach the Good News to you in Rome.

¹⁶I am not ashamed of the Good News, because it is the power God uses to save everyone who believes—to save the Jews first, and then to save non-Jews. ¹⁷The Good News shows how God makes people right with himself—that it begins and ends with faith. As the Scripture says, "But those who are right with God will live by faith."

All People Have Done Wrong

¹⁸God's anger is shown from heaven against all the evil and wrong things people do. By their own evil lives they hide the truth. ¹⁹God shows his anger because some knowledge of him has been made clear to them. Yes, God has shown himself to them. ²⁰There are things about him that people cannot see—his eternal power and all the things that make him God. But since the beginning of the world those things have been easy to understand by what God has made. So people have no excuse for the bad things they do. ²¹They knew God, but they did not give glory to God or thank him. Their thinking became useless. Their foolish minds were filled with darkness. ²²They said they were wise, but they became fools. ²³They traded the glory of God who lives forever for the worship of idols made to look like earthly people, birds, animals, and snakes.

²⁴Because they did these things, God left them

and let them go their sinful way, wanting only to do evil. As a result, they became full of sexual sin, using their bodies wrongly with each other. **25**They traded the truth of God for a lie. They worshiped and served what had been created instead of the God who created those things, who should be praised forever. Amen.

26Because people did those things, God left them and let them do the shameful things they wanted to do. Women stopped having natural sex and started having sex with other women. **27**In the same way, men stopped having natural sex and began wanting each other. Men did shameful things with other men, and in their bodies they received the punishment for those wrongs.

OLD TESTAMENT READING

The heavens declare the glory of God,
   and the skies announce what his hands
      have made.
2Day after day they tell the story;
   night after night they tell it again.
3They have no speech or words;
   they have no voice to be heard.
4But their message goes out through all the
      world;
   their words go everywhere on earth.

Psalm 19:1–4a

INSIGHTS

This is my Father's world,
And to my listening ears
All nature sings, and round me rings
The music of the spheres.
This is my Father's world:
I rest me in the thought
Of rocks and trees, of skies and seas—
His hand the wonders wrought.

This is my Father's world,
The birds their carols raise,
The morning light, the lily white,
Declare their Maker's praise.
This is my Father's world:
He shines in all that's fair;
In the rustling grass I hear Him pass,
He speaks to me everywhere.

This is my Father's world,
O let me ne'er forget
That though the wrong seems oft so
   strong,
God is the Ruler yet.
This is my Father's world:
The battle is not done;
Jesus who died shall be satisfied,
And earth and heav'n be one.

MALTBIE BABCOCK

PAUSE FOR REFLECTION
According to Paul, what excuses do people have for not knowing God? What testifies to God's glory and goodness? Describe how God's creation has influenced your beliefs about God.

ROMANS 1:28 — 2:16

28People did not think it was important to have a true knowledge of God. So God left them and allowed them to have their own worthless thinking and to do things they should not do. **29**They are filled with every kind of sin, evil, selfishness, and hatred. They are full of jealousy, murder, fighting, lying, and thinking the worst about each other. They gossip **30**and say evil things about each other. They hate God. They are rude and conceited and brag about themselves. They invent ways of doing evil. They do not obey their parents. **31**They are foolish, they do not keep their promises, and they show no kindness or mercy to others. **32**They know God's law says that those who live like this should die. But they themselves not only continue to do these evil things, they applaud others who do them.

You People Also Are Sinful

If you think you can judge others, you are wrong. When you judge them, you are really judging yourself guilty, because you do the same things they do. **2**God judges those who do wrong things, and we know that his judging is right. **3**You judge those who do wrong, but you do wrong yourselves. Do you think you will be able to escape the judgment of God? **4**He has been very kind and patient, waiting for you to change, but you think nothing of his kindness. Perhaps you do not understand that God is kind to you so you will change your hearts and lives. **5**But you are stubborn and refuse to change, so you are making

your own punishment even greater on the day he shows his anger. On that day everyone will see God's right judgments. **6**God will reward or punish every person for what that person has done. **7**Some people, by always continuing to do good, live for God's glory, for honor, and for life that has no end. God will give them life forever. **8**But other people are selfish. They refuse to follow truth and, instead, follow evil. God will give them his punishment and anger. **9**He will give trouble and suffering to everyone who does evil—to the Jews first and also to those who are not Jews. **10**But he will give glory, honor, and peace to everyone who does good—to the Jews first and also to those who are not Jews. **11**For God judges all people in the same way.

12People who do not have the law and who are sinners will be lost, although they do not have the law. And, in the same way, those who have the law and are sinners will be judged by the law. **13**Hearing the law does not make people right with God. It is those who obey the law who will be right with him. **14**(Those who are not Jews do not have the law, but when they freely do what the law commands, they are the law for themselves. This is true even though they do not have the law. **15**They show that in their hearts they know what is right and wrong, just as the law commands. And they show this by their consciences. Sometimes their thoughts tell them they did wrong, and sometimes their thoughts tell them they did right.) **16**All these things will happen on the day when God, through Christ Jesus, will judge people's secret thoughts. The Good News that I preach says this.

OLD TESTAMENT READING

The LORD hates what evil people do,
but he loves those who do what is right.

¹⁰The person who quits doing what is right will
be punished,

and the one who hates to be corrected will
die.

¹¹The LORD knows what is happening in the
world of the dead,
so he surely knows the thoughts of the living.

Proverbs 15:9–11

INSIGHTS

The Bible's proclamation of God's work as Judge is part of its witness to His character. It confirms what is said elsewhere of His moral perfection, His righteousness and justice, His wisdom, omniscience, and omnipotence. It shows us also that the heart of the justice which expresses God's nature is retribution, the rendering to men what they have deserved; for this is the essence of the judge's task. To reward good with good, and evil with evil, is natural to God. So, when the New Testament speaks of the final judgment, it always represents it in terms of retribution. God will judge all men, it says, 'according to their works' (Matthew 16:27; Revelation 20:12f.). Paul amplifies. 'God . . . will render to every man according to his deeds: to them who by patient continuance in well doing seek for glory and honour and immortality, eternal life; but unto them that are contentious, and do not obey the truth, but obey unrighteousness, indignation and wrath; tribulation and anguish, upon every soul of man that doeth evil . . . but glory, honour, and peace, to every man that worketh good' . . . for there is no respect of persons throughout: Christians, as well as non-Christians, will receive 'according to their works'. . . .

Thus retribution appears as a natural and predetermined expression of the divine character. God has resolved to be every man's Judge, rewarding every man according to his works. Retribution is the inescapable moral law of creation; God will see that each man sooner or later receives what he deserves—if not here, then hereafter.

J. I. PACKER

PAUSE FOR REFLECTION

What do people do when God gives them freedom to do as they please? What does God, in his kindness, wait for people to do? What will God, the Judge of the earth, do when people refuse to change their hearts and live in obedience to him?

ROMANS 2:17 — 3:18

The Jews and the Law

17 What about you? You call yourself a Jew. You trust in the law of Moses and brag that you are close to God. **18** You know what he wants you to do and what is important, because you have learned the law. **19** You think you are a guide for the blind and a light for those who are in darkness. **20** You think you can show foolish people what is right and teach those who know nothing. You have the law; so you think you know everything and have all truth. **21** You teach others, so why don't you teach yourself? You tell others not to steal, but you steal. **22** You say that others must not take part in adultery, but you are guilty of that sin. You hate idols, but you steal from temples. **23** You brag about having God's law, but you bring shame to God by breaking his law, **24** just as the Scriptures say: "Those who are not Jews speak against God's name because of you."

25 If you follow the law, your circumcision has meaning. But if you break the law, it is as if you were never circumcised. **26** People who are not Jews are not circumcised, but if they do what the law says, it is as if they were circumcised. **27** You Jews have the written law and circumcision, but you break the law. So those who are not circumcised in their bodies, but still obey the law, will show that you are guilty. **28** They can do this because a person is not a true Jew if he is only a Jew in his physical body; true circumcision is not only on the outside of the body. **29** A person is a Jew only if he is a Jew inside; true circumcision is

done in the heart by the Spirit, not by the written law. Such a person gets praise from God rather than from people.

3 So, do Jews have anything that other people do not have? Is there anything special about being circumcised? **2** Yes, of course, there is in every way. The most important thing is this: God trusted the Jews with his teachings. **3** If some Jews were not faithful to him, will that stop God from doing what he promised? **4** No! God will continue to be true even when every person is false. As the Scriptures say:

"So you will be shown to be right when you
     speak,
     and you will win your case."   *Psalm 51:4*

5 When we do wrong, that shows more clearly that God is right. So can we say that God is wrong to punish us? (I am talking as people might talk.) **6** No! If God could not punish us, he could not judge the world.

7 A person might say, "When I lie, it really gives him glory, because my lie shows God's truth. So why am I judged a sinner?" **8** It would be the same to say, "We should do evil so that good will come." Some people find fault with us and say we teach this, but they are wrong and deserve the punishment they will receive.

All People Are Guilty

9 So are we Jews better than others? No! We have already said that Jews and those who are not Jews are all guilty of sin. **10** As the Scriptures say:

"There is no one who always does what is
     right,
     not even one.

11 There is no one who understands.
  There is no one who looks to God for
      help.
12 All have turned away.
  Together, everyone has become useless.
There is no one who does anything good;
      there is not even one." *Psalm 14:1–3*
13 "Their throats are like open graves;
  they use their tongues for telling lies."
                              Psalm 5:9
  "Their words are like snake poison."
                              Psalm 140:3
14 "Their mouths are full of cursing and
      hate." *Psalm 10:7*
15 "They are always ready to kill people.
16 Everywhere they go they cause ruin and
      misery.
17 They don't know how to live in peace."
                              Isaiah 59:7–8
18 "They have no fear of God." *Psalm 36:1*

OLD TESTAMENT READING

This is what the LORD All-Powerful, the God of Israel, says: Change your lives and do what is right! Then I will let you live in this place. **5** You must change your lives and do what is right. Be fair to each other. **6** You must not be hard on strangers, orphans, and widows. Don't kill innocent people in this place! Don't follow other gods, or they will ruin your lives.

                              Jeremiah 7:3, 5–6

INSIGHTS

Everywhere Jesus went He proclaimed the twofold message of repentance and faith in God (Mark 1:15). The faith He proclaimed was not mere mental assent, but the kind of faith that produces change in people's lives. There is no such thing as biblical faith that does not produce obedience. . . .

It is important to note that the Bible identifies both a true and a false repentance. Second Corinthians 7:10 says, "Godly grief produces a repentance that leads to salvation and brings no regret, but worldly grief produces death." Godly grief is true repentance, and true repentance is more than contrition. A person may be sorrowful over his sins yet unrepentant because he is sorrowing for the wrong reasons. Instead of sorrowing because his sins have hurt and disappointed God, he may just feel bad because his sins have been personally painful, stressful, or costly, or because his sins have been found out. If there is no change in character, there has been no true repentance. . . .

The results of false repentance are seen everywhere in the church. Hearts are unbroken. Sin is covered up. . . . And many professing Christians do not walk in the light with God and one another. The fruit of true repentance is a change of mind, heart, and behavior.

                              FLOYD MCCLUNG

PAUSE FOR REFLECTION

What value does God place on outward signs of obedience to his law? How does God want his people to live?

ROMANS 3:19 — 4:12

¹⁹We know that the law's commands are for those who have the law. This stops all excuses and brings the whole world under God's judgment, ²⁰because no one can be made right with God by following the law. The law only shows us our sin.

How God Makes People Right

²¹But God has a way to make people right with him without the law, and he has now shown us that way which the law and the prophets told us about. ²²God makes people right with himself through their faith in Jesus Christ. This is true for all who believe in Christ, because all people are the same: ²³Everyone has sinned and fallen short of God's glorious standard, ²⁴and all need to be made right with God by his grace, which is a free gift. They need to be made free from sin through Jesus Christ. ²⁵God sent him to die in our place to take away our sins. We receive forgiveness through faith in the blood of Jesus' death. This showed that God always does what is right and fair, as in the past when he was patient and did not punish people for their sins. ²⁶And God gave Jesus to show today that he does what is right. God did this so he could judge rightly and so he could make right any person who has faith in Jesus.

²⁷So do we have a reason to brag about ourselves? No! And why not? It is the way of faith that stops all bragging, not the way of trying to obey the law. ²⁸A person is made right with God through faith, not through obeying the law. ²⁹Is

God only the God of the Jews? Is he not also the God of those who are not Jews? ³⁰Of course he is, because there is only one God. He will make Jews right with him by their faith, and he will also make those who are not Jews right with him through their faith. ³¹So do we destroy the law by following the way of faith? No! Faith causes us to be what the law truly wants.

The Example of Abraham

4 So what can we say that Abraham, the father of our people, learned about faith? ²If Abraham was made right by the things he did, he had a reason to brag. But this is not God's view, ³because the Scripture says, "Abraham believed God, and God accepted Abraham's faith, and that faith made him right with God."

⁴When people work, their pay is not given as a gift, but as something earned. ⁵But people cannot do any work that will make them right with God. So they must trust in him, who makes even evil people right in his sight. Then God accepts their faith, and that makes them right with him. ⁶David said the same thing. He said that people are truly blessed when God, without paying attention to their deeds, makes people right with himself.

⁷"Blessed are they
  whose sins are forgiven,
  whose wrongs are pardoned.
⁸Blessed is the person
  whom the Lord does not consider guilty."

Psalm 32:1–2

⁹Is this blessing only for those who are circumcised or also for those who are not circumcised? We have already said that God accepted Abraham's faith and that faith made him right with

God. **10**So how did this happen? Did God accept Abraham before or after he was circumcised? It was before his circumcision. **11**Abraham was circumcised to show that he was right with God through faith before he was circumcised. So Abraham is the father of all those who believe but are not circumcised; he is the father of all believers who are accepted as being right with God. **12**And Abraham is also the father of those who have been circumcised and who live following the faith that our father Abraham had before he was circumcised.

OLD TESTAMENT READING

Wicked people have many troubles,
    but the LORD's love surrounds those who
        trust him.
11Good people, rejoice and be happy in the
    LORD.
    Sing all you whose hearts are right.

Psalm 32:10–11

INSIGHTS

Faith is believing that Christ is what He is said to be and that He will do what He has promised to do, and then to expect this of Him. The Scriptures speak of Jesus Christ as being God in human flesh, as being perfect in His character, as being made a sin offering on our behalf, as bearing our sins in His own body on the tree. . . . The sacred records further tell us that He "rose again" (1 Co 15:4) from the dead, that He "ever liveth to make intercession for us" (Heb 7:25), that He has gone up into glory and has taken possession of heaven on the behalf of His people, and that he will shortly come again "to judge the . . . world with righteousness, and the peoples with equity" (Ps 98:9, ASV). . . .

. . . Jesus is what He is said to be. Jesus will do what He says He will do. Therefore, we must each trust Him, saying, "He will be to me what He says He is, and He will do to me what He has promised to do. I leave myself in the hands of Him who is appointed to save, that he may save me. I rest upon His promise that He will do even as He has said." This is saving faith, and he that has it has everlasting life. Whatever his dangers and difficulties, whatever his darkness and depression, whatever his infirmities and sins, he that believes thus on Christ Jesus is not condemned, and shall never come into condemnation.

CHARLES SPURGEON

PAUSE FOR REFLECTION

How are people made right with God? Who can be made right with God? How did God enable us to be made right with him? How does God bless those who trust him? Have you received that blessing?

ROMANS 4:13 – 5:11

God Keeps His Promise

13Abraham and his descendants received the promise that they would get the whole world. He did not receive that promise through the law, but through being right with God by his faith. **14**If people could receive what God promised by following the law, then faith is worthless. And God's promise to Abraham is worthless, **15**because the law can only bring God's anger. But if there is no law, there is nothing to disobey.

16So people receive God's promise by having faith. This happens so the promise can be a free gift. Then all of Abraham's children can have that promise. It is not only for those who live under the law of Moses but for anyone who lives with faith like that of Abraham, who is the father of us all. **17**As it is written in the Scriptures: "I am making you a father of many nations." This is true before God, the God Abraham believed, the God who gives life to the dead and who creates something out of nothing.

18There was no hope that Abraham would have children. But Abraham believed God and continued hoping, and so he became the father of many nations. As God told him, "Your descendants also will be too many to count." **19**Abraham was almost a hundred years old, much past the age for having children, and Sarah could not have children. Abraham thought about all this, but his faith in God did not become weak. **20**He never doubted that God would keep his promise, and he never stopped believing. He grew stronger in his faith

and gave praise to God. **21**Abraham felt sure that God was able to do what he had promised. **22**So, "God accepted Abraham's faith, and that faith made him right with God." **23**Those words ("God accepted Abraham's faith") were written not only for Abraham **24**but also for us. God will accept us also because we believe in the One who raised Jesus our Lord from the dead. **25**Jesus was given to die for our sins, and he was raised from the dead to make us right with God.

Right with God

Since we have been made right with God by our faith, we have peace with God. This happened through our Lord Jesus Christ, **2**who through our faith has brought us into that blessing of God's grace that we now enjoy. And we are happy because of the hope we have of sharing God's glory. **3**We also have joy with our troubles, because we know that these troubles produce patience. **4**And patience produces character, and character produces hope. **5**And this hope will never disappoint us, because God has poured out his love to fill our hearts. He gave us his love through the Holy Spirit, whom God has given to us.

6When we were unable to help ourselves, at the right time, Christ died for us, although we were living against God. **7**Very few people will die to save the life of someone else. Although perhaps for a good person someone might possibly die. **8**But God shows his great love for us in this way: Christ died for us while we were still sinners.

9So through Christ we will surely be saved from God's anger, because we have been made right with God by the blood of Christ's death.

[10]While we were God's enemies, he made us his friends through the death of his Son. Surely, now that we are his friends, he will save us through his Son's life. [11]And not only that, but now we are also very happy in God through our Lord Jesus Christ. Through him we are now God's friends again.

OLD TESTAMENT READING

But I pray to you, LORD, for favor.
  God, because of your great love, answer
    me.
  You are truly able to save.

Psalm 69:13

I will tell about the LORD's kindness
  and praise him for everything he has done.
I will praise the LORD for the many good
    things he has given us
  and for his goodness to the people of
    Israel.
He has shown great mercy to us
  and has been very kind to us.
[8]He said, "These are my people;
  my children will not lie to me."
So he saved them.
[9]When they suffered, he suffered also.
  He sent his own angel to save them.
Because of his love and kindness, he saved
    them.

Isaiah 63:7–9c

INSIGHTS

May God through His Holy Spirit teach you to cherish the unfathomable mystery of His love. Jesus said, "None is good save one, even God." The glory of God in heaven is that everything He wills and does is good. . . .

The God who wills only good is a God of love. He does not seek His own. He does not live for himself. He pours out His love upon all living creatures. . . .

Love "seeketh not her own." Love finds happiness in giving to others. Love sacrifices wholly for others. Therefore, God offered himself to us in the person of His Son. And the Son offered himself upon the cross to bring love to us and to win our hearts. The everlasting love with which the Father loves the Son is the same love with which the Son loves us. This same love of the Father, Jesus Christ has poured into our hearts through the Holy Spirit. God desires that our whole life be permeated with this love's vital power. . . .

. . . Love is the power of the Godhead: in the Father, Son, and Holy Spirit. All who are members of the body of Christ possess the love of God, and this love streams forth from them to take the whole world within its compass.

ANDREW MURRAY

ACTION POINT

When we place our faith in God's love, what are the results? Write your own psalm of thanksgiving, praising God for his gift of love.

ROMANS 5:12 – 6:14

Adam and Christ Compared

12Sin came into the world because of what one man did, and with sin came death. This is why everyone must die—because everyone sinned. **13**Sin was in the world before the law of Moses, but sin is not counted against us as breaking a command when there is no law. **14**But from the time of Adam to the time of Moses, everyone had to die, even those who had not sinned by breaking a command, as Adam had.

Adam was like the One who was coming in the future. **15**But God's free gift is not like Adam's sin. Many people died because of the sin of that one man. But the grace from God was much greater; many people received God's gift of life by the grace of the one man, Jesus Christ. **16**After Adam sinned once, he was judged guilty. But the gift of God is different. God's free gift came after many sins, and it makes people right with God. **17**One man sinned, and so death ruled all people because of that one man. But now those people who accept God's full grace and the great gift of being made right with him will surely have true life and rule through the one man, Jesus Christ.

18So as one sin of Adam brought the punishment of death to all people, one good act that Christ did makes all people right with God. And that brings true life for all. **19**One man disobeyed God, and many became sinners. In the same way, one man obeyed God, and many will be made right. **20**The law came to make sin worse. But when sin grew worse, God's grace increased. **21**Sin once used death to rule us, but God gave people more of his grace so that grace could rule by making people right with him. And this brings life forever through Jesus Christ our Lord.

Dead to Sin but Alive in Christ

So do you think we should continue sinning so that God will give us even more grace? **2**No! We died to our old sinful lives, so how can we continue living with sin? **3**Did you forget that all of us became part of Christ when we were baptized? We shared his death in our baptism. **4**When we were baptized, we were buried with Christ and shared his death. So, just as Christ was raised from the dead by the wonderful power of the Father, we also can live a new life.

5Christ died, and we have been joined with him by dying too. So we will also be joined with him by rising from the dead as he did. **6**We know that our old life died with Christ on the cross so that our sinful selves would have no power over us and we would not be slaves to sin. **7**Anyone who has died is made free from sin's control.

8If we died with Christ, we know we will also live with him. **9**Christ was raised from the dead, and we know that he cannot die again. Death has no power over him now. **10**Yes, when Christ died, he died to defeat the power of sin one time— enough for all time. He now has a new life, and his new life is with God. **11**In the same way, you should see yourselves as being dead to the power of sin and alive with God through Christ Jesus.

12So, do not let sin control your life here on earth so that you do what your sinful self wants to do. **13**Do not offer the parts of your body to serve sin, as things to be used in doing evil. Instead, offer yourselves to God as people who have died and now live. Offer the parts of your body to God to be used in doing good. ¹⁴Sin will not be your master, because you are not under law but under God's grace.

INSIGHTS

If we would know what Christ wants to be to us, we must first of all know Him as our Saviour from sin. When the angel came down from heaven to proclaim that He was to be born into the world, you remember he gave His name, "He shall be called Jesus, for he shall save his people from their sins." HAVE WE BEEN DELIVERED FROM SIN? He did not come to save us in our sins, but from our sins. . . .

Let us look at Him as He hangs upon the Cross, and see how He has put away sin. He was manifested that He might take away our sins. . . .

But Christ is not only a Saviour. I might save a man from drowning and rescue him from an untimely grave; but I might probably not be able to do any more for him. Christ is something more than a Saviour. When the children of Israel were placed behind the blood, that blood was their salvation; but they would still have heard the crack of the slave-driver's whip, if they had not been delivered from the Egyptian yoke of bondage: then it was that God delivered them from the hand of the King of Egypt. I have little sympathy with the idea that God comes down to save us, and then leaves us in prison, the slaves of our besetting sins. No; He has come to deliver us, and to give us victory over our evil tempers, our passions, and our lusts. Are you a professed Christian, but one who is a slave to some besetting sin? If you want to get victory over that temper or that lust, go on to know Christ more intimately. He brings deliverance for the past, the present, and the future.

D. L. MOODY

OLD TESTAMENT READING

So, say this to the people of Judah and those who live in Jerusalem: 'This is what the LORD says: I am preparing disaster for you and making plans against you. So stop doing evil. Change your ways and do what is right.' ¹²But the people of Judah will answer, 'It won't do any good to try! We will continue to do what we want. Each of us will do what his stubborn, evil heart wants!' "

Jeremiah 18:11–12

APPLICATION

In your own words, describe what the burden of sin does to people. How have you been enslaved to sin? Does your life give evidence that you are no longer a slave to sin? What can you do so that God will truly be your master?

ROMANS 6:15 – 7:13

Be Slaves of Righteousness

15So what should we do? Should we sin because we are under grace and not under law? No! **16**Surely you know that when you give yourselves like slaves to obey someone, then you are really slaves of that person. The person you obey is your master. You can follow sin, which brings spiritual death, or you can obey God, which makes you right with him. **17**In the past you were slaves to sin—sin controlled you. But thank God, you fully obeyed the things that you were taught. **18**You were made free from sin, and now you are slaves to goodness. **19**I use this example because this is hard for you to understand. In the past you offered the parts of your body to be slaves to sin and evil; you lived only for evil. In the same way now you must give yourselves to be slaves of goodness. Then you will live only for God.

20In the past you were slaves to sin, and goodness did not control you. **21**You did evil things, and now you are ashamed of them. Those things only bring death. **22**But now you are free from sin and have become slaves of God. This brings you a life that is only for God, and this gives you life forever. **23**The payment for sin is death. But God gives us the free gift of life forever in Christ Jesus our Lord.

An Example from Marriage

7 Brothers and sisters, all of you understand the law of Moses. So surely you know that the law rules over people only while they are alive. **2**For example, a woman must stay married to her husband as long as he is alive. But if her husband dies, she is free from the law of marriage. **3**But if she marries another man while her husband is still alive, the law says she is guilty of adultery. But if her husband dies, she is free from the law of marriage. Then if she marries another man, she is not guilty of adultery.

4In the same way, my brothers and sisters, your old selves died, and you became free from the law through the body of Christ. This happened so that you might belong to someone else—the One who was raised from the dead—and so that we might be used in service to God. **5**In the past, we were ruled by our sinful selves. The law made us want to do sinful things that controlled our bodies, so the things we did were bringing us death. **6**In the past, the law held us like prisoners, but our old selves died, and we were made free from the law. So now we serve God in a new way with the Spirit, and not in the old way with written rules.

Our Fight Against Sin

7You might think I am saying that sin and the law are the same thing. That is not true. But the law was the only way I could learn what sin meant. I would never have known what it means to want to take something belonging to someone else if the law had not said, "You must not want to take your neighbor's things." **8**And sin found a way to use that command and cause me to want all kinds of things I should not want. But without the law, sin has no power. **9**I was alive before I knew the law. But when the law's command came to me, then sin began to live, **10**and I died. The command was meant to bring life, but for me it brought death. **11**Sin found a way to fool me by using the command to make me die.

¹²So the law is holy, and the command is holy and right and good. ¹³Does this mean that something that is good brought death to me? No! Sin used something that is good to bring death to me. This happened so that I could see what sin is really like; the command was used to show that sin is very evil.

OLD TESTAMENT READING

You are holy people who belong to the LORD your God. He has chosen you from all the people on earth to be his very own.

⁷The LORD did not care for you and choose you because there were many of you—you are the smallest nation of all. ⁸But the LORD chose you because he loved you, and he kept his promise to your ancestors. So he brought you out of Egypt by his great power and freed you from the land of slavery, from the power of the king of Egypt.

Deuteronomy 7:6–8

INSIGHTS

We are chosen to be holy. This is what the word "saint" means. In Greek, the word is hagios, meaning holy, set apart, and belonging to God. It does not mean the spiritual elitism of a "Holy Joe" or the aloof smugness of a "Perfect Pat." Rather, it indicates ownership. God says to us, "You belong to Me!"

When Paul addressed the saints, he was not writing to church leaders or to spiritually advanced people. Rather, Paul wrote to all of God's people who stood equally with him as those chosen, called, and cherished.

We, then, can also enjoy our status as loved and forgiven people.

This is a lofty thought, but what does it mean practically? Nothing less than that all we are and have belongs to God. This means our minds, emotions, will and bodies belong to God. We expand God's reign in our lives to include the people, the possessions, and the plans of our lives. And we don't stop here. Our list grows to include the memories that shape our present and the values that etch our future. . . . We must also remember that our money is holy, too.

Choosing to be chosen means accepting Christ's lordship over our total lives. This requires our committed surrender to Him.

LLOYD OGILVIE

APPLICATION

Describe as fully as you can what it means to be a slave to sin. Describe what it means to belong to God. What difference does belonging to God make in a person's life? In your life? Have you surrendered to him as your Lord?

ROMANS 7:14 — 8:17

The War Within Us

14We know that the law is spiritual, but I am not spiritual since sin rules me as if I were its slave. **15**I do not understand the things I do. I do not do what I want to do, and I do the things I hate. **16**And if I do not want to do the hated things I do, that means I agree that the law is good. **17**But I am not really the one who is doing these hated things; it is sin living in me that does them. **18**Yes, I know that nothing good lives in me—I mean nothing good lives in the part of me that is earthly and sinful. I want to do the things that are good, but I do not do them. **19**I do not do the good things I want to do, but I do the bad things I do not want to do. **20**So if I do things I do not want to do, then I am not the one doing them. It is sin living in me that does those things.

21So I have learned this rule: When I want to do good, evil is there with me. **22**In my mind, I am happy with God's law. **23**But I see another law working in my body, which makes war against the law that my mind accepts. That other law working in my body is the law of sin, and it makes me its prisoner. **24**What a miserable man I am! Who will save me from this body that brings me death? **25**I thank God for saving me through Jesus Christ our Lord!

So in my mind I am a slave to God's law, but in my sinful self I am a slave to the law of sin.

Be Ruled by the Spirit

 So now, those who are in Christ Jesus are not judged guilty. **2**Through Christ Jesus the law of the Spirit that brings life made you free from the law that brings sin and death. **3**The law was without power, because the law was made weak by our sinful selves. But God did what the law could not do. He sent his own Son to earth with the same human life that others use for sin. By sending his Son to be an offering for sin, God used a human life to destroy sin. **4**He did this so that we could be the kind of people the law correctly wants us to be. Now we do not live following our sinful selves, but we live following the Spirit.

5Those who live following their sinful selves think only about things that their sinful selves want. But those who live following the Spirit are thinking about the things the Spirit wants them to do. **6**If people's thinking is controlled by the sinful self, there is death. But if their thinking is controlled by the Spirit, there is life and peace. **7**When people's thinking is controlled by the sinful self, they are against God, because they refuse to obey God's law and really are not even able to obey God's law. **8**Those people who are ruled by their sinful selves cannot please God.

9But you are not ruled by your sinful selves. You are ruled by the Spirit, if that Spirit of God really lives in you. But the person who does not have the Spirit of Christ does not belong to Christ. **10**Your body will always be dead because of sin. But if Christ is in you, then the Spirit gives you life, because Christ made you right with God. **11**God raised Jesus from the dead, and if God's Spirit is living in you, he will also give life to your bodies that die. God is the One who raised Christ from the dead, and he will give life through his Spirit that lives in you.

12So, my brothers and sisters, we must not be

ruled by our sinful selves or live the way our sinful selves want. **13**If you use your lives to do the wrong things your sinful selves want, you will die spiritually. But if you use the Spirit's help to stop doing the wrong things you do with your body, you will have true life.

14The true children of God are those who let God's Spirit lead them. **15**The Spirit we received does not make us slaves again to fear; it makes us children of God. With that Spirit we cry out, "Father." **16**And the Spirit himself joins with our spirits to say we are God's children. **17**If we are God's children, we will receive blessings from God together with Christ. But we must suffer as Christ suffered so that we will have glory as Christ has glory.

OLD TESTAMENT READING

Then Joshua said to the people, "Now respect the LORD and serve him fully and sincerely. Throw away the gods that your ancestors worshiped on the other side of the Euphrates River and in Egypt. Serve the LORD. **15**But if you don't want to serve the LORD, you must choose for yourselves today whom you will serve. You may serve the gods that your ancestors worshiped when they lived on the other side of the Euphrates River, or you may serve the gods of the Amorites who lived in this land. As for me and my family, we will serve the LORD."

Joshua 24:14–15

INSIGHTS

The Bible does not leave us floundering as to what is right and what is wrong in the basic areas of life. . . .

. . . Through Joshua God challenged the Israelites to choose among "the gods . . . on the other side of the River, or the gods of the Amorites," or the Lord. Elijah presented the choice on Mount Carmel, and made the difference very vivid. Choice continues to be important time after time for each of us, but there are crisis moments in each of our lives when we are tempted to make a tremendously wrong choice. . . .

What are your choices? Whom are your choices for? Not just for yourself. Choose now whom you will serve, and that choice is going to affect the next generation, and the next generation, and the next. Choice never affects one single person alone. It goes on and on and the effect goes out into geography and history. You are a part of history and your choices become a part of history.

EDITH SCHAEFFER

ACTION POINT

In what ways are you aware of your life struggle between choosing God or the way of sin? Pray that you will see clearly the choices you must make and that you will unfailingly obey God's way of life.

ROMANS 8:18-39

Our Future Glory

18The sufferings we have now are nothing compared to the great glory that will be shown to us. 19Everything God made is waiting with excitement for God to show his children's glory completely. 20Everything God made was changed to become useless, not by its own wish but because God wanted it and because all along there was this hope: 21that everything God made would be set free from ruin to have the freedom and glory that belong to God's children.

22We know that everything God made has been waiting until now in pain, like a woman ready to give birth. 23Not only the world, but we also have been waiting with pain inside us. We have the Spirit as the first part of God's promise. So we are waiting for God to finish making us his own children, which means our bodies will be made free. 24We were saved, and we have this hope. If we see what we are waiting for, that is not really hope. People do not hope for something they already have. 25But we are hoping for something we do not have yet, and we are waiting for it patiently.

26Also, the Spirit helps us with our weakness. We do not know how to pray as we should. But the Spirit himself speaks to God for us, even begs God for us with deep feelings that words cannot explain. 27God can see what is in people's hearts. And he knows what is in the mind of the Spirit, because the Spirit speaks to God for his people in the way God wants.

28We know that in everything God works for the good of those who love him. They are the people he called, because that was his plan. 29God knew them before he made the world, and he chose them to be like his Son so that Jesus would be the firstborn of many brothers and sisters. 30God planned for them to be like his Son; and those he planned to be like his Son, he also called; and those he called, he also made right with him; and those he made right, he also glorified.

God's Love in Christ Jesus

31So what should we say about this? If God is for us, no one can defeat us. 32He did not spare his own Son but gave him for us all. So with Jesus, God will surely give us all things. 33Who can accuse the people God has chosen? No one, because God is the One who makes them right. 34Who can say God's people are guilty? No one, because Christ Jesus died, but he was also raised from the dead, and now he is on God's right side, appealing to God for us. 35Can anything separate us from the love Christ has for us? Can troubles or problems or sufferings or hunger or nakedness or danger or violent death? 36As it is written in the Scriptures:

> "For you we are in danger of death all the time.
> People think we are worth no more than sheep to be killed."   Psalm 44:22

37But in all these things we are completely victorious through God who showed his love for us. 38Yes, I am sure that neither death, nor life, nor angels, nor ruling spirits, nothing now, nothing in the future, no powers, 39nothing above us, nothing below us, nor anything else in the whole world will ever be able to separate us from the love of God that is in Christ Jesus our Lord.

OLD TESTAMENT READING

The LORD looked and could not find any justice,
and he was displeased.
[16]He could not find anyone to help the people,
and he was surprised that there was no one to help.

So he used his own power to save the people;
his own goodness gave him strength.
[17]He covered himself with goodness like armor.
He put the helmet of salvation on his head.
He put on his clothes for punishing
and wrapped himself in the coat of his strong love.

[21]The LORD says, "This is my agreement with these people: My Spirit and my words that I give you will never leave you or your children or your grandchildren, now and forever."

Isaiah 59:15b–17, 21

INSIGHTS

In the very nature of things we soon discover in life that in order to be loved either in a physical or filial dimension we must show ourselves lovable. Somehow we have to demonstrate to others that we are worth loving. We have to prove that we are worthy of their love. And, sad to say, in most cases, the moment we fail to do this we discover that we are being cut off. . . .

Now, amazing as it may sound, and incredible as it may seem, there is none of this in the love of God. The simple truth is that His love for me does not in any way depend on my worthiness of it. In other words, I do not have to merit His love. I do not, so to speak, have to earn His love.

Scripture repeats this theme again and again. For example, in that most poignant of all the stories told by Jesus, the account of the prodigal son, we see clearly portrayed for us what the love of God is like. . . .

No doubt the dear old man had died a thousand deaths after his son's departure. . . .

Yet his attitude of devotion, affection, and utter selflessness never altered. It mattered not what happened to himself as long as his son could be restored and redeemed and remade. His care and concern for this one's welfare never abated.

This is the love of God.

W. PHILLIP KELLER

ACTION POINT

List the things (as many as you want) that, powerful and dreadful as they may be, cannot separate us from the love of God. Thank God that his love for you is greater than every one of those things!

ROMANS 9:1-29

God and the Jewish People

9 I am in Christ, and I am telling you the truth; I do not lie. My conscience is ruled by the Holy Spirit, and it tells me I am not lying. **2**I have great sorrow and always feel much sadness. **3**I wish I could help my Jewish brothers and sisters, my people. I would even wish that I were cursed and cut off from Christ if that would help them. **4**They are the people of Israel, God's chosen children. They have seen the glory of God, and they have the agreements that God made between himself and his people. God gave them the law of Moses and the right way of worship and his promises. **5**They are the descendants of our great ancestors, and they are the earthly family into which Christ was born, who is God over all. Praise him forever! Amen.

6It is not that God failed to keep his promise to them. But only some of the people of Israel are truly God's people, **7**and only some of Abraham's descendants are true children of Abraham. But God said to Abraham: "The descendants I promised you will be from Isaac." **8**This means that not all of Abraham's descendants are God's true children. Abraham's true children are those who become God's children because of the promise God made to Abraham. **9**God's promise to Abraham was this: "At the right time I will return, and Sarah will have a son." **10**And that is not all. Rebekah's sons had the same father, our father Isaac. **11-12**But before the two boys were born, God told Rebekah, "The older will serve the younger." This was be-

fore the boys had done anything good or bad. God said this so that the one chosen would be chosen because of God's own plan. He was chosen because he was the one God wanted to call, not because of anything he did. **13**As the Scripture says, "I loved Jacob, but I hated Esau."

14So what should we say about this? Is God unfair? In no way. **15**God said to Moses, "I will show kindness to anyone to whom I want to show kindness, and I will show mercy to anyone to whom I want to show mercy." **16**So God will choose the one to whom he decides to show mercy; his choice does not depend on what people want or try to do. **17**The Scripture says to the king of Egypt: "I made you king for this reason: to show my power in you so that my name will be talked about in all the earth." **18**So God shows mercy where he wants to show mercy, and he makes stubborn the people he wants to make stubborn.

19So one of you will ask me: "Then why does God blame us for our sins? Who can fight his will?" **20**You are only human, and human beings have no right to question God. An object should not ask the person who made it, "Why did you make me like this?" **21**The potter can make anything he wants to make. He can use the same clay to make one thing for special use and another thing for daily use.

22It is the same way with God. He wanted to show his anger and to let people see his power. But he patiently stayed with those people he was angry with—people who were made ready to be destroyed. **23**He waited with patience so that he could make known his rich glory to the people who receive his mercy. He has prepared these people to have his glory, **24**and we are those people whom God called. He called us not from the Jews only but also from those who are not Jews. **25**As the Scripture says in Hosea:

"I will say, 'You are my people'
to those I had called 'not my people.'
And I will show my love
to those people I did not love."

Hosea 2:1, 23

26"They were called,
'You are not my people,'
but later they will be called
'children of the living God.'" *Hosea 1:10*

27And Isaiah cries out about Israel:
"The people of Israel are many,
like the grains of sand by the sea.
But only a few of them will be saved,
28 because the Lord will quickly and
completely punish the people on the
earth." *Isaiah 10:22–23*

29It is as Isaiah said:
"The Lord All-Powerful
allowed a few of our descendants to live.
Otherwise we would have been completely
destroyed
like the cities of Sodom and Gomorrah."

Isaiah 1:9

OLD TESTAMENT READING

The clay does not ask the potter,
'What are you doing?'
The thing that is made doesn't say
to its maker,
'You have no hands.'"

Isaiah 45:9c–d

INSIGHTS

Child, don't try to understand Me. Just love Me. Just let Me love you. You don't have to understand Me to open yourself to My love.

You're right—I do ride the wild winds into town sometimes. I do appear in forms you have never seen, sound notes you have never heard. This makes you wonder if I get My signals crossed, if I take you south in order to get you north. I seem to have plopped you down, reasonable creature that you are, into an unreasonable world. You do not understand all this because I am God and you are you.

May I remind you how different we really are? You are human; I am divine. You are finite; I am infinite. You need love; I delight in love but do not need it. You need to be understood; I am above the need to be understood. You cannot understand; I understand perfectly. You are of time; I am of eternity. You are of reason; I am above reason. You are blown by the wind; I blow the wind.

RUTH SENTER

➤ ACTION POINT

Are you comfortable with the fact that God is the potter and you are the clay? Pray for the humility to accept God's love for you in the way that he gives it.

ROMANS 9:30 – 10:21

30So what does all this mean? Those who are not Jews were not trying to make themselves right with God, but they were made right with God because of their faith. 31The people of Israel tried to follow a law to make themselves right with God. But they did not succeed, 32because they tried to make themselves right by the things they did instead of trusting in God to make them right. They stumbled over the stone that causes people to stumble. 33As it is written in the Scripture:

"I will put in Jerusalem a stone that causes
     people to stumble,
  a rock that makes them fall.
Anyone who trusts in him will never be
     disappointed."   *Isaiah 8:14; 28:16*

10 Brothers and sisters, the thing I want most is for all the Jews to be saved. That is my prayer to God. 2I can say this about them: They really try to follow God, but they do not know the right way. 3Because they did not know the way that God makes people right with him, they tried to make themselves right in their own way. So they did not accept God's way of making people right. 4Christ ended the law so that everyone who believes in him may be right with God.

5Moses writes about being made right by following the law. He says, "A person who obeys these things will live because of them." 6But this is what the Scripture says about being made right through faith: "Don't say to yourself, 'Who will go up into heaven?'" (That means, "Who will go up to heaven and bring Christ down to earth?") 7"And do not say, 'Who will go down into the world below?'" (That means, "Who will go down and bring Christ up from the dead?") 8This is what the Scripture says: "The word is near you; it is in your mouth and in your heart." That is the teaching of faith that we are telling. 9If you declare with your mouth, "Jesus is Lord," and if you believe in your heart that God raised Jesus from the dead, you will be saved. 10We believe with our hearts, and so we are made right with God. And we declare with our mouths that we believe, and so we are saved. 11As the Scripture says, "Anyone who trusts in him will never be disappointed." 12That Scripture says "anyone" because there is no difference between those who are Jews and those who are not. The same Lord is the Lord of all and gives many blessings to all who trust in him, 13as the Scripture says, "Anyone who calls on the Lord will be saved."

14But before people can ask the Lord for help, they must believe in him; and before they can believe in him, they must hear about him; and for them to hear about the Lord, someone must tell them; 15and before someone can go and tell them, that person must be sent. It is written, "How beautiful is the person who comes to bring good news." 16But not all the Jews accepted the good news. Isaiah said, "Lord, who believed what we told them?" 17So faith comes from hearing the Good News, and people hear the Good News when someone tells them about Christ.

18But I ask: Didn't people hear the Good News? Yes, they heard—as the Scripture says:

"Their message went out through all the world;

their words go everywhere on earth."

Psalm 19:4

19Again I ask: Didn't the people of Israel understand? Yes, they did understand. First, Moses says:

"I will use those who are not a nation to make you jealous.

I will use a nation that does not understand to make you angry."

Deuteronomy 32:21

20Then Isaiah is bold enough to say:

"I was found by those who were not asking me for help.

I made myself known to people who were not looking for me." *Isaiah 65:1*

21But about Israel God says,

"All day long I stood ready to accept people who disobey and are stubborn."

Isaiah 65:2

OLD TESTAMENT READING

The LORD said to Moses, **2**"Tell the people of Israel: 'I am the LORD your God. **3**In the past you lived in Egypt, but you must not do what was done in that country. And you must not do as they do in the land of Canaan, where I am bringing you. Do not follow their customs. **4**You must obey my rules and follow them. I am the LORD your God. **5**Obey my laws and rules; a person who obeys them will live because of them. I am the LORD."

Leviticus 18:1–5

INSIGHTS

It's not through wisdom that people come to the knowledge of God and their absolute equality before Him. It's not through endless arguments of fine points of theology that they will find a humble heart. The doorway into the kingdom is so low down that one must bend in humility to get through. I've never known a single person who has been convinced of the kingdom of God through head knowledge—a person just can't think his or her way into the kingdom of God. Nor can anyone come into the kingdom of God based on a religious experience. It is knowledge of and faith in Christ that enables the equality of life in the kingdom to be real. "For Jews request a sign, and Greeks seek after wisdom; but we preach Christ crucified, to the Jews a stumbling block and to the Greeks foolishness, but to those who are called, both Jews and Greeks, Christ the power of God and the wisdom of God" (1 Cor 1:22–25).

TERRY FULLAM

PAUSE FOR REFLECTION

Can a person successfully follow God in his or her own way (Romans 10:1–4)? What is the way of salvation? To whom does God offer it?

ROMANS 11:1-21

God Shows Mercy to All People

11 So I ask: Did God throw out his people? No! I myself am an Israelite from the family of Abraham, from the tribe of Benjamin. **2**God chose the Israelites to be his people before they were born, and he has not thrown his people out. Surely you know what the Scripture says about Elijah, how he prayed to God against the people of Israel. **3**"Lord," he said, "they have killed your prophets, and they have destroyed your altars. I am the only prophet left, and now they are trying to kill me, too." **4**But what answer did God give Elijah? He said, "But I have left seven thousand people in Israel who have never bowed down before Baal." **5**It is the same now. There are a few people that God has chosen by his grace. **6**And if he chose them by grace, it is not for the things they have done. If they could be made God's people by what they did, God's gift of grace would not really be a gift.

7So this is what has happened: Although the Israelites tried to be right with God, they did not succeed, but the ones God chose did become right with him. The others were made stubborn and refused to listen to God. **8**As it is written in the Scriptures:

"God gave the people a dull mind so they
could not understand."   *Isaiah 29:10*
"He closed their eyes so they could not
see
and their ears so they could not hear.
This continues until today."   *Deuteronomy 29:4*

9And David says:

"Let their own feasts trap them and cause
their ruin;
let their feasts cause them to stumble and
be paid back.
10Let their eyes be closed so they cannot see
and their backs be forever weak from
troubles."   *Psalm 69:22–23*

11So I ask: When the Jews fell, did that fall destroy them? No! But their failure brought salvation to those who are not Jews, in order to make the Jews jealous. **12**The Jews' failure brought rich blessings for the world, and the Jews' loss brought rich blessings for the non-Jewish people. So surely the world will receive much richer blessings when enough Jews become the kind of people God wants.

13Now I am speaking to you who are not Jews. I am an apostle to those who are not Jews, and since I have that work, I will make the most of it. **14**I hope I can make my own people jealous and, in that way, help some of them to be saved. **15**When God turned away from the Jews, he became friends with other people in the world. So when God accepts the Jews, surely that will bring them life after death.

16If the first piece of bread is offered to God, then the whole loaf is made holy. If the roots of a tree are holy, then the tree's branches are holy too.

17It is as if some of the branches from an olive tree have been broken off. You non-Jewish people are like the branch of a wild olive tree that has been joined to that first tree. You now share the strength and life of the first tree, the Jews. **18**So do not brag about those branches that were broken off. If you brag, remember that you do not support the root, but the root supports you. **19**You will say, "Branches were broken off so that I could be joined to their tree." **20**That is true. But those branches were broken off because they did not believe, and you continue to be part of the tree only because you believe. Do not be proud, but be afraid. **21**If God did not let the natural branches of that tree stay, then he will not let you stay if you don't believe.

OLD TESTAMENT READING

But suppose the wicked stop doing all the sins they have done and obey all my rules and do what is fair and right. Then they will surely live; they will not die. **22**Their sins will be forgotten. Because they have done what is right, they will live. **23**I do not really want the wicked to die, says the Lord GOD. I want them to stop their bad ways and live."

Ezekiel 18:21–23

INSIGHTS

Kindness is invariably associated with mercy. It is impossible to be kind without being merciful. Likewise to be merciful is to be kind. it implies that there is a deep and genuine concern for another. This concern is one of compassion and mercy. . . .

Throughout the Scriptures the great theme of God's unrelenting kindness throbs like a powerful heartbeat. . . .

The kindness of God has drawn me to Him with bonds of love stronger than steel. The mercy of my Lord has endeared me to Him with enormous gratitude and thanksgiving. . . .

It is the kindness of God, expressed in Christ and revealed to us by His Spirit that supplies my salvation. His kindness makes provision for my pardon from sins and self-ishness at the cost of His own laid down life. It is His kindness that forgives my faults and accepts me into His family as His dearly beloved child. His kindness enables me to stand acquitted of my wrongdoing, justified freely in His presence. God's kindness removes my guilt and I am at one with Him and others in peace. It is the kindness of God that enables Him to share Himself with me in the inner sanctuary of my spirit, soul, and body. His kindness enables me to be re-made, refashioned, re-formed gently into His likeness. His kindness gives enormous meaning and dignity to this life and endless delight in the life yet to come.

It is the constant, enduring, unchanging kindness of God that gives me every reason to rejoice and revel in life . . . all of life . . . this one and the next.

W. PHILLIP KELLER

PAUSE FOR REFLECTION

Is there anyone to whom God doesn't want to offer his forgiveness? In what ways has God shown his forgiveness and mercy to the Jews? To non-Jews? Describe how God's unfailing kindness has touched your heart.

ROMANS 11:22 – 12:8

22So you see that God is kind and also very strict. He punishes those who stop following him. But God is kind to you, if you continue following in his kindness. If you do not, you will be cut off from the tree. **23**And if the Jews will believe in God again, he will accept them back. God is able to put them back where they were. **24**It is not natural for a wild branch to be part of a good tree. And you who are not Jews are like a branch cut from a wild olive tree and joined to a good olive tree. But since those Jews are like a branch that grew from the good tree, surely they can be joined to their own tree again.

25I want you to understand this secret, brothers and sisters, so you will understand that you do not know everything: Part of Israel has been made stubborn, but that will change when many who are not Jews have come to God. **26**And that is how all Israel will be saved. It is written in the Scriptures:

"The Savior will come from Jerusalem;
he will take away all evil from the family of Jacob.
27And I will make this agreement
with those people
when I take away their sins."

Isaiah 59:20–21; 27:9

28The Jews refuse to accept the Good News, so they are God's enemies. This has happened to help you who are not Jews. But the Jews are still God's chosen people, and he loves them very much be-cause of the promises he made to their ancestors. **29**God never changes his mind about the people he calls and the things he gives them. **30**At one time you refused to obey God. But now you have received mercy, because those people refused to obey. **31**And now the Jews refuse to obey, because God showed mercy to you. But this happened so that they also can receive mercy from him. **32**God has given all people over to their stubborn ways so that he can show mercy to all.

Praise to God

33Yes, God's riches are very great, and his wisdom and knowledge have no end! No one can explain the things God decides or understand his ways. **34**As the Scripture says,

"Who has known the mind of the Lord,
or who has been able to give him advice?"

Isaiah 40:13

35"No one has ever given God anything
that he must pay back." *Job 41:11*

36Yes, God made all things, and everything continues through him and for him. To him be the glory forever! Amen.

Give Your Lives to God

12 So brothers and sisters, since God has shown us great mercy, I beg you to offer your lives as a living sacrifice to him. Your offering must be only for God and pleasing to him, which is the spiritual way for you to worship. **2**Do not be shaped by this world; instead be changed within by a new way of thinking. Then you will be able to decide what God wants for you; you will know what is good and pleasing to him and what is perfect. **3**Because God has given me a special gift, I have something to say to everyone among you. Do not think you are better than you are. You must decide what you really are by the amount of faith God has given you. **4**Each one of us has a body with many parts, and these parts all have different uses. **5**In the same way, we are many, but in Christ we are all one body. Each one is a part of that body, and each part belongs to all the other parts. **6**We all have different gifts, each of which came because of the grace God gave us. The person who has the gift of prophecy should use that gift in agreement with the faith. **7**Anyone who has the gift of serving should serve. Anyone who has the gift of teaching should teach. **8**Whoever has the gift of encouraging others should encourage. Whoever has the gift of giving to others should give freely. Anyone who has the gift of being a leader should try hard when he leads. Whoever has the gift of showing mercy to others should do so with joy.

OLD TESTAMENT READING

ut Samuel answered,
"What pleases the LORD more:
    burnt offerings and sacrifices
    or obedience to his voice?
It is better to obey than to sacrifice.
    It is better to listen to God than to offer the
        fat of sheep."

1 Samuel 15:22

ACTION POINT

In what ways is your life an offering to God? In what ways are you tempted to fall short of full obedience? Pray that your deepest desire will be to give yourself fully as a living sacrifice to God.

ROMANS 12:9 – 13:14

9Your love must be real. Hate what is evil, and hold on to what is good. **10**Love each other like brothers and sisters. Give each other more honor than you want for yourselves. **11**Do not be lazy but work hard, serving the Lord with all your heart. **12**Be joyful because you have hope. Be patient when trouble comes, and pray at all times. **13**Share with God's people who need help. Bring strangers in need into your homes.

14Wish good for those who harm you; wish them well and do not curse them. **15**Be happy with those who are happy, and be sad with those who are sad. **16**Live in peace with each other. Do not be proud, but make friends with those who seem unimportant. Do not think how smart you are.

17If someone does wrong to you, do not pay him back by doing wrong to him. Try to do what everyone thinks is right. **18**Do your best to live in peace with everyone. **19**My friends, do not try to punish others when they wrong you, but wait for God to punish them with his anger. It is written: "I will punish those who do wrong; I will repay them," says the Lord. **20**But you should do this:

"If your enemy is hungry, feed him;
> if he is thirsty, give him a drink.
Doing this will be like pouring burning coals
> on his head."   *Proverbs 25:21–22*

21Do not let evil defeat you, but defeat evil by doing good.

Christians Should Obey the Law

 13 All of you must yield to the government rulers. No one rules unless God has given him the power to rule, and no one rules now without that power from God. **2**So those who are against the government are really against what God has commanded. And they will bring punishment on themselves. **3**Those who do right do not have to fear the rulers; only those who do wrong fear them. Do you want to be unafraid of the rulers? Then do what is right, and they will praise you. **4**The ruler is God's servant to help you. But if you do wrong, then be afraid. He has the power to punish; he is God's servant to punish those who do wrong. **5**So you must yield to the government, not only because you might be punished, but because you know it is right.

6This is also why you pay taxes. Rulers are working for God and give their time to their work. **7**Pay everyone, then, what you owe. If you owe any kind of tax, pay it. Show respect and honor to them all.

Loving Others

8Do not owe people anything, except always owe love to each other, because the person who loves others has obeyed all the law. **9**The law says, "You must not be guilty of adultery. You must not murder anyone. You must not steal. You must not want to take your neighbor's things." All these commands and all others are really only one rule: "Love your neighbor as you love yourself." **10**Love never hurts a neighbor, so loving is obeying all the law.

11Do this because we live in an important time. It is now time for you to wake up from your sleep, because our salvation is nearer now than when we first believed. **12**The "night" is almost finished, and the "day" is almost here. So we should stop doing things that belong to darkness and take up the weapons used for fighting in the light. **13**Let us live in a right way, like people who belong to the day. We should not have wild parties or get drunk. There should be no sexual sins of any kind, no fighting or jealousy. **14**But clothe yourselves with the Lord Jesus Christ and forget about satisfying your sinful self.

INSIGHTS

The context of this passage does . . . set up a principle that says, "If I owe anyone anything, I am not free to give love to that person." Anyone who has borrowed money from another person, and especially another Christian, realizes the wall that immediately goes up from being in a debtor/lender relationship. Debtors and lenders are not really free to love one another. This verse suggests principles for both sides. Lending to another Christian needs to be considered very, very seriously before it is done. On the other side, before you borrow from anyone for anything, consider the ramifications of being in bondage to that person. Are you, in fact, free to love that person? . . .

. . . The reality is that whenever you have borrowed from anyone, you are a servant to that person. . . .

. . . "Why is so much written about debt in God's Word?" I believe there are three reasons. First of all, debt is extremely deceptive. As we said earlier, getting into debt is easy—getting out is next to impossible. Second, debt creates bondage, and if that bondage is to the world system, we are no longer free to be the witnesses in this world that God has called us to be. Third, debt is almost blasphemous when we use it and deny God an opportunity to work. . . .

. . . Being in debt is never the real problem; it is only symptomatic of the real problem, which is usually greed, self-indulgence, impatience, fear, poor self-image, lack of self-discipline, and perhaps others. So, if you find yourself in debt, your first question is not, "How do I get out of debt?" Ask first of all, "Why am I in this situation?" and answer that question. Then getting out of debt will become much easier.

RON BLUE

OLD TESTAMENT READING

The wicked borrow and don't pay back,
but those who do right give freely to
others.
26Good people always lend freely to others,
and their children are a blessing.

Psalm 37:21, 26

PAUSE FOR REFLECTION

What is Jesus' greatest commandment? Examine the relationships between love, debt, ministry, and giving in your life. How do your lifestyle choices hinder your obedience to Christ's commandment to love one another?

ROMANS 14:1 – 15:3

Do Not Criticize Other People

14 Accept into your group someone who is weak in faith, and do not argue about opinions. **2**One person believes it is right to eat all kinds of food. But another, who is weak, believes it is right to eat only vegetables. **3**The one who knows that it is right to eat any kind of food must not reject the one who eats only vegetables. And the person who eats only vegetables must not think that the one who eats all foods is wrong, because God has accepted that person. **4**You cannot judge another person's servant. The master decides if the servant is doing well or not. And the Lord's servant will do well because the Lord helps him do well.

5Some think that one day is more important than another, and others think that every day is the same. Let all be sure in their own mind. **6**Those who think one day is more important than other days are doing that for the Lord. And those who eat all kinds of food are doing that for the Lord, and they give thanks to God. Others who refuse to eat some foods do that for the Lord, and they give thanks to God. **7**We do not live or die for ourselves. **8**If we live, we are living for the Lord, and if we die, we are dying for the Lord. So living or dying, we belong to the Lord.

9The reason Christ died and rose from the dead to live again was so he would be Lord over both the dead and the living. **10**So why do you judge your brothers or sisters in Christ? And why do you think you are better than they are? We will all stand before God to be judged, **11**because it is written in the Scriptures:

> "'As surely as I live,' says the Lord,
> 'Everyone will bow before me;
> everyone will say that I am God.'"
>
> *Isaiah 45:23*

12So each of us will have to answer to God.

Do Not Cause Others to Sin

13For that reason we should stop judging each other. We must make up our minds not to do anything that will make another Christian sin. **14**I am in the Lord Jesus, and I know that there is no food that is wrong to eat. But if a person believes something is wrong, that thing is wrong for him. **15**If you hurt your brother's or sister's faith because of something you eat, you are not really following the way of love. Do not destroy someone's faith by eating food he thinks is wrong, because Christ died for him. **16**Do not allow what you think is good to become what others say is evil. **17**In the kingdom of God, eating and drinking are not important. The important things are living right with God, peace, and joy in the Holy Spirit. **18**Anyone who serves Christ by living this way is pleasing God and will be accepted by other people.

19So let us try to do what makes peace and helps one another. **20**Do not let the eating of food destroy the work of God. All foods are all right to eat, but it is wrong to eat food that causes someone else to sin. **21**It is better not to eat meat or drink wine or do anything that will cause your brother or sister to sin.

22Your beliefs about these things should be kept secret between you and God. People are happy if they can do what they think is right without feeling guilty. **23**But those who eat something without being sure it is right are wrong because they did not believe it was right. Anything that is done without believing it is right is a sin.

15 We who are strong in faith should help the weak with their weaknesses, and not please only ourselves. **2**Let each of us please our neighbors for their good, to help them be stronger in faith. **3**Even Christ did not live to please himself. It was as the Scriptures said: "When people insult you, it hurts me."

INSIGHTS

When we please God, we have peace. We're not trying to juggle a dozen different things in order to please everyone around us. Instead, we have a single purpose—to please God.

When we try to please ourselves or others, however, things get out of balance. Far too many of us have become overly involved in various causes and have lost our perspective. Our priorities no longer are established by God, but by all the voices—many of which are sincere and good—clamoring around us. We have forgotten that our purpose is to please God.

But as spiritually renewed Christians who aim to please God, we can walk with security and confidence. We no longer view life and its problems with the short-sighted limitations of a merely human perspective. Instead, we view life with the long-term assurance that comes only from God's eternal perspective.

LUIS PALAU

OLD TESTAMENT READING

People will be rewarded for what they say,
and they will also be rewarded for what
they do.

Proverbs 12:14

Now, everything has been heard,
so I give my final advice:
Honor God and obey his commands,
because this is all people must do.
14God will judge everything,
even what is done in secret,
the good and the evil.

Ecclesiastes 12:13–14

Bring to me all the people who are mine,
whom I made for my glory,
whom I formed and made."

Isaiah 43:7

PAUSE FOR REFLECTION

For whom do believers live and die? How does that affect our lifestyle? What is our guideline for living in a way that pleases God? Who exemplifies such a lifestyle? How are we to treat those whose faith is weak? Why?

ROMANS 15:4-29

4Everything that was written in the past was written to teach us. The Scriptures give us patience and encouragement so that we can have hope. **5**May the patience and encouragement that come from God allow you to live in harmony with each other the way Christ Jesus wants. **6**Then you will all be joined together, and you will give glory to God the Father of our Lord Jesus Christ. **7**Christ accepted you, so you should accept each other, which will bring glory to God. **8**I tell you that Christ became a servant of the Jews to show that God's promises to the Jewish ancestors are true. **9**And he also did this so that those who are not Jews could give glory to God for the mercy he gives to them. It is written in the Scriptures:

"So I will praise you among the non-Jewish people.
I will sing praises to your name."

Psalm 18:49

10 The Scripture also says,

"Be happy, you who are not Jews, together with his people." *Deuteronomy 32:43*

11Again the Scripture says,

"All you who are not Jews, praise the Lord.
All you people, sing praises to him."

Psalm 117:1

12And Isaiah says,

"A new king will come from the family of Jesse.
He will come to rule over the non-Jewish people,

and they will have hope because of him."

Isaiah 11:10

13I pray that the God who gives hope will fill you with much joy and peace while you trust in him. Then your hope will overflow by the power of the Holy Spirit.

Paul Talks About His Work

14My brothers and sisters, I am sure that you are full of goodness. I know that you have all the knowledge you need and that you are able to teach each other. **15**But I have written to you very openly about some things I wanted you to remember. I did this because God gave me this special gift: **16**to be a minister of Christ Jesus to those who are not Jews. I served God by teaching his Good News, so that the non-Jewish people could be an offering that God would accept—an offering made holy by the Holy Spirit.

17So I am proud of what I have done for God in Christ Jesus. **18**I will not talk about anything except what Christ has done through me in leading those who are not Jews to obey God. They have obeyed God because of what I have said and done, **19**because of the power of miracles and the great things they saw, and because of the power of the Holy Spirit. I preached the Good News from Jerusalem all the way around to Illyricum, and so I have finished that part of my work. **20**I always want to preach the Good News in places where people have never heard of Christ, because I do not want to build on the work someone else has already started. **21**But it is written in the Scriptures:

"Those who were not told about him will see,
and those who have not heard about him will understand." *Isaiah 52:15*

Paul's Plan to Visit Rome

22This is the reason I was stopped many times from coming to you. **23**Now I have finished my work here. Since for many years I have wanted to come to you, **24**I hope to visit you on my way to Spain. After I enjoy being with you for a while, I hope you can help me on my trip. **25**Now I am going to Jerusalem to help God's people. **26**The believers in Macedonia and Southern Greece were happy to give their money to help the poor among God's people at Jerusalem. **27**They were happy to do this, and really they owe it to them. These who are not Jews have shared in the Jews' spiritual blessings, so they should use their material possessions to help the Jews. **28**After I am sure the poor in Jerusalem get the money that has been given for them, I will leave for Spain and stop and visit you. **29**I know that when I come to you I will bring Christ's full blessing.

OLD TESTAMENT READING

So our hope is in the LORD.
    He is our help, our shield to protect us.
21We rejoice in him,
    because we trust his holy name.
22LORD, show your love to us
    as we put our hope in you.

Psalm 33:20–22

INSIGHTS

As Jesus was entering into the last days of his life on earth, he prayed for his disciples and for all disciples to come. His petitions were for union with the Father, joy, protection, and usefulness. The sequence of those petitions is significant (John 17:11–17).

Friendship with Christ is the first priority and is basic for the qualities that follow. Out of that intimate, love relationship, joy is a logical consequence. Jesus knew, as he prayed for his disciples, that if they did indeed come into fellowship with him and exhibit the kind of full-fledged joy that he gives, there would be opposition from the world, and so he prayed not that his disciples would be protected from the world or taken out of it into a kind of insulated, holy huddle, but that they would be protected from anything that would destroy that union and joy. Then, out of that dynamic partnership, usefulness would naturally flow.

. . . The more I know Him, the more I experience that deep inner well of joy that is not dependent on external circumstances. This joy is present even in the midst of suffering and sorrow; it is a motivating power even in discouragement and dismay.

JEANIE MILEY

ACTION POINT

Who does God fill with hope and joy? Why is God worthy of our trust and hope? What has God done that comforts you and brings you hope, even when life is difficult? Thank him. Rejoice in his unfailing love!

ROMANS 15:30 – 16:27

30Brothers and sisters, I beg you to help me in my work by praying to God for me. Do this because of our Lord Jesus and the love that the Holy Spirit gives us. **31**Pray that I will be saved from the nonbelievers in Judea and that this help I bring to Jerusalem will please God's people there. **32**Then, if God wants me to, I will come to you with joy, and together you and I will have a time of rest. **33**The God who gives peace be with you all. Amen.

Greetings to the Christians

 I recommend to you our sister Phoebe, who is a helper in the church in Cenchrea. **2**I ask you to accept her in the Lord in the way God's people should. Help her with anything she needs, because she has helped me and many other people also.

3Give my greetings to Priscilla and Aquila, who work together with me in Christ Jesus **4**and who risked their own lives to save my life. I am thankful to them, and all the non-Jewish churches are thankful as well. **5**Also, greet for me the church that meets at their house.

Greetings to my dear friend Epenetus, who was the first person in Asia to follow Christ. **6**Greetings to Mary, who worked very hard for you. **7**Greetings to Andronicus and Junia, my relatives, who were in prison with me. They are very important apostles. They were believers in Christ before I was. **8**Greetings to Ampliatus, my dear friend in the Lord. **9**Greetings to Urbanus, a worker together with me for Christ. And greetings to my dear friend Stachys. **10**Greetings to Apelles, who was tested and proved that he truly loves Christ. Greetings to all those who are in the family of Aristobulus. **11**Greetings to Herodion, my fellow citizen. Greetings to all those in the family of Narcissus who belong to the Lord. **12**Greetings to Tryphena and Tryphosa, women who work very hard for the Lord. Greetings to my dear friend Persis, who also has worked very hard for the Lord. **13**Greetings to Rufus, who is a special person in the Lord, and to his mother, who has been like a mother to me also. **14**Greetings to Asyncritus, Phlegon, Hermes, Patrobas, Hermas, and all the brothers and sisters who are with them. **15**Greetings to Philologus and Julia, Nereus and his sister, and Olympas, and to all God's people with them. **16**Greet each other with a holy kiss. All of Christ's churches send greetings to you.

17Brothers and sisters, I ask you to look out for those who cause people to be against each other and who upset other people's faith. They are against the true teaching you learned, so stay away from them. **18**Such people are not serving our Lord Christ but are only doing what pleases themselves. They use fancy talk and fine words to fool the minds of those who do not know about evil. **19**All the believers have heard that you obey, so I am very happy because of you. But I want you to be wise in what is good and innocent in what is evil.

20The God who brings peace will soon defeat Satan and give you power over him.

The grace of our Lord Jesus be with you.

21Timothy, a worker together with me, sends greetings, as well as Lucius, Jason, and Sosipater, my relatives.

22I am Tertius, and I am writing this letter from Paul. I send greetings to you in the Lord.

23Gaius is letting me and the whole church here use his home. He also sends greetings to you, as do Erastus, the city treasurer, and our brother Quartus. [**24**The grace of our Lord Jesus Christ be with all of you. Amen.]

25Glory to God who can make you strong in faith by the Good News that I tell people and by the message about Jesus Christ. The message about Christ is the secret that was hidden for long ages past but is now made known. **26**It has been made clear through the writings of the prophets. And by the command of the eternal God it is made known to all nations that they might believe and obey.

27To the only wise God be glory forever through Jesus Christ! Amen.

OLD TESTAMENT READING

This is what the Lord GOD says: How terrible it will be for the foolish prophets who follow their own ideas and have not seen a vision from me! **7**You said, "This is the message of the LORD," but that is a false vision. Your prophecies are lies, because I have not spoken.

Ezekiel 13:3, 7

INSIGHTS

For the last sixty or so years professors and teachers in centers of theological training have had Satan's special attention, and so successful has he been that modernism has thoroughly penetrated the church. His ministers—yes, the devil's ministers, for he has many in the ministry!—are masquerading as ministers of truth and righteousness.

. . . Modern heresies and criticism are pitted against the infallible Word, the infallible Christ, the fact of sin, the redemptive works of the cross, the witness of the Holy Spirit. Knowing how completely the deity and death of Christ destroyed his works, Satan, through religious teachers, has been attacking the virgin birth, the sinlessness, the efficacious death, and the resurrection of our blessed Lord. . . .

By modernism, Satan has succeeded in robbing the church of her power in the world. With a humanized Christ, a mutilated Bible, and a glorified self, modernism is bankrupt. Nothing can damn evangelism like modernism, and Satan knows that—hence his untiring efforts to create an ever-increasing army of false teachers. . . . Let us pray for spiritual perception, whereby we can detect, and that immediately, the subtle error in a good deal we hear from some of the pulpits of our land.

HERBERT LOCKYER

APPLICATION

How seriously does God want his people to view the problem of false teachers? How can we guard against their deception?

1 CORINTHIANS
1:1-25

1 From Paul. God called me to be an apostle of Christ Jesus because that is what God wanted. Also from Sosthenes, our brother in Christ.

2To the church of God in Corinth, to you who have been made holy in Christ Jesus. You were called to be God's holy people with all people everywhere who pray in the name of the Lord Jesus Christ—their Lord and ours:

3Grace and peace to you from God our Father and the Lord Jesus Christ.

Paul Gives Thanks to God

4I always thank my God for you because of the grace God has given you in Christ Jesus. **5**I thank God because in Christ you have been made rich in every way, in all your speaking and in all your knowledge. **6**Just as our witness about Christ has been guaranteed to you, **7**so you have every gift from God while you wait for our Lord Jesus Christ to come again. **8**Jesus will keep you strong until the end so that there will be no wrong in you on the day our Lord Jesus Christ comes again. **9**God, who has called you into fellowship with his Son, Jesus Christ our Lord, is faithful.

Problems in the Church

10I beg you, brothers and sisters, by the name of our Lord Jesus Christ that all of you agree with each other and not be split into groups. I beg that you be completely joined together by having the same kind of thinking and the same purpose. **11**My brothers and sisters, some people from Chloe's family have told me quite plainly that there are quarrels among you. **12**This is what I mean: One of you says, "I follow Paul"; another says, "I follow Apollos"; another says, "I follow Peter"; and another says, "I follow Christ." **13**Christ has been divided up into different groups! Did Paul die on the cross for you? No! Were you baptized in the name of Paul? No! **14**I thank God I did not baptize any of you except Crispus and Gaius **15**so that now no one can say you were baptized in my name. **16**(I also baptized the family of Stephanas, but I do not remember that I baptized anyone else.) **17**Christ did not send me to baptize people but to preach the Good News. And he sent me to preach the Good News without using words of human wisdom so that the cross of Christ would not lose its power.

Christ Is God's Power and Wisdom

18The teaching about the cross is foolishness to those who are being lost, but to us who are being saved it is the power of God. **19**It is written in the Scriptures:

"I will cause the wise to lose their wisdom;
I will make the wise unable to
understand."   *Isaiah 29:14*

20Where is the wise person? Where is the educated person? Where is the skilled talker of this world? God has made the wisdom of the world foolish. **21**In the wisdom of God the world did not know God through its own wisdom. So God chose to use the message that sounds foolish to save those who believe. **22**The Jews ask for miracles, and the Greeks want wisdom. **23**But we preach a crucified Christ. This causes the Jews to stumble and is foolishness to non-Jews. **24**But Christ is the power of God and the wisdom of God to those people God has called—Jews and Greeks. **25**Even the foolishness of God is wiser than human wisdom, and the weakness of God is stronger than human strength.

OLD TESTAMENT READING

I, the LORD, made everything,
  stretching out the skies by myself
  and spreading out the earth all alone.
25I show that the signs of the lying prophets are
    false;
  I make fools of those who do magic.
  I confuse even the wise;
    they think they know much, but I make
      them look foolish.
26I make the messages of my servants come
    true;
  I make the advice of my messengers come
    true."

Isaiah 44:24b–26a

INSIGHTS

The Jews sought after wonders, but the Greeks sought after wisdom. The Greeks were known for their great philosophers and their knowledge. They had come to the point where they literally deified wisdom. They were worshiping at the shrine of science and knowledge. Does that sound familiar today in the twentieth century?

We have people today who say, "If you can't put it into the test tube or in a mathematical equation, we will not believe it." But you can't put the Cross in a crucible, and you can't put faith in a formula. The great philosopher, Pascal, said, "The heart has its reasons that reason knows nothing of." . . .

. . . God is too wise to let man come to know Him by his own wisdom. Man cannot solve his problems because he will not recognize their source, which is sin. Furthermore, he will not recognize the solution, which is salvation. God is so wise that He is not going to let man come to Him by his own wisdom.

As a matter of fact, we are told in 1 Corinthians 3:19 that "the wisdom of this world is foolishness with God." Think about it, a world full of wisdom is just a thimble full of foolishness to God. The Prophet Jeremiah said, "The wise men are ashamed. They are dismayed and taken. Behold they have rejected the Word of the Lord; so what wisdom do they have?" (Jer. 8:9). . . .

. . . If a person is going to come to God, he or she will have to come as a little child (Matt. 18:3).

JAMES MERRITT

PAUSE FOR REFLECTION

Why would using worldly wisdom to tell the Good News cause the cross of Christ to lose its power? Why would God, the source of all wisdom, turn the world's wisdom into foolishness?

1 CORINTHIANS 1:26 – 2:16

26Brothers and sisters, look at what you were when God called you. Not many of you were wise in the way the world judges wisdom. Not many of you had great influence. Not many of you came from important families. 27But God chose the foolish things of the world to shame the wise, and he chose the weak things of the world to shame the strong. 28He chose what the world thinks is unimportant and what the world looks down on and thinks is nothing in order to destroy what the world thinks is important. 29God did this so that no one can brag in his presence. 30Because of God you are in Christ Jesus, who has become for us wisdom from God. In Christ we are put right with God, and have been made holy, and have been set free from sin. 31So, as the Scripture says, "If people want to brag, they should brag only about the Lord."

The Message of Christ's Death

Dear brothers and sisters, when I came to you, I did not come preaching God's secret with fancy words or a show of human wisdom. 2I decided that while I was with you I would forget about everything except Jesus Christ and his death on the cross. 3So when I came to you, I was weak and fearful and trembling. 4My teaching and preaching were not with words of human wisdom that persuade people but with proof of the power that the Spirit gives. 5This was so that your faith would be in God's power and not in human wisdom.

God's Wisdom

6However, I speak a wisdom to those who are mature. But this wisdom is not from this world or from the rulers of this world, who are losing their power. 7I speak God's secret wisdom, which he has kept hidden. Before the world began, God planned this wisdom for our glory. 8None of the rulers of this world understood it. If they had, they would not have crucified the Lord of glory. 9But as it is written in the Scriptures:

"No one has ever seen this,
　and no one has ever heard about it.
No one has ever imagined
　what God has prepared for those who love
　　him."　　　　　　　　　*Isaiah 64:4*

10But God has shown us these things through the Spirit.

The Spirit searches out all things, even the deep secrets of God. 11Who knows the thoughts that another person has? Only a person's spirit that lives within him knows his thoughts. It is the same with God. No one knows the thoughts of God except the Spirit of God. 12Now we did not receive the spirit of the world, but we received the Spirit that is from God so that we can know all that God has given us. 13And we speak about these things, not with words taught us by human wisdom but with words taught us by the Spirit. And so we explain spiritual truths to spiritual people. 14A person who does not have the Spirit does not accept the truths that come from the Spirit of God. That person thinks they are foolish and cannot understand them, because they can only be judged to be true by the Spirit. **15**The spiritual person is able to judge all things, but no one can judge him. The Scripture says:

16"Who has known the mind of the Lord?
Who has been able to teach him?"

Isaiah 40:13

But we have the mind of Christ.

OLD TESTAMENT READING

So where does wisdom come from,
and where does understanding live?
21It is hidden from the eyes of every living thing,
even from the birds of the air.
22The places of destruction and death say,
'We have heard reports about it.'
23Only God understands the way to wisdom,
and he alone knows where it lives,
24because he looks to the farthest parts of the earth
and sees everything under the sky.
25When God gave power to the wind
and measured the water,
26when he made rules for the rain
and set a path for a thunderstorm to follow,
27then he looked at wisdom and decided its worth;
he set wisdom up and tested it.
28Then he said to humans,
'The fear of the Lord is wisdom;
to stay away from evil is understanding.'"

Job 28:20–28

INSIGHTS

Men are always seeking for greater wisdom, but they usually bypass the Ultimate Source of wisdom. The Scriptures clearly point this direction. They reveal, "The fear of the Lord is the beginning of wisdom, and the knowledge of the Holy One is understanding" (Prov. 9:10). But what has man done with this tremendous resource at his fingertips? Ignored it! "For even though they knew God, they did not honor Him as God, or give thanks; but they became futile in their speculations, and their foolish heart was darkened. Professing to be wise, they became fools" (Rom. 1:21–22).

Since God's wisdom resides in His Word, it is imperative to know what He has revealed, but even many Christians ignore a regular time reading and studying the Scriptures. Therefore, many of their decisions are foolish, because they've not consulted the Ultimate Source of wisdom.

RICK YOHN

APPLICATION

How does Scripture define wisdom? How does a person gain wisdom? Does God need educated and wise teachers to communicate his message? What kind of person does God use? Are you willing to be that kind of person? How will you gain God's wisdom?

1 CORINTHIANS 3:1—4:5

Following People Is Wrong

3 Brothers and sisters, in the past I could not talk to you as I talk to spiritual people. I had to talk to you as I would to people without the Spirit—babies in Christ. **2** The teaching I gave you was like milk, not solid food, because you were not able to take solid food. And even now you are not ready. **3** You are still not spiritual, because there is jealousy and quarreling among you, and this shows that you are not spiritual. You are acting like people of the world. **4** One of you says, "I belong to Paul," and another says, "I belong to Apollos." When you say things like this, you are acting like people of the world.

5 Is Apollos important? No! Is Paul important? No! We are only servants of God who helped you believe. Each one of us did the work God gave us to do. **6** I planted the seed, and Apollos watered it. But God is the One who made it grow. **7** So the one who plants is not important, and the one who waters is not important. Only God, who makes things grow, is important. **8** The one who plants and the one who waters have the same purpose, and each will be rewarded for his own work. **9** We are God's workers, working together; you are like God's farm, God's house.

10 Using the gift God gave me, I laid the foundation of that house like an expert builder. Others are building on that foundation, but all people should be careful how they build on it. **11** The foundation that has already been laid is Jesus Christ, and no one can lay down any other foundation. **12** But if people build on that foundation, using gold, silver, jewels, wood, grass, or straw, **13** their work will be clearly seen, because the Day of Judgment will make it visible. That Day will appear with fire, and the fire will test everyone's work to show what sort of work it was. **14** If the building that has been put on the foundation still stands, the builder will get a reward. **15** But if the building is burned up, the builder will suffer loss. The builder will be saved, but it will be as one who escaped from a fire.

16 Don't you know that you are God's temple and that God's Spirit lives in you? **17** If anyone destroys God's temple, God will destroy that person, because God's temple is holy and you are that temple.

18 Do not fool yourselves. If you think you are wise in this world, you should become a fool so that you can become truly wise, **19** because the wisdom of this world is foolishness with God. It is written in the Scriptures, "He catches those who are wise in their own clever traps." **20** It is also written in the Scriptures, "The Lord knows what wise people think. He knows their thoughts are just a puff of wind." **21** So you should not brag about human leaders. All things belong to you: **22** Paul, Apollos, and Peter; the world, life, death, the present, and the future—all these belong to you. **23** And you belong to Christ, and Christ belongs to God.

Apostles Are Servants of Christ

4 People should think of us as servants of Christ, the ones God has trusted with his secrets. **2** Now in this way those who are trusted with something valuable must show they are worthy of that trust. **3**As for myself, I do not care if I am judged by you or by any human court. I do not even judge myself. **4**I know of no wrong I have done, but this does not make me right before the Lord. The Lord is the One who judges me. **5**So do not judge before the right time; wait until the Lord comes. He will bring to light things that are now hidden in darkness, and will make known the secret purposes of people's hearts. Then God will praise each one of them.

OLD TESTAMENT READING

The LORD says, "Two-thirds of the people through all the land will die. They will be gone,
   and one-third will be left.
9The third that is left I will test with fire,
   purifying them like silver,
   testing them like gold.
Then they will call on me,
   and I will answer them.
I will say, 'You are my people,'
   and they will say, 'The LORD is our God.'"

Zechariah 13:8–9

The stone that the builders rejected became the cornerstone.

Psalm 118:22

INSIGHTS

What does it mean to build your house on the rock or to dig deeply and lay a foundation? . . . It is a matter of building on Jesus Himself. . . . To practice His words means . . . to believe that He is who He says He is and to turn from sin to faith in Him as the way of salvation. . . .

Isaiah writes, "This is what the Sovereign LORD says: 'See I lay a stone in Zion, a tested stone, a precious cornerstone for a sure foundation'" (Isa. 28:16). Paul declares, "You are . . . built on the foundation of the apostles and prophets, with Christ Jesus himself as the chief cornerstone" (Eph 2:19–20). . . . That is the true sense of Christ's teaching: "If you want a life that will last for eternity, build on Me." We sing:

My hope is built on nothing less
Than Jesus' blood and righteousness;
I dare not trust the sweetest frame,
But wholly lean on Jesus' name.

On Christ, the solid rock, I stand;
All other ground is sinking sand. . . .

. . . A life built on Jesus and His teachings will stand—it will stand in the trials and testings of this life, and it will stand in eternity.

JAMES BOICE

ACTION POINT

On what foundation are you building your life's work? Is your work worthy of the foundation; will it stand the test? Pray that your works will be proven worthy.

1 CORINTHIANS 4:6 – 5:8

⁶Brothers and sisters, I have used Apollos and myself as examples so you could learn through us the meaning of the saying, "Follow only what is written in the Scriptures." Then you will not be more proud of one person than another. ⁷Who says you are better than others? What do you have that was not given to you? And if it was given to you, why do you brag as if you did not receive it as a gift?

⁸You think you already have everything you need. You think you are rich. You think you have become kings without us. I wish you really were kings so we could be kings together with you. ⁹But it seems to me that God has put us apostles in last place, like those sentenced to die. We are like a show for the whole world to see—angels and people. ¹⁰We are fools for Christ's sake, but you are very wise in Christ. We are weak, but you are strong. You receive honor, but we are shamed. ¹¹Even to this very hour we do not have enough to eat or drink or to wear. We are often beaten, and we have no homes in which to live. ¹²We work hard with our own hands for our food. When people curse us, we bless them. When they hurt us, we put up with it. ¹³When they tell evil lies about us, we speak nice words about them. Even today, we are treated as though we were the garbage of the world—the filth of the earth.

¹⁴I am not trying to make you feel ashamed. I am writing this to give you a warning as my own dear children. ¹⁵For though you may have ten thousand teachers in Christ, you do not have many fathers. Through the Good News I became your father in Christ Jesus, ¹⁶so I beg you, please follow my example. ¹⁷That is why I am sending to you Timothy, my son in the Lord. I love Timothy, and he is faithful. He will help you remember my way of life in Christ Jesus, just as I teach it in all the churches everywhere.

¹⁸Some of you have become proud, thinking that I will not come to you again. ¹⁹But I will come to you very soon if the Lord wishes. Then I will know what the proud ones do, not what they say, ²⁰because the kingdom of God is present not in talk but in power. ²¹Which do you want: that I come to you with punishment or with love and gentleness?

Wickedness in the Church

It is actually being said that there is sexual sin among you. And it is a kind that does not happen even among people who do not know God. A man there has his father's wife. ²And you are proud! You should have been filled with sadness so that the man who did this should be put out of your group. ³I am not there with you in person, but I am with you in spirit. And I have already judged the man who did that sin as if I were really there. ⁴When you meet together in the name of our Lord Jesus, and I meet with you in spirit with the power of our Lord Jesus, ⁵then hand this man over to Satan. So his sinful self will be destroyed, and his spirit will be saved on the day of the Lord.

⁶Your bragging is not good. You know the saying, "Just a little yeast makes the whole batch of dough rise." ⁷Take out all the old yeast so that you

will be a new batch of dough without yeast, which you really are. For Christ, our Passover lamb, has been sacrificed. **⁸**So let us celebrate this feast, but not with the bread that has the old yeast—the yeast of sin and wickedness. Let us celebrate this feast with the bread that has no yeast—the bread of goodness and truth.

INSIGHTS

Can a Christian get away with sin? Some people seem to think so. However, a closer look points to another answer. God is always opposed to sin. He is never deceived and cannot be outwitted. He may allow sin to continue for a time, but there will be a day of accountability.

Nothing leads to evil quite as much as the idea that this world is all there is. Those who commit violent crimes and who harm the innocent have usually first convinced themselves that there will never be a day of judgment. Even the motorist speeding down the highway has convinced himself he will not receive a speeding ticket.

However, Jesus says that people who believe they will never be found out are wrong: "There is nothing covered up that will not be revealed, and hidden that will not be known" (Luke 12:2). . . .

. . . God totally opposes sin. Take a favorable attitude toward sin and God must take an unfavorable attitude toward you. No Christian can entertain sin and get away with it.

The Royal Canadian Mounted Police have taken as their motto, "We always get our man." The implication is that no matter where a wanted man runs, he will be found. Sin is the same way. No matter how hard we try, we cannot hide our sins. Regardless of how much good we do, it will not cover our disobedience.

God will not allow sin in the lives of His children to go unchecked.

GEORGE SWEETING
DONALD SWEETING

OLD TESTAMENT READING

A man or woman in one of the towns the LORD gave you might be found doing something evil and breaking the Agreement. **⁴**If it is true that such a hateful thing has happened in Israel, **⁵**take the man or woman who has done the evil thing to the city gates and throw stones at that person until he dies.

¹²The person who does not show respect for the judge or priest who is there serving the LORD your God must be put to death. You must get rid of that evil from Israel.

Deuteronomy 17:2, 4b–5, 12

APPLICATION

Why does God tell his people to punish the sinners among them? What was Paul's response to sin in the Corinthian church? What is your response to sin? How might your response be more pleasing to God?

1 CORINTHIANS 5:9 – 6:20

9I wrote you in my earlier letter not to associate with those who sin sexually. **10**But I did not mean you should not associate with those of this world who sin sexually, or with the greedy, or robbers, or those who worship idols. To get away from them you would have to leave this world. **11**I am writing to tell you that you must not associate with those who call themselves believers in Christ but who sin sexually, or are greedy, or worship idols, or abuse others with words, or get drunk, or cheat people. Do not even eat with people like that.

12-13 It is not my business to judge those who are not part of the church. God will judge them. But you must judge the people who are part of the church. The Scripture says, "You must get rid of the evil person among you."

Judging Problems Among Christians

6When you have something against another Christian, how can you bring yourself to go before judges who are not right with God? Why do you not let God's people decide who is right? **2**Surely you know that God's people will judge the world. So if you are to judge the world, are you not able to judge small cases as well? **3**You know that in the future we will judge angels, so surely we can judge the ordinary things of this life. **4**If you have ordinary cases that must be judged, are you going to appoint people as judges who mean nothing to the church? **5**I say this to shame you. Surely there is someone among you wise enough to judge a complaint between believers. **6**But now one believer goes to court against another believer—and you do this in front of unbelievers!

7The fact that you have lawsuits against each other shows that you are already defeated. Why not let yourselves be wronged? Why not let yourselves be cheated? **8**But you yourselves do wrong and cheat, and you do this to other believers!

9-10 Surely you know that the people who do wrong will not inherit God's kingdom. Do not be fooled. Those who sin sexually, worship idols, take part in adultery, those who are male prostitutes, or men who have sexual relations with other men, those who steal, are greedy, get drunk, lie about others, or rob—these people will not inherit God's kingdom. **11**In the past, some of you were like that, but you were washed clean. You were made holy, and you were made right with God in the name of the Lord Jesus Christ and in the Spirit of our God.

Use Your Bodies for God's Glory

12"I am allowed to do all things," but not all things are good for me to do. "I am allowed to do all things," but I will not let anything make me its slave. **13**"Food is for the stomach, and the stomach for food," but God will destroy them both. The body is not for sexual sin but for the Lord, and the Lord is for the body. **14**By his power God has raised the Lord from the dead and will also raise us from the dead. **15**Surely you know that your bodies are parts of Christ himself. So I must never take the parts of Christ and join them to a prostitute! **16**It is written in the Scriptures, "The two will become one body." So you should know that anyone who joins with a prostitute becomes one body with the prostitute. **17**But the one who joins with the Lord is one spirit with the Lord.

18So run away from sexual sin. Every other sin people do is outside their bodies, but those who sin sexually sin against their own bodies. **19**You should know that your body is a temple for the Holy Spirit who is in you. You have received the Holy Spirit from God. So you do not belong to yourselves, **20**because you were bought by God for a price. So honor God with your bodies.

OLD TESTAMENT READING

You cannot carry hot coals against your chest
　　without burning your clothes,
28and you cannot walk on hot coals
　　without burning your feet.
29The same is true if you have sexual relations
　　with another man's wife.
　　Anyone who does so will be punished.

Proverbs 6:27–29

INSIGHTS

It's often said that people "fall" into immorality. The expression is as revealing as it is faulty and dangerous. The very term fall betrays a victim mentality. It sounds as if we were walking down a street and someone tripped us or kicked our feet out from under us. It implies that moral collapse comes out of nowhere, that there is little or nothing we could have done to prevent what happened.

We do not fall into immorality. We walk into it. Indeed, sometimes we run headlong into it. We must realize from the beginning that immorality is a choice. It is not something that happens to people. . . .

Sexual sin never comes out of the clear blue sky. It is often the result of a long process in which a mind susceptible to sin is granted unguarded exposure to immoral input.

"Sow a thought, reap an action. Sow an action, reap a habit. Sow a habit, reap a character. Sow a character, reap a destiny." Our thoughts are the fabric with which we weave our character and destiny. We must actively fight off thoughts of impurity. But the key to doing this is not simply saying "I will not lust, I will not lust"—that often has the same effect as saying, "I will not think of purple elephants." We must cultivate our hearts and minds with what is godly and pure. These better thoughts will displace others (Phil 4:8).

RANDY ALCORN

PAUSE FOR REFLECTION

What does Paul say about judging the lifestyles of other Christians? What sins, in addition to sexual sins, does Paul take a hard line against? Why are we to run away from sin? What are the penalties for continuing in sin?

1 CORINTHIANS 7:1-24

About Marriage

7 Now I will discuss the things you wrote me about. It is good for a man not to have sexual relations with a woman. **2**But because sexual sin is a danger, each man should have his own wife, and each woman should have her own husband. **3**The husband should give his wife all that he owes her as his wife. And the wife should give her husband all that she owes him as her husband. **4**The wife does not have full rights over her own body; her husband shares them. And the husband does not have full rights over his own body; his wife shares them. **5**Do not refuse to give your bodies to each other, unless you both agree to stay away from sexual relations for a time so you can give your time to prayer. Then come together again so Satan cannot tempt you because of a lack of self-control. **6**I say this to give you permission to stay away from sexual relations for a time. It is not a command to do so. **7**I wish that everyone were like me, but each person has his own gift from God. One has one gift, another has another gift.

8Now for those who are not married and for the widows I say this: It is good for them to stay unmarried as I am. **9**But if they cannot control themselves, they should marry. It is better to marry than to burn with sexual desire.

10Now I give this command for the married people. (The command is not from me; it is from the Lord.) A wife should not leave her husband. **11**But if she does leave, she must not marry again, or she should make up with her husband. Also the husband should not divorce his wife.

12For all the others I say this (I am saying this, not the Lord): If a Christian man has a wife who is not a believer, and she is happy to live with him, he must not divorce her. **13**And if a Christian woman has a husband who is not a believer, and he is happy to live with her, she must not divorce him. **14**The husband who is not a believer is made holy through his believing wife. And the wife who is not a believer is made holy through her believing husband. If this were not true, your children would not be clean, but now your children are holy.

15But if those who are not believers decide to leave, let them leave. When this happens, the Christian man or woman is free. But God called us to live in peace. **16**Wife, you don't know; maybe you will save your husband. And husband, you don't know; maybe you will save your wife.

Live as God Called You

17But in any case each one of you should continue to live the way God has given you to live—the way you were when God called you. This is a rule I make in all the churches. **18**If a man was already circumcised when he was called, he should not undo his circumcision. If a man was without circumcision when he was called, he should not be circumcised. **19**It is not important if a man is circumcised or not. The important thing is obeying God's commands. **20**Each one of you should stay the way you were when God called you. **21**If you were a slave when God called you, do not let that bother you. But if you can be free, then make good use of your freedom. **22**Those who were slaves when the Lord called them are free persons who belong to the Lord. In the same way, those who were free when they were called are now Christ's slaves. **23**You all were bought at a great price, so do not become slaves of people. **24**Brothers and sisters, each of you should stay as you were when you were called, and stay there with God.

OLD TESTAMENT READING

God made husbands and wives to become one body and one spirit for his purpose—so they would have children who are true to God.

So be careful, and do not break your promise to the wife you married when you were young.

16The LORD God of Israel says, "I hate divorce. And I hate people who do cruel things as easily as they put on clothes," says the LORD All-Powerful.

Malachi 2:15–16b

INSIGHTS

If Paul is writing anything . . . , he is writing this, "When you marry, you marry for life." He has permanence in mind.

• The wife should not leave her husband (v. 10).
• The husband should not leave his wife (v. 11).
• Let him not send her away (v. 12).
• Let her not send him away (v. 13).

To write it once would be sufficient. Twice would be extremely and unmistakably clear. Three times would be more than enough. But four times? The man means business!

Years ago Cynthia and I took the ugly word divorce out of our dialogues. We agreed we would not even store it in the arsenal of our argument vocabulary. No matter how heated our disagreements may be, we'd not threaten each other with that term. It does something to a marriage when you can count on your partner to stick around and hammer out your differences with each other instead of walking away from them.

What does it take to stick it out . . . to be permanently committed to each other? I repeat, it takes grace! It takes an enormous amount of grace to negotiate through the mine field of disagreements. It takes grace to forgive and go on. Grace to hang tough even though the same mistake is made over and over or the same sin committed again and again. A marriage well-oiled by grace is durable, longlasting—protected against the wear and tear of friction.

CHARLES SWINDOLL

APPLICATION

What do you learn about the seriousness of marriage from these Scripture readings? What adjustments need to be made in your thinking toward marriage? Will you make them?

1 CORINTHIANS 7:25 – 8:8

Questions About Getting Married

25Now I write about people who are not married. I have no command from the Lord about this; I give my opinion. But I can be trusted, because the Lord has shown me mercy. **26**The present time is a time of trouble, so I think it is good for you to stay the way you are. **27**If you have a wife, do not try to become free from her. If you are not married, do not try to find a wife. **28**But if you decide to marry, you have not sinned. And if a girl who has never married decides to marry, she has not sinned. But those who marry will have trouble in this life, and I want you to be free from trouble.

29Brothers and sisters, this is what I mean: We do not have much time left. So starting now, those who have wives should live as if they had no wives. **30**Those who are crying should live as if they were not crying. Those who are happy should live as if they were not happy. Those who buy things should live as if they own nothing. **31**Those who use the things of the world should live as if they were not using them, because this world in its present form will soon be gone.

32I want you to be free from worry. A man who is not married is busy with the Lord's work, trying to please the Lord. **33**But a man who is married is busy with things of the world, trying to please his wife. **34**He must think about two things—pleasing his wife and pleasing the Lord. A woman who is not married or a girl who has never married is busy with the Lord's work. She wants to be holy in body and spirit. But a married woman is busy with things of the world, as to how she can please her husband. **35**I am saying this to help you, not to limit you. But I want you to live in the right way, to give yourselves fully to the Lord without concern for other things.

36If a man thinks he is not doing the right thing with the girl he is engaged to, if she is almost past the best age to marry and he feels he should marry her, he should do what he wants. They should get married. It is no sin. **37**But if a man is sure in his mind that there is no need for marriage, and has his own desires under control, and has decided not to marry the one to whom he is engaged, he is doing the right thing. **38**So the man who marries his girl does right, but the man who does not marry will do better.

39A woman must stay with her husband as long as he lives. But if her husband dies, she is free to marry any man she wants, but she must marry another believer. **40**The woman is happier if she does not marry again. This is my opinion, but I believe I also have God's Spirit.

About Food Offered to Idols

8 Now I will write about meat that is sacrificed to idols. We know that "we all have knowledge." Knowledge puffs you up with pride, but love builds up. **2**If you think you know something, you do not yet know anything as you should. **3**But if any person loves God, that person is known by God.

4So this is what I say about eating meat sacrificed to idols: We know that an idol is really nothing in the world, and we know there is only one

God. **5**Even though there are things called gods, in heaven or on earth (and there are many "gods" and "lords"), **6**for us there is only one God—our Father. All things came from him, and we live for him. And there is only one Lord—Jesus Christ. All things were made through him, and we also were made through him.

7But not all people know this. Some people are still so used to idols that when they eat meat, they still think of it as being sacrificed to an idol. Because their conscience is weak, when they eat it, they feel guilty. **8**But food will not bring us closer to God. Refusing to eat does not make us less pleasing to God, and eating does not make us better in God's sight.

OLD TESTAMENT READING

The LORD spoke his word to me, saying: **5**"Before I made you in your mother's womb, I chose you.

Before you were born, I set you apart for a special work
I appointed you as a prophet to the nations."

9Then the LORD reached out his hand and touched my mouth. He said to me, "See, I am putting my words in your mouth. **10**Today I have put you in charge of nations and kingdoms. You will pull up and tear down, destroy and overthrow, build up and plant."

Then the LORD spoke his word to me: **2**"You must not get married or have sons or daughters in this place."

Jeremiah 1:4–5, 9–10; 16:1–2

INSIGHTS

Jesus declared that there were those who were single "for the sake of the kingdom of heaven" (Matt. 19:12). And Paul builds on this foundation by suggesting that the unmarried can focus their energies toward the work of God in a way that the married simply cannot (1 Cor. 7:32–35).

Some have railed at Paul for urging people to seriously consider the single life, but the truth is that his words are filled with practical wisdom. He was not against marriage—in fact his great contribution to Christian sexual theology is the way he compares the sexual union in marriage to the union of Christ and his Church. But Paul did insist that we count the cost. You see, no one should enter the covenant of marriage without realizing the immense time and energy required to make that relationship work.

Richard Foster

APPLICATION

What does a person's marital status have to do with his or her spiritual service? What is more important than whether a person is married or single? Pray that you will be true to God's calling for you.

1 CORINTHIANS
8:9 — 9:18

9But be careful that your freedom does not cause those who are weak in faith to fall into sin. **10**Suppose one of you who has knowledge eats in an idol's temple. Someone who is weak in faith might see you eating there and be encouraged to eat meat sacrificed to idols while thinking it is wrong to do so. **11**This weak believer for whom Christ died is ruined because of your "knowledge." **12**When you sin against your brothers and sisters in Christ like this and cause them to do what they feel is wrong, you are also sinning against Christ. **13**So if the food I eat causes them to fall into sin, I will never eat meat again so that I will not cause any of them to sin.

Paul Is like the Other Apostles

9 I am a free man. I am an apostle. I have seen Jesus our Lord. You people are all an example of my work in the Lord. **2**If others do not accept me as an apostle, surely you do, because you are proof that I am an apostle in the Lord.

3This is the answer I give people who want to judge me: **4**Do we not have the right to eat and drink? **5**Do we not have the right to bring a believing wife with us when we travel as do the other apostles and the Lord's brothers and Peter? **6**Are Barnabas and I the only ones who must work to earn our living? **7**No soldier ever serves in the army and pays his own salary. No one ever plants a vineyard without eating some of the grapes. No person takes care of a flock without drinking some of the milk.

8I do not say this by human authority; God's law also says the same thing. **9**It is written in the law of Moses: "When an ox is working in the grain, do not cover its mouth to keep it from eating." When God said this, was he thinking only about oxen? No. **10**He was really talking about us. Yes, that Scripture was written for us, because it goes on to say: "The one who plows and the one who works in the grain should hope to get some of the grain for their work." **11**Since we planted spiritual seed among you, is it too much if we should harvest material things? **12**If others have the right to get something from you, surely we have this right, too. But we do not use it. No, we put up with everything ourselves so that we will not keep anyone from believing the Good News of Christ. **13**Surely you know that those who work at the Temple get their food from the Temple, and those who serve at the altar get part of what is offered at the altar. **14**In the same way, the Lord has commanded that those who tell the Good News should get their living from this work.

15But I have not used any of these rights. And I am not writing this now to get anything from you. I would rather die than to have my reason for bragging taken away. **16**Telling the Good News does not give me any reason for bragging. Telling the Good News is my duty—something I must do. And how terrible it will be for me if I do not tell the Good News. **17**If I preach because it is my own choice, I have a reward. But if I preach and it is not my choice to do so, I am only doing the duty that was given to me. **18**So what reward do I get? This is my reward: that when I tell the Good News I can offer it freely. I do not use my full rights in my work of preaching the Good News.

OLD TESTAMENT READING

made some of your children to be prophets
and some of your young people to be
Nazirites.
People of Israel, isn't this true?" says the LORD.

12"But you made the Nazirites drink wine
and told the prophets not to prophesy.
13Now I will make you get stuck,
as a wagon loaded with grain gets
stuck.
14No one will escape, not even the fastest
runner.
Strong people will not be strong enough;
warriors will not be able to save
themselves."

Amos 2:11–14

INSIGHTS

Few would question the assertion that we should renounce the wrong things in our lives. It is self-evident that such things mar our lives, spoil our enjoyment of life, and limit our usefulness to God and man. But not everyone is equally convinced that in the interest of the gospel the disciple of Christ may need to renounce some things that are perfectly right and legitimate. . . .

Four times in 1 Corinthians 9 Paul asserts his rights in the gospel. Three times he claims that he has refrained from exercising these rights in the higher interests of spreading the gospel. He affirms that he is ready to forgo any right he may have, and forsake any privilege, out of love for Christ and in the interests of the progress of the gospel. . . .

Oswald Chambers had some trenchant words to say in this connection: "If we are willing to give up only wrong things for Jesus, never let us talk about being in love with Him. Anyone will give up wrong things if he knows how, but are we prepared to give up the best we have for Jesus Christ? The only right a Christian has is the right to give up his rights. If we are to be the best for God, there must be victory in the realm of legitimate desire as well as in the realm of unlawful indulgence." . . .

. . . The disciple must choose his priorities very carefully, even in things that are right in themselves. If we are aiming at the heights of Christian experience, there will always come the challenge to voluntary renunciation of some rights.

J. OSWALD SANDERS

APPLICATION

Define Christian freedom in your own words. What is the objective of Christian freedom? What legitimate freedoms did Paul sacrifice for the sake of the Gospel? How much freedom will you sacrifice for the cause of Christ?

1 CORINTHIANS 9:19 – 10:22

¹⁹I am free and belong to no one. But I make myself a slave to all people to win as many as I can. ²⁰To the Jews I became like a Jew to win the Jews. I myself am not ruled by the law. But to those who are ruled by the law I became like a person who is ruled by the law. I did this to win those who are ruled by the law. ²¹To those who are without the law I became like a person who is without the law. I did this to win those people who are without the law. (But really, I am not without God's law—I am ruled by Christ's law.) ²²To those who are weak, I became weak so I could win the weak. I have become all things to all people so I could save some of them in any way possible. ²³I do all this because of the Good News and so I can share in its blessings.

²⁴You know that in a race all the runners run, but only one gets the prize. So run to win! ²⁵All those who compete in the games use self-control so they can win a crown. That crown is an earthly thing that lasts only a short time, but our crown will never be destroyed. ²⁶So I do not run without a goal. I fight like a boxer who is hitting something—not just the air. ²⁷I treat my body hard and make it my slave so that I myself will not be disqualified after I have preached to others.

Warnings from Israel's Past

10 Brothers and sisters, I want you to know what happened to our ancestors who followed Moses. They were all under the cloud and all went through the sea. ²They were all baptized as followers of Moses in the cloud and in the sea. ³They all ate the same spiritual food, ⁴and all drank the same spiritual drink. They drank from that spiritual rock that followed them, and that rock was Christ. ⁵But God was not pleased with most of them, so they died in the desert.

⁶And these things happened as examples for us, to stop us from wanting evil things as those people did. ⁷Do not worship idols, as some of them did. Just as it is written in the Scriptures: "They sat down to eat and drink, and then they got up and sinned sexually." ⁸We must not take part in sexual sins, as some of them did. In one day twenty-three thousand of them died because of their sins. ⁹We must not test Christ as some of them did; they were killed by snakes. ¹⁰Do not complain as some of them did; they were killed by the angel that destroys.

¹¹The things that happened to those people are examples. They were written down to teach us, because we live in a time when all these things of the past have reached their goal. ¹²If you think you are strong, you should be careful not to fall. ¹³The only temptation that has come to you is that which everyone has. But you can trust God, who will not permit you to be tempted more than you can stand. But when you are tempted, he will also give you a way to escape so that you will be able to stand it.

¹⁴So, my dear friends, run away from the worship of idols. ¹⁵I am speaking to you as to reasonable people; judge for yourselves what I say. ¹⁶We give thanks for the cup of blessing, which is a

sharing in the blood of Christ. And the bread that we break is a sharing in the body of Christ. **17**Because there is one loaf of bread, we who are many are one body, because we all share that one loaf.

18Think about the Israelites: Do not those who eat the sacrifices share in the altar? **19**I do not mean that the food sacrificed to an idol is important. I do not mean that an idol is anything at all. **20**But I say that what is sacrificed to idols is offered to demons, not to God. And I do not want you to share anything with demons. **21**You cannot drink the cup of the Lord and the cup of demons also. You cannot share in the Lord's table and the table of demons. **22**Are we trying to make the Lord jealous? We are not stronger than he is, are we?

OLD TESTAMENT READING

Then the LORD said to Satan, "Have you noticed my servant Job? No one else on earth is like him. He is an honest and innocent man, honoring God and staying away from evil. You caused me to ruin him for no good reason, but he continues to be without blame."

4"One skin for another!" Satan answered. "A man will give all he has to save his own life. **5**But reach out your hand and destroy his flesh and bones, and he will curse you to your face."

6The LORD said to Satan, "All right, then. Job is in your power, but you may not take his life."

7So Satan left the LORD's presence. He put painful sores on Job's body, from the top of his head to the soles of his feet. **8**Job took a piece of broken pottery to scrape himself, and he sat in ashes in misery.

9Job's wife said to him, "Why are you trying to stay innocent? Curse God and die!"

10Job answered, "You are talking like a foolish woman. Should we take only good things from God and not trouble?" In spite of all this Job did not sin in what he said.

Job 2:3–10

INSIGHTS

I have often heard my husband tell our teenagers, "Temptation is not only an opportunity to do the wrong thing, but an opportunity to do the right!" Although we usually consider temptation in negative terms, God allows us to be tempted in order to provide us with a chance to be obedient. If we are to learn to say no, and we are certainly supposed to say no sometimes to some things, then circumstances become life's workshop to that end. Saying no when you want to say yes strengthens you, produces endurance, and builds character—Christian character.

JILL BRISCOE

APPLICATION

What did Paul mean when he said he made his body a slave? Why did he do that? What things does the example of the Israelites in the desert warn us against? How seriously do you take that warning?

1 CORINTHIANS 10:23 — 11:22

How to Use Christian Freedom

23"We are allowed to do all things," but not all things are good for us to do. "We are allowed to do all things," but not all things help others grow stronger. **24**Do not look out only for yourselves. Look out for the good of others also.

25Eat any meat that is sold in the meat market. Do not ask questions about it. **26**You may eat it, "because the earth belongs to the Lord, and everything in it."

27Those who are not believers may invite you to eat with them. If you want to go, eat anything that is put before you. Do not ask questions about it. **28**But if anyone says to you, "That food was offered to idols," do not eat it. Do not eat it because of that person who told you and because eating it might be thought to be wrong. **29**I don't mean you think it is wrong, but the other person might. But why, you ask, should my freedom be judged by someone else's conscience? **30**If I eat the meal with thankfulness, why am I criticized because of something for which I thank God?

31The answer is, if you eat or drink, or if you do anything, do it all for the glory of God. **32**Never do anything that might hurt others—Jews, Greeks, or God's church— **33**just as I, also, try to please everybody in every way. I am not trying to do what is good for me but what is good for most people so they can be saved.

11 Follow my example, as I follow the example of Christ.

Being Under Authority

2I praise you because you remember me in everything, and you follow closely the teachings just as I gave them to you. **3**But I want you to understand this: The head of every man is Christ, the head of a woman is the man, and the head of Christ is God. **4**Every man who prays or prophesies with his head covered brings shame to his head. **5**But every woman who prays or prophesies with her head uncovered brings shame to her head. She is the same as a woman who has her head shaved. **6**If a woman does not cover her head, she should have her hair cut off. But since it is shameful for a woman to cut off her hair or to shave her head, she should cover her head. **7**But a man should not cover his head, because he is the likeness and glory of God. But woman is man's glory. **8**Man did not come from woman, but woman came from man. **9**And man was not made for woman, but woman was made for man. **10**So that is why a woman should have a symbol of authority on her head, because of the angels.

11But in the Lord women are not independent of men, and men are not independent of women. **12**This is true because woman came from man, but also man is born from woman. But everything comes from God. **13**Decide this for yourselves: Is it right for a woman to pray to God with her head uncovered? **14**Even nature itself teaches you that wearing long hair is shameful for a man. **15**But long hair is a woman's glory. Long hair is given to her as a covering. [16]Some people may still want to argue about this, but I would add that neither we nor the churches of God have any other practice.

The Lord's Supper

[17]In the things I tell you now I do not praise you, because when you come together you do more harm than good. [18]First, I hear that when you meet together as a church you are divided, and I believe some of this. [19](It is necessary to have differences among you so that it may be clear which of you really have God's approval.) [20]When you come together, you are not really eating the Lord's Supper. [21]This is because when you eat, each person eats without waiting for the others. Some people do not get enough to eat, while others have too much to drink. [22]You can eat and drink in your own homes! You seem to think God's church is not important, and you embarrass those who are poor. What should I tell you? Should I praise you? I do not praise you for doing this.

OLD TESTAMENT READING

Now Eli's sons were evil men; they did not care about the LORD.

[30]"So the LORD, the God of Israel, says: 'I promised that your family and your ancestor's family would serve me always.' But now the LORD says: 'This must stop! I will honor those who honor me, but I will dishonor those who ignore me. [31]The time is coming when I will destroy the descendants of both you and your ancestors. No man will grow old in your family.'"

1 Samuel 2:12, 30–31

INSIGHTS

Everything created was through Christ and His power, and furthermore, it was created for His honor. That includes everyday things today. You have a good job? It's to be enjoyed for Him. . . . You have good health? It is for Him. You have a family? The family members are for Him. . . . That is true because He's the ruler of our kingdom. He is Lord. And that's not simply the title of a chorus Christians sing; it's a statement of faith. He has the right to take charge of our decisions so that He might be honored through them. Every day I live I must address that. Again, it is a matter of priorities. . . .

. . . Those who are really committed to excellence give Him top priority.

CHARLES SWINDOLL

APPLICATION

Think about Jesus' commandment to love God and to love one another. Notice how Paul's instructions fulfill his command. In what practical ways can you obey Christ's commandments and honor God in your daily life?

1 CORINTHIANS
11:23 — 12:13

23The teaching I gave you is the same teaching I received from the Lord: On the night when the Lord Jesus was handed over to be killed, he took bread **24**and gave thanks for it. Then he broke the bread and said, "This is my body; it is for you. Do this to remember me." **25**In the same way, after they ate, Jesus took the cup. He said, "This cup is the new agreement that is sealed with the blood of my death. When you drink this, do it to remember me." **26**Every time you eat this bread and drink this cup you are telling others about the Lord's death until he comes.

27So a person who eats the bread or drinks the cup of the Lord in a way that is not worthy of it will be guilty of sinning against the body and the blood of the Lord. **28**Look into your own hearts before you eat the bread and drink the cup, **29**because all who eat the bread and drink the cup without recognizing the body eat and drink judgment against themselves. **30**That is why many in your group are sick and weak, and some of you have died. **31**But if we judged ourselves in the right way, God would not judge us. **32**But when the Lord judges us, he disciplines us so that we will not be destroyed along with the world.

33So my brothers and sisters, when you come together to eat, wait for each other. **34**Anyone who is too hungry should eat at home so that in meeting together you will not bring God's judgment on yourselves. I will tell you what to do about the other things when I come.

Gifts from the Holy Spirit

12 Now, brothers and sisters, I want you to understand about spiritual gifts. **2**You know the way you lived before you were believers. You let yourselves be influenced and led away to worship idols—things that could not speak. **3**So I want you to understand that no one who is speaking with the help of God's Spirit says, "Jesus be cursed." And no one can say, "Jesus is Lord," without the help of the Holy Spirit.

4There are different kinds of gifts, but they are all from the same Spirit. **5**There are different ways to serve but the same Lord to serve. **6**And there are different ways that God works through people but the same God. God works in all of us in everything we do. **7**Something from the Spirit can be seen in each person, for the common good. **8**The Spirit gives one person the ability to speak with wisdom, and the same Spirit gives another the ability to speak with knowledge. **9**The same Spirit gives faith to one person. And, to another, that one Spirit gives gifts of healing. **10**The Spirit gives to another person the power to do miracles, to another the ability to prophesy. And he gives to another the ability to know the difference between good and evil spirits. The Spirit gives one person the ability to speak in different kinds of languages and to another the ability to interpret those languages. **11**One Spirit, the same Spirit, does all these things, and the Spirit decides what to give each person.

The Body of Christ Works Together

12A person's body is one thing, but it has many parts. Though there are many parts to a body, all those parts make only one body. Christ is like that also. **13**Some of us are Jews, and some are Greeks. Some of us are slaves, and some are free. But we were all baptized into one body through one Spirit. And we were all made to share in the one Spirit.

OLD TESTAMENT READING

Joshua son of Nun was then filled with wisdom, because Moses had put his hands on him. So the Israelites listened to Joshua, and they did what the LORD had commanded Moses.

Deuteronomy 34:9

Then the LORD said to Moses, **2**"See, I have chosen Bezalel son of Uri from the tribe of Judah. (Uri was the son of Hur.) **3**I have filled Bezalel with the Spirit of God and have given him the skill, ability, and knowledge to do all kinds of work. **4**He is able to design pieces to be made from gold, silver, and bronze, **5**to cut jewels and put them in metal, to carve wood, and to do all kinds of work. **6**I have also chosen Oholiab son of Ahisamach from the tribe of Dan to work with Bezalel. I have given skills to all the craftsmen, and they will be able to make all these things I have commanded you: **7**the Meeting Tent, the Ark of the Agreement, the lid that covers the Ark, and everything in the Tent."

Exodus 31:1–7

INSIGHTS

It may take another Christian to pinpoint for us a particular talent we have. For instance, in the course of speaking at a meeting, I started, "I'm a one-talent person." . . . The meeting was scarcely over when a young woman dashed up to me and said, "That's not true what you said tonight. . . . I know about your writing and other things you do, but the best part is that you're good at sitting by the fire and being a friend."

It's evident, then, that we can be using a talent even when we do not recognize that we possess it. . . .

Perhaps we wish we could have had some choice as to which gift or ability would be ours. Maybe we would gladly trade ours off for something that has more appeal for us. But our all-wise God has apportioned His gifts as He wills, and one day He will require from each of us an accounting of our use of those gifts. . . .

If you and I really want to be used by our Lord, it will pay us to ferret out what our particular ability is, then get busy putting it to use.

JEANETTE LOCKERBIE

PAUSE FOR REFLECTION

How are the gifts that the Spirit gives to different individuals intended to work together (1 Cor. 12:1–13)? What do the Scriptures reveal to you about the purpose of spiritual gifts?

1 CORINTHIANS 12:14 — 13:13

14The human body has many parts. **15**The foot might say, "Because I am not a hand, I am not part of the body." But saying this would not stop the foot from being a part of the body. **16**The ear might say, "Because I am not an eye, I am not part of the body." But saying this would not stop the ear from being a part of the body. **17**If the whole body were an eye, it would not be able to hear. If the whole body were an ear, it would not be able to smell. **18-19**If each part of the body were the same part, there would be no body. But truly God put all the parts, each one of them, in the body as he wanted them. **20**So then there are many parts, but only one body.

21The eye cannot say to the hand, "I don't need you!" And the head cannot say to the foot, "I don't need you!" **22**No! Those parts of the body that seem to be the weaker are really necessary. **23**And the parts of the body we think are less deserving are the parts to which we give the most honor. We give special respect to the parts we want to hide. **24**The more respectable parts of our body need no special care. But God put the body together and gave more honor to the parts that need it **25**so our body would not be divided. God wanted the different parts to care the same for each other. **26**If one part of the body suffers, all the other parts suffer with it. Or if one part of our body is honored, all the other parts share its honor.

27Together you are the body of Christ, and each one of you is a part of that body. **28**In the church God has given a place first to apostles, second to prophets, and third to teachers. Then God has given a place to those who do miracles, those who have gifts of healing, those who can help others, those who are able to govern, and those who can speak in different languages. **29**Not all are apostles. Not all are prophets. Not all are teachers. Not all do miracles. **30**Not all have gifts of healing. Not all speak in different languages. Not all interpret those languages. **31**But you should truly want to have the greater gifts.

Love Is the Greatest Gift

And now I will show you the best way of all.

13 I may speak in different languages of people or even angels. But if I do not have love, I am only a noisy bell or a crashing cymbal. **2**I may have the gift of prophecy. I may understand all the secret things of God and have all knowledge, and I may have faith so great I can move mountains. But even with all these things, if I do not have love, then I am nothing. **3**I may give away everything I have, and I may even give my body as an offering to be burned. But I gain nothing if I do not have love.

4Love is patient and kind. Love is not jealous, it does not brag, and it is not proud. **5**Love is not rude, is not selfish, and does not get upset with others. Love does not count up wrongs that have been done. **6**Love takes no pleasure in evil but rejoices over the truth. **7**Love patiently accepts all things. It always trusts, always hopes, and always endures.

8Love never ends. There are gifts of prophecy, but they will be ended. There are gifts of speaking in different languages, but those gifts will stop.

There is the gift of knowledge, but it will come to an end. **9**The reason is that our knowledge and our ability to prophesy are not perfect. **10**But when perfection comes, the things that are not perfect will end. **11**When I was a child, I talked like a child, I thought like a child, I reasoned like a child. When I became a man, I stopped those childish ways. **12**It is the same with us. Now we see a dim reflection, as if we were looking into a mirror, but then we shall see clearly. Now I know only a part, but then I will know fully, as God has known me. **13**So these three things continue forever: faith, hope, and love. And the greatest of these is love.

OLD TESTAMENT READING

At mealtime Boaz told Ruth, "Come here. Eat some of our bread and dip it in our sauce."

So Ruth sat down beside the workers. Boaz handed her some roasted grain, and she ate until she was full; she even had some food left over. **15**When Ruth rose and went back to work, Boaz commanded his workers, "Let her gather even around the piles of cut grain. Don't tell her to go away. **16**In fact, drop some full heads of grain for her from what you have in your hands, and let her gather them. Don't tell her to stop."

Ruth 2:14–16

INSIGHTS

Jesus never wrote a book, yet the nature of his love was indelibly impressed upon the minds of his followers. They could never forget their three years experience with the Master. He was the Model. His very life clearly defined love for them. . . .

- Jesus was concerned about their families, homes, and health.
- Jesus was willing to take time for people in need even though he was engaged in a busy ministry.
- Jesus provided faithful support in the spiritual battle by intercessory prayer.
- Jesus extended complete forgiveness, even when it seemed undeserved.
- Jesus humbly served his followers, exemplified in his washing their feet.
- Jesus ultimately gave himself in his death on Calvary's cross.

In all of these acts of compassion, Jesus modeled a practical brand of love. His was a love that ministered to his disciples' pressing needs. Calvary, of course, tied it all together: The cross dealt finally with their sins and opened the way for them to experience all the blessings of God. . . .

So it is with us. If we are to love our brothers and sisters as Jesus commanded, we must learn to express a practical love for the whole person. It must be the kind of love our Master has shown to us.

WILLIAM FLETCHER

APPLICATION

What examples of Christian love that you have experienced stand out in your mind? What did those experiences teach you about love? What example of Jesus' love do you want to put into practice in your life?

1 CORINTHIANS 14:1-25

Desire Spiritual Gifts

14 You should seek after love, and you should truly want to have the spiritual gifts, especially the gift of prophecy. **2**I will explain why. Those who have the gift of speaking in different languages are not speaking to people; they are speaking to God. No one understands them; they are speaking secret things through the Spirit. **3**But those who prophesy are speaking to people to give them strength, encouragement, and comfort. **4**The ones who speak in different languages are helping only themselves, but those who prophesy are helping the whole church. **5**I wish all of you had the gift of speaking in different kinds of languages, but more, I wish you would prophesy. Those who prophesy are greater than those who can only speak in different languages—unless someone is there who can explain what is said so that the whole church can be helped.

6Brothers and sisters, will it help you if I come to you speaking in different languages? No! It will help you only if I bring you a new truth or some new knowledge, or prophecy, or teaching. **7**It is the same as with lifeless things that make sounds—like a flute or a harp. If they do not make clear musical notes, you will not know what is being played. **8**And in a war, if the trumpet does not give a clear sound, who will prepare for battle? **9**It is the same with you. Unless you speak clearly with your tongue, no one can understand what you are saying. You will be talking into the air! **10**It may be true that there are all kinds of sounds in the world, and none is without meaning. **11**But unless I understand the meaning of what someone says to me, we will be like foreigners to each other. **12**It is the same with you. Since you want spiritual gifts very much, seek most of all to have the gifts that help the church grow stronger.

13The one who has the gift of speaking in a different language should pray for the gift to interpret what is spoken. **14**If I pray in a different language, my spirit is praying, but my mind does nothing. **15**So what should I do? I will pray with my spirit, but I will also pray with my mind. I will sing with my spirit, but I will also sing with my mind. **16**If you praise God with your spirit, those persons there without understanding cannot say amen to your prayer of thanks, because they do not know what you are saying. **17**You may be thanking God in a good way, but the other person is not helped.

18I thank God that I speak in different kinds of languages more than all of you. **19**But in the church meetings I would rather speak five words I understand in order to teach others than thousands of words in a different language.

20Brothers and sisters, do not think like children. In evil things be like babies, but in your thinking you should be like adults. **21**It is written in the Scriptures:

> "With people who use strange words and foreign languages
> I will speak to these people.

But even then they will not listen to me,"

Isaiah 28:11–12

says the Lord.

22So the gift of speaking in different kinds of languages is a sign for those who do not believe, not for those who do believe. And prophecy is for people who believe, not for those who do not believe. **23**Suppose the whole church meets together and everyone speaks in different languages. If some people come in who do not understand or do not believe, they will say you are crazy. **24**But suppose everyone is prophesying and some people come in who do not believe or do not understand. If everyone is prophesying, their sin will be shown to them, and they will be judged by all that they hear. **25**The secret things in their hearts will be made known. So they will bow down and worship God saying, "Truly, God is with you."

OLD TESTAMENT READING

Josiah also broke down the altar at Bethel— the place of worship made by Jeroboam son of Nebat, who had led Israel to sin. Josiah burned that place, broke the stones of the altar into pieces, then beat them into dust. He also burned the Asherah idol. **16**When he turned around, he saw the graves on the mountain. He had the bones taken from the graves, and he burned them on the altar to ruin it. This happened as the LORD had said it would through the man of God.

2 Kings 23:15–16

INSIGHTS

The gifts of the Spirit . . . come to us from the Holy Spirit. He chooses who gets which gifts, and He dispenses them at His good pleasure. While we are held accountable for the use of any gifts He gives us, we have no responsibility for gifts we have not been given. Nor are we to covet what someone else has or be envious of that person. We may wish to have certain gifts and even ask for them, but if it is not the will of the Holy Spirit, we will not get what we ask for. And if we are dissatisfied because the Holy Spirit does not give us the gifts we want, we sin. . . .

Paul says that the purpose of these spiritual gifts is, "for the equipping of the saints for the work of service, to the building up of the body of Christ" (Eph. 4:12). In other words, God has given each of us a task to do, and supernatural gifts to equip us for it. . . .

In 1 Corinthians 12:7, the apostle Paul says the gifts are given "for the common good," so we are not to use them selfishly. Instead, we are to use them to help each other. . . .

God has also designed the gifts to help "unite" the body of Christ. . . .

Thus the gifts of the Spirit should never divide the body of Christ; they should unify it.

BILLY GRAHAM

APPLICATION

What is the purpose of spiritual gifts? What is the difference between prophesying and speaking in tongues? Why do you desire spiritual gifts? Pray that you will use your gift to God's glory.

1 CORINTHIANS 14:26 – 15:11

Meetings Should Help the Church

26So, brothers and sisters, what should you do? When you meet together, one person has a song, and another has a teaching. Another has a new truth from God. Another speaks in a different language, and another person interprets that language. The purpose of all these things should be to help the church grow strong. **27**When you meet together, if anyone speaks in a different language, it should be only two, or not more than three, who speak. They should speak one after the other, and someone should interpret. **28**But if there is no interpreter, then those who speak in a different language should be quiet in the church meeting. They should speak only to themselves and to God.

29Only two or three prophets should speak, and the others should judge what they say. **30**If a message from God comes to another person who is sitting, the first speaker should stop. **31**You can all prophesy one after the other. In this way all the people can be taught and encouraged. **32**The spirits of prophets are under the control of the prophets themselves. **33**God is not a God of confusion but a God of peace.

As is true in all the churches of God's people, **34**women should keep quiet in the church meetings. They are not allowed to speak, but they must yield to this rule as the law says. **35**If they want to learn something, they should ask their own husbands at home. It is shameful for a woman to speak in the church meeting. **36**Did God's teach-

ing come from you? Or are you the only ones to whom it has come?

37Those who think they are prophets or spiritual persons should understand that what I am writing to you is the Lord's command. **38**Those who ignore this will be ignored by God.

39So my brothers and sisters, you should truly want to prophesy. But do not stop people from using the gift of speaking in different kinds of languages. **40**But let everything be done in a right and orderly way.

The Good News About Christ

15Now, brothers and sisters, I want you to remember the Good News I brought to you. You received this Good News and continue strong in it. **2**And you are being saved by it if you continue believing what I told you. If you do not, then you believed for nothing.

3I passed on to you what I received, of which this was most important: that Christ died for our sins, as the Scriptures say; **4**that he was buried and was raised to life on the third day as the Scriptures say; **5**and that he was seen by Peter and then by the twelve apostles. **6**After that, Jesus was seen by more than five hundred of the believers at the same time. Most of them are still living today, but some have died. **7**Then he was seen by James and later by all the apostles. **8**Last of all he was seen by me—as by a person not born at the normal time. **9**All the other apostles are greater than I am. I am not even good enough to be called an apostle, because I persecuted the church of God. **10**But God's grace has made me what I am, and his grace to me was not wasted. I worked harder than all the other apostles. (But it was not I really; it was God's grace that was with me.) **11**So if I preached to you or the other apostles preached to you, we all preach the same thing, and this is what you believed.

OLD TESTAMENT READING

He was put to death;
he was punished for the sins of my people.
9He was buried with wicked men,
and he died with the rich.

Isaiah 53:8c–9a

God has risen with a shout of joy;
the LORD has risen as the trumpets
sounded.
6Sing praises to God. Sing praises.
Sing praises to our King. Sing praises.
7God is King of all the earth,
so sing a song of praise to him.
8God is King over the nations.
God sits on his holy throne.

Psalm 47:5–8

INSIGHTS

In the guise of a man, Jesus the Christ, was born, lived, grew up, worked, was crucified, and rose from the grave among us, He ascended back to His splendor among us.

In all of this, though subject to the strains and stresses of our human society, he never sinned. His was a perfect performance. His was a life without a single stain. His was the "perfect doing" and "perfect dying" required to redeem all men for all time from all their wrongs and sins and stains. . . .

It was in my stead He did all this: He paid the penalty for all my wrongs. He bled and suffered and died for me. He took my sins to set me free. It was to satisfy His own righteousness that He became my substitute. He did this to impute to me His own wondrous righteousness.

This is a titanic transaction of eternal dimensions. God, very God, in Christ takes my sins and gives me His goodness . . . His own righteousness.

Nothing else can satisfy my searching spirit. I look away from myself to see the splendor of His supreme self-sacrifice for my salvation. I see that He has made me whole. He has enfolded and filled me with His righteousness. He has accepted me as His own son. He is my living Lord and Savior. He is my Father!

My spirit leaps for joy, where before it was sunk with sin and despair. His Spirit bears witness with my spirit that I am now His son. In overwhelming appreciation and gratitude, I look up and my spirit cries, "Abba Father!"

W. PHILLIP KELLER

APPLICATION

What are the essential elements of the Christian faith? How fully was the Good News foretold in the Old Testament? Why must we continue believing the Good News? Pray that your faith will continue strong!

1 CORINTHIANS 15:12-44a

We Will Be Raised from the Dead

12Now since we preached that Christ was raised from the dead, why do some of you say that people will not be raised from the dead? **13**If no one is ever raised from the dead, then Christ has not been raised. **14**And if Christ has not been raised, then our preaching is worth nothing, and your faith is worth nothing. **15**And also, we are guilty of lying about God, because we testified of him that he raised Christ from the dead. But if people are not raised from the dead, then God never raised Christ. **16**If the dead are not raised, Christ has not been raised either. **17**And if Christ has not been raised, then your faith has nothing to it; you are still guilty of your sins. **18**And those in Christ who have already died are lost. **19**If our hope in Christ is for this life only, we should be pitied more than anyone else in the world.

20But Christ has truly been raised from the dead—the first one and proof that those who sleep in death will also be raised. **21**Death has come because of what one man did, but the rising from death also comes because of one man. **22**In Adam all of us die. In the same way, in Christ all of us will be made alive again. **23**But everyone will be raised to life in the right order. Christ was first to be raised. When Christ comes again, those who belong to him will be raised to life, **24**and then the end will come. At that time Christ will destroy all rulers, authorities, and powers, and he will hand over the kingdom to God the Father. **25**Christ must rule until he puts all enemies under his control. **26**The last enemy to be destroyed will be death. **27**The Scripture says that God put all things under his control. When it says "all things" are under him, it is clear this does not include God himself. God is the One who put everything under his control. **28**After everything has been put under the Son, then he will put himself under God, who had put all things under him. Then God will be the complete ruler over everything.

29If the dead are never raised, what will people do who are being baptized for the dead? If the dead are not raised at all, why are people being baptized for them?

30And what about us? Why do we put ourselves in danger every hour? **31**I die every day. That is true, brothers and sisters, just as it is true that I brag about you in Christ Jesus our Lord. **32**If I fought wild animals in Ephesus only with human hopes, I have gained nothing. If the dead are not raised, "Let us eat and drink, because tomorrow we will die."

33Do not be fooled: "Bad friends will ruin good habits." **34**Come back to your right way of thinking and stop sinning. Some of you do not know God—I say this to shame you.

What Kind of Body Will We Have?

35But someone may ask, "How are the dead raised? What kind of body will they have?" **36**Foolish person! When you sow a seed, it must die in the ground before it can live and grow. **37**And when you sow it, it does not have the same "body" it will have later. What you sow is only a bare seed, maybe wheat or something else. **38**But God gives it a body that he has planned for it, and God gives each kind of seed its own body. **39**All things made of flesh are not the same: People have one kind of flesh, animals have another, birds have another, and fish have another. **40**Also there are heavenly bodies and earthly bodies. But the beauty of the heavenly bodies is one kind, and the beauty of the earthly bodies is another. **41**The sun has one kind of beauty, the moon has another beauty, and the stars have another. And each star is different in its beauty.

42It is the same with the dead who are raised to life. The body that is "planted" will ruin and decay, but it is raised to a life that cannot be destroyed. **43**When the body is "planted," it is without honor, but it is raised in glory. When the body is "planted," it is weak, but when it is raised, it is powerful. **44**The body that is "planted" is a physical body. When it is raised, it is a spiritual body.

OLD TESTAMENT READING

Many people who have already died will live again. Some of them will wake up to have life forever, but some will wake up to find shame and disgrace forever. **3**The wise people will shine like the brightness of the sky. Those who teach others to live right will shine like stars forever and ever."

Daniel 12:2–3

INSIGHTS

Often when we are racked with pain and unable to think or worship, we feel that this indeed is "the body of our humiliation," and when we are tempted by the passions which rise from the flesh we do not think the word "vile" at all too vigorous a translation. Our bodies humble us; and that is about the best thing they do for us. Oh, that we were duly lowly, because our bodies ally us with animals and even link us with the dust!

But our Savior, the Lord Jesus, shall change all this. We shall be fashioned like His own body of glory. This will take place in all who believe in Jesus. By faith their souls have been transformed, and their bodies will undergo such a renewal as shall fit them for their regenerated spirits. How soon this grand transformation will happen we cannot tell; but the thought of it should help us to bear the trials of today and all the woes of the flesh. In a little while we shall be as Jesus now is. No more aching brows, no more swollen limbs, no more dim eyes, no more fainting hearts. The old man shall be no more a bundle of infirmities, nor the sick man a mass of agony. "Like unto his glorious body" [Phil. 3:21]. What an expression! Even our flesh shall rest in hope of such a resurrection!

CHARLES SPURGEON

PAUSE FOR REFLECTION
What is the significance and what are the results of Christ's resurrection? What will all those who rise up in Christ be given? What about the resurrection gives you the greatest hope?

1 CORINTHIANS 15:44b – 16:24

There is a physical body, and there is also a spiritual body. **45**It is written in the Scriptures: "The first man, Adam, became a living person." But the last Adam became a spirit that gives life. **46**The spiritual did not come first, but the physical and then the spiritual. **47**The first man came from the dust of the earth. The second man came from heaven. **48**People who belong to the earth are like the first man of earth. But those people who belong to heaven are like the man of heaven. **49**Just as we were made like the man of earth, so we will also be made like the man of heaven.

50I tell you this, brothers and sisters: Flesh and blood cannot have a part in the kingdom of God. Something that will ruin cannot have a part in something that never ruins. **51**But look! I tell you this secret: We will not all sleep in death, but we will all be changed. **52**It will take only a second— as quickly as an eye blinks—when the last trumpet sounds. The trumpet will sound, and those who have died will be raised to live forever, and we will all be changed. **53**This body that can be destroyed must clothe itself with something that can never be destroyed. And this body that dies must clothe itself with something that can never die. **54**So this body that can be destroyed will clothe itself with that which can never be destroyed, and this body that dies will clothe itself with that which can never die. When this happens, this Scripture will be made true:

"Death is destroyed forever in victory."

Isaiah 25:8

55"Death, where is your victory?
Death, where is your pain?" *Hosea 13:14*
56Death's power to hurt is sin, and the power of sin is the law. **57**But we thank God! He gives us the victory through our Lord Jesus Christ.

58So my dear brothers and sisters, stand strong. Do not let anything move you. Always give yourselves fully to the work of the Lord, because you know that your work in the Lord is never wasted.

The Gift for Other Believers

16 Now I will write about the collection of money for God's people. Do the same thing I told the Galatian churches to do: **2**On the first day of every week, each one of you should put aside money as you have been blessed. Save it up so you will not have to collect money after I come. **3**When I arrive, I will send whomever you approve to take your gift to Jerusalem. I will send them with letters of introduction, **4**and if it seems good for me to go also, they will go along with me.

Paul's Plans

5I plan to go through Macedonia, so I will come to you after I go through there. **6**Perhaps I will stay with you for a time or even all winter. Then you can help me on my trip, wherever I go. **7**I do not want to see you now just in passing. I hope to stay a longer time with you if the Lord allows it. **8**But I will stay at Ephesus until Pentecost, **9**because a good opportunity for a great and growing work has been given to me now. And there are many people working against me.

10If Timothy comes to you, see to it that he has nothing to fear with you, because he is working for the Lord just as I am. **11**So none of you should treat Timothy as unimportant, but help him on his trip in peace so that he can come back to me. I am expecting him to come with the brothers.

12Now about our brother Apollos: I strongly encouraged him to visit you with the other brothers. He did not at all want to come now; he will come when he has the opportunity.

Paul Ends His Letter

13Be alert. Continue strong in the faith. Have courage, and be strong. **14**Do everything in love.

15You know that the family of Stephanas were the first believers in Southern Greece and that they have given themselves to the service of God's people. I ask you, brothers and sisters, **16**to follow the leading of people like these and anyone else who works and serves with them.

17I am happy that Stephanas, Fortunatus, and Achaicus have come. You are not here, but they have filled your place. **18**They have refreshed my spirit and yours. You should recognize the value of people like these.

19The churches in Asia send greetings to you. Aquila and Priscilla greet you in the Lord, as does the church that meets in their house. **20**All the brothers and sisters here send greetings. Give each other a holy kiss when you meet.

21I, Paul, am writing this greeting with my own hand.

22If anyone does not love the Lord, let him be separated from God—lost forever!

Come, O Lord!

23The grace of the Lord Jesus be with you. **24**My love be with all of you in Christ Jesus.

OLD TESTAMENT READING

LORD, battle with those who battle with me.
Fight against those who fight against me.

7For no reason they spread out their net to trap me;
for no reason they dug a pit for me.

Psalm 35:1, 7

INSIGHTS

For many years as a struggling young Christian I was led to believe that if I was just good enough, and kind enough, and loving enough, the whole of the world would be bound to hug me to its heart. Unfortunately and unhappily one learns in time that simply is not so. It is one of the sobering shocks that comes to us as mature Christians.

If God, very God, who was all perfection, suffered such abuse at the hands of His adversaries when He was here among us as the Man Christ Jesus, how can we expect less? . . .

If in truth persecution does come to me because of my righteous character and commendable, Christlike conduct, it is proof positive that I am indeed God's person. . . .

W. PHILLIP KELLER

APPLICATION

Why did Paul plan to stay in Ephesus? Do you gain or lose enthusiasm for the Lord's work when you face opposition?

2 CORINTHIANS 1:1–17

1 From Paul, an apostle of Christ Jesus. I am an apostle because that is what God wanted. Also from Timothy our brother in Christ.

To the church of God in Corinth, and to all of God's people everywhere in Southern Greece:

2Grace and peace to you from God our Father and the Lord Jesus Christ.

Paul Gives Thanks to God

3Praise be to the God and Father of our Lord Jesus Christ. God is the Father who is full of mercy and all comfort. **4**He comforts us every time we have trouble, so when others have trouble, we can comfort them with the same comfort God gives us. **5**We share in the many sufferings of Christ. In the same way, much comfort comes to us through Christ. **6**If we have troubles, it is for your comfort and salvation, and if we have comfort, you also have comfort. This helps you to accept patiently the same sufferings we have. **7**Our hope for you is strong, knowing that you share in our sufferings and also in the comfort we receive.

8Brothers and sisters, we want you to know about the trouble we suffered in Asia. We had great burdens there that were beyond our own strength. We even gave up hope of living. **9**Truly, in our own hearts we believed we would die. But this happened so we would not trust in ourselves but in God, who raises people from the dead. **10**God saved us from these great dangers of death, and he will continue to save us. We have put our hope in him, and he will save us again. **11**And you can help us with your prayers. Then many people will give thanks for us—that God blessed us because of their many prayers.

The Change in Paul's Plans

12This is what we are proud of, and I can say it with a clear conscience: In everything we have done in the world, and especially with you, we have had an honest and sincere heart from God. We did this by God's grace, not by the kind of wisdom the world has. **13-14**We write to you only what you can read and understand. And I hope that as you have understood some things about us, you may come to know everything about us. Then you can be proud of us, as we will be proud of you on the day our Lord Jesus Christ comes again.

15I was so sure of all this that I made plans to visit you first so you could be blessed twice. **16**I planned to visit you on my way to Macedonia and again on my way back. I wanted to get help from you for my trip to Judea. **17**Do you think that I made these plans without really meaning it? Or maybe you think I make plans as the world does, so that I say yes, yes and at the same time no, no.

OLD TESTAMENT READING

G od, be merciful to me because people are chasing me;
the battle has pressed me all day long.
2My enemies have chased me all day;
there are many proud people fighting me.
3When I am afraid,

I will trust you.
4 I praise God for his word.
I trust God, so I am not afraid.
What can human beings do to me?

Psalm 56:1–4

LORD, your love fills the earth.
Teach me your demands.

65 You have done good things for your servant,
as you have promised, LORD.
66 Teach me wisdom and knowledge
because I trust your commands.

67 Before I suffered, I did wrong,
but now I obey your word.
68 You are good, and you do what is
good.
Teach me your demands.

76 Comfort me with your love,
as you promised me, your servant.
77 Have mercy on me so that I may live.
I love your teachings.

Psalm 119:64–68, 76–77

INSIGHTS

It has been well said that "earthly cares are a heavenly discipline." But they are even something better than discipline,—they are God's chariots, sent to take the soul to its high places of triumph. . . .

Everything that comes to us becomes a chariot the moment we treat it as such; and on the other hand, even the smallest trials may be a Juggernaut car to crush us into misery or despair if we so consider them. It lies with each of us to choose which they shall be. . . .

Look upon your chastenings then, no matter how grievous they may be for the present, as God's chariots sent to carry your souls into the "high places" of spiritual achievement and uplifting, and you will find that they are, after all, "paved with love."

The Bible tells us that when God went forth for the salvation of His people, then He "did ride upon His horses and chariots of salvation." And it is the same now. Everything becomes a "chariot of salvation" when God rides upon it. He maketh even the "clouds his chariot," we are told, and "rideth on the wings of the wind." Therefore the clouds and storms that darken our skies and seem to shut out the shining of the sun of righteousness are really only God's chariots, into which we may mount with Him, and "ride prosperously" over all the darkness.

HANNAH WHITALL SMITH

ACTION POINT

How well acquainted are you with the God Paul describes in 2 Corinthians 1:3? The next time you are ready to give up hope, why not trust the God of comfort to turn your troubles into triumphs of his making?

2 CORINTHIANS 1:18 — 3:3

18But since you can believe God, you can believe that what we tell you is never both yes and no. **19**The Son of God, Jesus Christ, that Silas and Timothy and I preached to you, was not yes and no. In Christ it has always been yes. **20**The yes to all of God's promises is in Christ, and through Christ we say yes to the glory of God. **21**Remember, God is the One who makes you and us strong in Christ. God made us his chosen people. **22**He put his mark on us to show that we are his, and he put his Spirit in our hearts to be a guarantee for all he has promised.

23I tell you this, and I ask God to be my witness that this is true: The reason I did not come back to Corinth was to keep you from being punished or hurt. **24**We are not trying to control your faith. You are strong in faith. But we are workers with you for your own joy.

So I decided that my next visit to you would not be another one to make you sad. **2**If I make you sad, who will make me glad? Only you can make me glad—particularly the person whom I made sad. **3**I wrote you a letter for this reason: that when I came to you I would not be made sad by the people who should make me happy. I felt sure of all of you, that you would share my joy. **4**When I wrote to you before, I was very troubled and unhappy in my heart, and I wrote with many tears. I did not write to make you sad, but to let you know how much I love you.

Forgive the Sinner

5Someone there among you has caused sadness, not to me, but to all of you. I mean he caused sadness to all in some way. (I do not want to make it sound worse than it really is.) **6**The punishment that most of you gave him is enough for him. **7**But now you should forgive him and comfort him to keep him from having too much sadness and giving up completely. **8**So I beg you to show that you love him. **9**I wrote you to test you and to see if you obey in everything. **10**If you forgive someone, I also forgive him. And what I have forgiven—if I had anything to forgive—I forgave it for you, as if Christ were with me. **11**I did this so that Satan would not win anything from us, because we know very well what Satan's plans are.

Paul's Concern in Troas

12When I came to Troas to preach the Good News of Christ, the Lord gave me a good opportunity there. **13**But I had no peace, because I did not find my brother Titus. So I said good-bye to them at Troas and went to Macedonia.

Victory Through Christ

14But thanks be to God, who always leads us as captives in Christ's victory parade. God uses us to spread his knowledge everywhere like a sweet-smelling perfume. **15**Our offering to God is this: We are the sweet smell of Christ among those who are being saved and among those who are being lost. **16**To those who are lost, we are the smell of death that brings death, but to those who are being saved, we are the smell of life that brings life. So who is able to do this work? **17**We do not sell the word of God for a profit as many other people do. But in Christ we speak the truth before God, as messengers of God.

Servants of the New Agreement

3 Are we starting to brag about ourselves again? Do we need letters of introduction to you or from you, like some other people? **2** You yourselves are our letter, written on our hearts, known and read by everyone. **3** You show that you are a letter from Christ sent through us. This letter is not written with ink but with the Spirit of the living God. It is not written on stone tablets but on human hearts.

OLD TESTAMENT READING

S o they sent a message to Joseph that said, "Your father gave this command before he died. **17** He said to us, 'You have done wrong and have sinned and done evil to Joseph. Tell Joseph to forgive you, his brothers.' So now, Joseph, we beg you to forgive our wrong. We are the servants of the God of your father." When Joseph received the message, he cried.

19 Then Joseph said to them, "Don't be afraid. Can I do what only God can do? **20** You meant to hurt me, but God turned your evil into good to save the lives of many people, which is being done. **21** So don't be afraid. I will take care of you and your children." So Joseph comforted his brothers and spoke kind words to them.

Genesis 50:16–17, 19–21

INSIGHTS

Forgiveness of sins is a great all-embracing gift of God. In His mercy, God sets the sinner free and receives him back into His love and favor. When we are forgiven, we have confidence toward God in prayer. We can be thankful every day of our lives because we are free and nothing stands between us and God. With the door open to communion with Him, God desires that we spend time with Him in His Word each day as people whose sins are forgiven. We need to live in the light of His countenance daily.

And God desires that this assurance affect our relationship with others. Those who are forgiven are free to forgive others. If it is difficult to forgive, we should consider how freely God has forgiven us of every offense toward Him. . . .

Remember these words daily: "As I need God's forgiveness each day, so let me be ready each day to forgive my brother." God grant you grace to do it!

ANDREW MURRAY

APPLICATION

What healing has God's forgiveness accomplished in your life? What are the consequences when God's people don't forgive one another? Who do you need to forgive? Pray that you will always follow God's merciful example in forgiving others.

2 CORINTHIANS
3:4 – 4:15

4We can say this, because through Christ we feel certain before God. **5**We are not saying that we can do this work ourselves. It is God who makes us able to do all that we do. **6**He made us able to be servants of a new agreement from himself to his people. This new agreement is not a written law, but it is of the Spirit. The written law brings death, but the Spirit gives life.

7The law that brought death was written in words on stone. It came with God's glory, which made Moses' face so bright that the Israelites could not continue to look at it. But that glory later disappeared. **8**So surely the new way that brings the Spirit has even more glory. **9**If the law that judged people guilty of sin had glory, surely the new way that makes people right with God has much greater glory. **10**That old law had glory, but it really loses its glory when it is compared to the much greater glory of this new way. **11**If that law which disappeared came with glory, then this new way which continues forever has much greater glory.

12We have this hope, so we are very bold. **13**We are not like Moses, who put a covering over his face so the Israelites would not see it. The glory was disappearing, and Moses did not want them to see it end. **14**But their minds were closed, and even today that same covering hides the meaning when they read the old agreement. That covering is taken away only through Christ. **15**Even today, when they read the law of Moses, there is a covering over their minds. **16**But when a person changes and follows the Lord, that covering is taken away. **17**The Lord is the Spirit, and where the Spirit of the Lord is, there is freedom. **18**Our faces, then, are not covered. We all show the Lord's glory, and we are being changed to be like him. This change in us brings ever greater glory, which comes from the Lord, who is the Spirit.

Preaching the Good News

4God, with his mercy, gave us this work to do, so we don't give up. **2**But we have turned away from secret and shameful ways. We use no trickery, and we do not change the teaching of God. We teach the truth plainly, showing everyone who we are. Then they can know in their hearts what kind of people we are in God's sight. **3**If the Good News that we preach is hidden, it is hidden only to those who are lost. **4**The devil who rules this world has blinded the minds of those who do not believe. They cannot see the light of the Good News—the Good News about the glory of Christ, who is exactly like God. **5**We do not preach about ourselves, but we preach that Jesus Christ is Lord and that we are your servants for Jesus. **6**God once said, "Let the light shine out of the darkness!" This is the same God who made his light shine in our hearts by letting us know the glory of God that is in the face of Christ.

Spiritual Treasure in Clay Jars

7We have this treasure from God, but we are like clay jars that hold the treasure. This shows that the great power is from God, not from us. **8**We have troubles all around us, but we are not defeated. We do not know what to do, but we do not give up the hope of living. 9We are persecuted, but God does not leave us. We are hurt sometimes, but we are not destroyed. 10We carry the death of Jesus in our own bodies so that the life of Jesus can also be seen in our bodies. 11We are alive, but for Jesus we are always in danger of death so that the life of Jesus can be seen in our bodies that die. 12So death is working in us, but life is working in you.

13It is written in the Scriptures, "I believed, so I spoke." Our faith is like this, too. We believe, and so we speak. 14God raised the Lord Jesus from the dead, and we know that God will also raise us with Jesus. God will bring us together with you, and we will stand before him. 15All these things are for you. And so the grace of God that is being given to more and more people will bring increasing thanks to God for his glory.

OLD TESTAMENT READING

Those who fight against the light
   do not know God's ways
   or stay in his paths.

23"God may let these evil people feel safe,
   but he is watching their ways.
24For a little while they are important,
      and then they die;
   they are laid low and buried like
      everyone else;
   they are cut off like the heads of grain."

Job 24:13, 23–24

INSIGHTS

Glory, I've learned, is what God is all about. His essential being. Whenever you talk about His character or attributes—like holiness, love, compassion, justice, truth, or mercy—that's God's glory. . . .

So how is it that you and I can glorify God? It happens every time we reveal His attributes in the course of our daily lives. Every time you share the good news of Christ with another. Every time you reflect patience in the middle of an upsetting or perplexing problem. Every time you smile from the heart or offer an encouraging word. Whenever those around you see God's character displayed in your attitudes and responses, you are displaying His glory.

. . . God's glory isn't reserved for a temple of stone or some heavenly vista. It can shine out clearly while you're changing a flat on the freeway . . . or counseling an angry co-worker . . . or lying in a hospital bed . . . or balancing two crying babies in the church nursery.

JONI EARECKSON TADA

APPLICATION

How is God's glory shown through believers different from that shown by Moses? How has God's Spirit opened up your mind? How is God's glory shining in your life?

2 CORINTHIANS 4:16 — 6:2

Living by Faith

16So we do not give up. Our physical body is becoming older and weaker, but our spirit inside us is made new every day. 17We have small troubles for a while now, but they are helping us gain an eternal glory that is much greater than the troubles. 18We set our eyes not on what we see but on what we cannot see. What we see will last only a short time, but what we cannot see will last forever.

We know that our body—the tent we live in here on earth—will be destroyed. But when that happens, God will have a house for us. It will not be a house made by human hands; instead, it will be a home in heaven that will last forever. 2But now we groan in this tent. We want God to give us our heavenly home, 3because it will clothe us so we will not be naked. 4While we live in this body, we have burdens, and we groan. We do not want to be naked, but we want to be clothed with our heavenly home. Then this body that dies will be fully covered with life. 5This is what God made us for, and he has given us the Spirit to be a guarantee for this new life.

6So we always have courage. We know that while we live in this body, we are away from the Lord. 7We live by what we believe, not by what we can see. 8So I say that we have courage. We really want to be away from this body and be at home with the Lord. 9Our only goal is to please God whether we live here or there, 10because we must all stand before Christ to be judged. Each of us will receive what we should get—good or bad—for the things we did in the earthly body.

Becoming Friends with God

11Since we know what it means to fear the Lord, we try to help people accept the truth about us. God knows what we really are, and I hope that in your hearts you know, too. 12We are not trying to prove ourselves to you again, but we are telling you about ourselves so you will be proud of us. Then you will have an answer for those who are proud about things that can be seen rather than what is in the heart. 13If we are out of our minds, it is for God. If we have our right minds, it is for you. 14The love of Christ controls us, because we know that One died for all, so all have died. 15Christ died for all so that those who live would not continue to live for themselves. He died for them and was raised from the dead so that they would live for him.

16From this time on we do not think of anyone as the world does. In the past we thought of Christ as the world thinks, but we no longer think of him in that way. 17If anyone belongs to Christ, there is a new creation. The old things have gone; everything is made new! 18All this is from God. Through Christ, God made peace between us and himself, and God gave us the work of telling everyone about the peace we can have with him. 19God was in Christ, making peace between the world and himself. In Christ, God did not hold the world guilty of its sins. And he gave us this message of peace. 20So we have been sent to speak for Christ. It is as if God is calling to you through us.

We speak for Christ when we beg you to be at peace with God. **21**Christ had no sin, but God made him become sin so that in Christ we could become right with God.

 We are workers together with God, so we beg you: Do not let the grace that you received from God be for nothing. **2**God says,

"At the right time I heard your prayers.
On the day of salvation I helped you."

Isaiah 49:8

I tell you that the "right time" is now, and the "day of salvation" is now.

OLD TESTAMENT READING

Who may go up on the mountain of the LORD?
Who may stand in his holy Temple?
4Only those with clean hands and pure hearts,
who have not worshiped idols,
who have not made promises in the name
of a false god.
5They will receive a blessing from the LORD;
the God who saves them will declare them
right.
6They try to follow God;
they look to the God of Jacob for help. *Selah*

Psalm 24:3–6

INSIGHTS

Man's place in creation was very remarkable. The Psalmist says, "For thou hast made him a little lower than the angels, and hast crowned him with glory and honor. Thou madest him to have dominion over the works of thy hands; thou hast put all things under his feet: all sheep and oxen, yea, and the beasts of the field; the fowl of the air, and the fish of the sea, and whatsoever passeth through the paths of the seas." . . .

What a man will become we can scarcely tell when he is remade in the image of God, and made like unto our divine Lord who is "the firstborn among many brethren." Our bodies are to be developed into something infinitely brighter and better than the bodies of men here below: and as for the soul, we cannot guess to what an elevation it shall be raised in Christ Jesus. There is room for the largest expectation here, as we conjecture what will be the full accomplishment of the vast intent of eternal love, an intent which has involved the sacrifice of the only-begotten Son of God. That can be no mean design which has been carried on at the expense of the best that heaven itself possessed.

CHARLES SPURGEON

ACTION POINT

Stop now and focus your eyes on what you cannot yet see. Imagine yourself standing in God's temple with clean hands and a pure heart. Imagine God as your glory and light forever. Praise him for his eternal glory that is to come!

2 CORINTHIANS 6:3 – 7:7

3We do not want anyone to find fault with our work, so nothing we do will be a problem for anyone. **4**But in every way we show we are servants of God: in accepting many hard things, in troubles, in difficulties, and in great problems. **5**We are beaten and thrown into prison. We meet those who become upset with us and start riots. We work hard, and sometimes we get no sleep or food. **6**We show we are servants of God by our pure lives, our understanding, patience, and kindness, by the Holy Spirit, by true love, **7**by speaking the truth, and by God's power. We use our right living to defend ourselves against everything. **8**Some people honor us, but others blame us. Some people say evil things about us, but others say good things. Some people say we are liars, but we speak the truth. **9**We are not known, but we are well known. We seem to be dying, but we continue to live. We are punished, but we are not killed. **10**We have much sadness, but we are always rejoicing. We are poor, but we are making many people rich in faith. We have nothing, but really we have everything.

11We have spoken freely to you in Corinth and have opened our hearts to you. **12**Our feelings of love for you have not stopped, but you have stopped your feelings of love for us. **13**I speak to you as if you were my children. Do to us as we have done—open your hearts to us.

Warning About Non-Christians

14You are not the same as those who do not believe. So do not join yourselves to them. Good and bad do not belong together. Light and darkness cannot share together. **15**How can Christ and Belial, the devil, have any agreement? What can a believer have together with a nonbeliever? **16**The temple of God cannot have any agreement with idols, and we are the temple of the living God. As God said: "I will live with them and walk with them. And I will be their God, and they will be my people."

17"Leave those people,
> and be separate, says the Lord.
Touch nothing that is unclean,
> and I will accept you."
>
> *Isaiah 52:11; Ezekiel 20:34, 41*

18"I will be your father,
> and you will be my sons and daughters,
> says the Lord Almighty." *2 Samuel 7:14*

7Dear friends, we have these promises from God, so we should make ourselves pure—free from anything that makes body or soul unclean. We should try to become holy in the way we live, because we respect God.

Paul's Joy

2Open your hearts to us. We have not done wrong to anyone, we have not ruined the faith of anyone, and we have not cheated anyone. **3**I do not say this to blame you. I told you before that we love you so much we would live or die with you. **4**I feel very sure of you and am very proud of you. You give me much comfort, and in all of our troubles I have great joy.

⁵When we came into Macedonia, we had no rest. We found trouble all around us. We had fighting on the outside and fear on the inside. ⁶But God, who comforts those who are troubled, comforted us when Titus came. ⁷We were comforted, not only by his coming but also by the comfort you gave him. Titus told me about your wish to see me and that you are very sorry for what you did. He also told me about your great care for me, and when I heard this, I was much happier.

OLD TESTAMENT READING

Don't follow the ways of the wicked;
    don't do what evil people do.
¹⁵Avoid their ways, and don't follow them.
    Stay away from them and keep on going.

Proverbs 4:14–15

INSIGHTS

Someone has said, "a belief is what you hold; a conviction is what holds you." A conviction is not truly a conviction unless it includes a commitment to live by what we claim to believe. A commitment is not a vow but a resolution—a determined purpose to live by God's word as he applies it to our lives. First, we need a commitment to holiness as a total way of life. We must decide that holiness is so important to God that it deserves priority attention in our lives. We must commit ourselves to obeying God in all of his commands. We cannot pick and choose according to our own values. A little bit of fudging on one's income tax return is sin just as much as outright theft; an unforgiving spirit toward someone else is sin just as much as murder. I am not suggesting that all sin is equally offensive to God; I am saying that all sin is offensive to God. The measure of sin is not just in its effect upon our neighbor, but in its affront to the majesty and holiness of a sovereign God.

Sin is serious to God, and it becomes serious business to us when we reflect upon the fact that every sin, regardless of how seemingly insignificant it appears to us, is an expression of contempt toward the sovereign authority of God. . . .

The psalmist recognized the seriousness of any and all sin when he said, "You have laid down precepts that are to be fully obeyed" (Psalm 119:4). He recognized that partial obedience—for example, refraining from outright theft of our neighbor's property while allowing our heart to covet it—is actually disobedience. God's precepts are to be fully obeyed.

JERRY BRIDGES

APPLICATION

List the lifestyle traits that are to characterize those who serve God. Why is purity so important to God? Why must God's people seek purity? What is the way to live a pure life? Is your desire for purity a belief or a conviction?

2 CORINTHIANS 7:8 – 8:15

8Even if my letter made you sad, I am not sorry I wrote it. At first I was sorry, because it made you sad, but you were sad only for a short time. **9**Now I am happy, not because you were made sad, but because your sorrow made you change your lives. You became sad in the way God wanted you to, so you were not hurt by us in any way. **10**The kind of sorrow God wants makes people change their hearts and lives. This leads to salvation, and you cannot be sorry for that. But the kind of sorrow the world has brings death. **11**See what this sorrow—the sorrow God wanted you to have—has done to you: It has made you very serious. It made you want to restore yourselves. It made you angry and afraid. It made you want to see me. It made you care. It made you want to do the right thing. In every way you have regained your innocence. **12**I wrote that letter, not because of the one who did the wrong or because of the person who was hurt. I wrote the letter so you could see, before God, the great care you have for us. **13**That is why we were comforted.

Not only were we very comforted, we were even happier to see that Titus was so happy. All of you made him feel much better. **14**I bragged to Titus about you, and you showed that I was right. Everything we said to you was true, and you have proved that what we bragged about to Titus is true. **15**And his love for you is stronger when he remembers that you were all ready to obey. You welcomed him with respect and fear. **16**I am very happy that I can trust you fully.

Christian Giving

8And now, brothers and sisters, we want you to know about the grace God gave the churches in Macedonia. **2**They have been tested by great troubles, and they are very poor. But they gave much because of their great joy. **3**I can tell you that they gave as much as they were able and even more than they could afford. No one told them to do it. **4**But they begged and pleaded with us to let them share in this service for God's people. **5**And they gave in a way we did not expect: They first gave themselves to the Lord and to us. This is what God wants. **6**So we asked Titus to help you finish this special work of grace since he is the one who started it. **7**You are rich in everything—in faith, in speaking, in knowledge, in truly wanting to help, and in the love you learned from us. In the same way, be strong also in the grace of giving.

8I am not commanding you to give. But I want to see if your love is true by comparing you with others that really want to help. **9**You know the grace of our Lord Jesus Christ. You know that Christ was rich, but for you he became poor so that by his becoming poor you might become rich.

10This is what I think you should do: Last year you were the first to want to give, and you were the first who gave. **11**So now finish the work you started. Then your "doing" will be equal to your "wanting to do." Give from what you have. **12**If you want to give, your gift will be accepted. It will be judged by what you have, not by what you do not have. **13**We do not want you to have troubles while other people are at ease, but we want everything to be equal. **14**At this time you have plenty. What you have can help others who are in need. Then later, when they have plenty, they can help you when you are in need, and all will be equal. **15**As it is written in the Scriptures, "The person who gathered more did not have too much, nor did the person who gathered less have too little."

INSIGHTS

Repentance is simply and precisely a change of mind. The original term denotes, a thinking again—a turning of the mind—as when one finds himself going wrong and turns about to pursue the opposite course. The term, when applied to evangelical repentance, means not merely a turning of the mind, but a change of the entire purposes of action, change in the entire attitude of the will. . . .

Conviction of sin as a wrong committed against God is implied in repentance. Without this there can be no rational repentance.

The sinner must become truly honest with God. He must honestly admit the truths affirmed by his reason and pressed on his soul by his conscience. Especially must he recognize God's rights: that he himself is God's property and belongs truly to God. . . .

Repentance implies a universal reformation of life, a reformation extending to all forms of sin. Penitent men turn from all sin as sin, because they regard it as sin, and therefore can have no sympathy with it. All known sin therefore they at once abandon. . . .

When I speak of abandoning sin, I do not imply that the penitent man never for even a moment relapses into it; but I imply that he sets himself against it in real honest earnestness.

CHARLES FINNEY

OLD TESTAMENT READING

As Ezra was praying and confessing and crying and throwing himself down in front of the Temple, a large group of Israelite men, women, and children gathered around him who were also crying loudly. **2**Then Shecaniah son of Jehiel the Elamite said to Ezra, "We have been unfaithful to our God by marrying women from the peoples around us. But even so, there is still hope for Israel. **3**Now let us make an agreement before our God. We will send away all these women and their children as you and those who respect the commands of our God advise."

Ezra 10:1–3b

▶ APPLICATION

What is the difference between godly sorrow and the world's sorrow? What feelings and actions does godly sorrow bring about? Pray that you will always respond appropriately to godly sorrow!

2 CORINTHIANS 8:16 – 9:15

Titus and His Companions Help

16I thank God because he gave Titus the same love for you that I have. **17**Titus accepted what we asked him to do. He wanted very much to go to you, and this was his own idea. **18**We are sending with him the brother who is praised by all the churches because of his service in preaching the Good News. **19**Also, this brother was chosen by the churches to go with us when we deliver this gift of money. We are doing this service to bring glory to the Lord and to show that we really want to help.

20We are being careful so that no one will criticize us for the way we are handling this large gift. **21**We are trying hard to do what the Lord accepts as right and also what people think is right.

22Also, we are sending with them our brother, who is always ready to help. He has proved this to us in many ways, and he wants to help even more now, because he has much faith in you.

23Now about Titus—he is my partner who is working with me to help you. And about the other brothers—they are sent from the churches, and they bring glory to Christ. **24**So show these men the proof of your love and the reason we are proud of you. Then all the churches can see it.

Help for Fellow Christians

I really do not need to write you about this help for God's people. **2**I know you want to help. I have been bragging about

this to the people in Macedonia, telling them that you in Southern Greece have been ready to give since last year. And your desire to give has made most of them ready to give also. **3**But I am sending the brothers to you so that our bragging about you in this will not be empty words. I want you to be ready, as I said you would be. **4**If any of the people from Macedonia come with me and find that you are not ready, we will be ashamed that we were so sure of you. (And you will be ashamed, too!) **5**So I thought I should ask these brothers to go to you before we do. They will finish getting in order the generous gift you promised so it will be ready when we come. And it will be a generous gift—not one that you did not want to give.

6Remember this: The person who plants a little will have a small harvest, but the person who plants a lot will have a big harvest. **7**Each of you should give as you have decided in your heart to give. You should not be sad when you give, and you should not give because you feel forced to give. God loves the person who gives happily. **8**And God can give you more blessings than you need. Then you will always have plenty of everything—enough to give to every good work. **9**It is written in the Scriptures:

"He gives freely to the poor.
    The things he does are right and will
        continue forever."   *Psalm 112:9*

10God is the One who gives seed to the farmer and bread for food. He will give you all the seed you need and make it grow so there will be a great harvest from your goodness. **11**He will make you rich in every way so that you can always give freely. And your giving through us will cause many to give thanks to God. **12** This service you do not only helps the needs of God's people, it also brings many more thanks to God. **13** It is a proof of your faith. Many people will praise God because you obey the Good News of Christ—the gospel you say you believe—and because you freely share with them and with all others. **14** And when they pray, they will wish they could be with you because of the great grace that God has given you. **15** Thanks be to God for his gift that is too wonderful for words.

OLD TESTAMENT READING

Whoever gives to the poor will have everything
    he needs,
      but the one who ignores the poor will
        receive many curses.

Proverbs 28:27

Lazy people's desire for sleep will kill them,
    because they refuse to work.
26 All day long they wish for more,
      but good people give without holding back.

Proverbs 21:25–26

INSIGHTS

We all know how subtle the materialistic temptations are and how convincing the rationalizations. Only by God's grace and with great effort can we escape the shower of luxuries which has almost suffocated our Christian compassion. All of us face this problem. Some years ago I spent about fifty dollars on an extra suit. That's not much of course. Besides, I persuaded myself, it was a wise investment (thanks to the 75 percent discount). But that money would have fed a starving child in India for about a year. In all honesty we have to ask ourselves: Dare we care at all about current fashions if that means reducing our ability to help hungry neighbors? Dare we care more about obtaining a secure economic future for our family than for living an uncompromisingly Christian lifestyle? . . .

. . . We have been brainwashed to believe that bigger houses, more prosperous businesses, more luxurious gadgets, are worthy goals in life. As a result, we are caught in an absurd, materialistic spiral. The more we make, the more we think we need in order to live decently and respectably. Somehow we have to break this cycle because it makes us sin against our needy brothers and sisters and, therefore, against our Lord. And it also destroys us. Sharing with others is the way to real joy.

RONALD SIDER

APPLICATION

List what God promises those who give generously. What do you think it means to be made "rich in every way so that you can always give freely"? Is your giving such that it brings praise to God from others?

2 CORINTHIANS 10:1 – 11:4

Paul Defends His Ministry

10 I, Paul, am begging you with the gentleness and the kindness of Christ. Some people say that I am easy on you when I am with you and bold when I am away. **2**They think we live in a worldly way, and I plan to be very bold with them when I come. I beg you that when I come I will not need to use that same boldness with you. **3**We do live in the world, but we do not fight in the same way the world fights. **4**We fight with weapons that are different from those the world uses. Our weapons have power from God that can destroy the enemy's strong places. We destroy people's arguments **5**and every proud thing that raises itself against the knowledge of God. We capture every thought and make it give up and obey Christ. **6**We are ready to punish anyone there who does not obey, but first we want you to obey fully.

7You must look at the facts before you. If you feel sure that you belong to Christ, you must remember that we belong to Christ just as you do. **8**It is true that we brag freely about the authority the Lord gave us. But this authority is to build you up, not to tear you down. So I will not be ashamed. **9**I do not want you to think I am trying to scare you with my letters. **10**Some people say, "Paul's letters are powerful and sound important, but when he is with us, he is weak. And his speaking is nothing." **11**They should know this: We are not there with you now, so we say these things in letters. But when we are there with you, we will show the same authority that we show in our letters.

12We do not dare to compare ourselves with those who think they are very important. They use themselves to measure themselves, and they judge themselves by what they themselves are. This shows that they know nothing. **13**But we will not brag about things outside the work that was given us to do. We will limit our bragging to the work that God gave us, and this includes our work with you. **14**We are not bragging too much, as we would be if we had not already come to you. But we have come to you with the Good News of Christ. **15**We limit our bragging to the work that is ours, not what others have done. We hope that as your faith continues to grow, you will help our work to grow much larger. **16**We want to tell the Good News in the areas beyond your city. We do not want to brag about work that has already been done in another person's area. **17**But, "If people want to brag, they should brag only about the Lord." **18**It is not those who say they are good who are accepted but those the Lord thinks are good.

Paul and the False Apostles

11 I wish you would be patient with me even when I am a little foolish, but you are already doing that. **2**I am jealous over you with a jealousy that comes from God. I promised to give you to Christ, as your only husband. I want to give you as his pure bride. **3**But I am afraid that your minds will be led away from your true and pure following of Christ just as Eve was tricked by the snake with his evil ways. **4**You are very patient with anyone who comes to you and preaches a different Jesus from the one we preached. You are very willing to accept a spirit or gospel that is different from the Spirit and Good News you received from us.

OLD TESTAMENT READING

Jehoshaphat's army went out into the Desert of Tekoa early in the morning. As they were starting out, Jehoshaphat stood and said, "Listen to me, people of Judah and Jerusalem. Have faith in the LORD your God, and you will stand strong. Have faith in his prophets, and you will succeed." [21]Jehoshaphat listened to the people's advice. Then he chose men to be singers to the LORD, to praise him because he is holy and wonderful. As they marched in front of the army, they said,

"Thank the LORD,

because his love continues forever."

[22]As they began to sing and praise God, the LORD set ambushes for the people of Ammon, Moab, and Edom who had come to attack Judah. And they were defeated.

2 Chronicles 20:20–22

INSIGHTS

We have no enemies but the enemies of God. Our fights are not against men but against spiritual wickednesses. We war with the devil and the blasphemy and error and despair which he brings into the field of battle. We fight with all the armies of sin—impurity, drunkenness, oppression, infidelity, and ungodliness. With these we contend earnestly, but not with sword or spear; the weapons of our warfare are not carnal.

Jehovah, our God, abhors everything which is evil, and, therefore, He goeth with us to fight for us in this crusade. He will save us, and He will give us grace to war a good warfare and win the victory. We may depend upon it that if we are on God's side God is on our side. With such an august ally the conflict is never in the least degree doubtful. It is not that truth is mighty and must prevail but that might lies with the Father who is almighty, with Jesus who has all power in heaven and in earth, and with the Holy Spirit who worketh His will among men.

Soldiers of Christ, gird on your armor. Strike home in the name of the God of holiness, and by faith grasp His salvation. Let not this day pass without striking a blow for Jesus and holiness.

CHARLES SPURGEON

ACTION POINT

Against what enemy does the believer fight? What weapons are in your spiritual arsenal? Are your weapons ready for battle and armed with the power of God? Pray that you will faithfully obey God and diligently fight against the enemy.

2 CORINTHIANS 11:5-33

5I do not think that those "great apostles" are any better than I am. **6**I may not be a trained speaker, but I do have knowledge. We have shown this to you clearly in every way.

7I preached God's Good News to you without pay. I made myself unimportant to make you important. Do you think that was wrong? **8**I accepted pay from other churches, taking their money so I could serve you. **9**If I needed something when I was with you, I did not trouble any of you. The brothers who came from Macedonia gave me all that I needed. I did not allow myself to depend on you in any way, and I will never depend on you. **10**No one in Southern Greece will stop me from bragging about that. I say this with the truth of Christ in me. **11**And why do I not depend on you? Do you think it is because I do not love you? God knows that I love you.

12And I will continue doing what I am doing now, because I want to stop those people from having a reason to brag. They would like to say that the work they brag about is the same as ours. **13**Such men are not true apostles but are workers who lie. They change themselves to look like apostles of Christ. **14**This does not surprise us. Even Satan changes himself to look like an angel of light. **15**So it does not surprise us if Satan's servants also make themselves look like servants who work for what is right. But in the end they will be punished for what they do.

Paul Tells About His Sufferings

16I tell you again: No one should think I am a fool. But if you think so, accept me as you would accept a fool. Then I can brag a little, too. **17**When I brag because I feel sure of myself, I am not talking as the Lord would talk but as a fool. **18**Many people are bragging about their lives in the world. So I will brag too. **19**You are wise, so you will gladly be patient with fools! **20**You are even patient with those who order you around, or use you, or trick you, or think they are better than you, or hit you in the face. **21**It is shameful to me to say this, but we were too "weak" to do those things to you!

But if anyone else is brave enough to brag, then I also will be brave and brag. (I am talking as a fool.) **22**Are they Hebrews? So am I. Are they Israelites? So am I. Are they from Abraham's family? So am I. **23**Are they serving Christ? I am serving him more. (I am crazy to talk like this.) I have worked much harder than they. I have been in prison more often. I have been hurt more in beatings. I have been near death many times. **24**Five times the Jews have given me their punishment of thirty-nine lashes with a whip. **25**Three different times I was beaten with rods. One time I was almost stoned to death. Three times I was in ships that wrecked, and one of those times I spent a night and a day in the sea. **26**I have gone on many travels and have been in danger from rivers, thieves, my own people, the Jews, and those who are not Jews. I have been in danger in cities, in places where no one lives, and on the sea. And I have been in danger with false Christians. **27**I have done hard and tiring work, and many times I did not sleep. I have been hungry and thirsty, and many times I have been without food. I have been cold and without clothes. **28**Besides all this, there is on me every day the load of my concern for all the churches. **29**I feel weak every time someone is weak, and I feel upset every time someone is led into sin.

30If I must brag, I will brag about the things that show I am weak. **31**God knows I am not lying. He is the God and Father of the Lord Jesus Christ, and he is to be praised forever. **32**When I was in Damascus, the governor under King Aretas wanted to arrest me, so he put guards around the city. **33**But my friends lowered me in a basket through a hole in the city wall. So I escaped from the governor.

OLD TESTAMENT READING

So the king commanded all his people, "Every time a boy is born to the Hebrews, you must throw him into the Nile River, but let all the girl babies live."

Exodus 1:22

The king's daughter said to the woman, "Take this baby and nurse him for me, and I will pay you." So the woman took her baby and nursed him. **10**When the child grew older, the woman took him to the king's daughter, and she adopted the baby as her own son. The king's daughter named him Moses, because she had pulled him out of the water.

Exodus 2:9–10

INSIGHTS

We grow in our understanding through difficulties, as God opens to us that which we could not have understood with any other background or in any other set of circumstances. Our assurance as children of the Living God is that He is able to bring beauty from ashes and to give the "oil of joy" for the spirit of mourning (see Isaiah 61:3). And, in addition, He refines, purifies, proves, and causes to grow in us something very precious and lasting in our attitudes toward Him and in our actions to other human beings. As He removed the hedge protecting Job (or any one of us . . .) he is also able to give us the grace to come through the onslaught that follows. However, there is much more than just "coming through," still hanging on to our trust and love of God. There is a "coming through," with a shinier, more gleaming sheen on our surface. We have the possibility during the hard time to have skimmed off more of the specks and scum which are hindering the more beautiful reality of love, joy, peace, long-suffering, and meekness.

EDITH SCHAEFFER

APPLICATION

For Paul, preaching the Good News was "good" enough to willingly bear great suffering, wasn't it? Pray for total confidence that God is bringing about good through the suffering in your life, too.

2 CORINTHIANS 12:1 – 13:4

A Special Blessing in Paul's Life

12 I must continue to brag. It will do no good, but I will talk now about visions and revelations from the Lord. **2** I know a man in Christ who was taken up to the third heaven fourteen years ago. I do not know whether the man was in his body or out of his body, but God knows. **3-4** And I know that this man was taken up to paradise. I don't know if he was in his body or away from his body, but God knows. He heard things he is not able to explain, things that no human is allowed to tell. **5** I will brag about a man like that, but I will not brag about myself, except about my weaknesses. **6** But if I wanted to brag about myself, I would not be a fool, because I would be telling the truth. But I will not brag about myself. I do not want people to think more of me than what they see me do or hear me say.

7 So that I would not become too proud of the wonderful things that were shown to me, a painful physical problem was given to me. This problem was a messenger from Satan, sent to beat me and keep me from being too proud. **8** I begged the Lord three times to take this problem away from me. **9** But he said to me, "My grace is enough for you. When you are weak, my power is made perfect in you." So I am very happy to brag about my weaknesses. Then Christ's power can live in me. **10** For this reason I am happy when I have weaknesses, insults, hard times, sufferings, and all kinds of troubles for Christ. Because when I am weak, then I am truly strong.

Paul's Love for the Christians

11 I have been talking like a fool, but you made me do it. You are the ones who should say good things about me. I am worth nothing, but those "great apostles" are not worth any more than I am! **12** When I was with you, I patiently did the things that prove I am an apostle—signs, wonders, and miracles. **13** So you received everything that the other churches have received. Only one thing was different: I was not a burden to you. Forgive me for this!

14 I am now ready to visit you the third time, and I will not be a burden to you. I want nothing from you, except you. Children should not have to save up to give to their parents. Parents should save to give to their children. **15** So I am happy to give everything I have for you, even myself. If I love you more, will you love me less?

16 It is clear I was not a burden to you, but you think I was tricky and lied to catch you. **17** Did I cheat you by using any of the messengers I sent to you? No, you know I did not. **18** I asked Titus to go to you, and I sent our brother with him. Titus did not cheat you, did he? No, you know that Titus and I did the same thing and with the same spirit.

19 Do you think we have been defending ourselves to you all this time? We have been speaking in Christ and before God. You are our dear friends, and everything we do is to make you stronger. **20** I am afraid that when I come, you will not be what I want you to be, and I will not be what you want me to be. I am afraid that among you there may be arguing, jealousy, anger, selfish fighting, evil talk, gossip, pride, and confusion. **21**I am afraid that when I come to you again, my God will make me ashamed before you. I may be saddened by many of those who have sinned because they have not changed their hearts or turned from their sexual sins and the shameful things they have done.

Final Warnings and Greetings

13 I will come to you for the third time. "Every case must be proved by two or three witnesses." **2**When I was with you the second time, I gave a warning to those who had sinned. Now I am away from you, and I give a warning to all the others. When I come to you again, I will not be easy with them. **3**You want proof that Christ is speaking through me. My proof is that he is not weak among you, but he is powerful. **4**It is true that he was weak when he was killed on the cross, but he lives now by God's power. It is true that we are weak in Christ, but for you we will be alive in Christ by God's power.

OLD TESTAMENT READING

Each man was sad and angry because his sons and daughters had been captured, but David found strength in the LORD his God.

8Then David asked the LORD, "Should I chase the people who took our families? Will I catch them?"

The LORD answered, "Chase them. You will catch them, and you will succeed in saving your families."

1 Samuel 30:6b, 8

INSIGHTS

Upon examining the life of the apostle Paul, one hardly gets the impression that he was a weak man. On the contrary, he debated against Christ's apostles over the question of gentile salvation, and he won! He spent his life preaching in the most hostile of circumstances. He planted churches throughout the major cities of Asia Minor and in the port cities along the Aegean Sea. Paul trained the first pastors and elders of these early congregations. And to top it all off, he wrote half of the New Testament!

I don't know what you think, but that certainly doesn't sound like a weak man to me. . . . He was a mover and a shaker.

So how do we reconcile Paul's claim to weakness with his amazing accomplishments? Simple, the answer is in the phrase, "when I am weak, then I am strong." A paraphrase of his comment would go something like this: "When I, Paul, in and of my own strength, am weak, then I, Paul, relying on the power of Christ in me, become strong, capable of whatever the Lord requires of me, full of energy and zeal to accomplish His will."

Charles Stanley

APPLICATION

Why does Paul say that God allowed him to become weak? How did Paul respond to his weakness? What did David do in his time of weakness? What does this example of faith teach you?

2 CORINTHIANS 13:5 — GALATIANS 1:21

5Look closely at yourselves. Test yourselves to see if you are living in the faith. You know that Jesus Christ is in you—unless you fail the test. **6**But I hope you will see that we ourselves have not failed the test. **7**We pray to God that you will not do anything wrong. It is not important to see that we have passed the test, but it is important that you do what is right, even if it seems we have failed. **8**We cannot do anything against the truth, but only for the truth. **9**We are happy to be weak, if you are strong, and we pray that you will become complete. **10**I am writing this while I am away from you so that when I come I will not have to be harsh in my use of authority. The Lord gave me this authority to build you up, not to tear you down.

11Now, brothers and sisters, I say good-bye. Live in harmony. Do what I have asked you to do. Agree with each other, and live in peace. Then the God of love and peace will be with you.

12Greet each other with a holy kiss. **13**All of God's holy people send greetings to you.

14The grace of the Lord Jesus Christ, the love of God, and the fellowship of the Holy Spirit be with you all.

1 From Paul, an apostle. I was not chosen to be an apostle by human beings, nor was I sent from human beings. I was made an apostle through Jesus Christ and God the Father who raised Jesus from the dead. **2**This letter is also from all those of God's family who are with me.

To the churches in Galatia:

3Grace and peace to you from God our Father and the Lord Jesus Christ. **4**Jesus gave himself for our sins to free us from this evil world we live in, as God the Father planned. **5**The glory belongs to God forever and ever. Amen.

The Only Good News

6God, by his grace through Christ, called you to become his people. So I am amazed that you are turning away so quickly and believing something different than the Good News. **7**Really, there is no other Good News. But some people are confusing you; they want to change the Good News of Christ. **8**We preached to you the Good News. So if we ourselves, or even an angel from heaven, should preach to you something different, we should be judged guilty! **9**I said this before, and now I say it again: You have already accepted the Good News. If anyone is preaching something different to you, let that person be judged guilty!

10Do you think I am trying to make people accept me? No, God is the One I am trying to please. Am I trying to please people? If I still wanted to please people, I would not be a servant of Christ.

Paul's Authority Is from God

11Brothers and sisters, I want you to know that the Good News I preached to you was not made up by human beings. **12**I did not get it from humans, nor did anyone teach it to me, but Jesus Christ showed it to me.

13You have heard about my past life in the Jewish religion. I attacked the church of God and tried to destroy it. **14**I was becoming a leader in the Jewish religion, doing better than most other Jews of my age. I tried harder than anyone else to follow the teachings handed down by our ancestors.

15But God had special plans for me and set me apart for his work even before I was born. He called me through his grace 16and showed his son to me so that I might tell the Good News about him to those who are not Jewish. When God called me, I did not get advice or help from any person. 17I did not go to Jerusalem to see those who were apostles before I was. But, without waiting, I went away to Arabia and later went back to Damascus.

18After three years I went to Jerusalem to meet Peter and stayed with him for fifteen days. 19I met no other apostles, except James, the brother of the Lord. 20God knows that these things I write are not lies. 21Later, I went to the areas of Syria and Cilicia.

INSIGHTS

It is better we should not know our future. If we did, we should often spoil God's plan for our life. If we could see into tomorrow and know the troubles it will bring, we might be tempted to seek some way of avoiding them, while really they are God's way to new honor and blessing. God's thoughts for us are always thoughts of love, good, promotion; but sometimes the path to the hilltop lies through dark valleys or up rough paths. Yet to miss the hard bit of road is to fail of gaining the lofty height. It is better, therefore, to walk, not knowing, with God, than it would be to see the way and choose for ourselves. God's way for us is always better than our own.

J. R. MILLER

OLD TESTAMENT READING

Now, tell my servant David: 'This is what the LORD All-Powerful says: I took you from the pasture and from tending the sheep and made you king of my people Israel. 8I have been with you everywhere you have gone. I have defeated your enemies for you. I will make you as famous as any of the great people on the earth. 9I will choose a place for my people Israel, and I will plant them so they can live in their own homes. They will not be bothered anymore. Wicked people will no longer hurt them as they have in the past 10when I chose judges for my people Israel. I will defeat all your enemies.'"

1 Chronicles 17:7–10a

When Samuel first saw Saul, the LORD said to Samuel, "This is the man I told you about. He will organize my people."

1 Samuel 9:17

ACTION POINT

David, Samuel, Saul, and Paul all knew that they were called by God to fulfill his plans. Is there any reason to believe that God has planned your life to a lesser degree? Are you willing to test yourself to see if you are following his plan for you? Pray that you will be faithful to his plan and calling for your life.

GALATIANS
1:22 – 2:21

²²In Judea the churches in Christ had never met me. ²³They had only heard it said, "This man who was attacking us is now preaching the same faith that he once tried to destroy." ²⁴And these believers praised God because of me.

Other Apostles Accepted Paul

After fourteen years I went to Jerusalem again, this time with Barnabas. I also took Titus with me. ²I went because God showed me I should go. I met with the believers there, and in private I told their leaders the Good News that I preach to the non-Jewish people. I did not want my past work and the work I am now doing to be wasted. ³Titus was with me, but he was not forced to be circumcised, even though he was a Greek. ⁴We talked about this problem because some false believers had come into our group secretly. They came in like spies to overturn the freedom we have in Christ Jesus. They wanted to make us slaves. ⁵But we did not give in to those false believers for a minute. We wanted the truth of the Good News to continue for you.

⁶Those leaders who seemed to be important did not change the Good News that I preach. (It doesn't matter to me if they were "important" or not. To God everyone is the same.) ⁷But these leaders saw that I had been given the work of telling the Good News to those who are not Jewish, just as Peter had the work of telling the Jews.

⁸God gave Peter the power to work as an apostle for the Jewish people. But he also gave me the power to work as an apostle for those who are not Jews. ⁹James, Peter, and John, who seemed to be the leaders, understood that God had given me this special grace, so they accepted Barnabas and me. They agreed that they would go to the Jewish people and that we should go to those who are not Jewish. ¹⁰The only thing they asked us was to remember to help the poor—something I really wanted to do.

Paul Shows that Peter Was Wrong

¹¹When Peter came to Antioch, I challenged him to his face, because he was wrong. ¹²Peter ate with the non-Jewish people until some Jewish people sent from James came to Antioch. When they arrived, Peter stopped eating with those who weren't Jewish, and he separated himself from them. He was afraid of the Jews. ¹³So Peter was a hypocrite, as were the other Jewish believers who joined with him. Even Barnabas was influenced by what these Jewish believers did. ¹⁴When I saw they were not following the truth of the Good News, I spoke to Peter in front of them all. I said, "Peter, you are a Jew, but you are not living like a Jew. You are living like those who are not Jewish. So why do you now try to force those who are not Jewish to live like Jews?"

¹⁵We were not born as non-Jewish "sinners," but as Jews. ¹⁶Yet we know that a person is made right with God not by following the law, but by trusting in Jesus Christ. So we, too, have put our faith in Christ Jesus, that we might be made right with God because we trusted in Christ. It is not

because we followed the law, because no one can be made right with God by following the law.

17We Jews came to Christ, trying to be made right with God, and it became clear that we are sinners, too. Does this mean that Christ encourages sin? No! **18**But I would really be wrong to begin teaching again those things that I gave up. **19**It was the law that put me to death, and I died to the law so that I can now live for God. **20**I was put to death on the cross with Christ, and I do not live anymore—it is Christ who lives in me. I still live in my body, but I live by faith in the Son of God who loved me and gave himself to save me. **21**By saying these things I am not going against God's grace. Just the opposite, if the law could make us right with God, then Christ's death would be useless.

OLD TESTAMENT READING

Whoever ignores the poor when they cry for help

will also cry for help and not be answered.

Proverbs 21:13

If anyone from your country becomes too poor to support himself, help him to live among you as you would a stranger or foreigner. **36**Do not charge him any interest on money you loan to him, but respect your God; let the poor live among you.'"

Leviticus 25:35–36

INSIGHTS

The Bible specifically commands believers to imitate God's special concern for the poor and oppressed. In the Old Testament, Yahweh frequently reminded the Israelites of their former oppression in Egypt when he commanded them to care for the poor. . . .

When Paul took up the collection for the poor in Jerusalem, he pointedly reminded the Corinthians that the Lord Jesus became poor so that they might become rich (2 Cor. 8:9). When the author of 1 John called on Christians to share with the needy, he first mentioned the example of Christ: "By this we know love, that he laid down his life for us; and we ought to lay down our lives for the brethren" (1 John 3:16). Then, in the very next verse, he urged Christians to give generously to the needy. It is the amazing self-sacrifice of Christ which Christians are to imitate as they relate to the poor and oppressed.

. . . God's Word commands believers to care for the poor. In fact the Bible underlines the command by teaching that when God's people care for the poor, they imitate God himself. But that is not all. God's Word teaches that those who neglect the poor and oppressed are really not God's people at all—no matter how frequent their religious rituals or how orthodox their creeds and confessions.

RONALD SIDER

► ACTION POINT

What do these passages reveal to you about God's attitude toward the poor? Deep in your heart, do you really want to help the poor? What more can you do to show God's compassion for the poor? Will you do it?

GALATIANS 3:1-20

Blessing Comes Through Faith

3 You people in Galatia were told very clearly about the death of Jesus Christ on the cross. But you were foolish; you let someone trick you. **2**Tell me this one thing: How did you receive the Holy Spirit? Did you receive the Spirit by following the law? No, you received the Spirit because you heard the Good News and believed it. **3**You began your life in Christ by the Spirit. Now are you trying to make it complete by your own power? That is foolish. **4**Were all your experiences wasted? I hope not! **5**Does God give you the Spirit and work miracles among you because you follow the law? No, he does these things because you heard the Good News and believed it.

6The Scriptures say the same thing about Abraham: "Abraham believed God, and God accepted Abraham's faith, and that faith made him right with God." **7**So you should know that the true children of Abraham are those who have faith. **8**The Scriptures, telling what would happen in the future, said that God would make the non-Jewish people right through their faith. This Good News was told to Abraham beforehand, as the Scripture says: "All nations will be blessed through you." **9**So all who believe as Abraham believed are blessed just as Abraham was. **10**But those who depend on following the law to make them right are under a curse, because the Scriptures say, "Anyone will be cursed who does not always obey what is written in the Book of the Law." **11**Now it is clear that no one can be made right

with God by the law, because the Scriptures say, "Those who are right with God will live by faith." **12**The law is not based on faith. It says, "A person who obeys these things will live because of them." **13**Christ took away the curse the law put on us. He changed places with us and put himself under that curse. It is written in the Scriptures, "Anyone whose body is displayed on a tree is cursed." **14**Christ did this so that God's blessing promised to Abraham might come through Jesus Christ to those who are not Jews. Jesus died so that by our believing we could receive the Spirit that God promised.

The Law and the Promise

15Brothers and sisters, let us think in human terms: Even an agreement made between two persons is firm. After that agreement is accepted by both people, no one can stop it or add anything to it. **16**God made promises both to Abraham and to his descendant. God did not say, "and to your descendants." That would mean many people. But God said, "and to your descendant." That means only one person; that person is Christ. **17**This is what I mean: God had an agreement with Abraham and promised to keep it. The law, which came four hundred thirty years later, cannot change that agreement and so destroy God's promise to Abraham. **18**If the law could give us Abraham's blessing, then the promise would not be necessary. But that is not possible, because God freely gave his blessings to Abraham through the promise he had made.

19So what was the law for? It was given to show that the wrong things people do are against God's will. And it continued until the special descendant, who had been promised, came. The law was given through angels who used Moses for a mediator to give the law to people. **20**But a mediator is not needed when there is only one side, and God is only one.

INSIGHTS

When upon life's billows you are
  tempest tossed,
When you are discouraged, thinking
  all is lost,
Count your many blessings, name
  them one by one,
And it will surprise you what the Lord hath done.

Are you ever burdened with a load of care?
Does the cross seem heavy you are called to bear?
Count your many blessings, ev'ry doubt will fly,
And you will be singing as the days go by.

When you look at others with their lands and gold,
Think that Christ has promised you His wealth untold;
Count your many blessings, money cannot buy
Your reward in heaven, nor your home on high.

So, amid the conflict, whether great or small,
Do not be discouraged, God is over all;
Count your many blessings, angels will attend,
Help and comfort give you to your journey's end.

Count your blessings, name them one by one;
Count your blessings, see what God hath done;
Count your blessings, name them one by one;
Count your many blessings, see what God hath done.

JOHNSON OATMAN, JR.

OLD TESTAMENT READING

The angel of the LORD called to Abraham from heaven a second time **16**and said, "The LORD says, 'Because you did not keep back your son, your only son, from me, I make you this promise by my own name: **17**I will surely bless you and give you many descendants.'"

Genesis 22:15–17a

ACTION POINT

What are the differences between obeying the law and believing the Good News? What was the purpose of the law? What is promised to all who believe? Name the blessings God has bestowed on you!

GALATIANS
3:21 — 4:20

The Purpose of the Law of Moses

21Does this mean that the law is against God's promises? Never! That would be true only if the law could make us right with God. But God did not give a law that can bring life. **22**Instead, the Scriptures showed that the whole world is bound by sin. This was so the promise would be given through faith to people who believe in Jesus Christ.

23Before this faith came, we were all held prisoners by the law. We had no freedom until God showed us the way of faith that was coming. **24**In other words, the law was our guardian leading us to Christ so that we could be made right with God through faith. **25**Now the way of faith has come, and we no longer live under a guardian.

26-27 You were all baptized into Christ, and so you were all clothed with Christ. This means that you are all children of God through faith in Christ Jesus. **28**In Christ, there is no difference between Jew and Greek, slave and free person, male and female. You are all the same in Christ Jesus. **29**You belong to Christ, so you are Abraham's descendants. You will inherit all of God's blessings because of the promise God made to Abraham.

4 I want to tell you this: While those who will inherit their fathers' property are still children, they are no different from slaves. It does not matter that the children own everything. **2**While they are children, they must obey those who are chosen to care for them. But when the children reach the age set by their fathers, they are free. **3**It is the same for us. We were once like children, slaves to the useless rules of this world. **4**But when the right time came, God sent his Son who was born of a woman and lived under the law. **5**God did this so he could buy freedom for those who were under the law and so we could become his children.

6Since you are God's children, God sent the Spirit of his Son into your hearts, and the Spirit cries out, "Father." **7**So now you are not a slave; you are God's child, and God will give you the blessing he promised, because you are his child.

Paul's Love for the Christians

8In the past you did not know God. You were slaves to gods that were not real. **9**But now you know the true God. Really, it is God who knows you. So why do you turn back to those weak and useless rules you followed before? Do you want to be slaves to those things again? **10**You still follow teachings about special days, months, seasons, and years. **11**I am afraid for you, that my work for you has been wasted.

12Brothers and sisters, I became like you, so I beg you to become like me. You were very good to me before. **13**You remember that it was because of an illness that I came to you the first time, preaching the Good News. **14**Though my sickness was a trouble for you, you did not hate me or make me leave. But you welcomed me as an angel from God, as if I were Jesus Christ himself! **15**You were very happy then, but where is that joy now?

I am ready to testify that you would have taken out your eyes and given them to me if that were possible. **16**Now am I your enemy because I tell you the truth?

17Those people are working hard to persuade you, but this is not good for you. They want to persuade you to turn against us and follow only them. **18**It is good for people to show interest in you, but only if their purpose is good. This is always true, not just when I am with you. **19**My little children, again I feel the pain of childbirth for you until you truly become like Christ. **20**I wish I could be with you now and could change the way I am talking to you, because I do not know what to think about you.

OLD TESTAMENT READING

But LORD, you are our father.
    We are like clay, and you are the potter;
    your hands made us all.
9LORD, don't continue to be angry with us;
    don't remember our sins forever.
Please, look at us,
    because we are your people.

Isaiah 64:8–9

You are holy people, who belong to the LORD your God. He has chosen you from all the people on earth to be his very own.

Deuteronomy 14:2

INSIGHTS

Adoption, by its very nature, is an act of free kindness to the persons adopted. If you become a father by adopting a child, you do so because you choose to, not because you are bound to. Similarly, God adopts because he chooses to. He has no duty to do so. He need not have done anything about our sins save punish us as we deserved. But he loved us; he redeemed us, forgave us . . . gave himself to us as our Father.

Nor does his grace stop short with that initial act, any more than the love of human parents who adopt stops short with the completing of the legal process that makes the child theirs. The establishing of the child's status as a member of the family is only a beginning. The real task remains: to establish a filial relationship between your adopted child and yourself to win the child's love by loving it. You seek to excite affection by showing affection. And so it is with God. Throughout our life in this world, and to all eternity beyond, he will constantly be showing us in one way or another more and more of his love, and thereby increasing our love to him continually.

J. I. PACKER

ACTION POINT

Think carefully about the implications of being made a child of God. How does one live as a child of a living, holy God? Pray that you will live like a child of God, not like a child of the world.

GALATIANS 4:21 — 5:15

The Example of Hagar and Sarah

21Some of you still want to be under the law. Tell me, do you know what the law says? **22**The Scriptures say that Abraham had two sons. The mother of one son was a slave woman, and the mother of the other son was a free woman. **23**Abraham's son from the slave woman was born in the normal human way. But the son from the free woman was born because of the promise God made to Abraham.

24This story teaches something else: The two women are like the two agreements between God and his people. One agreement is the law that God made on Mount Sinai, and the people who are under this agreement are like slaves. The mother named Hagar is like that agreement. **25**She is like Mount Sinai in Arabia and is a picture of the earthly city of Jerusalem. This city and its people are slaves to the law. **26**But the heavenly Jerusalem, which is above, is like the free woman. She is our mother. **27**It is written in the Scriptures:

"Be happy, Jerusalem.

You are like a woman who never gave birth to children.

Start singing and shout for joy.

You never felt the pain of giving birth,
but you will have more children

than the woman who has a husband."

Isaiah 54:1

28My brothers and sisters, you are God's children because of his promise, as Isaac was then. **29**The son who was born in the normal way treated the other son badly. It is the same today. **30**But what does the Scripture say? "Throw out the slave woman and her son. The son of the slave woman should not inherit anything. The son of the free woman should receive it all." **31**So, my brothers and sisters, we are not children of the slave woman, but of the free woman.

Keep Your Freedom

5 We have freedom now, because Christ made us free. So stand strong. Do not change and go back into the slavery of the law. **2**Listen, I Paul tell you that if you go back to the law by being circumcised, Christ does you no good. **3**Again, I warn every man: If you allow yourselves to be circumcised, you must follow all the law, **4**If you try to be made right with God through the law, your life with Christ is over—you have left God's grace. **5**But we have the true hope that comes from being made right with God, and by the Spirit we wait eagerly for this hope. **6**When we are in Christ Jesus, it is not important if we are circumcised or not. The important thing is faith—the kind of faith that works through love.

7You were running a good race. Who stopped you from following the true way? **8**This change did not come from the One who chose you. **9**Be careful! "Just a little yeast makes the whole batch of dough rise." **10**But I trust in the Lord that you will not believe those different ideas. Whoever is confusing you with such ideas will be punished.

11My brothers and sisters, I do not teach that a man must be circumcised. If I teach circumcision, why am I still being attacked? If I still taught circumcision, my preaching about the cross would not be a problem. **12** I wish the people who are bothering you would castrate themselves!

13 My brothers and sisters, God called you to be free, but do not use your freedom as an excuse to do what pleases your sinful self. Serve each other with love. **14** The whole law is made complete in this one command: "Love your neighbor as you love yourself." **15** If you go on hurting each other and tearing each other apart, be careful, or you will completely destroy each other.

INSIGHTS

Freedom is the privilege of those who are willing to obey. It is a privilege which carries many responsibilities. It is not an automatic right. . . .

Jesus said, ". . . You shall know the truth, and the truth shall make you free" (John 8:32). Truth makes us free because it gives understanding. Understanding helps us accept the necessary conditions, restrictions, and discipline which must prevail if there is to be true freedom. To obey the truth of God's Word makes us free from the slavery of evil habits, desires which harm us, and behavior which dishonors the Lord. Liberty is not the result of human achievement. It is the result of obedience to God. Disobedience means loss of freedom.

If freedom is to be real and lasting, it must be controlled by love. Freedom to do as one pleases, without regard for others or for the circumstances, is destructive. Christian liberty is freedom to love and to serve. It is abused when it is made an excuse for loveless behavior or inconsiderate action.

Real freedom is found in serving God. With our minds centered on Christ and what He would have us do, the self-centered desires and degrading habits of life are crowded out. Life is complete and happy when we surrender ourselves to God, whose yoke is easy and burden is light (Matthew 11:30).

LUCILLE SOLLENBERGER

OLD TESTAMENT READING

Isaac grew, and when he became old enough to eat food, Abraham gave a great feast. **9** But Sarah saw Ishmael making fun of Isaac. (Ishmael was the son of Abraham by Hagar, Sarah's Egyptian slave.) **10** So Sarah said to Abraham, "Throw out this slave woman and her son. Her son should not inherit anything; my son Isaac should receive it all."

11 This troubled Abraham very much because Ishmael was also his son. **12** But God said to Abraham, "Don't be troubled about the boy and the slave woman. Do whatever Sarah tells you. The descendants I promised you will be from Isaac."

Genesis 21:8–12

PAUSE FOR REFLECTION

What are the differences between the children of the slave woman and the free woman? Who gives true freedom? What privileges does freedom in Christ provide? Do you fully enjoy those privileges?

GALATIANS
5:16 — 6:18

The Spirit and Human Nature

16So I tell you: Live by following the Spirit. Then you will not do what your sinful selves want. **17**Our sinful selves want what is against the Spirit, and the Spirit wants what is against our sinful selves. The two are against each other, so you cannot do just what you please. **18**But if the Spirit is leading you, you are not under the law.

19The wrong things the sinful self does are clear: being sexually unfaithful, not being pure, taking part in sexual sins, **20**worshiping gods, doing witchcraft, hating, making trouble, being jealous, being angry, being selfish, making people angry with each other, causing divisions among people, **21**feeling envy, being drunk, having wild and wasteful parties, and doing other things like these. I warn you now as I warned you before: Those who do these things will not inherit God's kingdom. **22**But the Spirit produces the fruit of love, joy, peace, patience, kindness, goodness, faithfulness, **23**gentleness, self-control. There is no law that says these things are wrong. **24**Those who belong to Christ Jesus have crucified their own sinful selves. They have given up their old selfish feelings and the evil things they wanted to do. **25**We get our new life from the Spirit, so we should follow the Spirit. **26**We must not be proud or make trouble with each other or be jealous of each other.

Help Each Other

Brothers and sisters, if someone in your group does something wrong, you who are spiritual should go to that person and gently help make him right again. But be careful, because you might be tempted to sin, too. **2**By helping each other with your troubles, you truly obey the law of Christ. **3**If anyone thinks he is important when he really is not, he is only fooling himself. **4**Each person should judge his own actions and not compare himself with others. Then he can be proud for what he himself has done. **5**Each person must be responsible for himself.

6Anyone who is learning the teaching of God should share all the good things he has with his teacher.

Life Is like Planting a Field

7Do not be fooled: You cannot cheat God. People harvest only what they plant. **8**If they plant to satisfy their sinful selves, their sinful selves will bring them ruin. But if they plant to please the Spirit, they will receive eternal life from the Spirit. **9**We must not become tired of doing good. We will receive our harvest of eternal life at the right time if we do not give up. **10**When we have the opportunity to help anyone, we should do it. But we should give special attention to those who are in the family of believers.

Paul Ends His Letter

11See what large letters I use to write this myself. **12**Some people are trying to force you to be circumcised so the Jews will accept them. They are afraid they will be attacked if they follow only the cross of Christ. **13**Those who are circumcised do not obey the law themselves, but they want you to be circumcised so they can brag about what they forced you to do. **14**I hope I will never brag about things like that. The cross of our Lord Jesus Christ is my only reason for bragging. Through the cross of Jesus my world was crucified, and I died to the world. **15**It is not important if a man is circumcised or uncircumcised. The important thing is being the new people God has made. **16**Peace and mercy to those who follow this rule—and to all of God's people.

17So do not give me any more trouble. I have scars on my body that show I belong to Christ Jesus.

18My brothers and sisters, the grace of our Lord Jesus Christ be with your spirit. Amen.

OLD TESTAMENT READING

If people please God, God will give them wisdom, knowledge, and joy. But sinners will get only the work of gathering and storing wealth that they will have to give to the ones who please God. So all their work is useless, like chasing the wind.

Ecclesiastes 2:26

INSIGHTS

Our dividends in heaven are determined by what we invest in on earth. We can invest in eternal sureties, or we can invest in wind. . . .

. . . According to the law of the harvest you reap what you sow. If you sow wheat, you reap wheat; if you sow weeds, you reap weeds; if you sow wind, you reap wind. The law of the harvest operates in the spiritual and moral realms as well as the physical. "Do not be deceived, God is not mocked; for whatever a man sows, this he will also reap" (Galatians 6:7). . . . We should guard against sowing too much time, energy, and money on clothes and recreation and parties and other means of self-indulgence. We will reap nothing in terms of our eternal well-being from these seeds. No wonder growing Christians are exhorted to "guard yourselves from idols" (1 John 5:21). Idols are not just the wood and stone types that Israel turned to, but anything that steals our hearts and minds away from total commitment to the Lord. . . .

. . . If we invest our lives in the nothingness of what this world has to offer, we not only reap a harvest of nothing but we destroy our lives as well. Many Christians have lives that are disordered, chaotic, and shattered because of their investment in the wind of this world. . . .

. . . We must have a steady diet of the solid food of the Word of God now if we are going to avoid the stunted growth, starvation, and emptiness that are associated with feeding on wind.

DAVID REID

ACTION POINT

Examine your life and list what you have sown. Does what you have sown please the Spirit (Gal. 5:16–25)? What do you need to sow on earth in order to receive the heavenly dividends you desire?

EPHESIANS 1:1 – 2:3

1 From Paul, an apostle of Christ Jesus. I am an apostle because that is what God wanted. To God's holy people living in Ephesus, believers in Christ Jesus:

2 Grace and peace to you from God our Father and the Lord Jesus Christ.

Spiritual Blessings in Christ

3 Praise be to the God and Father of our Lord Jesus Christ. In Christ, God has given us every spiritual blessing in the heavenly world. **4** That is, in Christ, he chose us before the world was made so that we would be his holy people—people without blame before him. **5** Because of his love, God had already decided to make us his own children through Jesus Christ. That was what he wanted and what pleased him, **6** and it brings praise to God because of his wonderful grace. God gave that grace to us freely, in Christ, the One he loves. **7** In Christ we are set free by the blood of his death, and so we have forgiveness of sins. How rich is God's grace, **8** which he has given to us so fully and freely. God, with full wisdom and understanding, **9** let us know his secret purpose. This was what God wanted, and he planned to do it through Christ. **10** His goal was to carry out his plan, when the right time came, that all things in heaven and on earth would be joined together in Christ as the head.

11 In Christ we were chosen to be God's people, because from the very beginning God had decided this in keeping with his plan. And he is the One who makes everything agree with what he decides and wants. **12** We are the first people who hoped in Christ, and we were chosen so that we would bring praise to God's glory. **13** So it is with you. When you heard the true teaching—the Good News about your salvation—you believed in Christ. And in Christ, God put his special mark of ownership on you by giving you the Holy Spirit that he had promised. **14** That Holy Spirit is the guarantee that we will receive what God promised for his people until God gives full freedom to those who are his—to bring praise to God's glory.

Paul's Prayer

15 That is why since I heard about your faith in the Lord Jesus and your love for all God's people, **16** I have not stopped giving thanks to God for you. I always remember you in my prayers, **17** asking the God of our Lord Jesus Christ, the glorious Father, to give you a spirit of wisdom and revelation so that you will know him better. **18** I pray also that you will have greater understanding in your heart so you will know the hope to which he has called us and that you will know how rich and glorious are the blessings God has promised his holy people. **19** And you will know that God's power is very great for us who believe. That power is the same as the great strength **20** God used to raise Christ from the dead and put him at his right side in the heavenly world. **21** God has put Christ over all rulers, authorities, powers, and kings, not only in this world but also in the next. **22** God put everything under his power and made him the head over everything for the church, **23** which is Christ's body. The church is filled with Christ, and Christ fills everything in every way.

We Now Have Life

In the past you were spiritually dead because of your sins and the things you did against God. **2**Yes, in the past you lived the way the world lives, following the ruler of the evil powers that are above the earth. That same spirit is now working in those who refuse to obey God. **3**In the past all of us lived like them, trying to please our sinful selves and doing all the things our bodies and minds wanted. We should have suffered God's anger because we were sinful by nature. We were the same as all other people.

OLD TESTAMENT READING

My servant Job will pray for you, and I will listen to his prayer. Then I will not punish you for being foolish. You have not said what is right about me, as my servant Job did." **9**So Eliphaz the Temanite, Bildad the Shuhite, and Zophar the Naamathite did as the LORD said, and the LORD listened to Job's prayer.

Job 42:8b–9

INSIGHTS

Compassion lies at the heart of intercession. . . .

When we promise to pray for someone, how often do we truly enter into the reality of what that means? The story of the paralytic borne by four friends to Jesus for healing is a powerful illustration of intercessory love. We "carry" those for whom we pray (we even speak sometimes of having "a burden" in prayer). Self is out of the picture, for we have become that other person experiencing his pain with him, suffering his fears for him, consumed with the same longings.

"Blessed are the merciful," said Jesus (Matt 5:7). Part of the meaning of being merciful is to get inside the skin of someone else, to feel as he feels, think as he thinks, see as he sees, to understand life the way he understands it. That, of course, is at the heart of the incarnation. It is precisely what Jesus did when he "got inside the skin" of a human being and experienced life as we do.

This kind of intercession is contemplative rather than petitionary. It is gathered up in compassion and empathy more often than words—though words are sometimes helpful to us in focusing on a particular person or need. We can bear people to the Lord, as the friends of the paralytic did, and leave them with him. We do not need to inform him of all the facts or suggest how he should act. We are not able to pray, but the Holy Spirit can pray through and in us. We cannot heal, but God can heal through us.

MARGARET MAGDALEN

PAUSE FOR REFLECTION

Do you feel the passion with which Paul prayed? Such prayers go far deeper than cursory "Lord bless" and "Lord forgive" prayers, don't they? Could your prayers perhaps flow from deeper in your heart?

EPHESIANS 2:4 — 3:6

4But God's mercy is great, and he loved us very much. **5**Though we were spiritually dead because of the things we did against God, he gave us new life with Christ. You have been saved by God's grace. **6**And he raised us up with Christ and gave us a seat with him in the heavens. He did this for those in Christ Jesus **7**so that for all future time he could show the very great riches of his grace by being kind to us in Christ Jesus. **8**I mean that you have been saved by grace through believing. You did not save yourselves; it was a gift from God. **9**It was not the result of your own efforts, so you cannot brag about it. **10**God has made us what we are. In Christ Jesus, God made us to do good works, which God planned in advance for us to live our lives doing.

One in Christ

11You were not born Jewish. You are the people the Jews call "uncircumcised." Those who call you "uncircumcised" call themselves "circumcised." (Their circumcision is only something they themselves do on their bodies.) **12**Remember that in the past you were without Christ. You were not citizens of Israel, and you had no part in the agreements with the promise that God made to his people. You had no hope, and you did not know God. **13**But now in Christ Jesus, you who were far away from God are brought near through the blood of Christ's death. **14**Christ himself is our peace. He made both Jewish people and those who are not Jews one people. They were separated as if there were a wall between them, but Christ broke down that wall of hate by giving his own body. **15**The Jewish law had many commands and rules, but Christ ended that law. His purpose was to make the two groups of people become one new people in him and in this way make peace. **16**It was also Christ's purpose to end the hatred between the two groups, to make them into one body, and to bring them back to God. Christ did all this with his death on the cross. **17**Christ came and preached peace to you who were far away from God, and to those who were near to God. **18**Yes, it is through Christ we all have the right to come to the Father in one Spirit.

19Now you who are not Jewish are not foreigners or strangers any longer, but are citizens together with God's holy people. You belong to God's family. **20**You are like a building that was built on the foundation of the apostles and prophets. Christ Jesus himself is the most important stone in that building, **21**and that whole building is joined together in Christ. He makes it grow and become a holy temple in the Lord. **22**And in Christ you, too, are being built together with the Jews into a place where God lives through the Spirit.

Paul's Work in Telling the Good News

3 So I, Paul, am a prisoner of Christ Jesus for you who are not Jews. **2**Surely you have heard that God gave me this work to tell you about his grace. **3**He let me know his secret by showing it to me. I have already written a little about this. **4**If you read what I wrote then, you can see that I truly understand the secret about the Christ. **5**People who lived in other times were not told that secret. But now, through the Spirit, God has shown that secret to his holy apostles and prophets. ⁶This is that secret: that through the Good News those who are not Jews will share with the Jews in God's blessing. They belong to the same body, and they share together in the promise that God made in Christ Jesus.

INSIGHTS

In my own life I am acutely aware that I am a roughhewn man. Because of my rather tough, rough upbringing in a frontier environment, I simply do not possess the polish of the "man about the town." There are characteristics in my makeup which may seem harsh and unyielding. But, despite this, my life has been deeply touched by the mercy of those who took the time to try and understand me—who cared enough to forgive so many faults and who in mercy made me their friend.

Often these were people to whom I had shown no special kindness. Their bestowal of mercy on me was something totally unexpected and undeserved. Because of this, it has been a double delight. More than that, it has been an enormous inspiration that lifted and challenged me to respond in a measure beyond my wildest dreams.

Mercy does just that to people. It excites and stimulates their hope. It reassures them that life can be beautiful. It convinces them that there is good reason to carry on and push for better things if others care that much.

This all implies that if someone has extended mercy to me, surely I, in turn, can and must extend mercy to others.

But, to really find the true source of inner inspiration for this sort of conduct, the Christian simply must look beyond his fellow man. He must look away to the mercy of God our Father. Nothing else in all the world will so humble us. Nothing else will so move our stony spirits to extend mercy. Nothing else will so powerfully induce us to do the proper thing in extending genuine mercy to our contemporaries.

W. PHILLIP KELLER

OLD TESTAMENT READING

There is no God like you.
    You forgive those who are guilty of sin;
you don't look at the sins of your people
    who are left alive.
You will not stay angry forever,
    because you enjoy being kind.
¹⁹You will have mercy on us again;
    you will conquer our sins.

Micah 7:18–19a

PAUSE FOR REFLECTION

What has God's mercy, as described in Ephesians, accomplished for all people? How has God's mercy touched your life? What has been the result of his merciful touch? How will you thank him?

EPHESIANS 3:7 – 4:16

7 By God's special gift of grace given to me through his power, I became a servant to tell that Good News. **8** I am the least important of all God's people, but God gave me this gift—to tell those who are not Jews the Good News about the riches of Christ, which are too great to understand fully. **9** And God gave me the work of telling all people about the plan for his secret, which has been hidden in him since the beginning of time. He is the One who created everything. **10** His purpose was that through the church all the rulers and powers in the heavenly world will now know God's wisdom, which has so many forms. **11** This agrees with the purpose God had since the beginning of time, and he carried out his plan through Christ Jesus our Lord. **12** In Christ we can come before God with freedom and without fear. We can do this through faith in Christ. **13** So I ask you not to become discouraged because of the sufferings I am having for you. My sufferings are for your glory.

The Love of Christ

14 So I bow in prayer before the Father **15** from whom every family in heaven and on earth gets its true name. **16** I ask the Father in his great glory to give you the power to be strong inwardly through his Spirit. **17** I pray that Christ will live in your hearts by faith and that your life will be strong in love and be built on love. **18** And I pray that you and all God's holy people will have the power to

understand the greatness of Christ's love—how wide and how long and how high and how deep that love is. **19** Christ's love is greater than anyone can ever know, but I pray that you will be able to know that love. Then you can be filled with the fullness of God.

20 With God's power working in us, God can do much, much more than anything we can ask or imagine. **21** To him be glory in the church and in Christ Jesus for all time, forever and ever. Amen.

The Unity of the Body

4 I am in prison because I belong to the Lord. Therefore I urge you who have been chosen by God to live up to the life to which God called you. **2** Always be humble, gentle, and patient, accepting each other in love. **3** You are joined together with peace through the Spirit, so make every effort to continue together in this way. **4** There is one body and one Spirit, and God called you to have one hope. **5** There is one Lord, one faith, and one baptism. **6** There is one God and Father of everything. He rules everything and is everywhere and is in everything.

7 Christ gave each one of us the special gift of grace, showing how generous he is. **8** That is why it says in the Scriptures,

"When he went up to the heights,

he led a parade of captives,

and he gave gifts to people."   *Psalm 68:18*

9 When it says, "He went up," what does it mean? It means that he first came down to the earth. **10** So Jesus came down, and he is the same One who went up above all the heaven. Christ did that to fill everything with his presence. **11** And Christ gave gifts to people —he made some to be apostles, some to be prophets, some to go and tell the Good News, and some to have the work of caring for and teaching God's people. **12**Christ gave those gifts to prepare God's holy people for the work of serving, to make the body of Christ stronger. **13**This work must continue until we are all joined together in the same faith and in the same knowledge of the Son of God. We must become like a mature person, growing until we become like Christ and have his perfection.

14Then we will no longer be babies. We will not be tossed about like a ship that the waves carry one way and then another. We will not be influenced by every new teaching we hear from people who are trying to fool us. They make plans and try any kind of trick to fool people into following the wrong path. **15**No! Speaking the truth with love, we will grow up in every way into Christ, who is the head. **16**The whole body depends on Christ, and all the parts of the body are joined and held together. Each part does its own work to make the whole body grow and be strong with love.

OLD TESTAMENT READING

Give thanks to the LORD because
     he is good.
  His love continues forever.

4Only he can do great miracles.
  His love continues forever.

Psalm 136:1, 4

INSIGHTS

Before we can have any right idea of the love of Jesus, we must understand His previous glory in its height of majesty, and His incarnation upon the earth in all its depths of shame. But who can tell us the majesty of Christ? When He was enthroned in the highest heavens He was very God of very God; by Him were the heavens made, and all the hosts thereof. His own almighty arm upheld the spheres; the praises of cherubim and seraphim perpetually surrounded Him; the full chorus of the hallelujahs of the universe unceasingly flowed to the foot of his throne: He reigned supreme above all His creatures, God over all, blessed for ever. Who can tell His height of glory then? And who, on the other hand, can tell how low He descended? To be a man was something, to be a man of sorrows was far more; to bleed, and die, and suffer, these were much for Him who was the Son of God; but to suffer such unparalleled agony—to endure a death of shame and desertion by His Father, this is a depth of condescending love which the most inspired mind must utterly fail to fathom. Herein is love! and truly it is love that "passeth knowledge." O let this love fill our hearts with adoring gratitude, and lead us to practical manifestations of its power.

CHARLES SPURGEON

ACTION POINT

Describe in the best way you can, how wide, long, high, and deep Christ's love is. Pray that you will know the fullness of God's love in your life.

EPHESIANS 4:17 – 5:14

The Way You Should Live

17In the Lord's name, I tell you this. Do not continue living like those who do not believe. Their thoughts are worth nothing. **18**They do not understand, and they know nothing, because they refuse to listen. So they cannot have the life that God gives. **19**They have lost all feeling of shame, and they use their lives for doing evil. They continually want to do all kinds of evil. **20**But what you learned in Christ was not like this. **21**I know that you heard about him, and you are in him, so you were taught the truth that is in Jesus. **22**You were taught to leave your old self—to stop living the evil way you lived before. That old self becomes worse, because people are fooled by the evil things they want to do. **23**But you were taught to be made new in your hearts, **24**to become a new person. That new person is made to be like God—made to be truly good and holy.

25So you must stop telling lies. Tell each other the truth, because we all belong to each other in the same body. **26**When you are angry, do not sin, and be sure to stop being angry before the end of the day. **27**Do not give the devil a way to defeat you. **28**Those who are stealing must stop stealing and start working. They should earn an honest living for themselves. Then they will have something to share with those who are poor.

29When you talk, do not say harmful things, but say what people need—words that will help others become stronger. Then what you say will do good to those who listen to you. **30**And do not make the Holy Spirit sad. The Spirit is God's proof that you belong to him. God gave you the Spirit to show that God will make you free when the final day comes. **31**Do not be bitter or angry or mad. Never shout angrily or say things to hurt others. Never do anything evil. **32**Be kind and loving to each other, and forgive each other just as God forgave you in Christ.

Living in the Light

You are God's children whom he loves, so try to be like him. **2**Live a life of love just as Christ loved us and gave himself for us as a sweet-smelling offering and sacrifice to God.

3But there must be no sexual sin among you, or any kind of evil or greed. Those things are not right for God's holy people. **4**Also, there must be no evil talk among you, and you must not speak foolishly or tell evil jokes. These things are not right for you. Instead, you should be giving thanks to God. **5**You can be sure of this: No one will have a place in the kingdom of Christ and of God who sins sexually, or does evil things, or is greedy. Anyone who is greedy is serving a false god.

6Do not let anyone fool you by telling you things that are not true, because these things will bring God's anger on those who do not obey him. **7**So have nothing to do with them. **8**In the past you were full of darkness, but now you are full of light in the Lord. So live like children who belong to the light. **9**Light brings every kind of goodness, right living, and truth. **10**Try to learn what pleases the Lord. **11**Have nothing to do with the things done in darkness, which are not worth anything.

But show that they are wrong. ¹²It is shameful even to talk about what those people do in secret. ¹³But the light makes all things easy to see, ¹⁴and everything that is made easy to see can become light. This is why it is said:

"Wake up, sleeper!
    Rise from death,
and Christ will shine on you."

OLD TESTAMENT READING

Greed has two daughters
    named 'Give' and 'Give.'
There are three things that are never satisfied,
    really four that never say, 'I've had
        enough!':
¹⁶the cemetery, the childless mother,
    the land that never gets enough rain,
    and fire that never says, 'I've had enough!'"

Proverbs 30:15–16

INSIGHTS

Someone has well said, "Our pocketbooks have more to do with heaven and hell than our hymnbooks." Jesus told the story of the rich man who had everything, and a beggar who had nothing. The rich man, blinded by his abundance, neither saw his need for righteousness nor prepared himself for eternity. Lazarus, who had received only bad things, "crumbs from the rich man's table," had prepared well for his future. And their roles in the future life were completely reversed! (Luke 16:19–31) . . .

Cyprian, the third-century bishop of Carthage, wrote an amazingly up-to-date description of the affluent:

Their property held them in chains . . . which shackled their courage and choked their faith and hampered their judgment and throttled their souls. . . . If they stored up their treasure in heaven, they would not now have an enemy and a thief within their household. . . . They think of themselves as owners, whereas it is they rather who are owned: enslaved as they are to their own property, they are not the masters of their money but its slaves.

How we need to hear the voice of the New Testament as it calls us to a life of responsible stewardship of our resources.

ART BEALS

APPLICATION

Why is greed such a hindrance to spiritual growth? What other lifestyle choices are wrong for God's holy people? Why? What does your handling of possessions reveal about your heart?

EPHESIANS
5:15 — 6:4

15So be very careful how you live. Do not live like those who are not wise, but live wisely. **16**Use every chance you have for doing good, because these are evil times. **17**So do not be foolish but learn what the Lord wants you to do. **18**Do not be drunk with wine, which will ruin you, but be filled with the Spirit. **19**Speak to each other with psalms, hymns, and spiritual songs, singing and making music in your hearts to the Lord. **20**Always give thanks to God the Father for everything, in the name of our Lord Jesus Christ.

Wives and Husbands

21Yield to obey each other as you would to Christ.

22Wives, yield to your husbands, as you do to the Lord, **23**because the husband is the head of the wife, as Christ is the head of the church. And he is the Savior of the body, which is the church. **24**As the church yields to Christ, so you wives should yield to your husbands in everything.

25Husbands, love your wives as Christ loved the church and gave himself for it **26**to make it belong to God. Christ used the word to make the church clean by washing it with water. **27**He died so that he could give the church to himself like a bride in all her beauty. He died so that the church could be pure and without fault, with no evil or sin or any other wrong thing in it. **28**In the same way, husbands should love their wives as they love their own bodies. The man who loves his wife loves himself. **29**No one ever hates his own body, but feeds and takes care of it. And that is what Christ does for the church, **30**because we are parts of his body. **31**The Scripture says, "So a man will leave his father and mother and be united with his wife, and the two will become one body." **32**That secret is very important—I am talking about Christ and the church. **33**But each one of you must love his wife as he loves himself, and a wife must respect her husband.

Children and Parents

Children, obey your parents as the Lord wants, because this is the right thing to do. **2**The command says, "Honor your father and mother." This is the first command that has a promise with it— **3**"Then everything will be well with you, and you will have a long life on the earth."

4Fathers, do not make your children angry, but raise them with the training and teaching of the Lord.

OLD TESTAMENT READING

Be happy with the wife you married when you were young.

She gives you joy, as your fountain gives you water.

19She is as lovely and graceful as a deer.
Let her love always make you happy;
let her love always hold you captive.

20My son, don't be held captive by a woman
who takes part in adultery.
Don't fondle a woman who is not your wife.

Proverbs 5:18–20

My lover is mine, and I am his.
He feeds among the lilies
17until the day dawns
and the shadows disappear.
Turn, my lover.
Be like a gazelle or a young deer
on the mountain valleys.

Song of Songs 2:16–17

Laban and Bethuel answered, "This is clearly from the LORD, and we cannot change what must happen. **51**Rebekah is yours. Take her and go. Let her marry your master's son as the LORD has commanded."

66The servant told Isaac everything that had happened. **67**Then Isaac brought Rebekah into the tent of Sarah, his mother, and she became his wife. Isaac loved her very much, and so he was comforted after his mother's death.

Genesis 24:50–51, 66–67

INSIGHTS

If you could enter a time machine and emerge back in the first century when Paul's letters hit the culture of the day, you would be in for some real excitement. His instruction to husbands in Ephesians 5:25–27 must have caused a riot! They went contrary to the way men treated women at that time. Paul's writing called the husband to a ministry of loving servanthood to his wife in a culture which treated women as little better than household furnishings!

A husband is to love his wife with the same sacrificial self-abandonment that Christ adopted toward each of us. When a man considers hardship in marriage, he needs to look at the life of Jesus. Jesus said, "The Son of Man came not to be served, but to serve" (Matthew 20:28). Jesus is presented in Scripture as both Head and Servant. He is the "head over everything for the church" (Ephesians 1:22) who took "the very nature of a servant" (Philippians 2:7). And Jesus instructed us, "The greatest among you will be your servant" (Matthew 23:11).

As believers, we are all called to servanthood as an expression of our new life in Christ. However, when it comes to marriage, modeling this attribute of God's Son is a calling extended to husbands. A husband expresses love to his wife by regarding her as a completely equal partner in everything that concerns their life together. He asserts his headship to see that this equal partnership works. Loving headship affirms and defers; it encourages and stimulates. Loving headship delights to delegate without demanding.

H. NORMAN WRIGHT

PAUSE FOR REFLECTION

How do Paul's instructions about marriage fit in with the broader scope of instructions on Christian living that he offers in this passage (Ephesians 5:15–21)? What do his instructions reveal about God's desired intent for marriage?

EPHESIANS 6:5-24

Slaves and Masters

5Slaves, obey your masters here on earth with fear and respect and from a sincere heart, just as you obey Christ. **6**You must do this not only while they are watching you, to please them. With all your heart you must do what God wants as people who are obeying Christ. **7**Do your work with enthusiasm. Work as if you were serving the Lord, not as if you were serving only men and women. **8**Remember that the Lord will give a reward to everyone, slave or free, for doing good.

9Masters, in the same way, be good to your slaves. Do not threaten them. Remember that the One who is your Master and their Master is in heaven, and he treats everyone alike.

Wear the Full Armor of God

10Finally, be strong in the Lord and in his great power. **11**Put on the full armor of God so that you can fight against the devil's evil tricks. **12**Our fight is not against people on earth but against the rulers and authorities and the powers of this world's darkness, against the spiritual powers of evil in the heavenly world. **13**That is why you need to put on God's full armor. Then on the day of evil you will be able to stand strong. And when you have finished the whole fight, you will still be standing. **14**So stand strong, with the belt of truth tied around your waist and the protection of right living on your chest. **15**On your feet wear the Good News of peace to help you stand strong. **16**And also use the shield of faith with which you can stop all the burning arrows of the Evil One. **17**Accept God's salvation as your helmet, and take the sword of the Spirit, which is the word of God. **18**Pray in the Spirit at all times with all kinds of prayers, asking for everything you need. To do this you must always be ready and never give up. Always pray for all God's people.

19Also pray for me that when I speak, God will give me words so that I can tell the secret of the Good News without fear. **20**I have been sent to preach this Good News, and I am doing that now, here in prison. Pray that when I preach the Good News I will speak without fear, as I should.

Final Greetings

21I am sending to you Tychicus, our brother whom we love and a faithful servant of the Lord's work. He will tell you everything that is happening with me. Then you will know how I am and what I am doing. **22**I am sending him to you for this reason—so that you will know how we are, and he can encourage you.

23Peace and love with faith to you brothers and sisters from God the Father and the Lord Jesus Christ. **24**Grace to all of you who love our Lord Jesus Christ with love that never ends.

OLD TESTAMENT READING

One day the angels came to show themselves before the LORD, and Satan was with them. **7**The LORD said to Satan, "Where have you come from?"

Satan answered the LORD, "I have been wandering around the earth, going back and forth in it."

8 Then the LORD said to Satan, "Have you noticed my servant Job? No one else on earth is like him. He is an honest and innocent man, honoring God and staying away from evil."

9 But Satan answered the LORD, "Job honors God for a good reason. **10** You have put a wall around him, his family, and everything he owns. You have blessed the things he has done. His flocks and herds are so large they almost cover the land."

— Job 1:6–10

You must destroy all the people the LORD your God hands over to you. Do not feel sorry for them, and do not worship their gods, or they will trap you.

Deuteronomy 7:16

INSIGHTS

Awareness that we are involved in a cosmic battle which is supernatural, personal, and futile if fought with natural weapons is the beginning of conquering wisdom. We must be convinced of these things if we are to succeed. We must go beyond evangelical lip service to a deep-souled conviction which bursts our simplistic religious shackles.

Paul is specific about the nature of our evil opponents: "our struggle is . . . against the rulers, against the authorities, against the powers of this dark world and against the spiritual forces of evil in the heavenly realms" (v. 12). . . .

The immediate implication is that Satan is terribly powerful. To be sure he does not possess anything near the power of God, but in God's inscrutable arrangement he temporarily dominates and drives the world, which on the whole is separated from God's grace. . . .

. . . If we are filled with the Spirit (5:18), Satan's forces cannot subdue us. But those of us who neglect our resources, and especially those who give the enemies room in our lives, place ourselves in harm's way. . . .

. . . We cannot fight Satan ourselves. All our own doing will be in vain. Nevertheless there is something we can do, and that is to avail ourselves of the Lord's strength. . . . We are to acknowledge our weakness and invite his power. We must imitate Gideon's going from 32,000 warriors to 10,000 to 300 armed only with trumpets and lanterns (Judges 7). This divestment of natural strength enabled the putting on of God's power—and a mighty victory!

R. KENT HUGHES

APPLICATION

What does Scripture say you need in order to fight spiritual battles? Identify the spiritual battlefields in your life. List the battles you most frequently fail to recognize as spiritual. How can you better avail yourself of God's resources to fight those battles?

PHILIPPIANS
1:1 — 2:4

1 From Paul and Timothy, servants of Christ Jesus.

To all of God's holy people in Christ Jesus who live in Philippi, including your overseers and deacons:

²Grace and peace to you from God our Father and the Lord Jesus Christ.

Paul's Prayer

³I thank my God every time I remember you, ⁴always praying with joy for all of you. ⁵I thank God for the help you gave me while I preached the Good News—help you gave from the first day you believed until now. ⁶God began doing a good work in you, and I am sure he will continue it until it is finished when Jesus Christ comes again.

⁷And I know that I am right to think like this about all of you, because I have you in my heart. All of you share in God's grace with me while I am in prison and while I am defending and proving the truth of the Good News. ⁸God knows that I want to see you very much, because I love all of you with the love of Christ Jesus.

⁹This is my prayer for you: that your love will grow more and more; that you will have knowledge and understanding with your love; ¹⁰that you will see the difference between good and bad and will choose the good; that you will be pure and without wrong for the coming of Christ; ¹¹that you will be filled with the good things produced in your life by Christ to bring glory and praise to God.

Paul's Troubles Help the Work

¹²I want you brothers and sisters to know that what has happened to me has helped to spread the Good News. ¹³All the palace guards and everyone else knows that I am in prison because I am a believer in Christ. ¹⁴Because I am in prison, most of the believers have become more bold in Christ and are not afraid to speak the word of God.

¹⁵It is true that some preach about Christ because they are jealous and ambitious, but others preach about Christ because they want to help. ¹⁶They preach because they have love, and they know that God gave me the work of defending the Good News. ¹⁷But the others preach about Christ for selfish and wrong reasons, wanting to make trouble for me in prison.

¹⁸But it doesn't matter. The important thing is that in every way, whether for right or wrong reasons, they are preaching about Christ. So I am happy, and I will continue to be happy. ¹⁹Because you are praying for me and the Spirit of Jesus Christ is helping me, I know this trouble will bring my freedom. ²⁰I expect and hope that I will not fail Christ in anything but that I will have the courage now, as always, to show the greatness of Christ in my life here on earth, whether I live or die. ²¹To me the only important thing about living is Christ, and dying would be profit for me. ²²If I continue living in my body, I will be able to work for the Lord. I do not know what to choose—living or dying. ²³It is hard to choose between the two. I want to leave this life and be with Christ, which is much better, ²⁴but you need me here in my body. ²⁵Since I am sure of this, I know I will stay with you to help you grow and have joy in

your faith. **26**You will be very happy in Christ Jesus when I am with you again.

27Only one thing concerns me: Be sure that you live in a way that brings honor to the Good News of Christ. Then whether I come and visit you or am away from you, I will hear that you are standing strong with one purpose, that you work together as one for the faith of the Good News, **28**and that you are not afraid of those who are against you. All of this is proof that your enemies will be destroyed but that you will be saved by God. **29**God gave you the honor not only of believing in Christ but also of suffering for him, both of which bring glory to Christ. **30**When I was with you, you saw the struggles I had, and you hear about the struggles I am having now. You yourselves are having the same kind of struggles.

Does your life in Christ give you strength? Does his love comfort you? Do we share together in the spirit? Do you have mercy and kindness? **2**If so, make me very happy by having the same thoughts, sharing the same love, and having one mind and purpose. **3**When you do things, do not let selfishness or pride be your guide. Instead, be humble and give more honor to others than to yourselves. **4**Do not be interested only in your own life, but be interested in the lives of others.

OLD TESTAMENT READING

The LORD has told you, human, what is good;
he has told you what he wants from you:
to do what is right to other people,
love being kind to others,
and live humbly, obeying your God.

Micah 6:8

INSIGHTS

The humble person will renounce all the glory of the good he has or does and give it all to God. If there is anything good in him or any good done by him, he is not disposed to glorify himself or boast about it before God. . . . The disposition of the humble person is to wholly submit himself to God. He is content to be subject to the commands and laws of God, for he sees it is right and good that the creature be subject to His Creator. He wants to give God the honor that belongs to Him, and that is to reign over him and subject him to certain laws and commands that are designed for his own best interests.

Humility tends to prevent an inordinate aspiring to wealth or position—in short, ambitious behavior among people. A humble person is content with such a situation among others as God is pleased to allot to him and is not greedy for honor. Nor does he try to appear uppermost and exalted above his neighbors.

JONATHAN EDWARDS

▶ PAUSE FOR REFLECTION

Why is God opposed to the proud? What does God promise to the humble? In what ways is humility part of obeying Christ's commandment to love one another?

PHILIPPIANS 2:5-30

Be Unselfish Like Christ

5In your lives you must think and act like Christ Jesus.

6Christ himself was like God in everything.

But he did not think that being equal with God was something to be used for his own benefit.

7But he gave up his place with God and made himself nothing.

He was born as a man and became like a servant.

8And when he was living as a man, he humbled himself and was fully obedient to God,

even when that caused his death—death on a cross.

9So God raised him to the highest place.

God made his name greater than every other name

10so that every knee will bow to the name of Jesus—

everyone in heaven, on earth, and under the earth.

11And everyone will confess that Jesus Christ is Lord

and bring glory to God the Father.

Be the People God Wants You to Be

12My dear friends, you have always obeyed God when I was with you. It is even more important that you obey now while I am away from you.

Keep on working to complete your salvation with fear and trembling, **13**because God is working in you to help you want to do and be able to do what pleases him.

14Do everything without complaining or arguing. **15**Then you will be innocent and without any wrong. You will be God's children without fault. But you are living with crooked and mean people all around you, among whom you shine like stars in the dark world. **16**You offer the teaching that gives life. So when Christ comes again, I can be happy because my work was not wasted. I ran the race and won.

17Your faith makes you offer your lives as a sacrifice in serving God. If I have to offer my own blood with your sacrifice, I will be happy and full of joy with all of you. **18**You also should be happy and full of joy with me.

Timothy and Epaphroditus

19I hope in the Lord Jesus to send Timothy to you soon. I will be happy to learn how you are. **20**I have no one else like Timothy, who truly cares for you. **21**Other people are interested only in their own lives, not in the work of Jesus Christ. **22**You know the kind of person Timothy is. You know he has served with me in telling the Good News, as a son serves his father. **23**I plan to send him to you quickly when I know what will happen to me. **24**I am sure that the Lord will help me to come to you soon.

25Epaphroditus, my brother in Christ, works and serves with me in the army of Christ. When I needed help, you sent him to me. I think now that I must send him back to you, **26**because he wants very much to see all of you. He is worried because you heard that he was sick. **27**Yes, he was sick, and nearly died, but God had mercy on him and me too so that I would not have more sadness. **28**I want very much to send him to you so that when you see him you can be happy, and I can stop worrying about you. **29**Welcome him in the Lord with much joy. Give honor to people like him, **30**because he almost died for the work of Christ. He risked his life to give me the help you could not give in your service to me.

INSIGHTS

Whether we admit it or not, unbelief and disobedience are the underlying reasons for a complaining spirit.

God's Word is clear: "Do everything without complaining or arguing." This is a command, not an option. He doesn't qualify the statement and excuse us if things suddenly go wrong and it's not our fault. He says everything—and I take that to be all-inclusive. He is talking about every single circumstance whether desirable or not. When I complain, I am in essence saying, "I really don't believe God has arranged these circumstances or that He could change them if He desired." If I did believe it, I wouldn't need to complain. I'd know my only safety is in the center of His will no matter what happens.

The same God who told me not to complain also said, "In everything give thanks, for this is the will of God in Christ Jesus concerning you." How is it possible to give thanks and complain at the same time?

Is it hypocritical to say I'm thankful for my problems when I don't feel thankful? Not really, because God assures us that ". . . all things work together for good. . . ." Even when it looks disastrous, I can be certain that these self-same predicaments will be miraculously transformed under the skilled knife of the divine surgeon. He might do a little hurtful cutting on me through the process, but it will only be for my good.

MADALENE HARRIS

OLD TESTAMENT READING

Foolish people are always fighting,
but avoiding quarrels will bring you honor.

Proverbs 20:3

Pleasant words are like a honeycomb,
making people happy and healthy.

Proverbs 16:24

People without good sense find fault with their neighbors,
but those with understanding keep quiet.

Proverbs 11:12

PAUSE FOR REFLECTION

Did you realize that arguing and complaining are sins against God? Reread these Scripture passages and list the results of resisting the temptation to complain or argue—in your own life and in the lives of those around you.

PHILIPPIANS 3:1-21

The Importance of Christ

3 My brothers and sisters, be full of joy in the Lord. It is no trouble for me to write the same things to you again, and it will help you to be more ready. **2**Watch out for those who do evil, who are like dogs, who demand to cut the body. **3**We are the ones who are truly circumcised. We worship God through his Spirit, and our pride is in Christ Jesus. We do not put trust in ourselves or anything we can do, **4**although I might be able to put trust in myself. If anyone thinks he has a reason to trust in himself, he should know that I have greater reason for trusting in myself. **5**I was circumcised eight days after my birth. I am from the people of Israel and the tribe of Benjamin. I am a Hebrew, and my parents were Hebrews. I had a strict view of the law, which is why I became a Pharisee. **6**I was so enthusiastic I tried to hurt the church. No one could find fault with the way I obeyed the law of Moses. **7**Those things were important to me, but now I think they are worth nothing because of Christ. **8**Not only those things, but I think that all things are worth nothing compared with the greatness of knowing Christ Jesus my Lord. Because of him, I have lost all those things, and now I know they are worthless trash. This allows me to have Christ **9**and to belong to him. Now I am right with God, not because I followed the law, but because I believed in Christ. God uses my faith to make me right with him. **10**I want to know Christ and the power that raised him from the dead. I want to share in his sufferings and become like him in his death. **11**Then I have hope that I myself will be raised from the dead.

Continuing Toward Our Goal

12I do not mean that I am already as God wants me to be. I have not yet reached that goal, but I continue trying to reach it and to make it mine. Christ wants me to do that, which is the reason he made me his. **13**Brothers and sisters, I know that I have not yet reached that goal, but there is one thing I always do. Forgetting the past and straining toward what is ahead, **14**I keep trying to reach the goal and get the prize for which God called me through Christ to the life above.

15All of us who are spiritually mature should think this way, too. And if there are things you do not agree with, God will make them clear to you. **16**But we should continue following the truth we already have.

17Brothers and sisters, all of you should try to follow my example and to copy those who live the way we showed you. **18**Many people live like enemies of the cross of Christ. I have often told you about them, and it makes me cry to tell you about them now. **19**In the end, they will be destroyed. They do whatever their bodies want, they are proud of their shameful acts, and they think only about earthly things. **20**But our homeland is in heaven, and we are waiting for our Savior, the Lord Jesus Christ, to come from heaven. **21**By his power to rule all things, he will change our humble bodies and make them like his own glorious body.

OLD TESTAMENT READING

As a deer thirsts for streams of water,
  so I thirst for you, God.
²I thirst for the living God.
  When can I go to meet with him?

Psalm 42:1–2

God, you are my God.
  I search for you.
  I thirst for you
like someone in a dry, empty land
  where there is no water.
²I have seen you in the Temple
  and have seen your strength and glory.
³Because your love is better than life,
  I will praise you.
⁴I will praise you as long as I live.
  I will lift up my hands in prayer to your
    name.

Psalm 63:1–4b

INSIGHTS

Recently, I saw a young New Zealand cyclist win a grueling race in which he broke the national record. In a subsequent interview by the TV sports commentator, he was asked the question, "And what do you aim at for the future?" With not a moment's hesitation the reply came back: "I aim to be one of the best cyclists in the world."

In order to realize his ambition, he was prepared to pay any price in training—grueling discipline, forfeiture of social life, self-denial in many areas—and all for a piece of gold, or even bronze. Why is it that so few disciples have a similar, fixed ambition to excel for Christ? Are we "taking time and trouble to keep spiritually fit," or have we grown soft and flabby? . . .

. . . Winning a race makes great demands on the stamina and perseverance of the athlete.

Once the race has begun, the athlete cannot afford to look back. He must press on to the tape without distraction. His eyes must be fixed on the umpire's stand at the end of the track if he is to win the prize. . . .

So must the disciple run his race with eyes steadfastly fixed on his encouraging Lord, who is at once Judge, Umpire, and Awarder. He is not to look back either wistfully or hopelessly but to resolutely forget what is behind—failures and disappointments as well as successes and victories. He must strain forward to the tape with eyes fixed on his welcoming Lord. It was He who initiated our faith, and it is He who will strengthen us to complete the course.

J. OSWALD SANDERS

PAUSE FOR REFLECTION

In what way does Paul say spiritual maturity changes a person's thinking? How diligently are you pursuing God's calling? May the psalmist's words be your prayer and praise to the Lord!

PHILIPPIANS 4:1-23

What the Christians Are to Do

4 My dear brothers and sisters, I love you and want to see you. You bring me joy and make me proud of you, so stand strong in the Lord as I have told you.

2 I ask Euodia and Syntyche to agree in the Lord. **3** And I ask you, my faithful friend, to help these women. They served with me in telling the Good News, together with Clement and others who worked with me, whose names are written in the book of life.

4 Be full of joy in the Lord always. I will say again, be full of joy.

5 Let everyone see that you are gentle and kind. The Lord is coming soon. **6** Do not worry about anything, but pray and ask God for everything you need, always giving thanks. **7** And God's peace, which is so great we cannot understand it, will keep your hearts and minds in Christ Jesus.

8 Brothers and sisters, think about the things that are good and worthy of praise. Think about the things that are true and honorable and right and pure and beautiful and respected. **9** Do what you learned and received from me, what I told you, and what you saw me do. And the God who gives peace will be with you.

Paul Thanks the Christians

10 I am very happy in the Lord that you have shown your care for me again. You continued to care about me, but there was no way for you to show it. **11** I am not telling you this because I need anything. I have learned to be satisfied with the things I have and with everything that happens.

12 I know how to live when I am poor, and I know how to live when I have plenty. I have learned the secret of being happy at any time in everything that happens, when I have enough to eat and when I go hungry, when I have more than I need and when I do not have enough. **13** I can do all things through Christ, because he gives me strength.

14 But it was good that you helped me when I needed it. **15** You Philippians remember when I first preached the Good News there. When I left Macedonia, you were the only church that gave me help. **16** Several times you sent me things I needed when I was in Thessalonica. **17** Really, it is not that I want to receive gifts from you, but I want you to have the good that comes from giving. **18** And now I have everything, and more. I have all I need, because Epaphroditus brought your gift to me. It is like a sweet-smelling sacrifice offered to God, who accepts that sacrifice and is pleased with it. **19** My God will use his wonderful riches in Christ Jesus to give you everything you need. **20** Glory to our God and Father forever and ever! Amen.

21 Greet each of God's people in Christ Jesus. Those who are with me send greetings to you. **22** All of God's people greet you, particularly those from the palace of Caesar.

23 The grace of the Lord Jesus Christ be with you all.

OLD TESTAMENT READING

Give your worries to the LORD,
and he will take care of you.
He will never let good people down.

Psalm 55:22

Give thanks to the LORD and pray to him.
    Tell the nations what he has done.
2 Sing to him; sing praises to him.
    Tell about all his miracles.
3 Be glad that you are his;
    let those who seek the LORD be happy.
4 Depend on the LORD and his strength;
    always go to him for help.

Psalm 105:1–4

Trust the LORD and do good.
    Live in the land and feed on truth.
4 Enjoy serving the LORD,
    and he will give you what you
        want.
5 Depend on the LORD;
    trust him, and he will take care of you.

Psalm 37:3–5

INSIGHTS

During the Great Depression the bank in which my father was an officer was forced to close. . . .

I was convinced my father would be out of work. I knew I had to get a job as a boy of twelve to help support the family. A nearby corner grocer hired me after school and Saturdays for a dollar a week to sweep the floors and deliver groceries.

When I told my father, he replied, "I appreciate your concern and desire to help, son, but I am trusting the Lord to meet our needs. We belong to Him and He will take care of His own."

God honored my father's faith. He never went a day without employment through the entire Depression.

With similar confidence Paul wrote to the Philippian Christians, "My God will meet all your needs" (4:19). This was the encouragement those believers needed because they were far from affluent (2 Cor. 8:1–5). Out of their meager resources they had sent an offering to Paul in Rome (Phil. 4:14–18). Paul assured them that God would reimburse them.

Two important details about this promise must be observed. First, God will meet "all your needs," not your desires. Jesus said, "Your Father knows what you need" (Matt. 6:8), and His understanding of our needs may be different from ours.

Second, God will meet our needs "according to His glorious riches in Christ Jesus." God's supply is not "out of" but "according to His glorious riches." God is "able to do immeasurably more than we ask or imagine" (Eph. 3:20). . . .

Whatever your needs are right now, trust God to meet them and look for His supply.

JOHN WITMER

ACTION POINT

What does God's peace enable us to do? List the things on which God wants you to focus your thoughts. Will you ask God for what you need and trust him to care for you?

COLOSSIANS 1:1-23

1 From Paul, an apostle of Christ Jesus. I am an apostle because that is what God wanted. Also from Timothy, our brother.

2To the holy and faithful brothers and sisters in Christ that live in Colossae:

Grace and peace to you from God our Father.

3In our prayers for you we always thank God, the Father of our Lord Jesus Christ, **4**because we have heard about the faith you have in Christ Jesus and the love you have for all of God's people. **5**You have this faith and love because of your hope, and what you hope for is kept safe for you in heaven. You learned about this hope when you heard the message about the truth, the Good News **6**that was told to you. Everywhere in the world that Good News is bringing blessings and is growing. This has happened with you, too, since you heard the Good News and understood the truth about the grace of God. **7**You learned about God's grace from Epaphras, whom we love. He works together with us and is a faithful servant of Christ for us. **8**He also told us about the love you have from the Holy Spirit.

9Because of this, since the day we heard about you, we have continued praying for you, asking God that you will know fully what he wants. We pray that you will also have great wisdom and understanding in spiritual things **10**so that you will live the kind of life that honors and pleases the Lord in every way. You will produce fruit in every good work and grow in the knowledge of God. **11**God will strengthen you with his own great power so that you will not give up when troubles come, but you will be patient. **12**And you will joyfully give thanks to the Father who has made you able to have a share in all that he has prepared for his people in the kingdom of light. **13**God has freed us from the power of darkness, and he brought us into the kingdom of his dear Son. **14**The Son paid for our sins, and in him we have forgiveness.

The Importance of Christ

15No one can see God, but Jesus Christ is exactly like him. He ranks higher than everything that has been made. **16**Through his power all things were made—things in heaven and on earth, things seen and unseen, all powers, authorities, lords, and rulers. All things were made through Christ and for Christ. **17**He was there before anything was made, and all things continue because of him. **18**He is the head of the body, which is the church. Everything comes from him. He is the first one who was raised from the dead. So in all things Jesus has first place. **19**God was pleased for all of himself to live in Christ. **20**And through Christ, God has brought all things back to himself again—things on earth and things in heaven. God made peace through the blood of Christ's death on the cross.

21At one time you were separated from God. You were his enemies in your minds, and the evil things you did were against God. **22**But now God has made you his friends again. He did this through Christ's death in the body so that he might bring you into God's presence as people who are holy, with no wrong, and with nothing of which God can judge you guilty. **23**This will happen if you continue strong and sure in your faith. You must not be moved away from the hope brought to you by the Good News that you heard. That same Good News has been told to everyone in the world, and I, Paul, help in preaching that Good News.

OLD TESTAMENT READING

Who caused the one to come from the east?
Who gives him victories everywhere he goes?
The one who brought him gives nations over to him
and defeats kings.
[4]Who caused this to happen?
Who has controlled history since the beginning?
I, the LORD, am the one. I was here at the beginning,
and I will be here when all things are finished."

Isaiah 41:2a–b, 4

INSIGHTS

Right through the Old Testament the conviction runs that God is managing all human history for the good of his people and that the climax will be the setting up of the kingdom of God under the Messiah, God's anointed King. In the New Testament, Jesus of Nazareth is shown to be that Messiah or Christ. But his role is not only a kingly one, but prophetic and priestly too. Jesus as prophet preached in God's name; as priest, he offered himself in sacrifice for the sins of the people; as king, having risen triumphantly from the dead, he now reigns at God's right hand. "All authority in heaven and on earth has been given to me," he told his disciples (Matt. 28:18). So the early Christians came to see Jesus of Nazareth as the Christ of God, their Teacher, Savior, and living Lord.

. . . As Christians we know that Christ is reigning until all things are put under his feet and that we are living in the last days—the period between his first coming, to bring salvation and set up his kingdom, and his second coming, to complete the work of his kingdom in royal triumph and final judgment.

There is increasing chaos and confusion as human history moves to its close, but as Christians we can find stability and hope in Jesus who is the sovereign Lord of history. The Father has promised the Son, "Thy throne, O God, is forever and ever" (Heb. 1:8), and the promise will never fail.

J. I. PACKER

ACTION POINT

How does Christ's management of heaven and earth affect your view of history? Your hope for the future? Spend time in prayer, praising God for his incomparable greatness and his awesome love for you.

COLOSSIANS 1:24 — 2:15

Paul's Work for the Church

24I am happy in my sufferings for you. There are things that Christ must still suffer through his body, the church. I am accepting, in my body, my part of these things that must be suffered. **25**I became a servant of the church because God gave me a special work to do that helps you, and that work is to tell fully the message of God. **26**This message is the secret that was hidden from everyone since the beginning of time, but now it is made known to God's holy people. **27**God decided to let his people know this rich and glorious secret which he has for all people. This secret is Christ himself, who is in you. He is our only hope for glory. **28**So we continue to preach Christ to each person, using all wisdom to warn and to teach everyone, in order to bring each one into God's presence as a mature person in Christ. **29**To do this, I work and struggle, using Christ's great strength that works so powerfully in me.

 I want you to know how hard I work for you, those in Laodicea, and others who have never seen me. **2**I want them to be strengthened and joined together with love so that they may be rich in their understanding. This leads to their knowing fully God's secret, that is, Christ himself. **3**In him all the treasures of wisdom and knowledge are safely kept.

4I say this so that no one can fool you by arguments that seem good, but are false. **5**Though I am absent from you in my body, my heart is with you, and I am happy to see your good lives and your strong faith in Christ.

Continue to Live in Christ

6As you received Christ Jesus the Lord, so continue to live in him. **7**Keep your roots deep in him and have your lives built on him. Be strong in the faith, just as you were taught, and always be thankful.

8Be sure that no one leads you away with false and empty teaching that is only human, which comes from the ruling spirits of this world, and not from Christ. **9**All of God lives fully in Christ (even when Christ was on earth), **10**and you have a full and true life in Christ, who is ruler over all rulers and powers.

11Also in Christ you had a different kind of circumcision, a circumcision not done by hands. It was through Christ's circumcision, that is, his death, that you were made free from the power of your sinful self. **12**When you were baptized, you were buried with Christ, and you were raised up with him through your faith in God's power that was shown when he raised Christ from the dead. **13**When you were spiritually dead because of your sins and because you were not free from the power of your sinful self, God made you alive with Christ, and he forgave all our sins. **14**He canceled the debt, which listed all the rules we failed to follow. He took away that record with its rules and nailed it to the cross. **15**God stripped the spiritual rulers and powers of their authority. With the cross, he won the victory and showed the world that they were powerless.

OLD TESTAMENT READING

I waited patiently for the LORD.
He turned to me and heard my cry.
²He lifted me out of the pit of destruction,
out of the sticky mud.
He stood me on a rock
and made my feet steady.
³He put a new song in my mouth,
a song of praise to our God.
Many people will see this and worship him.
Then they will trust the LORD.

⁴Happy is the person
who trusts the LORD,
who doesn't turn to those who are
proud
or to those who worship false gods.

Psalm 40:1–4

Always remember what you have been taught,
and don't let go of it.
Keep all that you have learned;
it is the most important thing in life.
¹⁴Don't follow the ways of the wicked.

Proverbs 4:13–14a

INSIGHTS

It is a grand thing to have a faith which cannot be shaken. I saw one day a number of beech trees which had formed a wood: they had all fallen to the ground through a storm. The fact was they leaned upon one another to a great extent, and the thickness of the wood prevented each tree from getting a firm hold of the soil. They kept each other up and also constrained each other to grow up tall and thin, to the neglect of root growth. When the tempest forced down the first few trees the others readily followed one after the other. Close to that same spot I saw another tree in the open, bravely defying the blast, in solitary strength. The hurricane had beaten upon it but it had endured all its force unsheltered. That lone, brave tree seemed to be better rooted than before the storm.

I thought, "Is it not so with professors?" They often hold together, and help each other to grow up, but if they have not firm personal roothold, when a storm arises they fall in rows. A minister dies, or certain leaders are taken away, and over go the members by departure from the faith and from holiness. I would have you be self-contained, growing each man into Christ for himself, rooted and grounded in love and faith and every holy grace. Then when the worst storm that ever blew on mortal man shall come, it will be said of your faith, "It could not shake it."

CHARLES SPURGEON

PAUSE FOR REFLECTION

Why must believers know and understand God's truth? How deep and strong are your roots in the faith? Can you clearly separate the ideas of humans from the teachings of God? Are his teachings safe within your heart?

COLOSSIANS
2:16 – 3:17

Don't Follow People's Rules

16So do not let anyone make rules for you about eating and drinking or about a religious feast, a New Moon Festival, or a Sabbath day. **17**These things were like a shadow of what was to come. But what is true and real has come and is found in Christ. **18**Do not let anyone disqualify you by making you humiliate yourself and worship angels. Such people enter into visions, which fill them with foolish pride because of their human way of thinking. **19**They do not hold tightly to Christ, the head. It is from him that all the parts of the body are cared for and held together. So it grows in the way God wants it to grow.

20Since you died with Christ and were made free from the ruling spirits of the world, why do you act as if you still belong to this world by following rules like these: **21**"Don't handle this," "Don't taste that," "Don't even touch that thing"? **22**These rules refer to earthly things that are gone as soon as they are used. They are only human commands and teachings. **23**They seem to be wise, but they are only part of a human religion. They make people pretend not to be proud and make them punish their bodies, but they do not really control the evil desires of the sinful self.

Your New Life in Christ

3 Since you were raised from the dead with Christ, aim at what is in heaven, where Christ is sitting at the right hand of God. **2**Think only about the things in heaven, not the things on earth. **3**Your old sinful self has died, and your new life is kept with Christ in God. **4**Christ is your life, and when he comes again, you will share in his glory.

5So put all evil things out of your life: sexual sinning, doing evil, letting evil thoughts control you, wanting things that are evil, and greed. This is really serving a false god. **6**These things make God angry. **7**In your past, evil life you also did these things.

8But now also put these things out of your life: anger, bad temper, doing or saying things to hurt others, and using evil words when you talk. **9**Do not lie to each other. You have left your old sinful life and the things you did before. **10**You have begun to live the new life, in which you are being made new and are becoming like the One who made you. This new life brings you the true knowledge of God. **11**In the new life there is no difference between Greeks and Jews, those who are circumcised and those who are not circumcised, or people who are foreigners, or Scythians. There is no difference between slaves and free people. But Christ is in all believers, and Christ is all that is important.

12God has chosen you and made you his holy people. He loves you. So you should always clothe yourselves with mercy, kindness, humility, gentleness, and patience. **13**Bear with each other, and forgive each other. If someone does wrong to you, forgive that person because the Lord forgave you. **14**Even more than all this, clothe yourself in love. Love is what holds you all together in perfect unity. **15**Let the peace that Christ gives control your thinking, because you were all called together in one body to have peace. Always be thankful. **16**Let the teaching of Christ live in you richly. Use all wisdom to teach and instruct each other by singing psalms, hymns, and spiritual songs with thankfulness in your hearts to God. **17**Everything you do or say should be done to obey Jesus your Lord. And in all you do, give thanks to God the Father through Jesus.

OLD TESTAMENT READING

B e my holy people. Be holy because I am the LORD your God. **8**Remember and obey my laws. I am the LORD, and I have made you holy.'"

26"'So you must be holy to me because I, the LORD, am holy, and I have set you apart from other people to be my own.'"

Leviticus 20:7–8, 26

INSIGHTS

The New Testament leaves no doubt that holiness is our responsibility. If we are to pursue holiness, we must take some decisive action. . . .

The action we are to take is to put to death the misdeeds of the body (Romans 8:13). Paul uses the same expression in another book: "Put to death, therefore, whatever belongs to your earthly nature" (Colossians 3:5). . . . To put to death the misdeeds of the body, then, is to destroy the strength and vitality of sin as it tries to reign in our bodies.

It must be clear to us that mortification, though it is something we do, cannot be carried out in our own strength. . . . Mortification must be done by the strength and under the direction of the Holy Spirit. . . .

. . . "How do we destroy the strength and vitality of sin?" If we are to work at this difficult task, we must first have conviction. We must be persuaded that a holy life of God's will for every Christian is important. . . .

Not only must we develop conviction for living a holy life in general, but we must also develop convictions in specific areas of obedience.

These convictions are developed through exposure to the Word of God. . . .

. . . Obedience is the pathway to holiness, but it is only as we have His commands that we can obey them. God's Word must be so strongly fixed in our minds that it becomes the dominant influence in our thoughts, our attitudes, and our actions.

JERRY BRIDGES

PAUSE FOR REFLECTION

What is the one and only reason that God's people are to be holy? What does a person need to know to be holy? What must a person do to be holy? How does a person have the strength to be holy? What do you need to focus on as you pursue holiness?

COLOSSIANS 3:18 – 4:18

Your New Life with Other People

18Wives, yield to the authority of your husbands, because this is the right thing to do in the Lord.

19Husbands, love your wives and be gentle with them.

20Children, obey your parents in all things, because this pleases the Lord.

21Fathers, do not nag your children. If you are too hard to please, they may want to stop trying.

22Slaves, obey your masters in all things. Do not obey just when they are watching you, to gain their favor, but serve them honestly, because you respect the Lord. **23**In all the work you are doing, work the best you can. Work as if you were doing it for the Lord, not for people. **24**Remember that you will receive your reward from the Lord, which he promised to his people. You are serving the Lord Christ. **25**But remember that anyone who does wrong will be punished for that wrong, and the Lord treats everyone the same.

4 Masters, give what is good and fair to your slaves. Remember that you have a Master in heaven.

What the Christians Are to Do

2Continue praying, keeping alert, and always thanking God. **3**Also pray for us that God will give us an opportunity to tell people his message. Pray that we can preach the secret that God has made known about Christ. This is why I am in prison. **4**Pray that I can speak in a way that will make it clear, as I should.

5Be wise in the way you act with people who are not believers, making the most of every opportunity. **6**When you talk, you should always be kind and pleasant so you will be able to answer everyone in the way you should.

News About the People with Paul

7Tychicus is my dear brother in Christ and a faithful minister and servant with me in the Lord. He will tell you all the things that are happening to me. **8**This is why I am sending him: so you may know how we are and he may encourage you. **9**I send him with Onesimus, a faithful and dear brother in Christ, and one of your group. They will tell you all that has happened here.

10Aristarchus, a prisoner with me, and Mark, the cousin of Barnabas, greet you. (I have already told you what to do about Mark. If he comes, welcome him.) **11**Jesus, who is called Justus, also greets you. These are the only Jewish believers who work with me for the kingdom of God, and they have been a comfort to me.

12Epaphras, a servant of Jesus Christ, from your group, also greets you. He always prays for you that you will grow to be spiritually mature and have everything God wants for you. **13**I know he has worked hard for you and the people in Laodicea and in Hierapolis. **14**Demas and our dear friend Luke, the doctor, greet you.

15Greet the brothers and sisters in Laodicea. And greet Nympha and the church that meets in her house. **16**After this letter is read to you, be sure it is also read to the church in Laodicea. And you read the letter that I wrote to Laodicea. ¹⁷Tell Archippus, "Be sure to finish the work the Lord gave you."

¹⁸I, Paul, greet you and write this with my own hand. Remember me in prison. Grace be with you.

OLD TESTAMENT READING

My son, keep your father's commands,
and don't forget your mother's teaching.
²¹Keep their words in mind forever
as though you had them tied around your neck.
²²They will guide you when you walk.
They will guard you when you sleep.
They will speak to you when you are awake.

Proverbs 6:20–22

INSIGHTS

Much is being said and written these days about the care of the elderly. But what is being done in practical ways to relieve them of their ongoing fears for their future? Such fears as:

• financial problems in a day of rising costs and a fixed income

• fears of sickness with no one to take care of them, in a day when families can be so scattered as to be unavailable to one another . . .

Each of us, whatever our age, needs to remind himself that we are of great worth in the sight of God, that He has plans for each one. Speaking of the righteous, the psalmist writes, "They shall still bring forth fruit in old age" (Psalm 92:14).

Ironically, some countries to which we send missionaries with the gospel message can teach us much about honoring our fathers and our mothers. For example, a woman whom I met on one of my teaching trips to Asian countries confided to me, "My sister, who is much wealthier than I, felt that she should have the pleasure of taking care of our aged mother. But, as the youngest daughter, it is my privilege." . . .

. . . God knows our heart and our intentions. Where we treat the elderly around us with love and care, it will be counted as our obeying the fifth commandment.

And obedience is its own reward.

The Lord Jesus Himself set the pattern. From the cross, in the midst of His own agony, He remembered His mother and committed her to the care of "the disciple . . . whom he loved" (John 19:26–27).

JEANETTE LOCKERBIE

PAUSE FOR REFLECTION

It is good to honor one's parents by caring for them, but Scripture reveals a broader perspective on what it means to honor one's parents. How does this reading expand your picture of honoring one's parents? How do you measure up?

1 THESSALONIANS 1:1 – 2:16

1 From Paul, Silas, and Timothy.

To the church in Thessalonica, the church in God the Father and the Lord Jesus Christ: Grace and peace to you.

The Faith of the Thessalonians

2 We always thank God for all of you and mention you when we pray. **3** We continually recall before God our Father the things you have done because of your faith and the work you have done because of your love. And we thank him that you continue to be strong because of your hope in our Lord Jesus Christ.

4 Brothers and sisters, God loves you, and we know he has chosen you, **5** because the Good News we brought to you came not only with words, but with power, with the Holy Spirit, and with sure knowledge that it is true. Also you know how we lived when we were with you in order to help you. **6** And you became like us and like the Lord. You suffered much, but still you accepted the teaching with the joy that comes from the Holy Spirit. **7** So you became an example to all the believers in Macedonia and Southern Greece. **8** And the Lord's teaching spread from you not only into Macedonia and Southern Greece, but now your faith in God has become known everywhere. So we do not need to say anything about it. **9** People everywhere are telling about the way you accepted us when we were there with you. They tell how you stopped worshiping idols and began serving the living and true God. **10** And you wait for God's Son, whom God raised from the dead, to come from heaven. He is Jesus, who saves us from God's angry judgment that is sure to come.

Paul's Work in Thessalonica

2 Brothers and sisters, you know our visit to you was not a failure. **2** Before we came to you, we suffered in Philippi. People there insulted us, as you know, and many people were against us. But our God helped us to be brave and to tell you his Good News. **3** Our appeal does not come from lies or wrong reasons, nor were we trying to trick you. **4** But we speak the Good News because God tested us and trusted us to do it. When we speak, we are not trying to please people, but God, who tests our hearts. **5** You know that we never tried to influence you by saying nice things about you. We were not trying to get your money; we had no selfishness to hide from you. God knows that this is true. **6** We were not looking for human praise, from you or anyone else, **7** even though as apostles of Christ we could have used our authority over you.

But we were very gentle with you, like a mother caring for her little children. **8** Because we loved you, we were happy to share not only God's Good News with you, but even our own lives. You had become so dear to us! **9** Brothers and sisters, I know you remember our hard work and difficulties. We worked night and day so we would not burden any of you while we preached God's Good News to you.

10 When we were with you, we lived in a holy and honest way, without fault. You know this is true, and so does God. **11**You know that we treated each of you as a father treats his own children. **12**We encouraged you, we urged you, and we insisted that you live good lives for God, who calls you to his glorious kingdom.

13Also, we always thank God because when you heard his message from us, you accepted it as the word of God, not the words of humans. And it really is God's message which works in you who believe. **14**Brothers and sisters, your experiences have been like those of God's churches in Christ that are in Judea. You suffered from the people of your own country, as they suffered from the Jews **15**who killed both the Lord Jesus and the prophets and forced us to leave that country. They do not please God and are against all people. **16**They try

to stop us from teaching those who are not Jews so they may be saved. By doing this, they are increasing their sins to the limit. The anger of God has come to them at last.

OLD TESTAMENT READING

The LORD did not care for you and choose you because there were many of you—you are the smallest nation of all. **8**But the LORD chose you because he loved you, and he kept his promise to your ancestors.

Deuteronomy 7:7–8a

INSIGHTS

If there be one place where our Lord Jesus most fully becomes the joy and comfort of His people, it is where He plunged deepest into the depths of woe. Come hither, gracious souls, and behold the Man in the garden of Gethsemane; behold His heart so brimming with love that He cannot hold it in—so full of sorrow that it must find a vent. Behold the Man as they drive the nails into His hands and feet. . . .

Most of us know what it is to be overwhelmed in heart. Disappointments and heartbreaks will do this when billow after billow rolls over us, and we are like a broken shell hurled to and fro by the surf. Blessed be God, at such seasons we are not without an all-sufficient solace; our Savior is the harbor of weather-beaten sails, the hospice of forlorn pilgrims. Higher than we are is our God, His mercy higher than our sins, His love higher than our thoughts. A rock He is since He changes not, and a high rock, because the tempests which overwhelm us roll far beneath at His feet. O Lord, our God, by Your Holy Spirit, teach us your way of faith, lead us unto Your rest.

CHARLES SPURGEON

ACTION POINT

How do you think Paul's words encouraged the Thessalonians? When has someone encouraged you with the assurance of God's love? Who can you encourage today?

> ## 1 THESSALONIANS
> ## 2:17 – 4:12

Paul Wants to Visit Them Again

17 Brothers and sisters, though we were separated from you for a short time, our thoughts were still with you. We wanted very much to see you and tried hard to do so. 18 We wanted to come to you. I, Paul, tried to come more than once, but Satan stopped us. 19 You are our hope, our joy, and the crown we will take pride in when our Lord Jesus Christ comes. 20 Truly you are our glory and our joy.

3 When we could not wait any longer, we decided it was best to stay in Athens alone 2 and send Timothy to you. Timothy, our brother, works with us for God and helps us tell people the Good News about Christ. We sent him to strengthen and encourage you in your faith 3 so none of you would be upset by these troubles. You yourselves know that we must face these troubles. 4 Even when we were with you, we told you we all would have to suffer, and you know it has happened. 5 Because of this, when I could wait no longer, I sent Timothy to you so I could learn about your faith. I was afraid the devil had tempted you, and perhaps our hard work would have been wasted.

6 But Timothy now has come back to us from you and has brought us good news about your faith and love. He told us that you always remember us in a good way and that you want to see us just as much as we want to see you. 7 So, brothers and sisters, while we have much trouble and suffering, we are encouraged about you because of your faith. 8 Our life is really full if you stand strong in the Lord. 9 We have so much joy before our God because of you. We cannot thank him enough for all the joy we feel. 10 Night and day we continue praying with all our heart that we can see you again and give you all the things you need to make your faith strong.

11 Now may our God and Father himself and our Lord Jesus prepare the way for us to come to you. 12 May the Lord make your love grow more and multiply for each other and for all people so that you will love others as we love you. 13 May your hearts be made strong so that you will be holy and without fault before our God and Father when our Lord Jesus comes with all his holy ones.

A Life that Pleases God

4 Brothers and sisters, we taught you how to live in a way that will please God, and you are living that way. Now we ask and encourage you in the Lord Jesus to live that way even more. 2 You know what we told you to do by the authority of the Lord Jesus. 3 God wants you to be holy and to stay away from sexual sins. 4 He wants each of you to learn to control your own body in a way that is holy and honorable. 5 Don't use your body for sexual sin like the people who do not know God. 6 Also, do not wrong or cheat another Christian in this way. The Lord will punish people who do those things as we have already told you and warned you. 7 God called us to be holy and does not want us to live in sin. 8 So the person who refuses to obey this teaching is disobeying God, not simply a human teaching. And God is the One who gives us his Holy Spirit.

9We do not need to write you about having love for your Christian family, because God has already taught you to love each other. **10**And truly you do love the Christians in all of Macedonia. Brothers and sisters, now we encourage you to love them even more.

11Do all you can to live a peaceful life. Take care of your own business, and do your own work as we have already told you. **12**If you do, then people who are not believers will respect you, and you will not have to depend on others for what you need.

OLD TESTAMENT READING

Remember my commands and obey them; I am the LORD. **32**Show respect for my holy name. You Israelites must remember that I am holy; I am the LORD, who has made you holy. **33**I brought you out of Egypt to be your God, I am the LORD."

Leviticus 22:31–33

I am the LORD your God. Keep yourselves holy for me because I am holy. Don't make yourselves unclean with any of these crawling animals. **45**I am the LORD who brought you out of Egypt to be your God; you must be holy because I am holy."

Leviticus 11:44–45

INSIGHTS

Our daily expression of holiness is a reflection of our faith in Christ. If we have no desire to be holy, we should seriously question the genuineness of our faith in the Lord Jesus.

Christ not only died to save us from the punishment for our sins, but also from slavery to sin in this worldly culture. To continue to live in sin as a Christian is contradictory to the most basic meaning of Christianity. Christ died to save us from our sins, not to let us remain in our sins (Matthew 1:21; 1 John 1:6, 7). What kind of person would want to follow Christ and not desire to live a holy life? . . .

Holiness, then, is not an option for the believer. Paul wrote to Titus, "For the grace of God has appeared for the salvation of all men, training us to renounce irreligion and worldly passions, and to live sober, upright, and godly lives in this world" (Titus 2:11, 12). Though holiness is not a condition for salvation, it is the natural consequence of salvation. We do not become holy in order to be saved, but because we are saved. We do not do good works to get to heaven, but because heaven has already come into our hearts.

To trust Christ for salvation is to trust him for holiness. If there is no desire for holiness within, then it is doubtful that the Holy Spirit has come to dwell within. The Holy Spirit does not save us without giving us the desire to live a holy life.

FLOYD MCCLUNG

APPLICATION

What instruction does Paul give to those who please God? How does Scripture define holy living? If you are to live in a way that pleases God more and more, what is your next step?

1 THESSALONIANS 4:13 – 5:28

The Lord's Coming

13Brothers and sisters, we want you to know about those Christians who have died so you will not be sad, as others who have no hope. 14We believe that Jesus died and that he rose again. So, because of him, God will raise with Jesus those who have died. 15What we tell you now is the Lord's own message. We who are living when the Lord comes again will not go before those who have already died. 16The Lord himself will come down from heaven with a loud command, with the voice of the archangel, and with the trumpet call of God. And those who have died believing in Christ will rise first. 17After that, we who are still alive will be gathered up with them in the clouds to meet the Lord in the air. And we will be with the Lord forever. 18So encourage each other with these words.

Be Ready for the Lord's Coming

Now, brothers and sisters, we do not need to write you about times and dates. 2You know very well that the day the Lord comes again will be a surprise, like a thief that comes in the night. 3While people are saying, "We have peace and we are safe," they will be destroyed quickly. It is like pains that come quickly to a woman having a baby. Those people will not escape. 4But you, brothers and sisters, are not living in darkness, and so that day will not surprise you like a thief. 5You are all people who belong to the light and to the day. We do not belong to the night or to darkness. 6So we should not be like other people who are sleeping, but we should be alert and have self-control. 7Those who sleep, sleep at night. Those who get drunk, get drunk at night. 8But we belong to the day, so we should control ourselves. We should wear faith and love to protect us, and the hope of salvation should be our helmet. 9God did not choose us to suffer his anger but to have salvation through our Lord Jesus Christ. 10Jesus died for us so that we can live together with him, whether we are alive or dead when he comes. 11So encourage each other and give each other strength, just as you are doing now.

Final Instructions and Greetings

12Now, brothers and sisters, we ask you to appreciate those who work hard among you, who lead you in the Lord and teach you. 13Respect them with a very special love because of the work they do.

Live in peace with each other. 14We ask you, brothers and sisters, to warn those who do not work. Encourage the people who are afraid. Help those who are weak. Be patient with everyone. 15Be sure that no one pays back wrong for wrong, but always try to do what is good for each other and for all people.

16Always be joyful. 17Pray continually, 18and give thanks whatever happens. That is what God wants for you in Christ Jesus.

19Do not hold back the work of the Holy Spirit. 20Do not treat prophecy as if it were unimportant. 21But test everything. Keep what is good, 22and stay away from everything that is evil.

²³Now may God himself, the God of peace, make you pure, belonging only to him. May your whole self—spirit, soul, and body—be kept safe and without fault when our Lord Jesus Christ comes. ²⁴You can trust the One who calls you to do that for you.

²⁵Brothers and sisters, pray for us.

²⁶Give each other a holy kiss when you meet. ²⁷I tell you by the authority of the Lord to read this letter to all the believers.

²⁸The grace of our Lord Jesus Christ be with you.

OLD TESTAMENT READING

I know that my Defender lives,
    and in the end he will stand upon the earth.
²⁶Even after my skin has been destroyed,
    in my flesh I will see God.
²⁷I will see him myself;
    I will see him with my very own eyes.
    How my heart wants that to happen!"

Job 19:25–27

INSIGHTS

What would you say about a person who had made a hundred promises to you and kept ninety-nine of them? You probably would think that he was honest enough to fulfill the last promise as well, wouldn't you?

Jesus Christ has fulfilled every promise He ever made, except one. He has not yet returned. Will He?

In both the Old and New Testaments there are references to the return of the Lord. . . . Ezekiel tells of a Jerusalem which is to be restored, a temple which is to be rebuilt, and a land which is to be reclaimed and blessed with prosperity at the Lord's return. Zephaniah gives us the new song that He will teach to Israel and describes the overthrow of the false Christ.

In the New Testament, Matthew likens Christ to a bridegroom coming to receive His bride. Mark sees Him as a householder going on a long journey and entrusting certain tasks to his servants until his return. To Luke, Jesus is a nobleman going to a far country to transact business and leaving his possessions with his servants that they may trade with them until he comes.

John quotes Christ as saying, "I go to prepare a place for you. I will come again to receive you unto myself." The entire book of Revelation tells of the glorious return of Christ. And we can say with the apostle John, who wrote that book, "Amen, even so, come, Lord Jesus."

BILLY GRAHAM

PAUSE FOR REFLECTION

What about Christ's second coming gives you hope? What difference does Paul say the hope of Christ's second coming should make in the believer's life? What difference does that hope make in your life?

2 THESSALONIANS
1:1 – 2:12

1 From Paul, Silas, and Timothy.
To the church in Thessalonica in God our Father and the Lord Jesus Christ:

2Grace and peace to you from God the Father and the Lord Jesus Christ.

Paul Talks About God's Judgment

3We must always thank God for you, brothers and sisters. This is only right, because your faith is growing more and more, and the love that every one of you has for each other is increasing. **4**So we brag about you to the other churches of God. We tell them about the way you continue to be strong and have faith even though you are being treated badly and are suffering many troubles.

5This is proof that God is right in his judgment. He wants you to be counted worthy of his kingdom for which you are suffering. **6**God will do what is right. He will give trouble to those who trouble you. **7**And he will give rest to you who are troubled and to us also when the Lord Jesus appears with burning fire from heaven with his powerful angels. **8**Then he will punish those who do not know God and who do not obey the Good News about our Lord Jesus Christ. **9**Those people will be punished with a destruction that continues forever. They will be kept away from the Lord and from his great power. **10**This will happen on the day when the Lord Jesus comes to receive glory because of his holy people. And all the people who have believed will be amazed at Jesus. You will be in that group, because you believed what we told you.

11That is why we always pray for you, asking our God to help you live the kind of life he called you to live. We pray that with his power God will help you do the good things you want and perform the works that come from your faith. **12**We pray all this so that the name of our Lord Jesus Christ will have glory in you, and you will have glory in him. That glory comes from the grace of our God and the Lord Jesus Christ.

Evil Things Will Happen

2 Brothers and sisters, we have something to say about the coming of our Lord Jesus Christ and the time when we will meet together with him. **2**Do not become easily upset in your thinking or afraid if you hear that the day of the Lord has already come. Someone may have said this in a prophecy or in a message or in a letter as if it came from us. **3**Do not let anyone fool you in any way. That day of the Lord will not come until the turning away from God happens and the Man of Evil, who is on his way to hell, appears. **4**He will be against and put himself above any so-called god or anything that people worship. And that Man of Evil will even go into God's Temple and sit there and say that he is God.

5I told you when I was with you that all this would happen. Do you not remember? **6**And now you know what is stopping that Man of Evil so he will appear at the right time. **7**The secret power of evil is already working in the world, but there is one who is stopping that power. And he will continue to stop it until he is taken out of the way.

8Then that Man of Evil will appear, and the Lord Jesus will kill him with the breath that comes from his mouth and will destroy him with the glory of his coming. **9**The Man of Evil will come by the power of Satan. He will have great power, and he will do many different false miracles, signs, and wonders. **10**He will use every kind of evil to trick those who are lost. They will die, because they refused to love the truth. (If they loved the truth, they would be saved.) **11**For this reason God sends them something powerful that leads them away from the truth so they will believe a lie. **12**So all those will be judged guilty who did not believe the truth, but enjoyed doing evil.

OLD TESTAMENT READING

By doing what is fair,
    Jerusalem will be free again.
By doing what is right,
    her people who come back to the LORD will
        have freedom.
28But sinners and those who turn against him
    will be destroyed;
    those who have left the LORD will die.

Isaiah 1:27–28

INSIGHTS

Death is the "wages of sin." It is just what sin deserves. Labour earns wages, and creates a rightful claim to such remuneration. So men are conceived as earning wages when they sin. They become entitled to their pay. God deems Himself holden to give them their well-deserved wages. . . .

We are informed that in the final consummation of earthly scenes, "the judgment shall sit and the books shall be opened." We shall be there, and what is more, there to close up our account with our Lord and receive our allotment. Which will you have on that final settlement day? The wages of sin? . . .

. . . O, sinner, think of hell, and of yourself thrust into it. It pours forth its volumes of smoke and flame forever, never ceasing, never exhausted. Upon that spectacle the universe can look and read—"The wages of sin is death! O, sin not, since such is the doom of the unpardoned sinner!" Think what a demonstration this is in the government of God! What an exhibition of His holy justice, of His inflexible purpose to sustain the interests of holiness and happiness in all His vast dominions! . . .

Sinner, you may now escape this fearful doom. This is the reason why God has revealed hell in His faithful Word.

CHARLES FINNEY

PAUSE FOR REFLECTION

When will God punish those who don't know him? How can one escape God's punishment? How will God treat those who believe? What will happen before Jesus comes again? How are believers to live until he comes?

2 THESSALONIANS 2:13 – 3:18

You Are Chosen for Salvation

¹³Brothers and sisters, whom the Lord loves, God chose you from the beginning to be saved. So we must always thank God for you. You are saved by the Spirit that makes you holy and by your faith in the truth. ¹⁴God used the Good News that we preached to call you to be saved so you can share in the glory of our Lord Jesus Christ. ¹⁵So, brothers and sisters, stand strong and continue to believe the teachings we gave you in our speaking and in our letter.

¹⁶⁻¹⁷May our Lord Jesus Christ himself and God our Father encourage you and strengthen you in every good thing you do and say. God loved us, and through his grace he gave us a good hope and encouragement that continues forever.

Pray for Us

And now, brothers and sisters, pray for us that the Lord's teaching will continue to spread quickly and that people will give honor to that teaching, just as happened with you. ²And pray that we will be protected from stubborn and evil people, because not all people believe.

³But the Lord is faithful and will give you strength and will protect you from the Evil One. ⁴The Lord makes us feel sure that you are doing and will continue to do the things we told you. ⁵May the Lord lead your hearts into God's love and Christ's patience.

The Duty to Work

⁶Brothers and sisters, by the authority of our Lord Jesus Christ we command you to stay away from any believer who refuses to work and does not follow the teaching we gave you. ⁷You yourselves know that you should live as we live. We were not lazy when we were with you. ⁸And when we ate another person's food, we always paid for it. We worked very hard night and day so we would not be an expense to any of you. ⁹We had the right to ask you to help us, but we worked to take care of ourselves so we would be an example for you to follow. ¹⁰When we were with you, we gave you this rule: "Anyone who refuses to work should not eat."

¹¹We hear that some people in your group refuse to work. They do nothing but busy themselves in other people's lives. ¹²We command those people and beg them in the Lord Jesus Christ to work quietly and earn their own food. ¹³But you, brothers and sisters, never become tired of doing good.

¹⁴If some people do not obey what we tell you in this letter, then take note of them. Have nothing to do with them so they will feel ashamed. ¹⁵But do not treat them as enemies. Warn them as fellow believers.

Final Words

¹⁶Now may the Lord of peace give you peace at all times and in every way. The Lord be with all of you.

¹⁷I, Paul, end this letter now in my own handwriting. All my letters have this to show they are from me. This is the way I write.

¹⁸The grace of our Lord Jesus Christ be with you all.

OLD TESTAMENT READING

It is hard to find a good wife,
    because she is worth more than rubies.
11Her husband trusts her completely.
    With her, he has everything he needs.
12She does him good and not harm
    for as long as she lives.

13She looks for wool and flax
    and likes to work with her hands.
14She is like a trader's ship,
    bringing food from far away.
15She gets up while it is still dark
    and prepares food for her family
    and feeds her servant girls.
16She inspects a field and buys it.
    With money she earned, she plants a
        vineyard.

Proverbs 31:10–16

INSIGHTS

The common drudgery of daily life can be a Divine Calling. We often speak of a young man as "being called to the Ministry"; but it is as fitting to speak of a carpenter being called to the bench, the blacksmith to the forge, and the shoemaker to his last. "Brethren," said the Apostle, "let every man wherein he is called, therein abide with God."

Remember that your life has been appointed by God's wise providence. God as much sent Joseph to the drudgery and discipline of the prison as to the glory and responsibility of the palace. Nothing happens to us which is not included in His plan for us; and the incidents which seem most tiresome are often contrived to give us opportunities to become nobler, stronger characters.

We are called to be faithful in performing our assigned duties. Not brilliance, not success, not notoriety which attracts the world's notice, but the regular, quiet, and careful performance of trivial and common duties; faithfulness in that which is least is as great an attainment in God's sight as in the greatest. . . .

Take up your work, then, you who seem to be the nobodies. . . . Do it with a brave heart, looking up to Him who for many years toiled at the carpenter's bench. Amid the many scenes and actions of life, set the Lord always before your face. Do all as in His presence, and to win His smile; and be sure to cultivate a spirit of love to God and man. Look out for opportunities of cheering your fellow-workers. Do not murmur or grumble, but let your heart rise from your toil to God your Maker, Saviour, and Friend. So the lowliest service will glisten, as grass-blades do when sun and dew-drops garnish them.

F. B. MEYER

ACTION POINT

Study these readings and describe what it means to be a diligent and faithful worker for God's service today. How well do you measure up? What changes will you make to bring greater honor to God?

1 TIMOTHY 1:1-20

1 From Paul, an apostle of Christ Jesus, by the command of God our Savior and Christ Jesus our hope.

2 To Timothy, a true child to me because you believe:

Grace, mercy, and peace from God the Father and Christ Jesus our Lord.

Warning Against False Teaching

3 I asked you to stay longer in Ephesus when I went into Macedonia so you could command some people there to stop teaching false things. **4** Tell them not to spend their time on stories that are not true and on long lists of names in family histories. These things only bring arguments; they do not help God's work, which is done in faith. **5** The purpose of this command is for people to have love, a love that comes from a pure heart and a good conscience and a true faith. **6** Some people have missed these things and turned to useless talk. **7** They want to be teachers of the law, but they do not understand either what they are talking about or what they are sure about.

8 But we know that the law is good if someone uses it lawfully. **9** We also know that the law is not made for good people but for those who are against the law and for those who refuse to follow it. It is for people who are against God and are sinful, who are unholy and ungodly, who kill their fathers and mothers, who murder, **10** who take part in sexual sins, who have sexual relations with people of the same sex, who sell slaves, who tell lies, who speak falsely, and who do anything against the true teaching of God. **11** That teaching is part of the Good News of the blessed God that he gave me to tell.

Thanks for God's Mercy

12 I thank Christ Jesus our Lord, who gave me strength, because he trusted me and gave me this work of serving him. **13** In the past I spoke against Christ and persecuted him and did all kinds of things to hurt him. But God showed me mercy, because I did not know what I was doing. I did not believe. **14** But the grace of our Lord was fully given to me, and with that grace came the faith and love that are in Christ Jesus.

15 What I say is true, and you should fully accept it: Christ Jesus came into the world to save sinners, of whom I am the worst. **16** But I was given mercy so that in me, the worst of all sinners, Christ Jesus could show that he has patience without limit. His patience with me made me an example for those who would believe in him and have life forever. **17** To the King that rules forever, who will never die, who cannot be seen, the only God, be honor and glory forever and ever. Amen.

18 Timothy, my child, I am giving you a command that agrees with the prophecies that were given about you in the past. I tell you this so you can follow them and fight the good fight. **19** Continue to have faith and do what you know is right. Some people have rejected this, and their faith has been shipwrecked. **20** Hymenaeus and Alexander have done that, and I have given them to Satan so they will learn not to speak against God.

OLD TESTAMENT READING

The wicked should stop doing wrong,
  and they should stop their evil thoughts.
They should return to the LORD so he may
    have mercy on them.
  They should come to our God, because he
    will freely forgive them.

Isaiah 55:7

The LORD shows mercy and is kind.
  He does not become angry quickly, and he
    has great love.
9He will not always accuse us,
  and he will not be angry forever.
10He has not punished us as our sins should be
    punished;
  he has not repaid us for the evil we have
    done.

Psalm 103:8–10

INSIGHTS

In amateur baseball, there is a rule known as the "mercy rule." This rule terminates a game after a certain number of innings (usually seven) when one team is ahead by a certain number of runs (usually ten). The "mercy rule" has relieved the misery of many inferior teams or of a team that just had a bad day.

Mercy is an attribute of God for which we should be especially thankful. How wonderful that He has not given us what we really deserve! We all have our "bad days." So many times we've "blown it" with God. But He is merciful! His patience is astounding! It's hard to fathom God's mercy as He looks down upon this wicked world. How many chances He has given us! How many times we have failed to obey! . . .

. . . It is God's mercy that gives us hope for a continued relationship with Him.

Because of his mercy, we are still here! We should be so grateful that God is merciful toward His children. Our God promises to complete what He began in us (Philippians 1:6), and by His mercy He shows compassion toward us in our weaknesses. Psalms 103:14 says, "For He knows how we are formed, He remembers that we are dust." God sees us in our lowly estate and extends His mercy. Our hearts should praise the God of mercy. . . .

. . . It's only by His mercy that we are not destroyed totally and completely. Therefore, we . . . should be imitators of God and show mercy to those God brings our way.

ELLIOT JOHNSON / AL SCHIERBAUM

APPLICATION

Review the evidence in these readings that God is not begrudgingly merciful, but abundantly merciful! The next time someone accuses God of being harsh or unforgiving, tell about the evidence you have found of God's awesome, unfailing mercy.

1 TIMOTHY 2:1 – 3:13

Some Rules for Men and Women

First, I tell you to pray for all people, asking God for what they need and being thankful to him. [2]Pray for rulers and for all who have authority so that we can have quiet and peaceful lives full of worship and respect for God. [3]This is good, and it pleases God our Savior, [4]who wants all people to be saved and to know the truth. [5]There is one God and one mediator so that human beings can reach God. That way is through Christ Jesus, who is himself human. [6]He gave himself as a payment to free all people. He is proof that came at the right time. [7]That is why I was chosen to tell the Good News and to be an apostle. (I am telling the truth; I am not lying.) I was chosen to teach those who are not Jews to believe and to know the truth.

[8]So, I want the men everywhere to pray, lifting up their hands in a holy manner, without anger and arguments.

[9]Also, women should wear proper clothes that show respect and self-control, not using braided hair or gold or pearls or expensive clothes. [10]Instead, they should do good deeds, which is right for women who say they worship God.

[11]Let a woman learn by listening quietly and being ready to cooperate in everything. [12]But I do not allow a woman to teach or to have authority over a man, but to listen quietly, [13]because Adam was formed first and then Eve. [14]And Adam was not tricked, but the woman was tricked and became a sinner. [15]But she will be saved through having children if she continues in faith, love, and holiness, with self-control.

Elders in the Church

What I say is true: Anyone wanting to become an overseer desires a good work. [2]An overseer must not give people a reason to criticize him, and he must have only one wife. He must be self-controlled, wise, respected by others, ready to welcome guests, and able to teach. [3]He must not drink too much wine or like to fight, but rather be gentle and peaceable, not loving money. [4]He must be a good family leader, having children who cooperate with full respect. [5](If someone does not know how to lead the family, how can that person take care of God's church?) [6]But an elder must not be a new believer, or he might be too proud of himself and be judged guilty just as the devil was. [7]An elder must also have the respect of people who are not in the church so he will not be criticized by others and caught in the devil's trap.

Deacons in the Church

[8]In the same way, deacons must be respected by others, not saying things they do not mean. They must not drink too much wine or try to get rich by cheating others. [9]With a clear conscience they must follow the secret of the faith that God made known to us. [10]Test them first. Then let them serve as deacons if you find nothing wrong in them. [11]In the same way, women must be respected by others. They must not speak evil of others. They must be self-controlled and trustworthy in everything. [12]Deacons must have only one wife and be good leaders of their children and

their own families. [13]Those who serve well as deacons are making an honorable place for themselves, and they will be very bold in their faith in Christ Jesus.

OLD TESTAMENT READING

No other god has ever taken for himself one nation out of another. But the LORD your God did this for you in Egypt, right before your own eyes. He did it with tests, signs, miracles, war, and great sights, by his great power and strength.

[35]He showed you things so you would know that the LORD is God, and there is no other God besides him. [36]He spoke to you from heaven to teach you. He showed you his great fire on earth, and you heard him speak from the fire. [37]Because the LORD loved your ancestors, he chose you, their descendants, and he brought you out of Egypt himself by his great strength. [38]He forced nations out of their land ahead of you, nations that were bigger and stronger than you were. The LORD did this so he could bring you into their land and give it to you as your own, and this land is yours today.

Deuteronomy 4:34–38

INSIGHTS

Men have always stumbled over the simplicity of salvation. That is why there are so many cults. Each one has a unique slant on the doctrine of salvation, each corrupting the simplicity of the gospel revealed in God's Word (cf. 2 Corinthians 11:3) by espousing salvation by human works. . . .

From start to finish, God's Word disproves them all, and in a wonderfully consistent way. Its message, woven through sixty-six books, written over a span of fifteen hundred years by more than forty different authors, is marvelously unified and congruous. The message is simply that God graciously saves repentant sinners who come to Him in faith. There is no secret here, no mystery, no obscurity, no complexity. . . .

. . . God has come down from heaven and spoken to us by His Son (Hebrews 1:1–2). We can never gain the right to climb to heaven and find the answers for ourselves. . . .

. . . Jesus is the only source of salvation. Those who do not believe in His name are condemned, excluded from eternal life. No matter how sincere, how religious, how immersed in good works, everyone must be born again. There is no promise of life—only a guarantee of condemnation—for those who will not . . . turn from sin in obedient faith to the One who was lifted up so that they would not have to perish.

JOHN F. MacARTHUR, JR.

APPLICATION

What truth does God want all people to know? What evidence does Scripture give that God is the only true God? What is the one way of salvation? Do you personally know that way?

1 TIMOTHY
3:14 — 4:16

The Secret of Our Life

¹⁴Although I hope I can come to you soon, I am writing these things to you now. ¹⁵Then, even if I am delayed, you will know how to live in the family of God. That family is the church of the living God, the support and foundation of the truth. ¹⁶Without doubt, the secret of our life of worship is great:

He was shown to us in a human body,
    proved right in spirit,
and seen by angels.

He was proclaimed to the nations,
believed in by the world,
    and taken up in glory

A Warning About False Teachers

4 Now the Holy Spirit clearly says that in the later times some people will stop believing the faith. They will follow spirits that lie and teachings of demons. ²Such teachings come from the false words of liars whose consciences are destroyed as if by a hot iron. ³They forbid people to marry and tell them not to eat certain foods which God created to be eaten with thanks by people who believe and know the truth. ⁴Everything God made is good, and nothing should be refused if it is accepted with thanks, ⁵because it is made holy by what God has said and by prayer.

Be a Good Servant of Christ

⁶By telling these things to the brothers and sisters, you will be a good servant of Christ Jesus. You will be made strong by the words of the faith and the good teaching which you have been following. ⁷But do not follow foolish stories that disagree with God's truth, but train yourself to serve God. ⁸Training your body helps you in some ways, but serving God helps you in every way by bringing you blessings in this life and in the future life, too. ⁹What I say is true, and you should fully accept it. ¹⁰This is why we work and struggle: We hope in the living God who is the Savior of all people, especially of those who believe.

¹¹Command and teach these things. ¹²Do not let anyone treat you as if you are unimportant because you are young. Instead, be an example to the believers with your words, your actions, your love, your faith, and your pure life. ¹³Until I come, continue to read the Scriptures to the people, strengthen them, and teach them. ¹⁴Use the gift you have, which was given to you through prophecy when the group of elders laid their hands on you. ¹⁵Continue to do those things; give your life to doing them so your progress may be seen by everyone. ¹⁶Be careful in your life and in your teaching. If you continue to live and teach rightly, you will save both yourself and those who listen to you.

OLD TESTAMENT READING

The king stood by the pillar and made an agreement in the presence of the LORD to follow the LORD and obey his commands, rules, and laws with his whole being, and to obey the words of the agreement written in this book. Then all the people promised to obey the agreement.

²⁴Josiah destroyed the mediums, fortune-tellers, house gods, and idols. He also destroyed all the hated gods seen in the land of Judah and Jerusalem. This was to obey the words of the teachings written in the book Hilkiah the priest had found in the Temple of the LORD.

²⁵There was no king like Josiah before or after him. He obeyed the LORD with all his heart, soul, and strength, following all the Teachings of Moses.

2 Kings 23:3, 24–25

INSIGHTS

I frequently hear that the call to be holy and the call to demonstrate love to sinners are mutually exclusive. (As if love is the antithesis to holiness!) Jesus welcomed and loved sinners; he did not drive them away by too much affectation of righteousness. He showed genuine compassion for people, but he was also direct and uncompromising in denouncing sin. Jesus had compassion, but there was also toughness in this love. He won them without sacrificing the purity of his life.

The paradox of agape love is that we accept our neighbor unconditionally and with open arms and at the same time desire moral purity for their lives. If Jesus is our Lord, our compassion will be shaped by his moral absolutes. Christ both was merciful and made judgments. Some things, he said, were immoral and destructive, but he never ceased to love. Indeed, it was his love that prompted his judgment. The enemy of our age is our desire to be tolerant and open-minded. . . .

I know a Christian woman who has cared deeply for a non-Christian woman who has had every variety of sexual experience. One day the non-Christian woman said to the Christian, "It's funny, my non-Christian friends accept me. They say it doesn't matter what I do. I'm free. But it's only with you that I feel loved, that I know I could always come to you. But it's also only when I'm with you that I feel shame and remorse for what I'm doing."

That is holiness. It never abandons; it identifies deeply with individual people. But it also brings the reality of God's presence, the purity of his holiness.

REBECCA PIPPERT

► PAUSE FOR REFLECTION

List the areas of life in which the believer ought to be an example. What happens when people have a godly example before them? To whom are you an example of godly living? Do you know what impact your example is having?

1 TIMOTHY 5:1-25

Rules for Living with Others

5 Do not speak angrily to an older man, but plead with him as if he were your father. Treat younger men like brothers, **2**older women like mothers, and younger women like sisters. Always treat them in a pure way.

3Take care of widows who are truly widows. **4**But if a widow has children or grandchildren, let them first learn to do their duty to their own family and to repay their parents or grandparents. That pleases God. **5**The true widow, who is all alone, puts her hope in God and continues to pray night and day for God's help. **6**But the widow who uses her life to please herself is really dead while she is alive. **7**Tell the believers to do these things so that no one can criticize them. **8**Whoever does not care for his own relatives, especially his own family members, has turned against the faith and is worse than someone who does not believe in God.

9To be on the list of widows, a woman must be at least sixty years old. She must have been faithful to her husband. **10**She must be known for her good works—works such as raising her children, welcoming strangers, washing the feet of God's people, helping those in trouble, and giving her life to do all kinds of good deeds.

11But do not put younger widows on that list. After they give themselves to Christ, they are pulled away from him by their physical desires, and then they want to marry again. **12**They will be judged for not doing what they first promised to do. **13**Besides that, they learn to waste their time, going from house to house. And they not only waste their time but also begin to gossip and busy themselves with other people's lives, saying things they should not say. **14**So I want the younger widows to marry, have children, and manage their homes. Then no enemy will have any reason to criticize them. **15**But some have already turned away to follow Satan.

16If any woman who is a believer has widows in her family, she should care for them herself. The church should not have to care for them. Then it will be able to take care of those who are truly widows.

17The elders who lead the church well should receive double honor, especially those who work hard by speaking and teaching, **18**because the Scripture says: "When an ox is working in the grain, do not cover its mouth to keep it from eating," and "A worker should be given his pay."

19Do not listen to someone who accuses an elder, without two or three witnesses. **20**Tell those who continue sinning that they are wrong. Do this in front of the whole church so that the others will have a warning.

21Before God and Christ Jesus and the chosen angels, I command you to do these things without showing favor of any kind to anyone.

22Think carefully before you lay your hands on anyone, and don't share in the sins of others. Keep yourself pure.

23Stop drinking only water, but drink a little wine to help your stomach and your frequent sicknesses.

24The sins of some people are easy to see even

before they are judged, but the sins of others are seen only later. **25**So also good deeds are easy to see, but even those that are not easily seen cannot stay hidden.

OLD TESTAMENT READING

Then Nathan said to David, "You are the man! This is what the LORD, the God of Israel, says: 'I appointed you king of Israel and saved you from Saul. **9**So why did you ignore the LORD's command? Why did you do what he says is wrong? You killed Uriah the Hittite with the sword of the Ammonites and took his wife to be your wife!'"

13Then David said to Nathan, "I have sinned against the LORD."

Nathan answered, "The LORD has taken away your sin. You will not die. **14**But what you did caused the LORD's enemies to lose all respect for him. For this reason the son who was born to you will die."

2 Samuel 12:7, 9, 13–14

INSIGHTS

Too often I have seen marriages go down the drain, relationships deteriorate to the point of destruction, people with glaring personal limitations go unchecked—all because Christians who know precisely what is wrong will not love sufficiently to tackle the problem.

"I was afraid I would hurt their future," is one lame excuse. But that is exactly what happens.

My mind recalls the words of our Lord to Peter when he veered off course; it seems a harsh slash to the disciple who had a short time before confessed him as Lord. "Out of my sight, Satan! You are a stumbling block to me; you do not have in mind the things of God, but the things of men." (Matthew 16:23) These words came from the lips of the One who loves with everlasting love.

A former pastor told me about his experience of sinking into an illicit sexual relationship. He said he felt like an exhausted swimmer battling alone in the pounding surf, unable to escape the strong undertow, about to go down for the last time. On shore he could see all the people of his church. Some were shaking their heads in weeping and despair; others were shouting and shaking their fists in anger and frustration. There were words of encouragement and gestures of good will. There they were, all lined up, watching and waiting for something to happen. Only one man stepped forward and risked everything to plunge into the water and help the victim to safety.

HOWARD AND JEANNE HENDRICKS

PAUSE FOR REFLECTION

In what ways does Paul urge Christians to hold one another accountable? What are the results of a proper response to correction? Who holds you accountable to live in obedience to God?

TUESDAY

A GODLY ATTITUDE TOWARD RICHES

1 TIMOTHY 6:1-21

All who are slaves under a yoke should show full respect to their masters so no one will speak against God's name and our teaching. ²The slaves whose masters are believers should not show their masters any less respect because they are believers. They should serve their masters even better, because they are helping believers they love.

You must teach and preach these things.

False Teaching and True Riches

³Anyone who has a different teaching does not agree with the true teaching of our Lord Jesus Christ and the teaching that shows the true way to serve God. ⁴This person is full of pride and understands nothing, but is sick with a love for arguing and fighting about words. This brings jealousy, fighting, speaking against others, evil mistrust, ⁵and constant quarrels from those who have evil minds and have lost the truth. They think that serving God is a way to get rich.

⁶Serving God does make us very rich, if we are satisfied with what we have. ⁷We brought nothing into the world, so we can take nothing out. ⁸But, if we have food and clothes, we will be satisfied with that. ⁹Those who want to become rich bring temptation to themselves and are caught in a trap. They want many foolish and harmful things that ruin and destroy people. ¹⁰The love of money causes all kinds of evil. Some people have left the faith, because they wanted to get more money, but they have caused themselves much sorrow.

Some Things to Remember

¹¹But you, man of God, run away from all those things. Instead, live in the right way, serve God, have faith, love, patience, and gentleness. ¹²Fight the good fight of faith, grabbing hold of the life that continues forever. You were called to have that life when you confessed the good confession before many witnesses. ¹³In the sight of God, who gives life to everything, and of Christ Jesus, I give you a command. Christ Jesus made the good confession when he stood before Pontius Pilate. ¹⁴Do what you were commanded to do without wrong or blame until our Lord Jesus Christ comes again. ¹⁵God will make that happen at the right time. He is the blessed and only Ruler, the King of all kings and the Lord of all lords. ¹⁶He is the only One who never dies. He lives in light so bright no one can go near it. No one has ever seen God, or can see him. May honor and power belong to God forever. Amen.

¹⁷Command those who are rich with things of this world not to be proud. Tell them to hope in God, not in their uncertain riches. God richly gives us everything to enjoy. ¹⁸Tell the rich people to do good, to be rich in doing good deeds, to be generous and ready to share. ¹⁹By doing that, they will be saving a treasure for themselves as a strong foundation for the future. Then they will be able to have the life that is true life.

²⁰Timothy, guard what God has trusted to you. Stay away from foolish, useless talk and from the arguments of what is falsely called "knowledge." ²¹By saying they have that "knowledge," some have missed the true faith.

Grace be with you.

OLD TESTAMENT READING

Be careful not to forget the LORD your God so that you fail to obey his commands, laws, and rules that I am giving to you today. **12**When you eat all you want and build nice houses and live in them, **13**when your herds and flocks grow large and your silver and gold increase, when you have more of everything, **14**then your heart will become proud. You will forget the LORD your God, who brought you out of the land of Egypt, where you were slaves. **17**You might say to yourself, "I am rich because of my own power and strength," **18**but remember the LORD your God! It is he who gives you the power to become rich, keeping the agreement he promised to your ancestors, as it is today.

Deuteronomy 8:11–14, 17–18

God gives some people the ability to enjoy the wealth and property he gives them, as well as the ability to accept their state in life and enjoy their work. **20**They do not worry about how short life is, because God keeps them busy with what they love to do.

Ecclesiastes 5:19–20

INSIGHTS

There will be this difference between the rich that loves his riches and the poor that hates his poverty. When they die, the heart of the one will still be crowded with things and their pleasures, while the heart of the other will be relieved of their lack. The one has had his good things; the other, his sorrowful things.

But the rich man, on the other hand, who held his things lightly and who did not let them nestle in his heart, who was a channel and not a cistern, who was ever and always forsaking his money—this rich man starts in the new world side by side with the man who accepted, not hated, his poverty. Each will say, "I am free."

GEORGE MACDONALD

God often allows people to accumulate property so they may have an opportunity to extend the cause of truth and righteousness in the earth. . . . Professing Christians acknowledge themselves to be but stewards for God, that everything they possess is His; consequently, their possessions are at His disposal. Now, is it a fact that these people act in harmony with what they profess? Well, God often tries them to see if they are hypocrites or not.

CHARLES FINNEY

PAUSE FOR REFLECTION

What traps await those who accumulate riches? Who is the source of wealth? Write down what it means for you to have a godly attitude toward riches. In what ways do riches tempt you? How well are you handling what God has given to you?

2 TIMOTHY 1:1 – 2:13

1 From Paul, an apostle of Christ Jesus by the will of God. God sent me to tell about the promise of life that is in Christ Jesus.

²To Timothy, a dear child to me:

Grace, mercy, and peace to you from God the Father and Christ Jesus our Lord.

Encouragement for Timothy

³I thank God as I always mention you in my prayers, day and night. I serve him, doing what I know is right as my ancestors did. ⁴Remembering that you cried for me, I want very much to see you so I can be filled with joy. ⁵I remember your true faith. That faith first lived in your grandmother Lois and in your mother Eunice, and I know you now have that same faith. ⁶This is why I remind you to keep using the gift God gave you when I laid my hands on you. Now let it grow, as a small flame grows into a fire. ⁷God did not give us a spirit that makes us afraid but a spirit of power and love and self-control.

⁸So do not be ashamed to tell people about our Lord Jesus, and do not be ashamed of me, in prison for the Lord. But suffer with me for the Good News. God, who gives us the strength to do that, ⁹saved us and made us his holy people. That was not because of anything we did ourselves but because of God's purpose and grace. That grace was given to us through Christ Jesus before time began, ¹⁰but it is now shown to us by the coming of our Savior Christ Jesus. He destroyed death, and through the Good News he showed us the way to have life that cannot be destroyed. ¹¹I was cho-

sen to tell that Good News and to be an apostle and a teacher. ¹²I am suffering now because I tell the Good News, but I am not ashamed, because I know Jesus, the One in whom I have believed. And I am sure he is able to protect what he has trusted me with until that day. ¹³Follow the pattern of true teachings that you heard from me in faith and love, which are in Christ Jesus. ¹⁴Protect the truth that you were given; protect it with the help of the Holy Spirit who lives in us.

¹⁵You know that everyone in Asia has left me, even Phygelus and Hermogenes. ¹⁶May the Lord show mercy to the family of Onesiphorus, who has often helped me and was not ashamed that I was in prison. ¹⁷When he came to Rome, he looked eagerly for me until he found me. ¹⁸May the Lord allow him to find mercy from the Lord on that day. You know how many ways he helped me in Ephesus.

A Loyal Soldier of Christ Jesus

2 You then, Timothy, my child, be strong in the grace we have in Christ Jesus. ²You should teach people whom you can trust the things you and many others have heard me say. Then they will be able to teach others. ³Share in the troubles we have like a good soldier of Christ Jesus. ⁴A soldier wants to please the enlisting officer, so no one serving in the army wastes time with everyday matters. ⁵Also an athlete who takes part in a contest must obey all the rules in order to win. ⁶The farmer who works hard should be the first person to get some of the food that was grown. ⁷Think about what I am saying, because the Lord will give you the ability to understand everything.

⁸Remember Jesus Christ, who was raised from the dead, who is from the family of David. This is

the Good News I preach, **9**and I am suffering because of it to the point of being bound with chains like a criminal. But God's teaching is not in chains. **10**So I patiently accept all these troubles so that those whom God has chosen can have the salvation that is in Christ Jesus. With that salvation comes glory that never ends.

11This teaching is true:

If we died with him, we will also live with him.
12If we accept suffering, we will also rule with
him.
If we say we don't know him, he will say he
doesn't know us.
13If we are not faithful, he will still be faithful,
because he must be true to who he is.

OLD TESTAMENT READING

But be careful! Watch out and don't forget the things you have seen. Don't forget them as long as you live, but teach them to your children and grandchildren. **10**Remember the day you stood before the LORD your God at Mount Sinai. He said to me, "Bring the people together so I can tell them what I have to say. Then they will respect me as long as they live in the land, and they will teach these things to their children."

Deuteronomy 4:9–10

INSIGHTS

The discipling ministry lacks the glamour and excitement of the platform or large meeting type of ministry. But we can hardly overemphasize the importance of investing the right kind of person, one of vision and discipline, totally committed to Jesus Christ, willing to pay any price to have the will of God fulfilled in his life. . . .

. . . The Great Commission given to us in Matthew 28:19–20 says, "Go therefore, and teach [make disciples of] all nations." It takes a disciple-maker to make disciples. Historically, the Church has believed that the Great Commission was not given to a select few people, but to all believers. If this is true, then all believers can be disciple-makers. . . .

. . . If you are not a disciple-maker, then I would suggest that you do the same thing that Timothy did with Paul, or that Peter, James, and John did with the Lord Jesus. Make yourself available to a disciple-maker who can help you to become a disciple-maker. Latch on to them. Learn from them the "how to" involved in developing those qualities needed to spiritually reproduce yourself in the lives of others.

WALTER HENRICHSEN

PAUSE FOR REFLECTION

Is disciple-making a new phenomenon? What principles of discipleship did Moses outline for the Israelites? In what ways do those principles apply today?

2 TIMOTHY
2:14 – 3:11

A Worker Pleasing to God

14Continue teaching these things, warning people in God's presence not to argue about words. It does not help anyone, and it ruins those who listen. **15**Make every effort to give yourself to God as the kind of person he will approve. Be a worker who is not ashamed and who uses the true teaching in the right way. **16**Stay away from foolish, useless talk, because that will lead people further away from God. **17**Their evil teaching will spread like a sickness inside the body. Hymenaeus and Philetus are like that. **18**They have left the true teaching, saying that the rising from the dead has already taken place, and so they are destroying the faith of some people. **19**But God's strong foundation continues to stand. These words are written on the seal: "The Lord knows those who belong to him," and "Everyone who wants to belong to the Lord must stop doing wrong."

20In a large house there are not only things made of gold and silver, but also things made of wood and clay. Some things are used for special purposes, and others are made for ordinary jobs. **21**All who make themselves clean from evil will be used for special purposes. They will be made holy, useful to the Master, ready to do any good work.

22But run away from the evil desires of youth. Try hard to live right and to have faith, love, and peace, together with those who trust in the Lord from pure hearts. **23**Stay away from foolish and stupid arguments, because you know they grow into quarrels. **24**And a servant of the Lord must not quarrel but must be kind to everyone, a good teacher, and patient. **25**The Lord's servant must gently teach those who disagree. Then maybe God will let them change their minds so they can accept the truth. **26**And they may wake up and escape from the trap of the devil, who catches them to do what he wants.

The Last Days

3 Remember this! In the last days there will be many troubles, **2**because people will love themselves, love money, brag, and be proud. They will say evil things against others and will not obey their parents or be thankful or be the kind of people God wants. **3**They will not love others, will refuse to forgive, will gossip, and will not control themselves. They will be cruel, will hate what is good, **4**will turn against their friends, and will do foolish things without thinking. They will be conceited, will love pleasure instead of God, **5**and will act as if they serve God but will not have his power. Stay away from those people. **6**Some of them go into homes and get control of silly women who are full of sin and are led by many evil desires. **7**These women are always learning new teachings, but they are never able to understand the truth fully. **8**Just as Jannes and Jambres were against Moses, these people are against the truth. Their thinking has been ruined, and they have failed in trying to follow the faith. **9**But they will not be successful in what they do, because as with Jannes and Jambres, everyone will see that they are foolish.

Obey the Teachings

10But you have followed what I teach, the way I live, my goal, faith, patience, and love. You know I never give up. **11**You know how I have been hurt and have suffered, as in Antioch, Iconium, and Lystra. I have suffered, but the Lord saved me from all those troubles.

OLD TESTAMENT READING

I will sing of your love and fairness;
  LORD, I will sing praises to you.
2I will be careful to live an innocent life.
  When will you come to me?

I will live an innocent life in my house.
3 I will not look at anything wicked.
I hate those who turn against you;
  they will not be found near me.
4Let those who want to do wrong stay away
    from me;
  I will have nothing to do with evil.
5If anyone secretly says things against his
    neighbor,
  I will stop him.
I will not allow people
  to be proud and look down on others.

Psalm 101:1–5

INSIGHTS

The practice of godliness involves the pursuit of holiness because God has said, "Be holy, because I am holy" (1 Peter 1:16). Paul tells us that we have been called to a holy life; we have been redeemed for that purpose. Any Christian who is not earnestly pursuing holiness in every aspect of his life is flying in the face of God's purpose in saving him.

What is holiness? The best practical definition that I have heard is simply "without sin." . . .

John said he wrote his first letter so that his readers would not sin (1 John 2:1). Most Christians seem content not to sin very much, but John's goal was that we not sin at all. Every sin, no matter how small it may seem to us, is an affront to God's authority, a disregard for his law, a spurning of his love. Because of this, sin cannot be tolerated in any form, to any degree. . . .

. . . When Paul was instructing the Ephesian Christians about the importance of holiness he said, "So I tell you this, and insist on it in the Lord, that you must no longer live as the Gentiles do" (4:17). He insisted on holiness, and he did so with the Lord's authority. Holiness is not an option but a must for every Christian. . . .

. . . If we want to train ourselves to be godly, it must be holiness in every area of our lives.

JERRY BRIDGES

PAUSE FOR REFLECTION

What must everyone who believes in God stop doing—and start doing? How important is this teaching for Christians today? In what ways do you share the psalmist's delight in innocence and pure living expressed in Psalm 101?

2 TIMOTHY 3:12 — 4:22

12Everyone who wants to live as God desires, in Christ Jesus, will be persecuted. **13**But people who are evil and cheat others will go from bad to worse. They will fool others, but they will also be fooling themselves.

14But you should continue following the teachings you learned. You know they are true, because you trust those who taught you. **15**Since you were a child you have known the Holy Scriptures which are able to make you wise. And that wisdom leads to salvation through faith in Christ Jesus. **16**All Scripture is inspired by God and is useful for teaching, for showing people what is wrong in their lives, for correcting faults, and for teaching how to live right. **17**Using the Scriptures, the person who serves God will be capable, having all that is needed to do every good work.

4 I give you a command in the presence of God and Christ Jesus, the One who will judge the living and the dead, and by his coming and his kingdom: **2**Preach the Good News. Be ready at all times, and tell people what they need to do. Tell them when they are wrong. Encourage them with great patience and careful teaching, **3**because the time will come when people will not listen to the true teaching but will find many more teachers who please them by saying the things they want to hear. **4**They will stop listening to the truth and will begin to follow false stories. **5**But you should control yourself at all times, accept troubles, do the work of telling the Good News, and complete all the duties of a servant of God.

6My life is being given as an offering to God, and the time has come for me to leave this life. **7**I have fought the good fight, I have finished the race, I have kept the faith. **8**Now, a crown is being held for me—a crown for being right with God. The Lord, the judge who judges rightly, will give the crown to me on that day—not only to me but to all those who have waited with love for him to come again.

Personal Words

9Do your best to come to me as soon as you can, **10**because Demas, who loved this world, left me and went to Thessalonica. Crescens went to Galatia, and Titus went to Dalmatia. **11**Luke is the only one still with me. Get Mark and bring him with you when you come, because he can help me in my work here. **12**I sent Tychicus to Ephesus. **13**When I was in Troas, I left my coat there with Carpus. So when you come, bring it to me, along with my books, particularly the ones written on parchment.

14Alexander the metalworker did many harmful things against me. The Lord will punish him for what he did. **15**You also should be careful that he does not hurt you, because he fought strongly against our teaching.

16The first time I defended myself, no one helped me; everyone left me. May they be forgiven. **17**But the Lord stayed with me and gave me strength so I could fully tell the Good News to all those who are not Jews. So I was saved from the lion's mouth. **18**The Lord will save me when anyone tries to hurt me, and he will bring me safely to his heavenly kingdom. Glory forever and ever be the Lord's. Amen.

Final Greetings

19Greet Priscilla and Aquila and the family of Onesiphorus. 20Erastus stayed in Corinth, and I left Trophimus sick in Miletus. 21Try as hard as you can to come to me before winter.

Eubulus sends greetings to you. Also Pudens, Linus, Claudia, and all the brothers and sisters in Christ greet you.

22The Lord be with your spirit. Grace be with you.

OLD TESTAMENT READING

They read from the Book of the Teachings of God and explained what it meant so the people understood what was being read.

14This is what they found written in the Teachings: The LORD commanded through Moses that the people of Israel were to live in shelters during the feast of the seventh month. 15The people were supposed to preach this message and spread it through all their towns and in Jerusalem: "Go out into the mountains, and bring back branches from olive and wild olive trees, myrtle trees, palms, and shade trees. Make shelters with them, as it is written."

Nehemiah 8:8, 14–15

INSIGHTS

There are few joys like the joy of sudden discovery. Instantly, there is forgotten the pain and expense of the search, the inconveniences, the hours, the sacrifices. Bathed in the ecstasy of discovery, time stands still. . . .

Solomon talks about the greatest discovery of all. . . .

"My son, if you will receive my sayings,
And treasure my commandments
    within you,
Make your ear attentive to wisdom,
Incline your heart to understanding;
For if you cry for discernment,
Lift your voice for understanding;
If you seek her as silver,
And search for her as for hidden
    treasures;
Then you will discern the fear of the
    LORD,
And discover the knowledge of God."

(Proverbs 2:1–5)

Talk about a discovery! Hidden in the Scriptures are priceless verbal vaults. Silent. Hard to find. Easy to miss if you're in a hurry. But they are there, awaiting discovery. God's Word, like a deep, deep mine, stands ready to yield its treasures.

Charles Swindoll

PAUSE FOR REFLECTION

What are the results of learning and obeying God's Word? What are the results of rejecting it? Have you discovered the rich treasures of God's Word for yourself?

З

TITUS 1:1 – 2:8

1 From Paul, a servant of God and an apostle of Jesus Christ. I was sent to help the faith of God's chosen people and to help them know the truth that shows people how to serve God. **2**That faith and that knowledge come from the hope for life forever, which God promised to us before time began. And God cannot lie. **3**At the right time God let the world know about that life through preaching. He trusted me with that work, and I preached by the command of God our Savior.

4To Titus, my true child in the faith we share:

Grace and peace from God the Father and Christ Jesus our Savior.

Titus' Work in Crete

5I left you in Crete so you could finish doing the things that still needed to be done and so you could appoint elders in every town, as I directed you. **6**An elder must not be guilty of doing wrong, must have only one wife, and must have believing children. They must not be known as children who are wild and do not cooperate. **7**As God's managers, overseers must not be guilty of doing wrong, being selfish, or becoming angry quickly. They must not drink too much wine, like to fight, or try to get rich by cheating others. **8**Overseers must be ready to welcome guests, love what is good, be wise, live right, and be holy and self-controlled. **9**By holding on to the trustworthy word just as we teach it, overseers can help people by using true teaching, and they can show those who are against the true teaching that they are wrong.

10There are many people who refuse to cooperate, who talk about worthless things and lead others into the wrong way—mainly those who insist on circumcision to be saved. **11**These people must be stopped, because they are upsetting whole families by teaching things they should not teach, which they do to get rich by cheating people. **12**Even one of their own prophets said, "Cretans are always liars, evil animals, and lazy people who do nothing but eat." **13**The words that prophet said are true. So firmly tell those people they are wrong so they may become strong in the faith, **14**not accepting Jewish false stories and the commands of people who reject the truth. **15**To those who are pure, all things are pure, but to those who are full of sin and do not believe, nothing is pure. Both their minds and their consciences have been ruined. **16**They say they know God, but their actions show they do not accept him. They are hateful people, they refuse to obey, and they are useless for doing anything good.

Following the True Teaching

2 But you must tell everyone what to do to follow the true teaching. **2**Teach older men to be self-controlled, serious, wise, strong in faith, in love, and in patience.

3In the same way, teach older women to be holy in their behavior, not speaking against others or enslaved to too much wine, but teaching what is good. **4**Then they can teach the young women to love their husbands, to love their children, **5**to be wise and pure, to be good workers at home, to be kind, and to yield to their husbands. Then no one will be able to criticize the teaching God gave us.

6In the same way, encourage young men to be

wise. **7**In every way be an example of doing good deeds. When you teach, do it with honesty and seriousness. **8**Speak the truth so that you cannot be criticized. Then those who are against you will be ashamed because there is nothing bad to say about us.

OLD TESTAMENT READING

If the priests keep all the rules I have given, they will not become guilty; if they are careful, they will not die. I am the LORD who has made them holy.'"

Leviticus 22:9

A priest should teach what he knows, and people should learn the teachings from him, because he is the messenger of the LORD All-Powerful. **8**But you priests have stopped obeying me. With your teachings you have caused many people to do wrong. You have broken the agreement with the tribe of Levi!" says the LORD All-Powerful. **9**"You have not been careful to do what I say, but instead you take sides in court cases. So I have caused you to be hated and disgraced in front of everybody."

Malachi 2:7–9

INSIGHTS

Luke recorded that believers from Lystra and Iconium "spoke well of him" (Acts 16:2). In other words Timothy had a good reputation as a Christian. He was "blameless" in the eyes of those in the Christian community. There were no specific flaws in his life that would bring reproach to the cause of Christ. So Paul invited Timothy to be his missionary companion, and this resulted in a deep, lasting relationship and ministry together.

Titus was also this kind of man. Mature in many ways, he maintained pure motives, evidencing compassion and concern for people (2 Cor. 8:16) and demonstrating a positive attitude toward the ministry (v. 17). There is no better way in which to develop a good reputation among Christians and non-Christians alike.

Be blameless. This quality and the other qualifications for elders are standards all of us should strive for, whether we are in positions of church leadership or not.

GENE GETZ

ACTION POINT

Why is it essential that those who teach others in the ways of God be blameless? How much do you want to be the kind of Christian Paul describes as an "elder"? What changes must you make to be blameless and trustworthy? Are you willing?

TITUS 2:9 — 3:15

⁹Slaves should yield to their own masters at all times, trying to please them and not arguing with them. ¹⁰They should not steal from them but should show their masters they can be fully trusted so that in everything they do they will make the teaching of God our Savior attractive.

¹¹That is the way we should live, because God's grace that can save everyone has come. ¹²It teaches us not to live against God nor to do the evil things the world wants to do. Instead, that grace teaches us to live in the present age in a wise and right way and in a way that shows we serve God. ¹³We should live like that while we wait for our great hope and the coming of the glory of our great God and Savior Jesus Christ. ¹⁴He gave himself for us so he might pay the price to free us from all evil and to make us pure people who belong only to him—people who are always wanting to do good deeds.

¹⁵Say these things and encourage the people and tell them what is wrong in their lives, with all authority. Do not let anyone treat you as if you were unimportant.

The Right Way to Live

3 Remind the believers to yield to the authority of rulers and government leaders, to obey them, to be ready to do good, ²to speak no evil about anyone, to live in peace, and to be gentle and polite to all people.

³In the past we also were foolish. We did not obey, we were wrong, and we were slaves to many things our bodies wanted and enjoyed. We spent our lives doing evil and being jealous. People hated us, and we hated each other. ⁴But when the kindness and love of God our Savior was shown, ⁵he saved us because of his mercy. It was not because of good deeds we did to be right with him. He saved us through the washing that made us new people through the Holy Spirit. ⁶God poured out richly upon us that Holy Spirit through Jesus Christ our Savior. ⁷Being made right with God by his grace, we could have the hope of receiving the life that never ends.

⁸This teaching is true, and I want you to be sure the people understand these things. Then those who believe in God will be careful to use their lives for doing good. These things are good and will help everyone.

⁹But stay away from those who have foolish arguments and talk about useless family histories and argue and quarrel about the law. Those things are worth nothing and will not help anyone. ¹⁰After a first and second warning, avoid someone who causes arguments. ¹¹You can know that such people are evil and sinful; their own sins prove them wrong.

Some Things to Remember

¹²When I send Artemas or Tychicus to you, make every effort to come to me at Nicopolis, because I have decided to stay there this winter. ¹³Do all you can to help Zenas the lawyer and Apollos on their journey so that they have everything they need. ¹⁴Our people must learn to use their lives for doing good deeds to provide what is necessary so that their lives will not be useless.

¹⁵All who are with me greet you. Greet those who love us in the faith.

Grace be with you all.

OLD TESTAMENT READING

D aniel answered, "O king, live forever! **22**My God sent his angel to close the lions' mouths. They have not hurt me, because my God knows I am innocent. I never did anything wrong to you, O king."

25Then King Darius wrote a letter to all people and all nations, to those who spoke every language in the world:

I wish you great peace and wealth.

26I am making a new law for people in every part of my kingdom. All of you must fear and respect the God of Daniel.

Daniel's God is the living God;
　he lives forever.
His kingdom will never be destroyed,
　and his rule will never end.
27God rescues and saves people
　and does mighty miracles
　in heaven and on earth.
He is the one who saved Daniel
　from the power of the lions.

Daniel 6:21–22, 25–27

INSIGHTS

. . . [T]here are unique things involved in your moment-by-moment work since you are a child of the Creator of the universe. . . .

You are to do well, whatever you are doing, to the glory of God (see 1 Peter 4:11). Just as flowers that grow on the Alpine peaks, beauty in the cracks of rocks with perhaps no one ever passing that way, are not growing in vain because God sees them, so it is true of the human being. A person may live alone, walk alone, and feel that no one is recognizing that he or she is being patient in the tribulation of loneliness . . . but God does know, and is aware of the whisper, "I love you, God. Please accept my praise as I walk alone today." This is true of people in prisons, in concentration camps, in hospital beds, or in wheelchairs. . . . "Work" to the glory of God can be done in every part of life . . . which is what makes it all so fair. No one gets a bigger opportunity than another. And no one is "out of work"!

EDITH SCHAEFFER

PAUSE FOR REFLECTION

What kind of people are we without Jesus? What kind of people does his death make us? How are believers supposed to use their lives? Who do you know who truly lives like a servant of the living God?

PHILEMON 1-25

1From Paul, a prisoner of Christ Jesus, and from Timothy, our brother.

To Philemon, our dear friend and worker with us; 2to Apphia, our sister; to Archippus, a worker with us; and to the church that meets in your home:

3Grace and peace to you from God our Father and the Lord Jesus Christ.

Philemon's Love and Faith

4I always thank my God when I mention you in my prayers, 5because I hear about the love you have for all God's holy people and the faith you have in the Lord Jesus. 6I pray that the faith you share may make you understand every blessing we have in Christ. 7I have great joy and comfort, my brother, because the love you have shown to God's people has refreshed them.

Accept Onesimus as a Brother

8So, in Christ, I could be bold and order you to do what is right. 9But because I love you, I am pleading with you instead. I, Paul, an old man now and also a prisoner for Christ Jesus, 10am pleading with you for my child Onesimus, who became my child while I was in prison. 11In the past he was useless to you, but now he has become useful for both you and me.

12I am sending him back to you, and with him I am sending my own heart. 13I wanted to keep him with me so that in your place he might help me while I am in prison for the Good News. 14But I did not want to do anything without asking you first so that any good you do for me will be be-cause you want to do it, not because I forced you. 15Maybe Onesimus was separated from you for a short time so you could have him back forever—16no longer as a slave, but better than a slave, as a loved brother. I love him very much, but you will love him even more, both as a person and as a believer in the Lord.

17So if you consider me your partner, welcome Onesimus as you would welcome me. 18If he has done anything wrong to you or if he owes you anything, charge that to me. 19I, Paul, am writing this with my own hand. I will pay it back, and I will say nothing about what you owe me for your own life. 20So, my brother, I ask that you do this for me in the Lord: Refresh my heart in Christ. 21I write this letter, knowing that you will do what I ask you and even more.

22One more thing—prepare a room for me in which to stay, because I hope God will answer your prayers and I will be able to come to you.

Final Greetings

23Epaphras, a prisoner with me for Christ Jesus, sends greetings to you. 24And also Mark, Aristarchus, Demas, and Luke, workers together with me, send greetings.

25The grace of our Lord Jesus Christ be with your spirit.

OLD TESTAMENT READING

So the king said to Joseph, "God has shown you all this. There is no one as wise and understanding as you are, so 40I will put you in charge of my palace. All the people will obey your orders, and only I will be greater than you."

42Then the king took off from his own finger his ring with the royal seal on it, and he put it on Joseph's finger. He gave Joseph fine linen clothes to wear, and he put a gold chain around Joseph's neck. **43**The king had Joseph ride in the second royal chariot, and people walked ahead of his chariot calling, "Bow down!" By doing these things, the king put Joseph in charge of all of Egypt.

Genesis 41:39–40, 42–43

So Joseph said to them, "Come close to me." When the brothers came close to him, he said to them, "I am your brother Joseph, whom you sold as a slave to go to Egypt. **5**Now don't be worried or angry with yourselves because you sold me here. God sent me here ahead of you to save people's lives.

9"So leave quickly and go to my father. Tell him, 'Your son Joseph says: God has made me master over all Egypt. Come down to me quickly. **10**Live in the land of Goshen where you will be near me. Your children, your grandchildren, your flocks and herds, and all that you have will also be near me. **11**I will care for you during the next five years of hunger so that you and your family and all that you have will not starve.'"

Genesis 45:4–5, 9–11

INSIGHTS

Are you still running around trying to milk acceptance and self-esteem out of the world like lost people when you've already got both? Are you still employing the same old methods, such as trying to perform up to your flesh's standards to generate and maintain self-esteem moment by moment? You are of infinite worth. You are accepted. Not by people, perhaps, but of God! If you're rejected by certain people, welcome to the club. So was Jesus. But He didn't go around with His head down. Why? Because He knew it's not a feeling that matters; it's what you know. He knew He was accepted.

Do you know that? . . . You are not to strive to get love; we don't live that way. We live from a posture of knowing that we are loved.

. . . You can accept yourself now as the new person you truly are in Him, just as the Father accepts you—perfectly.

BILL GILLHAM

PAUSE FOR REFLECTION

In biblical times, who had less value than a slave? In what ways did God affirm the value of Joseph and Onesimus? How was each one received? Who do you need to accept as a beloved brother or sister before God?

HEBREWS 1:1 – 2:4

God Spoke Through His Son

1 In the past God spoke to our ancestors through the prophets many times and in many different ways. **2** But now in these last days God has spoken to us through his Son. God has chosen his Son to own all things, and through him he made the world. **3** The Son reflects the glory of God and shows exactly what God is like. He holds everything together with his powerful word. When the Son made people clean from their sins, he sat down at the right side of God, the Great One in heaven. **4** The Son became much greater than the angels, and God gave him a name that is much greater than theirs.

5 This is because God never said to any of the angels,

"You are my Son.
Today I have become your Father."

Psalm 2:7

Nor did God say of any angel,

"I will be his Father,
and he will be my Son." *2 Samuel 7:14*

6 And when God brings his firstborn Son into the world, he says,

"Let all God's angels worship him." *Psalm 97:7*

7 This is what God said about the angels:

"God makes his angels become like winds.
He makes his servants become like flames
of fire." *Psalm 104:4*

8 But God said this about his Son:

"God, your throne will last forever and ever.
You will rule your kingdom with fairness.

9 You love right and hate evil,
so God has chosen you from among your
friends;
he has set you apart with much joy."

Psalm 45:6–7

10 God also says,

"Lord, in the beginning you made the earth,
and your hands made the skies.

11 They will be destroyed, but you will remain.
They will all wear out like clothes.

12 You will fold them like a coat.
And, like clothes, you will change them.
But you never change,
and your life will never end."

Psalm 102:25–27

13 And God never said this to an angel:

"Sit by me at my right side
until I put your enemies under your
control." *Psalm 110:1*

14 All the angels are spirits who serve God and are sent to help those who will receive salvation.

Our Salvation Is Great

2 So we must be more careful to follow what we were taught. Then we will not stray away from the truth. **2** The teaching God spoke through angels was shown to be true, and anyone who did not follow it or obey it received the punishment that was earned. **3** So surely we also will be punished if we ignore this great salvation. The Lord himself first told about this salvation, and those who heard him testified it was true. **4** God also testified to the truth of the message by using wonders, great signs, many kinds of miracles, and by giving people gifts through the Holy Spirit, just as he wanted.

He is my God,
and I will praise him."

Exodus 15:1b–2b

OLD TESTAMENT READING

I will sing to the LORD,
because he is worthy of great honor.
He has thrown the horse and its rider
into the sea.
2The LORD gives me strength and makes me
sing;
he has saved me.

LORD, teach me what you want me to do,
and I will live by your truth.
Teach me to respect you completely.
12Lord, my God, I will praise you with all my
heart,
and I will honor your name forever.
13You have great love for me.
You have saved me from death.

Psalm 86:11–13

INSIGHTS

Our salvation is good reason to rejoice. Hannah rejoiced because of salvation in a song that Mary echoed when Jesus was born and salvation had come. The magi rejoiced when they saw the star that led them to the infant Jesus and salvation (Matthew 2:10). The Ethiopian eunuch rejoiced in the discovery of salvation through Philip's ministry of the Word (Acts 8:39). Christians rejoice in hope and even in suffering since they have peace with God (Romans 5:2–3).

Rejoicing and salvation belong together. The coming of Jesus into this world can never be a matter of academic aloofness or objective study. Because it is real and because it means so much it goes right to the heart to make it leap with joy. It is the emotion felt when a woman finds a lost coin or a shepherd finds a lost sheep or a waiting Father sees his lost son on the horizon (read Luke 15). It is not like a student poring over a book in the library. It is more like a student with a thousand others, rejoicing over a touchdown on the field. It is like oil drillers watching their first wild fountain of black gold after days of hard and fruitless labor. It is a soldier seeing a light in the window or a returning prisoner finding yellow ribbons tied all over the tree. In prayer let us remember all the joy we have drawn from the wells of salvation. It should make quite a list.

WILLIAM STODDARD

ACTION POINT

If you risk living as if salvation were unimportant, take notice! What makes salvation great? Who revealed it? Who has proven it? Throughout the ages, God's people have rejoiced and celebrated his salvation. Go ahead, be amazed, and join them in praising God for his salvation!

HEBREWS 2:5 – 3:6

Christ Became Like Humans

5God did not choose angels to be the rulers of the new world that was coming, which is what we have been talking about. **6**It is written in the Scriptures,

"Why are people even important to you?
Why do you take care of human beings?
7You made them a little lower than the angels
and crowned them with glory and honor.
8You put all things under their control."

Psalm 8:4–6

When God put everything under their control, there was nothing left that they did not rule. Still, we do not yet see them ruling over everything. **9**But we see Jesus, who for a short time was made lower than the angels. And now he is wearing a crown of glory and honor because he suffered and died. And by God's grace, he died for everyone.

10God is the One who made all things, and all things are for his glory. He wanted to have many children share his glory, so he made the One who leads people to salvation perfect through suffering. **11**Jesus, who makes people holy, and those who are made holy are from the same family. So he is not ashamed to call them his brothers and sisters. **12**He says,

"Then, I will tell my brothers and sisters about you;
I will praise you in the public meeting."

Psalm 22:22

13He also says,

"I will trust in God." *Isaiah 8:17*

And he also says,

"I am here, and with me are the children God
has given me." *Isaiah 8:18*

14Since these children are people with physical bodies, Jesus himself became like them. He did this so that, by dying, he could destroy the one who has the power of death—the devil— **15**and free those who were like slaves all their lives because of their fear of death. **16**Clearly, it is not angels that Jesus helps, but the people who are from Abraham. **17**For this reason Jesus had to be made like his brothers and sisters in every way so he could be their merciful and faithful high priest in service to God. Then Jesus could die in their place to take away their sins. **18**And now he can help those who are tempted, because he himself suffered and was tempted.

Jesus Is Greater than Moses

3So all of you holy brothers and sisters, who were called by God, think about Jesus, who was sent to us and is the high priest of our faith. **2**Jesus was faithful to God as Moses was in God's family. **3**Jesus has more honor than Moses, just as the builder of a house has more honor than the house itself. **4**Every house is built by someone, but the builder of everything is God himself. **5**Moses was faithful in God's family as a servant, and he told what God would say in the future. **6**But Christ is faithful as a Son over God's house. And we are God's house if we confidently maintain our hope.

OLD TESTAMENT READING

I will make them one nation in the land, on the mountains of Israel. One king will rule all of them. They will never again be two nations; they will not be divided into two kingdoms anymore. **23b**I will save them from all the ways they sin and turn against me, and I will make them clean. Then they will be my people, and I will be their God.

24" 'My servant David will be their king, and they will all have one shepherd. They will live by my rules and obey my laws. **25**They will live on the land I gave to my servant Jacob, the land in which your ancestors lived. They will all live on the land forever: they, their children, and their grandchildren. David my servant will be their king forever. **26**I will make an agreement of peace with them, an agreement that continues forever. I will put them in their land and make them grow in number. Then I will put my Temple among them forever. **27**The place where I live will be with them. I will be their God, and they will be my people. **28**When my Temple is among them forever, the nations will know that I, the LORD, make Israel holy.' "

Ezekiel 37:22, 23b–28

INSIGHTS

Christ in us can manifest His holiness if we will yield our flesh to Him. This is not a human operation; it is a spiritual one. Jesus installs His holiness in us by grace. Not a once-for-all-time transaction, this is a daily, moment-by-moment striving to live more by the Spirit and less by the flesh.

Though becoming more holy is God's work in us, it is not a passive enterprise. Our part is active, to strive and strain toward the high calling we have received. God's part is to forgive our failings based on the merit of Christ's atoning death.

His will is that we become holy. . . . This kind of holiness is not the result of our own best effort. . . .

The forgiveness of Christ makes us holy; He washed away our sin. In reality, God in us—the Holy Spirit—makes us holy. There is no possibility of holiness apart from His grace. He calls us, He justifies us, He sanctifies us (makes us holy), and He will glorify us—all by His grace.

Our part is to surrender in faith; God's part is to implant the sanctifying Holy Spirit in us. "So I say, live by the Spirit, and you will not gratify the desires of the sinful nature" (Galatians 5:16). Because of His everlasting love, we know Him, and He is faithful to mold us into the character of His Son Jesus Christ—to make us holy.

PATRICK MORLEY

ACTION POINT

Meditate on what Jesus did to make his people holy. How significant is it that Jesus considers his holy people to be his family—his brothers? How do these truths inspire you to yield to his holiness?

HEBREWS 3:7 — 4:13

We Must Continue to Follow God

7So it is as the Holy Spirit says:

"Today listen to what he says.

8Do not be stubborn as in the past

when you turned against God,

when you tested God in the desert.

9There your ancestors tried me and tested me

and saw the things I did for forty years.

10I was angry with them.

I said, 'They are not loyal to me

and have not understood my ways.'

11I was angry and made a promise,

'They will never enter my rest.'"

Psalm 95:7–11

12So brothers and sisters, be careful that none of you has an evil, unbelieving heart that will turn you away from the living God. **13**But encourage each other every day while it is "today." Help each other so none of you will become hardened because sin has tricked you. **14**We all share in Christ if we keep till the end the sure faith we had in the beginning. **15**This is what the Scripture says:

"Today listen to what he says.

Do not be stubborn as in the past

when you turned against God."

Psalm 95:7–8

16Who heard God's voice and was against him? It was all those people Moses led out of Egypt. **17**And with whom was God angry for forty years? He was angry with those who sinned, who died in the desert. **18**And to whom was God talking when he promised that they would never enter his rest? He was talking to those who did not obey him. **19**So we see they were not allowed to enter and have God's rest, because they did not believe.

4 Now, since God has left us the promise that we may enter his rest, let us be very careful so none of you will fail to enter. **2**The Good News was preached to us just as it was to them. But the teaching they heard did not help them, because they heard it but did not accept it with faith. **3**We who have believed are able to enter and have God's rest. As God has said,

"I was angry and made a promise,

'They will never enter my rest.'"

Psalm 95:11

But God's work was finished from the time he made the world. **4**In the Scriptures he talked about the seventh day of the week: "And on the seventh day God rested from all his works." **5**And again in the Scripture God said, "They will never enter my rest."

6It is still true that some people will enter God's rest, but those who first heard the way to be saved did not enter, because they did not obey. **7**So God planned another day, called "today." He spoke about that day through David a long time later in the same Scripture used before:

"Today listen to what he says.

Do not be stubborn." *Psalm 95:7–8*

8We know that Joshua did not lead the people into that rest, because God spoke later about another day. **9**This shows that the rest for God's people is still coming. **10**Anyone who enters God's rest will rest from his work as God did. **11**Let us try as hard as we can to enter God's rest so that no one will fail by following the example of those who refused to obey.

¹²God's word is alive and working and is sharper than a double-edged sword. It cuts all the way into us, where the soul and the spirit are joined, to the center of our joints and bones. And it judges the thoughts and feelings in our hearts. ¹³Nothing in all the world can be hidden from God. Everything is clear and lies open before him, and to him we must explain the way we have lived.

OLD TESTAMENT READING

If the LORD is pleased with us, he will lead us into that land and give us that fertile land. ⁹Don't turn against the LORD! Don't be afraid of the people in that land! We will chew them up. They have no protection, but the LORD is with us. So don't be afraid of them."

²⁰The LORD answered, "I have forgiven them as you asked. ²¹But, as surely as I live and as surely as my glory fills the whole earth, I make this promise: ²²All these people saw my glory and the miracles I did in Egypt and in the desert, but they disobeyed me and tested me ten times. ²³So not one of them will see the land I promised to their ancestors. No one who rejected me will see that land."

Numbers 14:8–9, 20–23

INSIGHTS

How do we find God and grow in him? Jesus was adamant at this point. He said we must do what he says. We must put into practical obedience the knowledge that we have. He continually asked people to drop their nets, to sell all they had and to follow him.

We might say that Jesus had a theology of obedience. And the object of this obedience was a living person, not a historical norm, not a code of laws, but himself. He called people to be accountable to God whether they were believers or skeptics who were searching. For example, he told his disciples, "What is the point of calling me, 'Lord, Lord,' without doing what I tell you to do?" (Lk. 6:46 Phillips). . . .

Jesus knew that obedience to his and his Father's words yielded faith. . . . If I had to sum up one's response to the gospel message, I would say as William Pannell has said, "It's paint—or get off the ladder." Jesus approached people exactly like that. He told them to pick up their brush and paint something.

Do you want to discover who Jesus is and deal honestly with your doubts? Jesus' style is not to suggest that you go and ponder the virgin birth for three months but to begin doing what he says.

REBECCA PIPPERT

APPLICATION

What does an unbelieving heart lead us to do? What is the relationship between obedience and belief? When our life is over, what will God ask us to explain? Are you ready to answer him?

HEBREWS 4:14 — 6:8

Jesus Is Our High Priest

14Since we have a great high priest, Jesus the Son of God, who has gone into heaven, let us hold on to the faith we have. **15**For our high priest is able to understand our weaknesses. He was tempted in every way that we are, but he did not sin. **16**Let us, then, feel very sure that we can come before God's throne where there is grace. There we can receive mercy and grace to help us when we need it.

5 Every high priest is chosen from among other people. He is given the work of going before God for them to offer gifts and sacrifices for sins. **2**Since he himself is weak, he is able to be gentle with those who do not understand and who are doing wrong things. **3**Because he is weak, the high priest must offer sacrifices for his own sins and also for the sins of the people.

4To be a high priest is an honor, but no one chooses himself for this work. He must be called by God as Aaron was. **5**So also Christ did not choose himself to have the honor of being a high priest, but God chose him. God said to him,

"You are my Son.
Today I have become your Father."

Psalm 2:7

6And in another Scripture God says,

"You are a priest forever,
a priest like Melchizedek." *Psalm 110:4*

7While Jesus lived on earth, he prayed to God and asked God for help. He prayed with loud cries and tears to the One who could save him from death, and his prayer was heard because he trusted God. **8**Even though Jesus was the Son of God, he learned obedience by what he suffered. **9**And because his obedience was perfect, he was able to give eternal salvation to all who obey him. **10**In this way God made Jesus a high priest, a priest like Melchizedek.

Warning Against Falling Away

11We have much to say about this, but it is hard to explain because you are so slow to understand. **12**By now you should be teachers, but you need someone to teach you again the first lessons of God's message. You still need the teaching that is like milk. You are not ready for solid food. **13**Anyone who lives on milk is still a baby and knows nothing about right teaching. **14**But solid food is for those who are grown up. They are mature enough to know the difference between good and evil.

6 So let us go on to grown-up teaching. Let us not go back over the beginning lessons we learned about Christ. We should not again start teaching about faith in God and about turning away from those acts that lead to death. **2**We should not return to the teaching about baptisms, about laying on of hands, about the raising of the dead and eternal judgment. **3**And we will go on to grown-up teaching if God allows.

4Some people cannot be brought back again to a changed life. They were once in God's light, and enjoyed heaven's gift, and shared in the Holy Spirit. **5**They found out how good God's word is, and they received the powers of his new world. **6**But they fell away from Christ. It is impossible to bring them back to a changed life again, because they are nailing the Son of God to a cross again and are shaming him in front of others.

⁷Some people are like land that gets plenty of rain. The land produces a good crop for those who work it, and it receives God's blessings. ⁸Other people are like land that grows thorns and weeds and is worthless. It is about to be cursed by God and will be destroyed by fire.

OLD TESTAMENT READING

Tell your brother Aaron to come to you, along with his sons Nadab, Abihu, Eleazar, and Ithamar. Separate them from the other Israelites to serve me as priests. ²Make holy clothes for your brother Aaron to give him honor and beauty. ³Tell all the skilled craftsmen to whom I have given wisdom to make special clothes for Aaron— clothes to show that he belongs to me so that he may serve me as a priest."

Exodus 28:1–3

INSIGHTS

At one time in history a "NO ACCESS" sign was posted at the gates of Paradise. Even in the Old Testament temple there was no access to the throne of God by the ordinary person. Even for the High Priest his access was "limited" to once a year under very guarded circumstances. A thick veil separated the Holy of Holies from the rest of the temple. It was off-limits. Restricted. No admission was permitted to the rank-and-file believer.

The moment Jesus was slain, the instant the Just One died for the unjust, the veil in the temple was torn. The presence of God became accessible to us. For the Christian the "NO ACCESS" sign was removed from the gates of Paradise. We may now trespass freely on holy ground. We have access to His grace, but even more, we have access to Him. Justified men need no longer say to the Holy, "Depart from me, for I am a sinful man." Now we can be comfortable in the presence of a holy God. We can take our questions to Him. He is not too remote to hear our cries. We come as those covered by the righteousness of Christ. I repeat: We can be comfortable in the presence of God. To be sure we still come in awe, in a spirit of reverence and adoration, but the tremendous news is that we can . . . approach the throne of grace with confidence.

R. C. SPROUL

PAUSE FOR REFLECTION

From the Old Testament reading, do you begin to sense the vital role of God's priests? In what ways does your understanding of Christ's role as high priest (explained in Hebrews) help you realize how much he has done to save us?

HEBREWS 6:9 – 7:10

9Dear friends, we are saying this to you, but we really expect better things from you that will lead to your salvation. **10**God is fair; he will not forget the work you did and the love you showed for him by helping his people. And he will remember that you are still helping them. **11**We want each of you to go on with the same hard work all your lives so you will surely get what you hope for. **12**We do not want you to become lazy. Be like those who through faith and patience will receive what God has promised.

13God made a promise to Abraham. And as there is no one greater than God, he used himself when he swore to Abraham, **14**saying, "I will surely bless you and give you many descendants." **15**Abraham waited patiently for this to happen, and he received what God promised.

16People always use the name of someone greater than themselves when they swear. The oath proves that what they say is true, and this ends all arguing. **17**God wanted to prove that his promise was true to those who would get what he promised. And he wanted them to understand clearly that his purposes never change, so he made an oath. **18**These two things cannot change: God cannot lie when he makes a promise, and he cannot lie when he makes an oath. These things encourage us who came to God for safety. They give us strength to hold on to the hope we have been given. **19**We have this hope as an anchor for the soul, sure and strong. It enters behind the cur-

tain in the Most Holy Place in heaven, **20**where Jesus has gone ahead of us and for us. He has become the high priest forever, a priest like Melchizedek.

The Priest Melchizedek

7 Melchizedek was the king of Salem and a priest for God Most High. He met Abraham when Abraham was coming back after defeating the kings. When they met, Melchizedek blessed Abraham, **2**and Abraham gave him a tenth of everything he had brought back from the battle. First, Melchizedek's name means "king of goodness," and he is king of Salem, which means "king of peace." **3**No one knows who Melchizedek's father or mother was, where he came from, when he was born, or when he died. Melchizedek is like the Son of God; he continues being a priest forever.

4You can see how great Melchizedek was. Abraham, the great father, gave him a tenth of everything that he won in battle. **5**Now the law says that those in the tribe of Levi who become priests must collect a tenth from the people—their own people—even though the priests and the people are from the family of Abraham. **6**Melchizedek was not from the tribe of Levi, but he collected a tenth from Abraham. And he blessed Abraham, the man who had God's promises. **7**Now everyone knows that the more important person blesses the less important person. **8**Priests receive a tenth, even though they are only men who live and then die. But Melchizedek, who received a tenth from Abraham, continues living, as the Scripture says. **9**We might even say that Levi, who receives a tenth, also paid it when Abraham paid Melchizedek a tenth.

10Levi was not yet born, but he was in the body of his ancestor when Melchizedek met Abraham.

OLD TESTAMENT READING

The LORD your God will force out the people living there. The LORD will push them out ahead of you. And you will own the land, as he has promised you.

6"Be strong. You must be careful to obey everything commanded in the Book of the Teachings of Moses. Do not stray from it either from the left or the right.

14"It's almost time for me to die. You know and fully believe that the LORD has done great things for you. You know that he has not failed to keep any of his promises. **15**Every good promise that the LORD your God made has come true, and in the same way, his other promises will come true. He promised that evil will come to you and that he will destroy you from this good land that he gave you. **16**This will happen if you don't keep your agreement with the LORD your God. If you go and serve other gods and worship them, the LORD will become very angry with you. Then none of you will be left in this good land he has given you."

Joshua 23:5–6, 14–16

INSIGHTS

The Bible is filled with the promises of God. We need to claim each one by faith and activate its truth in our lives. Some folks like to say, "If God said it, I believe it, and that settles it!" The fact of the matter is, if God said it, that settles it, whether we believe it or not.

Someone will question, "How can I be sure God really said this?" or, "How can I be sure this is what it means?" I realize we must interpret each promise in its proper context. But I also believe that we need to take those promises which apply to us and activate them by faith.

In Hebrews 4:3, we read an amazing truth. It says there that God's works were "finished from the foundation of the world." In other words, God had already provided the answer to your every need before the world was ever formed. With His divine foreknowledge He looked down the corridor of time to come, saw your coming problem and provided just exactly what you would need. . . .

. . . Think on the majesty and magnitude of God. Focus on the promises He has given you in His Word. Turn your attention to fulfilling His purpose for your life. Live in the confidence that He is in control. Now you can relax, for there is nothing to worry about. God cares and He keeps His promises to help.

RICHARD LEE

APPLICATION

What about God's character encourages us to trust in his promises? Of what did Joshua remind the Israelites before he died? Why is it important to remember that God keeps his promises? Will you remember to live by his promises?

HEBREWS 7:11 – 8:6

11The people were given the law concerning the system of priests from the tribe of Levi, but they could not be made perfect through that system. So there was a need for another priest to come, a priest like Melchizedek, not Aaron. **12**And when a different kind of priest comes, the law must be changed, too. **13**We are saying these things about Christ, who belonged to a different tribe. No one from that tribe ever served as a priest at the altar. **14**It is clear that our Lord came from the tribe of Judah, and Moses said nothing about priests belonging to that tribe.

Jesus Is like Melchizedek

15And this becomes even more clear when we see that another priest comes who is like Melchizedek. **16**He was not made a priest by human rules and laws but through the power of his life, which continues forever. **17**It is said about him,

"You are a priest forever,
    a priest like Melchizedek."   *Psalm 110:4*

18The old rule is now set aside, because it was weak and useless. **19**The law of Moses could not make anything perfect. But now a better hope has been given to us, and with this hope we can come near to God. **20**It is important that God did this with an oath. Others became priests without an oath, **21**but Christ became a priest with God's oath. God said:

"The Lord has made a promise
    and will not change his mind.
'You are a priest forever.'"   *Psalm 110:4*

22This means that Jesus is the guarantee of a better agreement from God to his people.

23When one of the other priests died, he could not continue being a priest. So there were many priests. **24**But because Jesus lives forever, he will never stop serving as priest. **25**So he is able always to save those who come to God through him because he always lives, asking God to help them.

26Jesus is the kind of high priest we need. He is holy, sinless, pure, not influenced by sinners, and he is raised above the heavens. **27**He is not like the other priests who had to offer sacrifices every day, first for their own sins, and then for the sins of the people. Christ offered his sacrifice only once and for all time when he offered himself. **28**The law chooses high priests who are people with weaknesses, but the word of God's oath came later than the law. It made God's Son to be the high priest, and that Son has been made perfect forever.

Jesus Is Our High Priest

8 Here is the point of what we are saying: We have a high priest who sits on the right side of God's throne in heaven. **2**Our high priest serves in the Most Holy Place, the true place of worship that was made by God, not by humans.

3Every high priest has the work of offering gifts and sacrifices to God. So our high priest must also offer something to God. **4**If our high priest were now living on earth, he would not be a priest, because there are already priests here who follow the law by offering gifts to God. **5**The work they do as priests is only a copy and a shadow of what is in heaven. This is why God warned Moses when he was ready to build the Holy Tent: "Be very careful to make everything by the plan I showed you on the mountain." **6**But the priestly work that has been given to Jesus is much greater than the work that was given to the other priests. In the same way, the new agreement that Jesus brought from God to his people is much greater than the old one. And the new agreement is based on promises of better things.

OLD TESTAMENT READING

The LORD said to my Lord,
"Sit by me at my right side
until I put your enemies under your
control."
2The LORD will enlarge your kingdom beyond
Jerusalem,
and you will rule over your enemies.

3Your people will join you on your day of
battle.
You have been dressed in holiness from
birth;
you have the freshness of a child.

4The LORD has made a promise
and will not change his mind.
He said, "You are a priest forever,
a priest like Melchizedek."

Psalm 110:1–4

This is the agreement I will make
with the people of Israel at that time," says
the LORD:
"I will put my teachings in their minds
and write them on their hearts.
I will be their God,
and they will be my people."

Jeremiah 31:33

INSIGHTS

We need a priest such as Jesus is, to represent us in heaven. Although we are so completely absolved from guilt, and so fully "accepted in the beloved", yet in ourselves, while down here, we are still erring, sinning, feeble, needy creatures, exposed to trials and temptations, liable to stumble, and encompassed by infirmities. How we need the high priestly mediation of our dear heavenly Advocate, whose presence yonder keeps us in all the benefits of the New Covenant, maintains our standing in grace, and releases to us the paraclete ministries of the Holy Spirit. It has been well said, "We could not stand for a moment down here, if He were not living for us up there."

Thank God, "we have such an high priest"!

J. SIDLOW BAXTER

ACTION POINT

Identify the unique aspects of Christ's priesthood and describe why his unique role as high priest is significant. Pray now and thank God that he has sent a high priest—like no other—to offer the only perfect sacrifice for your sins.

HEBREWS 8:7 – 9:12

7 If there had been nothing wrong with the first agreement, there would have been no need for a second agreement. **8** But God found something wrong with his people. He says:

"Look, the time is coming, says the Lord,
　when I will make a new agreement
with the people of Israel
　and the people of Judah.
9 It will not be like the agreement
　I made with their ancestors
when I took them by the hand
　to bring them out of Egypt.
But they broke that agreement,
　and I turned away from them, says the Lord.
10 This is the agreement I will make
　with the people of Israel at that time, says
　　the Lord.
I will put my teachings in their minds
　and write them on their hearts.
I will be their God,
　and they will be my people.
11 People will no longer have to teach their
　　neighbors and relatives
　to know the Lord,
because all people will know me,
　from the least to the most important.
12 I will forgive them for the wicked things they
　did,
　and I will not remember their sins
　　anymore."　　　　*Jeremiah 31:31–34*
13 God called this a new agreement, so he has

made the first agreement old. And anything that is old and worn out is ready to disappear.

The Old Agreement

The first agreement had rules for worship and a place on earth for worship. **2** The Holy Tent was set up for this. The first area in the Tent was called the Holy Place. In it were the lamp and the table with the bread that was made holy for God. **3** Behind the second curtain was a room called the Most Holy Place. **4** In it was a golden altar for burning incense and the Ark covered with gold that held the old agreement. Inside this Ark was a golden jar of manna, Aaron's rod that once grew leaves, and the stone tablets of the old agreement. **5** Above the Ark were the creatures that showed God's glory, whose wings reached over the lid. But we cannot tell everything about these things now.

6 When everything in the Tent was made ready in this way, the priests went into the first room every day to worship. **7** But only the high priest could go into the second room, and he did that only once a year. He could never enter the inner room without taking blood with him, which he offered to God for himself and for sins the people did without knowing they did them. **8** The Holy Spirit uses this to show that the way into the Most Holy Place was not open while the system of the old Holy Tent was still being used. **9** This is an example for the present time. It shows that the gifts and sacrifices offered cannot make the conscience of the worshiper perfect. **10** These gifts and sacrifices were only about food and drink and special washings. They were rules for the body, to be followed until the time of God's new way.

The New Agreement

11But when Christ came as the high priest of the good things we now have, he entered the greater and more perfect tent. It is not made by humans and does not belong to this world. **12**Christ entered the Most Holy Place only once—and for all time. He did not take with him the blood of goats and calves. His sacrifice was his own blood, and by it he set us free from sin forever.

OLD TESTAMENT READING

But it was the LORD who decided
to crush him and make him suffer.
The LORD made his life a penalty offering,
but he will still see his descendants and live a
long life.
He will complete the things the LORD wants
him to do.
11"After his soul suffers many things,
he will see life and be satisfied.
My good servant will make many people right
with God;
he will carry away their sins."

Isaiah 53:10–11

INSIGHTS

"If we confess our sins, he is faithful and just and will forgive us our sins and purify us from all unrighteousness" (1 John 1:9). This verse tells us what to do when we've sinned—we must confess that we have sinned and need forgiveness.

Then if we confess, God promises to forgive. He takes care of that sin once and for all. He restores our relationship with him. . . .

. . . At the center of forgiveness is always the cross of Christ. Without his body on the cross, forgiveness would not even be available. Forgiveness is costly, and we need to see it from that perspective. There is no forgiveness without tears, without a price to be paid, without the sacrifice of Christ.

Because of Christ's sacrifice, sin need not defeat us. . . .

Though we cannot eliminate the temptation to sin, we are not left without redemptive resources. God is on our side, Jesus is advocating for us, and the Holy Spirit is making us aware of our weaknesses as our Teacher and Guide.

DAVID MCKENNA

PAUSE FOR REFLECTION

Describe the many differences between the old and new agreements. What difference does it make that Jesus is now our high priest? Pray and thank God that the blood of Jesus takes away our sins forever.

HEBREWS
9:13 — 10:10

13The blood of goats and bulls and the ashes of a cow are sprinkled on the people who are unclean, and this makes their bodies clean again. **14**How much more is done by the blood of Christ. He offered himself through the eternal Spirit as a perfect sacrifice to God. His blood will make our consciences pure from useless acts so we may serve the living God.

15For this reason Christ brings a new agreement from God to his people. Those who are called by God can now receive the blessings he has promised, blessings that will last forever. They can have those things because Christ died so that the people who lived under the first agreement could be set free from sin.

16When there is a will, it must be proven that the one who wrote that will is dead. **17**A will means nothing while the person is alive; it can be used only after the person dies. **18**This is why even the first agreement could not begin without blood to show death. **19**First, Moses told all the people every command in the law. Next he took the blood of calves and mixed it with water. Then he used red wool and a branch of the hyssop plant to sprinkle it on the book of the law and on all the people. **20**He said, "This is the blood that begins the Agreement that God commanded you to obey." **21**In the same way, Moses sprinkled the blood on the Holy Tent and over all the things used in worship. **22**The law says that almost everything must be made clean by blood, and sins cannot be forgiven without blood to show death.

Christ's Death Takes Away Sins

23So the copies of the real things in heaven had to be made clean by animal sacrifices. But the real things in heaven need much better sacrifices. **24**Christ did not go into the Most Holy Place made by humans, which is only a copy of the real one. He went into heaven itself and is there now before God to help us. **25**The high priest enters the Most Holy Place once every year with blood that is not his own. But Christ did not offer himself many times. **26**Then he would have had to suffer many times since the world was made. But Christ came only once and for all time at just the right time to take away all sin by sacrificing himself. **27**Just as everyone must die once and then be judged, **28**so Christ was offered as a sacrifice one time to take away the sins of many people. And he will come a second time, not to offer himself for sin, but to bring salvation to those who are waiting for him.

10 The law is only an unclear picture of the good things coming in the future; it is not the real thing. The people under the law offer the same sacrifices every year, but these sacrifices can never make perfect those who come near to worship God. **2**If the law could make them perfect, the sacrifices would have already stopped. The worshipers would be made clean, and they would no longer have a sense of sin. **3**But these sacrifices remind them of their sins every year, **4**because it is impossible for the blood of bulls and goats to take away sins.

⁵So when Christ came into the world, he said:
"You do not want sacrifices and offerings,
but you have prepared a body for me.
⁶You do not ask for burnt offerings
and offerings to take away sins.
⁷Then I said, 'Look, I have come.
It is written about me in the book.
God, I have come to do what you want.'"

Psalm 40:6–8

⁸In this Scripture he first said, "You do not want sacrifices and offerings. You do not ask for burnt offerings and offerings to take away sins." (These are all sacrifices that the law commands.) ⁹Then he said, "Look, I have come to do what you want." God ends the first system of sacrifices so he can set up the new system. ¹⁰And because of this, we are made holy through the sacrifice Christ made in his body once and for all time.

OLD TESTAMENT READING

Then Aaron must kill the goat of the sin offering for the people and bring its blood into the room behind the curtain. He must do with the goat's blood as he did with the bull's blood, sprinkling it on the lid and in front of the lid. ¹⁷ᵇSo Aaron will perform the acts to remove sins from himself, his family, and all the people of Israel, so they will belong to the LORD.

³⁴"That law for removing the sins of the Israelites so they will belong to the LORD will continue forever. You will do these things once a year."

So they did the things the LORD had commanded Moses.

Leviticus 16:15, 17b, 34

INSIGHTS

When we sin, our only option is repentance. Without repentance there is no forgiveness. We must come before God in contrition. David put it this way:

"For thou has no delight in sacrifice. . . . The sacrifice acceptable to God is a broken spirit; a broken and contrite heart, O God, thou wilt not despise" [Psalm 51:16, 17].

Here David's profound thoughts reveal his understanding of what many Old Testament persons failed to grasp—that the offering of sacrifices in the temple did not gain merit for the sinner. Sacrifices pointed beyond themselves to the perfect Sacrifice. The perfect atonement was offered by the perfect Lamb without blemish. The blood of bulls and goats does not take away sin. The blood of Jesus does. To avail ourselves of the atonement of Christ, to gain that covering, requires that we come before God in brokenness and contrition. The true sacrifices of God are a broken spirit and a contrite heart.

R. C. SPROUL

APPLICATION

What does the sacrifice of Christ's blood accomplish that no other sacrifice can do? What kind of sacrifice does God want from his people? What has Christ's sacrifice done for you personally?

HEBREWS 10:11-39

¹¹Every day the priests stand and do their religious service, often offering the same sacrifices. Those sacrifices can never take away sins. ¹²But after Christ offered one sacrifice for sins, forever, he sat down at the right side of God. ¹³And now Christ waits there for his enemies to be put under his power. ¹⁴With one sacrifice he made perfect forever those who are being made holy.

¹⁵The Holy Spirit also tells us about this. First he says:

¹⁶ "This is the agreement I will make
 with them at that time, says the Lord.
I will put my teachings in their hearts
 and write them on their minds."

Jeremiah 31:33

¹⁷ Then he says:

"Their sins and the evil things they do—
 I will not remember anymore."

Jeremiah 31:34

¹⁸Now when these have been forgiven, there is no more need for a sacrifice for sins.

Continue to Trust God

¹⁹So, brothers and sisters, we are completely free to enter the Most Holy Place without fear because of the blood of Jesus' death. ²⁰We can enter through a new and living way that Jesus opened for us. It leads through the curtain—Christ's body. ²¹And since we have a great priest over God's house, ²²let us come near to God with a sincere heart and a sure faith, because we have been made free from a guilty conscience, and our bodies have been washed with pure water. ²³Let us hold firmly to the hope that we have confessed, because we can trust God to do what he promised.

²⁴Let us think about each other and help each other to show love and do good deeds. ²⁵You should not stay away from the church meetings, as some are doing, but you should meet together and encourage each other. Do this even more as you see the day coming.

²⁶If we decide to go on sinning after we have learned the truth, there is no longer any sacrifice for sins. ²⁷There is nothing but fear in waiting for the judgment and the terrible fire that will destroy all those who live against God. ²⁸Anyone who refused to obey the law of Moses was found guilty from the proof given by two or three witnesses. He was put to death without mercy. ²⁹So what do you think should be done to those who do not respect the Son of God, who look at the blood of the agreement that made them holy as no different from others' blood, who insult the Spirit of God's grace? Surely they should have a much worse punishment. ³⁰We know that God said, "I will punish those who do wrong; I will repay them." And he also said, "The Lord will judge his people." ³¹It is a terrible thing to fall into the hands of the living God.

³²Remember those days in the past when you first learned the truth. You had a hard struggle with many sufferings, but you continued strong. ³³Sometimes you were hurt and attacked before crowds of people, and sometimes you shared with those who were being treated that way. ³⁴You helped the prisoners. You even had joy when all

that you owned was taken from you, because you knew you had something better and more lasting.

35So do not lose the courage you had in the past, which has a great reward. 36You must hold on, so you can do what God wants and receive what he has promised. 37For in a very short time,

"The One who is coming will come
and will not be delayed.
38 Those who are right with me
will live by faith.
But if they turn back with fear,
I will not be pleased with them."

Habakkuk 2:3–4

39But we are not those who turn back and are lost. We are people who have faith and are saved.

OLD TESTAMENT READING

The LORD will judge the people with fire,
and he will destroy many people with his
sword;
he will kill many people.

Isaiah 66:16

Try to do good, not evil,
so that you will live,
and the LORD God All-Powerful will be with
you
just as you say he is.

Amos 5:14

INSIGHTS

Without a physical order in the universe, there could be no science.

Much of the genius of our space program involves achieving the most precise knowledge and conformity to this order. Failure means disaster.

Tens of thousands of man-hours, the most sophisticated technology, and the latest advances in space science are involved. . . . But all of it is helpless without an orderly universe to count on, and conform to.

God, who ordained physical order, also ordained moral and spiritual order. Conformity guarantees fulfillment. Disobedience spells destruction. . . .

One can reject God's moral absolutes. But that does not get rid of them. The law of sin and death is just as inviolable as the law of gravity. Morality isn't arbitrary. It's part of the natural law of the universe. God's law stands whether we like it or not.

We ignore this fact to our doom. Violating God's physical law is destructive, but violating His moral law is infinitely more serious—for it has eternal consequences.

Every malfunction of the social order in America derives from our transgression of God's moral law. If we refuse to turn to God for mercy and grace, we condemn ourselves to His inexorable justice and judgment.

RICHARD HALVERSON

APPLICATION

What will happen to everyone who lives against God? What is promised to those who continue living by faith? Pray for the courage to live as God wants his people to live.

HEBREWS 11:1-22

What Is Faith?

11 Faith means being sure of the things we hope for and knowing that something is real even if we do not see it. **2** Faith is the reason we remember great people who lived in the past.

3 It is by faith we understand that the whole world was made by God's command so what we see was made by something that cannot be seen.

4 It was by faith that Abel offered God a better sacrifice than Cain did. God said he was pleased with the gifts Abel offered and called Abel a good man because of his faith. Abel died, but through his faith he is still speaking.

5 It was by faith that Enoch was taken to heaven so he would not die. He could not be found, because God had taken him away. Before he was taken, the Scripture says that he was a man who truly pleased God. **6** Without faith no one can please God. Anyone who comes to God must believe that he is real and that he rewards those who truly want to find him.

7 It was by faith that Noah heard God's warnings about things he could not yet see. He obeyed God and built a large boat to save his family. By his faith, Noah showed that the world was wrong, and he became one of those who are made right with God through faith.

8 It was by faith Abraham obeyed God's call to go to another place God promised to give him. He left his own country, not knowing where he was to go. **9** It was by faith that he lived like a foreigner in the country God promised to give him. He lived in tents with Isaac and Jacob, who had received that same promise from God. **10** Abraham was waiting for the city that has real foundations—the city planned and built by God.

11 He was too old to have children, and Sarah could not have children. It was by faith that Abraham was made able to become a father, because he trusted God to do what he had promised. **12** This man was so old he was almost dead, but from him came as many descendants as there are stars in the sky. Like the sand on the seashore, they could not be counted.

13 All these great people died in faith. They did not get the things that God promised his people, but they saw them coming far in the future and were glad. They said they were like visitors and strangers on earth. **14** When people say such things, they show they are looking for a country that will be their own. **15** If they had been thinking about the country they had left, they could have gone back. **16** But they were waiting for a better country—a heavenly country. So God is not ashamed to be called their God, because he has prepared a city for them.

17 It was by faith that Abraham, when God tested him, offered his son Isaac as a sacrifice. God made the promises to Abraham, but Abraham was ready to offer his own son as a sacrifice. **18** God had said, "The descendants I promised you will be from Isaac." **19** Abraham believed that God could raise the dead, and really, it was as if Abraham got Isaac back from death.

20 It was by faith that Isaac blessed the future of Jacob and Esau. **21** It was by faith that Jacob, as he was dying, blessed each one of Joseph's sons. Then he worshiped as he leaned on the top of his walking stick.

²²It was by faith that Joseph, while he was dying, spoke about the Israelites leaving Egypt and gave instructions about what to do with his body.

OLD TESTAMENT READING

Then God led Abram outside and said, "Look at the sky. There are so many stars you cannot count them. Your descendants also will be too many to count."

⁶Abram believed the LORD. And the LORD accepted Abram's faith, and that faith made him right with God.

Genesis 15:5–6

INSIGHTS

Faith is my deliberate and positive response to the good in another to the extent that I will act on his behalf in a personal, powerful way. . . .

. . . It means that I am willing to share my life along with all its capacities (time, strength, attention, talents, means, energy, affection, acceptance) with another. It means that I actively, energetically give of my best to another outside of and apart from myself.

To speak of faith in any other way than this is to indulge in mere "believism." It is to play around with pious platitudes that pack no punch at all. This sort of superficial spirituality is actually the great bane of Christianity. Literally hundreds of thousands of people claim they trust in God; they claim to have faith in Christ; they claim to be believers, yet their lives and personal conduct are a denial and travesty of true faith. . . .

. . . When our Lord lived amongst us He was continually looking for this dynamic trust and response to Himself. Whenever He found even the tiniest fragment of faith being exercised in Him He was delighted.

W. PHILLIP KELLER

ACTION POINT

Is faith for things in the past, present, or future? In what ways is faith a catalyst in your life? Pray that your faith will be a delight to God.

HEBREWS 11:23 — 12:6

23It was by faith that Moses' parents hid him for three months after he was born. They saw that Moses was a beautiful baby, and they were not afraid to disobey the king's order.

24It was by faith that Moses, when he grew up, refused to be called the son of the king of Egypt's daughter. **25**He chose to suffer with God's people instead of enjoying sin for a short time. **26**He thought it was better to suffer for the Christ than to have all the treasures of Egypt, because he was looking for God's reward. **27**It was by faith that Moses left Egypt and was not afraid of the king's anger. Moses continued strong as if he could see the God that no one can see. **28**It was by faith that Moses prepared the Passover and spread the blood on the doors so the one who brings death would not kill the firstborn sons of Israel.

29It was by faith that the people crossed the Red Sea as if it were dry land. But when the Egyptians tried it, they were drowned.

30It was by faith that the walls of Jericho fell after the people had marched around them for seven days.

31It was by faith that Rahab, the prostitute, welcomed the spies and was not killed with those who refused to obey God.

32Do I need to give more examples? I do not have time to tell you about Gideon, Barak, Samson, Jephthah, David, Samuel, and the prophets. **33**Through their faith they defeated kingdoms. They did what was right, received God's promises, and shut the mouths of lions. **34**They stopped great fires and were saved from being killed with swords. They were weak, and yet were made strong. They were powerful in battle and defeated other armies. **35**Women received their dead relatives raised back to life. Others were tortured and refused to accept their freedom so they could be raised from the dead to a better life. **36**Some were laughed at and beaten. Others were put in chains and thrown into prison. **37**They were stoned to death, they were cut in half, and they were killed with swords. Some wore the skins of sheep and goats. They were poor, abused, and treated badly. **38**The world was not good enough for them! They wandered in deserts and mountains, living in caves and holes in the earth.

39All these people are known for their faith, but none of them received what God had promised. **40**God planned to give us something better so that they would be made perfect, but only together with us.

Follow Jesus' Example

12 We are surrounded by a great cloud of people whose lives tell us what faith means. So let us run the race that is before us and never give up. We should remove from our lives anything that would get in the way and the sin that so easily holds us back. **2**Let us look only to Jesus, the One who began our faith and who makes it perfect. He suffered death on the cross. But he accepted the shame as if it were nothing because of the joy that God put before him. And now he is sitting at the right side of God's throne. **3**Think about Jesus' example. He held on while wicked people were doing evil things to him. So do not get tired and stop trying.

God Is like a Father

⁴You are struggling against sin, but your struggles have not yet caused you to be killed. ⁵You have forgotten the encouraging words that call you his children:

"My child, don't think the Lord's discipline is worth nothing,
and don't stop trying when he corrects you.
⁶The Lord disciplines those he loves,
and he punishes everyone he accepts as his child." *Proverbs 3:11–12*

OLD TESTAMENT READING

The one whom God corrects is happy,
so do not hate being corrected by the Almighty.
¹⁸God hurts, but he also bandages up;
he injures, but his hands also heal." *Job 5:17–18*

INSIGHTS

Most of us don't want to be broken in the storms of life. We much prefer to protect our personalities from the stresses and strains of our days. We would rather, much rather, be tough and rugged and self-assured than contrite before Christ, repentant in soul before His Spirit. . . .

Many of us would like to avoid the mills of God. We are tempted to ask Him to deliver us from the upsetting, tumbling tides of time that knock off our rough corners and shape us to His design. We plead for release from the discipline of difficulties, the rub of routine responsibilities, the polish that comes from long perseverance.

We are a restless generation. We of the West want and insist on instant results. We demand a quick fix. We look for shortcuts and immediate results. We are quite sure we can be a rough slab of stone today and a polished gemstone tomorrow.

But God's ways and our ways are not the same. His patience is persistent. His work is meticulous. His years know no end. His perception of time is that one day is as a thousand years and a thousand years as but a single day.

The shattering of rock, the smoothing of stone, the polishing of a jewel in the sea requires eons of time. Can I then expect the breaking of my hard heart, the smoothing of my spirit, the shaping of my character as it is conformed to His own to be any less time-consuming?

W. PHILLIP KELLER

APPLICATION

What is the relationship between having faith and receiving God's correction? In what way does correction help us remove sin from our lives? Pray that you will feel God's great love as he corrects you!

HEBREWS 12:7-29

7So hold on through your sufferings, because they are like a father's discipline. God is treating you as children. All children are disciplined by their fathers. 8If you are never disciplined (and every child must be disciplined), you are not true children. 9We have all had fathers here on earth who disciplined us, and we respected them. So it is even more important that we accept discipline from the Father of our spirits so we will have life. 10Our fathers on earth disciplined us for a short time in the way they thought was best. But God disciplines us to help us, so we can become holy as he is. 11We do not enjoy being disciplined. It is painful at the time, but later, after we have learned from it, we have peace, because we start living in the right way.

Be Careful How You Live

12You have become weak, so make yourselves strong again. 13Keep on the right path, so the weak will not stumble but rather be strengthened.

14Try to live in peace with all people, and try to live free from sin. Anyone whose life is not holy will never see the Lord. 15Be careful that no one fails to receive God's grace and begins to cause trouble among you. A person like that can ruin many of you. 16Be careful that no one takes part in sexual sin or is like Esau and never thinks about God. As the oldest son, Esau would have received everything from his father, but he sold all that for a single meal. 17You remember that after Esau did this, he wanted to get his father's blessing, but his

father refused. Esau could find no way to change what he had done, even though he wanted the blessing so much that he cried.

18You have not come to a mountain that can be touched and that is burning with fire. You have not come to darkness, sadness, and storms. 19You have not come to the noise of a trumpet or to the sound of a voice like the one the people of Israel heard and begged not to hear another word. 20They did not want to hear the command: "If anything, even an animal, touches the mountain, it must be put to death with stones." 21What they saw was so terrible that Moses said, "I am shaking with fear."

22But you have come to Mount Zion, to the city of the living God, the heavenly Jerusalem. You have come to thousands of angels gathered together with joy. 23You have come to the meeting of God's firstborn children whose names are written in heaven. You have come to God, the judge of all people, and to the spirits of good people who have been made perfect. 24You have come to Jesus, the One who brought the new agreement from God to his people, and you have come to the sprinkled blood that has a better message than the blood of Abel.

25So be careful and do not refuse to listen when God speaks. Others refused to listen to him when he warned them on earth, and they did not escape. So it will be worse for us if we refuse to listen to God who warns us from heaven. 26When he spoke before, his voice shook the earth, but now he has promised, "Once again I will shake not only the earth but also the heavens." 27The words "once again" clearly show us that everything that was made—things that can be shaken—will be destroyed. Only the things that cannot be shaken will remain.

28So let us be thankful, because we have a kingdom that cannot be shaken. We should worship God in a way that pleases him with respect and fear, **29**because our God is like a fire that burns things up.

OLD TESTAMENT READING

David felt ashamed after he had counted the people. He said to the LORD, "I have sinned greatly by what I have done. LORD, I beg you to forgive me, your servant, because I have been very foolish."

15So the LORD sent a terrible disease on Israel.

17When David saw the angel that killed the people, he said to the LORD, "I am the one who sinned and did wrong. These people only followed me like sheep. They did nothing wrong. Please punish me and my family."

18That day Gad came to David and said, "Go and build an altar to the LORD on the threshing floor of Araunah the Jebusite." **19**So David did what Gad told him to do, just as the LORD commanded.

25b Then the LORD answered his prayer for the country, and the disease in Israel stopped.

2 Samuel 24:10, 15a, 17–19, 25b

INSIGHTS

Just as a caring parent will lovingly discipline and train his child, so God lovingly disciplines us. We live in a world of mystery and unexplained enigmas, so it is not surprising that the element of mystery should invade this realm too. Indeed, our Lord indicated that it would be so. "What I do you do not realize now; but you shall understand hereafter" (John 13:7). If we are to experience serenity in this turbulent world, we will need to take firmer grasp of God's sovereignty and trust His love even when we cannot discern His purpose. We must remember that the hand molding the clay is nail-pierced, and that our God's sovereignty will never clash with His paternity. "But now, O LORD, Thou art our Father, we are the clay, and Thou our potter" (Isa. 64:8). If we are to enjoy a deepening intimacy with God, we must react to His providential dealings in a spiritual way, even though they may be inscrutable. These dealings may take various forms, but all are planned in love, and with a view to cultivating a deeper intimacy with God.

J. OSWALD SANDERS

PAUSE FOR REFLECTION

Why does God punish his people? What did God's punishment accomplish in David's life (2 Samuel 24)? Do you think David realized how seriously he had sinned before God punished him? What causes you to recognize the seriousness of your sin?

HEBREWS 13:1-25

13 Keep on loving each other as brothers and sisters. **2** Remember to welcome strangers, because some who have done this have welcomed angels without knowing it. **3** Remember those who are in prison as if you were in prison with them. Remember those who are suffering as if you were suffering with them.

4 Marriage should be honored by everyone, and husband and wife should keep their marriage pure. God will judge as guilty those who take part in sexual sins. **5** Keep your lives free from the love of money, and be satisfied with what you have. God has said,

"I will never leave you;
I will never abandon you."

Deuteronomy 31:6

6 So we can be sure when we say,

"I will not be afraid, because the Lord is my helper.
People can't do anything to me."

Psalm 118:6

7 Remember your leaders who taught God's message to you. Remember how they lived and died, and copy their faith. **8** Jesus Christ is the same yesterday, today, and forever.

9 Do not let all kinds of strange teachings lead you into the wrong way. Your hearts should be strengthened by God's grace, not by obeying rules about foods, which do not help those who obey them.

10 We have a sacrifice, but the priests who serve in the Holy Tent cannot eat from it. **11** The high priest carries the blood of animals into the Most Holy Place where he offers this blood for sins. But the bodies of the animals are burned outside the camp. **12** So Jesus also suffered outside the city to make his people holy with his own blood. **13** So let us go to Jesus outside the camp, holding on as he did when we are abused.

14 Here on earth we do not have a city that lasts forever, but we are looking for the city that we will have in the future. **15** So through Jesus let us always offer to God our sacrifice of praise, coming from lips that speak his name. **16** Do not forget to do good to others, and share with them, because such sacrifices please God.

17 Obey your leaders and act under their authority. They are watching over you, because they are responsible for your souls. Obey them so that they will do this work with joy, not sadness. It will not help you to make their work hard.

18 Pray for us. We are sure that we have a clear conscience, because we always want to do the right thing. **19** I especially beg you to pray so that God will send me back to you soon.

20-21 I pray that the God of peace will give you every good thing you need so you can do what he wants. God raised from the dead our Lord Jesus, the Great Shepherd of the sheep, because of the blood of his death. His blood began the eternal agreement that God made with his people. I pray that God will do in us what pleases him, through Jesus Christ, and to him be glory forever and ever. Amen.

22 My brothers and sisters, I beg you to listen

patiently to this message I have written to encourage you, because it is not very long. **23**I want you to know that our brother Timothy has been let out of prison. If he arrives soon, we will both come to see you.

24Greet all your leaders and all of God's people. Those from Italy send greetings to you.

25Grace be with you all.

OLD TESTAMENT READING

Respect the LORD your God, and do what he has told you to do. Love him. Serve the LORD your God with your whole being, **13**and obey the LORD's commands and laws that I am giving you today for your own good.

16Give yourselves completely to serving him, and do not be stubborn any longer. **18**He helps orphans and widows, and he loves foreigners and gives them food and clothes. **19**You also must love foreigners, because you were foreigners in Egypt. **20**Respect the LORD your God and serve him. Be loyal to him and make your promises in his name. **21**He is the one you should praise; he is your God, who has done great and wonderful things for you, which you have seen with your own eyes.

Deuteronomy 10:12b–13, 16, 18–21

INSIGHTS

In recent decades the phrase "easy believism" has surfaced. Unfortunately, it describes a large number of contemporary Christians who have received Christ as Savior but do not, in practice, regard Him as Lord. They seem to have received Him in order to reach heaven someday or to get help for their problems, but they have never fully committed to trust, obey, honor and serve Him as a way of life.

Our Lord never intended that we be His casual acquaintances. He wants us to be His disciples, fully dedicated to following Him and lifting up His holy name to the world. . . . Our Lord is repulsed by mediocre commitment. . . .

. . . When we acknowledge Christ as our Lord, we affirm that He is our Master for life and that we are dedicated to serving and glorifying Him. In all things, large and small, our deepest desire is to do what our Lord would want us to do. We ask for His guidance—not for our gain, but for His glory. We discipline ourselves in studying and obeying His written Word. We proclaim His love to the world around us. We try to think, speak and act in a way that will attract others to Him.

The misguided person who thinks all this is too difficult or irrelevant misses the point. The Christian life is far more than a fire escape from hell; it is the life of submission and obedience which result in joy and victory.

BILL BRIGHT

ACTION POINT

Describe the kind of life God has called his people to live (in both Old and New Testaments). Pray that living such a life will be of utmost importance to you. Make that commitment today!

JAMES 1:1-27

1 From James, a servant of God and of the Lord Jesus Christ.

To all of God's people who are scattered everywhere in the world:

Greetings.

Faith and Wisdom

2My brothers and sisters, when you have many kinds of troubles, you should be full of joy, **3**because you know that these troubles test your faith, and this will give you patience. **4**Let your patience show itself perfectly in what you do. Then you will be perfect and complete and will have everything you need. **5**But if any of you needs wisdom, you should ask God for it. He is generous to everyone and will give you wisdom without criticizing you. **6**But when you ask God, you must believe and not doubt. Anyone who doubts is like a wave in the sea, blown up and down by the wind. **7-8**Such doubters are thinking two different things at the same time, and they cannot decide about anything they do. They should not think they will receive anything from the Lord.

True Riches

9Believers who are poor should take pride that God has made them spiritually rich. **10**Those who are rich should take pride that God has shown them that they are spiritually poor. The rich will die like a wild flower in the grass. **11**The sun rises with burning heat and dries up the plants. The flower falls off, and its beauty is gone. In the same way the rich will die while they are still taking care of business.

Temptation Is Not from God

12When people are tempted and still continue strong, they should be happy. After they have proved their faith, God will reward them with life forever. God promised this to all those who love him. **13**When people are tempted, they should not say, "God is tempting me." Evil cannot tempt God, and God himself does not tempt anyone. **14**But people are tempted when their own evil desire leads them away and traps them. **15**This desire leads to sin, and then the sin grows and brings death.

16My dear brothers and sisters, do not be fooled about this. **17**Every good action and every perfect gift is from God. These good gifts come down from the Creator of the sun, moon, and stars, who does not change like their shifting shadows. **18**God decided to give us life through the word of truth so we might be the most important of all the things he made.

Listening and Obeying

19My dear brothers and sisters, always be willing to listen and slow to speak. Do not become angry easily, **20**because anger will not help you live the right kind of life God wants. **21**So put out of your life every evil thing and every kind of wrong. Then in gentleness accept God's teaching that is planted in your hearts, which can save you.

22Do what God's teaching says; when you only listen and do nothing, you are fooling yourselves. **23**Those who hear God's teaching and do nothing are like people who look at themselves in a mirror.

24They see their faces and then go away and quickly forget what they looked like. **25**But the truly happy people are those who carefully study God's perfect law that makes people free, and they continue to study it. They do not forget what they heard, but they obey what God's teaching says. Those who do this will be made happy.

The True Way to Worship God

26People who think they are religious but say things they should not say are just fooling themselves. Their "religion" is worth nothing. **27**Religion that God accepts as pure and without fault is this: caring for orphans or widows who need help, and keeping yourself free from the world's evil influence.

OLD TESTAMENT READING

The Lord was pleased that Solomon had asked this. **11**So God said to him, "You did not ask for a long life, or riches for yourself, or the death of your enemies. Since you asked for wisdom to make the right decisions, **12**I will do what you asked. I will give you wisdom and understanding that is greater than anyone has had in the past or will have in the future. **13**I will also give you what you did not ask for: riches and honor. During your life no other king will be as great as you."

1 Kings 3:10–13

INSIGHTS

It has been said that the wisest man in the world is the man who knows he doesn't know.

In the midst of trials how often we say, "If only I knew what to do"; or we may say, "I don't know which way to turn or what to do."

God has promised to give us His wisdom. "If any of you is deficient in wisdom, let him ask of the giving God [Who gives] to every one liberally and ungrudgingly, without reproaching or faultfinding, and it will be given him" (Amplified). . . .

Not only are we to ask God for wisdom but we are to ask in faith. Someone has said, "Doubt is a non-conductor of grace."

We are not to be double-minded, wanting partly our way and partly God's way.

As we ask of God and ask in faith, God has promised to give liberally. We are to ask for wisdom to face serenely the trials of today, unwaveringly trusting in Him. We are to ask for wisdom to meet each trial of life and to face it triumphantly.

MILLIE STAMM

PAUSE FOR REFLECTION

For what reasons did Solomon and Daniel ask for God's wisdom? Did God's answer meet or exceed their expectations? For what in your life do you need God's wisdom? Have you asked him for it?

JAMES 2:1-26

Love All People

My dear brothers and sisters, as believers in our glorious Lord Jesus Christ, never think some people are more important than others. **2**Suppose someone comes into your church meeting wearing nice clothes and a gold ring. At the same time a poor person comes in wearing old, dirty clothes. **3**You show special attention to the one wearing nice clothes and say, "Please, sit here in this good seat." But you say to the poor person, "Stand over there," or, "Sit on the floor by my feet." **4**What are you doing? You are making some people more important than others, and with evil thoughts you are deciding that one person is better.

5Listen, my dear brothers and sisters! God chose the poor in the world to be rich with faith and to receive the kingdom God promised to those who love him. **6**But you show no respect to the poor. The rich are always trying to control your lives. They are the ones who take you to court. **7**And they are the ones who speak against Jesus, who owns you.

8This royal law is found in the Scriptures: "Love your neighbor as you love yourself." If you obey this law, you are doing right. **9**But if you treat one person as being more important than another, you are sinning. You are guilty of breaking God's law. **10**A person who follows all of God's law but fails to obey even one command is guilty of breaking all the commands in that law. **11**The same God who said, "You must not be guilty of adultery," also said, "You must not murder anyone." So if you do not take part in adultery but you murder someone, you are guilty of breaking all of God's law. **12**In everything you say and do, remember that you will be judged by the law that makes people free. **13**So you must show mercy to others, or God will not show mercy to you when he judges you. But the person who shows mercy can stand without fear at the judgment.

Faith and Good Works

14My brothers and sisters, if people say they have faith, but do nothing, their faith is worth nothing. Can faith like that save them? **15**A brother or sister in Christ might need clothes or food. **16**If you say to that person, "God be with you! I hope you stay warm and get plenty to eat," but you do not give what that person needs, your words are worth nothing. **17**In the same way, faith by itself—that does nothing—is dead.

18Someone might say, "You have faith, but I have deeds." Show me your faith without doing anything, and I will show you my faith by what I do. **19**You believe there is one God. Good! But the demons believe that, too, and they tremble with fear.

20You foolish person! Must you be shown that faith that does nothing is worth nothing? **21**Abraham, our ancestor, was made right with God by what he did when he offered his son Isaac on the altar. **22**So you see that Abraham's faith and the things he did worked together. His faith was made perfect by what he did. **23**This shows the full meaning of the Scripture that says: "Abraham believed God, and God accepted Abraham's faith, and that faith made him right with God." And

Abraham was called God's friend. **24**So you see that people are made right with God by what they do, not by faith only.

25Another example is Rahab, a prostitute, who was made right with God by something she did. She welcomed the spies into her home and helped them escape by a different road.

26Just as a person's body that does not have a spirit is dead, so faith that does nothing is dead!

INSIGHTS

My life has been deeply touched by the mercy of those who took the time to try and understand me—who cared enough to forgive so many of my faults and who in mercy made me their friend.

Often these were people to whom I had shown no special kindness. Their bestowal of mercy on me was something totally unexpected and undeserved. Because of this, it has been a double delight. More than that, it has been an enormous inspiration that lifted and challenged me to respond in a measure beyond my wildest dreams. . . .

. . . To really find the true source of inner inspiration for this sort of conduct, the Christian simply must look beyond his fellow man. He must look away to the mercy of God our Father. Nothing else in all the world will so humble us. Nothing else will so move our stony spirits to extend mercy. Nothing else will so powerfully induce us to do the proper thing in extending genuine mercy to our contemporaries. . . .

Christ calls us to be merciful. He calls us to be forgiving and compassionate. This does not mean we wink at wrong and sweep sin under the carpet. Rather it demands that we care enough to bring others to the God of all mercy. And it is He who will cleanse, re-create, and renew them in His loving-kindness and tender mercy. Bless His dear name!

W. PHILLIP KELLER

OLD TESTAMENT READING

Do not enter the city gate of my people
    in their time of trouble
or laugh at their problems
    in their time of trouble.
Do not take their treasures
    in their time of trouble.
14Do not stand at the crossroads
    to destroy those who are trying to escape.
Do not capture those who escape alive and
        turn them over to their enemy
    in their time of trouble."

Obadiah 13–14

ACTION POINT

In what situations does James plead for believers to show mercy? In what ways does your normal human behavior lack God's mercy? How will you seek to demonstrate his mercy?

JAMES 3:1 — 4:10

Controlling the Things We Say

3 My brothers and sisters, not many of you should become teachers, because you know that we who teach will be judged more strictly. ²We all make many mistakes. If people never said anything wrong, they would be perfect and able to control their entire selves, too. ³When we put bits into the mouths of horses to make them obey us, we can control their whole bodies. ⁴Also a ship is very big, and it is pushed by strong winds. But a very small rudder controls that big ship, making it go wherever the pilot wants. ⁵It is the same with the tongue. It is a small part of the body, but it brags about great things.

A big forest fire can be started with only a little flame. ⁶And the tongue is like a fire. It is a whole world of evil among the parts of our bodies. The tongue spreads its evil through the whole body. The tongue is set on fire by hell, and it starts a fire that influences all of life. ⁷People can tame every kind of wild animal, bird, reptile, and fish, and they have tamed them, ⁸but no one can tame the tongue. It is wild and evil and full of deadly poison. ⁹We use our tongues to praise our Lord and Father, but then we curse people, whom God made like himself. ¹⁰Praises and curses come from the same mouth! My brothers and sisters, this should not happen. ¹¹Do good and bad water flow from the same spring? ¹²My brothers and sisters, can a fig tree make olives, or can a grapevine make figs? No! And a well full of salty water cannot give good water.

True Wisdom

¹³Are there those among you who are truly wise and understanding? Then they should show it by living right and doing good things with a gentleness that comes from wisdom. ¹⁴But if you are selfish and have bitter jealousy in your hearts, do not brag. Your bragging is a lie that hides the truth. ¹⁵That kind of "wisdom" does not come from God but from the world. It is not spiritual; it is from the devil. ¹⁶Where jealousy and selfishness are, there will be confusion and every kind of evil. ¹⁷But the wisdom that comes from God is first of all pure, then peaceful, gentle, and easy to please. This wisdom is always ready to help those who are troubled and to do good for others. It is always fair and honest. ¹⁸People who work for peace in a peaceful way plant a good crop of right-living.

Give Yourselves to God

4 Do you know where your fights and arguments come from? They come from the selfish desires that war within you. ²You want things, but you do not have them. So you are ready to kill and are jealous of other people, but you still cannot get what you want. So you argue and fight. You do not get what you want, because you do not ask God. ³Or when you ask, you do not receive because the reason you ask is wrong. You want things so you can use them for your own pleasures.

⁴So, you are not loyal to God! You should know that loving the world is the same as hating God. Anyone who wants to be a friend of the world becomes God's enemy. ⁵Do you think the Scripture

means nothing that says, "The Spirit that God made to live in us wants us for himself alone"? ⁶But God gives us even more grace, as the Scripture says,

"God is against the proud,
    but he gives grace to the humble."

Proverbs 3:34

⁷So give yourselves completely to God. Stand against the devil, and the devil will run from you. ⁸Come near to God, and God will come near to you. You sinners, clean sin out of your lives. You who are trying to follow God and the world at the same time, make your thinking pure. ⁹Be sad, cry, and weep! Change your laughter into crying and your joy into sadness. ¹⁰Humble yourself in the Lord's presence, and he will honor you.

OLD TESTAMENT READING

People will be rewarded for what they say;
    they will be rewarded by how they speak.

²¹What you say can mean life or death.
    Those who speak with care will be
    rewarded.

Proverbs 18:20–21

INSIGHTS

No man can tame the tongue, but the Word of God encourages us to recognize that the Holy Spirit can transform and tie the tongue. . . .

. . . The tongue is the temperature gauge on the heart's engine. If the engine overheats, then the temperature gauge warns us of engine trouble. If the tongue gets out of control, it is a sure sign that we need to check our heart. . . . We need to constantly fill the heart with good things from God's Word in order to tie our tongues.

One must also concede to the Spirit's control to tie the tongue successfully. It always interested me that when James describes the tongue as a horse's bit that controls the horse or a ship's rudder that directs the ship, he, perhaps purposefully, fails to mention that a horse's bit must, in reality, be controlled by the rider and the ship's rudder must be controlled by the helmsman. I daily remind myself that the Lord, through the Holy Spirit, must be the rider or the helmsman controlling my tongue. Who is your helmsman?

If you have difficulty yielding control to the Lord, ask Him for the desire to give Him control. . . . When you have the willingness to concede control of your tongue, you'll soon discover you also have the strength to do it as well.

VICKI LAKE

PAUSE FOR REFLECTION

What does your tongue reveal about your heart? Think about your experiences with the good and evil things people have said, and write your own proverb about the tongue.

JAMES 4:11–5:20

You Are Not the Judge

11Brothers and sisters, do not tell evil lies about each other. If you speak against your fellow believers or judge them, you are judging and speaking against the law they follow. And when you are judging the law, you are no longer a follower of the law. You have become a judge. **12**God is the only Lawmaker and Judge. He is the only One who can save and destroy. So it is not right for you to judge your neighbor.

Let God Plan Your Life

13Some of you say, "Today or tomorrow we will go to some city. We will stay there a year, do business, and make money." **14**But you do not know what will happen tomorrow! Your life is like a mist. You can see it for a short time, but then it goes away. **15**So you should say, "If the Lord wants, we will live and do this or that." **16**But now you are proud and you brag. All of this bragging is wrong. **17**Anyone who knows the right thing to do, but does not do it, is sinning.

A Warning to the Rich

You rich people, listen! Cry and be very sad because of the troubles that are coming to you. **2**Your riches have rotted, and your clothes have been eaten by moths. **3**Your gold and silver have rusted, and that rust will be a proof that you were wrong. It will eat your bodies like fire. You saved your treasure for the last days. **4**The pay you did not give the workers who mowed your fields cries out against you, and the cries of the workers have been heard by the Lord All-Powerful. **5**Your life on earth was full of rich living and pleasing yourselves with everything you wanted. You made yourselves fat, like an animal ready to be killed. **6**You have judged guilty and then murdered innocent people, who were not against you.

Be Patient

7Brothers and sisters, be patient until the Lord comes again. A farmer patiently waits for his valuable crop to grow from the earth and for it to receive the autumn and spring rains. **8**You, too, must be patient. Do not give up hope, because the Lord is coming soon. **9**Brothers and sisters, do not complain against each other or you will be judged guilty. And the Judge is ready to come! **10**Brothers and sisters, follow the example of the prophets who spoke for the Lord. They suffered many hard things, but they were patient. **11**We say they are happy because they did not give up. You have heard about Job's patience, and you know the Lord's purpose for him in the end. You know the Lord is full of mercy and is kind.

Be Careful What You Say

12My brothers and sisters, above all, do not use an oath when you make a promise. Don't use the name of heaven, earth, or anything else to prove what you say. When you mean yes, say only yes, and when you mean no, say only no so you will not be judged guilty.

The Power of Prayer

13Anyone who is having troubles should pray. Anyone who is happy should sing praises.

14Anyone who is sick should call the church's elders. They should pray for and pour oil on the person in the name of the Lord. **15**And the prayer that is said with faith will make the sick person well; the Lord will heal that person. And if the person has sinned, the sins will be forgiven. **16**Confess your sins to each other and pray for each other so God can heal you. When a believing person prays, great things happen. **17**Elijah was a human being just like us. He prayed that it would not rain, and it did not rain on the land for three and a half years! **18**Then Elijah prayed again, and the rain came down from the sky, and the land produced crops again.

Saving a Soul

19My brothers and sisters, if one of you wanders away from the truth, and someone helps that person come back, **20**remember this: Anyone who brings a sinner back from the wrong way will save that sinner's soul from death and will cause many sins to be forgiven.

OLD TESTAMENT READING

Then Esther sent this answer to Mordecai: **16**"Go and get all the Jewish people in Susa together. For my sake, fast; do not eat or drink for three days, night and day. I and my servant girls will also fast. Then I will go to the king, even though it is against the law, and if I die, I die."

Esther 4:15–16

INSIGHTS

God honors prayer. . . . He longs to demonstrate His power in the tremendous trials that jar us like thunder, and in the pinprick troubles that annoy us. Giant needs are never too great for His power; dwarf-sized ones are never too small for His love. . . .

God can answer prayer because He is the supreme ruler of all. . . . He governs both world events and our individual lives, ready at our request to act, to intervene, to overrule for our good, His glory, and the progress of the gospel. He has decreed that prayer is the way to secure His aid and move His mighty hand. Therefore even in sickness, failure, rejection, or financial distress, we can pray and experience His peace which transcends human understanding. Through prayer we can open a window to let God's love shine into our lives; we can open our hands to receive His riches; we can open our hearts to let His presence fill and empower us. Through it we can also allow Him to provide answers to prayer that are important to Him and to us.

WARREN MYERS

PAUSE FOR REFLECTION

What great powers does James attribute to prayer? Do you believe God answers prayer—enough to risk your life on the power of prayer as Esther did?

1 PETER 1:1-21

1 From Peter, an apostle of Jesus Christ.
To God's chosen people who are away from their homes and are scattered all around Pontus, Galatia, Cappadocia, Asia, and Bithynia. **2**God planned long ago to choose you by making you his holy people, which is the Spirit's work. God wanted you to obey him and to be made clean by the blood of the death of Jesus Christ.

Grace and peace be yours more and more.

We Have a Living Hope

3Praise be to the God and Father of our Lord Jesus Christ. In God's great mercy he has caused us to be born again into a living hope, because Jesus Christ rose from the dead. **4**Now we hope for the blessings God has for his children. These blessings, which cannot be destroyed or be spoiled or lose their beauty, are kept in heaven for you. **5**God's power protects you through your faith until salvation is shown to you at the end of time. **6**This makes you very happy, even though now for a short time different kinds of troubles may make you sad. **7**These troubles come to prove that your faith is pure. This purity of faith is worth more than gold, which can be proved to be pure by fire but will ruin. But the purity of your faith will bring you praise and glory and honor when Jesus Christ is shown to you. **8**You have not seen Christ, but still you love him. You cannot see him now, but you believe in him. So you are filled with a joy that cannot be explained, a joy full of glory. **9**And you are receiving the goal of your faith—the salvation of your souls.

10The prophets searched carefully and tried to learn about this salvation. They prophesied about the grace that was coming to you. **11**The Spirit of Christ was in the prophets, telling in advance about the sufferings of Christ and about the glory that would follow those sufferings. The prophets tried to learn about what the Spirit was showing them, when those things would happen, and what the world would be like at that time. **12**It was shown them that their service was not for themselves but for you, when they told about the truths you have now heard. Those who preached the Good News to you told you those things with the help of the Holy Spirit who was sent from heaven—things into which angels desire to look.

A Call to Holy Living

13So prepare your minds for service and have self-control. All your hope should be for the gift of grace that will be yours when Jesus Christ is shown to you. **14**Now that you are obedient children of God do not live as you did in the past. You did not understand, so you did the evil things you wanted. **15**But be holy in all you do, just as God, the One who called you, is holy. **16**It is written in the Scriptures: "You must be holy, because I am holy."

17You pray to God and call him Father, and he judges each person's work equally. So while you are here on earth, you should live with respect for God. **18**You know that in the past you were living in a worthless way, a way passed down from the people who lived before you. But you were saved from that useless life. You were bought, not with something that ruins like gold or silver, **19**but with the precious blood of Christ, who was like a pure and perfect lamb. **20**Christ was chosen before the world was made, but he was shown to the world in these last times for your sake. **21**Through Christ you believe in God, who raised Christ from the dead and gave him glory. So your faith and your hope are in God.

INSIGHTS

What is trouble but that very influence that brings you nearer to the heart of God than prayers or hymns? I think sorrows usually bring us closer to God than joys do. But sorrows, to be of use, must be borne, as Christ's were, victoriously, carrying with them intimations and sacred prophecies to the heart of hope. This is not only so we will not be overcome by them, but also so we will be strengthened and ennobled and enlarged by them. . . .

. . . By fire, by anvil-strokes, by the hammer that breaks the flinty rock, you are made what you are. You were gold in the rock, and God played miner, and blasted you out of the rock. Then He played stamper, and crushed you. Then He played smelter, and melted you.

Now you are gold, free from the rock by the grace of God's severity to you. As you look back upon those experiences . . . and see what they have done for you, and what you are now, you say, "I would not exchange what I learned from these things for all the world." . . .

When God comes to you wrapped and wreathed in clouds, and in storms, why should we not recognize Him, and say, "I know you, God; and I will not flee you; though you slay me, I will trust thee"? If a man could see God in his troubles and take sorrow to be the . . . sweet discipline of a bitter medicine that brings health, though the taste is not agreeable—if one could so look upon his God, how sorrows would make him strong!

HENRY BEECHER

OLD TESTAMENT READING

The third that is left I will test with fire,
    purifying them like silver,
    testing them like gold.
Then they will call on me,
    and I will answer them.
I will say, 'You are my people,'
    and they will say, 'The LORD is our God.'"

Zechariah 13:9

APPLICATION

What is the value of a pure faith? What are its rewards? How does our faith become pure? How is God purifying your faith today? Welcome his testing!

1 PETER 1:22 — 2:17

22Now that your obedience to the truth has purified your souls, you can have true love for your Christian brothers and sisters. So love each other deeply with all your heart. **23**You have been born again, and this new life did not come from something that dies, but from something that cannot die. You were born again through God's living message that continues forever. **24**The Scripture says,

"All people are like the grass,
and all their glory is like the flowers of the
field.
The grass dies and the flowers fall,
25 but the word of the Lord will live forever."
Isaiah 40:6–8

And this is the word that was preached to you.

Jesus Is the Living Stone

So then, rid yourselves of all evil, all lying, hypocrisy, jealousy, and evil speech. **2**As newborn babies want milk, you should want the pure and simple teaching. By it you can mature in your salvation, **3**because you have already examined and seen how good the Lord is.

4Come to the Lord Jesus, the "stone" that lives. The people of the world did not want this stone, but he was the stone God chose, and he was precious. **5**You also are like living stones, so let yourselves be used to build a spiritual temple—to be holy priests who offer spiritual sacrifices to God.

He will accept those sacrifices through Jesus Christ. **6**The Scripture says:

"I will put a stone in the ground in Jerusalem.
Everything will be built on this important
and precious rock.
Anyone who trusts in him
will never be disappointed." *Isaiah 28:16*

7 This stone is worth much to you who believe. But to the people who do not believe,

"the stone that the builders rejected
has become the cornerstone."
Psalm 118:22

8Also, he is

"a stone that causes people to stumble,
a rock that makes them fall." *Isaiah 8:14*

They stumble because they do not obey what God says, which is what God planned to happen to them.

9But you are a chosen people, royal priests, a holy nation, a people for God's own possession. You were chosen to tell about the wonderful acts of God, who called you out of darkness into his wonderful light. **10**At one time you were not a people, but now you are God's people. In the past you had never received mercy, but now you have received God's mercy.

Live for God

11Dear friends, you are like foreigners and strangers in this world. I beg you to avoid the evil things your bodies want to do that fight against your soul. **12**People who do not believe are living all around you and might say that you are doing wrong. Live such good lives that they will see the good things you do and will give glory to God on the day when Christ comes again.

Yield to Every Human Authority

13For the Lord's sake, yield to the people who have authority in this world: the king, who is the highest authority, 14and the leaders who are sent by him to punish those who do wrong and to praise those who do right. 15It is God's desire that by doing good you should stop foolish people from saying stupid things about you. 16Live as free people, but do not use your freedom as an excuse to do evil. Live as servants of God. 17Show respect for all people: Love the brothers and sisters of God's family, respect God, honor the king.

OLD TESTAMENT READING

Then Nebuchadnezzar said, "Praise the God of Shadrach, Meshach, and Abednego. Their God has sent his angel and saved his servants from the fire! These three men trusted their God and refused to obey my command. They were willing to die rather than serve or worship any god other than their own. 29So I now give this command: Anyone from any nation or language who says anything against the God of Shadrach, Meshach, and Abednego will be torn apart and have his house turned into a pile of stones. No other god can save his people like this."

Daniel 3:28–29

INSIGHTS

God considers himself honored by the high attainments of His children and dishonored by their low attainments. He is honored in the fact that their graces so shine forth that it shall be seen by all around that they have partaken largely of His Spirit.

Exalted piety is honorable to God. Manifestations of great grace and spirituality of mind honor God. He is greatly honored by the fruits of righteousness His people bring forth. Christ himself says, "Herein is my Father glorified that ye bring forth much fruit." Ministers should be greatly fruitful. They should bring forth the fruits of the Spirit in their tempers, in their lives, in the strength of their faith and labors of love. Can you doubt that God has great interest in these things? Indeed His great desire, that you should bring forth fruit to His glory, is shown in the fact that He says, "open thy mouth wide, and I will fill it."

CHARLES FINNEY

PAUSE FOR REFLECTION

What do you think it means to be made "pure by obeying the truth"? What purpose is served when believers live good lives? What have you learned from the lives of those who honor God in such a way? Are you willing to get rid of everything in your life that doesn't bring honor to the King?

1 PETER 2:18 — 3:12

Follow Christ's Example

18Slaves, yield to the authority of your masters with all respect, not only those who are good and kind, but also those who are dishonest. **19**A person might have to suffer even when it is unfair, but if he thinks of God and can stand the pain, God is pleased. **20**If you are beaten for doing wrong, there is no reason to praise you for being patient in your punishment. But if you suffer for doing good, and you are patient, then God is pleased. **21**This is what you were called to do, because Christ suffered for you and gave you an example to follow. So you should do as he did.

22"He had never sinned,

and he had never lied."   *Isaiah 53:9*

23People insulted Christ, but he did not insult them in return. Christ suffered, but he did not threaten. He let God, the One who judges rightly, take care of him. **24**Christ carried our sins in his body on the cross so we would stop living for sin and start living for what is right. And you are healed because of his wounds. **25**You were like sheep that wandered away, but now you have come back to the Shepherd and Overseer of your souls.

Wives and Husbands

3 In the same way, you wives should yield to your husbands. Then, if some husbands do not obey God's teaching, they will be persuaded to believe without anyone's saying a word to them. They will be persuaded by the way their wives live. **2**Your husbands will see the pure lives you live with your respect for God. **3**It is not fancy hair, gold jewelry, or fine clothes that should make you beautiful. **4**No, your beauty should come from within you—the beauty of a gentle and quiet spirit that will never be destroyed and is very precious to God. **5**In this same way the holy women who lived long ago and followed God made themselves beautiful, yielding to their own husbands. **6**Sarah obeyed Abraham, her husband, and called him her master. And you women are true children of Sarah if you always do what is right and are not afraid.

7In the same way, you husbands should live with your wives in an understanding way, since they are weaker than you. But show them respect, because God gives them the same blessing he gives you—the grace that gives true life. Do this so that nothing will stop your prayers.

Suffering for Doing Right

8Finally, all of you should be in agreement, understanding each other, loving each other as family, being kind and humble. **9**Do not do wrong to repay a wrong, and do not insult to repay an insult. But repay with a blessing, because you yourselves were called to do this so that you might receive a blessing. **10**The Scripture says,

"A person must do these things

to enjoy life and have many happy days.

He must not say evil things,

and he must not tell lies.

11He must stop doing evil and do good.

He must look for peace and work for it.

12The Lord sees the good people

and listens to their prayers.

But the Lord is against

those who do evil."   *Psalm 34:12–16*

OLD TESTAMENT READING

Abimelech came from Gerar to see Isaac. He brought with him Ahuzzath, who advised him, and Phicol, the commander of his army. **27**Isaac asked them, "Why have you come to see me? You were my enemy and forced me to leave your country."

28They answered, "Now we know that the LORD is with you. Let us swear an oath to each other. Let us make an agreement with you **29**that since we did not hurt you, you will not hurt us. We were good to you and sent you away in peace. Now the LORD has blessed you."

30So Isaac prepared food for them, and they all ate and drank. **31**Early the next morning the men swore an oath to each other. Then Isaac sent them away, and they left in peace.

Genesis 26:26–31

INSIGHTS

If the life is opened to receive the divine presence of the risen Christ, He comes in, speaking peace—just as He came again and again to His distraught disciples after His resurrection, saying, "Peace be unto you!"

He comes into our lives there to shed abroad a new love, His own life, that expresses itself in peace. When He enters my experience; when He penetrates my personality; when He becomes Sovereign in my spirit, I in turn become a person of peace. It is then that I begin to know what it means to be at peace with God, at peace with others, at peace with myself.

Increasingly as He is given control of my life the entire complexion of my character, conduct, and conversation alters. I discover that He can change me dramatically. Peace, good will, good cheer, and serenity replace animosity, bitterness, hostility, belligerence, jealousy, bad temper, quarreling, and rivalry. . . .

. . . The peace of God, which is self-sacrificing and self-foregoing, produces healing. It comes to bind up the wounds; to pour in the oil of consolation; to bring repose and quietness; to still the troubled soul; to speak peace to stormy spirits. This peace comes only from Christ. It is one of the genuine, indisputable marks of God's presence in a person's life.

W. PHILLIP KELLER

ACTION POINT

Who set the standard for living in peace? What does living in peace look like? How full of Christ's peace is your life? Pray that God will give you a fuller love and more intimate understanding of his peace and that it will touch every area of your life.

1 PETER 3:13 — 4:11

¹³If you are trying hard to do good, no one can really hurt you. ¹⁴But even if you suffer for doing right, you are blessed.

"Don't be afraid of what they fear;

do not dread those things." *Isaiah 8:12–13*
¹⁵But respect Christ as the holy Lord in your hearts. Always be ready to answer everyone who asks you to explain about the hope you have, ¹⁶but answer in a gentle way and with respect. Keep a clear conscience so that those who speak evil of your good life in Christ will be made ashamed. ¹⁷It is better to suffer for doing good than for doing wrong if that is what God wants. ¹⁸Christ himself suffered for sins once. He was not guilty, but he suffered for those who are guilty to bring you to God. His body was killed, but he was made alive in the spirit, ¹⁹And in the spirit he went and preached to the spirits in prison ²⁰who refused to obey God long ago in the time of Noah. God was waiting patiently for them while Noah was building the boat. Only a few people—eight in all—were saved by water. ²¹And that water is like baptism that now saves you—not the washing of dirt from the body, but the promise made to God from a good conscience. And this is because Jesus Christ was raised from the dead. ²²Now Jesus has gone into heaven and is at God's right side ruling over angels, authorities, and powers.

Change Your Lives

4 Since Christ suffered while he was in his body, strengthen yourselves with the same way of thinking Christ had. The person who has suffered in the body is finished with sin. ²Strengthen yourselves so that you will live here on earth doing what God wants, not the evil things people want. ³In the past you wasted too much time doing what nonbelievers enjoy. You were guilty of sexual sins, evil desires, drunkenness, wild and drunken parties, and hateful idol worship. ⁴Nonbelievers think it is strange that you do not do the many wild and wasteful things they do, so they insult you. ⁵But they will have to explain this to God, who is ready to judge the living and the dead. ⁶For this reason the Good News was preached to those who are now dead. Even though they were judged like all people, the Good News was preached to them so they could live in the spirit as God lives.

Use God's Gifts Wisely

⁷The time is near when all things will end. So think clearly and control yourselves so you will be able to pray. ⁸Most importantly, love each other deeply, because love will cause people to forgive each other for many sins. ⁹Open your homes to each other, without complaining. ¹⁰Each of you has received a gift to use to serve others. Be good servants of God's various gifts of grace. ¹¹Anyone who speaks should speak words from God. Anyone who serves should serve with the strength God gives so that in everything God will be praised through Jesus Christ. Power and glory belong to him forever and ever. Amen.

OLD TESTAMENT READING

God, don't be far off.
My God, hurry to help me.

¹³Let those who accuse me
  be ashamed and destroyed.
Let those who are trying to hurt me
  be covered with shame and
    disgrace.
¹⁴But I will always have hope
  and will praise you more and more.
¹⁵I will tell how you do what is right.

I will tell about your salvation all day long,
  even though it is more than I can tell.
¹⁶I will come and tell about your powerful
    works, Lord GOD.
I will remind people that only you do what
    is right.

Psalm 71:12–16

INSIGHTS

Christians have a corner on hope. Why? Because the basis of all hope is knowing who God is. There is no hope without a God who controls the universe and promises to bring us to heaven.

Hope designates a future—that is what we hope in. Time, our period on this earth, can be seen in various ways, but only one way offers hope. Some see time as cyclical: history repeats itself and will continue to repeat itself only to get worse (and finally burn itself up). Others see time in the modern secular view that immortality exists as each generation gives birth to the next, which then gives birth to the next. But Christians see time in a straight line—God began time, has a specific purpose for each person within his divine plan, and he will bring it to an end when he returns as he promised.

Hope is not in most of the things our fellow humans hope in. It cannot be found in possessions, in our own strength or supposed "immortality," in people's love, in the past. Neither can it be found in human achievement, in who we are or what we have done, or in this life itself.

So where is hope? Our hope lies in our Christian growth here on earth—that we are doing what God wants for us in our particular place in time. We hope in the new heaven and new earth God has promised for us (Hebrews 13:14). We hope in Christ's second coming, in eternal life, and in resurrection (1 John 3:2, 3). We hope in the fact that this world is not all there is (Revelation 21:2, 3). And the great thing about our hope is that it is based on fact. It will happen because our hope is based on God, not on us.

YFC EDITORS

ACTION POINT

Describe the hope of your salvation. Be specific. How might your hope affect the heart of a nonbeliever? What should be your purpose in everything you do? Ask God to fulfill his purpose through you.

1 PETER 4:12 — 5:14

Suffering as a Christian

12My friends, do not be surprised at the terrible trouble which now comes to test you. Do not think that something strange is happening to you. **13**But be happy that you are sharing in Christ's sufferings so that you will be happy and full of joy when Christ comes again in glory. **14**When people insult you because you follow Christ, you are blessed, because the glorious Spirit, the Spirit of God, is with you. **15**Do not suffer for murder, theft, or any other crime, nor because you trouble other people. **16**But if you suffer because you are a Christian, do not be ashamed. Praise God because you wear that name. **17**It is time for judgment to begin with God's family. And if that judging begins with us, what will happen to those people who do not obey the Good News of God?

18"If it is very hard for a good person to be
saved,

the wicked person and the sinner will
surely be lost!"

19So those who suffer as God wants should trust their souls to the faithful Creator as they continue to do what is right.

The Flock of God

5 Now I have something to say to the elders in your group. I also am an elder. I have seen Christ's sufferings, and I will share in the glory that will be shown to us. I beg you to **2**shepherd God's flock, for whom you are responsible. Watch over them because you want to, not because you are forced. That is how God wants it. Do it because you are happy to serve, not because you want money. **3**Do not be like a ruler over people you are responsible for, but be good examples to them. **4**Then when Christ, the Chief Shepherd, comes, you will get a glorious crown that will never lose its beauty.

5In the same way, younger people should be willing to be under older people. And all of you should be very humble with each other.

"God is against the proud,

but he gives grace to the humble."

Proverbs 3:34

6Be humble under God's powerful hand so he will lift you up when the right time comes. **7**Give all your worries to him, because he cares about you.

8Control yourselves and be careful! The devil, your enemy, goes around like a roaring lion looking for someone to eat. **9**Refuse to give in to him, by standing strong in your faith. You know that your Christian family all over the world is having the same kinds of suffering.

10And after you suffer for a short time, God, who gives all grace, will make everything right. He will make you strong and support you and keep you from falling. He called you to share in his glory in Christ, a glory that will continue forever. **11**All power is his forever and ever. Amen.

Final Greetings

12I wrote this short letter with the help of Silas, who I know is a faithful brother in Christ. I wrote to encourage you and to tell you that this is the true grace of God. Stand strong in that grace.

13The church in Babylon, who was chosen like you, sends you greetings. Mark, my son in Christ, also greets you. 14Give each other a kiss of Christian love when you meet.

Peace to all of you who are in Christ.

OLD TESTAMENT READING

Then the LORD spoke his word to Elijah: 3"Leave this place and go east and hide near Kerith Ravine east of the Jordan River. 4You may drink from the stream, and I have commanded ravens to bring you food there." 6The birds brought Elijah bread and meat every morning and evening, and he drank water from the stream.

7After a while the stream dried up because there was no rain. 8Then the LORD spoke his word to Elijah, 9"Go to Zarephath in Sidon and live there. I have commanded a widow there to take care of you."

1 Kings 17:2–4, 6–9

INSIGHTS

One winter I worked as secretary and receptionist at a mortuary. . . .

My husband had just been affected by a large company layoff, so I had needed to work. One particularly dark and dreary day I sat all by myself in the large office of the mortuary. While I typed a letter, my thoughts drifted to the house payment and utility bills. I soon felt overwhelmed. Tears came as I thought about the fact that we also needed groceries. Furthermore, Christmas was coming.

Suddenly, my thoughts were interrupted by a noise at the window. I walked over to see what it was. Through my tears, I saw that a sparrow had flown into the window and, stunned by the blow, had fallen to the ground.

This little incident reminded me of what God has to say in His Word about the birds of the air. He's aware of and provides for all of their needs. How much more is He aware of His children in need.

I felt so encouraged as I recalled sermons on this topic. I could almost hear the gospel singer: "His Eye Is On the Sparrow." I hummed the song the rest of the day. My faith increased, as I learned to trust God for my every need.

Then one morning a friend stood at the front door. "The Lord laid it on my heart to give you this money," he said. He didn't know it, but it was our house payment. Later, several checks came in the mail from a loving friend, signed, "Love, Jesus." One week we were invited out to dinner every night. And the children ended up having a delightful Christmas.

BARBARA HYATT

APPLICATION

What worry did Peter's readers face? For what reasons does he tell them not to worry? What reassurance of God's loving care does the Old Testament reading provide? Will you trust in his care?

2 PETER 1:1-21

1 From Simon Peter, a servant and apostle of Jesus Christ.

To you who have received a faith as valuable as ours, because our God and Savior Jesus Christ does what is right.

2Grace and peace be given to you more and more, because you truly know God and Jesus our Lord.

God Has Given Us Blessings

3Jesus has the power of God, by which he has given us everything we need to live and to serve God. We have these things because we know him. Jesus called us by his glory and goodness. 4Through these he gave us the very great and precious promises. With these gifts you can share in God's nature, and the world will not ruin you with its evil desires.

5Because you have these blessings, do your best to add these things to your lives: to your faith, add goodness; and to your goodness, add knowledge; 6and to your knowledge, add self-control; and to your self-control, add patience; and to your patience, add service for God; 7and to your service for God, add kindness for your brothers and sisters in Christ; and to this kindness, add love. 8If all these things are in you and are growing, they will help you to be useful and productive in your knowledge of our Lord Jesus Christ. 9But anyone who does not have these things cannot see clearly. He is blind and has forgotten that he was made clean from his past sins.

10My brothers and sisters, try hard to be certain that you really are called and chosen by God. If you do all these things, you will never fall. 11And you will be given a very great welcome into the eternal kingdom of our Lord and Savior Jesus Christ.

12You know these things, and you are very strong in the truth, but I will always help you remember them. 13I think it is right for me to help you remember as long as I am in this body. 14I know I must soon leave this body, as our Lord Jesus Christ has shown me. 15I will try my best so that you may be able to remember these things even after I am gone.

We Saw Christ's Glory

16When we told you about the powerful coming of our Lord Jesus Christ, we were not telling just clever stories that someone invented. But we saw the greatness of Jesus with our own eyes. 17Jesus heard the voice of God, the Greatest Glory, when he received honor and glory from God the Father. The voice said, "This is my Son, whom I love, and I am very pleased with him." 18We heard that voice from heaven while we were with Jesus on the holy mountain.

19This makes us more sure about the message the prophets gave. It is good for you to follow closely what they said as you would follow a light shining in a dark place, until the day begins and the morning star rises in your hearts. 20Most of all, you must understand this: No prophecy in the Scriptures ever comes from the prophet's own interpretation. 21No prophecy ever came from what a person wanted to say, but people led by the Holy Spirit spoke words from God.

OLD TESTAMENT READING

Only the LORD gives wisdom;
  he gives knowledge and understanding.

Proverbs 2:6

These are the wise words of Solomon son of David, king of Israel.

³They will teach you how to be wise and
    self-controlled
  and will teach you to do what is honest and
    fair and right.

⁷Knowledge begins with respect for the LORD,
  but fools hate wisdom and discipline.

Proverbs 1:1, 3, 7

INSIGHTS

We are to make every effort to increase our faith, knowledge, self-control, steadfastness and brotherly affection. Each of us is expected to be spiritually self-sustaining. We cannot rely on pastors or Christian leaders to keep our faith propped up.

Some Christians live from Sunday to Sunday. They start their week ready for action, but by Saturday are drained of their enthusiasm and can barely drag themselves to church the next day for another boost. Paul talks of digesting the milk of the Word (1 Cor 3:2). Babies need someone to feed them milk, and in the same way, new Christians need someone to help them understand biblical truth. Yet, we have all seen [challenged] adults who are incapable of feeding themselves. Behavior that is natural and cute in an infant is saddening to watch in these adults. Sadly, there are Christians who have not made "every effort to supplement their faith," and they too are [challenged] in their spiritual development.

Prayer and Bible study are important in supplementing our faith. God reveals himself to us in the Bible, and through prayer we have direct access to him with our problems and questions. . . .

. . . Once Bible study is a regular part of our lives, we will begin to reap the rewards of a more stable and mature relationship with the Lord. We will also have the personal confidence to go to the Bible and find our own answers to life's questions.

God does not want us to be spiritually [challenged] and unable to sustain the new life he has given us. He wants us to reach a place of maturity where we can spiritually feed ourselves and be able to stand firm in the face of any adversity.

FLOYD MCCLUNG

PAUSE FOR REFLECTION

What things does Peter say to add to your faith? What is the purpose and the result of doing these things? Consider your own life, and write down what you think will be accomplished if you add each of these things to your faith. Be specific.

2 PETER 2:1-22

False Teachers

2 There used to be false prophets among God's people, just as you will have some false teachers in your group. They will secretly teach things that are wrong—teachings that will cause people to be lost. They will even refuse to accept the Master, Jesus, who bought their freedom. So they will bring quick ruin on themselves. **2**Many will follow their evil ways and say evil things about the way of truth. **3**Those false teachers only want your money, so they will use you by telling you lies. Their judgment spoken against them long ago is still coming, and their ruin is certain.

4When angels sinned, God did not let them go free without punishment. He sent them to hell and put them in caves of darkness where they are being held for judgment. **5**And God punished the world long ago when he brought a flood to the world that was full of people who were against him. But God saved Noah, who preached about being right with God, and seven other people with him. **6**And God also destroyed the evil cities of Sodom and Gomorrah by burning them until they were ashes. He made those cities an example of what will happen to those who are against God. **7**But he saved Lot from those cities. Lot, a good man, was troubled because of the filthy lives of evil people. **8**(Lot was a good man, but because he lived with evil people every day, his good heart was hurt by the evil things he saw and heard.) **9**So the Lord knows how to save those who serve him when troubles come. He will hold evil people and punish them, while waiting for the Judgment Day. **10**That punishment is especially for those who live by doing the evil things their sinful selves want and who hate authority.

These false teachers are bold and do anything they want. They are not afraid to speak against the angels. **11**But even the angels, who are much stronger and more powerful than false teachers, do not accuse them with insults before the Lord. **12**But these people speak against things they do not understand. They are like animals that act without thinking, animals born to be caught and killed. And, like animals, these false teachers will be destroyed. **13**They have caused many people to suffer, so they themselves will suffer. That is their pay for what they have done. They take pleasure in openly doing evil, so they are like dirty spots and stains among you. They delight in deceiving you while eating meals with you. **14**Every time they look at a woman they want her, and their desire for sin is never satisfied. They lead weak people into the trap of sin, and they have taught their hearts to be greedy. God will punish them! **15**These false teachers left the right road and lost their way, following the way Balaam went. Balaam was the son of Beor, who loved being paid for doing wrong. **16**But a donkey, which cannot talk, told Balaam he was sinning. It spoke with a man's voice and stopped the prophet's crazy thinking.

17Those false teachers are like springs without water and clouds blown by a storm. A place in the blackest darkness has been kept for them. **18**They brag with words that mean nothing. By their evil desires they lead people into the trap of sin—

people who are just beginning to escape from others who live in error. **19**They promise them freedom, but they themselves are not free. They are slaves of things that will be destroyed. For people are slaves of anything that controls them. **20**They were made free from the evil in the world by knowing our Lord and Savior Jesus Christ. But if they return to evil things and those things control them, then it is worse for them than it was before. **21**Yes, it would be better for them to have never known the right way than to know it and to turn away from the holy teaching that was given to them. **22**What they did is like this true saying: "A dog goes back to what it has thrown up," and,

"After a pig is washed, it goes back and rolls in the mud."

OLD TESTAMENT READING

They are like hungry dogs
   that are never satisfied.
They are like shepherds
   who don't know what they are doing.
They all have gone their own way;
   all they want to do is satisfy themselves.

Isaiah 56:11

INSIGHTS

Deception is on the rise within the Christian church and we ignore it to our peril. Sometimes it is difficult—even for a Christian—to recognize the deceivers. Jesus spoke of false prophets who "perform great signs and miracles to deceive even the elect." . . .

Satan does not want to build a church and call it "The First Church of Satan." He is far too clever for that. He invades the Sunday school, the youth department, the Christian education program, the pulpit and the seminary classroom.

The apostle Paul warned that many will follow false teachers, not knowing that in feeding upon what these people say they are taking the devil's poison into their own lives. Thousands of uninstructed Christians are being deceived today. False teachers use high-sounding words that seem like the height of logic, scholarship and culture. They are intellectually clever and crafty in their sophistry. They are adept at beguiling thoughtless, untaught men and women. . . .

The best advice against deception that I can give is to urge you to spend your time looking at the real Christ. Then, when a counterfeit appears, you'll have less trouble spotting him.

BILLY GRAHAM

ACTION POINT

List the lifestyle patterns that serve as clues that a false teacher is at work. How can a person guard against the practiced deception of false teachers? How do you plan to learn God's truth?

2 PETER 3:1-18

Jesus Will Come Again

3 My friends, this is the second letter I have written you to help your honest minds remember. **2**I want you to think about the words the holy prophets spoke in the past, and remember the command our Lord and Savior gave us through your apostles. **3**It is most important for you to understand what will happen in the last days. People will laugh at you. They will live doing the evil things they want to do. **4**They will say, "Jesus promised to come again. Where is he? Our fathers have died, but the world continues the way it has been since it was made." **5**But they do not want to remember what happened long ago. By the word of God heaven was made, and the earth was made from water and with water. **6**Then the world was flooded and destroyed with water. **7**And that same word of God is keeping heaven and earth that we now have in order to be destroyed by fire. They are being kept for the Judgment Day and the destruction of all who are against God.

8But do not forget this one thing, dear friends: To the Lord one day is as a thousand years, and a thousand years is as one day. **9**The Lord is not slow in doing what he promised—the way some people understand slowness. But God is being patient with you. He does not want anyone to be lost, but he wants all people to change their hearts and lives.

10But the day of the Lord will come like a thief. The skies will disappear with a loud noise. Every-thing in them will be destroyed by fire, and the earth and everything in it will be exposed. **11**In that way everything will be destroyed. So what kind of people should you be? You should live holy lives and serve God, **12**as you wait for and look forward to the coming of the day of God. When that day comes, the skies will be destroyed with fire, and everything in them will melt with heat. **13**But God made a promise to us, and we are waiting for a new heaven and a new earth where goodness lives.

14Dear friends, since you are waiting for this to happen, do your best to be without sin and without fault. Try to be at peace with God. **15**Remember that we are saved because our Lord is patient. Our dear brother Paul told you the same thing when he wrote to you with the wisdom that God gave him. **16**He writes about this in all his letters. Some things in Paul's letters are hard to understand, and people who are ignorant and weak in faith explain these things falsely. They also falsely explain the other Scriptures, but they are destroying themselves by doing this.

17Dear friends, since you already know about this, be careful. Do not let those evil people lead you away by the wrong they do. Be careful so you will not fall from your strong faith. **18**But grow in the grace and knowledge of our Lord and Savior Jesus Christ. Glory be to him now and forever! Amen.

OLD TESTAMENT READING

Y ou sit as the Holy One.
The praises of Israel are your throne.

⁴Our ancestors trusted you;
 they trusted, and you saved
  them.
⁵They called to you for help
 and were rescued.
They trusted you
 and were not disappointed.

⁶But I am like a worm instead of a man.
 People make fun of me and hate me.

⁷Those who look at me laugh.
 They stick out their tongues and shake
  their heads.
⁸They say, "Turn to the LORD for help.
 Maybe he will save you.
If he likes you,
 maybe he will rescue you."

Psalm 22:3–8

INSIGHTS

"They laughed at me and made fun of me because I wouldn't participate in what they were doing."

. . . "I lost several 'friends' because I didn't go along with their gossiping when we got together."

Modern day persecution because of our faith? Perhaps. It hurts to be misunderstood and not accepted. Believers in China and other parts of the world still face intense persecution. They lose their homes, some end up in prison, and many are killed because of their faith.

Most of us have never really felt the piercing sting of persecution. It could happen to us as it does in other countries like China. It could happen in ways hard to imagine if our democratic society were overturned. You never know. But whatever type of persecution you experience, do you know how Jesus wants you to respond? It's quite simple. Rejoice and be glad. That's all. Be glad. Don't retaliate. Don't sulk. Don't complain. Don't just grin and bear it. Rejoice and actually "leap for joy" (Luke 6:23).

. . . Expect opposition to your Christian stance. That's normal. If you are persecuted because of your stance for Jesus Christ, it means you are really committed to Him and your commitment is evident to others. You are having an impact in the world around you. Isn't it strange that living for Him brings discomfort? But why not? Living for Christ means confronting a world that is living contrary to the way God intended. Your Christian life bothers them. It's convicting. So they will react to you. But I guess Jesus understands that pretty well, doesn't He? Look at what it cost Him.

H. NORMAN WRIGHT

APPLICATION

What perspective does Peter offer to help his readers bear persecution? Will God hurry to fulfill his plan for anyone? In what ways does focusing on God—his eternal timelessness and omnipotent power—help you face the challenges of unbelievers?

1 JOHN 1:1 – 2:14

1 We write you now about what has always existed, which we have heard, we have seen with our own eyes, we have looked at, and we have touched with our hands. We write to you about the Word that gives life. **2**He who gives life was shown to us. We saw him and can give proof about it. And now we announce to you that he has life that continues forever. He was with God the Father and was shown to us. **3**We announce to you what we have seen and heard, because we want you also to have fellowship with us. Our fellowship is with God the Father and with his Son, Jesus Christ. **4**We write this to you so we may be full of joy.

God Forgives Our Sins

5Here is the message we have heard from Christ and now announce to you: God is light, and in him there is no darkness at all. **6**So if we say we have fellowship with God, but we continue living in darkness, we are liars and do not follow the truth. **7**But if we live in the light, as God is in the light, we can share fellowship with each other. Then the blood of Jesus, God's Son, cleanses us from every sin.

8If we say we have no sin, we are fooling ourselves, and the truth is not in us. **9**But if we confess our sins, he will forgive our sins, because we can trust God to do what is right. He will cleanse us from all the wrongs we have done. **10**If we say we have not sinned, we make God a liar, and we do not accept God's teaching.

Jesus Is Our Helper

2 My dear children, I write this letter to you so you will not sin. But if anyone does sin, we have a helper in the presence of the Father—Jesus Christ, the One who does what is right. **2**He died in our place to take away our sins, and not only our sins but the sins of all people.

3We can be sure that we know God if we obey his commands. **4**Anyone who says, "I know God," but does not obey God's commands is a liar, and the truth is not in that person. **5**But if someone obeys God's teaching, then in that person God's love has truly reached its goal. This is how we can be sure we are living in God: **6**Whoever says that he lives in God must live as Jesus lived.

The Command to Love Others

7My dear friends, I am not writing a new command to you but an old command you have had from the beginning. It is the teaching you have already heard. **8**But also I am writing a new command to you, and you can see its truth in Jesus and in you, because the darkness is passing away, and the true light is already shining.

9Anyone who says, "I am in the light," but hates a brother or sister, is still in the darkness. **10**Whoever loves a brother or sister lives in the light and will not cause anyone to stumble in his faith. **11**But whoever hates a brother or sister is in darkness, lives in darkness, and does not know where to go, because the darkness has made that person blind.

12I write to you, dear children,
  because your sins are forgiven through
    Christ.

13 I write to you, fathers,
  because you know the One who existed
    from the beginning.
I write to you, young people,
  because you have defeated the Evil
    One.
14 I write to you, children,
  because you know the Father.
I write to you, fathers,
  because you know the One who existed
    from the beginning.
I write to you, young people,
  because you are strong;
  the teaching of God lives in you,
  and you have defeated the Evil One.

OLD TESTAMENT READING

Send me your light and truth
  to guide me.
Let them lead me to your holy mountain,
  to where you live.
4 Then I will go to the altar of God,
  to God who is my joy and happiness.
I will praise you with a harp,
  God, my God.

Psalm 43:3–4

Light is not given to evil people."

Job 38:15a

INSIGHTS

Servants of Christ shine with His light in a society that is hopelessly lost.

. . .

We pose a weird phenomenon to those in darkness. They cannot figure us out! And that is exactly as Jesus planned it. Think of some distinctive characteristics of light:

• Light is silent. No noise, no big splash, no banners—light simply shines. It's like a single lighthouse along a rugged shoreline. All it does is shine as it turns.

• Light gives direction. No words, no sermon. Jesus says that others "see" our actions—but nothing is said of their hearing.

• Light attracts attention. You don't have to ask people to look at you when you turn a light on in a dark room. It happens automatically. . . . If you are a Christian family in a non-Christian neighborhood, you are the light in that darkness. The same is true if you are the only Christian nurse on your floor, or student in your school, or professional in your firm or group, or salesman in your district. You are a light in darkness—a servant of God who is being watched, who gives off a very distinct message . . . often with hardly a word being said. . . . Let it shine! Don't attempt to show off how bright and sparkling you are, just shine!

CHARLES SWINDOLL

APPLICATION

What feelings does the God of light bring into your life? Describe what it means for you to "live in the light." What corners of darkness in your life do you need to open up to God's cleansing light?

1 JOHN 2:15 — 3:10

15Do not love the world or the things in the world. If you love the world, the love of the Father is not in you. **16**These are the ways of the world: wanting to please our sinful selves, wanting the sinful things we see, and being too proud of what we have. None of these come from the Father, but all of them come from the world. **17**The world and everything that people want in it are passing away, but the person who does what God wants lives forever.

Reject the Enemies of Christ

18My dear children, these are the last days. You have heard that the enemy of Christ is coming, and now many enemies of Christ are already here. This is how we know that these are the last days. **19**These enemies of Christ were in our fellowship, but they left us. They never really belonged to us; if they had been a part of us, they would have stayed with us. But they left, and this shows that none of them really belonged to us.

20You have the gift that the Holy One gave you, so you all know the truth. **21**I do not write to you because you do not know the truth but because you do know the truth. And you know that no lie comes from the truth.

22Who is the liar? It is the person who does not accept Jesus as the Christ. This is the enemy of Christ: the person who does not accept the Father and his Son. **23**Whoever does not accept the Son does not have the Father. But whoever confesses the Son has the Father, too.

24Be sure you continue to follow the teaching you heard from the beginning. If you continue to follow what you heard from the beginning, you will stay in the Son and in the Father. **25**And this is what the Son promised to us—life forever.

26I am writing this letter about those people who are trying to lead you the wrong way. **27**Christ gave you a special gift that is still in you, so you do not need any other teacher. His gift teaches you about everything, and it is true, not false. So continue to live in Christ, as his gift taught you.

28Yes, my dear children, live in him so that when Christ comes back, we can be without fear and not be ashamed in his presence. **29**Since you know that Christ is righteous, you know that all who do right are God's children.

We Are God's Children

3 The Father has loved us so much that we are called children of God. And we really are his children. The reason the people in the world do not know us is that they have not known him. **2**Dear friends, now we are children of God, and we have not yet been shown what we will be in the future. But we know that when Christ comes again, we will be like him, because we will see him as he really is. **3**Christ is pure, and all who have this hope in Christ keep themselves pure like Christ.

4The person who sins breaks God's law. Yes, sin is living against God's law. **5**You know that Christ came to take away sins and that there is no sin in Christ. **6**So anyone who lives in Christ does not go on sinning. Anyone who goes on sinning has never really understood Christ and has never known him.

7Dear children, do not let anyone lead you the

wrong way. Christ is righteous. So to be like Christ a person must do what is right. **8**The devil has been sinning since the beginning, so anyone who continues to sin belongs to the devil. The Son of God came for this purpose: to destroy the devil's work.

9Those who are God's children do not continue sinning, because the new life from God remains in them. They are not able to go on sinning, because they have become children of God. **10**So we can see who God's children are and who the devil's children are: Those who do not do what is right are not God's children, and those who do not love their brothers and sisters are not God's children.

OLD TESTAMENT READING

Anything I saw and wanted, I got for myself;
   I did not miss any pleasure I desired.
I was pleased with everything I did,
      and this pleasure was the reward for all my
      hard work.
11But then I looked at what I had done,
      and I thought about all the hard work.
   Suddenly I realized it was useless, like chasing
      the wind.
      There is nothing to gain from anything we
      do here on earth.

Ecclesiastes 2:10–11

INSIGHTS

When I look back on my life nowadays, which I sometimes do, what strikes me forcibly about it is that what seemed at the time most significant and seductive, seems now most futile and absurd. For instance, success in all of its various guises; being known and being praised; ostensible pleasures, like acquiring money . . . or travelling, going to and fro in the world and up and down in it like Satan, exploring and experiencing whatever Vanity Fair has to offer.

In retrospect all these exercises in self-gratification seem pure fantasy, what Pascal called "licking the earth." They are diversions designed to distract our attention from the true purpose of our existence in this world, which is, quite simply, to look for God, and, in looking, to find Him, and having found Him, to love Him, thereby establishing a harmonious relationship with His purposes for His creation.

MALCOLM MUGGERIDGE

ACTION POINT

Write down what you believe to be your true purpose in life. What things are important according to that purpose? Pray that God will help you focus on the important things and put aside everything else—no matter how tempting it may appear!

1 JOHN 3:11 — 4:12

We Must Love Each Other

11This is the teaching you have heard from the beginning: We must love each other. **12**Do not be like Cain who belonged to the Evil One and killed his brother. And why did he kill him? Because the things Cain did were evil, and the things his brother did were good.

13Brothers and sisters, do not be surprised when the people of the world hate you. **14**We know we have left death and have come into life because we love each other. Whoever does not love is still dead. **15**Everyone who hates a brother or sister is a murderer, and you know that no murderers have eternal life in them. **16**This is how we know what real love is: Jesus gave his life for us. So we should give our lives for our brothers and sisters, **17**Suppose someone has enough to live and sees a brother or sister in need, but does not help. Then God's love is not living in that person. **18**My children, we should love people not only with words and talk, but by our actions and true caring.

19-20 This is the way we know that we belong to the way of truth. When our hearts make us feel guilty, we can still have peace before God. God is greater than our hearts, and he knows everything. **21**My dear friends, if our hearts do not make us feel guilty, we can come without fear into God's presence. **22**And God gives us what we ask for because we obey God's commands and do what pleases him. **23**This is what God commands: that we believe in his Son, Jesus Christ, and that we love each other, just as he commanded. **24**The people who obey God's commands live in God, and God lives in them. We know that God lives in us because of the Spirit God gave us.

Warning Against False Teachers

4 My dear friends, many false prophets have gone out into the world. So do not believe every spirit, but test the spirits to see if they are from God. **2**This is how you can know God's Spirit: Every spirit who confesses that Jesus Christ came to earth as a human is from God. **3**And every spirit who refuses to say this about Jesus is not from God. It is the spirit of the enemy of Christ, which you have heard is coming, and now he is already in the world.

4My dear children, you belong to God and have defeated them; because God's Spirit, who is in you, is greater than the devil, who is in the world. **5**And they belong to the world, so what they say is from the world, and the world listens to them. **6**But we belong to God, and those who know God listen to us. But those who are not from God do not listen to us. That is how we know the Spirit that is true and the spirit that is false.

Love Comes from God

7Dear friends, we should love each other, because love comes from God. Everyone who loves has become God's child and knows God. **8**Whoever does not love does not know God, because God is love. **9**This is how God showed his love to us: He sent his one and only Son into the world so that we could have life through him. **10**This is what real love is: It is not our love for God; it is God's love for us. He sent his Son to die in our place to take away our sins.

¹¹Dear friends, if God loved us that much we also should love each other. ¹²No one has ever seen God, but if we love each other, God lives in us, and his love is made perfect in us.

OLD TESTAMENT READING

The king asked, "Is anyone left in Saul's family? I want to show God's kindness to that person." ⁵Then King David had servants bring Jonathan's son from the house of Makir son of Ammiel in Lo Debar. ⁶Mephibosheth, Jonathan's son, came before David and bowed facedown on the floor.

David said, "Mephibosheth!"

Mephibosheth said, "I am your servant."

⁷David said to him, "Don't be afraid. I will be kind to you for your father Jonathan's sake. I will give you back all the land of your grandfather Saul, and you will always eat at my table."

2 Samuel 9:3, 5–7

INSIGHTS

There is more to becoming a Christian than accepting a set of doctrines and striving to live out a particular lifestyle. Being a Christian involves allowing God to become a living presence in your life. . . . A Christian is a person who is possessed by Christ in such a way that feelings, thoughts, and attitudes are all changed. For the Christian person, loving becomes a spiritual exercise because God is love, and the Christian knows that "every one that loveth is born of God." God wants to indwell you and affect your consciousness for many reasons, but above them all is His desire to be able to reach other people with His love through you. . . . If you will pray and ask Him to be an indwelling reality and if you are willing to yield to His will in all things, He will enter into your consciousness and begin to effect a transformation in your life. Most important, you will, little by little, begin to relate to other people as He would relate to them. You will recognize that being a Christian involves a commitment to treat others as He would treat them. . . .

If you want to do something that will cause you to become a more loving person, surrender yourself to Jesus. He has a way of making lovers out of people.

TONY CAMPOLO

APPLICATION

Why is love characteristic of God's children? What does a lack of love reveal about a person's heart? How much should God's children love each other? In what ways do God's children demonstrate their love? To whom can you show the kind of godly love that David showed Mephibosheth?

1 JOHN 4:13 – 5:21

13We know that we live in God and he lives in us, because he gave us his Spirit. 14We have seen and can testify that the Father sent his Son to be the Savior of the world. 15Whoever confesses that Jesus is the Son of God has God living inside, and that person lives in God. 16And so we know the love that God has for us, and we trust that love.

God is love. Those who live in love live in God, and God lives in them. 17This is how love is made perfect in us: that we can be without fear on the day God judges us, because in this world we are like him. 18Where God's love is, there is no fear, because God's perfect love drives out fear. It is punishment that makes a person fear, so love is not made perfect in the person who fears.

19We love because God first loved us. 20If people say, "I love God," but hate their brothers or sisters, they are liars. Those who do not love their brothers and sisters, whom they have seen, cannot love God, whom they have never seen. 21And God gave us this command: Those who love God must also love their brothers and sisters.

Faith in the Son of God

5Everyone who believes that Jesus is the Christ is God's child, and whoever loves the Father also loves the Father's children. 2This is how we know we love God's children: when we love God and obey his commands. 3Loving God means obeying his commands. And God's commands are not too hard for us, 4because everyone who is a child of God conquers the world. And this is the victory that conquers the world—our faith. 5So the one who conquers the world is the person who believes that Jesus is the Son of God.

6Jesus Christ is the One who came by water and blood. He did not come by water only, but by water and blood. And the Spirit says that this is true, because the Spirit is the truth. 7So there are three witnesses: 8the Spirit, the water, and the blood; and these three witnesses agree. 9We believe people when they say something is true. But what God says is more important, and he has told us the truth about his own Son. 10Anyone who believes in the Son of God has the truth that God told us. Anyone who does not believe makes God a liar, because that person does not believe what God told us about his Son. 11This is what God told us: God has given us eternal life, and this life is in his Son. 12Whoever has the Son has life, but whoever does not have the Son of God does not have life.

We Have Eternal Life Now

13I write this letter to you who believe in the Son of God so you will know you have eternal life. 14And this is the boldness we have in God's presence: that if we ask God for anything that agrees with what he wants, he hears us. 15If we know he hears us every time we ask him, we know we have what we ask from him.

16If anyone sees a brother or sister sinning (sin that does not lead to eternal death), that person should pray, and God will give the sinner life. I am talking about people whose sin does not lead to eternal death. There is sin that leads to death. I do not mean that a person should pray about that sin. **17**Doing wrong is always sin, but there is sin that does not lead to eternal death.

18We know that those who are God's children do not continue to sin. The Son of God keeps them safe, and the Evil One cannot touch them. **19**We know that we belong to God, but the Evil One controls the whole world. **20**We also know that the Son of God has come and has given us understanding so that we can know the True One. And our lives are in the True One and in his Son, Jesus Christ. He is the true God and the eternal life.

21So, dear children, keep yourselves away from false gods.

OLD TESTAMENT READING

ut God has listened;
he has heard my prayer.
20Praise God,
who did not ignore my prayer
or hold back his love from me.

Psalm 66:19–20

INSIGHTS

PLEASE INTERRUPT

Sometimes I feel like an interruption,
and then I want to shrink
back into my shell
and never come out again.
I want to walk away and say,
"I'm sorry I took your time."

Being an interruption hurts.
It tells me
something is more important than
I am.
It tells me
to hurry up and move along.
It tells me
you are looking
but don't see me.
It tells me
you are listening

but don't hear me.
And so I move along.

But, God says,
"Don't hurry away.
Stick around.
Tell me how it is with you.
Tell me what you're feeling
right this minute.
Tell me why you feel that way.
I want to know you.
You count with me.
I care about you.
Tell me what I can do for you."

And I go away feeling
He was glad I called.

RUTH SENTER

PAUSE FOR REFLECTION

Who listens to you every time you speak? How do you know that God hears your prayers? What would you tell others that he has done for you?

➤ # 2 JOHN 1—
3 JOHN 15

¹From the Elder.

To the chosen lady and her children:

I love all of you in the truth, and all those who know the truth love you. ²We love you because of the truth that lives in us and will be with us forever. ³Grace, mercy, and peace from God the Father and his Son, Jesus Christ, will be with us in truth and love.

⁴I was very happy to learn that some of your children are following the way of truth, as the Father commanded us. ⁵And now, dear lady, this is not a new command but is the same command we have had from the beginning. I ask you that we all love each other. ⁶And love means living the way God commanded us to live. As you have heard from the beginning, his command is this: Live a life of love.

⁷Many false teachers are in the world now who do not confess that Jesus Christ came to earth as a human. Anyone who does not confess this is a false teacher and an enemy of Christ. ⁸Be careful yourselves that you do not lose everything you have worked for, but that you receive your full reward.

⁹Anyone who goes beyond Christ's teaching and does not continue to follow only his teaching does not have God. But whoever continues to follow the teaching of Christ has both the Father and the Son. ¹⁰If someone comes to you and does not bring this teaching, do not welcome or accept that person into your house. ¹¹If you welcome such a person, you share in the evil work.

¹²I have many things to write to you, but I do not want to use paper and ink. Instead, I hope to come to you and talk face to face so we can be full of joy. ¹³The children of your chosen sister greet you.

3 JOHN

¹From the Elder.

To my dear friend Gaius, whom I love in the truth:

²My dear friend, I know your soul is doing fine, and I pray that you are doing well in every way and that your health is good. ³I was very happy when some brothers and sisters came and told me about the truth in your life and how you are following the way of truth. ⁴Nothing gives me greater joy than to hear that my children are following the way of truth.

⁵My dear friend, it is good that you help the brothers and sisters, even those you do not know. ⁶They told the church about your love. Please help them to continue their trip in a way worthy of God. ⁷They started out in service to Christ, and they have been accepting nothing from nonbelievers. ⁸So we should help such people; when we do, we share in their work for the truth.

⁹I wrote something to the church, but Diotrephes, who loves to be their leader, will not listen to us. ¹⁰So if I come, I will talk about what Diotrephes is doing, about how he lies and says evil things about us. But more than that, he refuses to accept the other brothers and sisters; he even stops those who do want to accept them and puts them out of the church.

¹¹My dear friend, do not follow what is bad; follow what is good. The one who does good belongs to God. But the one who does evil has never known God.

¹²Everyone says good things about Demetrius, and the truth agrees with what they say. We also speak well of him, and you know what we say is true.

¹³I have many things I want to write you, but I do not want to use pen and ink. ¹⁴I hope to see you soon and talk face to face. ¹⁵Peace to you. The friends here greet you. Please greet each friend there by name.

OLD TESTAMENT READING

Then Moses called Joshua and said to him in front of the people, "Be strong and brave, because you will lead these people into the land the LORD promised to give their ancestors, and help them take it as their own. ⁸The LORD himself will go before you. He will be with you; he will not leave you or forget you. Don't be afraid and don't worry."

Deuteronomy 31:7–8

INSIGHTS

I decided to take a break and hit the slopes (emphasis on hit, since it was my first time in all my life to attempt to ski). . . .

It was unbelievable! . . . It is doubtful that anyone else on planet earth has ever come down any ski slope more ways than I did. Or landed in more positions. Or did more creative things in the air before landing. . . .

Working with me that humiliating day was the world's most encouraging ski instructor (yes, I had an instructor!) who set the new record in patience. . . .

Never once did she lose her cool.

Never once did she laugh at me.

Never once did she yell, scream, threaten, or swear.

Never once did she call me "dummy." . . .

. . . That day God gave me a living, never-to-be-forgotten illustration of the value of encouragement. . . .

What is true for a novice on the snow once a year is all the more true for the people we meet every day. Harassed by demands and deadlines; bruised by worry, adversity, and failure; broken by disillusionment; and defeated by sin, they live somewhere between dull discouragement and sheer panic. Even Christians are not immune! We may give off this "I've got it all together" air of confidence, much like I did when I first snapped on the skis. But realistically, we also struggle, lose our balance, slip and slide, tumble, and fall flat on our faces.

All of us need encouragement—somebody to believe in us. To reassure and reinforce us. To help us pick up the pieces and go on. To provide us with increased determination in spite of the odds.

CHARLES SWINDOLL

APPLICATION

Describe the kinds of encouragement in faith revealed through these Scripture readings. When have you been blessed by spiritual encouragement? Who could use your encouragement today?

JUDE 1-13

1From Jude, a servant of Jesus Christ and a brother of James.

To all who have been called by God. God the Father loves you, and you have been kept safe in Jesus Christ:

2Mercy, peace, and love be yours richly.

God Will Punish Sinners

3Dear friends, I wanted very much to write you about the salvation we all share. But I felt the need to write you about something else: I want to encourage you to fight hard for the faith that was given the holy people of God once and for all time. **4**Some people have secretly entered your group. Long ago the prophets wrote about these people who will be judged guilty. They are against God and have changed the grace of our God into a reason for sexual sin. They also refuse to accept Jesus Christ, our only Master and Lord.

5I want to remind you of some things you already know: Remember that the Lord saved his people by bringing them out of the land of Egypt. But later he destroyed all those who did not believe. **6**And remember the angels who did not keep their place of power but left their proper home. The Lord has kept these angels in darkness, bound with everlasting chains, to be judged on the great day. **7**Also remember the cities of Sodom and Gomorrah and the other towns around them. In the same way they were full of sexual sin and people who desired sexual relations that God does not allow. They suffer the punishment of eternal fire, as an example for all to see.

8It is the same with these people who have entered your group. They are guided by dreams and make themselves filthy with sin. They reject God's authority and speak against the angels. **9**Not even the archangel Michael, when he argued with the devil about who would have the body of Moses, dared to judge the devil guilty. Instead, he said, "The Lord punish you." **10**But these people speak against things they do not understand. And what they do know, by feeling, as dumb animals know things, are the very things that destroy them. **11**It will be terrible for them. They have followed the way of Cain, and for money they have given themselves to doing the wrong that Balaam did. They have fought against God as Korah did, and like Korah, they surely will be destroyed. **12**They are like dirty spots in your special Christian meals you share. They eat with you and have no fear, caring only for themselves. They are clouds without rain, which the wind blows around. They are autumn trees without fruit that are pulled out of the ground. So they are twice dead. **13**They are like wild waves of the sea, tossing up their own shameful actions like foam. They are like stars that wander in the sky. A place in the blackest darkness has been kept for them forever.

OLD TESTAMENT READING

Cry, because the Lord's day of judging is near;
  the Almighty is sending destruction.
7People will be weak with fear,
  and their courage will melt away.
8Everyone will be afraid.
  Pain and hurt will grab them;

they will hurt like a woman giving birth to
a baby.
They will look at each other in fear,
with their faces red like fire.
⁹Look, the LORD's day of judging is
coming—
a terrible day, a day of God's anger.
He will destroy the land
and the sinners who live in it.
¹⁰The stars will not show their light;
the skies will be dark.

The sun will grow dark as it rises,
and the moon will not give its light.

¹¹The LORD says, "I will punish the world for its
evil
and wicked people for their sins.
I will cause proud people to lose their pride,
and I will destroy the pride of those who
are cruel to others."

Isaiah 13:6–11

INSIGHTS

You have a "lake of fire and brimstone," and you see lost sinners thrown into its waves of rolling fire; and they lash its burning shore, and gnaw their tongues for pain. There the worm dieth not, and their fire is not quenched, and "not one drop of water" can reach them to "cool their tongues"—"tormented in that flame."

What think you? Has God said these things to frighten our poor souls? Did He mean to play on our fears for His own amusement? Can you think so? Nay, does it not rather grieve His heart that He must build such a hell, and must plunge therein the sinners who will not honour His law—will not embrace salvation from sinning through His grace? Ah, the waves of death roll darkly under the eye of the Holy and compassionate One! He has no pleasure in the death of the sinner! But He must sustain His throne, and save His loyal subjects if He can. . . .

God would have us understand what an awful thing sin is, and what fearful punishment it deserves. He would fain show us by such figures how terrible must be the doom of the determined sinner.

CHARLES FINNEY

PAUSE FOR REFLECTION

Why must God punish those who are against him? List the sins of those who are against God. How can God's people stand strong against them? How are God's people to treat those who have doubts?

JUDE 14-25

14Enoch, the seventh descendant from Adam, said about these people: "Look, the Lord is coming with many thousands of his holy angels to **15**judge every person. He is coming to punish all who are against God for all the evil they have done against him. And he will punish the sinners who are against God for all the evil they have said against him."

16These people complain and blame others, doing the evil things they want to do. They brag about themselves, and they flatter others to get what they want.

A Warning and Things to Do

17Dear friends, remember what the apostles of our Lord Jesus Christ said before. **18**They said to you, "In the last times there will be people who laugh about God, following their own evil desires which are against God." **19**These are the people who divide you, people whose thoughts are only of this world, who do not have the Spirit.

20But dear friends, use your most holy faith to build yourselves up, praying in the Holy Spirit. **21**Keep yourselves in God's love as you wait for the Lord Jesus Christ with his mercy to give you life forever.

22Show mercy to some people who have doubts. **23**Take others out of the fire, and save them. Show mercy mixed with fear to others, hating even their clothes which are dirty from sin.

Praise God

24God is strong and can help you not to fall. He can bring you before his glory without any wrong in you and can give you great joy. **25**He is the only God, the One who saves us. To him be glory, greatness, power, and authority through Jesus Christ our Lord for all time past, now, and forever. Amen.

OLD TESTAMENT READING

This is what the LORD says:
"The wise must not brag about their
wisdom.
The strong must not brag about their
strength.
The rich must not brag about their money.
24But if people want to brag, let them brag
that they understand and know me.
Let them brag that I am the LORD,
and that I am kind and fair,
and that I do things that are right on earth.
This kind of bragging pleases me," says the
LORD.

Jeremiah 9:23-24

Give happiness to me, your servant,
because I give my life to you, Lord.
5Lord, you are kind and forgiving
and have great love for those who call to
you.

11LORD, teach me what you want me to do,
and I will live by your truth.
Teach me to respect you completely.
12Lord, my God, I will praise you with all my
heart,
and I will honor your name forever.
13You have great love for me.

You have saved me from death.

14God, proud people are attacking me;
a gang of cruel people is trying to kill me.
They do not respect you.

16Turn to me and have mercy.
Give me, your servant, strength.

Psalm 86:4–5; 11–14, 16a

INSIGHTS

God is a just God, One who shows no partiality. Outside of grace, God's penalty falls on all. "The wages of sin is death" (Romans 6:23). Sin is sin. The consequences have been posted; He gives fair warning. No excuses accepted. No variations on the rules. Man is accountable. Rebellion, be it active or passive, calls for justice.

I understand God's justice because I remember rebellion—ten-year-old rebellion. My father was the dispenser of justice. "No swimming in the creek today," he said. I had plenty of excuses: "Jimmy went in." "I was so hot." "It isn't fair when everybody else's dad lets them go."

Excuses didn't matter because the standard had been violated. The penalty was swift and sure. Justice was done. But then the father who had just administered justice reached for his big white handkerchief and wiped the tears from his eyes. That day, justice and love were forever linked in my mind.

My father's actions pointed me toward a heavenly Father who sits in the hall of justice, calls His creation to accountability, but weeps over waywardness even as He pronounces sentence. "Oh, Jerusalem, Jerusalem . . . how often I have longed to gather your children together, as a hen gathers her chicks under her wings, but you were not willing!" (Luke 13:34, NIV). Justice and love exist in the same person.

. . . I can be at peace about God's system of justice, for I have confidence in the Judge. There will be no payoffs. He judges clean.

As a sinner who knew where to find grace, I know God today not as my judge but as a loving Father who continually calls me to accountability. One day He was my judge. But I can almost see a white handkerchief dabbing tears as He wept over my rebellion, issued the sentence, and then took my penalty upon Himself. I am acquitted. Justice has been done. My debt has been paid. I can rest my case. . . .

"God is fair," I said to myself, "whether or not I understand His ways. For He is a God of justice."

RUTH SENTER

APPLICATION

How does God want his people to treat those who have doubts? Do you have complete trust in God, who is both Judge and Savior? Are you at rest in his love?

REVELATION 1:1-20

John Tells About This Book

1 This is the revelation of Jesus Christ, which God gave to him, to show his servants what must soon happen. And Jesus sent his angel to show it to his servant John, **2**who has told everything he has seen. It is the word of God; it is the message from Jesus Christ. **3**Blessed is the one who reads the words of God's message, and blessed are the people who hear this message and do what is written in it. The time is near when all of this will happen.

Jesus' Message to the Churches

4From John.

To the seven churches in Asia:

Grace and peace to you from the One who is and was and is coming, and from the seven spirits before his throne, **5**and from Jesus Christ. Jesus is the faithful witness, the first among those raised from the dead. He is the ruler of the kings of the earth.

He is the One who loves us, who made us free from our sins with the blood of his death. **6**He made us to be a kingdom of priests who serve God his Father. To Jesus Christ be glory and power forever and ever! Amen.

7Look, Jesus is coming with the clouds, and everyone will see him, even those who stabbed him. And all peoples of the earth will cry loudly because of him. Yes, this will happen! Amen.

8The Lord God says, "I am the Alpha and the Omega. I am the One who is and was and is coming. I am the Almighty."

9I, John, am your brother. All of us share with Christ in suffering, in the kingdom, and in patience to continue. I was on the island of Patmos, because I had preached the word of God and the message about Jesus. **10**On the Lord's day I was in the Spirit, and I heard a loud voice behind me that sounded like a trumpet. **11**The voice said, "Write what you see in a book and send it to the seven churches: to Ephesus, Smyrna, Pergamum, Thyatira, Sardis, Philadelphia, and Laodicea."

12I turned to see who was talking to me. When I turned, I saw seven golden lampstands **13**and someone among the lampstands who was "like a Son of Man." He was dressed in a long robe and had a gold band around his chest. **14**His head and hair were white like wool, as white as snow, and his eyes were like flames of fire. **15**His feet were like bronze that glows hot in a furnace, and his voice was like the noise of flooding water. **16**He held seven stars in his right hand, and a sharp double-edged sword came out of his mouth. He looked like the sun shining at its brightest time.

17When I saw him, I fell down at his feet like a dead man. He put his right hand on me and said, "Do not be afraid. I am the First and the Last. **18**I am the One who lives; I was dead, but look, I am alive forever and ever! And I hold the keys to death and to the place of the dead. **19**So write the things you see, what is now and what will happen later. **20**Here is the secret of the seven stars that you saw in my right hand and the seven golden lampstands: The seven lampstands are the seven churches, and the seven stars are the angels of the seven churches."

OLD TESTAMENT READING

People of Jacob, listen to me.
　　People of Israel, I have called you to be my
　　　people.

I am God;
　　I am the beginning and the end.
13 I made the earth with my own hands.
　　　With my right hand I spread out the
　　　　skies.
　　When I call them,
　　　they come together before me."

Isaiah 48:12–13

INSIGHTS

I am the beginning;
　I am the end.
You are very concerned with
　　beginnings.
　You hesitate to reach
　　the end.
The Alpha/beginning,
　the Omega/end,
　means that I am your all-in-all.
Do you want to stay
　an Alpha person—
　always at the starting line of faith?
　That is a safe place—
　where you say you believe Me,
　where you champion truth,
　but you don't move.
Move, I say!
　Feel the wind of trials and victories in
　　Me.
I am the Finisher, the Omega.
Lift your eyes from the starting line
　and focus on all that lies before
　　you—

on the intelligent golden faith
　awaiting you at the finish.

Learn of me; digest My Word,
　always in communion with Me.
I am your health, your energy:
　I bring you to a "finish"
　that is not the end of all things;
　not a place where you collapse,
　emptied out, done.
It is the place where you
　allow Me freely
　to live through you.

My finish means new development,
　new discoveries,
　new victories,
　new holy charges.
My dearest and most effective
　　servants
　are those who move
　in "finished" faith.

MARIE CHAPIAN

APPLICATION

As you read about the awesome power and greatness of God, the I AM, fear seems to be an appropriate response, doesn't it? Yet when John fell down in fear before God, God gently and compassionately reached out to him and told him what he was to do (Rev. 1:17–20). What is the great I AM moving you to do today?

REVELATION 2:1-17

To the Church in Ephesus

"Write this to the angel of the church in Ephesus:

"The One who holds the seven stars in his right hand and walks among the seven golden lampstands says this: **2**I know what you do, how you work hard and never give up. I know you do not put up with the false teachings of evil people. You have tested those who say they are apostles but really are not, and you found they are liars. **3**You have patience and have suffered troubles for my name and have not given up.

4"But I have this against you: You have left the love you had in the beginning. **5**So remember where you were before you fell. Change your hearts and do what you did at first. If you do not change, I will come to you and will take away your lampstand from its place. **6**But there is something you do that is right: You hate what the Nicolaitans do, as much as I.

7"Every person who has ears should listen to what the Spirit says to the churches. To those who win the victory I will give the right to eat the fruit from the tree of life, which is in the garden of God.

To the Church in Smyrna

8"Write this to the angel of the church in Smyrna:

"The One who is the First and the Last, who died and came to life again, says this: **9**I know your troubles and that you are poor, but really you are rich! I know the bad things some people say about you. They say they are Jews, but they are not true Jews. They are a synagogue that belongs to Satan. **10**Do not be afraid of what you are about to suffer. I tell you, the devil will put some of you in prison to test you, and you will suffer for ten days. But be faithful, even if you have to die, and I will give you the crown of life.

11"Everyone who has ears should listen to what the Spirit says to the churches. Those who win the victory will not be hurt by the second death.

To the Church in Pergamum

12"Write this to the angel of the church in Pergamum:

"The One who has the sharp, double-edged sword says this: **13**I know where you live. It is where Satan has his throne. But you are true to me. You did not refuse to tell about your faith in me even during the time of Antipas, my faithful witness who was killed in your city, where Satan lives.

14"But I have a few things against you: You have some there who follow the teaching of Balaam. He taught Balak how to cause the people of Israel to sin by eating food offered to idols and by taking part in sexual sins. **15**You also have some who follow the teaching of the Nicolaitans. **16**So change your hearts and lives. If you do not, I will come to you quickly and fight against them with the sword that comes out of my mouth.

17"Everyone who has ears should listen to what the Spirit says to the churches.

"I will give some of the hidden manna to everyone who wins the victory. I will also give to each one who wins the victory a white stone with a new name written on it. No one knows this new name except the one who receives it."

OLD TESTAMENT READING

G o and speak this message toward the north:
'Come back, unfaithful people of Israel,'
   says the LORD.

'I will stop being angry at you,
because I am full of mercy,' says the
LORD.
'I will not be angry with you forever.'"

Jeremiah 3:12

INSIGHTS

A few years ago, in a commencement address at Harvard University, Alexander Solzhenitsyn tried to summarize the root problem facing capitalism and Marxism. He said that the trouble with both systems is that men have forgotten God. One system does it by its materialist philosophy; the other system by its materialist economy.

But "the sin of forgetting God" is not just the sin of economics and governments. It can be the sin of religion as well. Religious people forget God by setting up a religious system in His place.

Stephen was up against such a system in Acts 7. Stephen charged that the religion of Jerusalem had turned bad. The supreme court of that city did not take Stephen's words lightly. They were furious. They tried to silence him by running him out of town, and finally they killed him by stoning. Stephen's hot piety was a threat to the council's cold religion.

A fire dies unless it is fed. The most natural thing in this world is for a person to lose his zeal, fervor, and drive. . . .

Each of us forgets too soon. We all have the inherent tendency to drift from God.

The constant call of the Bible is to be on guard—to remember! Continually we are told to turn around, to repent, to draw near to God and submit to Him. . . .

The first lesson we must learn is the one Stephen tried to teach the Sanhedrin: "The Most High does not dwell in houses [or structures, or systems] made by human hands" (v. 48). He is God, Maker of heaven and earth, Alpha and Omega. He is the One to whom every man shall one day give account.

The second lesson that Stephen preached, by his words and life, is that God wants a personal relationship with His people. He does not want a system or a dead religion. He wants you. He wants to be your God and your friend. He wants a partnership with His creatures. He wants them to love Him and enjoy Him forever.

GEORGE SWEETING
DONALD SWEETING

ACTION POINT

How much does God treasure the faithful love of his followers? What does he promise to those who love him faithfully? What is his warning to those who forsake him? In what ways have you forsaken God? How will you regain your love for him?

REVELATION 2:18 – 3:6

To the Church in Thyatira

18"Write this to the angel of the church in Thyatira:

"The Son of God, who has eyes that blaze like fire and feet like shining bronze, says this: **19**I know what you do. I know about your love, your faith, your service, and your patience. I know that you are doing more now than you did at first.

20"But I have this against you: You let that woman Jezebel spread false teachings. She says she is a prophetess, but by her teaching she leads my people to take part in sexual sins and to eat food that is offered to idols. **21**I have given her time to change her heart and turn away from her sin, but she does not want to change. **22**So I will throw her on a bed of suffering. And all those who take part in adultery with her will suffer greatly if they do not turn away from the wrongs she does. **23**I will also kill her followers. Then all the churches will know I am the One who searches hearts and minds, and I will repay each of you for what you have done.

24"But others of you in Thyatira have not followed her teaching and have not learned what some call Satan's deep secrets. I say to you that I will not put any other load on you. **25**Only continue in your loyalty until I come.

26"I will give power over the nations to everyone who wins the victory and continues to be obedient to me until the end.

27'You will rule over them with an iron rod,
as when pottery is broken into pieces.'

Psalm 2:9

28This is the same power I received from my Father. I will also give him the morning star. **29**Everyone who has ears should listen to what the Spirit says to the churches.

To the Church in Sardis

3 "Write this to the angel of the church in Sardis:

"The One who has the seven spirits and the seven stars says this: I know what you do. People say that you are alive, but really you are dead. **2**Wake up! Strengthen what you have left before it dies completely. I have found that what you are doing is less than what my God wants. **3**So do not forget what you have received and heard. Obey it, and change your hearts and lives. So you must wake up, or I will come like a thief, and you will not know when I will come to you. **4**But you have a few there in Sardis who have kept their clothes unstained, so they will walk with me and will wear white clothes, because they are worthy. **5**Those who win the victory will be dressed in white clothes like them. And I will not erase their names from the book of life, but I will say they belong to me before my Father and before his angels. **6**Everyone who has ears should listen to what the Spirit says to the churches."

OLD TESTAMENT READING

Now, Israel, this is what the LORD your God wants you to do: Respect the LORD your God, and do what he has told you to do. Love him. Serve the LORD your God with your whole being.

Deuteronomy 10:12

Today you have said that the LORD is your God, and you have promised to do what he wants you to do—to keep his rules, commands, and laws. You have said you will obey him. **18**And today the LORD has said that you are his very own people, as he has promised you. But you must obey his commands.

Deuteronomy 26:17–18

Prophets or those who tell the future with dreams might come to you and say they will show you a miracle or a sign. **2**The miracle or sign might even happen, and then they might say, "Let's serve other gods" (gods you have not known) "and let's worship them." **5**The prophets or dreamers must be killed, because they said you should turn against the LORD your God, who brought you out of Egypt and saved you from the land where you were slaves. They tried to turn you from doing what the LORD your God commanded you to do. You must get rid of the evil among you.

Deuteronomy 13:1–2, 5

INSIGHTS

The older I get and the better acquainted I am with Christ, the more I'm aware of His insistence on holiness. This seems to be a matter about which He's not open to negotiation even in the slightest.

I guess somebody could consider bringing up this subject for discussion, "Ah, Jesus, I feel You're a bit too stubborn on this righteousness issue. I mean, I figure I've made some pretty big concessions Your way. On the matter of this one pet sin, couldn't You compromise a little? Accommodate me? Maybe 3 or 4 percent darkness allowable, and all the rest light?"

I warn you, the Lord won't budge even one millimeter. . . .

The absolute truth is: Anyone who wants to be close friends with Christ needs to achieve this victory-over-sin mindset, needs to learn to keep short accounts with God, needs to refuse to allow sins of long standing to go unconfessed day after day, week after week, even year after year. . . .

The hour must come when the church as a body and the individuals who compose the corporate entity reach for holiness. We must ask God for determination to overcome sin; we must pray for conviction for our unrighteousness. We must understand that we will never experience that overwhelming sense of the presence of Christ if we are not intent on striving to be 100 percent light-walkers.

DAVID MAINS

APPLICATION

What attitude do these readings say God's people must have toward sin? What action does he require? What does God promise to those who win the victory? How determined are you to overcome the sin in your life?

REVELATION
3:7 — 4:5

To the Church in Philadelphia

7"Write this to the angel of the church in Philadelphia:

"This is what the One who is holy and true, who holds the key of David, says. When he opens a door, no one can close it. And when he closes it, no one can open it. **8**I know what you do. I have put an open door before you, which no one can close. I know you have little strength, but you have obeyed my teaching and were not afraid to speak my name. **9**Those in the synagogue that belongs to Satan say they are Jews, but they are not true Jews; they are liars. I will make them come before you and bow at your feet, and they will know that I have loved you. **10**You have obeyed my teaching about not giving up your faith. So I will keep you from the time of trouble that will come to the whole world to test those who live on earth.

11"I am coming soon. Continue strong in your faith so no one will take away your crown. **12**I will make those who win the victory pillars in the temple of my God, and they will never have to leave it. I will write on them the name of my God and the name of the city of my God, the new Jerusalem, that comes down out of heaven from my God. I will also write on them my new name. **13**Everyone who has ears should listen to what the Spirit says to the churches.

To the Church in Laodicea

14"Write this to the angel of the church in Laodicea:

"The Amen, the faithful and true witness, the ruler of all God has made, says this: **15**I know what you do, that you are not hot or cold. I wish that you were hot or cold! **16**But because you are lukewarm—neither hot, nor cold—I am ready to spit you out of my mouth. **17**You say, 'I am rich, and I have become wealthy and do not need anything.' But you do not know that you are really miserable, pitiful, poor, blind, and naked. **18**I advise you to buy from me gold made pure in fire so you can be truly rich. Buy from me white clothes so you can be clothed and so you can cover your shameful nakedness. Buy from me medicine to put on your eyes so you can truly see.

19"I correct and punish those whom I love. So be eager to do right, and change your hearts and lives. **20**Here I am! I stand at the door and knock. If you hear my voice and open the door, I will come in and eat with you, and you will eat with me.

21"Those who win the victory will sit with me on my throne in the same way that I won the victory and sat down with my Father on his throne. **22**Everyone who has ears should listen to what the Spirit says to the churches."

John Sees Heaven

4 After the vision of these things I looked, and there before me was an open door in heaven. And the same voice that spoke to me before, that sounded like a trumpet, said, "Come up here, and I will show you what must happen after this." **2**Immediately I was in the Spirit, and before me was a throne in heaven, and someone was sitting on it. **3**The One who sat on the throne looked like precious stones, like jasper and carnelian. All around the throne was a rainbow the color of an emerald. **4**Around the throne there were twenty-four other thrones with twenty-four elders sitting on them. They were dressed in white and had golden crowns on their heads. **5**Lightning flashes and noises and thunder came from the throne. Before the throne seven lamps were burning, which are the seven spirits of God.

OLD TESTAMENT READING

At that time Michael, the great prince who protects your people, will stand up. There will be a time of much trouble, the worst time since nations have been on earth, but your people will be saved. Everyone whose name is written in God's book will be saved. **2**Many people who have already died will live again. Some of them will wake up to have life forever, but some will wake up to find shame and disgrace forever. **3**The wise people will shine like the brightness of the sky. Those who teach others to live right will shine like stars forever and ever."

Daniel 12:1–3

INSIGHTS

Ray Stedman tells the story of an old missionary couple who had been working in Africa for many years and were returning to New York City to retire. With no pension and broken in health, they were discouraged, fearful of the future.

They happened to be booked on the same ship as Teddy Roosevelt, who was returning from a big-game hunting expedition. They watched the passengers trying to glimpse the great man, the crew fussing over him. . . .

At the dock in New York a band was waiting to greet the President. . . . But the missionary couple slipped off the ship unnoticed.

That night, in a cheap flat they found on the East Side, the man's spirit broke. He said to his wife, "I can't take this; God is not treating us fairly." His wife suggested he go in the bedroom and tell the Lord.

A short time later he came out of the bedroom with a face completely changed. His wife asked, "Dear, what happened?"

"The Lord settled it with me," he said. "I told him how bitter I was that the President should receive this tremendous homecoming, when no one met us as we returned home. And when I finished, it seemed as though the Lord put his hand on my shoulder and simply said, 'But you're not home yet!' "

DONALD MCCULLOUGH

APPLICATION

To whom does Jesus promise salvation? What kind of a "homecoming" does he promise to those who belong to him? Ask God to help you, like the old missionary, keep perspective on what is to come!

REVELATION
4:6 — 6:2

6Also before the throne there was something that looked like a sea of glass, clear like crystal.

In the center and around the throne were four living creatures with eyes all over them, in front and in back. **7**The first living creature was like a lion. The second was like a calf. The third had a face like a man. The fourth was like a flying eagle. **8**Each of these four living creatures had six wings and was covered all over with eyes, inside and out. Day and night they never stop saying:

"Holy, holy, holy is the Lord God Almighty.

He was, he is, and he is coming."

9These living creatures give glory, honor, and thanks to the One who sits on the throne, who lives forever and ever. **10**Then the twenty-four elders bow down before the One who sits on the throne, and they worship him who lives forever and ever. They put their crowns down before the throne and say:

11"You are worthy, our Lord and God,

to receive glory and honor and power,

because you made all things.

Everything existed and was made,

because you wanted it."

Then I saw a scroll in the right hand of the One sitting on the throne. The scroll had writing on both sides and was kept closed with seven seals. **2**And I saw a powerful angel calling in a loud voice, "Who is worthy to break the seals and open the scroll?" **3**But there was no one in heaven or on earth or under the earth who could open the scroll or look inside it. **4**I cried bitterly because there was no one who was worthy to open the scroll or look inside. **5**But one of the elders said to me, "Do not cry! The Lion from the tribe of Judah, David's descendant, has won the victory so that he is able to open the scroll and its seven seals."

6Then I saw a Lamb standing in the center of the throne and in the middle of the four living creatures and the elders. The Lamb looked as if he had been killed. He had seven horns and seven eyes, which are the seven spirits of God that were sent into all the world. **7**The Lamb came and took the scroll from the right hand of the One sitting on the throne. **8**When he took the scroll, the four living creatures and the twenty-four elders bowed down before the Lamb. Each one of them had a harp and golden bowls full of incense, which are the prayers of God's holy people. **9**And they all sang a new song to the Lamb:

"You are worthy to take the scroll

and to open its seals,

because you were killed,

and with the blood of your death you

bought people for God

from every tribe, language, people, and

nation.

10You made them to be a kingdom of priests for

our God,

and they will rule on the earth."

11Then I looked, and I heard the voices of many angels around the throne, and the four living creatures, and the elders. There were thousands and thousands of angels, **12**saying in a loud voice:

"The Lamb who was killed is worthy
to receive power, wealth, wisdom, and
strength,
honor, glory, and praise!"

13Then I heard all creatures in heaven and on earth and under the earth and in the sea saying:

"To the One who sits on the throne
and to the Lamb
be praise and honor and glory and power
forever and ever."

14The four living creatures said, "Amen," and the elders bowed down and worshiped.

Then I watched while the Lamb opened the first of the seven seals. I heard one of the four living creatures say with a voice like thunder, "Come!" **2**I looked, and there before me was a white horse. The rider on the horse held a bow, and he was given a crown, and he rode out, determined to win the victory.

OLD TESTAMENT READING

In the year that King Uzziah died, I saw the Lord sitting on a very high throne. His long robe filled the Temple. **2**Heavenly creatures of fire stood above him. Each creature had six wings: It used two wings to cover its face, two wings to cover its feet, and two wings for flying. **3**Each creature was calling to the others:

"Holy, holy, holy is the LORD All-Powerful.
His glory fills the whole earth."

4Their calling caused the frame around the door to shake, as the Temple filled with smoke.

5I said, "Oh, no! I will be destroyed. I am not pure, and I live among people who are not pure, but I have seen the King, the LORD All-Powerful."

Isaiah 6:1–5

INSIGHTS

For this one moment in time, the old apostle was ushered into the presence of the Mystery behind the universe. There is no way to describe God. John could only describe the response to God. . . . Even as he stood before Him, God remained a mystery to John and to us—the Mystery who was and is and will always be, the Mystery behind our creation and our preservation, the Mystery worthy of our glory and honor and power.

The risen Christ had called John into the presence of God so that the old man could know, and through him we could know, this fact: Behind the universe there is a Power worthy of our praise and of our trust. In spite of rumors to the contrary, we are not creatures abandoned on a planet spinning madly through the universe. . . . We are the children of a great and wonderful God who even now sits in power accomplishing His purposes in His creation.

BILLY GRAHAM

APPLICATION

Reread each detail John uses to describe heaven's holiness. Imagine the sights, the sounds, and magnitude of God's powerful holiness! Praise God for his holiness.

REVELATION
6:3 — 7:8

³When the Lamb opened the second seal, I heard the second living creature say, "Come!" ⁴Then another horse came out, a red one. Its rider was given power to take away peace from the earth and to make people kill each other, and he was given a big sword.

⁵When the Lamb opened the third seal, I heard the third living creature say, "Come!" I looked, and there before me was a black horse, and its rider held a pair of scales in his hand. ⁶Then I heard something that sounded like a voice coming from the middle of the four living creatures. The voice said, "A quart of wheat for a day's pay, and three quarts of barley for a day's pay, and do not damage the olive oil and wine!"

⁷When the Lamb opened the fourth seal, I heard the voice of the fourth living creature say, "Come!" ⁸I looked, and there before me was a pale horse. Its rider was named death, and Hades was following close behind him. They were given power over a fourth of the earth to kill people by war, by starvation, by disease, and by the wild animals of the earth.

⁹When the Lamb opened the fifth seal, I saw under the altar the souls of those who had been killed because they were faithful to the word of God and to the message they had received. ¹⁰These souls shouted in a loud voice, "Holy and true Lord, how long until you judge the people of the earth and punish them for killing us?" ¹¹Then each one of them was given a white robe and was told to wait a short time longer. There were still some of their fellow servants and brothers and sisters in the service of Christ who must be killed as they were. They had to wait until all of this was finished.

¹²Then I watched while the Lamb opened the sixth seal, and there was a great earthquake. The sun became black like rough black cloth, and the whole moon became red like blood. ¹³And the stars in the sky fell to the earth like figs falling from a fig tree when the wind blows. ¹⁴The sky disappeared as a scroll when it is rolled up, and every mountain and island was moved from its place.

¹⁵Then the kings of the earth, the rulers, the generals, the rich people, the powerful people, the slaves, and the free people hid themselves in caves and in the rocks on the mountains. ¹⁶They called to the mountains and the rocks, "Fall on us. Hide us from the face of the One who sits on the throne and from the anger of the Lamb! ¹⁷The great day for their anger has come, and who can stand against it?"

The 144,000 People of Israel

7 After the vision of these things I saw four angels standing at the four corners of the earth. The angels were holding the four winds of the earth to keep them from blowing on the land or on the sea or on any tree. ²Then I saw another angel coming up from the east who had the seal of the living God. And he called out in a loud voice to the four angels to whom God had given power to harm the earth and the sea. ³He said to them, "Do not harm the land or the sea or the trees until we mark with a sign the foreheads of the people who serve our God." **4**Then I heard how many people were marked with the sign. There were one hundred forty-four thousand from every tribe of the people of Israel.

5From the tribe of Judah twelve thousand were marked with the sign,

from the tribe of Reuben twelve thousand,

from the tribe of Gad twelve thousand,

6from the tribe of Asher twelve thousand,

from the tribe of Naphtali twelve thousand,

from the tribe of Manasseh twelve thousand,

7from the tribe of Simeon twelve thousand,

from the tribe of Levi twelve thousand,

from the tribe of Issachar twelve thousand,

8from the tribe of Zebulun twelve thousand,

from the tribe of Joseph twelve thousand,

and from the tribe of Benjamin twelve thousand were marked with the sign.

OLD TESTAMENT READING

The LORD is a jealous God who punishes; the LORD punishes and is filled with anger.

5The mountains shake in front of him, and the hills melt.

The earth trembles when he comes; the world and all who live in it shake with fear.

6No one can stay alive when he is angry; no one can survive his strong anger.

Nahum 1:2a, 5–6a

INSIGHTS

The Sixth Seal Judgment (Rev. 6:12–17) . . . unleashes universal havoc on the earth. . . .

These judgments will produce terror in the hearts of all living men. Their hearts will be filled with fear—not primarily because of the physical disturbances or the awful wars and pestilences, but because they will see God on His throne. Men will plead to be hidden "from the face of Him that sitteth on the throne, and from the wrath of the Lamb." They will go to any length to avoid facing their Creator and Judge, even to seeking death under the rocks and mountains in which they will try to hide. All classes of people (v. 15) will be affected. As has been true throughout history, there will be no general or mass turning to God in repentance, but only a turning from God's face.

CHARLES RYRIE

ACTION POINT

What does God promise to those who are guilty of sin? Pray that you will be faithful so you will not hide from God's presence.

REVELATION
7:9 – 8:13

The Great Crowd Worships God

9After the vision of these things I looked, and there was a great number of people, so many that no one could count them. They were from every nation, tribe, people, and language of the earth. They were all standing before the throne and before the Lamb, wearing white robes and holding palm branches in their hands. **10**They were shouting in a loud voice, "Salvation belongs to our God, who sits on the throne, and to the Lamb." **11**All the angels were standing around the throne and the elders and the four living creatures. They all bowed down on their faces before the throne and worshiped God, **12**saying, "Amen! Praise, glory, wisdom, thanks, honor, power, and strength belong to our God forever and ever. Amen!"

13Then one of the elders asked me, "Who are these people dressed in white robes? Where did they come from?"

14I answered, "You know, sir."

And the elder said to me, "These are the people who have come out of the great distress. They have washed their robes and made them white in the blood of the Lamb. **15**Because of this, they are before the throne of God. They worship him day and night in his temple. And the One who sits on the throne will be present with them. **16**Those people will never be hungry again, and they will never be thirsty again. The sun will not hurt them, and no heat will burn them, **17**because the Lamb

at the center of the throne will be their shepherd. He will lead them to springs of water that give life. And God will wipe away every tear from their eyes."

The Seventh Seal

8When the Lamb opened the seventh seal, there was silence in heaven for about half an hour. **2**And I saw the seven angels who stand before God and to whom were given seven trumpets.

3Another angel came and stood at the altar, holding a golden pan for incense. He was given much incense to offer with the prayers of all God's holy people. The angel put this offering on the golden altar before the throne. **4**The smoke from the incense went up from the angel's hand to God with the prayers of God's people. **5**Then the angel filled the incense pan with fire from the altar and threw it on the earth, and there were flashes of lightning, thunder and loud noises, and an earthquake.

The Seven Angels and Trumpets

6Then the seven angels who had the seven trumpets prepared to blow them.

7The first angel blew his trumpet, and hail and fire mixed with blood were poured down on the earth. And a third of the earth, and all the green grass, and a third of the trees were burned up.

8Then the second angel blew his trumpet, and something that looked like a big mountain, burning with fire, was thrown into the sea. And a third of the sea became blood, **9**a third of the living things in the sea died, and a third of the ships were destroyed.

[10]Then the third angel blew his trumpet, and a large star, burning like a torch, fell from the sky. It fell on a third of the rivers and on the springs of water. [11]The name of the star is Wormwood. And a third of all the water became bitter, and many people died from drinking the water that was bitter.

[12]Then the fourth angel blew his trumpet, and a third of the sun, and a third of the moon, and a third of the stars were struck. So a third of them became dark, and a third of the day was without light, and also the night.

[13]While I watched, I heard an eagle that was flying high in the air cry out in a loud voice, "Trouble! Trouble! Trouble for those who live on the earth because of the remaining sounds of the trumpets that the other three angels are about to blow!"

OLD TESTAMENT READING

The LORD makes me very happy;
   all that I am rejoices in my God.
He has covered me with clothes of salvation
   and wrapped me with a coat of goodness,
like a bridegroom dressed for his wedding,
   like a bride dressed in jewels.

Isaiah 61:10

INSIGHTS

How many achievements and how many blessings for men the Scripture ascribes to the power of the Blood of the Lord Jesus! By the power of His Blood peace is made between man and God. By its power there is forgiveness of sins and eternal life for all who put their faith in the Lord Jesus. By the power of His Blood Satan is overcome. By its power there is continual cleansing from all sin for us. By the power of His Blood we may be set free from the tyranny of an evil conscience to serve the living God. By its infinite power with God the most unworthy have liberty to enter the Holy of Holies of God's presence and live there all the day. . . .

. . . That which gives the precious Blood its power with God for men is the lamb-like disposition of the One who shed it. . . . The title "the Lamb" so frequently given to the Lord Jesus in Scripture is first of all descriptive of His work—that of being a sacrifice for our sin. . . . But the title "the Lamb" has a deeper meaning. It describes His character. He is the Lamb in that He is meek and lowly in heart, gentle and un-resisting, and all the time surrendering His own will to the Father's for the blessing and saving of men.

ROY AND REVEL HESSION

ACTION POINT

Who is the Lamb of God? What does the blood of the Lamb do? List the ways God will bless those who are washed clean by the blood of the Lamb. Pray now and thank him for such a glorious salvation!

REVELATION
9:1 – 10:4

9 Then the fifth angel blew his trumpet, and I saw a star fall from the sky to the earth. The star was given the key to the deep hole that leads to the bottomless pit. **2**Then it opened up the hole that leads to the bottomless pit, and smoke came up from the hole like smoke from a big furnace. Then the sun and sky became dark because of the smoke from the hole. **3**Then locusts came down to the earth out of the smoke, and they were given the power to sting like scorpions. **4**They were told not to harm the grass on the earth or any plant or tree. They could harm only the people who did not have the sign of God on their foreheads. **5**These locusts were not given the power to kill anyone, but to cause pain to the people for five months. And the pain they felt was like the pain a scorpion gives when it stings someone. **6**During those days people will look for a way to die, but they will not find it. They will want to die, but death will run away from them.

7The locusts looked like horses prepared for battle. On their heads they wore what looked like crowns of gold, and their faces looked like human faces. **8**Their hair was like women's hair, and their teeth were like lions' teeth. **9**Their chests looked like iron breastplates, and the sound of their wings was like the noise of many horses and chariots hurrying into battle. **10**The locusts had tails with stingers like scorpions, and in their tails was their power to hurt people for five months. **11**The locusts had a king who was the angel of the bottomless pit. His name in the Hebrew language is Abaddon and in the Greek language is Apollyon.

12The first trouble is past; there are still two other troubles that will come.

13Then the sixth angel blew his trumpet, and I heard a voice coming from the horns on the golden altar that is before God. **14**The voice said to the sixth angel who had the trumpet, "Free the four angels who are tied at the great river Euphrates." **15**And they let loose the four angels who had been kept ready for this hour and day and month and year so they could kill a third of all people on the earth. **16**I heard how many troops on horses were in their army—two hundred million.

17The horses and their riders I saw in the vision looked like this: They had breastplates that were fiery red, dark blue, and yellow like sulfur. The heads of the horses looked like heads of lions, with fire, smoke, and sulfur coming out of their mouths. **18**A third of all the people on earth were killed by these three terrible disasters coming out of the horses' mouths: the fire, the smoke, and the sulfur. **19**The horses' power was in their mouths and in their tails; their tails were like snakes with heads, and with them they hurt people.

20The other people who were not killed by these terrible disasters still did not change their hearts and turn away from what they had made with their own hands. They did not stop worshiping demons and idols made of gold, silver, bronze, stone, and wood—things that cannot see or hear or walk. **21**These people did not change their hearts and turn away from murder or evil magic, from their sexual sins or stealing.

The Angel and the Small Scroll

10 Then I saw another powerful angel coming down from heaven dressed in a cloud with a rainbow over his head. His face was like the sun, and his legs were like pillars of fire. **2** The angel was holding a small scroll open in his hand. He put his right foot on the sea and his left foot on the land. **3** Then he shouted loudly like the roaring of a lion. And when he shouted, the voices of seven thunders spoke. **4** When the seven thunders spoke, I started to write. But I heard a voice from heaven say, "Keep hidden what the seven thunders said, and do not write them down."

OLD TESTAMENT READING

Let all the people who live in the land shake with fear,
> because the LORD's day of judging is coming;
> it is near.

10 Before them, earth and sky shake.
> The sun and the moon become dark,
> and the stars stop shining.
11 The LORD shouts out orders
> to his army.
> His army is very large!
> Those who obey him are very strong!
> The LORD's day of judging
> is an overwhelming and terrible day.
> No one can stand up against it!
12 The LORD says, "Even now, come back to me with all your heart.
> Fast, cry, and be sad."

Joel 2:1b, 10–12

INSIGHTS

How terrible it is to witness the approach of a tempest: to note the forewarnings of the storm; to mark the birds of heaven as they droop their wings; to see the cattle as they lay their heads low in terror; to discern the face of the sky as it groweth black, and look to the sun which shineth not, and the heavens which are angry and frowning! . . . And yet, sinner, this is your present position. No hot drops have as yet fallen, but a shower of fire is coming. No terrible winds howl around you, but God's tempest is gathering its dread artillery. As yet the water-floods are dammed up by mercy, but the floodgates shall soon be opened: the thunderbolts of God are yet in His storehouse, but lo! the tempest hastens, and how awful shall that moment be when God, robed in vengeance, shall march forth in fury! Where, where, where, O sinner, wilt thou hide thy head, or whither wilt thou flee? O that the hand of mercy may now lead you to Christ! He is freely set before you in the gospel: His riven side is the rock of shelter. Thou knowest thy need of Him; believe in Him, cast thyself upon Him, and then the fury shall be overpast for ever.

CHARLES SPURGEON

PAUSE FOR REFLECTION

What is the sole reason for the horrible punishment that is promised on God's day of judgment? What does God want from every person?

REVELATION 10:5 – 11:14

5Then the angel I saw standing on the sea and on the land raised his right hand to heaven, **6**and he made a promise by the power of the One who lives forever and ever. He is the One who made the skies and all that is in them, the earth and all that is in it, and the sea and all that is in it. The angel promised, "There will be no more waiting! **7**In the days when the seventh angel is ready to blow his trumpet, God's secret will be finished. This secret is the Good News God told to his servants, the prophets."

8Then I heard the same voice from heaven again, saying to me: "Go and take the open scroll that is in the hand of the angel that is standing on the sea and on the land."

9So I went to the angel and told him to give me the small scroll. And he said to me, "Take the scroll and eat it. It will be sour in your stomach, but in your mouth it will be sweet as honey." **10**So I took the small scroll from the angel's hand and ate it. In my mouth it tasted sweet as honey, but after I ate it, it was sour in my stomach. **11**Then I was told, "You must prophesy again about many peoples, nations, languages, and kings."

The Two Witnesses

11 I was given a measuring stick like a rod, and I was told, "Go and measure the temple of God and the altar, and count the people worshiping there. **2**But do not measure the yard outside the temple. Leave it alone, because it has been given to those who are not God's people. And they will trample on the holy city for forty-two months. **3**And I will give power to my two witnesses to prophesy for one thousand two hundred sixty days, and they will be dressed in rough cloth to show their sadness."

4These two witnesses are the two olive trees and the two lampstands that stand before the Lord of the earth. **5**And if anyone tries to hurt them, fire comes from their mouths and kills their enemies. And if anyone tries to hurt them in whatever way, in that same way that person will die. **6**These witnesses have the power to stop the sky from raining during the time they are prophesying. And they have power to make the waters become blood, and they have power to send every kind of trouble to the earth as many times as they want.

7When the two witnesses have finished telling their message, the beast that comes up from the bottomless pit will fight a war against them. He will defeat them and kill them. **8**The bodies of the two witnesses will lie in the street of the great city where the Lord was killed. This city is named Sodom and Egypt, which has a spiritual meaning. **9**Those from every race of people, tribe, language, and nation will look at the bodies of the two witnesses for three and one-half days, and they will refuse to bury them. **10**People who live on the earth will rejoice and be happy because these two are dead. They will send each other gifts, because these two prophets brought much suffering to those who live on the earth.

11But after three and one-half days, God put the breath of life into the two prophets again. They stood on their feet, and everyone who saw them became very afraid. **12**Then the two prophets heard a loud voice from heaven saying, "Come up here!" And they went up into heaven in a cloud as their enemies watched.

13In the same hour there was a great earthquake, and a tenth of the city was destroyed. Seven thousand people were killed in the earthquake, and those who did not die were very afraid and gave glory to the God of heaven.

14The second trouble is finished. Pay attention: The third trouble is coming soon.

OLD TESTAMENT READING

Now Elijah the Tishbite was a prophet from the settlers in Gilead. "I serve the LORD, the God of Israel," Elijah said to Ahab. "As surely as the LORD lives, no rain or dew will fall during the next few years unless I command it."

During the third year without rain, the LORD spoke his word to Elijah: "Go and meet King Ahab, and I will soon send rain." **2**So Elijah went to meet Ahab.

By this time there was no food in Samaria.

1 Kings 17:1; 18:1–2

INSIGHTS

During the darkest ages, men have been raised up to testify against the prevailing corruption of their time, and especially the corruption of the apostate church. Their opponents have endeavored to silence their voice and blacken their character, but God has ever vindicated them and given life out of death. Always when the enemies of the truth have deemed themselves triumphant, there has been a rekindling of gospel testimony. A few years before Luther appeared, a medal was struck to commemorate the extinction of so-called heresy. Such witness-bearing as is suggested by the comparison with Zechariah's vision is fed from the heart of Christ. He is the root of the martyr line; his Spirit is the life-breath of his witnesses. All through the centuries, commonly called Christian though generally very un-Christian, there has been an unbroken succession of pure and noble souls who have stood for Jesus Christ even unto death. Let us dare to stand with them and our Lord, that he may not be ashamed of us at his coming.

F. B. MEYER

ACTION POINT

At what times does God call special prophets? What powers does he give them? Who controls their fate? What has God called you to do? Pray that you will trust him to care for you and enable you to accomplish his work.

REVELATION 11:15 — 12:12

The Seventh Trumpet

15Then the seventh angel blew his trumpet. And there were loud voices in heaven, saying:

"The power to rule the world now belongs to
our Lord and his Christ,
and he will rule forever and ever."

16Then the twenty-four elders, who sit on their thrones before God, bowed down on their faces and worshiped God. **17**They said:

"We give thanks to you, Lord God Almighty,
who is and who was,
because you have used your great power
and have begun to rule!
18 The people of the world were angry,
but your anger has come.
The time has come to judge the dead,
and to reward your servants the prophets
and your holy people,
all who respect you, great and small.
The time has come to destroy those who
destroy the earth!"

19Then God's temple in heaven was opened. The Ark that holds the agreement God gave to his people could be seen in his temple. Then there were flashes of lightning, noises, thunder, an earthquake, and a great hailstorm.

The Woman and the Dragon

12 And then a great wonder appeared in heaven: A woman was clothed with the sun, and the moon was under her feet, and a crown of twelve stars was on her head. **2**She was pregnant and cried out with pain, because she was about to give birth. **3**Then another wonder appeared in heaven: There was a giant red dragon with seven heads and seven crowns on each head. He also had ten horns. **4**His tail swept a third of the stars out of the sky and threw them down to the earth. He stood in front of the woman who was ready to give birth so he could eat her baby as soon as it was born. **5**Then the woman gave birth to a son who will rule all the nations with an iron rod. And her child was taken up to God and to his throne. **6**The woman ran away into the desert to a place God prepared for her where she would be taken care of for one thousand two hundred sixty days.

7Then there was a war in heaven. Michael and his angels fought against the dragon, and the dragon and his angels fought back. **8**But the dragon was not strong enough, and he and his angels lost their place in heaven. **9**The giant dragon was thrown down out of heaven. (He is that old snake called the devil or Satan, who tricks the whole world.) The dragon with his angels was thrown down to the earth.

10Then I heard a loud voice in heaven saying:

"The salvation and the power and the
kingdom of our God
and the authority of his Christ have now
come.
The accuser of our brothers and sisters,
who accused them day and night before
our God,
has been thrown down.
11And our brothers and sisters defeated
him

by the blood of the Lamb's death
and by the message they preached.
They did not love their lives so much
that they were afraid of death.
¹²So rejoice, you heavens
and all who live there!
But it will be terrible for the earth and the
sea,
because the devil has come down to you!
He is filled with anger,
because he knows he does not have much
time."

OLD TESTAMENT READING

As I watched, the little horn began making war against God's holy people and was defeating them ²²until God, who has been alive forever, came. He judged in favor of the holy people who belong to the Most High God; then the time came for them to receive the power to rule.

Daniel 7:21–22

INSIGHTS

What is this celestial conflict all about? The fact that Michael led God's angels to victory is significant, because Michael is identified with the nation Israel. . . . Apparently, the devil's hatred of Israel will spur him to make one final assault against the throne of God, but he will be defeated by Michael and a heavenly host. . . .

How does this future war apply to the church today? The same serpent who accuses the saints in heaven also deceives . . . the nations into thinking that the people of God are dangerous, deluded, even destructive. . . . God's people in every age must expect the world's opposition, but the church can always defeat the enemy by being faithful to Jesus Christ. . . .

. . . Satan is not equal to God; he is not omnipotent, omnipresent, or omniscient. His power is limited and his tactics must fail when God's people trust the power of the blood and of the Word. . . .

Believers in any age or situation can rejoice in this victory, no matter how difficult their experiences may be. Our warfare is not against flesh and blood, but against the spiritual forces of the wicked one; and these have been defeated by our Saviour (Eph. 6:10ff; note also 1:15–23).

WARREN WIERSBE

ACTION POINT

What perspective do you gain on your struggles today from this account of ultimate struggle in heaven? Thank God he has already won the battle! Pray that you will remain faithful to him as you fight the battles in your life.

REVELATION 12:13 – 13:18

¹³When the dragon saw he had been thrown down to the earth, he hunted for the woman who had given birth to the son. ¹⁴But the woman was given the two wings of a great eagle so she could fly to the place prepared for her in the desert. There she would be taken care of for three and one-half years, away from the snake. ¹⁵Then the snake poured water out of its mouth like a river toward the woman so the flood would carry her away. ¹⁶But the earth helped the woman by opening its mouth and swallowing the river that came from the mouth of the dragon. ¹⁷Then the dragon was very angry at the woman, and he went off to make war against all her other children—those who obey God's commands and who have the message Jesus taught.

¹⁸And the dragon stood on the seashore.

The Two Beasts

13 Then I saw a beast coming up out of the sea. It had ten horns and seven heads, and there was a crown on each horn. A name against God was written on each head. ²This beast looked like a leopard, with feet like a bear's feet and a mouth like a lion's mouth. And the dragon gave the beast all of his power and his throne and great authority. ³One of the heads of the beast looked as if it had been killed by a wound, but this death wound was healed. Then the whole world was amazed and followed the beast. ⁴People worshiped the dragon because he had given his power to the beast. And they also worshiped the beast, asking, "Who is like the beast? Who can make war against it?"

⁵The beast was allowed to say proud words and words against God, and it was allowed to use its power for forty-two months. ⁶It used its mouth to speak against God, against God's name, against the place where God lives, and against all those who live in heaven. ⁷It was given power to make war against God's holy people and to defeat them. It was given power over every tribe, people, language, and nation. ⁸And all who live on earth will worship the beast—all the people since the beginning of the world whose names are not written in the Lamb's book of life. The Lamb is the One who was killed.

⁹Anyone who has ears should listen:

¹⁰If you are to be a prisoner,
then you will be a prisoner.
If you are to be killed with the sword,
then you will be killed with the sword.

This means that God's holy people must have patience and faith.

¹¹Then I saw another beast coming up out of the earth. It had two horns like a lamb, but it spoke like a dragon. ¹²This beast stands before the first beast and uses the same power the first beast has. By this power it makes everyone living on earth worship the first beast, who had the death wound that was healed. ¹³And the second beast does great miracles so that it even makes fire come down from heaven to earth while people are watching. ¹⁴It fools those who live on earth by the miracles it has been given the power to do. It does these miracles to serve the first beast. The second beast orders people to make

an idol to honor the first beast, the one that was wounded by the deadly sword but sprang to life again. **15**The second beast was given power to give life to the idol of the first one so that the idol could speak. And the second beast was given power to command all who will not worship the image of the beast to be killed. **16**The second beast also forced all people, small and great, rich and poor, free and slave, to have a mark on their right hand or on their forehead. **17**No one could buy or sell without this mark, which is the name of the beast or the number of its name. **18**This takes wisdom. Let the one who has understanding find the meaning of the number, which is the number of a person. Its number is 666.

OLD TESTAMENT READING

The king of the North will tell lies and cause those who have not obeyed God to be ruined. But those who know God and obey him will be strong and fight back.

33"Those who are wise will help the others understand what is happening. But they will be killed with swords, or burned, or taken captive, or robbed of their homes and possessions. These things will continue for many days. **34**When the wise ones are suffering, they will get a little help, but many who join the wise ones will not help them in their time of need. **35**Some of the wise ones will be killed. But the hard times must come so they can be made stronger and purer and without faults until the time of the end comes. Then, at the right time, the end will come."

Daniel 11:32–35

INSIGHTS

We must be entrenched in the strength of the Lord. We must be enclosed "in the power of his might," or, as one has paraphrased it, "in the energy of him, the strong." It is in vain we engage in the conflict if that preliminary condition has not been fulfilled. In earthly warfare the soldier does not provide his own means of defense or weapons of assault. So in Christian conflict our whole equipment is divinely provided for us. He gives us a position that is impregnable—strength in the Lord; an armor that is impenetrable; and a weapon that is infallible—"the sword of the Spirit." We have by faith to take that position and continually to abide in it. We have by faith to put on that armor and wear it constantly.

EVAN HOPKINS

ACTION POINT

What difficulties will God's people face in the end times? How must they respond to Satan? What are their weapons, and what must they be prepared to give up? What will be accomplished by those who remain strong? Pray that your faith will be purified through the battles you face!

REVELATION 14:1-20

The Song of the Saved

14 Then I looked, and there before me was the Lamb standing on Mount Zion. With him were one hundred forty-four thousand people who had his name and his Father's name written on their foreheads. **2**And I heard a sound from heaven like the noise of flooding water and like the sound of loud thunder. The sound I heard was like people playing harps. **3**And they sang a new song before the throne and before the four living creatures and the elders. No one could learn the new song except the one hundred forty-four thousand who had been bought from the earth. **4**These are the ones who did not do sinful things with women, because they kept themselves pure. They follow the Lamb every place he goes. These one hundred forty-four thousand were bought from among the people of the earth as people to be offered to God and the Lamb. **5**They were not guilty of telling lies; they are without fault.

The Three Angels

6Then I saw another angel flying high in the air. He had the eternal Good News to preach to those who live on earth—to every nation, tribe, language, and people. **7**He preached in a loud voice, "Fear God and give him praise, because the time has come for God to judge all people. So worship God who made the heavens, and the earth, and the sea, and the springs of water."

8Then the second angel followed the first angel and said, "Ruined, ruined is the great city of Babylon! She made all the nations drink the wine of the anger of her adultery."

9Then a third angel followed the first two angels, saying in a loud voice: "If anyone worships the beast and his idol and gets the beast's mark on the forehead or on the hand, **10**that one also will drink the wine of God's anger, which is prepared with all its strength in the cup of his anger. And that person will be put in pain with burning sulfur before the holy angels and the Lamb. **11**And the smoke from their burning pain will rise forever and ever. There will be no rest, day or night, for those who worship the beast and his idol or who get the mark of his name." **12**This means God's holy people must be patient. They must obey God's commands and keep their faith in Jesus.

13Then I heard a voice from heaven saying, "Write this: Blessed are the dead who die from now on in the Lord."

The Spirit says, "Yes, they will rest from their hard work, and the reward of all they have done stays with them."

The Earth Is Harvested

14Then I looked, and there before me was a white cloud, and sitting on the white cloud was One who looked like a Son of Man. He had a gold crown on his head and a sharp sickle in his hand. **15**Then another angel came out of the temple and called out in a loud voice to the One who was sitting on the cloud, "Take your sickle and harvest from the earth, because the time to harvest has come, and the fruit of the earth is ripe." **16**So the One who was sitting on the cloud swung his sickle over the earth, and the earth was harvested.

17Then another angel came out of the temple in heaven, and he also had a sharp sickle. **18**And then another angel, who has power over the fire, came from the altar. This angel called to the angel with the sharp sickle, saying, "Take your sharp sickle and gather the bunches of grapes from the earth's vine, because its grapes are ripe." **19**Then the angel swung his sickle over the earth. He gathered the earth's grapes and threw them into the great winepress of God's anger. **20**They were trampled in the winepress outside the city, and blood flowed out of the winepress as high as horses' bridles for a distance of about one hundred eighty miles.

OLD TESTAMENT READING

The LORD, the God of Israel, said this to me: "My anger is like the wine in a cup. Take it from my hand and make all the nations, to whom I am sending you, drink all of my anger from this cup. **16**They will drink my anger and stumble about and act like madmen because of the war I am going to send among them."

17So I took the cup from the LORD's hand and went to those nations and made them drink from it. **26b**I made all the kingdoms on earth drink from the cup of the LORD's anger, but the king of Babylon will drink from this cup after all the others.

Jeremiah 25:15–17, 26b

INSIGHTS

The sinner's peace is that terribly prophetic calm that the traveler occasionally experiences on the higher Alps. Everything is still. The birds suspend their notes, fly low, and cower down with fear. The hum of bees among the flowers is hushed. A horrible stillness rules the hour, as if death had silenced all things by stretching his awful scepter over them. But the tempest is preparing—the lightning will soon cast abroad its flames of fire. Earth will rock with thunder-blasts; granite peaks will be dissolved. All nature will tremble beneath the fury of the storm. That calm is what the sinner is experiencing. He should not rejoice in it, because the hurricane of wrath is coming, the whirlwind and the tribulation that can sweep him away and utterly destroy him.

CHARLES SPURGEON

PAUSE FOR REFLECTION

In light of these Scripture readings, the "sinner's peace" that Spurgeon refers to certainly is ominous, isn't it? What does God's merciful forgiveness that he repeatedly offers to all people, contrasted with his guarantee of final, unchangeable punishment, teach you about the divine nature?

REVELATION
15:1 – 16:11

The Last Troubles

15 Then I saw another wonder in heaven that was great and amazing. There were seven angels bringing seven disasters. These are the last disasters, because after them, God's anger is finished.

2 I saw what looked like a sea of glass mixed with fire. All of those who had won the victory over the beast and his idol and over the number of his name were standing by the sea of glass. They had harps that God had given them. **3** They sang the song of Moses, the servant of God, and the song of the Lamb:

"You do great and wonderful things,

Psalm 111:2

Lord God Almighty.   *Amos 3:13*

Everything the Lord does is right and true,

Psalm 145:17

King of the nations.

4 Everyone will respect you, Lord,

Jeremiah 10:7

and will honor you.

Only you are holy.

All the nations will come

and worship you,   *Psalm 86:9–10*

because the right things you have done

are now made known."   *Deuteronomy 32:4*

5 After this I saw that the temple (the Tent of the Agreement) in heaven was opened. **6** And the seven angels bringing the seven disasters came out of the temple. They were dressed in clean, shining linen and wore golden bands tied around their chests. **7** Then one of the four living creatures gave to the seven angels seven golden bowls filled with the anger of God, who lives forever and ever. **8** The temple was filled with smoke from the glory and the power of God, and no one could enter the temple until the seven disasters of the seven angels were finished.

The Bowls of God's Anger

16 Then I heard a loud voice from the temple saying to the seven angels, "Go and pour out the seven bowls of God's anger on the earth."

2 The first angel left and poured out his bowl on the land. Then ugly and painful sores came upon all those who had the mark of the beast and who worshiped his idol.

3 The second angel poured out his bowl on the sea, and it became blood like that of a dead man, and every living thing in the sea died.

4 The third angel poured out his bowl on the rivers and the springs of water, and they became blood. **5** Then I heard the angel of the waters saying:

"Holy One, you are the One who is and who was.

You are right to decide to punish these evil people.

6 They have poured out the blood of your holy people and your prophets.

So now you have given them blood to drink as they deserve."

7 And I heard a voice coming from the altar saying:

"Yes, Lord God Almighty,
   the way you punish evil people is right and
      fair."

[8]The fourth angel poured out his bowl on the sun, and he was given power to burn the people with fire. [9]They were burned by the great heat, and they cursed the name of God, who had control over these disasters. But the people refused to change their hearts and lives and give glory to God.

[10]The fifth angel poured out his bowl on the throne of the beast, and darkness covered its kingdom. People gnawed their tongues because of the pain. [11]They also cursed the God of heaven because of their pain and the sores they had, but they refused to change their hearts and turn away from the evil things they did.

OLD TESTAMENT READING

The LORD saw this and rejected them;
   his sons and daughters had made him
      angry.
[20]He said, "I will turn away from them
   and see what will happen to them.
They are evil people,
   unfaithful children.

[23]"I will pile troubles upon them
   and shoot my arrows at them.
[24]They will be starved and sick,
   destroyed by terrible diseases.
I will send them vicious animals
   and gliding, poisonous snakes."

Deuteronomy 32:19–20, 23–24

INSIGHTS

How glorious must He [Christ] have been in the eyes of seraphs, when a cloud received Him out of mortal sight, and He ascended up to heaven! Now He wears the glory which He had with God or ever the earth was, and yet another glory above all—that which He has well earned in the fight against sin, death, and hell. As victor He wears the illustrious crown. . . . He wears the glory of an Intercessor who can never fail, of a Prince who can never be defeated, of a Conqueror who has vanquished every foe, of a Lord who has the heart's allegiance of every subject. Jesus wears all the glory which the pomp of heaven can bestow upon Him, which ten thousand times ten thousand angels can minister to Him. You cannot with your utmost stretch of imagination conceive His exceeding greatness; yet there will be a further revelation of it when He shall descend from heaven in great power, with all the holy angels—"Then shall He sit upon the throne of His glory." Oh, the splendour of that glory! It will ravish His people's hearts. Nor is this the close, for eternity shall sound His praise, "Thy throne, O God, is for ever and ever!" Reader, if you would joy in Christ's glory hereafter, He must be glorious in your sight now. Is He so?

CHARLES SPURGEON

APPLICATION

Study the contrasts between the praises of God's people and the evil of those who reject God and his salvation. On which side of the battle will you stand firm? Do you delight to sing God's praises?

REVELATION 16:12 – 17:8

12The sixth angel poured out his bowl on the great river Euphrates so that the water in the river was dried up to prepare the way for the kings from the east to come. **13**Then I saw three evil spirits that looked like frogs coming out of the mouth of the dragon, out of the mouth of the beast, and out of the mouth of the false prophet. **14**These evil spirits are the spirits of demons, which have power to do miracles. They go out to the kings of the whole world to gather them together for the battle on the great day of God Almighty.

15"Listen! I will come as a thief comes! Blessed are those who stay awake and keep their clothes on so that they will not walk around naked and have people see their shame."

16Then the evil spirits gathered the kings together to the place that is called Armageddon in the Hebrew language.

17The seventh angel poured out his bowl into the air. Then a loud voice came out of the temple from the throne, saying, "It is finished!" **18**Then there were flashes of lightning, noises, thunder, and a big earthquake—the worst earthquake that has ever happened since people have been on earth. **19**The great city split into three parts, and the cities of the nations were destroyed. And God remembered the sins of Babylon the Great, so he gave that city the cup filled with the wine of his terrible anger. **20**Then every island ran away, and mountains disappeared. **21**Giant hailstones, each weighing about a hundred pounds, fell from the sky upon people. People cursed God for the disaster of the hail, because this disaster was so terrible.

The Woman on the Animal

17 Then one of the seven angels who had the seven bowls came and spoke to me. He said, "Come, and I will show you the punishment that will be given to the great prostitute, the one sitting over many waters. **2**The kings of the earth sinned sexually with her, and the people of the earth became drunk from the wine of her sexual sin."

3Then the angel carried me away by the Spirit to the desert. There I saw a woman sitting on a red beast. It was covered with names against God written on it, and it had seven heads and ten horns. **4**The woman was dressed in purple and red and was shining with the gold, precious jewels, and pearls she was wearing. She had a golden cup in her hand, a cup filled with evil things and the uncleanness of her sexual sin. **5**On her forehead a title was written that was secret. This is what was written:

THE GREAT BABYLON

MOTHER OF PROSTITUTES

AND OF THE EVIL THINGS OF THE EARTH

6Then I saw that the woman was drunk with the blood of God's holy people and with the blood of those who were killed because of their faith in Jesus.

When I saw the woman, I was very amazed. **7**Then the angel said to me, "Why are you amazed? I will tell you the secret of this woman and the beast she rides—the one with seven heads and ten horns. **8**The beast you saw was once alive but is not alive now. But soon it will come up out of the bottomless pit and go away to be destroyed. There are people who live on earth whose names have not been written in the book of life since the beginning of the world. They will be amazed when they see the beast, because he was once alive, is not alive now, but will come again."

OLD TESTAMENT READING

This is what will happen: On the day Gog attacks the land of Israel, I will become very angry, says the Lord GOD. **19**With jealousy and great anger I tell you that at that time there will surely be a great earthquake in Israel. **20**The fish of the sea, the birds of the sky, the wild animals, everything that crawls on the ground, and all the people on the earth will shake with fear before me. Also, the mountains will be thrown down, the cliffs will fall, and every wall will fall to the ground. **21**Then I will call for a war against Gog on all my mountains, says the Lord GOD. Everyone's sword will attack the soldier next to him. **22**I will punish Gog with disease and death. I will send a heavy rain with hailstones and burning sulfur on Gog, his army, and the many nations with him. **23**Then I will show how great I am. I will show my holiness, and I will make myself known to the many nations that watch. Then they will know that I am the LORD.'"

Ezekiel 38:18–23

INSIGHTS

If men and women will not yield to the love of God, and be changed by the grace of God, then there is no way for them to escape the wrath of God.

Rank and wealth will not deliver anyone in that terrible day. John's list included kings, captains, and slaves, the rich and the poor. "Who shall be able to stand?"

. . . We are so accustomed to emphasizing the meekness and gentleness of Christ (Matt. 11:28–30) that we forget His holiness and justice. The same Christ who welcomed the children in the temple also drove merchants from that same temple. God's wrath is not like a child's temper tantrum or punishment meted out by an impatient parent. God's wrath is the evidence of His holy love for all that is right and His holy hatred for all that is evil. Only a soft and sentimental person would want to worship a God who did not deal justly with evil in the world.

WARREN WIERSBE

PAUSE FOR REFLECTION

What are God's purposes in punishing the evil nations? How will the people on earth respond when the last of God's angels pours out his anger? Pray that God will give you greater insight into his perfect holiness as you study these passages.

REVELATION 17:9 — 18:10

9"You need a wise mind to understand this. The seven heads on the beast are seven mountains where the woman sits. 10And they are seven kings. Five of the kings have already been destroyed, one of the kings lives now, and another has not yet come. When he comes, he must stay a short time. 11The beast that was once alive, but is not alive now, is also an eighth king. He belongs to the first seven kings, and he will go away to be destroyed.

12"The ten horns you saw are ten kings who have not yet begun to rule, but they will receive power to rule with the beast for one hour. 13All ten of these kings have the same purpose, and they will give their power and authority to the beast. 14They will make war against the Lamb, but the Lamb will defeat them, because he is Lord of lords and King of kings. He will defeat them with his called, chosen, and faithful followers."

15Then the angel said to me, "The waters that you saw, where the prostitute sits, are peoples, races, nations, and languages. 16The ten horns and the beast you saw will hate the prostitute. They will take everything she has and leave her naked. They will eat her body and burn her with fire. 17God made the ten horns want to carry out his purpose by agreeing to give the beast their power to rule, until what God has said comes about. 18The woman you saw is the great city that rules over the kings of the earth."

Babylon Is Destroyed

After the vision of these things, I saw another angel coming down from heaven. This angel had great power, and his glory made the earth bright. 2He shouted in a powerful voice:

"Ruined, ruined is the great city of Babylon!
She has become a home for demons
and a prison for every evil spirit,
and a prison for every unclean bird and
unclean beast.
3She has been ruined, because all the peoples
of the earth
have drunk the wine of the desire of her
sexual sin.
She has been ruined also because the kings of
the earth
have sinned sexually with her,
and the merchants of the earth
have grown rich from the great wealth of
her luxury."

4Then I heard another voice from heaven saying:
"Come out of that city, my people,
so that you will not share in her sins,
so that you will not receive the disasters
that will come to her.
5Her sins have piled up as high as the sky,
and God has not forgotten the wrongs she
has done.
6Give that city the same as she gave to others.
Pay her back twice as much as she did.
Prepare wine for her that is twice as strong
as the wine she prepared for others.
7She gave herself much glory and rich living.
Give her that much suffering and sadness.

She says to herself, 'I am a queen sitting on my
throne.
I am not a widow; I will never be sad.'
8So these disasters will come to her in one
day:
death, and crying, and great hunger,
and she will be destroyed by fire,
because the Lord God who judges her is
powerful."
9The kings of the earth who sinned sexually
with her and shared her wealth will see the smoke
from her burning. Then they will cry and be sad
because of her death. **10**They will be afraid of her
suffering and stand far away and say:

"Terrible! How terrible for you, great city,
powerful city of Babylon,
because your punishment has come in one
hour!"

OLD TESTAMENT READING

At dawn the next morning, the angels begged
Lot to hurry. They said, "Go! Take your wife
and your two daughters with you so you will not
be destroyed when the city is punished."

Genesis 19:15

INSIGHTS

Through our union with Christ in His death we are delivered from the dominion
of sin. But we still find sin struggling to gain mastery over us. . . . We may not like the
fact that we have this lifelong struggle with sin, but the more we realize and accept
it, the better equipped we will be to deal with it. . . .

The Bible tells us that the heart is deceitful and unsearchable to any but God
alone (Jeremiah 17:9–10). Even as believers we do not know our own hearts (1 Corinthians 4:3–5). . . .

Knowing that indwelling sin occupies a heart that is deceitful and unsearchable
should make us extremely wary. . . .

. . . Though sin no longer has dominion over us, it wages its guerrilla warfare
against us. If left unchecked, it will defeat us. Our recourse against this warfare is to
deal swiftly and firmly with the first motions of indwelling sin. . . .

. . . We must never consider that our fight against sin is at an end. The heart is
unsearchable, our evil desires are insatiable, and our reason is constantly in danger
of being deceived. Well did Jesus say, "Watch and pray so that you will not fall into
temptation" (Matthew 26:41).

JERRY BRIDGES

APPLICATION

Why is it important for God's people to do everything they can to separate themselves from sin? What punishment will come to those who linger when God tells
them to run? Are you listening for his warning?

REVELATION 18:11-24

11And the merchants of the earth will cry and be sad about her, because now there is no one to buy their cargoes— **12**cargoes of gold, silver, jewels, pearls, fine linen, purple cloth, silk, red cloth; all kinds of citron wood and all kinds of things made from ivory, expensive wood, bronze, iron, and marble; **13**cinnamon, spice, incense, myrrh, frankincense, wine, olive oil, fine flour, wheat, cattle, sheep, horses, carriages, slaves, and human lives.

14The merchants will say,
"Babylon, the good things you wanted are
          gone from you.
All your rich and fancy things have
          disappeared.
      You will never have them again."
15The merchants who became rich from selling to her will be afraid of her suffering and will stand far away. They will cry and be sad **16**and say:
"Terrible! How terrible for the great city!
      She was dressed in fine linen, purple and
          red cloth,
      and she was shining with gold, precious
          jewels, and pearls!
17All these riches have been destroyed in one
          hour!"
Every sea captain, every passenger, the sailors, and all those who earn their living from the sea stood far away from Babylon. **18**As they saw the smoke from her burning, they cried out loudly,

"There was never a city like this great city!" **19**And they threw dust on their heads and cried out, weeping and being sad. They said:
"Terrible! How terrible for the great city!
All the people who had ships on the sea
      became rich because of her wealth!
But she has been destroyed in one hour!
20Be happy because of this, heaven!
      Be happy, God's holy people and apostles
          and prophets!
God has punished her because of what she did
      to you."
21Then a powerful angel picked up a large stone, like one used for grinding grain, and threw it into the sea. He said:
"In the same way, the great city of Babylon
          will be thrown down,
      and it will never be found again.
22The music of people playing harps and other
          instruments, flutes, and trumpets,
      will never be heard in you again.
No workman doing any job
      will ever be found in you again.
The sound of grinding grain
      will never be heard in you again.
23The light of a lamp
      will never shine in you again,
and the voices of a bridegroom and bride
      will never be heard in you again.
Your merchants were the world's great people,
      and all the nations were tricked by your
          magic.
24You are guilty of the death of the prophets
          and God's holy people
      and all who have been killed on earth."

OLD TESTAMENT READING

The LORD says,
"Babylon, you are a destroying mountain,
   and I am against you.
   You have destroyed the whole land.
I will put my hand out against you.
   I will roll you off the cliffs,
   and I will make you a burned-out
      mountain.

26People will not find any rocks in Babylon big
      enough for cornerstones.
   People will not take any rocks from
         Babylon to use for the foundation of
         a building,
   because your city will be just a pile of
         ruins forever," says the LORD.

36So this is what the LORD says:
"I will soon defend you, Judah,
   and make sure that Babylon is punished."
                              Jeremiah 51:25–26, 36a

INSIGHTS

In spite of what people often think, no one is getting away with anything. Payday someday! God's vengeance will be revealed, even against false religion in whose name and under whose influence millions have suffered and died. God's judgment will fall and vindicate His people. . . .

The extent of Babylon's payment: The law of retribution is applied; what we sow, we shall reap. It is doubled to emphasize the enormity of the woman's sins and the justice behind her judgment and fall. The "cup which she has mixed," containing the wine of her wrath against the people of God, is now mixed for her with a double portion of God's wrath (14:10).

The experience of Babylon's sorrow: Like so many unbelievers today, this woman believes she will never experience sorrow or torment for her lifestyle and luxurious living. She boasts "I sit as queen, and am no widow." After all, she reasons, the kings of the earth are her lovers. But she is a widow in that God has forsaken her. . . .

Two things characterize the harlot's lifestyle: self-glorification and sensuous living. For this, she will receive torment and sorrow. So will all who choose to follow her path. . . .

The hunger for achievement and accumulation of wealth remains as the dominant factor of people's lifestyles and desires. The "fools" of this world are found daily in every marketplace and place of business. . . . But judgment day is coming! The merchants of the world, along with the kings of the earth, will mourn the sudden destruction of the woman who helped them become prosperous.

                              DAVID HOCKING

PAUSE FOR REFLECTION

Why is God against Babylon? Why will the people of earth mourn the destruction of Babylon? What does her defeat symbolize? Where is your heart's loyalty? Will you shed even one tear over Babylon's loss?

REVELATION 19:1-16

People in Heaven Praise God

19 After this vision and announcement I heard what sounded like a great many people in heaven saying:

"Hallelujah!

Salvation, glory, and power belong to our God,

2   because his judgments are true and right.

He has punished the prostitute

who made the earth evil with her sexual sin.

He has paid her back for the death of his servants."

3Again they said:

"Hallelujah!

She is burning, and her smoke will rise forever and ever."

4Then the twenty-four elders and the four living creatures bowed down and worshiped God, who sits on the throne. They said:

"Amen, Hallelujah!"

5Then a voice came from the throne, saying:

"Praise our God, all you who serve him

and all you who honor him, both small and great!"

6Then I heard what sounded like a great many people, like the noise of flooding water, and like the noise of loud thunder. The people were saying:

"Hallelujah!

Our Lord God, the Almighty, rules.

7Let us rejoice and be happy

and give God glory,

because the wedding of the Lamb has come,

and the Lamb's bride has made herself ready.

8Fine linen, bright and clean, was given to her to wear."

(The fine linen means the good things done by God's holy people.)

9And the angel said to me, "Write this: Blessed are those who have been invited to the wedding meal of the Lamb!" And the angel said, "These are the true words of God."

10Then I bowed down at the angel's feet to worship him, but he said to me, "Do not worship me! I am a servant like you and your brothers and sisters who have the message of Jesus. Worship God, because the message about Jesus is the spirit that gives all prophecy."

The Rider on the White Horse

11Then I saw heaven opened, and there before me was a white horse. The rider on the horse is called Faithful and True, and he is right when he judges and makes war. 12His eyes are like burning fire, and on his head are many crowns. He has a name written on him, which no one but himself knows. 13He is dressed in a robe dipped in blood, and his name is the Word of God. 14The armies of heaven, dressed in fine linen, white and clean, were following him on white horses. 15Out of the rider's mouth comes a sharp sword that he will use to defeat the nations, and he will rule them with a rod of iron. He will crush out the wine in the winepress of the terrible anger of God the Almighty. 16On his robe and on his upper leg was written this name: KING OF KINGS AND LORD OF LORDS.

OLD TESTAMENT READING

Are there any gods like you, LORD?
There are no gods like you.
You are wonderfully holy,
amazingly powerful,
a worker of miracles.
12 You reached out with your right hand,
and the earth swallowed our enemies.
13 You keep your loving promise
and lead the people you have saved.

With your strength you will guide them
to your holy place.
17 You will lead your people and place them
on your very own mountain,
the place that you, LORD, made for yourself to live,
the temple, Lord, that your hands have made.
18 The LORD will be king forever!"

Exodus 15:11–13, 17–18

INSIGHTS

There is a party in heaven because the party that meant destruction for so many has been ended. A new celebration sponsored by God has gotten under way. According to this scripture, those allied with the Lamb of God cannot help but shout, "Hallelujah!" at this incredible turn of events. . . .

. . . Many of the most credible biblical scholars have agreed that Babylon in the Book of Revelation always refers to the dominant society in which Christians have to live. . . .

. . . When our Babylon falls (and it, like all Babylons, will one day fall), how will you react? Will you react like the merchants described in Revelation 18:3 who "grew rich from her excessive luxuries" and those political potentates who conspired with her to exploit the weak and the poor? Or will you be able to join the angels on that day and sing praises to God?

. . . Have you given your time and energy to get those things that go with living in Babylon so that, when it falls, all that you have ever worked for will fall with it? Or have you so invested your life in the Kingdom of God that, even if heaven and earth shall pass away, what is important to you will endure? In the end, will you be able to shout and sing in that eternal party that will be shared by those who have laid up their treasures in heaven (Matt. 6:19–21)?

TONY CAMPOLO

PAUSE FOR REFLECTION

Reread the praises to God in these passages—several times, if you'd like. Can you imagine anything more wonderful than praising God in heaven? Have you accepted your invitation to join his everlasting party?

REVELATION
19:17 — 20:15

17Then I saw an angel standing in the sun, and he called with a loud voice to all the birds flying in the sky: "Come and gather together for the great feast of God **18**so that you can eat the bodies of kings, generals, mighty people, horses and their riders, and the bodies of all people—free, slave, small, and great."

19Then I saw the beast and the kings of the earth. Their armies were gathered together to make war against the rider on the horse and his army. **20**But the beast was captured and with him the false prophet who did the miracles for the beast. The false prophet had used these miracles to trick those who had the mark of the beast and worshiped his idol. The false prophet and the beast were thrown alive into the lake of fire that burns with sulfur. **21**And their armies were killed with the sword that came out of the mouth of the rider on the horse, and all the birds ate the bodies until they were full.

The Thousand Years

20 I saw an angel coming down from heaven. He had the key to the bottomless pit and a large chain in his hand. **2**The angel grabbed the dragon, that old snake who is the devil and Satan, and tied him up for a thousand years. **3**Then he threw him into the bottomless pit, closed it, and locked it over him. The angel did this so he could not trick the people of the earth anymore until the thousand years

were ended. After a thousand years he must be set free for a short time.

4Then I saw some thrones and people sitting on them who had been given the power to judge. And I saw the souls of those who had been killed because they were faithful to the message of Jesus and the message from God. They had not worshiped the beast or his idol, and they had not received the mark of the beast on their foreheads or on their hands. They came back to life and ruled with Christ for a thousand years. **5**(The others that were dead did not live again until the thousand years were ended.) This is the first raising of the dead. **6**Blessed and holy are those who share in this first raising of the dead. The second death has no power over them. They will be priests for God and for Christ and will rule with him for a thousand years.

7When the thousand years are over, Satan will be set free from his prison. **8**Then he will go out to trick the nations in all the earth—Gog and Magog—to gather them for battle. There are so many people they will be like sand on the seashore. **9**And Satan's army marched across the earth and gathered around the camp of God's people and the city God loves. But fire came down from heaven and burned them up. **10**And Satan, who tricked them, was thrown into the lake of burning sulfur with the beast and the false prophet. There they will be punished day and night forever and ever.

People of the World Are Judged

11Then I saw a great white throne and the One who was sitting on it. Earth and sky ran away from him and disappeared. **12**And I saw the dead, great and small, standing before the throne. Then books were opened, and the book of life was opened. The dead were judged by what they had done, which was written in the books. **13**The sea gave up the dead who were in it, and Death and Hades gave up the dead who were in them. Each person was judged by what he had done. **14**And Death and Hades were thrown into the lake of fire. The lake of fire is the second death. **15**And anyone whose name was not found written in the book of life was thrown into the lake of fire.

OLD TESTAMENT READING

Human, prophesy against Gog and say, 'This is what the Lord GOD says: I am against you, Gog, chief ruler of Meshech and Tubal. **4**You, all your troops, and the nations with you will fall dead on the mountains of Israel. I will let you be food for every bird that eats meat and for every wild animal. **5**You will lie fallen on the ground, because I have spoken, says the Lord GOD. **6**I will send fire on Magog and those who live in safety on the coastlands. Then they will know that I am the LORD.

7" 'I will make myself known among my people Israel, and I will not let myself be dishonored anymore. Then the nations will know that I am the LORD, the Holy One in Israel. **8**It is coming! It will happen, says the Lord GOD. The time I talked about is coming.'"

Ezekiel 39:1, 4–8

INSIGHTS

For thousands of years, Satan has seduced nations and people into thinking that they can build a world of peace and love without Christ. Sometimes he has deceived people into thinking that education or money would solve personal problems. But his dirty work is over, for a time. At the end of the thousand years "he must be set free for a short time" (Revelation 20:3).

During the Millennium, believers will continue to populate the earth. However, their offspring, living in an ideal environment with King Jesus as the loving, benevolent ruler, can still rebel against God, and some will.

When Satan is released for a time, he will gather some of his old cohorts, Gog and Magog, the nations that hated Israel, and march on Jerusalem once more. This battle will not last long, for fire will come down from heaven and zap them. Then Satan will have his final place of unrest; he will be thrown "into the lake of burning sulfur, where the beast and the false prophet had been thrown. They will be tormented day and night for ever and ever" (Revelation 20:10).

DAVID JEREMIAH

APPLICATION

What amazing events are promised for future times in this portion of Scripture? What is the penalty for those who are not faithful to God? Pray that you, no matter what happens in your lifetime, will remain faithful to your Lord.

REVELATION 21:1-27

The New Jerusalem

21 Then I saw a new heaven and a new earth. The first heaven and the first earth had disappeared, and there was no sea anymore. **2**And I saw the holy city, the new Jerusalem, coming down out of heaven from God. It was prepared like a bride dressed for her husband. **3**And I heard a loud voice from the throne, saying, "Now God's presence is with people, and he will live with them, and they will be his people. God himself will be with them and will be their God. **4**He will wipe away every tear from their eyes, and there will be no more death, sadness, crying, or pain, because all the old ways are gone."

5The One who was sitting on the throne said, "Look! I am making everything new!" Then he said, "Write this, because these words are true and can be trusted."

6The One on the throne said to me, "It is finished. I am the Alpha and the Omega, the Beginning and the End. I will give free water from the spring of the water of life to anyone who is thirsty. **7**Those who win the victory will receive this, and I will be their God, and they will be my children. **8**But cowards, those who refuse to believe, who do evil things, who kill, who sin sexually, who do evil magic, who worship idols, and who tell lies—all these will have a place in the lake of burning sulfur. This is the second death."

9Then one of the seven angels who had the seven bowls full of the seven last troubles came to me, saying, "Come with me, and I will show you the bride, the wife of the Lamb." **10**And the angel carried me away by the Spirit to a very large and high mountain. He showed me the holy city, Jerusalem, coming down out of heaven from God. **11**It was shining with the glory of God and was bright like a very expensive jewel, like a jasper, clear as crystal. **12**The city had a great high wall with twelve gates with twelve angels at the gates, and on each gate was written the name of one of the twelve tribes of Israel. **13**There were three gates on the east, three on the north, three on the south, and three on the west. **14**The walls of the city were built on twelve foundation stones, and on the stones were written the names of the twelve apostles of the Lamb.

15The angel who talked with me had a measuring rod made of gold to measure the city, its gates, and its wall. **16**The city was built in a square, and its length was equal to its width. The angel measured the city with the rod. The city was 1,500 miles long, 1,500 miles wide, and 1,500 miles high. **17**The angel also measured the wall. It was 216 feet high, by human measurements, which the angel was using. **18**The wall was made of jasper, and the city was made of pure gold, as pure as glass. **19**The foundation stones of the city walls were decorated with every kind of jewel. The first foundation was jasper, the second was sapphire, the third was chalcedony, the fourth was emerald, **20**the fifth was onyx, the sixth was carnelian, the seventh was chrysolite, the eighth was beryl, the ninth was topaz, the tenth was chrysoprase, the eleventh was jacinth, and the twelfth was amethyst. **21**The twelve gates were twelve pearls, each gate having been made from a single pearl. And the street of the city was made of pure gold as clear as glass.

²²I did not see a temple in the city, because the Lord God Almighty and the Lamb are the city's temple. ²³The city does not need the sun or the moon to shine on it, because the glory of God is its light, and the Lamb is the city's lamp. ²⁴By its light the people of the world will walk, and the kings of the earth will bring their glory into it. ²⁵The city's gates will never be shut on any day, because there is no night there. ²⁶The glory and the honor of the nations will be brought into it. ²⁷Nothing unclean and no one who does shameful things or tells lies will ever go into it. Only those whose names are written in the Lamb's book of life will enter the city.

OLD TESTAMENT READING

Shout and be glad, Jerusalem. I am coming, and I will live among you," says the LORD. ¹¹"At that time people from many nations will join with the LORD and will become my people. Then I will live among you, and you will know that the LORD All-Powerful has sent me to you. ¹²The LORD will take Judah as his own part of the holy land, and Jerusalem will be his chosen city again. ¹³Be silent, everyone, in the presence of the LORD. He is coming out of the holy place where he lives."

Zechariah 2:10–13

INSIGHTS

The longing for a future glorious city of God can be traced back as far as the Old Testament patriarchs. Abraham ". . . was looking forward to the city with foundations, whose architect and builder is God" (Hebrews 11:10).

Paul mentioned this city in his letter to the Galatians. He called it "the Jerusalem which is above" (Galatians 4:26).

The "New Jerusalem" (Revelation 21:2; 3:12) is just one of the several names given to this future city of God. It is also called The Holy City, the Heavenly Jerusalem, and Mount Zion. Whatever it is named, it will be a holy and beautiful place, more perfect than the Garden of Eden. . . .

Jesus is preparing the New Jerusalem for us now. . . .

. . . His light will be among us forevermore.

In our eternal home there will be no sadness, no more tears. . . .

. . . For all eternity He will be with us and we will know and see Him.

DAVID JEREMIAH

ACTION POINT

Study what God promises to his children in the New Jerusalem. Do you have any doubts that God deeply loves you and fully knows your every pain and sorrow? Trust your heavenly Father's promise. Thank him for his goodness.

REVELATION 22:1-21

 Then the angel showed me the river of the water of life. It was shining like crystal and was flowing from the throne of God and of the Lamb **2**down the middle of the street of the city. The tree of life was on each side of the river. It produces fruit twelve times a year, once each month. The leaves of the tree are for the healing of all the nations. **3**Nothing that God judges guilty will be in that city. The throne of God and of the Lamb will be there, and God's servants will worship him. **4**They will see his face, and his name will be written on their foreheads. **5**There will never be night again. They will not need the light of a lamp or the light of the sun, because the Lord God will give them light. And they will rule as kings forever and ever.

6The angel said to me, "These words can be trusted and are true." The Lord, the God of the spirits of the prophets, sent his angel to show his servants the things that must happen soon.

7"Listen! I am coming soon! Blessed is the one who obeys the words of prophecy in this book."

8I, John, am the one who heard and saw these things. When I heard and saw them, I bowed down to worship at the feet of the angel who showed these things to me. **9**But the angel said to me, "Do not worship me! I am a servant like you, your brothers the prophets, and all those who obey the words in this book. Worship God!"

10Then the angel told me, "Do not keep secret the words of prophecy in this book, because the time is near for all this to happen. **11**Let whoever is doing evil continue to do evil. Let whoever is unclean continue to be unclean. Let whoever is doing right continue to do right. Let whoever is holy continue to be holy."

12"Listen! I am coming soon! I will bring my reward with me, and I will repay each one of you for what you have done. **13**I am the Alpha and the Omega, the First and the Last, the Beginning and the End.

14"Blessed are those who wash their robes so that they will receive the right to eat the fruit from the tree of life and may go through the gates into the city. **15**Outside the city are the evil people, those who do evil magic, who sin sexually, who murder, who worship idols, and who love lies and tell lies.

16"I, Jesus, have sent my angel to tell you these things for the churches. I am the descendant from the family of David, and I am the bright morning star."

17The Spirit and the bride say, "Come!" Let the one who hears this say, "Come!" Let whoever is thirsty come; whoever wishes may have the water of life as a free gift.

18I warn everyone who hears the words of the prophecy of this book: If anyone adds anything to these words, God will add to that person the disasters written about in this book. **19**And if anyone takes away from the words of this book of prophecy, God will take away that one's share of the tree of life and of the holy city, which are written about in this book.

20Jesus, the One who says these things are true, says, "Yes, I am coming soon."

Amen. Come, Lord Jesus!

²¹The grace of the Lord Jesus be with all. Amen.

OLD TESTAMENT READING

The LORD says, "All you who are thirsty, come and drink.
Those of you who do not have money, come, buy and eat!
Come buy wine and milk without money and without cost.
³Come to me and listen; listen to me so you may live."

Isaiah 55:1, 3a

There is a river that brings joy to the city of God,
the holy place where God Most High lives.
⁵God is in that city, and so it will not be shaken.

Psalm 46:4–5a

INSIGHTS

Come celebrate the living water that flows for you from an eternal spring. You need not fear stagnation. You need only draw nearer—put your roots down deep, settle in, and be at home in My love. Then every day will be a new day. Every day you will wonder at the richness of life that has come to you by My grace. Every day you will watch eagerly for My sunrise, search eagerly for My presence in the mundane activities of your world. Every day you will know Me better, and every day you will want to know Me more.

And every day you will live in joyful anticipation of My presence. You will think of My love for you as it is now, and as it will be on that day when I carry you across the threshold into the New Jerusalem—the home I am preparing for you.

Every day you will count the days until the wedding, when you and I will sit down together at the marriage supper of the Lamb. . . .

On that day, child, I will call you by a new name. You will be a crown of splendor in My hand, a royal diadem in the hand of your God. I will delight in you, I will rejoice over you as a bridegroom rejoices over his bride.

Come to the spring and drink deeply of My love. Let it flow over you, bringing a foretaste of that day when the river of life will flow for you through the New Jerusalem and love will be forever fresh.

Until then, turn from your fears and relax in My love. Here at the source you will find your renewal.

RUTH SENTER

PAUSE FOR REFLECTION

What to you is the most meaningful aspect of God's salvation, of his endless river of life? Meditate on this glorious gift. Thank him for what he has done for you and for anyone who will forsake sin and come to him.

INDEX

Second Coming of Christ

Seeking God

Self-esteem (see Love)

Sensitivity to Other Christians' Beliefs

Servanthood

Sharing Christ

Sin

Alcorn, Randy C., taken from *Sexual Temptation*. © 1989 by Randy Alcorn. Used by permission of InterVarsity Press, P.O. Box 1400, Downers Grove, IL 60515.

Anderson, Lynn, *Finding the Heart to Go On*, Here's Life Publishers, San Bernardino, CA, © 1991.

Arnold, Duane W. H., taken from the book *Prayers of the Martyrs*. Copyright © 1991 by Duane W. H. Arnold. Used by permission of Zondervan Publishing House.

Augsburger, David W., taken from *Freedom of Forgiveness*. Copyright © 1970, 1988. Moody Bible Institute of Chicago. Moody Press. Used by permission.

Avila, St. Teresa of, from the book *A Life of Prayer*, copyright 1983 by Multnomah Press. Published by Multnomah Press, Portland, Oregon 97266. Used by permission.

Babcock, Maltbie, *This Is My Father's World* in *The Hymnal for Worship and Celebration*, copyright ©1986, Word Music, Waco, Texas.

Barna, George, *The Frog in the Kettle*, copyright © 1990 by Regal Books, a division of Gospel Light Publications. Used by permission.

Baxter, J. Sidlow, taken from the book *Awake My Heart*. Copyright © 1959 by J. Sidlow Baxter. Used by permission of the Zondervan Publishing House.

Beals, Art, *Beyond Hunger*, copyright © 1985, Multnomah Press, Portland, Oregon 97266.

Beckwith, Mary, *Still Moments*, copyright © 1989 by Regal Books, a division of Gospel Light Publications. Used by permission.

Blue, Ron, *Master Your Money*, copyright © 1986, Thomas Nelson Publishers, Nashville, TN.

Boice, James Montgomery, taken from *The Parables of Jesus*. Copyright © 1983. Moody Bible Institute of Chicago. Moody Press. Used by permission.

Bridges, Jerry, *The Practice of Godliness*, copyright © 1983 by Jerry Bridges, NavPress, Colorado Springs, Colorado.

Bridges, Jerry, *The Pursuit of Holiness*, copyright © 1978 by the Navigators, NavPress, Colorado Springs, Colorado.

Bright, Bill, *Promises—A Daily Guide to Supernatural Living*, Here's Life Publishers, San Bernadino, CA, © 1983.

Bright, Bill, *The Secret: How to Live with Purpose and Power*, Here's Life Publishers, San Bernadino, CA, © 1989.

Briscoe, Jill, *Running on Empty*, copyright © 1988, Word, Inc., Dallas, Texas.

Bruce, F. F., taken from *The Hard Sayings of Jesus*. © 1983 by F. F. Bruce. Used by permission of InterVarsity Press, P.O. Box 1400, Downers Grove, IL 60515. Worldwide permission granted by Hodder & Stoughton Limited, England.

Bryant, Al (Compiler), *Day By Day With C. H. Spurgeon*, copyright © 1980, Word, Inc., Dallas, Texas.

Bryant, Al, *Keep in Touch*, copyright © 1981, Word, Inc., Dallas, Texas.

Bryant, Al, *Strength for the Day: Daily Meditations with F. B. Meyer*, copyright © 1979, Word, Inc., Dallas, Texas.

Buechner, Frederick, excerpt from *Wishful Thinking*. Copyright © 1973 by Frederick Buechner. Reprinted by permission of HarperCollins Publishers.

Calkin, Ruth Harms, from *Tell Me Again Lord, I Forget*, © 1974. Used by permission of Tyndale House Publishers, Inc. All rights reserved.

Campolo, Anthony, *The Kingdom of God Is a Party*, copyright © 1990, Word, Inc., Dallas, Texas.

Campolo, Anthony, *Who Switched the Price Tags?*, copyright © 1986, Word, Inc., Dallas, Texas.

Chapian, Marie, *Discovering Joy*, Bethany House Publishers, © 1990.

Chisholm, Thomas O. (Words) and Runyan, William M. (Music), *Great Is Thy Faithfulness* in *The Hymnal for Worship and Celebration*, copyright © 1923. Renewal 1951 by Hope Publishing Co., Carol Stream, IL 60188. All rights reserved. Used by permission.

Crabb, Rachael, *The Personal Touch*, copyright © 1990 by Rachael Crabb and Raeann Hart, NavPress, Colorado Springs, Colorado.

Evans, Anthony T., taken from *America's Only Hope*. Copyright © 1990. Moody Bible Institute of Chicago. Moody Press. Used by permission.

Fickett, Harold L., *Walking What You're Talking (Principles of James)*, copyright © 1988 by Regal Books, a division of Gospel Light Publications. Used by permission.

Finney, Charles G., *God's Love for a Sinning World*. © 1966 by Kregel Publications: Grand Rapids, Michigan. Used by permission.

Finney, Charles G., *Principles of Consecration*, Bethany House Publishers, © 1990.

Finney, Charles Grandison, *Principles of Devotion*, Bethany House Publishers, © 1987.

Finney, Charles G., *Victory Over the World*. © 1966 by Kregel Publications: Grand Rapids, Michigan. Used by permission.

Fletcher, William M., *The Second Greatest Commandment*. Copyright © 1983. NavPress, Colorado Springs, Colorado. (Dr. William M. Fletcher is Minister-at-Large, Rocky Mountain Conservative Baptist Association.)

Foster, Richard J., excerpts from *Celebration of Discipline*. Copyright © 1978 by Richard J. Foster. Reprinted by permission of HarperCollins Publishers.

Foster, Richard J., excerpts from *Money, Sex and Power*. Copyright © 1985 by Richard J. Foster. Reprinted by permission of HarperCollins Publishers.

Fullam, Terry L., *Thirsting*, copyright © 1989, Thomas Nelson Publishers, Nashville, TN.

Gaither, Gloria, *We Have This Moment*, copyright © 1988, Word, Inc., Dallas, Texas.

Geisler, Norman L. (Editor), *What Augustine Says*, Baker Book House, © 1982.

Gillham, Bill, *Lifetime Guarantee*, Wolgemuth & Hyatt, Publishers, Inc. Used by permission.

Graham, Billy, *Answers to Life's Problems*, copyright © 1960, 1988, Word, Inc., Dallas, Texas.

Graham, Billy, *Approaching Hoofbeats*, copyright © 1983, Word, Inc., Dallas, Texas.

Graham, Billy, *The Holy Spirit*, copyright © 1978, 1988, Word, Inc., Dallas, Texas.

Graham, Billy, *Unto the Hills: A Devotional Treasury from Billy Graham*, copyright © 1986, Word, Inc., Dallas, Texas.

Gregory, Joel C., *Growing Pains of the Soul*, copyright © 1987, Word, Inc., Dallas, Texas.

Guinness, Os, taken from *The Devil's Gauntlet*. © 1989 by Os Guinness. Used by permission of InterVarsity Press, P.O. Box 1400, Downers Grove, IL 60515.

Halverson, Richard C., *No Greater Power*, copyright © 1986, Multnomah Press, Portland, Oregon 97266.

Harris, Madalene, *Climbing Higher*, Here's Life Publishers, San Bernadino, CA, © 1989.

Hayford, Jack, from *Daybreak*, © 1984. Used by permission of Tyndale House Publishers, Inc. All rights reserved.

Hendricks, Howard G. and Jeanne W., from the book *Footprints,* copyright © 1981, Multnomah Press, Portland, Oregon 97266. (Howard Hendricks is a distinguished professor at Dallas Theological Seminary; Jeanne Hendricks is an author, mother of four, and grandmother of six.)

Henrichsen, Walter A., Reprinted by permission from *Disciples Are Made—Not Born.* Published by Victor Books and © 1974 by SP Publications, Inc., Wheaton, IL.

Hession, Roy, from *The Calvary Road,* copyright 1952 Christian Literature Crusade, London (Ft. Washington, PA, and Alresford, Hants: Christian Literature Crusade). Used by permission.

Hocking, David L., from the book *The Coming World Leader,* copyright 1988 by Calvary Communications, Inc. Published by Multnomah Press, Portland, Oregon 97266. Used by permission.

Hughes, R. Kent, taken from *Ephesians,* copyright 1990. Used with permission by Good News Publishers/Crossway Books, Wheaton, IL.

Hybels, Bill, *Seven Wonders of the Spiritual World,* copyright © 1988, Word, Inc., Dallas, Texas.

Hybels, Bill, taken from *Too Busy Not to Pray.* © 1988 by Bill Hybels. Used by permission of InterVarsity Press, P.O. Box 1400, Downers Grove, IL 60515.

Jeremiah, David and Carlson, Carole C., *Escape the Coming Night,* copyright © 1990, Word, Inc., Dallas, Texas.

Johnson, Elliot and Schierbaum, Al, *Our Great and Awesome God: Meditations for Athletes.* Wolgemuth & Hyatt, Publishers, Inc. Used by permission.

Keller, W. Phillip, *A Gardener Looks at the Fruits of the Spirit,* copyright © 1986, Word, Inc., Dallas, Texas.

Keller, W. Phillip, *Salt for Society,* copyright © 1981, Word, Inc., Dallas, Texas.

Keller, W. Phillip, *Songs of My Soul,* copyright © 1989, Word, Inc., Dallas, Texas.

Keller, W. Phillip, *Taming Tension,* Baker Book House, © 1979.

Kempis, Thomas à, taken from *The Imitation of Christ.* Copyright © 1984. Moody Bible Institute of Chicago. Moody Press. Used by permission.

Kroll, Woodrow Michael, *Early in the Morning, Book Two.* Used by permission of Loizeaux Brothers, Inc., Neptune, New Jersey.

Lake, Vicki, reprinted by permission from *Firming Up Your Flabby Faith.* Published by Victor Books and © 1990 by SP Publications, Inc., Wheaton, IL.

Larson, Bruce, reprinted from *A Call to Holy Living,* copyright © 1988 Augsburg Publishing House. Used by permission of Augsburg Fortress.

Lee, Richard, *The Unfailing Promise,* copyright © 1988, Word, Inc., Dallas, Texas.

Lockerbie, Jeanette, taken from *Springtime of Faith.* Copyright © 1990. Moody Bible Institute of Chicago. Moody Press. Used by permission.

Lockyer, Herbert, *Satan: His Person and Power,* copyright © 1980, Word, Inc., Dallas, Texas.

Lucado, Max, *The Applause of Heaven,* copyright © 1990, Word, Inc., Dallas, Texas.

Lucado, Max, from *On the Anvil,* © 1985. Used by permission of Tyndale House Publishers, Inc. All rights reserved.

Luther, Martin, *A Mighty Fortress Is Our God* in *The Hymnal for Worship and Celebration,* copyright © 1986, Word Music, Waco, Texas.

MacArthur, John, Jr., taken from the book *The Gospel According to Jesus.* Copyright © 1988 by John F. MacArthur, Jr. Used by permission of Zondervan Publishing House.

MacDonald, George, *Knowing the Heart of God,* Bethany House Publishers, © 1990.

MacDonald, Gordon, *Ordering Your Private World,* copyright © 1984, 1985, Thomas Nelson Publishers, Nashville, TN.

MacDonald, Gordon, *Rebuilding Your Broken World,* copyright © 1988, 1990, Thomas Nelson Publishers, Nashville, TN.

McClung, Floyd, *Holiness and the Spirit of the Age.* Copyright © 1990 by Harvest House Publishers, Eugene, OR 97402.

McClung, Floyd, taken from *Wholehearted.* © 1988, 1990 by Floyd McClung. Used by permission of InterVarsity Press, P.O. Box 1400, Downers Grove, IL 60515. Worldwide permission granted by HarperCollins Publishers, London, England.

McCullough, Donald W., taken from *Finding Happiness in the Most Unlikely Places.* © 1990 by Donald W. McCullough. Used by permission of InterVarsity Press, P.O. Box 1400, Downers Grove, IL 60515.

McKenna, David, from *Practical Christianity;* LaVonne Neff, Ron Beers, Bruce Barton, Linda Taylor, Dave Veerman, and Jim Galvin (Compilers and Editors), © 1987 by Youth for Christ/USA. Used by permission of Tyndale House Publishers. All rights reserved.

Magdalen, Margaret, taken from *Jesus, Man of Prayer.* © 1987 by Sister Margaret Magdalen. Used by permission of InterVarsity Press, P.O. Box 1400, Downers Grove, IL 60515. Worldwide permission granted by Hodder & Stoughton Limited, England.

Mains, David R., *The Sense of His Presence,* copyright ©1988, Word, Inc., Dallas, Texas.

Mains, Karen Burton, taken from the book *You Are What You Say.* Copyright © 1988 by Karen Burton Mains. Used by permission of the Zondervan Publishing House.

Merritt, James Gregory, reprinted by permission from *God's Prescription for a Healthy Christian.* Published by Victor Books and © 1990 by SP Publications, Inc., Wheaton, IL.

Meyer, F. B., from *Devotional Commentary by F. B. Meyer* (1989) Tyndale House Publishers, Inc. Used by permission. All rights reserved.

Meyer, F. B., taken from *Our Daily Walk.* Copyright © 1951, 1972 by the Zondervan Publishing House. Used by permission.

Miley, Jeanie, *Creative Silence: Keys to the Deeper Life,* copyright © 1989, Word, Inc., Dallas, Texas.

Mitchell, John G., from the book *An Everlasting Love,* copyright 1982 by Multnomah Press. Published by Multnomah Press, Portland, Oregon 97266. Used by permission.

Moody, D. L., taken from *The Way to God and How to Find It.* Copyright © 1983. Moody Bible Institute of Chicago. Moody Press. Used by permission.

Morley, Patrick, *I Surrender.* Wolgemuth & Hyatt, Publishers, Inc. Used by permission.

Mote, Edward, *The Solid Rock* in *The Hymnal for Worship and Celebration,* copyright © 1986, Word Music, Waco, Texas.

Muggeridge, Malcolm, from *The End of Christendom,* copyright 1980 by William B. Eerdmans Publishing Co., pp. 51–54. Used by permission.

Muggeridge, Malcolm, *A Twentieth Century Testimony,* copyright © 1978, Thomas Nelson Publishers, Nashville, TN.

Murray, Andrew, from *Abide in Christ* (Ft. Washington, PA: Christian Literature Crusade).

Murray, Andrew, *The Believer's Secret of Living Like Christ,* Bethany House Publishers, © 1985.

Murray, Andrew, *The Believer's Secret of Waiting on God,* Bethany House Publishers, © 1986.

Murray, Andrew, taken from *The True Vine.* Copyright © 1983. Moody Bible Institute of Chicago. Moody Press. Used by permission.

Murray, Andrew and Edwards, Jonathan; Parkhurst, Louis Gifford (Compiler and Editor), *The Believer's Secret of Christian Love,* Bethany House Publishers, © 1990.

Murray, Andrew and Finney, Charles G.; Parkhurst, L. G. (Compiler and Editor), *The Believer's Secret of Spiritual Power,* Bethany House Publishers, © 1987.

Myers, Warren and Ruth, *Pray: How to Be Effective in Prayer,* copyright © 1983, NavPress, Colorado Springs, Colorado.

Oatman, Johnson Jr., *Count Your Blessings* in *The Hymnal for Worship and Celebration,* copyright © 1986, Word Music, Waco, Texas.

Ogilvie, Lloyd, *Enjoying God,* copyright © 1989, Word, Inc., Dallas, Texas.

Ogilvie, Lloyd John, taken from *Silent Strength for My Life.* Copyright © 1990 by Harvest House Publishers, Eugene, OR 97402. Used by permission.

Ortlund, Anne, *Disciplines of the Home,* copyright © 1990, Word, Inc., Dallas, Texas.

Packer, J. I., taken from *Knowing God.* © 1973 by J. I. Packer. Used by permission of InterVarsity Press, P.O. Box 1400, Downers Grove, IL 60515. Worldwide permission granted by Hodder & Stoughton Limited, England.

Packer, James and Watson, Jean, reprinted from *Your Father Loves You,* © 1986 by James Packer and Jean Watson. Used by permission of Harold Shaw Publishers, Wheaton, IL. Worldwide permission granted by Hodder & Stoughton Limited, England.

Palau, Luis, reprinted by permission from *Time to Stop Pretending.* Published by Victor Books and © 1985 by SP Publications, Inc., Wheaton, IL.

Pinnock, Clark H., from *Practical Christianity;* LaVonne Neff, Ron Beers, Bruce Barton, Linda Taylor, Dave Veerman, and Jim Galvin (Compilers and Editors), © 1987 by Youth for Christ/USA. Used by permission of Tyndale House Publishers. All rights reserved.

Pippert, Rebecca Manley, taken from *Out of the Saltshaker and Into the World.* © 1979 by Inter-Varsity Christian Fellowship of the USA. Used by permission of InterVarsity Press, P.O. Box 1400, Downers Grove, IL 60515.

Reid, David, *Devotions for Growing Christians.* Used by permission of Loizeaux Brothers, Inc., Neptune, New Jersey.

Ryrie, Charles C., reprinted by permission from *The Final Countdown.* Published by Victor Books and © 1982 by SP Publications, Inc., Wheaton, IL.

Sanders, J. Oswald, taken from *Enjoying Intimacy With God.* Copyright © 1980. Moody Bible Institute of Chicago. Moody Press. Used by permission.

Sanders, J. Oswald, taken from *Just Like Us.* Copyright © 1978. Moody Bible Institute of Chicago. Moody Press. Used by permission.

Sanders, J. Oswald, taken from *Shoe Leather Commitment.* Copyright © 1990. Moody Bible Institute of Chicago. Moody Press. Used by permission.

Schaeffer, Edith, from the book *Affliction,* copyright © 1978 by Edith Schaeffer. Used by permission of Fleming H. Revell Company.

Schaeffer, Edith, *Common Sense Christian Living,* copyright © 1983, Thomas Nelson Publishers, Nashville, TN.

Schmidt, Thomas E., taken from the book *Trying to Be Good.* Copyright © 1990 by Thomas E. Schmidt. Used by permission of the Zondervan Publishing House.

Senter, Ruth, taken from *The Attributes of God.* Copyright © 1987. Moody Bible Institute of Chicago. Moody Press. Used by permission.

Senter, Ruth, *Longing for Love,* copyright © 1991 by Ruth Senter, NavPress, Colorado Springs, Colorado.

Senter, Ruth, taken from the book *Startled by Silence.* Copyright © 1986 by Ruth Senter. Used by permission of the Zondervan Publishing House.

Shaw, Luci, reprinted from *Postcard from the Shore,* © 1985 by Luci Shaw. Used by permission of Harold Shaw Publishers, Wheaton, IL.

Sherman, Doug and Hendricks, William, *How to Succeed Where It Really Counts,* copyright © 1989 by Doug Sherman and William Hendricks, NavPress, Colorado Springs, Colorado.

Sider, Ronald J., *Rich Christians in an Age of Hunger,* copyright © 1990, Word, Inc., Dallas, Texas.

Simpson, A. B., taken from the book *Days of Heaven on Earth.* Copyright © 1984 by Christian Publications. Used by permission of the Zondervan Publishing House.

Smith, F. LaGard, *The Daily Gospels* (formerly *The Intimate Jesus*). Copyright © 1988 by Harvest House Publishers, Eugene, OR 97402.

Smith, Hannah Whitall, from the book *The Christian's Secret of a Happy Life.* Copyright © 1952 by Fleming H. Revell Company. Used by permission of Fleming H. Revell Company.

Sollenberger, Lucille Fern, *My Daily Appointment with God,* copyright © 1988, Word, Inc., Dallas, Texas.

Sproul, R. C., from *Effective Prayer,* © 1984. Used by permission of Tyndale House Publishers, Inc. All rights reserved.

Sproul, R. C., from *The Holiness of God,* © 1985. Used by permission of Tyndale House Publishers, Inc. All rights reserved.

Sproul, R. C., *One Holy Passion,* copyright © 1987, Thomas Nelson Publishers, Nashville, TN.

Spurgeon, C. H., taken from *All of Grace.* Copyright © 1984. Moody Bible Institute of Chicago. Moody Press. Used by permission.

Spurgeon, Charles H., taken from *Faith's Checkbook.* Copyright © 1987. Moody Bible Institute of Chicago. Moody Press. Used by permission.

Spurgeon, Charles H., *Morning and Evening,* copyright © 1991, Hendrickson Publishers, Inc. Peabody, MA.

Spurgeon, C. H., reprinted from *The Quotable Spurgeon,* © 1990 by Harold Shaw Publishers, Wheaton, IL. Used by permission.

Stamm, Mildred, taken from the book *Meditation Moments for Women.* Copyright © 1967 by the Zondervan Publishing House. Used by permission.

Stamm, Millie, taken from the book *Beside Still Waters.* Copyright © 1984 by Christian Women's Club. Used by permission of the Zondervan Publishing House.

Stamm, Millie, taken from the book *Be Still and Know.* Copyright © 1978 by Millie Stamm. Used by permission of the Zondervan Publishing House.

Stanley, Charles, *How to Handle Adversity,* copyright © 1989, Thomas Nelson Publishers, Nashville, TN.

Steer, Roger, reprinted from *Spiritual Secrets of George Müller,* © 1985 by Roger Steer. U.S.A. rights granted by permission of Harold Shaw Publishers, Wheaton, IL. Worldwide permission granted by Hodder & Stoughton Limited, England.

Steinberger, G., *In the Footprints of the Lamb,* Bethany House Publishers, © 1936.

Stoddard, William S., from the book *First Light,* copyright 1990 by Multnomah Press. Published by Multnomah Press, Portland, Oregon 97266. Used by permission.

Stott, John, from *Basic Christianity.* Copyright 1958, 1971. Inter-Varsity Press, London. Published in the U.S.A. by William B. Eerdmans Publishing Co. and in the U.K. by InterVarsity Press. Used by permission. Worldwide permission granted by Inter-Varsity Press, London, England. Second edition.

Sweeting, George, taken from *The Acts of God.* Copyright © 1986. Moody Bible Institute of Chicago. Moody Press. Used by permission.

Swindoll, Charles R., *The Grace Awakening,* copyright © 1990, Word, Inc., Dallas, Texas.

Swindoll, Charles R., *Improving Your Serve: The Art of Unselfish Living,* copyright © 1981, Word, Inc., Dallas, Texas.

Swindoll, Charles R., *Living Above the Level of Mediocrity: A Commitment to Excellence.* Copyright © 1987, Word, Inc., Dallas, Texas.

Swindoll, Charles R., from the book *Make Up Your Mind,* copyright 1981. Published by Multnomah Press, Portland, Oregon 97266. Used by permission.

Swindoll, Charles R., *Strengthening Your Grip: Essentials in an Aimless World,* copyright © 1982, Word, Inc., Dallas, Texas.

Tada, Joni Eareckson, from the book *Secret Strength,* copyright 1988 by Joni, Inc. Published by Multnomah Press, Portland, Oregon 97266. Used by permission.

Tamasy, Robert J. (General Editor), *The Complete Christian Businessman,* Wolgemuth & Hyatt, Publishers, Inc. Used by permission.

Tucker, Ruth A., taken from the book *Stories of Faith.* Copyright © 1989 by Ruth A. Tucker. Used by permission of Zondervan Publishing House.

Webber, Robert, *Worship is a Verb,* copyright © 1985, Word, Inc., Dallas, Texas. (Second edition by Abbott Martyn Press, Nashville, TN).

Wenham, David, taken from *The Parables of Jesus.* © 1989 by David Wenham. Used by permission of InterVarsity Press, P.O. Box 1400, Downers Grove, IL 60515. Worldwide permission granted by Hodder & Stoughton Limited, England.

White, John, taken from *The Fight.* © 1976 by Inter-Varsity Christian Fellowship of the U.S.A. Used by permission of InterVarsity Press, P.O. Box 1400, Downers Grove, IL 60515.

Wiersbe, Warren W., reprinted by permission from *Be Alert.* Published by Victor Books and © 1984 by SP Publications, Inc., Wheaton, IL.

Wiersbe, Warren W., reprinted by permission from *Be Victorious.* Published by Victor Books and © 1985 by SP Publications, Inc., Wheaton, IL.

Wiersbe, Warren W. (Compiler), *Classic Sermons on the Attributes of God.* © 1989 by Kregel Publications: Grand Rapids, Michigan. Used by permission.

Wiersbe, Warren W., taken from *Thoughts for Men on the Move.* Copyright © 1970, 1988. Moody Bible Institute of Chicago. Moody Press. Used by permission.

Wiersbe, Warren W., reprinted by permission from *Windows on the Parables.* Published by Victor Books and © 1979 by SP Publications, Inc., Wheaton, IL.

Wirt, Sherwood E., *Your Mighty Fortress: Cultivating Your Inner Life With God,* Here's Life Publishers, San Bernadino, CA, © 1989.

Wright, H. Norman, *Quiet Times for Couples.* Copyright © 1990 by Harvest House Publishers, Eugene, OR 97402.

YFC Editors, from *Practical Christianity;* LaVonne Neff, Ron Beers, Bruce Barton, Linda Taylor, Dave Veerman, and Jim Galvin (Compilers and Editors), © 1987 by Youth for Christ/USA. Used by permission of Tyndale House Publishers. All rights reserved.

Yancey, Philip, taken from the book *Where Is God When It Hurts?* Copyright © 1990, 1977 by Philip Yancey. Used by permission of the Zondervan Publishing House.

Yohn, Rick, *Finding Time,* copyright © 1984, Word, Inc., Dallas, Texas.

Zuck, Roy B. (Editor), reprinted by permission from *Devotions for Kindred Spirits.* Published by Victor Books and © 1990 by SP Publications, Inc., Wheaton, IL.